Netter's Orthopaedic Clinical Examination

An Evidence-Based Approach

2nd Edition

Joshua A. Cleland, PT, PhD

Associate Professor, Physical Therapy Program
Franklin Pierce University, Concord, New Hampshire
Rehabilitation Services of Concord Hospital, Concord, New Hampshire

Shane Koppenhaver, PT, PhD

Major, Army Medical Specialist Corps
Assistant Professor, U.S. Army–Baylor University Doctoral Physical Therapy Program
Fort Sam Houston, Texas

Illustrations by Frank H. Netter, MD

Contributing Illustrators
Carlos A. G. Machado, MD
John A. Craig, MD

SAUNDERS

ELSEVIER

SAUNDERS
ELSEVIER

Suite 1800
Philadelphia, Pennsylvania 19103

Notices

Knowledge and best practice in this field are constantly changing. As new research and experience broaden our
understanding, changes in research methods, professional practices, or medical treatment may become necessary.
Practitioners and researchers must always rely on their own experience and knowledge in evaluating and
using any information, methods, compounds, or experiments described herein. In using such information
or methods they should be mindful of their own safety and the safety of others, including parties for whom
they have a professional responsibility.

With respect to any drug or pharmaceutical products identified, readers are advised to check the most current information provided (i) on procedures featured or (ii) by the manufacturer of each product to be ad-
ministered, to verify the recommended dose or formula, the method and duration of administration, and
contraindications. It is the responsibility of practitioners, relying on their own experience and knowledge of
their patients, to make diagnoses, to determine dosages and the best treatment for each individual patient,
and to take all appropriate safety precautions.

To the fullest extent of the law, neither the Publisher nor the authors, contributors, or editors assume any liability
for any injury and/or damage to persons or property as a matter of products liability, negligence or otherwise, or
from any use or operation of any methods, products, instructions, or ideas contained in the material herein.

Library of Congress Cataloging-in-Publication Data
Cleland, Joshua.
    Netter's orthopaedic clinical examination: an evidence-based approach. — 2nd ed. / Joshua A. Cleland,
Shane Koppenhaver ; illustrations by Frank H. Netter ; contributing illustrators, Carlos A. G. Machado,
John A. Craig.
        p. ; cm.
    Rev. ed. of: Orthopaedic clinical examination : an evidence-based approach for physical therapists /
Joshua Cleland ; illustrations by Frank H. Netter. c2005.
    Includes bibliographical references and index.
    ISBN 978-1-4377-1384-8
    1. Physical orthopedic tests—Handbooks, manuals, etc. 2. Physical diagnosis—Handbooks, manuals, etc.
I. Koppenhaver, Shane. II. Netter, Frank H. (Frank Henry), 1906-1991. III. Orthopaedic clinical examination.
IV. Title. V. Title: Orthopaedic clinical examination.
    [DNLM: 1. Musculoskeletal Diseases—diagnosis—Handbooks. 2. Physical Examination—methods—Handbooks.
3. Evidence-Based Medicine—Handbooks. 4. Physical Therapy Modalities—Handbooks. WE 39 C624n 2011]
    RD 734.5P58C59 2011
616.7'075—dc22

2009039235

Acquisitions Editor: Elyse O'Grady
Developmental Editor: Marybeth Thiel
Publishing Services Manager: Frank Polizzano
Project Manager: Lee Ann Draud
Design Direction: Lou Forgione
Illustrations Manager: Karen Giacomucci

Printed in United States of America

Last digit is the print number: 9   8   7   6   5   4   3   2

*To our incredible mentors and colleagues
who have fostered our passion for
evidence-based practice and orthopaedics.*

*To our photography models (Jessica Palmer and
Nicole Koppenhaver) and photographers (Sara Randall,
Lindsey Browne, and Jeff Hebert) for spending more hours
and retakes than we'd like to admit.*

*To Dr. Frank Netter and the Elsevier editorial staff
who turned our ideas into a fantastic literary guide.*

*And, most important, to our wonderful families,
whose sacrifices and support
made this considerable endeavor possible.*

Frank H. Netter, MD

Frank H. Netter was born in 1906, in New York City. He studied art at the Art Student's League and the National Academy of Design before entering medical school at New York University, where he received his MD degree in 1931. During his student years, Dr. Netter's notebook sketches attracted the attention of the medical faculty and other physicians, allowing him to augment his income by illustrating articles and textbooks. He continued illustrating as a sideline after establishing a surgical practice in 1933, but he ultimately opted to give up his practice in favor of a full-time commitment to art. After service in the United States Army during World War II, Dr. Netter began his long collaboration with the CIBA Pharmaceutical Company (now Novartis Pharmaceuticals). This 45-year partnership resulted in the production of the extraordinary collection of medical art so familiar to physicians and other medical professionals worldwide.

In 2005, Elsevier, Inc., purchased the Netter Collection and all publications from Icon Learning Systems. There are now more than 50 publications featuring the art of Dr. Netter available through Elsevier, Inc. (in the U.S.: www.us.elsevierhealth.com/Netter and outside the U.S.: www.elsevierhealth.com).

Dr. Netter's works are among the finest examples of the use of illustration in the teaching of medical concepts. The 13-book *Netter Collection of Medical Illustrations*, which includes the greater part of the more than 20,000 paintings created by Dr. Netter, became and remains one of the most famous medical works ever published. *The Netter Atlas of Human Anatomy*, first published in 1989, presents the anatomical paintings from the Netter Collection. Now translated into 16 languages, it is the anatomy atlas of choice among medical and health professions students the world over.

The Netter illustrations are appreciated not only for their aesthetic qualities, but, more important, for their intellectual content. As Dr. Netter wrote in 1949, ". . . clarification of a subject is the aim and goal of illustration. No matter how beautifully painted, how delicately and subtly rendered a subject may be, it is of little value as a *medical illustration* if it does not serve to make clear some medical point." Dr. Netter's planning, conception, point of view, and approach are what inform his paintings and what makes them so intellectually valuable.

Frank H. Netter, MD, physician and artist, died in 1991.

Learn more about the physician-artist whose work has inspired the Netter Reference collection: http://www.netterimages.com/artist/netter.htm.

Carlos Machado, MD

Carlos Machado was chosen by Novartis to be Dr. Netter's successor. He continues to be the main artist who contributes to the Netter collection of medical illustrations.

Self-taught in medical illustration, cardiologist Carlos Machado has contributed meticulous updates to some of Dr. Netter's original plates and has created many paintings of his own in the style of Netter as an extension of the Netter collection. Dr. Machado's photorealistic expertise and his keen insight into the physician-patient relationship inform his vivid and unforgettable visual style. His dedication to researching each topic and subject he paints places him among the premier medical illustrators at work today.

Learn more about his background and see more of his art at http://www.netterimages.com/artist/machado.htm.

Joshua Cleland, PT, DPT, PhD, OCS, FAAOMPT

Dr. Cleland earned a Master of Physical Therapy degree from Notre Dame College in 2000 and the Doctor of Physical Therapy degree from Creighton University in 2001. In 2006, he received a PhD from Nova Southeastern University. He received board certification from the American Physical Therapy Association as an Orthopaedic Clinical Specialist in 2002 and completed a fellowship in manual therapy through Regis University in Denver, Colorado, in 2005. Josh is presently a Professor in the Physical Therapy Program at Franklin Pierce University. He practices clinically in outpatient orthopaedics at Rehabilitation Services of Concord Hospital, Concord, New Hampshire. He is actively involved in numerous clinical research studies investigating the effectiveness of manual physical therapy and exercise in the management of spine and extremities disorders. He has published more than 85 manuscripts in peer-reviewed journals. He is on the Editorial Board for *Physical Therapy* and is an Editorial Review Board Member for the *Journal of Orthopaedic and Sports Physical Therapy*. He is the recipient of the 2009 Eugene Michels New Investigator Award. He received the 2008 Jack Walker Award from the American Physical Therapy Association. In addition, Dr. Cleland was awarded the Excellence in Research Award from the American Academy of Orthopaedic Manual Physical Therapists on two separate occasions (2004 and 2006).

Shane Koppenhaver, PT, PhD, OCS, FAAOMPT

Dr. Koppenhaver received his Masters of Physical Therapy degree from the U.S. Army/Baylor University Graduate Program in 1998, and a PhD in Exercise Physiology from the University of Utah in 2009. He became board certified in Orthopedic Physical Therapy in 2001 and completed a fellowship in manual therapy through Regis University in 2009. Dr. Koppenhaver is a Major in the U.S. Army and an Assistant Professor in the U.S. Army/Baylor University Doctoral Program in Physical Therapy. He has published numerous studies on low back pain, spinal manipulation, and the use of ultrasound imaging in the measurement of trunk muscle function. His primary research interests concern mechanistic and clinical outcomes associated with manual therapy, especially as they apply to clinical reasoning and management of patients with neuromusculoskeletal conditions.

Foreword

Diagnosis is not the end, but the beginning of practice. —Martin H. Fischer

Physical examination and the ability to differentially diagnose accurately are critical components of orthopaedic medicine. However, the decisions that providers use to select their "preferred" evaluative tools are often based on tradition or what was learned during initial professional training rather than on science. Although some questions and examination procedures may be very helpful in establishing an accurate orthopaedic diagnosis, others may be utterly useless and serve only to distract both patients and providers. With the rapidly expanding amount of recent research investigating the diagnostic utility of tests and measures, it is essential for clinicians to use selective components of the history and physical examination that are supported by current best evidence.

This textbook is unique and easy to decipher for the audience for whom it is written. The authors should be commended for compiling the evidence currently available in the literature and applying it to the regional musculoskeletal examination. First, the authors outline in detail the relevant literature and clearly describe the psychometric properties of each historical and physical examination procedure. Second, the text provides a thorough evaluation of each subarea and highlights a variety of evaluative tests for the various regions of the body. This approach helps to present the material to medical professionals in a more focused and streamlined fashion. Third, if pictures represent a thousand words, the text should be considered a million pages. The combination of hand-drawn and photographic examples of anatomy, pathoanatomy, and special tests are invaluable to the reader as they help integrate the evidence into dynamic clinical practice. Finally, the authors must be commended for organizing and presenting all the material in such a logical format that makes it highly useful in both academic environments and in those of busy orthopaedic health care professionals.

As director of an accredited clinical health care program, I appreciate that this text provides a useful resource within the library regarding our professional domains: (1) Prevention, (2) Clinical Evaluation and Diagnosis, (3) Immediate Care, (4) Treatment/Rehabilitation and Reconditioning, (5) Organization and Administration, and (6) Professional Responsibility. This text is an example of the practical information we need along with the voluminous and technical literature available to us all. I believe the authors have succeeded in their objective, and our program will be using this resource now and into the future.

Well done, and thank you.

BRADLEY HAYES, PHD, ATC/L
Director, Athletic Training Education
University of Utah College of Health

Preface

Over the past several years, evidence-based practice has become the standard in the medical and health care professions. As described by Sackett and colleagues (*Evidence-Based Medicine: How to Practice and Teach EBM*, 2nd ed, London, 2000, Harcourt Publishers Limited), evidence-based practice is a combination of three elements: the best available evidence, clinical experience, and patient values. Sackett has further reported that "when these three elements are integrated, clinicians and patients form a diagnostic and therapeutic alliance which optimizes clinical outcomes and quality of life." Each element contributes significantly to the clinical reasoning process by helping to identify a diagnosis or prognosis or establish an effective and efficient plan of care. Unfortunately, the evidence-based approach confronts a number of barriers that may limit the clinician's ability to utilize the best available evidence to guide decisions about patient care, most significantly a lack of time and resources. Given the increasing prevalence of new clinical tests in the orthopaedic setting and the frequent omission from textbooks of information about their diagnostic utility, the need was clear for a quick reference guide for students and busy clinicians that would enhance their ability to incorporate evidence into clinical decision making.

The purpose of *Netter's Orthopaedic Clinical Examination: An Evidence Based Approach* is twofold: to serve as a textbook for musculoskeletal evaluation courses in an academic setting and to provide a quick, user-friendly guide and reference for clinicians who want to locate the evidence related to the diagnostic utility of commonly utilized tests and measures.

The first chapter is intended to introduce the reader to the essential concepts underlying evidence-based practice, including the statistical methods it employs and the critical analysis of research articles. The remainder of the book consists of chapters devoted to individual body regions. Each chapter begins with a review of the relevant osteology, arthrology, myology, and neurology and is liberally illustrated with images by the well-known medical artist Frank H. Netter, MD. The second portion of each chapter provides information related to patient complaints and physical examination findings. Reliability and diagnostic utility estimates (sensitivity, specificity, and likelihood ratios) are presented for each patient complaint and physical examination finding and are accompanied by quick access interpretation guides. Test descriptions and definitions of positive test findings are included as reported by the original study authors, both to minimize any alteration of information and to provide readers insight into difference values reported by different studies. At the end of each chapter are tables listing information on commonly used outcome measures and quality ratings for all the studies investigating tests' diagnostic utility.

We hope that clinicians will find *Netter's Orthopaedic Clinical Examination* a user-friendly clinical resource for determining the relevance of findings from the orthopaedic examination. We also hope that students and educators will find this a valuable guide to incorporate into courses related to musculoskeletal evaluation and treatment.

JOSHUA A. CLELAND, PT, PHD

SHANE KOPPENHAVER, PT, PHD

Contents

Contents

The Reliability and Diagnostic Utility of the Orthopaedic Clinical Examination

1

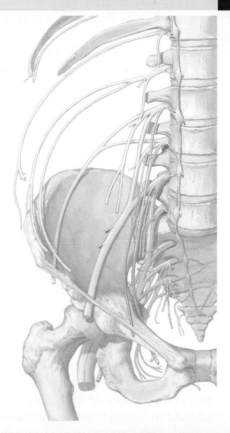

The health sciences and medical professions are undergoing a paradigm shift toward evidence-based practice, defined as the integration of the best available research evidence and clinical expertise with the patient's values.[1,2] Evidence should be incorporated into all aspects of physical therapy patient and client management including examination, evaluation, diagnosis, prognosis, and intervention. Perhaps the most crucial component is a careful, succinct clinical examination that can lead to an accurate diagnosis, the selection of appropriate interventions, and determination of a prognosis. Thus, incorporating evidence on the ability of clinical tests and measures to distinguish between patients who do and do not present with specific musculoskeletal disorders is of utmost importance.[1,2]

The diagnostic process entails obtaining a patient history, developing a working hypothesis, and selecting specific tests and measures to confirm or refute the formulated hypothesis. The clinician must determine the pretest (before the evaluation) probability that the patient has a particular disorder. Based on this information the clinician selects appropriate tests and measures that will help determine the post-test (after the evaluation) probability of the patient having the disorder, until a degree of certainty has been reached such that patient management can begin (the *treatment threshold*). The purpose of clinical tests is not to obtain diagnostic certainty but rather to reduce the level of uncertainty until the treatment threshold is reached.[2] The concepts of pretest and post-test probability and treatment threshold are elaborated later in this chapter.

As the number of reported clinical tests and measures continues to grow, it is essential to thoroughly evaluate a test's diagnostic properties before incorporating it into clinical practice.[3] Integrating the best evidence available for the diagnostic utility of each clinical test is essential in determining an accurate diagnosis and implementing effective, efficient treatment. It seems only sensible that clinicians and students should be aware of the diagnostic properties of tests and measures and know which have clinical utility. This text assists clinicians and students in selecting tests and measures to ensure the appropriate classification of patients and to allow for quick implementation of effective management strategies.

The assessment of diagnostic tests involves examining a number of properties, including reliability and diagnostic accuracy. A test is considered *reliable* if it produces precise and reproducible information. A test is considered to have *diagnostic accuracy* if it has the ability to discriminate between patients with and without a specific disorder.[4] Scientific evaluation of the clinical utility of physical therapy tests and measures involves comparing the examination results to reference standards such as radiographic studies (which represent the closest measure of the truth). Using statistical methods from the field of epidemiology, the diagnostic accuracy of the test—its ability to determine which patients have the disorder and which do not—is then calculated. This chapter focuses on the characteristics that define the reliability and diagnostic accuracy of specific tests and measures. The chapter concludes with a discussion of quality assessment of studies investigating diagnostic utility.

RELIABILITY

For a clinical test to provide information that can be used to guide clinical decision making, it must be reliable. Reliability is the degree of consistency to which an instrument or rater measures a particular attribute.[5] When we investigate the reliability of a measurement, we are determining the proportion of that measurement that is a true representation and the proportion that is the result of measurement error.[6]

When discussing the clinical examination process, it is important to consider two forms of reliability: intra-examiner and inter-examiner reliability. Intra-examiner reliability is the ability of a single rater to obtain the identical measurement during separate performances of the same test.

Inter-examiner reliability is a measure of the ability of two or more raters to obtain identical results with the same test.

The kappa coefficient (κ) is a measure of the proportion of potential agreement after chance is removed[1,5,7]; it is the reliability coefficient most often used for categorical data (positive or negative).[5] The correlation coefficient commonly used to determine the reliability of data that is continuous in nature (e.g., range of motion) is the intraclass correlation coefficient (ICC).[7] Although interpretations of reliability vary, coefficients are often evaluated by the criteria described by Shrout[8] with values less than 0.10 indicating no reliability, values between 0.11 and 0.40 indicating slight reliability, values between 0.61 and 0.80 indicating moderate reliability, and values greater than 0.81 indicating substantial reliability. "Acceptable reliability" must be decided by the clinician using the specific test or measure[9] and should be based on the variable being tested, why a particular test is important, and on whom the test will be used.[6] For example, 5% measurement error may be very acceptable when measuring joint range of motion, but is not nearly as acceptable when measuring pediatric core body temperature.

DIAGNOSTIC ACCURACY

Clinical tests and measures can never absolutely confirm or exclude the presence of a specific disease.[10] However, clinical tests can be used to alter the clinician's estimate of the probability that a patient has a specific musculoskeletal disorder. The accuracy of a test is determined by the measure of agreement between the clinical test and a reference standard.[11,12] A reference standard is the criterion considered the closest representation of the truth of a disorder being present.[1] The results obtained with the reference standard are compared with the results obtained with the test under investigation to determine the percentage of people correctly diagnosed, or diagnostic accuracy.[13] Because the diagnostic utility statistics are completely dependent on both the reference standard used and the population studied, we have specifically listed these within this text to provide information to consider when selecting the tests and measures reported. Diagnostic accuracy is often expressed in terms of positive and negative predictive values (PPVs and NPVs), sensitivity and specificity, and likelihood ratios (LRs).[1,14]

2×2 Contingency Table

To determine the clinical utility of a test or measure, the results of the reference standard are compared with the results of the test under investigation in a 2×2 contingency table, which provides direct comparison between the reference standard and the test under investigation.[15] It allows for the calculation of the values associated with diagnostic accuracy to assist with determining the utility of the clinical test under investigation (Table 1-1).

The 2×2 contingency table is divided into four cells (a, b, c, d) for the determination of the test's ability to correctly identify true positives (cell a) and rule out true negatives (cell d). Cell b represents the false-positive findings wherein the diagnostic test was found to be positive yet the reference standard obtained a negative result. Cell c represents the false-negative findings wherein the diagnostic test was found to be negative yet the reference standard obtained a positive result.

Once a study investigating the diagnostic utility of a clinical test has been completed and the comparison to the reference standard has been performed in the 2×2 contingency table, determination of the clinical utility in terms of overall accuracy, PPVs and NPVs, sensitivity and specificity, and LRs can be calculated. These statistics are useful in determining whether a diagnostic test is useful for either ruling in or ruling out a disorder.

Table 1-1 2×2 Contingency Table Used to Compare the Results of the Reference Standard to Those of the Test Under Investigation

	Reference Standard Positive	Reference Standard Negative
Clinical Test Positive	True-positive results a	False-positive results b
Clinical Test Negative	False-negative results c	True-negative results d

Overall Accuracy

The overall accuracy of a diagnostic test is determined by dividing the correct responses (true positives and true negatives) by the total number of patients.[16] Using the 2×2 contingency table, the overall accuracy is determined by the following equation:

$$\text{Overall accuracy} = 100\% \times (a + d)/(a + b + c + d)$$

A perfect test would exhibit an overall accuracy of 100%. This is most likely unobtainable in that no clinical test is perfect, and each will always exhibit at least a small degree of uncertainty. The accuracy of a diagnostic test should not be used to determine the clinical utility of the test because the overall accuracy can be a bit misleading. The accuracy of a test can be significantly influenced by the prevalence, or total instances of a disease in the population at a given time.[5,6]

Positive and Negative Predictive Values

Positive predictive values estimate the likelihood that a patient with a positive test actually has the disease.[5,6,17] PPVs are calculated horizontally in the 2×2 contingency table (Table 1-2) and indicate the percentage of patients accurately identified as having the disorder (true positive) divided by all the positive results of the test under investigation. A high PPV indicates that a positive result is a strong predictor that the patient has the disorder.[5,6] The formula for the PPV is:

$$\text{PPV} = 100\% \times a/(a + b)$$

NPVs estimate the likelihood that a patient with a negative test does not have the disorder.[5,6] NPVs are also calculated horizontally in the 2×2 contingency table (see Table 1-2) and indicate the percentage of patients accurately identified as not having the disorder (true negative) divided by all the negative results of the test under investigation.[11] The formula for the NPV is as follows:

$$\text{NPV} = 100\% \times d/(c + d)$$

Table 1-2 2×2 Contingency Showing the Calculation of Positive and Negative Predictive Values Horizontally and Sensitivity and Specificity Vertically

	Reference Standard Positive	Reference Standard Negative	
Clinical Test Positive	True positives a	False positives b	PPV = a/(a + b)
Clinical Test Negative	c False negatives	d True negatives	NPV = d/(c + d)
	Sensitivity = a/(a + c)	Specificity = d/(b + d)	

The predictive values are significantly influenced by the prevalence of the condition.[11] Hence, we have not specifically reported these in this text.

Sensitivity

The sensitivity of a diagnostic test indicates the test's ability to detect those patients who actually have the disorder as indicated by the reference standard. This is also referred to as the *true-positive rate*.[1] Tests with high sensitivity are good for ruling out a particular disorder. The acronym *SnNout* can be used to remember that a test with high *Sensitivity* and a *Negative* result is good for ruling *out* the disorder.[1]

Consider, for example, a clinical test that, compared with the reference standard, exhibits a high sensitivity for detecting lumbar spinal stenosis. Considering the rule above, if the test is negative it reliably rules out lumbar spinal stenosis. If the test is positive, it is likely to accurately identify a high percentage of patients presenting with stenosis. However, it also may identify as positive many of those without the disorder (false positives). Thus, although a negative result can be relied on, a positive test result does not allow us to draw any conclusions (Figs. 1-1 and 1-2).

The sensitivity of a test also can be calculated from the 2×2 contingency tables. However, it is calculated vertically (see Table 1-2). The formula for calculating a test's sensitivity is as follows:

$$\text{Sensitivity} = 100\% \times a/(a + c)$$

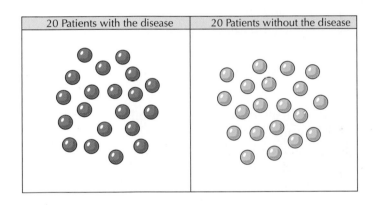

Figure 1-1 Sensitivity and specificity example. Twenty patients with and 20 patients without the disorder.

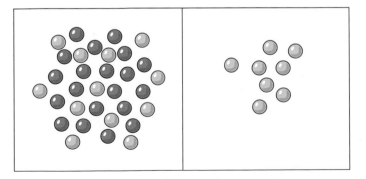

Figure 1-2 100% Sensitivity. One hundred percent sensitivity, inferring that if the test is positive, all those with the disease will be captured. However, although this test captured all those with the disease, it also captured many without. Yet if the test result is negative, we are confident that the disorder can be ruled out (SnNout).

The specificity of a diagnostic test simply indicates the test's ability to detect those patients who actually do not have the disorder as indicated by the reference standard. This is also referred to as the *true-negative rate*.[1] Tests with high specificity are good for ruling in a disorder. The acronym *SpPin* can be used to remember that a test with high *Sp*ecificity and a *P*ositive result is good for ruling *in* the disorder.[16,18,19]

Consider a test with high specificity. It would demonstrate a strong ability to accurately identify all patients who do not have the disorder. If a highly specific clinical test is negative, it is likely to identify a high percentage of those patients who do not have the disorder. However, it is also possible that the highly specific test with a negative result will identify a number of patients who actually have the disease as being negative (false negative). Therefore, we can be fairly confident that a highly specific test with a positive finding indicates that the disorder is present (Fig. 1-3).

The formula for calculating test specificity is as follows:

$$\text{Specificity} = 100\% \times d/(b + d)$$

Sensitivity and specificity have been used for decades to determine a test's diagnostic utility; however, they possess a few clinical limitations.[11] Although sensitivity and specificity can be useful to assist clinicians in selecting tests that are good for ruling in or out a particular disorder, few clinical tests demonstrate both high sensitivity and high specificity.[11] Also the sensitivity and specificity do not provide information regarding a change in the probability of a patient having a disorder if the test results are positive or negative.[18,20] Instead, LRs have been advocated as the optimal statistics for determining a shift in pretest probability that a patient has a specific disorder.

Likelihood Ratios

A test's result is valuable only if it alters the pretest probability of a patient having a disorder.[21] LRs combine a test's sensitivity and specificity to develop an indication in the shift of probability given the specific test result and are valuable in guiding clinical decision making.[20] LRs are a powerful measure that can significantly increase or reduce the probability of a patient having a disease.[22]

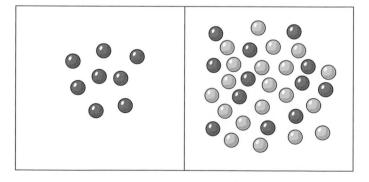

Figure 1-3 100% Specificity. One hundred percent specificity, inferring that if the test is negative all those without the disease will be captured. However, although this test captured all those without the disease, it also captured many with. Yet if the test is positive, we are confident that the patient has the disorder (SpPin).

LRs can be either positive or negative. A positive LR indicates a shift in probability favoring the existence of a disorder, whereas a negative LR indicates a shift in probability favoring the absence of a disorder. Although LRs are often not reported in studies investigating the diagnostic utility of the clinical examination, they can be calculated easily if a test's sensitivity and specificity are available. Throughout this text, for studies that did not report LRs but did document a test's sensitivity and specificity, the LRs were calculated by the authors.

The formula used to determine a positive LR is as follows:

$$LR = \text{Sensitivity}/(1 - \text{Specificity})$$

The formula used to determine a negative LR is as follows:

$$LR = (1 - \text{Sensitivity})/\text{Specificity}$$

A guide to interpreting test results can be found in Table 1-3. Positive LRs > 1 increase the odds of the disorder given a positive test, and negative LRs < 1 decrease the odds of the disorder given a negative test.[22] However, it is the magnitude of the shifts in probability that determines the usefulness of a clinical test. Positive LRs > 10 and negative LRs close to zero often represent large and conclusive shifts in probability. An LR of 1 (either positive or negative) does not alter the probability that the patient does or does not have the particular disorder and is of little clinical value.[22] Once the LRs have been calculated, they can be applied to the nomogram (Fig. 1-4),[23] or a mathematical equation[24] can be used to determine more precisely the shifts in probability given a specific test result. Both methods are described in further detail later in the chapter.

If a diagnostic test exhibits a specificity of 1, the positive LR cannot be calculated because the equation will result in a zero for the denominator. In these circumstances it has been suggested to modify the 2×2 contingency table by adding 0.5 to each cell in the table to allow for the calculation of LRs.[25]

Consider, for example, the diagnostic utility of the Crank test[5,26] in detecting labral tears compared with arthroscopic examination, the reference standard. This is revealed in a 2×2 contingency table (Table 1-4). The inability to calculate a positive LR becomes obvious in the following:

$$\text{Positive LR} = \text{Sensitivity}/(1 - \text{Specificity}) = 1/(1 - 1) = 1/0.$$

Because zero cannot be the denominator in a fraction, the 2×2 contingency table is modified by adding 0.5 to each cell.

Although the addition of 0.5 to each cell is the only reported method of modifying the contingency table to prevent zero in the denominator of an LR calculation, considering the changes that occur with the diagnostic properties of sensitivity, specificity, and predictive values, this technique has not been used in this text. In circumstances in which the specificity is zero and the positive LR cannot be calculated, it is documented as "undefined" (UD). In these cases, although we are not calculating the positive LR, the test is indicative of a large shift in probability.

Table 1-3 Interpretation of Likelihood Ratios

Positive Likelihood Ratio	Negative Likelihood Ratio	Interpretation
>10	<0.1	Generate large and often conclusive shifts in probability
5 to 10	0.1 to 0.2	Generate moderate shifts in probability
2 to 5	0.2 to 0.5	Generate small but sometimes important shifts in probability
1 to 2	0.5 to 1.0	Alter probability to a small and rarely important degree

Adapted from Jaeschke R, Guyatt GH, Sackett DL III. How to use an article about a diagnostic test. B. What are the results and will they help me in caring for my patients? *JAMA*. 1994;271:703-707.

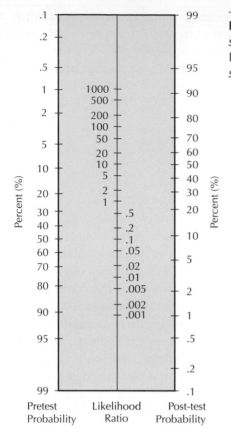

Figure 1-4 Fagan's nomogram. *(Adapted with permission from Fagan TJ. Nomogram for Baye's theorem. N Engl J Med. 1975;293:257. Copyright 2005, Massachusetts Medical Society. All rights reserved.)*

Table 1-4 Results of the Crank Test in Detecting Labral Tears When Compared with the Reference Standard of Arthroscopic Examination

	Arthroscopic Examination Positive (n = 12)	Arthroscopic Examination Negative (n = 3)	
Crank Test Positive	10 a	0 b	PPV = 100 × 10/10 = 100%
Crank Test Negative	c 2	d 3	NPV = 100 × 3/5 = 60%
	Sensitivity = 100% × 10/12 = 83%	Specificity = 100% × 3/3 = 100%	

CONFIDENCE INTERVALS

Calculations of sensitivity, specificity, and LRs are known as *point estimates*. That is, they are the single best estimates of the population values.[5] However, because point estimates are based on small subsets of people (samples), it is unlikely that they are a perfect representation of the larger population. It is more accurate, therefore, to include a range of values (interval estimate) in which the population value is likely to fall. A confidence interval (CI) is a range of scores around the point estimate that likely contains the population value.[27] Commonly, the 95% CI is calculated for studies investigating the diagnostic utility of the clinical examination. A 95% CI indicates the spread of scores that we can be 95% confident in to contain the population value.[5] In this text, 95% CI is reported for all studies that provided this information.

PRETEST AND POST-TEST PROBABILITY

Pretest probability is the likelihood that a patient exhibits a specific disorder before the clinical examination. Often prevalence rates are used as an indication of pretest probability, but when prevalence rates are unknown, the pretest probability is based on a combination of the patient's medical history, results of previous tests, and the clinician's experience.[16] Determining the pretest probability is the first step in the decision-making process for clinicians. Pretest probability is an estimate by the clinician and can be expressed as a percentage (e.g., 75%, 80%) or as a qualitative measure (e.g., somewhat likely, very likely).[11,16] Once the pretest probability of a patient having a particular disorder is identified, tests and measures that have the potential to alter the probability should be selected for the physical examination. Post-test probability is the likelihood that a patient has a specific disorder after the clinical examination procedures have been performed.

CALCULATING POST-TEST PROBABILITY

As previously mentioned, LRs can assist with determining the shifts in probability that would occur following a given test result and depend on the respective LR ratios of that given test. The quickest method of determining the shifts in probability once an LR is known for a specific test can be determined using the nomogram (Fig. 1-5).[23] The nomogram is a diagram that illustrates the pretest probability on the right and the post-test probability on the left, and the LRs are in the middle. To determine the shift in probability, a mark is placed on the nomogram representing the pretest probability. Then a mark is made on the nomogram at the level of the LR (either negative

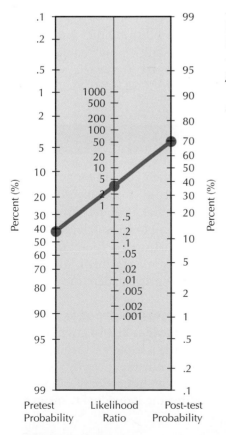

Figure 1-5 Nomogram representing the change in pretest probability from 42% if the test was positive (positive likelihood ratio = 4.2) to a post-test probability of 71%. *(Adapted with permission from Fagan TJ. Nomogram for Baye's theorem. N Engl J Med. 1975;293:257. Copyright 2005, Massachusetts Medical Society. All rights reserved.)*

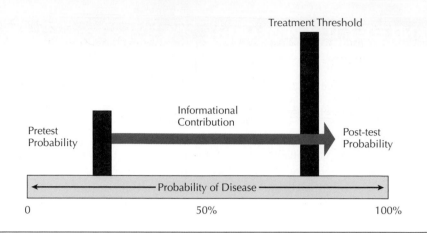

Figure 1-6 Treatment threshold. Clinicians must use the pretest probability and likelihood ratios to determine the treatment threshold as indicated in this illustration.

or positive). The two lines are connected with a straight line and the line is carried through the left of the diagram. The point at which the line crosses the post-test probability scale indicates the shift in probability.

A more precise determination of the shift in probability can be calculated algebraically with the following formula[16]:

$$\text{Step 1. Pretest odds} = \text{Pretest probability}/1 - \text{Pretest probability}$$

$$\text{Step 2. Pretest odds} \times \text{LR} = \text{Post-test odds}$$

$$\text{Step 3. Post-test odds}/\text{Post-test odds} + 1 = \text{Post-test probability}$$

The clinician must make a determination of when the post-test probability is either low enough to rule out the presence of a certain disease or when the post-test probability is high enough that the clinician feels confident in having established the presence of a disorder. The level at which evaluation ceases and treatment begins is known as the *treatment threshold* (Fig. 1-6).[16]

ASSESSMENT OF STUDY QUALITY

Once relevant articles are retrieved, the next step is critical analysis of their content for adequate methodological rigor. It has been reported that the methodologic quality of studies investigating the diagnostic utility of the clinical examination is generally inferior to that of studies investigating the effectiveness of therapies.[28,29] Unfortunately, studies with significant methodologic flaws reporting the usefulness of specific tests and measures can lead to premature incorporation of ineffective tests. This can result in inaccurate diagnoses and poor patient management. Alternatively, identification and use of rigorously appraised clinical tests can improve patient care and outcomes.[29]

The Quality Assessment of Diagnostic Accuracy Studies (QUADAS) was developed to assess the quality of diagnostic accuracy studies.[30] A four-round Delphi panel identified 14 criteria that are used to assess a study's methodologic quality (see tables at the end of Chapters 2 through 11). Each item is scored as "yes," "no," or "unclear." The QUADAS is not intended to quantify a score for each study but rather provides a qualitative assessment of the study with the identification of weaknesses.[30] The QUADAS has demonstrated adequate agreement for the individual items in the checklist.[31] We have used the QUADAS to evaluate each study referenced in this text and have included details of the quality assessments in the appendix of each chapter. Studies deemed to be of poor methodologic quality (represented by a red symbol) have not been included in the diagnostic utility tables throughout the chapters. Green symbols indicate a high level of methodologic quality and imply that readers can be confident in study results. Yellow symbols indicate fair methodologic quality and imply that readers should interpret such study results with caution.

SUMMARY

It is important to consider the reliability and diagnostic utility of tests and measures before including them as components of the clinical examination. Tests and measures should demonstrate adequate reliability before they are used to guide clinical decision making. Throughout this text, the reliability of many tests and measures are reported. It is essential that clinicians consider these reported levels of reliability in the context of their own practice.

Before implementing tests and measures into the orthopaedic examination, it is first essential to consider each test's diagnostic utility. Table 1-5 summarizes the statistics related to diagnostic accuracy as well as the mathematical equations and operational definitions for each. The useful-

Table 1-5 2×2 Contingency Table and Statistics Used to Determine the Diagnostic Utility of a Test or Measure

	Reference Standard Positive	Reference Standard Negative
Diagnostic Test Positive	**True-positive results** a	False-positive results b
Diagnostic Test Negative	c False-negative results	d **True-negative results**

Statistic	Formula	Description
Overall accuracy	$(a + d)/(a + b + c + d)$	The percentage of individuals who are correctly diagnosed
Sensitivity	$a/(a + c)$	The proportion of patients with the condition who have a positive test result
Specificity	$d/(b + d)$	The proportion of patients without the condition who have a negative test result
Positive predictive value	$a/(a + b)$	The proportion of individuals with a positive test result who have the condition
Negative predictive value	$d/(c + d)$	The proportion of individuals with a negative test result who do not have the condition
Positive likelihood ratio	Sensitivity/(1 − Specificity)	If the test is positive, the increase in odds favoring the condition
Negative likelihood ratio	(1 − Sensitivity)/Specificity	If the test is positive, the decrease in odds favoring the condition

ness of a test or measure is most commonly considered in terms of the respective test's diagnostic properties. These can be described in terms of sensitivity, specificity, PPVs, and NPVs. However, perhaps the most useful diagnostic property is the LR, which can assist in altering the probability that a patient has a specific disorder.

No clinical test or measure provides absolute certainty as to the presence or absence of disease. However, clinicians can determine when enough data have been collected to alter the probability beyond the treatment threshold where the evaluation can cease and therapeutic management can begin. Furthermore, careful methodologic assessment provides greater insight into the scientific rigor of each study and its performance, applicability, reliability, and reproducibility within a given clinical practice.

REFERENCES

1. Sackett DL, Straws SE, Richardson WS, et al. *Evidence-Based Medicine: How to Practice and Teach EBM.* 2nd ed. London: Harcourt Publishers Limited; 2000.
2. Kassirer JP. Our stubborn quest for diagnostic certainty a cause of excessive testing. *N Engl J Med.* 1989;320:1489-1491.
3. Lijmer JG, Mol BW, Heisterkamp S, et al. Empirical evidence of design-related bias in studies of diagnostic tests. *JAMA.* 1999;282:1061-1066.
4. Schwartz JS. Evaluating diagnostic tests: What is done–what needs to be done. *J G Intern Med.* 1986;1:266-267.
5. Portney LG, Watkins MP. *Foundations of Clinical Research: Applications to Practice.* 2nd ed. Upper Saddle River, NJ: Prentice Hall Health; 2000.
6. Rothstein JM, Echternach JL. *Primer on Measurement: An Introductory Guide to Measurement Issues.* Alexandria, VA: American Physical Therapy Association; 1999.
7. Domholdt E. *Physical Therapy Research.* 2nd ed. Philadelphia: WB Saunders; 2000.
8. Shrout PE. Measurement reliability and agreement in psychiatry. *Stat Methods Med Res.* 1998;7:301-317.
9. Van Genderen F, De Bie R, Helders P, Van Meeteren N. Reliability research: towards a more clinically relevant approach. *Physical Therapy Reviews.* 2003;8:169-176.
10. Bossuyt PMM, Reitsma JB, Bruns DE, et al. Towards complete and accurate reporting of studies of diagnostic accuracy: the STARD initiative. *Clin Chem.* 2003;49:1-6.
11. Fritz JM, Wainner RS. Examining diagnostic tests: an evidence-based perspective. *Phys Ther.* 2001;81:1546-1564.
12. Jaeschke R, Guyatt GH, Sackett DL III. How to use an article about a diagnostic test A. Are the results of the study valid? *JAMA.* 1994;271:389-391.
13. Bossuyt PMM, Reitsma JB, Bruns DE, et al. The STARD statement for reporting studies of diagnostic accuracy: explanation and elaboration. *Clin Chem.* 2003;49:7-18.
14. McGinn T, Guyatt G, Wyer P, et al. Users' guides to the medical literature XXII: how to use articles about clinical decision rules. *JAMA.* 2000;284:79-84.
15. Greenhalgh T. Papers that report diagnostic or screening tests. *BMJ.* 1997;315:540-543.
16. Bernstein J. Decision analysis (current concepts review). *J Bone Joint Surg.* 1997;79:1404-1414.
17. Potter NA, Rothstein JM. Intertester reliability for selected clinical tests of the sacroiliac joint. *Phys Ther.* 1985;65:1671-1675.
18. Boyko EJ. Ruling out or ruling in disease with the most sensitive or specific diagnostic test: short cut or wrong turn? *Med Decis Making.* 1994;14:175-180.
19. Riddle DL, Stratford PW. Interpreting validity indexes for diagnostic tests: an illustration using the Berg balance test. *Phys Ther.* 1999;79:939-948.
20. Hayden SR, Brown MD. Liklihood ratio: a powerful tool for incorporating the results of a diagnostic test into clinical decision making. *Ann Emerg Med.* 1999;33:575-580.
21. Simel DL, Samsa GP, Matchar DB. Liklihood ratios with confidence: sample size estimation for diagnostic test studies. *J Clin Epidem.* 1991;44:763-770.
22. Jaeschke R, Guyatt GH, Sackett DL III. How to use an article about a diagnostic test. B. What are the results and will they help me in caring for my patients? *JAMA.* 1994;271:703-707.
23. Fagan TJ. Nomogram for Bayes's theorem. *N Engl J Med.* 1975;293:257.
24. Sackett DL, Haynes RB, Guyatt GH, Tugwell P. *Clinical Epidemiology: A Basic Science for Clinical Medicine.* Boston: Little, Brown; 1991.
25. Wainner RS, Fritz JM, Irrgang JJ, et al. Reliability and diagnostic accuracy of the clinical examination and patient self-report measures for cervical radiculopathy. *Spine.* 2003;28:52-62.
26. Mimori K, Muneta T, Nakagawa T, Shinomiya K. A new pain provocation test for superior labral tears of the shoulder. *Am J Sports Med.* 1999;27:137-142.
27. Fidler F, Thomason N, Cumming G, et al. Editors can lead researchers to confidence intervals, but can't make them think. *Psychol Sci.* 2004;15:119-126.
28. Moons KGM, Biesheuvel CJ, Grobbee DE. Test research versus diagnostic research. *Clin Chem.* 2004;50:473-476.

29. Reid MC, Lachs MS, Feinstein AR. Use of methodological standards in diagnostic test research. *JAMA*. 1995;274:645-651.

30. Whiting P, Harbord R, Kleijnen J. No role for quality scores in systematic reviews of diagnostic accuracy studies. *BMC Med Res Methodol*. 2005;5:19.

31. Whiting PF, Weswood ME, Rutjes AW, et al. Evaluation of QUADAS, a tool for the quality assessment of diagnostic accuracy studies. *BMC Med Res Methodol*. 2006;6:9.

Temporomandibular Joint

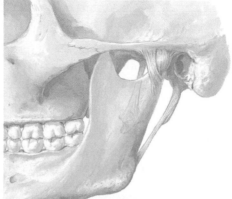

CLINICAL SUMMARY AND RECOMMENDATIONS

Patient History

Questions	• Self-report of temporomandibular joint (TMJ) pain has been shown to be very good at identifying temporomandibular dysfunction (TMD) as defined by a comprehensive clinical examination (+LR of 9.8).
	• A subject complaint of "periodic restriction" (the inability to open the mouth as wide as was previously possible) has been found to be the best single history item to identify anterior disc displacement, both in patients with reducing and nonreducing discs.

Physical Examination

Palpation	• Reproducing pain during palpation of the TMJ and related muscles has been found to be moderately reliable and appears to demonstrate good diagnostic utility for identifying TMJ effusion by magnetic resonance imaging (MRI) and TMD when compared with a comprehensive physical examination. We recommend that palpation at least include the TMJ (+LR = 4.87 to 5.67), the temporalis muscle (+LR = 2.73 to 4.12), and the masseter muscle (+LR = 3.65 to 4.87).
	• If clinically feasible, pressure pain threshold testing demonstrates superior diagnostic utility in identifying TMD when compared with a comprehensive physical examination.
Joint Sounds	• Detecting joint sounds (clicking and crepitus) during jaw motion is generally unreliable and demonstrates poor diagnostic utility except in the detection of moderate to severe osteoarthritis (+LR = 4.79) and nonreducing anterior disc displacement (+LR = 7.1 to 15.2).
Range of Motion and Dynamic Movement	• Measuring mouth range of motion appears to be highly reliable and, when restricted or deviated from midline, exhibits moderate diagnostic utility in identifying nonreducing anterior disc displacement.
	• Detecting pain during motion is less reliable, but also demonstrates moderate to good diagnostic utility in identifying nonreducing anterior disc displacement and self-reported TMJ pain.
	• The combination of *motion restriction* and *pain during assisted opening* has been found to be the best combination to identify nonreducing anterior disc displacement (+LR = 7.71).
	• Consistent with assessment of other body regions, assessment of "joint play" and "end-feel" are highly unreliable and have unknown diagnostic utility.
Interventions	• Patients with TMD who report *symptoms* ≥ 4/10 pain for ≤ 10 months' duration may benefit from nightly wear of an occlusal stabilization splint, especially if they have *nonreducing anterior disc displacement* and show *improvement after 2 months* (+LR = 10.8 if all four factors present).

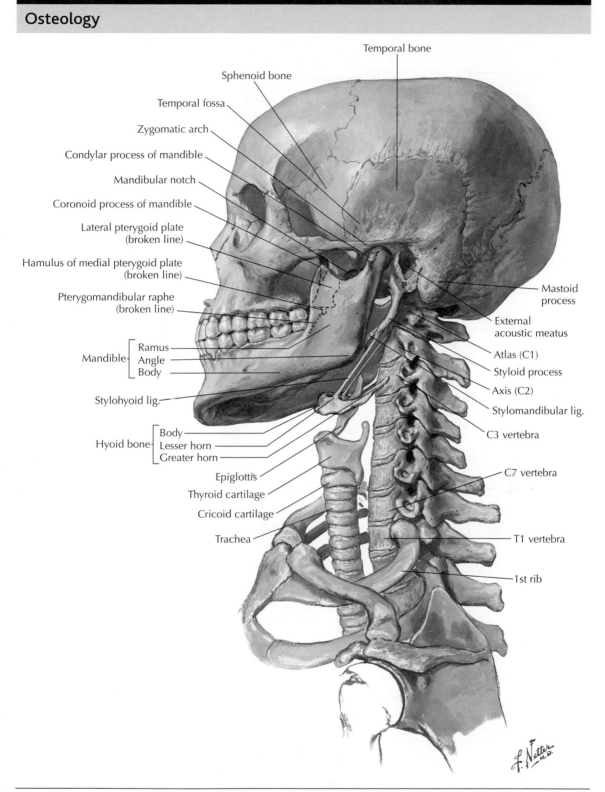

Figure 2-1

Bony framework of head and neck.

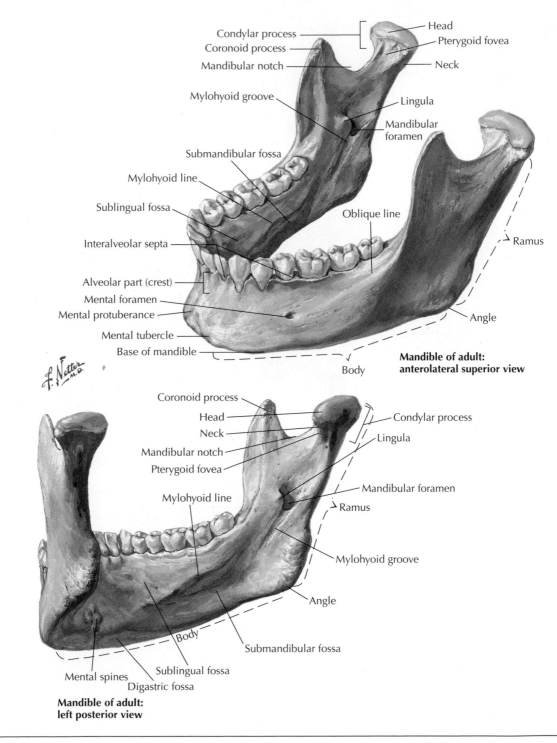

Condylar process
Coronoid process
Mandibular notch
Mylohyoid groove
Submandibular fossa
Mylohyoid line
Sublingual fossa
Interalveolar septa
Alveolar part (crest)
Mental foramen
Mental protuberance
Mental tubercle
Base of mandible

Head
Pterygoid fovea
Neck
Lingula
Mandibular foramen
Oblique line
Ramus
Angle
Body

**Mandible of adult:
anterolateral superior view**

Coronoid process
Head
Neck
Mandibular notch
Pterygoid fovea
Mylohyoid line
Condylar process
Lingula
Mandibular foramen
Ramus
Mylohyoid groove
Angle
Body
Submandibular fossa
Mental spines
Sublingual fossa
Digastric fossa

**Mandible of adult:
left posterior view**

Figure 2-2

Mandible.

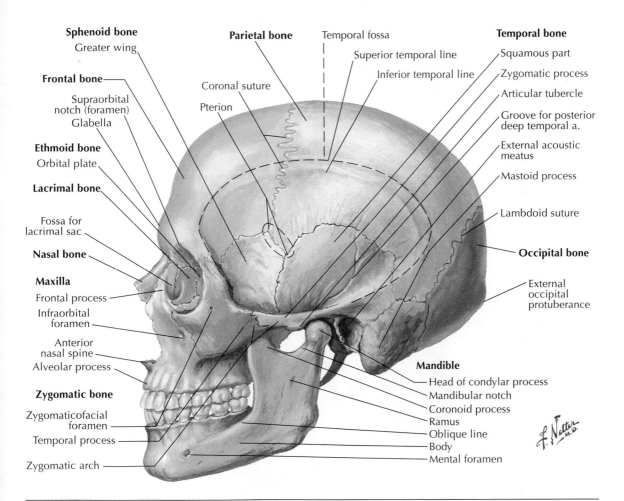

Sphenoid bone
Greater wing

Frontal bone
Supraorbital notch (foramen)
Glabella

Ethmoid bone
Orbital plate

Lacrimal bone

Fossa for lacrimal sac

Nasal bone

Maxilla
Frontal process
Infraorbital foramen
Anterior nasal spine
Alveolar process

Zygomatic bone
Zygomaticofacial foramen
Temporal process
Zygomatic arch

Parietal bone
Coronal suture
Pterion

Temporal fossa
Superior temporal line
Inferior temporal line

Temporal bone
Squamous part
Zygomatic process
Articular tubercle
Groove for posterior deep temporal a.
External acoustic meatus
Mastoid process
Lambdoid suture

Occipital bone

External occipital protuberance

Mandible
Head of condylar process
Mandibular notch
Coronoid process
Ramus
Oblique line
Body
Mental foramen

Figure 2-3
Lateral skull.

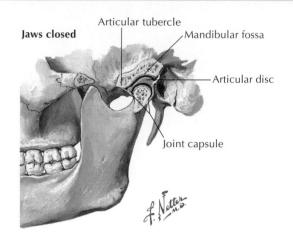

Figure 2-4

Temporomandibular joint.

The temporomandibular joint (TMJ) is divided by an intra-articular biconcave disc that separates the joint cavity into two distinct functional components. The upper joint is a plane-gliding joint that permits translation of the mandibular condyles. The lower joint is a hinge joint that permits rotation of the condyles. The closed pack position of the TMJ is full occlusion. A unilateral restriction pattern primarily limits contralateral excursion, but also affects mouth opening and protrusion.

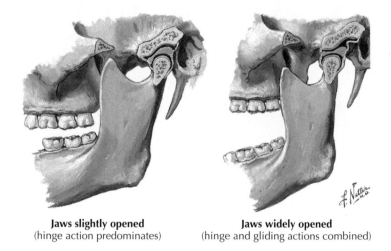

Figure 2-5

Temporomandibular joint mechanics.

During mandibular depression from a closed mouth position, the initial movement occurs at the lower joint as the condyles pivot on the intra-articular disc. This motion continues to approximately 11 mm of depression. With further mandibular depression, motion begins to occur at the upper joint and causes anterior translation of the disc on the articular eminence. Normal mandibular depression is between 40 and 50 mm.

Ligaments

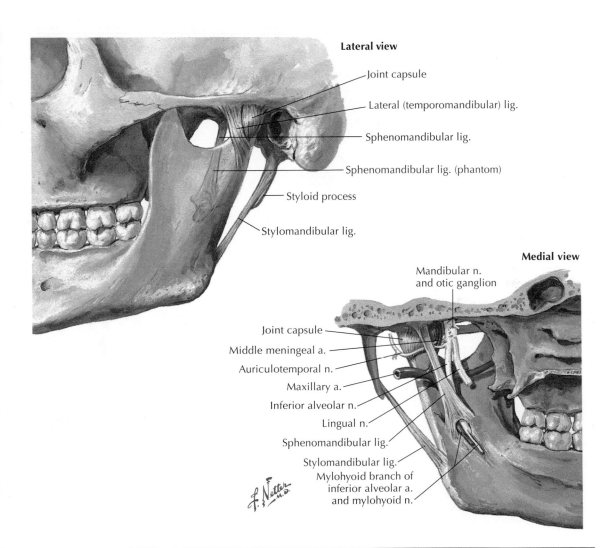

Lateral view

- Joint capsule
- Lateral (temporomandibular) lig.
- Sphenomandibular lig.
- Sphenomandibular lig. (phantom)
- Styloid process
- Stylomandibular lig.

Medial view

- Mandibular n. and otic ganglion
- Joint capsule
- Middle meningeal a.
- Auriculotemporal n.
- Maxillary a.
- Inferior alveolar n.
- Lingual n.
- Sphenomandibular lig.
- Stylomandibular lig.
- Mylohyoid branch of inferior alveolar a. and mylohyoid n.

Figure 2-6

Temporomandibular joint ligaments.

Ligaments	Attachments	Function
Temporomandibular	Thickening of anterior joint capsule extending from neck of mandible to zygomatic arch	Strengthen the TMJ laterally
Sphenomandibular	Sphenoid bone to mandible	Serve as a fulcrum and reinforcement to TMJ motion
Stylomandibular	Styloid process to angle of the mandible	Provide minimal support to the joint

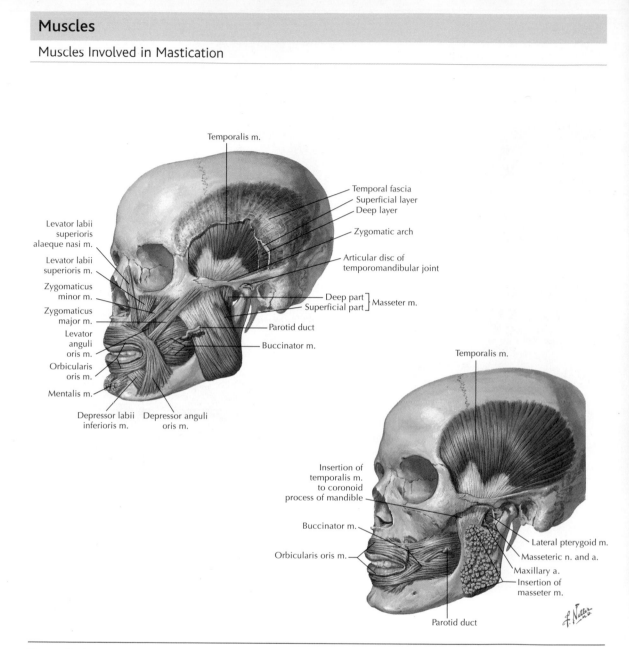

Figure 2-7

Muscles involved in mastication, lateral views.

Muscle	Proximal Attachment	Distal Attachment	Nerve and Segmental Level	Action
Temporalis	Temporal fossa	Coronoid process and anterior ramus of mandible	Deep temporal branches of mandibular nerve	Elevate mandible
Masseter	Inferior and medial aspects of zygomatic arch	Coronoid process and lateral ramus of mandible	Mandibular nerve via masseteric nerve	Elevate and protrude mandible

Muscles

Muscles Involved in Mastication (continued)

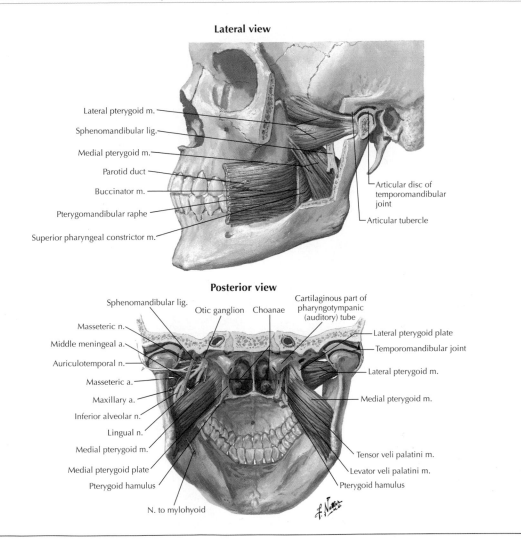

Lateral view

Lateral pterygoid m.
Sphenomandibular lig.
Medial pterygoid m.
Parotid duct
Buccinator m.
Pterygomandibular raphe
Superior pharyngeal constrictor m.

Articular disc of temporomandibular joint
Articular tubercle

Posterior view

Sphenomandibular lig.
Otic ganglion   Choanae
Cartilaginous part of pharyngotympanic (auditory) tube
Masseteric n.
Middle meningeal a.
Auriculotemporal n.
Masseteric a.
Maxillary a.
Inferior alveolar n.
Lingual n.
Medial pterygoid m.
Medial pterygoid plate
Pterygoid hamulus
N. to mylohyoid

Lateral pterygoid plate
Temporomandibular joint
Lateral pterygoid m.
Medial pterygoid m.
Tensor veli palatini m.
Levator veli palatini m.
Pterygoid hamulus

Figure 2-8

Muscles involved in mastication, lateral and posterior views.

Muscle	Proximal Attachment	Distal Attachment	Nerve and Segmental Level	Action
Medial pterygoid	Medial surface of lateral pterygoid plate, pyramidal process of palatine bone, and tuberosity of maxilla	Medial aspect of mandibular ramus	Mandibular nerve via medial pterygoid nerve	Elevate and protrude mandible
Lateral Pterygoid				
Superior head	Lateral surface of greater wing of sphenoid bone	Neck of mandible, articular disc, and TMJ capsule	Mandibular nerve via lateral pterygoid nerve	Acting bilaterally: protrude and depress mandible
Inferior head	Lateral surface of lateral pterygoid plate			Acting unilaterally: laterally deviate mandible

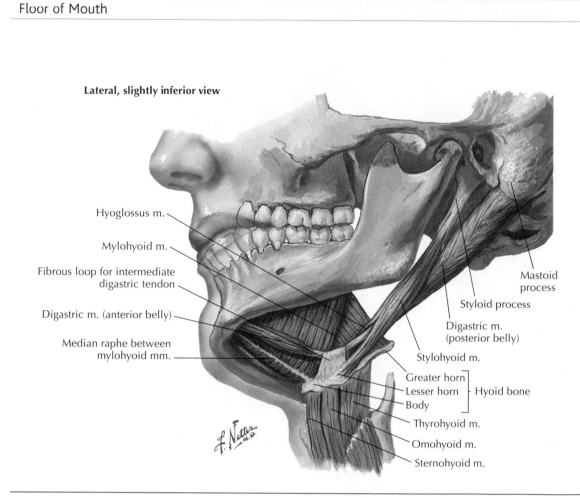

Lateral, slightly inferior view

Hyoglossus m.

Mylohyoid m.

Fibrous loop for intermediate digastric tendon

Digastric m. (anterior belly)

Median raphe between mylohyoid mm.

Mastoid process

Styloid process

Digastric m. (posterior belly)

Stylohyoid m.

Greater horn
Lesser horn — Hyoid bone
Body

Thyrohyoid m.

Omohyoid m.

Sternohyoid m.

Figure 2-9

Floor of mouth, inferior view.

Muscle	Proximal Attachment	Distal Attachment	Nerve and Segmental Level	Action
Mylohyoid	Mylohyoid line of mandible	Hyoid bone	Mylohyoid nerve (branch of cranial nerve [CN] V₃)	Elevates hyoid bone
Stylohyoid	Styloid process of temporal bone	Hyoid bone	Cervical branch of facial nerve	Elevates and retracts hyoid bone
Geniohyoid	Inferior mental spine of mandible	Hyoid bone	C1 via the hypoglossal nerve	Elevates hyoid bone anterosuperiorly
Digastric				
Anterior belly	Digastric fossa of mandible	Intermediate tendon to hyoid bone	Mylohyoid nerve	Depresses mandible; raises and stabilizes hyoid bone
Posterior belly	Mastoid notch of temporal bone		Facial nerve	

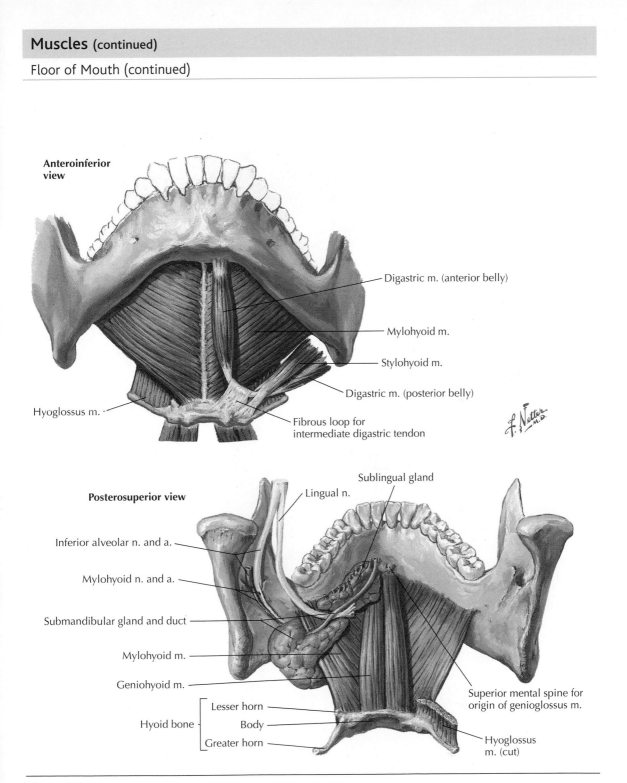

Anteroinferior view

Digastric m. (anterior belly)

Mylohyoid m.

Stylohyoid m.

Digastric m. (posterior belly)

Fibrous loop for intermediate digastric tendon

Hyoglossus m.

Posterosuperior view

Lingual n.

Sublingual gland

Inferior alveolar n. and a.

Mylohyoid n. and a.

Submandibular gland and duct

Mylohyoid m.

Geniohyoid m.

Hyoid bone — Lesser horn, Body, Greater horn

Superior mental spine for origin of genioglossus m.

Hyoglossus m. (cut)

Figure 2-10

Floor of mouth, anteroinferior and posterosuperior views.

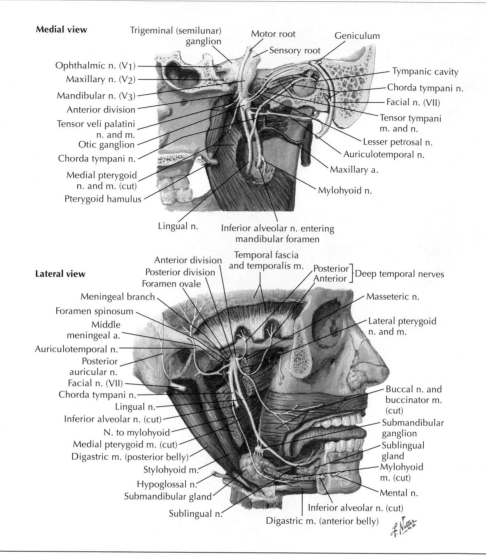

Figure 2-11

Mandibular nerve, medial and lateral views.

Nerves	Segmental Levels	Sensory	Motor
Mandibular	CN V$_3$	Skin of inferior third of face	Temporalis, masseter, lateral pterygoid, medial pterygoid, digastric, mylohyoid
Nerve to mylohyoid	CN V$_3$	No sensory	Mylohyoid
Buccal	CN V$_3$	Cheek lining and gingiva	No motor
Lingual	CN V$_3$	Anterior tongue and floor of mouth	No motor
Maxillary	CN V$_2$	Skin of middle third of face	No motor
Ophthalmic	CN V$_1$	Skin of superior third of face	No motor
CN V, trigeminal nerve.			

Initial Hypotheses Based on Patient History

Patient Reports	Initial Hypothesis
Patient reports jaw crepitus and pain during mouth opening and closing. Might also report limited opening with translation of the jaw to the affected side at the end range of opening	Possible osteoarthrosis Possible capsulitis Possible internal derangement consisting of an anterior disc displacement that does not reduce[1-3]
Patient reports jaw clicking and pain during opening and closing of the mouth	Possible internal derangement consisting of anterior disc displacement with reduction[1,4,5]
Patient reports of limited motion to about 20 mm with no joint noise	Possible capsulitis Possible internal derangement consisting of an anterior disc displacement that does not reduce[1]

The Association of Oral Habits with Temporomandibular Disorders

Figure 2-12
Frequent leaning of head on the palm.

Gavish and colleagues[6] investigated the association with oral habits and signs and symptoms of temporomandibular disorders in 248 randomly selected female high school students. Although sensitivity and specificity were not reported, the results demonstrated that chewing gum, jaw play (nonfunctional jaw movements), chewing ice, and frequent leaning of the head on the palm were associated with the presence on TMJ disorders.

ICC or κ	Interpretation
.81-1.0	Substantial agreement
.61-.80	Moderate agreement
.41-.60	Fair agreement
.11-.40	Slight agreement
.0-.10	No agreement

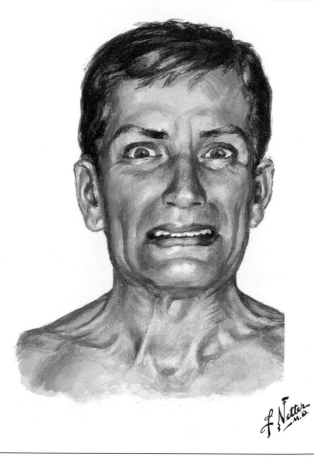

Figure 2-13

Temporomandibular joint pain.

Historical Finding and Study	Description and Positive Findings	Population	Test-Retest Reliability
Visual analog scale[7]	100-mm line with ends defined as "no pain" and "worst pain imaginable"		κ = **.38**
Numerical scale[7]	An 11-point scale with 0 indicating "no pain" and 10 representing "worst pain"	38 consecutive patients referred with TMD	κ = **.36**
Behavior rating scale[7]	A 6-point scale ranging from "minor discomfort" to "very strong discomfort"		κ = **.68**
Verbal scale[7]	A 5-point scale ranging from "no pain" to "very severe pain"		κ = **.44**

Diagnostic Utility of the Patient History in Identifying Anterior Disc Displacement

+LR	Interpretation	−LR
>10	Large	<.1
5.0-10.0	Moderate	.1-.2
2.0-5.0	Small	.2-.5
1.0-2.0	Rarely important	.5-1.0

Historical Finding and Study Quality	Description and Positive Findings	Population	Reference Standard	Sens	Spec	+LR	−LR
Clicking[8]	Momentary snapping sound during opening or functioning			In presence of reducing disc			
				.82	.19	1.01	.95
				In presence of nonreducing disc			
				.86	.24	1.13	.58
Locking[8]	Sudden onset of restricted movement during opening or closing			In presence of reducing disc			
				.53	.22	.68	2.14
				In presence of nonreducing disc			
				.86	.52	1.79	.27
Restriction after clicking[8]	Inability to open as wide as was previously possible after clicking			In presence of reducing disc			
				.26	.40	.43	1.85
				In presence of nonreducing disc			
				.66	.74	2.54	.46
Periodic restriction[8]	Periodic inability to open as wide as was previously possible			In presence of reducing disc			
				.60	.90	6.0	.44
				In presence of nonreducing disc			
				.12	.95	2.4	.93
Continuous restriction[8]	Continuous inability to open as wide as was previously possible	70 patients (90 TMJs) referred with complaints of cranio-mandibular pain	Anterior disc displacement via MRI	In presence of reducing disc			
				.35	.26	.47	2.5
				In presence of nonreducing disc			
				.78	.62	2.05	.35
Function related to joint pain[8]				In presence of reducing disc			
				.82	.10	.91	1.8
				In presence of nonreducing disc			
				.96	.24	1.26	.17
Complaint of clicking[8]				In presence of reducing disc			
				.28	.24	.37	3.00
				In presence of nonreducing disc			
				.82	.69	2.65	.26
Complaint of movement-related pain[8]	Not reported			In presence of reducing disc			
				.71	.31	1.03	.94
				In presence of nonreducing disc			
				.74	.36	1.16	.72
Complaint of severe restriction[8]				In presence of reducing disc			
				.60	.65	1.71	.62
				In presence of nonreducing disc			
				.38	.93	5.43	.67

Self-Reported Temporomandibular Pain

ICC or κ	Interpretation
.81-1.0	Substantial agreement
.61-.80	Moderate agreement
.41-.60	Fair agreement
.11-.40	Slight agreement
.0-.10	No agreement

Historical Finding and Study	Description and Positive Findings	Population	Reliability
Self-report of TMJ pain[9]	See diagnostic table on following page. Participants were asked same questions 2 weeks apart.	120 adolescents: 60 with self-reported TMJ pain, and 60 age- and sex-matched controls	Test-retest κ = **.83** (.74, .93)

+LR	Interpretation	−LR
>10	Large	<.1
5.0-10.0	Moderate	.1-.2
2.0-5.0	Small	.2-.5
1.0-2.0	Rarely important	.5-1.0

Historical Finding and Study Quality	Description and Positive Findings	Population	Reference Standard	Sens	Spec	+LR	−LR
Self-report of TMJ pain[9]	Participants were asked: (1) "Do you have pain in your temple, face, TMJ, or jaw once a week or more?" (2) "Do you have pain when you open your mouth wide or chew once a week or more?" If answer is "yes" to either question, test is positive.	120 adolescents: 60 with self-reported TMJ pain and 60 age- and sex-matched controls	RDC/TMD diagnosis of myofascial pain or arthralgia, arthritis, and arthrosis	.98	.90	9.8 (4.8, 20.0)	.02 (.00, .16)

RDC/TMD, Research Diagnostic Criteria for Temporomandibular Disorders (see next page).

Research Diagnostic Criteria for Temporomandibular Disorders

The Research Diagnostic Criteria for Temporomandibular Disorders (RDC/TMD) was developed in response to a general lack of standardization in TMD assessment and diagnosis.[10] The RDC/TMD is based on a biopsychosocial model and is comprised of a comprehensive set of history questions and physical examination procedures. The examination includes measurement of the range of mandibular motion, muscle and joint palpation with defined pressure, and recording of joint sounds. The specific examination questions, procedures, and scoring instructions are available at a website created by a consortium of worldwide researchers using the RDC/TMD (http://rdc-tmdinternational.org); they are summarized here.

RDC/TMD Examination Procedures		
Mandibular range of motion (measured in millimeters)	• Unassisted opening without pain • Maximum unassisted opening • Maximum assisted opening	• Lateral excursions • Protrusion
Joint sounds	• Clicking or crepitus during opening • Clicking or crepitus during closing • Joint sounds during lateral excursion (contralateral side)	• Joint sounds during lateral excursion (ipsilateral side) • Joint sounds during protrusion
Masticatory muscle and TMJ palpation tenderness	• Temporalis posterior • Temporalis middle • Temporalis anterior • Masseter superior • Masseter body • Masseter inferior	• Posterior mandibular region • Submandibular region • Lateral pterygoid area • Tendon of temporalis • TMJ lateral • TMJ posterior

Based on the findings from these tests, the RCD/TMD purports the following eight different temporomandibular diagnoses:
- Ia: Myofascial pain without limited mouth opening
- Ib: Myofascial pain with limited mouth opening
- IIa: Disc displacement with reduction
- IIb: Disc displacement without reduction and with limited mouth opening
- IIc: Disc displacement without reduction and without limited mouth opening
- IIIa: Arthralgia
- IIIb: Osteoarthritis
- IIIC: Osteoarthrosis

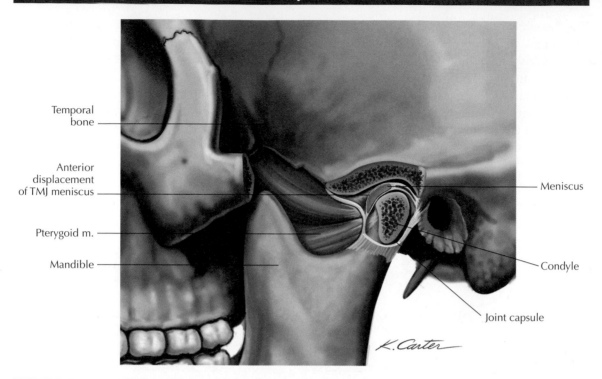

Figure 2-14

Anterior disc displacement.

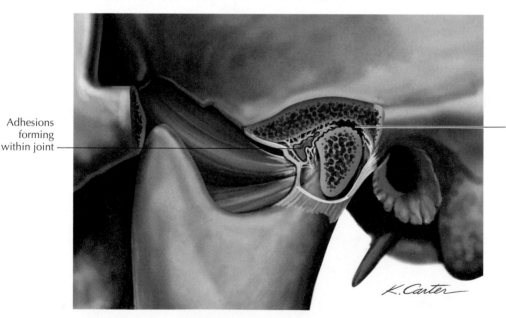

Figure 2-15

Temporomandibular arthrosis.

Reliability and Diagnostic Utility of RDC/TMD Diagnoses

ICC or κ	Interpretation
.81-1.0	Substantial agreement
.61-.80	Moderate agreement
.41-.60	Fair agreement
.11-.40	Slight agreement
.0-.10	No agreement

Diagnosis and Study	Description and Positive Findings	Population	Inter-examiner Reliability
Myofascial pain without limited mouth opening[11]			ICC = .51
Myofascial pain with limited mouth opening[11]			ICC = .58
Disc displacement with reduction[11]			ICC = .61
Disc displacement without reduction (acute)[11]			ICC = .31
Disc displacement without reduction (chronic)[11]	Used RDC/TMD examination and criteria (see previous page)	230 patients from 10 international TMD centers	ICC = .06
Arthralgia[11]			ICC = .47
Osteoarthritis[11]			ICC = .00
Osteoarthrosis[11]			ICC = .00
Group I diagnosis[11]			ICC = .75
Group II diagnosis[11]			ICC = .61
Group III diagnosis[11]			ICC = .54

Each ICC estimate represents the median value from multiple inter-examiner comparisons.

+LR	Interpretation	−LR
>10	Large	<.1
5.0-10.0	Moderate	.1-.2
2.0-5.0	Small	.2-.5
1.0-2.0	Rarely important	.5-1.0

Diagnosis and Study Quality	Description and Positive Findings	Population	Reference Standard	Sens	Spec	+LR	−LR
RDC/TMD diagnosis of myofascial pain *with* limited mouth opening[12] ◇	Used RDC/TMD examination and criteria (see previous page)	61 patients seeking treatment for orofacial muscle pain and/or TMJ pain and diagnosed with myofascial pain with or without limited mouth opening	TMJ pathosis via MRI	.29	.50	.57	1.43
RDC/TMD diagnosis of myofascial pain *without* limited mouth opening[12] ◇				1.0	.84	6.33	.00

Reliability in Determining the Presence of Pain during Muscle Palpation

ICC or κ	Interpretation
.81-1.0	Substantial agreement
.61-.80	Moderate agreement
.41-.60	Fair agreement
.11-.40	Slight agreement
.0-.10	No agreement

Finding and Study	Description and Positive Findings	Population	Inter-examiner Reliability
Extraoral[13]	Examiner palpates the temporalis, masseter, posterior cervical, and sternocleidomastoid muscles	64 healthy volunteers	κ = .91
Intraoral[13]	Examiner palpates tendon of the temporalis, lateral pterygoid, masseter, and body of the tongue		κ = .90
Masseter[14]	Examiner palpates the mid belly of the masseter muscle	79 randomly selected patients referred to a craniomandibular disorder department	κ = .33
Temporalis[14]	Examiner palpates the mid belly of the temporalis muscle		κ = .42
Medial pterygoid[14]	Examiner palpates the insertion of the medial pterygoid		κ = .23
Masseter[15]	Examiner palpates the superficial and deep portion of the masseter muscle	79 patients referred to a TMD and orofacial pain department	κ = .33
Temporalis[15]	Examiner palpates the anterior and posterior aspects of the temporalis muscle		κ = .42
Medial pterygoid[15] attachment	Examiner palpates the medial pterygoid muscles extraorally		κ = .23
Masseter[16]	Examiner palpates the origin, body, and insertion of the masseter muscle	27 TMD patients	κ (Right) = .78 (Left) = .56
Temporalis[16]	Examiner palpates the origin, body, and insertion of the temporalis muscle		κ (Right) = .87 (Left) = .91
Tendon of temporalis[16]	Examiner palpates the tendon of the temporalis muscle		κ (Right) = .53 (Left) = .48

Palpation

Reliability in Determining the Presence of Pain during TMJ Regional Palpation

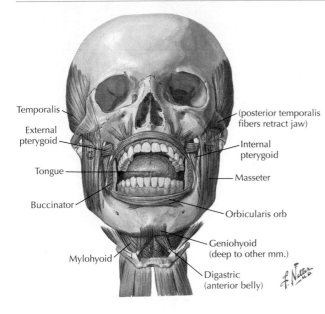

ICC or κ	Interpretation
.81-1.0	Substantial agreement
.61-.80	Moderate agreement
.41-.60	Fair agreement
.11-.40	Slight agreement
.0-.10	No agreement

Temporalis

External pterygoid

Tongue

Buccinator

Mylohyoid

(posterior temporalis fibers retract jaw)

Internal pterygoid

Masseter

Orbicularis orb

Geniohyoid (deep to other mm.)

Digastric (anterior belly)

Figure 2-16

Musculature of the temporomandibular joint.

Finding and Study	Description and Positive Findings	Population	Reliability
Lateral palpation[17]	Examiner palpates anterior to the ear over the TMJ	61 patients with TMJ pain	Intra-examiner κ = **.53**
Posterior palpation[17]	Examiner palpates TMJ through external meatus		Intra-examiner κ = **.48**
Palpation of TMJ[14]	Examiner palpates the lateral and dorsal aspects of the condyle	79 randomly selected patients referred to a craniomandibular disorder department	Inter-examiner κ = **.33**
Masseter[15]	Examiner palpates the superficial and deep portion of the masseter muscle	79 patients referred to a temporomandibular disorder and orofacial pain department	Inter-examiner κ = **.33**
Palpation of TMJ[15]	Examiner palpates the lateral pole of the condyle in open and closed mouth positions. The dorsal pole is palpated posteriorly through the external auditory meatus		Inter-examiner κ = **.33**
Retromandibular region[16]			Inter-examiner κ (Right) = **.56** (Left) = **.50**
Submandibular region[16]			Inter-examiner κ (Right) = **.73** (Left) = **.68**
Lateral pterygoid area[16]	Examiner palpation consistent with RDC/TMD guidelines	27 temporomandibular disorder patients	Inter-examiner κ (Right) = **.50** (Left) = **.37**
Lateral pole and posterior attachment of TMJ[16]			Inter-examiner κ (Right) = **.43** (Left) = **.46**

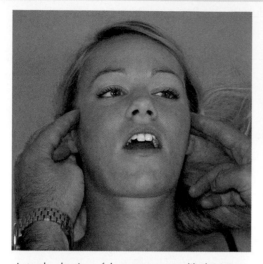

Lateral palpation of the temporomandibular joint

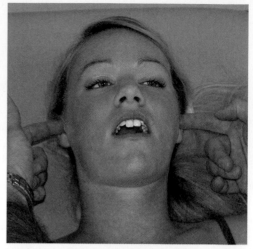

Posterior palpation of the temporomandibulor joint through external auditory meatus

Palpation of the temporalis

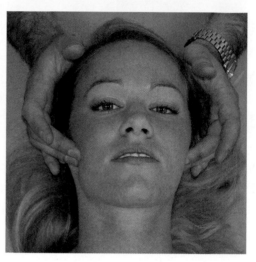

Palpation of the masseter

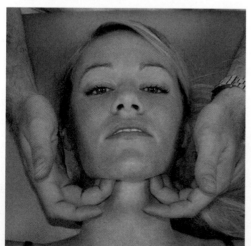

Palpation of the medial pterygoid

Figure 2-17
Palpation tests.

Palpation

Diagnostic Utility of Palpation in Identifying Temporomandibular Conditions

+LR	Interpretation	−LR
>10	Large	<.1
5.0–10.0	Moderate	.1–.2
2.0–5.0	Small	.2–.5
1.0–2.0	Rarely important	.5–1.0

Test and Study Quality	Description and Positive Findings	Population	Reference Standard	Sens	Spec	+LR	−LR
Lateral palpation[17] ◇	Examiner palpates the lateral pole of the condyle with the index finger. Positive if pain is present	61 patients with TMJ pain	Presence of TMJ effusion via MRI	.83	.69	2.68	.25
Posterior palpation[17] ◇	Examiner palpates the posterior portion of the condyle with the little finger in the patient's ear. Positive if pain is present			.85	.62	2.24	.24
Palpation[18] ○	Palpation of lateral and posterior aspects of the TMJ and assessment of pain response with active movements. Positive if patient reports pain	84 patients with symptoms of TMJ pain	TMJ synovitis via arthroscopic investigation	.92	.21	1.16	.38
Palpation[19] ○	Examiner palpates lateral and posterior aspects of the TMJ with one finger and determines the presence of tenderness	200 consecutive patients with TMJ disease	TMJ synovitis via arthroscopic investigation	.88	.36	1.38	.33
Tender joint on palpation[8] ○	Examiner palpates the lateral and posterior aspects of the joint. Positive if pain is present	70 patients (90 TMJs) referred with complaints of craniomandibular pain	Detecting anterior disc displacement via MRI	In presence of reducing disc			
				.38	.41	.64	1.51
				In presence of nonreducing disc			
				.66	.67	2.0	.51
Palpation[20] ○	Examiner palpated the TMJ laterally and posteriorly, the temporalis muscle, and the masseter muscle. Pain recorded via visual analog scale (VAS) using a cutoff value to maximize sensitivity and specificity	147 patients referred for craniomandibular complaints and 103 asymptomatic individuals	Patient report of tenderness in the masticatory muscles, the preauricular area, or TMJ in the past month	.75	.67	2.27	.37
Palpation of temporalis muscle[21] ○	Performed with index and middle fingers for 2 to 4 seconds with approximately 3 pounds of pressure on the muscle and 2 pounds of pressure on the joint. Pain recorded via VAS with cutoff values at 1 standard deviation from the mean*	40 patients diagnosed with TMD and 40 asymptomatic patients	TMD diagnosis from RCD/TMD evaluation	Right side*			
				.60	.78	2.73	.51
				Left side*			
				.70	.83	4.12	.36
Palpation of temporomandibular joint[21] ○				Right side*			
				.68	.88	5.67	.36
				Left side*			
				.73	.85	4.87	.32
Palpation of masseter muscle[21] ○				Right side*			
				.73	.85	4.87	.32
				Left side*			
				.73	.80	3.65	.34

*Gomes and colleagues[21] also calculated sensitivity and specificity for cutoff values of 1.5 and 2 standard deviations. Values showed almost perfect specificity, but poor sensitivity.

Palpation

Diagnostic Utility of Pressure Pain Thresholds in Identifying Temporomandibular Disorder

+LR	Interpretation	−LR
>10	Large	<.1
5.0-10.0	Moderate	.1-.2
2.0-5.0	Small	.2-.5
1.0-2.0	Rarely important	.5-1.0

Test and Study Quality	Description and Positive Findings	Population	Reference Standard	Sens	Spec	+LR	−LR
PPT temporalis muscle[21]				Right side			
				.68	.88	5.67	.36
				Left side			
				.63	.90	6.30	.41
PPT temporomandibular joint[21]	Used pressure algometer fitted with a rubber tip. PPT defined as the lightest pressure to cause pain. Cutoff values represent 1 standard deviation from the mean*	40 patients diagnosed with TMD and 40 asymptomatic patients		Right side			
				.56	.95	11.20	.46
				Left side			
				.75	.95	15.00	.26
PPT masseter muscle[21]			TMD diagnosis from RCD/TMD evaluation	Right side			
				.75	.90	7.50	.28
				Left side			
				.78	.90	7.80	.24
PPT anterior temporalis muscle[22]	Used pressure algometer pressed into relaxed muscle belly. PPT defined as the lightest pressure to cause pain. Cutoff values chosen from receiver operator curve when specificity was .91.	99 women with dental or intra-articular TMJ pain		.77	.91	8.37	.25
PPT middle temporalis muscle[22]				.73	.91	7.93	.30
PPT posterior temporalis muscle[22]				.67	.91	7.28	.36
PPT masseter muscle[22]				.55	.91	5.98	.50

PPT, pressure pain threshold.

*Gomes and colleagues[21] also calculated sensitivity and specificity for cutoff values of 1.5 and 2 standard deviations. Values showed almost perfect specificity, but poor sensitivity.

Joint Sounds

ICC or κ	Interpretation
.81-1.0	Substantial agreement
.61-.80	Moderate agreement
.41-.60	Fair agreement
.11-.40	Slight agreement
.0-.10	No agreement

Reliability of Detecting Joint Sounds during Active Motion

Test and Study	Description and Positive Findings	Population	Reliability
Click sounds during mouth opening[17]	During mouth opening, examiner records the presence of a click sound	61 patients with TMJ pain	Intra-examiner κ = .12
Crepitus sounds during mouth opening[17]	During mouth opening, examiner records the presence of a grating or grinding sound		Intra-examiner κ = .15
Clicking during active maximal mouth opening [14]	Intensity of clicking and crepitation is graded on a 0- to 2-scale from "none" to "clearly audible"	79 randomly selected patients referred to a craniomandibular disorder department	Inter-examiner κ = .70
Crepitation during active maximal mouth opening[14]			Inter-examiner κ = .29
Joint noise[14]	Presence of joint noises are recorded by examiner		Inter-examiner κ = .24
Opening[15]	Examiner records the presence of joint sounds during mandibular opening, lateral excursion, right and left and protrusion	79 patients referred to a temporomandibular disorder and orofacial pain department	Inter-examiner κ = .59
Lateral excursion, right[15]			Inter-examiner κ = .57
Lateral excursion, left[15]			Inter-examiner κ = .50
Protrusion[15]			Inter-examiner κ = .47
TMJ sounds[16]	Presence of joint noises are recorded by examiner during mouth opening	27 temporomandibular disorder patients	Inter-examiner κ (Right) = **.52** (Left) = **.25**

Reliability of Detecting Joint Sounds during Joint Play

Test and Study	Description and Positive Findings	Population	Reliability
Joint noise during joint play[14]	Examiner records presence of joint noise during traction and translation	79 randomly selected patients referred to a craniomandibular disorder department	Inter-examiner κ = −.01
Traction, right[15]	Examiner moves the mandibular condyle in an inferior direction for traction and in a medial-lateral direction for translation. Examiner records presence of joint sound during translation and traction	79 patients referred to a TMD and orofacial pain department	Inter-examiner κ = −.02
Traction, left[15]			Inter-examiner κ = .66
Translation, right[15]			Inter-examiner κ = .07
Translation, left[15]			Inter-examiner κ = −.02

Joint Sounds

Diagnostic Utility of Clicking in Identifying Temporomandibular Conditions

+LR	Interpretation	−LR
>10	Large	<.1
5.0-10.0	Moderate	.1-.2
2.0-5.0	Small	.2-.5
1.0-2.0	Rarely important	.5-1.0

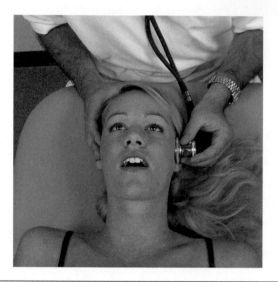

Figure 2-18

Auscultation performed with a stethoscope.

Test and Study Quality	Description and Positive Findings	Population	Reference Standard	Sens	Spec	+LR	−LR
Clicking[3] ◇	Examiner palpates the lateral aspect of the TMJ during opening and closing. Examiner records audible, palpable clicking	146 patients attending a TMJ and craniofacial pain clinic	Anterior disc displacement *with* reduction via MRI	.51	.83	3.0	.59
Clicking[17] ◇	Examiner auscultates for sounds during joint movement. Presence of a click sound is considered positive	61 patients with TMJ pain	Presence of TMJ effusion via MRI	.69	.51	1.41	.61
Reproducible clicking[8] ◯	Auscultation with a stethoscope. Considered positive if observed at least 4 times during 5 repetitions of mouth opening	70 patients (90 TMJs) referred with complaints of craniomandibular pain	Detecting anterior disc displacement via MRI	In presence of reducing disc			
				.10	.40	.17	2.25
				In presence of nonreducing disc			
				.71	.90	7.10	.32
Reciprocal clicking[8] ◯	Auscultation with a stethoscope. Considered positive if a click on opening is followed by a click on closing			In presence of reducing disc			
				.40	.52	.83	1.15
				In presence of nonreducing disc			
				.76	.95	15.2	.25

Joint Sounds

Diagnostic Utility of Crepitus in Identifying Temporomandibular Conditions

+LR	Interpretation	−LR
>10	Large	<.1
5.0-10.0	Moderate	.1-.2
2.0-5.0	Small	.2-.5
1.0-2.0	Rarely important	.5-1.0

Test and Study Quality	Description and Positive Findings	Population	Reference Standard	Sens	Spec	+LR	−LR
Presence of crepitus[17]	Examiner auscultates for sounds during joint movement. Presence of grating or grinding noise is considered positive	61 patients with TMJ pain	Presence of TMJ effusion via MRI	.85	.30	1.21	.50
Presence of crepitus[18]	Osteoarthritis based on the presence of crepitus during auscultation. Presence of crepitus is considered positive	84 patients with symptoms of TMJ pain	TMJ osteoarthritis via arthroscopic investigation	.70	.43	1.23	.70
Presence of crepitus[19]	Auscultation performed with stethoscope. Presence of crepitus is considered positive	200 consecutive patients with TMJ disease	TMJ osteoarthritis via arthroscopic investigation	Minor osteoarthritis*			
				.45	.84	2.81	.65
				Severe osteoarthritis*			
				.67	.86	4.79	.38

*Minor osteoarthritis is defined as smooth, glossy white surfaces of the disc and fibrocartilage. Severe osteoarthritis is defined as one or more of the following features: (1) pronounced fibrillation of the articular cartilage and disc; (2) exposure of subchondral bone; (3) disc perforation.

Reliability of Mouth Opening Range of Motion Measurements of the Temporomandibular Joint

ICC or κ	Interpretation
.81-1.0	Substantial agreement
.61-.80	Moderate agreement
.41-.60	Fair agreement
.11-.40	Slight agreement
.0-.10	No agreement

Figure 2-19

Measurement of mouth opening active range of motion.

Test and Study		Description and Positive Findings	Population	Reliability
Opening[23]	Without TMJ disorder	Patient is instructed to open mouth as much as possible without causing pain. Interincisal distance is measured to the nearest millimeter with a plastic ruler	15 subjects with a TMJ disorder and 15 subjects without this disorder	Inter-examiner ICC = .98 Intra-examiner ICC = .77-.89
	With TMJ disorder			Inter-examiner ICC = .99 Intra-examiner ICC = .94
Unassisted opening without pain[24]	In older adults	Measured in mm with ruler consistent with RMC/TMD guidelines	43 asymptomatic older adults (age 68 to 96 years) and 44 asymptomatic young adults (age 18 to 45 years)	Inter-examiner ICC = .88 (.78, .94)
	In young adults			Inter-examiner ICC = .91 (.83, .95)
Maximum unassisted opening[24]	In older adults			Inter-examiner ICC = .95 (.91, .97)
	In young adults			Inter-examiner ICC = .98 (.96, .99)
Maximum assisted opening[24]	In older adults			Inter-examiner ICC = .96 (.92, .98)
	In young adults			Inter-examiner ICC = .98 (.96, .99)
Unassisted opening without pain[16]			27 TMD patients	Inter-examiner ICC = .83
Maximum unassisted opening[16]				Inter-examiner ICC = .89
Maximum assisted opening[16]				Inter-examiner ICC = .93

Range of Motion

Reliability of Range of Motion Measurements of the Temporomandibular Joint

ICC or κ	Interpretation
.81-1.0	Substantial agreement
.61-.80	Moderate agreement
.41-.60	Fair agreement
.11-.40	Slight agreement
.0-.10	No agreement

Test and Study		Description and Positive Findings	Population	Reliability
Overbite[23]	Without TMJ disorder	A horizontal line is made on the lower incisor at the level of the upper incisor with the TMJ closed. The vertical distance between the line and the superior aspect of the lower incisor is measured	15 subjects with a TMJ disorder and 15 subjects without TMJ disorder	Inter-examiner ICC = .98 Intra-examiner ICC = .90-.96
	With TMJ disorder			Inter-examiner ICC = .95 Intra-examiner ICC = .90-.97
Excursion, left[23]	Without TMJ disorder	Vertical marks are made in the median plane on the anterior surface of the lower central incisors in relationship to the upper central incisors. Patient is instructed to move the jaw as far lateral as possible and the measurement is recorded		Inter-examiner ICC = .95 Intra-examiner ICC = .91-.92
	With TMJ disorder			Inter-examiner ICC = .94 Intra-examiner ICC = .85-.92
Excursion, right[23]	Without TMJ disorder			Inter-examiner ICC = .90 Intra-examiner ICC = .70-.87
	With TMJ disorder			Inter-examiner ICC = .96 Intra-examiner ICC = .75-.82
Protrusion[23]	Without TMJ disorder	Two vertical lines are made on the first upper and lower canine incisors. Subject is instructed to move the jaw as far forward as possible and a measurement is made between the two marks		Inter-examiner ICC = .95 Intra-examiner ICC = .85-.93
	With TMJ disorder			Inter-examiner ICC = .98 Intra-examiner ICC = .89-.93
Overjet[23]	Without TMJ disorder	The horizontal distance between the upper and lower incisors is measured when the mouth is closed		Inter-examiner ICC = 1.0 Intra-examiner ICC = .98
	With TMJ disorder			Inter-examiner ICC = .99 Intra-examiner ICC = .98-.99
Maximum laterotrusion[24]	In older adults	Measured in millimeters with ruler consistent with RMC/TMD guidelines	43 older asymptomatic adults (age 68 to 96 years) and 44 young asymptomatic adults (age 18 to 45 years)	Inter-examiner ICC = .71 (.45, .84)
	In young adults			Inter-examiner ICC = .77 (.57, .88)
Maximum protrusion[24]	In older adults			Inter-examiner ICC = .78 (.59, .88)
	In young adults			Inter-examiner ICC = .90 (.81, .95)
Lateral excursion, right[16]			27 TMD patients	Inter-examiner ICC = .41
Lateral excursion, left[16]				Inter-examiner ICC = .40
Horizontal overbite[16]				Inter-examiner ICC = .79
Vertical overlap[16]				Inter-examiner ICC = .70

Range of Motion

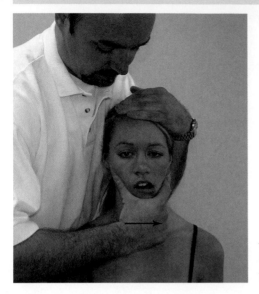

ICC or κ	Interpretation
.81-1.0	Substantial agreement
.61-.80	Moderate agreement
.41-.60	Fair agreement
.11-.40	Slight agreement
.0-.10	No agreement

Figure 2-20

Translation of mandible, left.

The Reliability of Joint Play and End-Feel Assessment of the TMJ

Test and Study		Description and Positive Findings	Population	Reliability
Traction and translation[14]	Restriction of movement	Examiner records the presence of restriction of movement at end-feel during traction and translation of the TMJ	79 randomly selected patients referred to a craniomandibular disorder department	Inter-examiner κ = .08
	End-feel			Inter-examiner κ = .07
Traction, right[15]	Joint play	Examiner moves the mandibular condyle in an inferior direction for traction and a medial-lateral direction for translation. The extent of joint play and end-feel are graded as "normal" or "abnormal"	79 patients referred to a temporomandibular disorder and orofacial pain department	Inter-examiner κ = −.03
	End-feel			Inter-examiner κ = −.05
Traction, left[15]	Joint play			Inter-examiner κ = .08
	End-feel			Inter-examiner κ = .20
Translation, right[15]	Joint play			Inter-examiner κ = −.05
	End-feel			Inter-examiner κ = −.05
Translation, left[15]	Joint play			Inter-examiner κ = −.10
	End-feel			Inter-examiner κ = −.13

Reliability of Measuring Mandibular Opening with Different Head Positions

Test and Study	Description and Positive Findings	Population	Reliability
Forward head position[25]	Patient is instructed to slide the jaw forward as far as possible and a measurement of vertical mandibular opening is recorded		Inter-examiner ICC = .92 Intra-examiner ICC = .97
Neutral head position[25]	Patient is placed in a position where a plumb line bisects the ear and a measurement of vertical mandibular opening is recorded	40 healthy subjects	Inter-examiner ICC = .93 Intra-examiner ICC = .93
Retracted head position[25]	Patient is instructed to slide the jaw backward as far as possible and a measurement of vertical mandibular opening is recorded		Inter-examiner ICC = .92 Intra-examiner ICC = .92

Range of Motion

Diagnostic Utility of Limited Range of Motion in Identifying Anterior Disc Displacement

+LR	Interpretation	−LR
>10	Large	<.1
5.0-10.0	Moderate	.1-.2
2.0-5.0	Small	.2-.5
1.0-2.0	Rarely important	.5-1.0

Test and Study Quality	Description and Positive Findings	Population	Reference Standard	Sens	Spec	+LR	−LR
Restriction of condylar translation[3] ◇	Examiner asks patient to maximally open mouth while palpating condylar movement. Examiner records any limitation of condylar translation	146 patients attending a TMJ and craniofacial pain clinic	Anterior disc displacement *without* reduction via MRI	.69	.81	3.63	.38
Restriction range functional opening[3] ◇	Examiner asks patient to maximally open mouth and measures the distance in millimeters. Less than 40 mm is considered a restriction			.32	.83	1.88	.82
Restriction range functional opening[8] ○	Measurement is taken at the end range of active mouth opening. Definition of positive not reported			In presence of reducing disc			
				.38	.21	.48	2.95
				In presence of nonreducing disc			
				.86	.62	2.26	.23
Restriction range passive opening[8] ○	Measurement is taken at the end range of passive mouth opening after 15 seconds. Definition of positive not reported			In presence of reducing disc			
				.29	.29	.41	2.45
				In presence of nonreducing disc			
				.76	.69	2.45	.35
Restricted translation[8] ○	Not reported	70 patients (90 TMJs) referred with complaints of craniomandibular pain	Anterior disc displacement via MRI	In presence of reducing disc			
				.15	.38	.24	2.24
				In presence of nonreducing disc			
				.66	.81	3.47	.42
Restricted protrusion[8] ○	Measurement is taken at the end range of active mandibular protrusion. Definition of positive not reported			In presence of reducing disc			
				.29	.38	.47	1.87
				In presence of nonreducing disc			
				.62	.64	1.72	.59
Restricted contralateral movement[8] ○	A measurement is taken at the end of contralateral movement from the midline. Definition of positive not reported			In presence of reducing disc			
				.15	.34	.23	2.50
				In presence of nonreducing disc			
				.66	.76	2.75	.45

Diagnostic Utility of Deviations in Movement in Identifying Anterior Disc Displacement

+LR	Interpretation	−LR
>10	Large	<.1
5.0-10.0	Moderate	.1-.2
2.0-5.0	Small	.2-.5
1.0-2.0	Rarely important	.5-1.0

Test and Study Quality	Description and Positive Findings	Population	Reference Standard	Sens	Spec	+LR	−LR
Deviation of mandible[3] ◆	Patient is asked to maximally open the mouth. If the midline of the upper and lower incisors does not line up, then the test is considered positive	146 patients attending a TMJ and craniofacial pain clinic	Anterior disc displacement *without* reduction via MRI	.32	.87	2.46	.78
Deviation of mandible with correction[8] ○	Examiner observes active mouth opening. Test is considered positive if a deviation occurs and the mandible returns to midline	70 patients (90 TMJs) referred with complaints of craniomandibular pain	Anterior disc displacement via MRI	In presence of reducing disc			
				.14	.57	.33	1.51
				In presence of nonreducing disc			
				.44	.83	2.59	.67
Deviation of mandible without correction[8] ○	Examiner observes active mouth opening. Test is considered positive if the mandible does not return to midline after deviation			In presence of reducing disc			
				.18	.41	.31	2.0
				In presence of nonreducing disc			
				.66	.83	3.88	.41

Dynamic Movements

Reliability of Determining the Presence of Pain during Dynamic Movements

ICC or κ	Interpretation
.81-1.0	Substantial agreement
.61-.80	Moderate agreement
.41-.60	Fair agreement
.11-.40	Slight agreement
.0-.10	No agreement

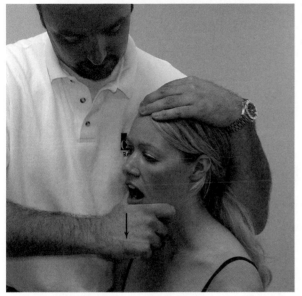

Figure 2-21

Assessment of pain during passive opening.

Test and Study	Description and Positive Findings	Population	Reliability
Mandibular movements[17]	Patient is asked if pain is felt during opening, closing, lateral excursion, protrusion, and retrusion	61 patients with TMJ pain	Intra-examiner κ = **.43**
Maximum assisted opening[17]	Examiner applies overpressure to the end-range of mandibular depression		Intra-examiner κ = **−.05**
Pain on opening[15]	Patient is asked to maximally open mouth	79 patients referred to a temporomandibular disorder and orofacial pain department	Inter-examiner κ = **.28**
Pain on lateral excursion, right[15]	Patient is asked to move the mandible in a lateral direction as far as possible		Inter-examiner κ = **.28**
Pain on lateral excursion, left[15]			Inter-examiner κ = **.28**
Pain on protrusion[15]	Patient is asked to actively protrude the jaw		Inter-examiner κ = **.36**
Passive opening[14]	At the end of active opening the examiner applies a passive stretch to increase mouth opening	79 randomly selected patients referred to a craniomandibular disorder department	Inter-examiner κ = **.34**
Active opening[14]	Patient is asked to open mouth as wide as possible		Inter-examiner κ = **.32**

ICC or κ	Interpretation
.81-1.0	Substantial agreement
.61-.80	Moderate agreement
.41-.60	Fair agreement
.11-.40	Slight agreement
.0-.10	No agreement

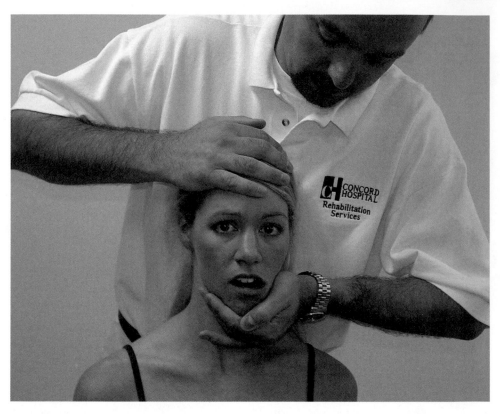

Figure 2-22

Manual resistance applied during lateral deviation.

Test and Study	Description and Positive Findings	Population	Reliability
Dynamic tests[17]	Patient performs opening, closing, lateral excursion, protrusion, and retrusion movements while examiner applies resistance	61 patients with TMJ pain	Intra-examiner κ = **.20**
Opening[15]	Examiner applies isometric resistance during opening, closing, and lateral excursions to the right and left of the TMJ. The presence of pain is recorded	79 patients referred to a TMD and orofacial pain department	Inter-examiner κ = **.24**
Closing[15]			Inter-examiner κ = **.30**
Lateral excursion, right[15]			Inter-examiner κ = **.28**
Lateral excursion, left[15]			Inter-examiner κ = **.26**
Static pain test[14]	The examiner applies resistance against the patient's mandible in an upward, downward, and lateral direction	79 randomly selected patients referred to a craniomandibular disorder department	Inter-examiner κ = **.15**

Reliability of Determining the Presence of Pain during Joint Play

ICC or κ	Interpretation
.81-1.0	Substantial agreement
.61-.80	Moderate agreement
.41-.60	Fair agreement
.11-.40	Slight agreement
.0-.10	No agreement

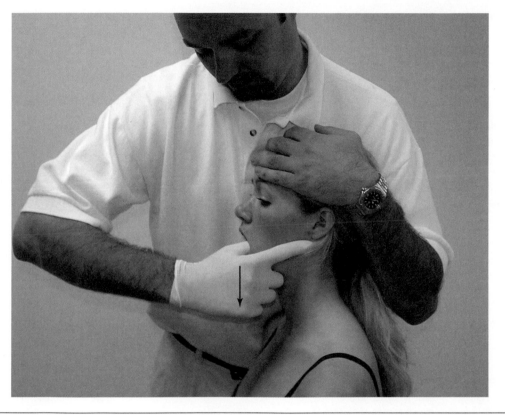

Figure 2-23

Temporomandibular traction.

Test and Study	Description and Positive Findings	Population	Reliability
Joint play[13]	Examiner performs passive traction and translation movements	61 patients with TMJ pain	Intra-examiner ICC = **.20**
Joint play test[15]	Examiner applies a traction and a translation (medial/lateral) force through the TMJ	79 randomly selected patients referred to a craniomandibular disorder department	Inter-examiner ICC = **.46**
Traction, right[16]	Examiner moves the mandibular condyle in an inferior direction for traction and a mediolateral direction for translation. The presence of pain is recorded	79 patients referred to a TMD and orofacial pain department	Inter-examiner ICC = **−.08**
Traction, left[16]			Inter-examiner ICC = **.25**
Translation, right[16]			Inter-examiner ICC = **.50**
Translation, left[16]			Inter-examiner ICC = **.28**

Diagnostic Utility of Pain in Identifying Temporomandibular Conditions

+LR	Interpretation	−LR
>10	Large	<.1
5.0-10.0	Moderate	.1-.2
2.0-5.0	Small	.2-.5
1.0-2.0	Rarely important	.5-1.0

Test and Study Quality	Description and Positive Findings	Population	Reference Standard	Sens	Spec	+LR	−LR
Pain during mandibular movements[17] ◇	Patient is asked to open, close, protrude, retrude, and perform lateral excursion of the mandible. Positive if pain present	61 patients with TMJ pain	Presence of TMJ effusion via MRI	.82	.61	2.10	.30
Pain during maximum opening and overpressure[17] ◇	Patient is asked to perform the movements above while examiner applies resistance. Positive if pain present			.93	.016	.95	4.38
Pain during dynamic tests[17] ◇	Patient is instructed to open the mouth as wide as possible and examiner applies overpressure. Positive if pain present			.74	.44	1.32	.59
Pain during joint play[17] ◇	Examiner passively performs translation and traction of the TMJ. Positive if pain present			.80	.39	1.31	.51
TMJ pain during assisted opening[3] ◇	At the end of maximal mouth opening, examiner applies 2 to 3 pounds of overpressure. The presence or absence of pain is recorded	146 patients attending a TMJ and craniofacial pain clinic	Anterior disc displacement *without* reduction via MRI	.55	.91	6.11	.49
Joint pain on opening[8] ○	Patient is asked to open mouth as wide as possible. Positive if pain present	70 patients (90 TMJs) referred with complaints of craniomandibular pain	Anterior disc displacement via MRI	In presence of reducing disc			
				.44	.31	.64	1.81
				In presence of nonreducing disc			
				.74	.57	1.72	.46
Pain with contralateral motion[8] ○	Patient is asked to perform lateral excursion contralateral to the side of joint involvement. Positive if pain present			In presence of reducing disc			
				.60	.69	1.94	.58
				In presence of nonreducing disc			
				.34	.93	4.86	.71

Dynamic Movements

Diagnostic Utility of Pain in Identifying Temporomandibular Conditions

+LR	Interpretation	−LR
>10	Large	<.1
5.0-10.0	Moderate	.1-.2
2.0-5.0	Small	.2-.5
1.0-2.0	Rarely important	.5-1.0

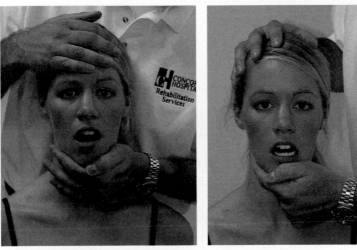

Mouth opening   Mouth closing

Figure 2-24
Manual resistance applied during mouth opening and closing.

Test and Study Quality	Description and Positive Findings	Population	Reference Standard	Sens	Spec	+LR	−LR
Dynamic/static[20] ◯	Manual resistance was applied during mouth opening, closing, protrusion, and lateral deviation. Pain was recorded via VAS using a cutoff value to maximize sensitivity and specificity			.63	.93	.90	.40
Active movements[20] ◯	Patient was asked to maximally depress mandible, protrude, and deviate right and left. Pain was recorded via VAS using a cutoff value to maximize sensitivity and specificity	147 patients referred for craniomandibular complaints and 103 asymptomatic individuals	Patient report of tenderness in the masticatory muscles, the preauricular area, or temporomandibular area in the past month	.87	.67	2.64	.19
Passive movements[20] ◯	At the end of maximal mouth opening, examiner gently applied overpressure. Pain was recorded via VAS using a cutoff value to maximize sensitivity and specificity			.80	.64	2.22	.31

ICC or κ	Interpretation
.81-1.0	Substantial agreement
.61-.80	Moderate agreement
.41-.60	Fair agreement
.11-.40	Slight agreement
.0-.10	No agreement

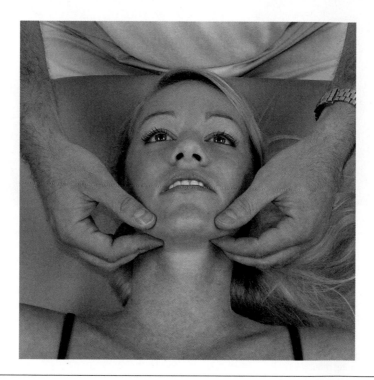

Figure 2-25

Bilateral temporomandibular compression.

Test and Study		Description and Positive Findings	Population	Reliability
Compression, right[15]	Pain	The examiner loads the intra-articular structures by moving the mandible in a dorsocranial direction. The presence of pain and joint sounds are recorded	79 patients referred to a TMD and orofacial pain department	Inter-examiner κ = **.19**
	Sounds			Not reported
Compression, left[15]	Pain			Inter-examiner κ = **.47**
	Sounds			Inter-examiner κ = **1.0**
Compression[14]	Pain		79 randomly selected patients referred to a craniomandibular disorder department	Inter-examiner κ = **.40**
	Joint noises			Inter-examiner κ = **.66**

Other Tests

Diagnostic Utility of Lower Extremity Measurements

ICC or κ	Interpretation
.81-1.0	Substantial agreement
.61-.80	Moderate agreement
.41-.60	Fair agreement
.11-.40	Slight agreement
.0-.10	No agreement

Test and Study	Description and Positive Findings	Population	Reliability
Leg length inequality[26]	With patient supine, examiner visually compares the position of the medial malleoli. Considered positive if leg length inequality ≥ .5 cm		Inter-examiner κ = **.33 to .39**
Internal foot rotation test[26]	With patient supine, examiner exerts forced internal rotation of the root and assesses the amount of end-play. Considered positive if difference in rotation ≥ 15 degrees	41 dental students	Inter-examiner κ = **.15 to .27**

+LR	Interpretation	−LR
>10	Large	<.1
5.0-10.0	Moderate	.1-.2
2.0-5.0	Small	.2-.5
1.0-2.0	Rarely important	.5-1.0

Test and Study Quality	Description and Positive Findings	Population	Reference Standard	Sens	Spec	+LR	−LR
Leg length inequality[26] ◯	With patient supine, examiner visually compares the position of the medial malleoli. Considered positive if leg length inequality ≥ .5 cm	41 dental students	Jaw muscle myofascial pain from RCD/TMD evaluation	.43	.41	.73	1.39
			Anterior TMJ disc displacement from RCD/TMD evaluation	.50	.41	.85	1.22
Internal foot rotation test[26] ◯	With patient supine, examiner exerts forced internal rotation of the root and assesses the amount of end-play. Considered positive if difference in rotation ≥ 15 degrees		Jaw muscle myofascial pain from RCD/TMD evaluation	.43	.47	.81	1.21
			Anterior TMJ disc displacement from RCD/TMD evaluation	.57	.52	1.19	.83

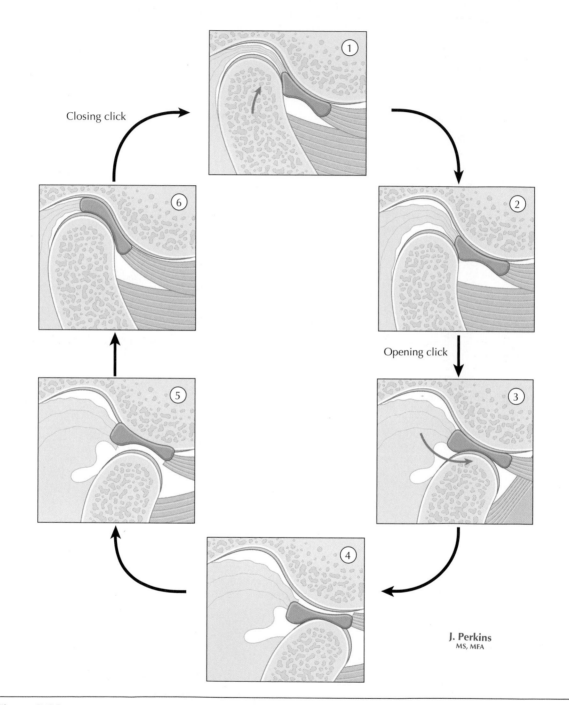

Closing click

Opening click

J. Perkins
MS, MFA

Figure 2-26

Anterior disc displacement with reduction.

Combinations of Tests (continued)

Diagnostic Utility of Combined Tests for Detecting Anterior Disc Displacement with Reduction

+LR	Interpretation	−LR
>10	Large	<.1
5.0-10.0	Moderate	.1-.2
2.0-5.0	Small	.2-.5
1.0-2.0	Rarely important	.5-1.0

Test and Study Quality	Description and Positive Findings	Population	Reference Standard	Sens	Spec	+LR	−LR
No deviation of the mandible; no pain during assisted opening[3] ◇	See previous descriptions under single test items	146 patients attending a TMJ and craniofacial pain clinic	Anterior disc displacement *with* reduction via MRI	.76	.30	1.09	.80
No deviation of the mandible; no limitation of opening[3] ◇				.76	.27	1.04	.89
No deviation of the mandible; no restriction of condylar translation[3] ◇				.75	.37	1.19	.68
No deviation of the mandible; clicking[3] ◇				.51	.85	3.40	.58
No deviation of the mandible; no pain during opening; no limitation of opening[3] ◇				.71	.35	1.09	.83
No deviation of the mandible; no pain during opening; no limitation of opening; no restriction of condylar translation[3] ◇				.68	.37	1.08	.86
No deviation of the mandible; no pain during opening; no limitation of opening; no restriction of condylar translation; clicking[3] ◇				.44	.86	3.14	.65

Diagnostic Utility of Combined Tests for Detecting Anterior Disc Displacement without Reduction

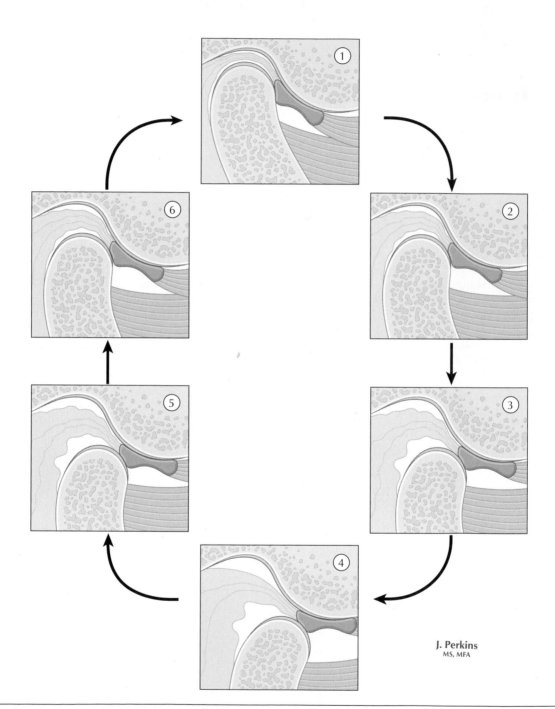

Figure 2-27

Anterior disc displacement without reduction.

Combinations of Tests (continued)

Diagnostic Utility of Combined Tests for Detecting Anterior Disc Displacement without Reduction

+LR	Interpretation	−LR
>10	Large	<.1
5.0-10.0	Moderate	.1-.2
2.0-5.0	Small	.2-.5
1.0-2.0	Rarely important	.5-1.0

Test and Study Quality	Description and Positive Findings	Population	Reference Standard	Sens	Spec	+LR	−LR
Motion restriction; no clicking[3] ◇	See previous descriptions under single test items	146 patients attending a TMJ and craniofacial pain clinic	Anterior disc displacement *without* reduction via MRI	.61	.82	3.39	.48
Motion restriction; pain during assisted opening[3] ◇				.54	.93	7.71	.49
Motion restriction; limitation of maximal mouth opening[3] ◇				.31	.87	2.38	.79
Motion restriction; deviation of the mandible[3] ◇				.30	.90	3.0	.78
Motion restriction; no clicking, TMJ pain with assistive opening[3] ◇				.46	.94	7.67	.59
Motion restriction; no clicking; TMJ pain with assistive opening; limitation of maximum mouth opening[3] ◇				.22	.96	5.50	.81
Motion restriction; no clicking; TMJ pain with assistive opening; limitation of maximum mouth opening; deviation of the mandible[3] ◇				.11	.98	5.5	.91
Clinical diagnosis using history and combined test[27] ◇	Examination using Clinical Diagnostic Criteria for Temporomandibular Disorders (CDC/TMD)	69 patients referred with TMD	Anterior disc displacement *without* reduction via MRI	.75	.83	4.41	.3

Combinations of Tests

Predicting Treatment Success with Nightly Wear of Occlusal Stabilization Splint

+LR	Interpretation	−LR
>10	Large	<.1
5.0-10.0	Moderate	.1-.2
2.0-5.0	Small	.2-.5
1.0-2.0	Rarely important	.5-1.0

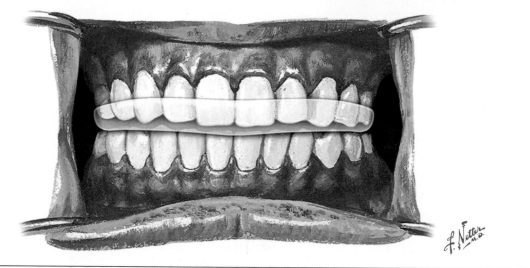

Figure 2-28

Occlusal stabilization splint.

Test and Study Quality	Description and Positive Findings	Population	Reference Standard	Sens	Spec	+LR	−LR*
Time since pain[28]	≤ 42 weeks			.62 (.49, .73)	.69 (.54, .80)	2.0 (1.3, 3.0)	.55
Baseline pain level[28]	≥40 mm on VAS			.48 (.35, .60)	.72 (.57, .83)	1.7 (1.0, 2.7)	.72
Change in VAS level at 2 months[28]	≥15 mm on VAS			.72 (.75, .93)	.91, (.64, .88)	3.9 (2.3, 6.5)	.31
Disc displacement without reduction[28]	As observed on MRI	119 consecutive patients referred to TMD clinic diagnosed with unilateral TMJ arthralgia	Treatment success (>70% reduction in VAS) after 6 months with nightly wear of occlusal stabilization splint	.25 (.15, .37)	.91 (.79, .97)	2.7 (1.0, 6.8)	.82
4 positive tests[28]	4/4 above			.10 (.04, .20)	.99 (.90, 1.00)	10.8 (.62, 188.1)	.91
≥3 positive tests[28]	≥3/4 above			.23, (.14, .36)	.91 (.79, .97)	2.5 (.97, 6.4)	.85
≥2 positive tests[28]	≥2/4 above			.49 (.37, .62)	.85 (.72, .93)	3.3 (1.7, 6.6)	.60

*−LRs not reported in study and, therefore, were calculated by authors of this book.
VAS, visual analog scale.

Combinations of Tests

Predicting Treatment Failure with Nightly Wear of Occlusal Stabilization Splint

+LR	Interpretation	−LR
>10	Large	<.1
5.0-10.0	Moderate	.1-.2
2.0-5.0	Small	.2-.5
1.0-2.0	Rarely important	.5-1.0

Test and Study Quality	Description and Positive Findings	Population	Reference Standard	Sens	Spec	+LR	−LR*
Time since pain[28] ◇	>43 weeks	119 consecutive patients referred to TMD clinic diagnosed with unilateral TMJ arthralgia	Treatment failure after 6 months with nightly wear of occlusal stabilization splint	.56 (.45, .67)	.65 (.47, .79)	1.68	.68 (.52, .89)
Baseline pain level[28] ◇	<40 mm on VAS			.76 (.65, .84)	.68 (.50, .82)	2.38	.36 (.24, .54)
Change in VAS level at 2 months[28] ◇	≤ 9 mm on VAS			.82 (.71, .89)	.97 (.84, .99)	27.33	.19 (.12, .30)
Disc displacement with reduction[28] ◇	As observed on MRI			.10 (.05, .19)	.57 (.40, .73)	.23	1.59 (1.42, 1.78)
4 positive tests[28] ◇	4/4 above			.96 (.67, 1.0)	.76 (.67, .84)	4.00	.05 (.00, .77)
≥3 positive tests[28] ◇	≥3/4 above			.19 (.09, .36)	.96 (.89, .99)	4.75	.84 (.72, .98)
≥2 positive tests[28] ◇	≥2/4 above			.38 (.23, .55)	.78 (.67, .86)	1.73	.80 (.62, 1.0)

*−LRs not reported in study and, therefore, were calculated by authors of this book.
VAS, visual analog scale.

Outcome Measure	Scoring and Interpretation	Test-Retest Reliability	MCID
Mandibular Function Impairment Questionnaire (MFIQ)	Users rate perceived level of difficulty on a Likert scale ranging from 0 (no difficulty) to 4 (very great difficulty or impossible without help) on a series of 17 questions about jaw function. The sum item score for function impairment ranges from 0 to 68 with higher scores representing more disability	Spearman's r = .69 to .96[29,30]	14[29]
Numeric Pain Rating Scale (NPRS)	Users rate their level of pain on an 11-point scale ranging from 0 to 10, with high scores representing more pain. Often asked as current pain, least, worst, and average pain in the past 24 hours	ICC = .72[31]	2[32,33]

MCID, minimum clinically important difference.

Quality Assessment of Diagnostic Studies for TMD Using QUADAS

	Riolo 1988	Schiffman 1989	Cacchiotti 1991	Stegenga 1992	Paesani 1992[34]	Holmund 1996	Israel 1998	Orsini 1999	Visscher 2000	Emshoff 2002
1. Was the spectrum of patients representative of the patients who will receive the test in practice?	U	U	N	Y	N	Y	Y	Y	N	Y
2. Were selection criteria clearly described?	N	N	N	Y	N	N	Y	Y	Y	Y
3. Is the reference standard likely to correctly classify the target condition?	U	U	N	Y	U	Y	Y	Y	U	Y
4. Is the time period between reference standard and index test short enough to be reasonably sure that the target condition did not change between the two tests?	U	U	U	U	U	U	U	U	U	Y
5. Did the whole sample, or a random selection of the sample, receive verification using a reference standard of diagnosis?	U	U	Y	Y	N	Y	Y	Y	Y	Y
6. Did patients receive the same reference standard regardless of the index test result?	U	Y	Y	Y	U	Y	Y	Y	Y	Y
7. Was the reference standard independent of the index test (i.e., the index test did not form part of the reference standard)?	Y	Y	Y	Y	Y	Y	Y	Y	Y	Y
8. Was the execution of the index test described in sufficient detail to permit replication of the test?	Y	U	Y	Y	Y	Y	Y	Y	Y	Y
9. Was the execution of the reference standard described in sufficient detail to permit its replication?	Y	N	N	Y	U	Y	U	Y	Y	Y
10. Were the index test results interpreted without knowledge of the results of the reference test?	U	U	U	U	U	U	U	Y	Y	Y
11. Were the reference standard results interpreted without knowledge of the results of the index test?	U	Y	U	U	U	U	U	Y	Y	Y
12. Were the same clinical data available when test results were interpreted as would be available when the test is used in practice?	U	U	U	U	U	U	Y	U	U	U
13. Were uninterpretable/intermediate test results reported?	U	U	Y	U	U	Y	Y	Y	U	Y
14. Were withdrawals from the study explained?	U	U	Y	U	U	Y	Y	U	U	Y
Quality summary rating:	▭	▭	▭	○	▭	○	○	◇	○	◇

Y = yes, N = no, U = unclear. ◇ Good quality (Y - N = 10 to 14)   ○ Fair quality (Y - N = 5 to 9)   ▭ Poor quality (Y - N ≤ 4)

Quality Assessment of Diagnostic Studies for TMD Using QUADAS

	Manfredini 2003	Schmitter 2004	Farella 2005	Silva 2005	Nilsson 2006	Emshoff 2008	Gomes 2008
1. Was the spectrum of patients representative of the patients who will receive the test in practice?	Y	Y	N	Y	Y	Y	Y
2. Were selection criteria clearly described?	U	Y	Y	Y	N	Y	U
3. Is the reference standard likely to correctly classify the target condition?	Y	Y	Y	Y	Y	Y	Y
4. Is the time period between reference standard and index test short enough to be reasonably sure that the target condition did not change between the two tests?	Y	N	U	U	Y	Y	U
5. Did the whole sample, or a random selection of the sample, receive verification using a reference standard of diagnosis?	Y	Y	U	Y	Y	Y	U
6. Did patients receive the same reference standard regardless of the index test result?	Y	Y	Y	Y	Y	Y	U
7. Was the reference standard independent of the index test (i.e., the index test did not form part of the reference standard)?	Y	Y	Y	U	Y	Y	N
8. Was the execution of the index test described in sufficient detail to permit replication of the test?	Y	Y	Y	Y	Y	Y	Y
9. Was the execution of the reference standard described in sufficient detail to permit its replication?	Y	Y	Y	Y	Y	Y	Y
10. Were the index test results interpreted without knowledge of the results of the reference test?	Y	Y	U	U	U	Y	Y
11. Were the reference standard results interpreted without knowledge of the results of the index test?	Y	Y	U	U	U	Y	Y
12. Were the same clinical data available when test results were interpreted as would be available when the test is used in practice?	Y	U	U	U	U	Y	U
13. Were uninterpretable/intermediate test results reported?	U	Y	U	U	Y	Y	U
14. Were withdrawals from the study explained?	Y	Y	U	U	Y	Y	Y
Quality summary rating:	◇	◇	○	○	○	◇	○

Y = yes, N = no, U = unclear. ◇ Good quality (Y − N = 10 to 14)   ○ Fair quality (Y − N = 5 to 9)   ▮ Poor quality (Y − N ≤ 4)

1. Barclay P, Hollender LG, Maravilla KR, Truelove EL. Comparison of clinical and magnetic resonance imaging diagnosis in patients with disc displacement in the temporomandibular joint. *Oral Surg Oral Med Oral Pathol Oral Radiol Endod.* 1999;88:37-43.

2. Cholitgul W, Nishiyama H, Sasai T, et al. Clinical and magnetic resonance imaging findings in temporomandibular joint disc displacement. *Dentomaxillofac Radiol.* 1997;26:183-188.

3. Orsini MG, Kuboki T, Terada S, et al. Clinical predictability of temporomandibular joint disc displacement. *J Dent Res.* 1999;78:650-660.

4. Gross AR, Haines T, Thomson MA, et al. Diagnostic tests for temporomandibular disorders: an assessment of the methodologic quality of research reviews. *Man Ther.* 1996;1:250-257.

5. Haley DP, Schiffman EL, Lindgren BR, et al. The relationship between clinical and MRI findings in patients with unilateral temporomandibular joint pain. *J Am Dent Assoc.* 2001;132:476-481.

6. Gavish A, Halachmi M, Winocur E, Gazit E. Oral habits and their association with signs and symptoms of temporomandibular disorders in adolescent girls. *J Oral Rehabil.* 2000;27:22-32.

7. Magnusson T, List T, Helkimo M. Self-assessment of pain and discomfort in patients with temporomandibular disorders: a comparison of five different scales with respect to their precision and sensitivity as well as their capacity to register memory of pain and discomfort. *J Oral Rehabil.* 1995;22:549-556.

8. Stegenga B, de Bont LG, van der Kuijl B, Boering G. Classification of temporomandibular joint osteoarthrosis and internal derangement. 1. Diagnostic significance of clinical and radiographic symptoms and signs. *Cranio.* 1992;10:96-106; discussion 116-117.

9. Nilsson IM, List T, Drangsholt M. The reliability and validity of self-reported temporomandibular disorder pain in adolescents. *J Orofac Pain.* 2006;20:138-144.

10. Dworkin SF, LeResche L. Research diagnostic criteria for temporomandibular disorders: review, criteria, examinations and specifications, critique. *J Craniomandib Disord.* 1992;6:301-355.

11. John MT, Dworkin SF, Mancl LA. Reliability of clinical temporomandibular disorder diagnoses. *Pain.* 2005;118:61-69.

12. Schmitter M, Kress B, Rammelsberg P. Temporomandibular joint pathosis in patients with myofascial pain: a comparative analysis of magnetic resonance imaging and a clinical examination based on a specific set of criteria. *Oral Surg Oral Med Oral Pathol Oral Radiol Endod.* 2004;97:318-324.

13. Dworkin SF, LeResche L, DeRouen T, et al. Assessing clinical signs of temporomandibular disorders: reliability of clinical examiners. *J Prosthet Dent.* 1990;63:574-579.v

14. Lobbezoo-Scholte AM, de Wijer A, Steenks MH, Bosman F. Interexaminer reliability of six orthopaedic tests in diagnostic subgroups of craniomandibular disorders. *J Oral Rehabil.* 1994;21:273-285.

15. de Wijer A, Lobbezoo-Scholte AM, Steenks MH, Bosman F. Reliability of clinical findings in temporomandibular disorders. *J Orofac Pain.* 1995;9:181-191.

16. Leher A, Graf K, PhoDuc JM, Rammelsberg P. Is there a difference in the reliable measurement of temporomandibular disorder signs between experienced and inexperienced examiners? *J Orofac Pain.* 2005;19:58-64.

17. Manfredini D, Tognini F, Zampa V, Bosco M. Predictive value of clinical findings for temporomandibular joint effusion. *Oral Surg Oral Med Oral Pathol Oral Radiol Endod.* 2003;96:521-526.

18. Israel HA, Diamond B, Saed-Nejad F, Ratcliffe A. Osteoarthritis and synovitis as major pathoses of the temporomandibular joint: comparison of clinical diagnosis with arthroscopic morphology. *J Oral Maxillofac Surg.* 1998;56:1023-1027; discussion 1028.

19. Holmlund AB, Axelsson S. Temporomandibular arthropathy: correlation between clinical signs and symptoms and arthroscopic findings. *Int J Oral Maxillofac Surg.* 1996;25:178-181.

20. Visscher CM, Lobbezoo F, de Boer W, et al. Clinical tests in distinguishing between persons with or without craniomandibular or cervical spinal pain complaints. *Eur J Oral Sci.* 2000;108:475-483.

21. Gomes MB, Guimaraes JP, Guimaraes FC, Neves AC. Palpation and pressure pain threshold: reliability and validity in patients with temporomandibular disorders. *Cranio.* 2008;26:202-210.

22. Silva RS, Conti PC, Lauris JR, et al. Pressure pain threshold in the detection of masticatory myofascial pain: an algometer-based study. *J Orofac Pain.* 2005;19:318-324.

23. Walker N, Bohannon RW, Cameron D. Discriminant validity of temporomandibular joint range of motion measurements obtained with a ruler. *J Orthop Sports Phys Ther.* 2000;30:484-492.

24. Hassel AJ, Rammelsberg P, Schmitter M. Inter-examiner reliability in the clinical examination of temporomandibular disorders: influence of age. *Community Dent Oral Epidemiol.* 2006;34:41-46.

25. Higbie EJ, Seidel-Cobb D, Taylor LF, Cummings GS. Effect of head position on vertical mandibular opening. *J Orthop Sports Phys Ther.* 1999;29:127-130.

26. Farella M, Michelotti A, Pellegrino G, et al. Interexaminer reliability and validity for diagnosis of temporomandibular disorders of visual leg measurements used in dental kinesiology. *J Orofac Pain.* 2005;19:285-290.

27. Emshoff R, Innerhofer K, Rudisch A, Bertram S. Clinical versus magnetic resonance imaging findings with internal derangement of the temporomandibular joint: an evaluation of anterior disc displacement

without reduction. *J Oral Maxillofac Surg.* 2002;60:36-41; discussion 42-43.

28. Emshoff R, Rudisch A. Likelihood ratio methodology to identify predictors of treatment outcome in temporomandibular joint arthralgia patients. *Oral Surg Oral Med Oral Pathol Oral Radiol Endod.* 2008;106:525-533.

29. Kropmans TJ, Dijkstra PU, van Veen A, et al. The smallest detectable difference of mandibular function impairment in patients with a painfully restricted temporomandibular joint. *J Dent Res.* 1999;78:1445-1449.

30. Undt G, Murakami K, Clark GT, et al. Cross-cultural adaptation of the JPF-Questionnaire for German-speaking patients with functional temporomandibular joint disorders. *J Craniomaxillofac Surg.* 2006;34:226-233.

31. Li L, Liu X, Herr K. Postoperative pain intensity assessment: a comparison of four scales in Chinese adults. *Pain Med.* 2007;8:223-234.

32. Farrar JT, Berlin JA, Strom BL. Clinically important changes in acute pain outcome measures: a validation study. *J Pain Symptom Manage.* 2003;25:406-411.

33. Farrar JT, Portenoy RK, Berlin JA, et al. Defining the clinically important difference in pain outcome measures. *Pain.* 2000;88:287-294.

34. Paesani D, Westesson PL, Hatala MP, et al. Accuracy of clinical diagnosis for TMJ internal derangement and arthrosis. *Oral Surg Oral Med Oral Pathol.* 1992;73:360-363.

Cervical Spine

CLINICAL SUMMARY AND RECOMMENDATIONS

Patient History

Complaints
- The utility of patient history has only been studied in identifying cervical radiculopathy. Subjective reports of symptoms were generally not helpful, with diagnoses including complaints of "weakness," "numbness," "tingling," "burning," or "arm pain."

- The patient complaints most useful in diagnosing cervical radiculopathy were *(1) a report of symptoms most bothersome in the scapular area* (+LR [likelihood ratio] = 2.30) and *(2) a report that symptoms improve with moving the neck* (+LR = 2.23).

Physical Examination

Screening
- Traditional neurological screening (sensation, reflex, and manual muscle testing [MMT]) is of moderate utility in identifying cervical radiculopathy. Sensation testing (pin prick at any location) and MMT of the muscles in the lower arm and hand are unhelpful. Muscle stretch reflex (MSR) and MMT of the muscles in the upper arm (especially the biceps brachii), exhibit good diagnostic utility and are recommended.

- Both the Canadian C-Spine Rule (CCR) and the NEXUS Low-Risk Criteria are excellent at ruling out clinically important cervical spine injuries that require radiography. Because both methods are simple and have been shown to be superior to both a general clinical examination and physician judgment, we recommend use of the CCR because it has been consistently shown to have perfect sensitivity (−LR = 0.0).

Range of Motion and Manual Assessment
- Measuring cervical range of motion is consistently reliable, but is of unknown diagnostic utility.

- The results of studies assessing the reliability of passive intervertebral motion are highly variable but generally report poor reliability when assessing limitations of movement and moderate reliability when assessing for pain.

- Assessing for both pain and limited movement during manual assessment is highly sensitive for zygopophyseal joint pain and is recommended to rule out zygopophyseal involvement (−LR = .00 to .23).

Special Tests
- Multiple studies demonstrate high diagnostic utility of Spurling's test to identify cervical radiculopathy, cervical disc prolapse, and neck pain (+LR = 1.9 to 18.6).

- Using a combination of *Spurling's A test, upper limb tension test A, a distraction test,* and assessing for *cervical rotation* < 60° to the ipsilateral side is very good at identifying cervical radiculopathy and is recommended (+LR = 30.3 if all four factors present).

Interventions
- Patients with *neck pain for < 30 days* have a high probability of rapid improvement if treated with thoracic manipulation (+LR = 6.4). Other factors associated with improved thoracic manipulation, especially in combination are *(1) no symptoms distal to the shoulder, (2) low fear avoidance behavior, (3) patient reports that looking up does not aggravate symptoms, (4) cervical extension ROM < 30°,* and *(5) decreased upper thoracic spine kyphosis* (+LR = 12 if any four of six factors present).

- Because the risks of thoracic manipulation are minimal, we recommend such treatment be considered a first-line intervention for patients with neck pain (and no contraindications).

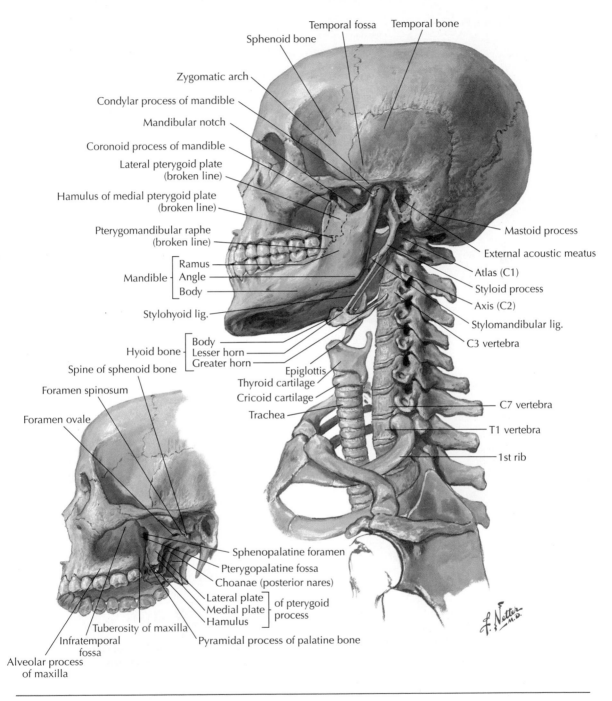

Figure 3-1

Bony framework of the head and neck.

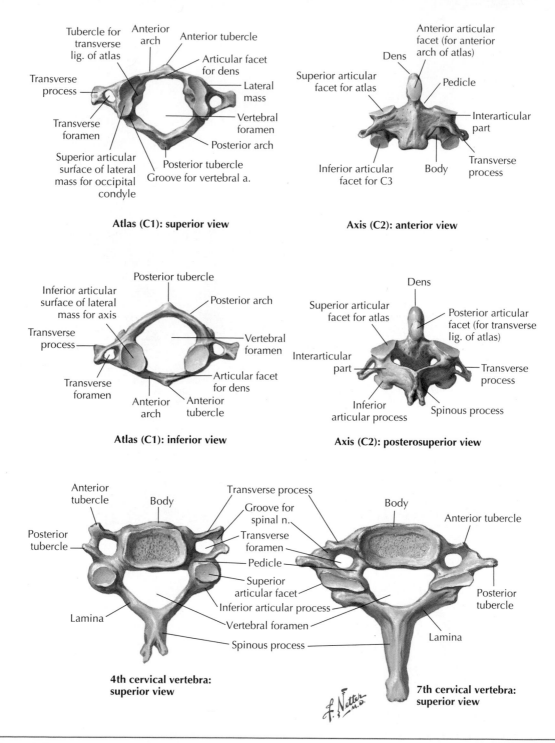

Atlas (C1): superior view

Axis (C2): anterior view

Atlas (C1): inferior view

Axis (C2): posterosuperior view

4th cervical vertebra: superior view

7th cervical vertebra: superior view

Figure 3-2

Cervical vertebrae.

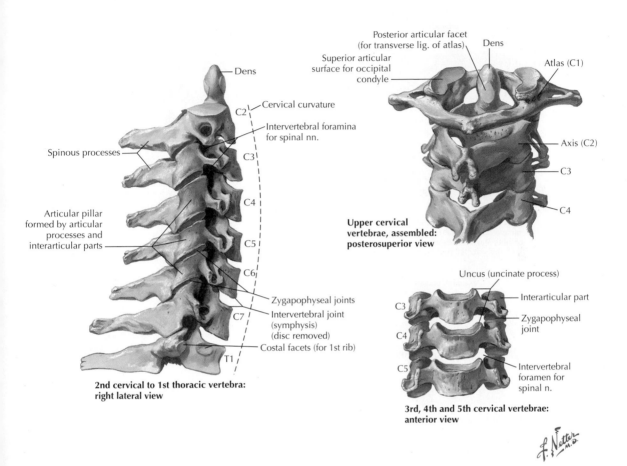

Figure 3-3

Joints of the cervical spine.

Joint	Type and Classification	Closed Packed Position	Capsular Pattern
Atlanto-occipital	Synovial: plane	Not Reported	Not Reported
Atlanto-odontoid/dens	Synovial: trochoid	Extension	Not Reported
Atlantoaxial Apophyseal joints	Synovial: plane	Extension	Not Reported
C3-C7 Apophyseal joints	Synovial: plane	Full extension	Limitation in sidebending = rotation = extension
C3-C7 Intervertebral joints	Amphiarthrodial	Not applicable	Not applicable

Ligaments

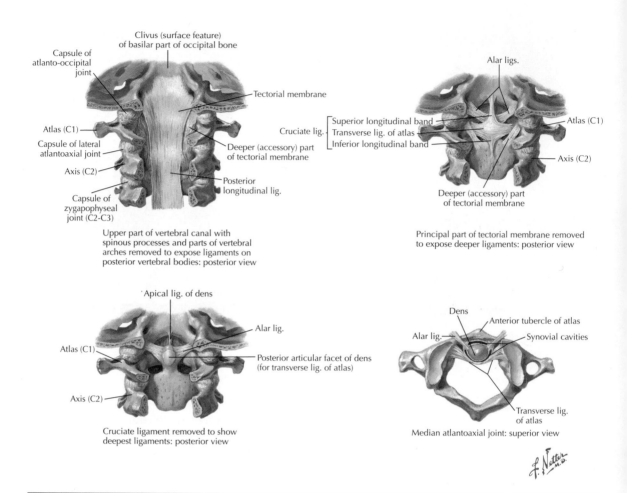

Figure 3-4

Ligaments of the atlanto-occipital joint.

Ligaments	Attachments	Function
Alar	Sides of dens to lateral aspects of foramen magnum	Limits ipsilateral head rotation and contralateral sidebending
Apical	Dens to posterior aspect of foramen magnum	Limits separation of dens from occiput
Tectorial membrane	Body of C2 to occiput	Limits forward flexion
Cruciform ligament • Superior longitudinal • Transverse • Inferior	• Transverse ligament to the occiput • Extends between lateral tubercles of C1 • Transverse ligament to the body of C2	Maintains contact between dens and anterior arch of atlas

Ligaments

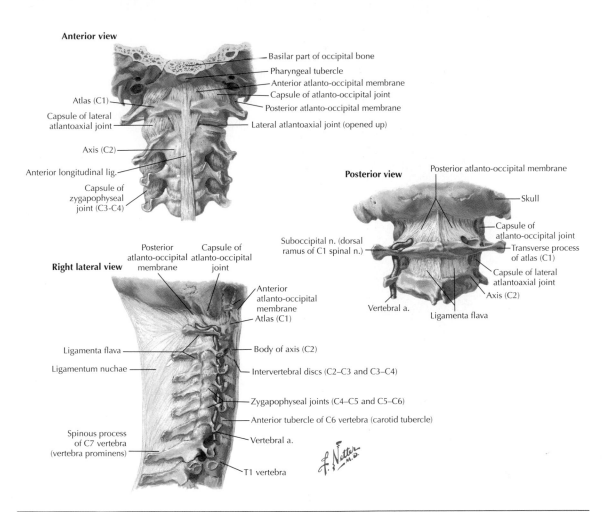

Anterior view

Basilar part of occipital bone
Pharyngeal tubercle
Anterior atlanto-occipital membrane
Capsule of atlanto-occipital joint
Posterior atlanto-occipital membrane
Lateral atlantoaxial joint (opened up)

Atlas (C1)
Capsule of lateral atlantoaxial joint
Axis (C2)
Anterior longitudinal lig.
Capsule of zygapophyseal joint (C3-C4)

Posterior view

Posterior atlanto-occipital membrane
Skull
Capsule of atlanto-occipital joint
Transverse process of atlas (C1)
Capsule of lateral atlantoaxial joint
Axis (C2)
Suboccipital n. (dorsal ramus of C1 spinal n.)
Vertebral a.
Ligamenta flava

Right lateral view

Posterior atlanto-occipital membrane
Capsule of atlanto-occipital joint
Anterior atlanto-occipital membrane
Atlas (C1)
Body of axis (C2)
Intervertebral discs (C2–C3 and C3–C4)
Zygapophyseal joints (C4–C5 and C5–C6)
Anterior tubercle of C6 vertebra (carotid tubercle)
Vertebral a.
T1 vertebra
Ligamenta flava
Ligamentum nuchae
Spinous process of C7 vertebra (vertebra prominens)

Figure 3-5

Spinal ligaments.

Ligaments	Attachments	Function
Anterior longitudinal	Extends from anterior sacrum to anterior tubercle of C1. Connects anterolateral vertebral bodies and discs	Maintains stability of vertebral body joints and prevents hyperextension of vertebral column
Posterior longitudinal	Extends from the sacrum to C2. Runs within the vertebral canal attaching the posterior vertebral bodies	Prevents hyperflexion of vertebral column and posterior disc protrusion
Ligamentum nuchae	An extension of the supraspinous ligament (occipital protuberance to C7)	Prevents cervical hyperflexion
Ligamenta flava	Attaches the lamina above each vertebra to the lamina below	Prevents separation of the vertebral lamina
Supraspinous	Connects apices of spinous processes C7-S1	Limits separation of spinous processes
Interspinous	Connects adjoining spinous processes C1-S1	Limits separation of spinous processes
Intertransverse	Connects adjacent transverse processes of vertebrae	Limits separation of transverse processes

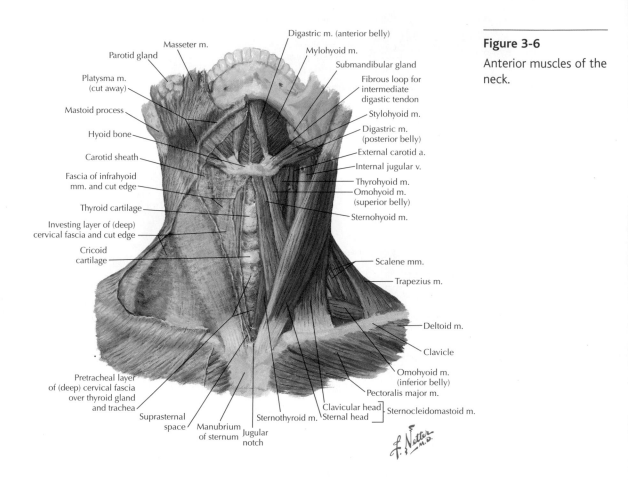

Figure 3-6

Anterior muscles of the neck.

Muscle	Proximal Attachment	Distal Attachment	Nerve and Segmental Level	Action
Sternocleidomastoid	Lateral aspect of mastoid process and lateral superior nuchal line	Sternal head: anterior aspect of manubrium Clavicular head: supero-medial aspect of clavicle	Spinal root of accessory nerve	Neck flexion, ipsilateral side-bending, and contralateral rotation
Scalenes				
• Anterior	Transverse processes of vertebrae C4-C6	1st rib	C4, C5, C6	Elevates first rib, ipsilateral sidebending, and contralateral rotation
• Middle	Transverse processes of vertebrae C1-C4	Superior aspect of 1st rib	Ventral rami of cervical spinal nerves	Elevates 1st rib, ipsilateral side-bending, contralateral rotation
• Posterior		External aspect of 2nd rib	Ventral rami of cervical spinal nerves C3, C4	Elevates 2nd rib, ipsilateral sidebending, contralateral rotation
Platysma	Inferior mandible	Fascia of pectoralis major and deltoid	Cervical branch of facial nerve	Draws skin of neck superiorly with clenched jaw, draws corners of the mouth inferiorly

Suprahyoid and Infrahyoid Muscles

Hyoid bone
Thyrohyoid membrane
External carotid a.
Internal jugular v.
Thyrohyoid m.
Thyroid cartilage
Omohyoid m. (superior belly)
Sternohyoid m.
Median cricothyroid lig.
Cricoid cartilage
Scalene mm.
Trapezius m.
Omohyoid m. (inferior belly)
Trachea

Digastric m. (anterior belly)
Mylohyoid m.
Hyoglossus m.
Stylohyoid m.
Digastric m. (posterior belly)
Fibrous loop for intermediate digastric tendon
Sternohyoid and omohyoid mm. (cut)
Thyrohyoid m.
Oblique line of thyroid cartilage
Cricothyroid m.
Sternothyroid m.
Omohyoid m. (superior belly) (cut)
Thyroid gland
Sternohyoid m. (cut)
Clavicle

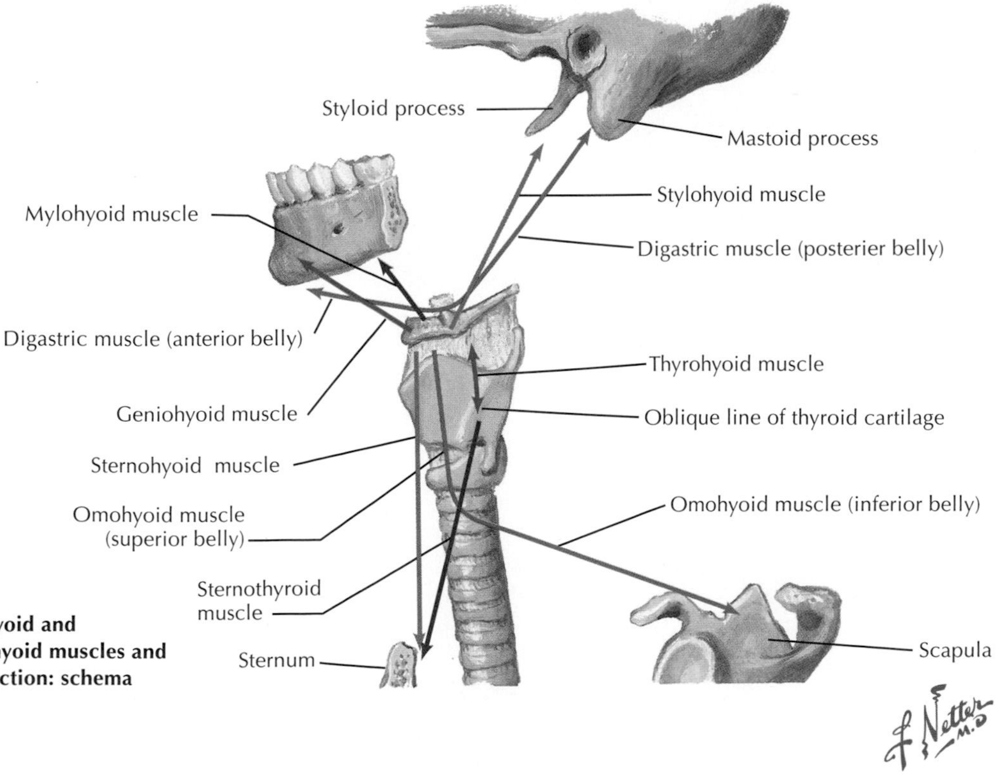

Styloid process
Mastoid process
Stylohyoid muscle
Digastric muscle (posterier belly)
Mylohyoid muscle
Digastric muscle (anterior belly)
Geniohyoid muscle
Sternohyoid muscle
Omohyoid muscle (superior belly)
Sternothyroid muscle
Thyrohyoid muscle
Oblique line of thyroid cartilage
Omohyoid muscle (inferior belly)
Scapula
Sternum

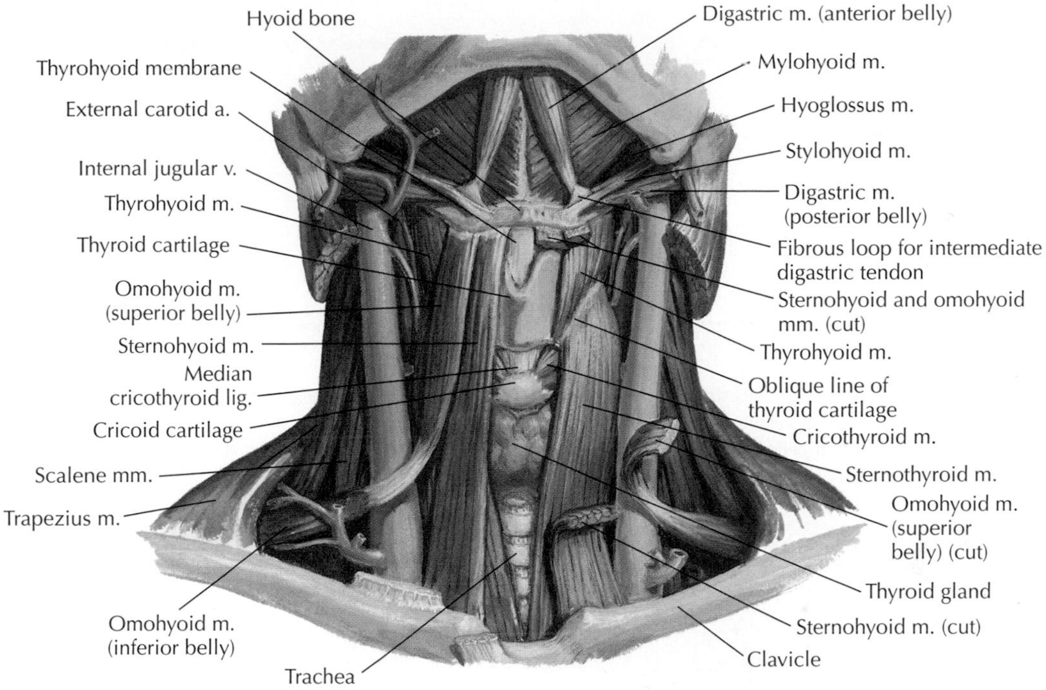

Infrahyoid and suprahyoid muscles and their action: schema

Figure 3-7
Suprahyoid and infrahyoid muscles.

Muscles (continued)

Suprahyoid and Infrahyoid Muscles

Muscle	Proximal Attachment	Distal Attachment	Nerve and Segmental Level	Action
Suprahyoids				
Mylohyoid	Mandibular mylohyoid line	Hyoid bone	Mylohyoid nerve	Elevates hyoid bone, floor of mouth, and tongue
Geniohyoid	Mental spine of mandible	Body of hyoid bone	Hypoglossal nerve	Elevates hyoid bone anterosuperiorly, widens pharynx
Stylohyoid	Styloid process of temporal bone	Body of hyoid bone	Cervical branch of facial nerve	Elevates and retracts hyoid bone
Digastric	Anterior belly: digastric fossa of mandible Posterior belly: mastoid notch of temporal bone	Greater horn of hyoid bone	Anterior belly: mylohyoid nerve Posterior belly: facial nerve	Depresses mandible and raises hyoid
Infrahyoids				
Sternohyoid	Manubrium and medial clavicle	Body of hyoid bone	Branch of ansa cervicalis (C1, C2, C3)	Depresses hyoid bone after it has been elevated
Omohyoid	Superior border of scapula	Inferior aspect of hyoid bone	Branch of ansa cervicalis (C1, C2, C3)	Depresses and retracts hyoid bone
Sternothyroid	Posterior aspect of manubrium	Thyroid cartilage	Branch of ansa cervicalis (C2, C3)	Depresses hyoid bone and larynx
Thyrohyoid	Thyroid cartilage	Body and greater horn of hyoid bone	Hypoglossal nerve (C1)	Depresses hyoid bone, elevates larynx

Muscles

Scalene and Prevertebral Muscles

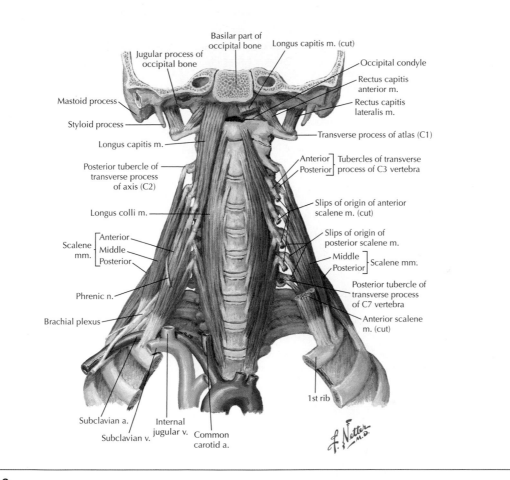

Figure 3-8

Scalene and prevertebral muscles.

Muscle	Proximal Attachment	Distal Attachment	Nerve and Segmental Level	Action
Longus capitis	Basilar aspect of occipital bone	Anterior tubercles of transverse processes C3-C6	Ventral rami of C1-C3 spinal nerves	Flexes head on neck
Longus colli	Anterior tubercle of C1, bodies of C1-C3, and transverse processes of C3-C6	Bodies of C3-T3 and transverse processes of C3-C5	Ventral rami of C2-C6 spinal nerves	Neck flexion, ipsilateral sidebending and rotation
Rectus capitis anterior	Base of skull anterior to occipital condyle	Anterior aspect of lateral mass of C1	Branches from loop between C1 and C2 spinal nerves	Flexes head on neck
Rectus capitis lateralis	Jugular process of occipital bone	Transverse process of C1		Flexes head and assists in stabilizing head on neck

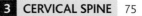

Muscles

Posterior Muscles of the Neck

Muscle	Proximal Attachment	Distal Attachment	Nerve and Segmental Level	Action
Upper trapezius	Superior nuchal line, occipital protuberance, nuchal ligament, spinous processes C7-C12	Lateral clavicle, acromion, and spine of scapula	Spinal root of accessory nerve	Elevates scapula
Levator scapulae	Transverse processes of C1-C4	Superomedial border of scapula	Dorsal scapular nerve (C3, C4, C5)	Elevates scapula and inferiorly rotates glenoid fossa
Semispinalis capitis and cervicis	Cervical and thoracic spinous processes	Superior spinous processes and occipital bone	Dorsal rami of spinal nerves	Bilaterally: extends the neck Unilaterally: ipsilateral sidebending
Splenius capitis and cervicis	Spinous processes T1-T6 and ligamentum nuchae	Mastoid process and lateral superior nuchal line	Dorsal rami of middle cervical spinal nerves	Bilaterally: head and neck extension Unilaterally: ipsilateral rotation
Longissimus capitis and cervicis	Superior thoracic transverse processes and cervical transverse processes	Mastoid process of temporal bone and cervical transverse processes	Dorsal rami of cervical spinal nerves	Head extension, ipsilateral sidebending, and rotation of head and neck
Spinalis cervicis	Lower cervical spinous processes of vertebrae	Upper cervical spinous processes of vertebrae	Dorsal rami of spinal nerves	Bilaterally: extends neck Unilaterally: ipsilateral sidebending of neck
Posterior Occipitals				
Rectus capitis posterior major	Spinous process of C2	Lateral inferior nuchal line of occipital bone	Suboccipital nerve (C1)	Head extension and ipsilateral rotation
Rectus capitis posterior minor	Posterior arch of C1	Medial inferior nuchal line	Suboccipital nerve (C1)	Head extension and ipsilateral rotation
Obliquus capitis superior	Transverse process of C1	Occipital bone	Suboccipital nerve (C1)	Head extension and sidebending
Obliquus capitis inferior	Spinous process of C2	Transverse process of C1	Suboccipital nerve (C1)	Ipsilateral neck rotation

Posterior Muscles of the Neck

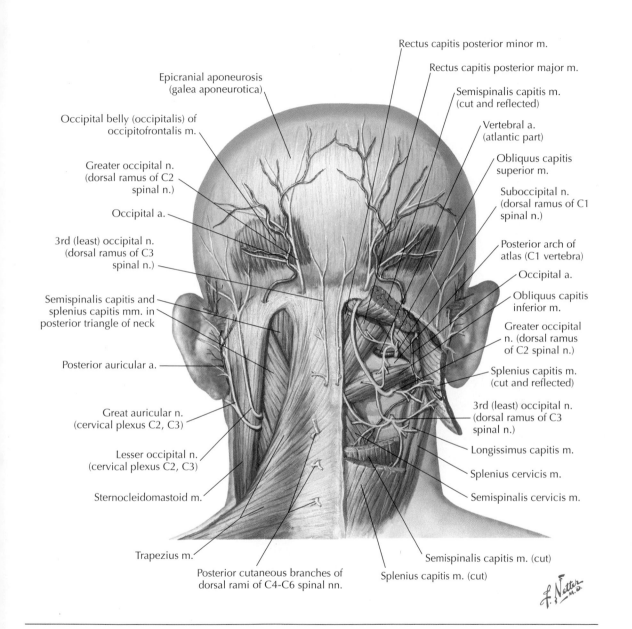

Rectus capitis posterior minor m.

Rectus capitis posterior major m.

Semispinalis capitis m. (cut and reflected)

Epicranial aponeurosis (galea aponeurotica)

Vertebral a. (atlantic part)

Occipital belly (occipitalis) of occipitofrontalis m.

Obliquus capitis superior m.

Greater occipital n. (dorsal ramus of C2 spinal n.)

Suboccipital n. (dorsal ramus of C1 spinal n.)

Occipital a.

Posterior arch of atlas (C1 vertebra)

3rd (least) occipital n. (dorsal ramus of C3 spinal n.)

Occipital a.

Obliquus capitis inferior m.

Semispinalis capitis and splenius capitis mm. in posterior triangle of neck

Greater occipital n. (dorsal ramus of C2 spinal n.)

Posterior auricular a.

Splenius capitis m. (cut and reflected)

3rd (least) occipital n. (dorsal ramus of C3 spinal n.)

Great auricular n. (cervical plexus C2, C3)

Longissimus capitis m.

Lesser occipital n. (cervical plexus C2, C3)

Splenius cervicis m.

Sternocleidomastoid m.

Semispinalis cervicis m.

Trapezius m.

Semispinalis capitis m. (cut)

Posterior cutaneous branches of dorsal rami of C4-C6 spinal nn.

Splenius capitis m. (cut)

Figure 3-9

Posterior muscles of the neck.

Nerves	Segmental Levels	Sensory	Motor
Dorsal scapular	C4, C5	No sensory	Rhomboids, levator scapulae
Suprascapular	C4, C5, C6	No sensory	Supraspinatus, infraspinatus
Nerve to subclavius	C5, C6	No sensory	Subclavius
Lateral pectoral	C5, C6, C7	No sensory	Pectoralis major
Medial pectoral	C8, T1	No sensory	Pectoralis major Pectoralis minor
Long thoracic	C5, C6, C7	No sensory	Serratus anterior
Medial cutaneous of arm	C8, T1	Medial aspect of arm	No motor
Medial cutaneous of forearm	C8, T1	Medial aspect of forearm	No motor
Upper subscapular	C5, C6	No sensory	Subscapularis
Lower subscapular	C5, C6, C7	No sensory	Subscapularis, teres major
Thoracodorsal	C6, C7, C8	No sensory	Latissimus dorsi
Axillary	C5, C6	Lateral shoulder	Deltoid, teres minor
Radial	C5, C6, C7, C8, T1	Dorsal lateral aspect of hand including the thumb and up to the base of digits 2 and 3	Triceps brachii, brachioradialis, anconeus, extensor carpi radialis longus, extensor carpi radialis brevis
Median	C5, C6, C7, C8, T1	Palmar aspect of lateral hand including lateral half of 4th digit and dorsal distal half of digits 1-3 and lateral border of 4	Pronator teres, flexor carpi radialis, palmaris longus, flexor digitorum superficialis, flexor pollicis longus, flexor digitorum profundus (lateral half), pronator quadratus, lumbricals to digits 2 and 3, thenar muscles
Ulnar	C8, T1	Medial border of both palmar and dorsal hand including medial half of 4th digit	Flexor carpi ulnaris, flexor digitorum profundus (medial half), palmar interossei, adductor pollicis, palmaris brevis, dorsal interossei, lumbricals to digits 4 and 5, hypothenar muscles
Musculocutaneous	C5, C6, C7	Lateral forearm	Coracobrachialis, biceps brachii, brachialis

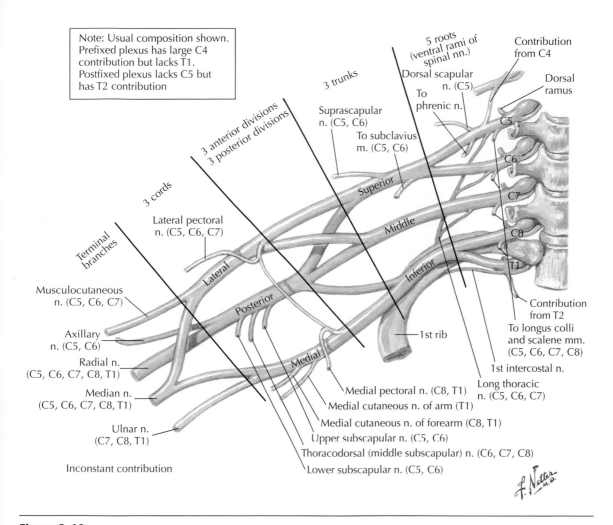

Note: Usual composition shown. Prefixed plexus has large C4 contribution but lacks T1. Postfixed plexus lacks C5 but has T2 contribution

5 roots (ventral rami of spinal nn.)

Contribution from C4

Dorsal scapular n. (C5)

Dorsal ramus

3 trunks

To phrenic n.

Suprascapular n. (C5, C6)

C5

3 anterior divisions
3 posterior divisions

To subclavius m. (C5, C6)

C6

C7

Superior

3 cords

Lateral pectoral n. (C5, C6, C7)

Middle

C8

T1

Terminal branches

Lateral

Inferior

Contribution from T2

Musculocutaneous n. (C5, C6, C7)

Posterior

1st rib

To longus colli and scalene mm. (C5, C6, C7, C8)

Axillary n. (C5, C6)

Medial

1st intercostal n.

Radial n. (C5, C6, C7, C8, T1)

Long thoracic n. (C5, C6, C7)

Median n. (C5, C6, C7, C8, T1)

Medial pectoral n. (C8, T1)

Medial cutaneous n. of arm (T1)

Ulnar n. (C7, C8, T1)

Medial cutaneous n. of forearm (C8, T1)

Upper subscapular n. (C5, C6)

Inconstant contribution

Thoracodorsal (middle subscapular) n. (C6, C7, C8)

Lower subscapular n. (C5, C6)

Figure 3-10

Nerves of the neck.

Initial Hypotheses Based on Patient History

History	Initial Hypotheses
Patient reports diffuse nonspecific neck pain that is exacerbated by neck movements	Mechanical neck pain[1] Cervical facet syndrome[2] Cervical muscle strain or sprain
Patient reports pain in certain postures that are alleviated by positional changes	Upper crossed postural syndrome
Traumatic mechanism of injury with complaint of nonspecific cervical symptoms that are exacerbated in the vertical positions and relieved with the head supported in the supine position	Cervical instability, especially if patient reports dysesthesias of the face occurring with neck movement
Reports of nonspecific neck pain with numbness and tingling into one upper extremity	Cervical radiculopathy
Reports of neck pain with bilateral upper extremity symptoms with occasional reports of loss of balance or lack of coordination of the lower extremities	Cervical myelopathy

Cervical Zygapophyseal Pain Syndromes

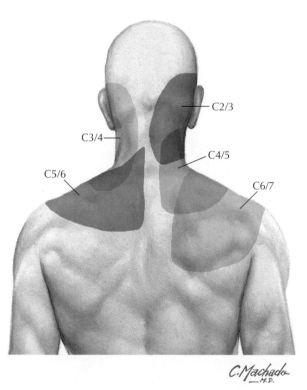

Figure 3-11

Pain referral patterns. Distribution of zygapophyseal pain referral patterns as described by Dwyer and colleagues.[3]

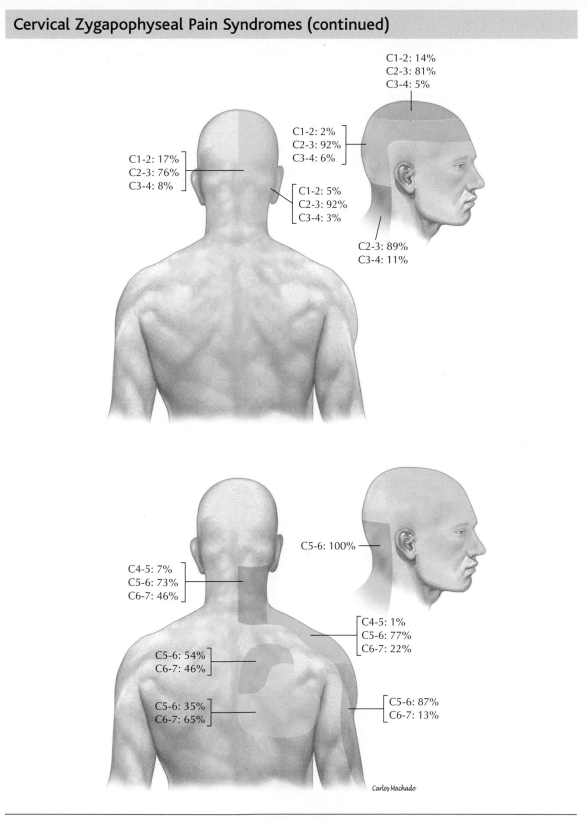

C1-2: 14%
C2-3: 81%
C3-4: 5%

C1-2: 2%
C2-3: 92%
C3-4: 6%

C1-2: 17%
C2-3: 76%
C3-4: 8%

C1-2: 5%
C2-3: 92%
C3-4: 3%

C2-3: 89%
C3-4: 11%

C5-6: 100%

C4-5: 7%
C5-6: 73%
C6-7: 46%

C4-5: 1%
C5-6: 77%
C6-7: 22%

C5-6: 54%
C6-7: 46%

C5-6: 87%
C6-7: 13%

C5-6: 35%
C6-7: 65%

Carlos Machado

Figure 3-12

Pain referral patterns. Probability of zygapophyseal joints at the segments indicated being the source of pain, as described by Cooper and colleagues.[5]

Reliability of the Cervical Spine Historical Examination

ICC or κ	Interpretation
.81-1.0	Substantial agreement
.61-.80	Moderate agreement
.41-.60	Fair agreement
.11-.40	Slight agreement
.0-.10	No agreement

Historical Question and Study	Possible Responses	Population	Inter-examiner Reliability
Mode of onset[6]	Gradual, sudden, or traumatic		κ = .72 (.47, .96)
Nature of neck symptoms[6]	Constant or intermittent		κ = .81 (.56, 1.0)
Prior episode of neck pain[6]	Yes or No		κ = .90 (.70, 1.0)
Turning the head aggravates symptoms[6]	Yes or No	22 patients with mechanical neck pain	(Right) κ = −.04 (2.11, .02)* (Left) κ = 1.0 (1.0, 1.0)
Looking up and down aggravates symptoms[6]	Yes or No		(Down) κ = .79 (.51, 1.0) (Up) κ = .80 (.55, 1.0)
Driving aggravates symptoms[6]	Yes or No		κ = −.06 (−.39, .26)*
Sleeping aggravates symptoms[6]	Yes or No		κ = .90 (.72, 1.0)
Which of the following symptoms are most bothersome for you?[7]	• Pain • Numbness and tingling • Loss of feeling		κ = .74 (.55, .93)
Where are your symptoms most bothersome?[7]	• Neck • Shoulder or shoulder blade • Arm above elbow • Arm below elbow • Hands and/or fingers	50 patients with suspected cervical radiculopathy or carpal tunnel syndrome	κ = .83 (.68, .96)
Which of the following best describes the behavior of your symptoms?[7]	• Constant • Intermittent • Variable		κ = .57 (.35, .79)
Does your entire affected limb and/or hand feel numb?[7]	Yes or No		κ = .53 (.26, .81)
Do your symptoms keep you from falling asleep?[7]	Yes or No		κ = .70 (.48, .92)
Do your symptoms improve with moving your neck?[7]	Yes or No		κ = .67 (.44, .90)

*Question had high percent agreement but low κ because 95% of participants answered "yes."

+LR	Interpretation	−LR
>10	Large	<.1
5.0-10.0	Moderate	.1-.2
2.0-5.0	Small	.2-.5
1.0-2.0	Rarely important	.5-1.0

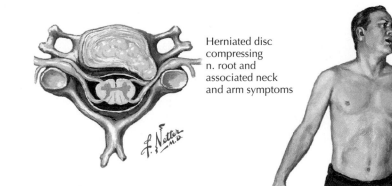

Herniated disc compressing n. root and associated neck and arm symptoms

Figure 3-13

Cervical radiculopathy.

Complaint and Study Quality	Description and Positive Findings	Population	Reference Standard	Sens	Spec	+LR	−LR
Weakness[8]	Not specifically described	183 patients referred to electro-diagnostic laboratories	Cervical radiculopathy via electrodiagnostics	.65	.39	1.07	.90
Numbness[8]				.79	.25	1.05	.84
Arm pain[8]				.65	.26	.88	1.35
Neck pain[8]				.62	.35	.95	1.09
Tingling[8]				.72	.25	.96	1.92
Burning[8]				.33	.63	.89	1.06

+LR	Interpretation	−LR
>10	Large	<.1
5.0-10.0	Moderate	.1-.2
2.0-5.0	Small	.2-.5
1.0-2.0	Rarely important	.5-1.0

Complaint and Study Quality	Description and Positive Findings	Population	Reference Standard	Sens	Spec	+LR	−LR
Which of the following symptoms are most bothersome for you?[7] ◇	Pain			.47 (.23, .71)	.52 (.41, .65)	.99 (.56, 1.7)	
	Numbness and tingling			.47 (.23, .71)	.56 (.42, .68)	1.1 (.6, 1.9)	
	Loss of feeling			.06 (.00, .17)	.92 (.85, .99)	.74 (.09, 5.9)	
Where are your symptoms most bothersome?[7] ◇	Neck			.19 (.00, .35)	.90 (.83, .98)	1.9 (.54, 6.9)	
	Shoulder or scapula			.38 (.19, .73)	.84 (.75, .93)	2.3 (1.0, 5.4)	
	Arm above elbow	82 consecutive patients referred to an electrophysiologic laboratory with suspected diagnosis of cervical radiculopathy or carpal tunnel syndrome.	Cervical radiculopathy via needle electromyography and nerve conduction studies	.03 (.14, .61)	.93 (.86, .99)	.41 (.02, 7.3)	Not reported
	Arm below elbow			.06 (.0, .11)	.84 (.75, .93)	.39 (.05, 2.8)	
	Hands and/or fingers			.38 (.14, .48)	.48 (.36, .61)	.73 (.37, 1.4)	
Which of the following best describes the behavior of your symptoms?[7] ◇	Constant			.12 (.00, .27)	.84 (.75, .93)	.74 (.18, 3.1)	
	Intermittent			.35 (.13, .58)	.62 (.50, .74)	.93 (.45, 1.9)	
	Variable			.53 (.29, .77)	.54 (.42, .66)	1.2 (.68, 1.9)	
Does your entire affected limb and/or hand feel numb?[7] ◇				.24 (.03, .44)	.73 (.62, .84)	.87 (.34, 2.3)	1.1 (.77, 1.4)
Do your symptoms keep you from falling asleep?[7] ◇	Yes or No			.47 (.23, .71)	.60 (.48, .72)	1.19 (.66, 2.1)	.88 (.54, 1.4)
Do your symptoms improve with moving your neck?[7] ◇				.65 (.42, .87)	.71 (.60, .82)	2.23 (1.3, 3.8)	.50 (.26, .97)

Neurological Examination

Reliability of Sensation Testing

ICC or κ	Interpretation
.81-1.0	Substantial agreement
.61-.80	Moderate agreement
.41-.60	Fair agreement
.11-.40	Slight agreement
.0-.10	No agreement

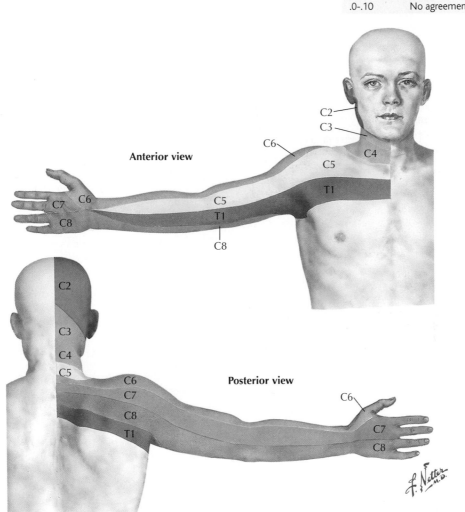

Figure 3-14

Dermatomes of the upper limb.

Test and Study	Description and Positive Findings	Population	Reliability
Identifying sensory deficits in the extremities[9]	No details given	8924 adult patients who presented to the emergency department after blunt trauma to the head/neck and had a Glasgow Coma Score of 15	Inter-examiner κ = **.60**

Diagnostic Utility of Pin Prick Sensation Testing for Cervical Radiculopathy

+LR	Interpretation	−LR
>10	Large	<.1
5.0-10.0	Moderate	.1-.2
2.0-5.0	Small	.2-.5
1.0-2.0	Rarely important	.5-1.0

Test and Study Quality	Description and Positive Findings	Population	Reference Standard	Sens	Spec	+LR	−LR
C5 Dermatome[7]	Pin prick sensation testing. Graded as "normal" or "abnormal"	82 consecutive patients referred to an electro-physiologic laboratory with suspected diagnosis of cervical radiculopathy or carpal tunnel syndrome	Cervical radiculopathy via needle electromyography and nerve conduction studies	.29 (.08, .51)	.86 (.77, .94)	2.1 (.79, 5.3)	.82 (.60, 1.1)
C6 Dermatome[7]				.24 (.03, .44)	.66 (.54, .78)	.69 (.28, 1.8)	1.16 (.84, 1.6)
C7 Dermatome[7]				.18 (.0, .36)	.77 (.66, .87)	.76 (.25, 2.3)	1.07 (.83, 1.4)
C8 Dermatome[7]				.12 (.0, .27)	.81 (.71, .90)	.61 (.15, 2.5)	1.09 (.88, 1.4)
T1 Dermatome[7]				.18 (.0, .36)	.79 (.68, .89)	.83 (.27, 2.6)	1.05 (.81, 1.4)
Decreased sensation to pin prick[8]	Not specifically described	183 patients referred to electrodiagnostic laboratories	Cervical radiculopathy via electrodiagnostics	.49	.64	1.36	.80

Neurological Examination

Reliability of Manual Muscle Testing

ICC or κ	Interpretation
.81-1.0	Substantial agreement
.61-.80	Moderate agreement
.41-.60	Fair agreement
.11-.40	Slight agreement
.0-.10	No agreement

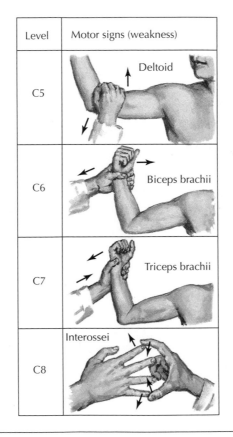

Level	Motor signs (weakness)
C5	Deltoid
C6	Biceps brachii
C7	Triceps brachii
C8	Interossei

Figure 3-15

Manual muscle testing of the upper limb.

Test and Study	Description and Positive Findings	Population	Reliability
Identifying motor deficits in the extremities[9]	No details given	8924 adult patients who presented to the emergency department after blunt trauma to the head/neck and had a Glasgow Coma Score of 15	Inter-examiner κ = **.93**

Diagnostic Utility of Manual Muscle Testing for Cervical Radiculopathy

+LR	Interpretation	−LR
>10	Large	<.1
5.0-10.0	Moderate	.1-.2
2.0-5.0	Small	.2-.5
1.0-2.0	Rarely important	.5-1.0

Test and Study Quality	Description and Positive Findings	Population	Reference Standard	Sens	Spec	+LR	−LR
MMT deltoid[7]	Standard strength testing using methods of Kendall and McCreary. Graded as "normal" or "abnormal"	82 consecutive patients referred to an electrophysiologic laboratory with suspected diagnosis of cervical radiculopathy or carpal tunnel syndrome	Cervical radiculopathy via needle electromyography and nerve conduction studies	.24 (.03, .44)	.89 (.81, .97)	2.1 (.70, 6.4)	.86 (.65, 1.1)
MMT biceps brachii[7]				.24 (.03, .44)	.94 (.88, 1.0)	3.7 (1.0, 13.3)	.82 (.62, 1.1)
MMT extensor carpi radialis longus/ brevis[7]				.12 (.00, .27)	.90 (.83, .98)	1.2 (.27, 5.6)	.98 (.81, 1.2)
MMT triceps brachii[7]				.12 (.00, .27)	.94 (.88, 1.0)	1.9 (.37, 9.3)	.94 (.78, 1.1)
MMT flexor carpi radialis[7]				.06 (.00, .17)	.89 (.82, .97)	.55 (.07, 4.2)	1.05 (.91, 1.2)
MMT abductor pollicis brevis[7]				.06 (.00, .17)	.84 (.75, .93)	.37 (.05, 2.7)	1.12 (.95, 1.3)
MMT first dorsal interosseus[7]				.03 (.00, .10)	.93 (.87, .99)	.40 (.02, 7.0)	1.05 (.94, 1.2)

Neurological Examination

Diagnostic Utility of Muscle Stretch Reflex Testing for Cervical Radiculopathy

+LR	Interpretation	−LR
>10	Large	<.1
5.0-10.0	Moderate	.1-.2
2.0-5.0	Small	.2-.5
1.0-2.0	Rarely important	.5-1.0

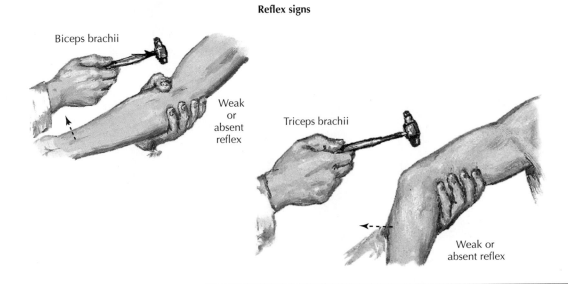

Reflex signs

Biceps brachii

Weak or absent reflex

Triceps brachii

Weak or absent reflex

Figure 3-16

Reflex testing.

Test and Study Quality	Description and Positive Findings	Population	Reference Standard	Sens	Spec	+LR	−LR
Biceps brachii MSR[7]	Tested bilaterally using a standard reflex hammer. Graded as "normal" or "abnormal"	82 consecutive patients referred to an electrophysiologic laboratory with suspected diagnosis of cervical radiculopathy or carpal tunnel syndrome	Cervical radiculopathy via needle electromyography and nerve conduction studies	.24 (.3, .44)	.95 (.90, 1.0)	4.9 (1.2, 20.0)	.80 (.61, 1.1)
Brachioradialis MSR[7]				.06 (.0, .17)	.95 (.90, 1.9)	1.2 (.14, 11.1)	.99 (.87, 1.1)
Triceps MSR[7]				.03 (.0, .10)	.93 (.87, .99)	.40 (.02, 7.0)	1.05 (.94, 1.2)
Biceps[8]	Not specifically described	183 patients referred to electrodiagnostic laboratories	Cervical radiculopathy via electrodiagnostics	.10	.99	10.0	.91
Triceps[8]				.10	.95	2.0	.95
Brachioradialis[8]				.08	.99	8.0	.93

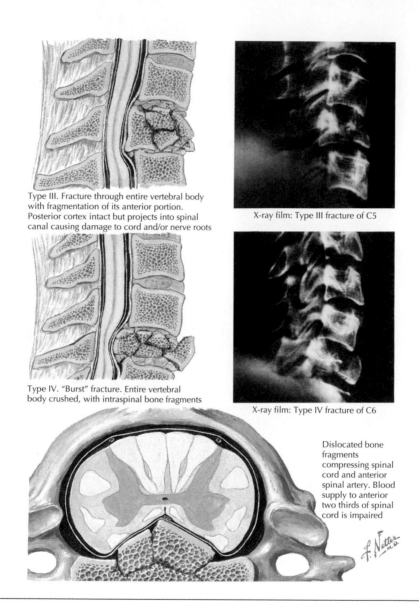

Type III. Fracture through entire vertebral body with fragmentation of its anterior portion. Posterior cortex intact but projects into spinal canal causing damage to cord and/or nerve roots

X-ray film: Type III fracture of C5

Type IV. "Burst" fracture. Entire vertebral body crushed, with intraspinal bone fragments

X-ray film: Type IV fracture of C6

Dislocated bone fragments compressing spinal cord and anterior spinal artery. Blood supply to anterior two thirds of spinal cord is impaired

Figure 3-17

Compression fracture of the cervical spine.

NEXUS Low-Risk Criteria[10]
Cervical spine radiography is indicated for patients with trauma unless they meet all of the following criteria: 1. No posterior midline cervical spine tenderness 2. No evidence of intoxication 3. Normal level of alertness 4. No focal neurological deficit 5. No painful distracting injuries

Canadian C-Spine Rule[10]

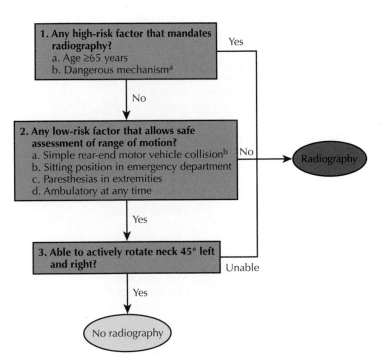

1. **Any high-risk factor that mandates radiography?**
   a. Age ≥65 years
   b. Dangerous mechanism[a]

Yes

No

2. **Any low-risk factor that allows safe assessment of range of motion?**
   a. Simple rear-end motor vehicle collision[b]
   b. Sitting position in emergency department
   c. Paresthesias in extremities
   d. Ambulatory at any time

No → Radiography

Yes

3. **Able to actively rotate neck 45° left and right?**

Unable

Yes

No radiography

[a]A dangerous mechanism is considered to be a fall from an elevation of 3 feet or greater or three to five stairs; an axial load to the head (e.g., diving); a motor vehicle collision at high speed (>100 km/hr) or with rollover or ejection.

[b]A simple rear-end motor vehicle collision excludes being pushed into oncoming traffic, being hit by a bus or a large truck, a rollover, or being hit by a high-speed vehicle.

Diagnostic Utility of the Clinical Examination for Identifying Cervical Spine Injury

+LR	Interpretation	−LR
>10	Large	<.1
5.0–10.0	Moderate	.1-.2
2.0–5.0	Small	.2-.5
1.0–2.0	Rarely important	.5-1.0

Test and Study Quality	Description and Positive Findings	Population	Reference Standard	Sens	Spec	+LR	−LR
NEXUS Low-Risk Criteria[11] ◇		34,069 patients who presented to the emergency department after blunt trauma and had cervical spine radiography	Clinically important cervical spine injury demonstrated by radiography, computed tomography (CT), or magnetic resonance imaging (MRI)	.99 (.98, 1.0)	.13 (.13, .13)	1.14	.08
NEXUS Low-Risk Criteria[12] ◇	See previous page	8924 alert adult patients who presented to the emergency department after blunt trauma to the head/neck		.93 (.87, .96)	.38 (.37, .39)	1.50	.18
NEXUS Low-Risk Criteria[10] ◇		7438 alert adult patients who presented to the emergency department after blunt trauma to the head/neck	Clinically important cervical spine injury defined as any fracture, dislocation, or ligamentous instability demonstrated by radiography, CT, and/or a telephone follow-up	.91 (.85, .94)	.37 (.36, .38)	1.44	.24
Canadian C-Spine Rule[10] ◇				.99 (.96, 1.0)	.45 (.44, .46)	1.80	.02
Canadian C-Spine Rule[9] ◇	See previous page	8924 alert adult patients who presented to the emergency department after blunt trauma to the head/neck		1.0 (.98, 1.0)	.43 (.40, .44)	1.75	.00
Canadian C-Spine Rule[13] ◯				1.0 (.94, 1.0)	.44 (.43, .45)	1.79	.00
Physician judgment[13] ◯	Physicians were asked to estimate the probability that the patient would have a clinically important cervical spine injury by circling one of the following: 0%, 1%, 2%, 3%, 4%, 5%, 10%, 20%, 30%, 40%, 50%, 75%, or 100%	6265 alert adult patients who presented to the emergency department after trauma to the head/neck	Clinically important cervical spine injury demonstrated by radiography, CT, and/or a telephone follow-up	.92 (.82, .96)	.54 (.53, .55)	2.00	.15

Diagnostic Utility of the Clinical Examination for Identifying Cervical Spine Injury

Test and Study Quality	Description and Positive Findings	Population	Reference Standard	Sens	Spec	+LR	−LR
Clinical examination[14] ◯	Patient history including mechanism of injury and subjective complaints of neck pain and/or neurological deficits followed by physical examination of tenderness to palpation, abnormalities to palpation, and neurological deficits	534 patients consulting a level I trauma center after blunt trauma to head/neck	Cervical fracture via CT	.77	.55	1.70	.42
	Among subset of patients with a Glasgow Coma Score of 15 (i.e., alert), who were not intoxicated, and who did not have a distracting injury			.67	.62	1.76	.54

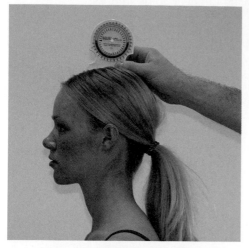

Positioning of inclinometer to measure
flexion and extension

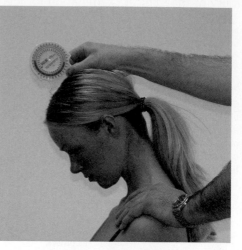

Measurement of flexion

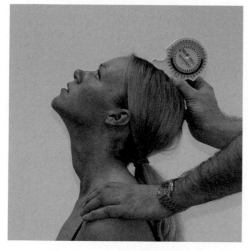

Measurement of extension

Positioning of inclinometer
to measure side bending

Measurement of side
bending to the right

Figure 3-18

Range of motion.

Range of Motion

Reliability of Measuring Range of Motion

ICC or κ	Interpretation
.81-1.0	Substantial agreement
.61-.80	Moderate agreement
.41-.60	Fair agreement
.11-.40	Slight agreement
.0-.10	No agreement

Test and Study	Instrumentation	Population	Inter-examiner Reliability
Extension[15]	Inclinometer	30 patients with neck pain	ICC = .86 (.73, .93)
Flexion[15]			ICC = .78 (.59, .89)
Rotation in flexion[15]			(Right) ICC = .78 (.60, .89) (Left) ICC = .89 (.78, .95)
Lateral bending[15]			(Right) ICC = .87 (.75, .94) (Left) ICC = .85 (.70, .92)
Rotation[15]			(Right) ICC = .86 (.74, .93) (Left) ICC = .91 (.82, .96)
Flexion[6]	Inclinometer	22 patients with mechanical neck pain	ICC = .75 (.50, .89)
Extension[6]			ICC = .74 (.48, .88)
Sidebending[6]			(Right) ICC = .66 (.33, .84) (Left) ICC = .69 (.40, .86)
Rotation[6]	Goniometer		(Right) ICC = .78 (.55, .90) (Left) ICC = .77 (.52, .90)
Flexion-Extension[16]	Digital inclinometer	32 patients with neck pain referred to physical therapy	Single measurement ICC = .89 (.77, .94) Mean of 2 measurements ICC = .95 (.90, .98)
Lateral-flexion[16]			Single measurement ICC = .77 (.58, .88) Mean of 2 measurements ICC = .89 (.77, .94)
Rotation[16]			Single measurement ICC = .88 (.78, .94) Mean of 2 measurements ICC = .95 (.90, .98)
Flexion[7]	Inclinometer	50 patients with suspected cervical radiculopathy or carpal tunnel syndrome	ICC = .79 (.65, .88)
Extension[7]			ICC = .84 (.70, .95)
Left rotation[7]	Goniometer		ICC = .75 (.59, .85)
Right rotation[7]			ICC = .63 (.22, .82)
Left sidebending[7]	Inclinometer		ICC = .63 (.40, .78)
Right sidebending[7]			ICC = .68 (.62, .87)

ICC, intraclass correlation coefficient.

Reliability of Measuring Range of Motion (continued)

ICC or κ	Interpretation
.81-1.0	Substantial agreement
.61-.80	Moderate agreement
.41-.60	Fair agreement
.11-.40	Slight agreement
.0-.10	No agreement

Test and Study	Instrumentation	Population	Inter-examiner Reliability
Flexion[17]	Cervical range-of-motion (CROM) instrument	60 patients with neck pain	ICC = .58
Extension[17]			ICC = .97
Right sidebending[17]			ICC = .96
Left sidebending[17]			ICC = .94
Right rotation[17]			ICC = .96
Left rotation[17]			ICC = .98
Protraction[17]			ICC = .49
Retraction[17]			ICC = .35
Flexion/Extension[18]	Inclinometer and CROM	30 asymptomatic subjects	Inclinometer ICC = .84 CROM ICC = .88
Sidebending[18]			Inclinometer ICC = .82 CROM ICC = .84
Rotation[18]			Inclinometer ICC = .81 CROM ICC = .92
Flexion[19]	CROM, universal goniometer, and visual estimation	60 patients in whom the assessment of cervical ROM testing would be appropriate during the PT evaluation	CROM ICC = .86 Goniometer ICC = .57 Visual estimation ICC = .42
Extension[19]			CROM ICC = .86 Goniometer ICC = .79 Visual estimation ICC = .42
Left sidebending[19]			CROM ICC = .73 Goniometer ICC = .79 Visual estimation ICC = .63
Right sidebending[19]			CROM ICC = .73 Goniometer ICC = .79 Visual estimation ICC = .63
Left rotation[19]			CROM ICC = .82 Goniometer ICC = .54 Visual estimation ICC = .70
Right rotation[19]			CROM ICC = .92 Goniometer ICC = .62 Visual estimation ICC = .82
Identifying ability to actively rotate neck 45° left and right[9]	No details given	8924 adult patients who presented to the emergency department after blunt trauma to the head/neck and had a Glasgow Coma Score of 15	κ = .67
Identifying ability to actively flex neck[9]			κ = .63

Range of Motion

Reliability of Pain Responses during Active Physiologic Range of Motion

ICC or κ	Interpretation
.81-1.0	Substantial agreement
.61-.80	Moderate agreement
.41-.60	Fair agreement
.11-.40	Slight agreement
.0-.10	No agreement

Test and Study	Description and Positive Findings	Population	Inter-examiner Reliability
Extension[15]	Symptom response recorded as "no effect," "increases symptoms," "decreases symptoms," "centralizes symptoms," or "peripheralizes symptoms"	30 patients with neck pain	κ = .65 (.54, .76)
Flexion[15]			κ = .87 (.81, .94)
Rotation in flexion[15]			(Right) κ = .25 (.12, .39) (Left) κ = .69 (.59, .78)
Lateral bending[15]			(Right) κ = .75 (.66, .84) (Left) κ = .28 (.15, .41)
Rotation[15]			(Right) κ = .76 (.67, .84) (Left) κ = .74 (.64, .84)
Flexion[6]	Patient asked about change in symptoms during active range of motion (AROM). Answers were "no change," "increased pain," or "decreased pain"	22 patients with mechanical neck pain	κ = .55 (.23, .87)
Extension[6]			κ = .23 (.09, .37)
Sidebending[6]			(Right) κ = .81 (.57, 1.0) (Left) κ = .00 (−.22, .23)
Rotation[6]			(Right) κ = .40 (−.07, .87) (Left) κ = .73 (.46, 1.0)
Flexion[6]	The effect of each movement on centralization (the movement caused the pain and/or paresthesias to move proximally) or peripheralization of symptoms (the movement causes the pain and/or paresthesias to move more distally) was recorded	22 patients with mechanical neck pain	κ = 1.0 (1.0, 1.0)
Extension[6]			κ = .44 (.17, .71)
Sidebending[6]			(Right) κ = −.06 (−.15, .03) (Left) κ = .02 (−.25, .66)
Rotation[6]			(Right) κ = −.05 (−.15, .03) (Left) κ = −.10 (−.21, .00)
Flexion[20]	Patient seated with back supported. Patient is asked to perform full flexion and pressure is applied by the examiner. Pain responses are recorded on an 11-point numeric pain rating scale (NPRS)	32 patients with neck pain	κ = .63
Extension[20]			κ = .71
Rotation, right[20]			κ = .70
Rotation, left[20]			κ = .66
Sidebending, right[20]			κ = .65
Sidebending, left[20]			κ = .45
Flexion C0-C1[20]	Patient is asked to perform high cervical flexion/extension by nodding. Pain responses are recorded on an 11-point NPRS		κ = .36
Extension C0-C1[20]			κ = .56
Flexion[21]	Patient performs AROM and pain is determined to be either present or not present	24 patients with headaches	κ = .53 (.17, .89)
Extension[21]			κ = .67 (.34, .99)
Rotation, right[21]			κ = .65 (.31, .99)
Rotation, left[21]			κ = .46 (.10, .79)

Diagnostic Utility of Pain Responses during Active Physiologic Range of Motion

+LR	Interpretation	−LR
>10	Large	<.1
5.0-10.0	Moderate	.1-.2
2.0-5.0	Small	.2-.5
1.0-2.0	Rarely important	.5-1.0

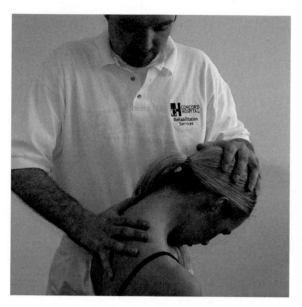

Testing flexion with overpressure

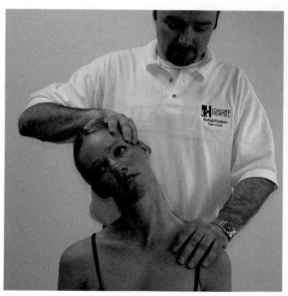

Testing sidebending with overpressure

Figure 3-19

Overpressure testing.

Test and Measure	Test Procedure and Determination of Positive Findings	Population	Reference Standard	Sens	Spec	+LR	−LR
Active flexion and extension of the neck[22]	Active flexion and extension performed to the extremes of the range. Positive if subject reported pain with procedure	75 males (22 with neck pain)	Patient reports of neck pain	.27	.90	2.70	.81

Cervical Strength and Endurance

Reliability of Cervical Strength and Endurance Testing

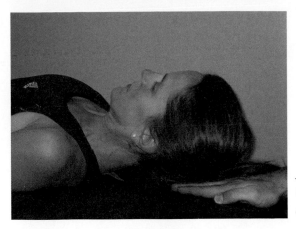

ICC or κ	Interpretation
.81-1.0	Substantial agreement
.61-.80	Moderate agreement
.41-.60	Fair agreement
.11-.40	Slight agreement
.0-.10	No agreement

Figure 3-20

Cervical flexor endurance.

Test and Study	Description and Positive Findings	Population	Reliability
Neck flexor muscle endurance test[23]	With patient supine with knees flexed, examiner's hand is placed behind occiput and the subject gently flexes the upper neck and lifts the head off the examiner's hand while retaining the upper neck flexion. The test was timed and terminated when the subject was unable to maintain the position of the head off the examiner's hand	21 patients with postural neck pain	Inter-examiner ICC = **.93 (.86, .97)**
Chin tuck neck flexion test[6]	With patient supine, subject tucks the chin and lifts the head approximately 1 inch. The test was timed with a stopwatch and terminated when the patient's position deviated	22 patients with mechanical neck pain	Inter-examiner ICC = **.57 (.14, .81)**
Cervical flexor endurance[24]	With patient supine, knees flexed, and chin maximally retracted, subject lifts the head slightly. The test was timed with a stopwatch and terminated when the subject lost maximal retraction, flexed the neck, or could not continue	27 asymptomatic subjects	Intra-examiner ICC = **0.74 (.50, .87)** Inter-examiner Test #1 ICC = **.54 (.31, .73)** Test #2 ICC = **.66 (.46, .81)**
Cervical flexor endurance[25]	With patient supine with knees flexed and chin maximally retracted, subject lifts the head approximately 1 inch. The test was timed with a stopwatch and terminated when the subject lost maximal retraction	20 asymptomatic subjects	Intra-examiner ICC = **.82−.91** Inter-examiner ICC = **.67−.78**
		20 patients with neck pain	Inter-examiner ICC = **.67**
Craniocervical flexion test[26]	With patient supine with a pressure biofeedback unit placed suboccipitally, subjects perform a gentle head-nodding action of craniocervical flexion for five 10-second incremental stages of increasing range (22, 24, 26, 28, and 30 mm Hg). Performance was measured by the highest level of pressure the individual could hold for 10 seconds	10 asymptomatic subjects	Intra-examiner κ = **.72**
Cervical flexor endurance[27]	With patient supine with knees flexed, subject holds the tongue on the roof of the mouth and breathes normally. Subject then lifts his or her head off the table and holds it as long as possible with the neck in a neutral position. The test was timed with a stopwatch and terminated when the head moved > 5° either forward or backward	30 patients with grade II whiplash-associated disorders	Inter-examiner ICC = **.96**

Passive Intervertebral Motion

Reliability of Assessing Limited Passive Intervertebral Motion

ICC or κ	Interpretation
.81-1.0	Substantial agreement
.61-.80	Moderate agreement
.41-.60	Fair agreement
.11-.40	Slight agreement
.0-.10	No agreement

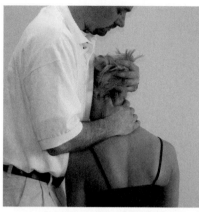

Testing rotation of C1-C2

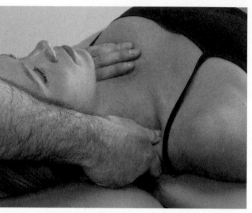

Testing of stiffness of 1st rib

Figure 3-21

Assessing limited passive intervertebral motion.

Test and Study	Description and Positive Findings	Population	Inter-examiner Reliability
Rotation of C1-C2[28]	With patient seated, C2 is stabilized while C1 is rotated on C2 until the end of passive ROM. Positive if decreased rotation on one side compared with contralateral side		κ = .28
Lateral flexion of C2-C3[28]	With patient supine, examiner's left hand stabilizes the patient's head while the right hand performs sidebending flexion of C2-C3 until the end of passive ROM. This is repeated in the contralateral direction. Positive if lateral flexion on one side is reduced compared with contralateral side	61 patients with nonspecific neck problems	κ = .43
Flexion and extension[28]	With patient sidelying, examiner stabilizes the patient's neck with one hand while palpating the movement at C7-T1 with the other. Positive if flexion and extension are "stiff" compared with the vertebrae superior and inferior		κ = .36
First rib[28]	With patient supine, the cervical spine is rotated toward the side being tested. The first rib is pressed in a ventral and caudal direction. Positive if the rib is more "stiff" than the contralateral side		κ = .35
Identification of hypomobile segment[29]	With subject sitting, examiner palpates passive physiologic intervertebral motion at each cervical vertebra in rotation and lateral flexion and determines the most hypomobile segment	3 asymptomatic patients with single-level congenital fusions in the cervical spine (2 at C2-C3 and 1 at C5-C6)	κ = .68

Passive Intervertebral Motion

Reliability of Assessing Limited and Painful Passive Intervertebral Motion

ICC or κ	Interpretation
.81-1.0	Substantial agreement
.61-.80	Moderate agreement
.41-.60	Fair agreement
.11-.40	Slight agreement
.0-.10	No agreement

Test and Study	Description and Positive Findings	Population	Inter-examiner Reliability			
			Limited Movements		Pain	
			Right	Left	Right	Left
C0-C1[6]	With patient supine, examiner cradles the occiput with both hands, rotates the head 30° toward the side to be tested, and an anterior to posterior glide is performed to assess the amount of available motion compared with the contralateral side	22 patients with mechanical neck pain	κ = −.26 (−.57, .07)	κ = .46 (.06, .86)	κ = −.52 (−.09, −.14)	κ = .08 (−.37, .54)
C1-C2[6]	With patient supine, examiner passively and maximally flexes the neck followed by passive cervical rotation to one side and then to the other. The amount of motion to each side was compared, and if one side was determined to have less motion, it was considered to be "hypomobile"		κ = .72 (.43, .91)	κ = .74 (.40, 1.0)	κ = .15 (−.05, .36)	κ = −.16 (−.56, .22)
C0-C1[20]	With patient supine, passive flexion is performed. Motion classified as "limited" or "not limited" and patient pain response assessed on 11-point numeric pain rating (NPR) scale		κ = .29	Not reported	ICC = .73	Not reported
C1-C2[20]	With patient supine, rotation is performed and classified as "limited" or "not limited." Patient pain response assessed on 11-point NPR scale	32 patients with neck pain	κ = .20	κ = .37	ICC = .56	ICC = .35
C2-C3[20]			κ = .34	κ = .63	ICC = .50	ICC = .78
C3-C4[20]	With patient supine, fixation of lower segment with side-bending to the right and left. Motion classified as "limited" or "not limited" and patient pain response assessed on 11-point NPR scale		κ = .20	κ = .26	ICC = .62	ICC = .75
C4-C5[20]			κ = .16	κ = −.09	ICC = .62	ICC = .55
C5-C6[20]			κ = .17	κ = .09	ICC = .66	ICC = .65
C6-C7[20]			κ = .34	κ = .03	ICC = .59	ICC = .22
C7-T1[20]			κ = .08	κ = .14	ICC = .45	ICC = .34
T1-T2[20]			κ = .33	κ = .46	ICC = .80	ICC = .54

Passive Intervertebral Motion

Reliability of Assessing Limited and Painful Passive Intervertebral Motion (continued)

ICC or κ	Interpretation
.81-1.0	Substantial agreement
.61-.80	Moderate agreement
.41-.60	Fair agreement
.11-.40	Slight agreement
.0-.10	No agreement

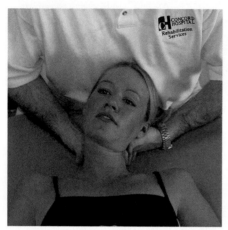

Testing side bending of C5-C6

Figure 3-22
Assessing limited and painful passive intervertebral motion.

Test and Study	Description and Positive Findings	Population	Inter-examiner Reliability	
			Limited Movements	**Pain**
C2[6]	Posterior to anterior (PA) spring testing centrally over the spinous process of the vertebrae. Mobility judged as "normal," "hypomobile," or "hypermobile" and as "painful" or "not painful"	22 patients with mechanical neck pain	κ = .01 (−.35, .38)	κ = .13 (−.04, .31)
C3[6]			κ = .10 (−.25, .44)	κ = .13 (−.21, .47)
C4[6]			κ = .10 (−.22, .40)	κ = .27 (−.12, .67)
C5[6]			κ = .10 (−.15, .35)	κ = .12 (−.09, .42)
C6[6]			κ = .01 (−.21, .24)	κ = .55 (.22, .88)
C7[6]			κ = .54 (0.2, .88)	κ = .90 (.72, 1.0)
C0-C1 lateral glide[15]	Mobility was recorded as "normal" or "hypomobile" when compared with the contralateral side. Pain reproduction recorded as "pain" or "no pain"	30 patients with neck pain	κ = .81 (.72, .91)	κ =32 (.15, .49)
C0-C1 lateral bend[15]			κ = .35 (.08, .62)	κ = .35 (.15, .55)
C1-C2 rotation in full flexion[15]			κ = .21 (.08, .34)	κ = .36 (.24, .49)
C1-C2- full lateral flexion[15]			κ = .30 (.17, .43)	κ = .61 (.5, .72)
C2 lateral glide[15]			κ = .46 (.33, .59)	κ = .42 (.28, .56)
C3 lateral glide[15]			κ = .25 (.12, .38)	κ = .29 (.16, .43)
C4 lateral glide[15]			κ = .27 (.13, .40)	κ = .65 (.54, .76)
C5 lateral glide[15]			κ = .18 (.03, .33)	κ = .55 (.43, .67)
C6 lateral glide[15]			κ = −.07 (−.34, .20)	κ = .76 (.64, .87)

Passive Intervertebral Motion

Diagnostic Utility of Assessing Limited and Painful Passive Intervertebral Motion

+LR	Interpretation	−LR
>10	Large	<..1
5.0-10.0	Moderate	.1-.2
2.0-5.0	Small	.2-.5
1.0-2.0	Rarely important	.5-1.0

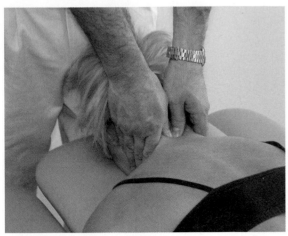

Posteroanterior central glides to the mid cervical spine

Figure 3-23

Assessing limited and painful passive intervertebral motion.

Test and Study Quality	Description and Positive Findings	Population	Reference Standard	Sens	Spec	+LR	−LR
Manual examination[30] ◇	Subjective examination, followed by central PA glides, followed by passive physiologic intervertebral movements of flexion, extension, sidebending, and rotation. Joint dysfunction was diagnosed if the examiner concluded that the joint demonstrated an abnormal end-feel, abnormal quality of resistance to motion, and the reproduction of pain	173 patients with cervical pain		.89 (.82, .96)	.47 (.37, .57)	1.7 (1.2, 2.5)	.23
Manual examination[31] ◇		20 patients with cervical pain	Level of zygapophyseal pain via radiologically controlled diagnostic nerve block	1.0 (.81, 1.0)*	1.0 (.51, 1.0)*	Undefined	.00
Identification of hypomobile segment[29] ○	With subject sitting, examiner palpates passive physiologic intervertebral motion at each cervical vertebra in rotation and lateral flexion and determines the most hypomobile segment	3 asymptomatic patients with single-level congenital fusions in the cervical spine (2 at C2-C3 and 1 at C5-C6).	Level of congenital cervical fusion	.98	.74	3.77	.03

*Confidence intervals were not originally reported by Jull and colleagues,[31] but were later calculated and presented by King and colleagues.[30]

Palpation

Reliability of Assessing Pain with Palpation

ICC or κ	Interpretation
.81-1.0	Substantial agreement
.61-.80	Moderate agreement
.41-.60	Fair agreement
.11-.40	Slight agreement
.0-.10	No agreement

Test and Study		Description and Positive Findings	Population	Inter-examiner Reliability
Upper cervical spinous process[32]		Patient supine. Graded as "no tenderness," "moderate tenderness," and "marked tenderness"	52 patients referred for cervical myelography	κ = .47
Lower cervical spinous process[32]				κ = .52
Right side of neck[32]				κ = .24
Suprascapular area[32]				(Right) κ = .42 (Left) κ = .44
Scapular area[32]				(Right) κ = .34 (Left) κ = .56
Zygapophyseal joint pressure[21]	High cervical	Method of classification for high, middle, and low not described		κ = .14 (−.12, .39)
	Middle cervical			κ = .37 (.12, .85)
	Low cervical			κ = .31 (.28, .90)
Occiput[21]		No details		(Right) κ = .00 (−1.00, .77) (Left) κ = .16 (−.31, .61)
Mastoid process[21]				κ = .77 (.34, 1.00)
Sternocleidomastoid (SCM) muscle[21]	Insertion	SCM insertion on occiput (minor occipital nerve)	24 patients with headaches	(Right) κ = .68 (.29, 1.00) (Left) κ = .35 (−.17, .86)
	Anterior	Just anterior to SCM muscle border		(Right) κ = .35 (−.17, .86) (Left) κ = .55 (.10, .99)
	Middle	At SCM muscle border		(Right) κ = .52 (.12, .92) (Left) κ = .42 (.01, .82)
	Posterior	Just posterior to SCM muscle border		(Right) κ = .60 (.19, 1.00) (Left) κ = .87 (.62, 1.00)
Midline neck tenderness[9]		No details given	8924 adult patients who presented to the emergency department after blunt trauma to the head/neck and had a Glasgow Coma Score of 15	κ = .78
Posterolateral neck tenderness[9]				κ = .32
Maximal tenderness at midline[9]				κ = .72

Palpation

Reliability of Assessing Pain with Palpation with and without a Patient History

ICC or κ	Interpretation
.81-1.0	Substantial agreement
.61-.80	Moderate agreement
.41-.60	Fair agreement
.11-.40	Slight agreement
.0-.10	No agreement

Test and Study	Description and Positive Findings	Population	Inter-examiner Reliability	
			Without knowledge of history	With knowledge of history
Spinous processes C2-C3[33]	No details given	100 patients with neck and/or shoulder problems with or without radiating pain	κ = .60	κ = .49
Spinous processes C4-C7[33]			κ = .42	κ = .50
Spinous processes T1-T3[33]			κ = .55	κ = .79
Paraspinal joints C1-C3[33]			κ = .32	κ = .22
Paraspinal joints C4-C7[33]			κ = .34	κ = .55
Paraspinal joints T1-T3[33]			κ = .41	κ = .51
Neck muscles[33]			κ = .32	κ = .46
Brachial plexus[33]			κ = .27	κ = .22
Paraspinal muscles[33]			κ = −.04	κ = .46

Diagnostic Utility of Assessing Pain with Palpation

+LR	Interpretation	−LR
>10	Large	<.1
5.0-10.0	Moderate	.1-.2
2.0-5.0	Small	.2-.5
1.0-2.0	Rarely important	.5-1.0

Test and Measure	Test Procedure and Determination of Positive Findings	Population	Reference Standard	Sens	Spec	+LR	−LR
Palpation over the facet joints in the cervical spine[22]	Articulations were palpated 2 cm lateral to the spinous process. Positive if patient reported pain with procedure	75 males (22 with neck pain)	Patient reports of neck pain	.82	.79	3.90	.23

ICC or κ	Interpretation
.81-1.0	Substantial agreement
.61-.80	Moderate agreement
.41-.60	Fair agreement
.11-.40	Slight agreement
.0-.10	No agreement

Unlike postural defect, kyphosis of Scheuermann's disease persists when patient is prone and thoracic spine extended or hyperextended (above) and accentuated when patient bends forward (below)

In adolescent, exaggerated thoracic kyphosis and compensatory lumbar lordosis due to Scheuermann's disease may be mistaken for postural defect

Figure 3-24

Thoracic kyphosis.

Test and Study	Description and Positive Findings	Population	Inter-examiner Reliability
Forward head[6]	Answered "yes" if the patient's external auditory meatus was anteriorly deviated (anterior to the lumbar spine)		κ = −.1 (−.2, −.00)
Excessive shoulder protraction[6]	Answered "yes" if the patient's acromions were anteriorly deviated (anterior to the lumbar spine)		κ = .83 (.51, 1.0)
C7-T2 excessive kyphosis[6]	Recorded as" normal" (no deviation), "excessive kyphosis," or "diminished kyphosis." *Excessive kyphosis* was defined as an increase in the convexity and a *diminished kyphosis* was defined as a flattening of the convexity of the thoracic spine (at each segmental group)	22 patients with mechanical neck pain	κ = .79 (.51, 1.0)
T3-5 excessive kyphosis[6]			κ = .69 (.3, 1.0)
T3-5 decreased kyphosis[6]			κ = .58 (.22, .95)
T6-10 excessive kyphosis[6]			κ = .9 (.74, 1.0)
T6-10 decreased kyphosis[6]			κ = .9 (.73, 1.0)

Postural and Muscle Length Assessment

Reliability of Muscle Length Assessment

ICC or κ	Interpretation
.81-1.0	Substantial agreement
.61-.80	Moderate agreement
.41-.60	Fair agreement
.11-.40	Slight agreement
.0-.10	No agreement

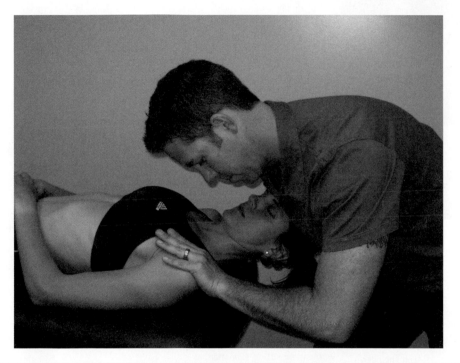

Figure 3-25

Muscle length assessment.

Test and Study	Description and Positive Findings	Population	Inter-examiner Reliability
Latissimus dorsi[6]			(Right) κ = .80 (.53, 1.0) (Left) κ = .69 (.30, 1.0)
Pectoralis minor[6]			(Right) κ = .81 (.57, 1.0) (Left) κ = .71 (.43, 1.0)
Pectoralis major[6]			(Right) κ = .90 (.72, 1.0) (Left) κ = .50 (.01, 1.0)
Levator scapulae[6]	Each muscle was recorded as "normal" or "restricted length"	22 patients with mechanical neck pain	(Right) κ = .61 (.26, .95) (Left) κ = .54 (.19, .90)
Upper trapezius[6]			(Right) κ = .79 (.52, 1.0) (Left) κ = .63 (.31, .96)
Anterior and middle scalenes[6]			(Right) κ = .81 (.57, 1.0) (Left) κ = .62 (.29, .96)
Suboccipitals[6]			(Right) κ = .63 (.26, 1.0) (Left) κ = .58 (.15, 1.0)

Spurling's and Neck Compression Tests

Reliability of Spurling's and Neck Compression Tests

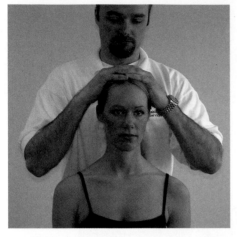

ICC or κ	Interpretation
.81-1.0	Substantial agreement
.61-.80	Moderate agreement
.41-.60	Fair agreement
.11-.40	Slight agreement
.0-.10	No agreement

Figure 3-26

Cervical compression test.

Test and Study		Description and Positive Findings	Population	Inter-examiner Reliability
Straight compression[33]		Patient seated with examiner standing behind patient. Examiner exerts pressure on head. Positive if pain is provoked	100 patients with neck and/or shoulder problems with or without radiating pain	κ = **.34** without knowledge of patient history κ = **.44** with knowledge of patient history
Neck compression with[32]:	Right shoulder/ arm pain	Cervical compression performed with patient sitting. Examiner passively rotates and sidebends the head to the right and/or left. A compression force of 7 kg is applied. Presence and location of pain, paresthesias, or numbness is recorded	52 patients referred for cervical myelography	(Right) κ = **.61** (Left) Not available
	Left shoulder/ arm pain			(Right) Not available (Left) κ = **.40**
	Right forearm/ hand pain			(Right) κ = **.77** (Left) κ = **.54**
	Left forearm/ hand pain			(Right) Not available (Left) κ = **.62**
Spurling's A[7]		Patient seated with neck sidebent toward ipsilateral side; 7 kg of overpressure is applied	50 patients with suspected cervical radiculopathy or carpal tunnel syndrome	κ = **.60 (.32, .87)**
Spurling's B[7]		Patient seated with extension and sidebending/rotation to ipsilateral side; 7 kg of overpressure is applied		κ = **.62 (.25, .99)**
Spurling to the right[33]		Cervical compression performed with patient seated. Examiner passively rotates and sidebends head to right or left and applies compression force of 7 kg. Presence and location of pain, paresthesias, or numbness is recorded	100 patients with neck and/or shoulder problems with or without radiating pain	κ = **.37** without knowledge of patient history κ = **.28** with knowledge of patient history
Spurling to the left[33]				κ = **.37** without knowledge of patient history κ = **.46** with knowledge of patient history

Spurling's and Neck Compression Tests

Diagnostic Utility of Spurling's Test

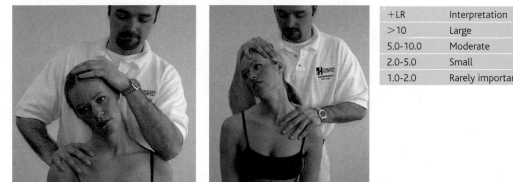

Spurling's A test

Spurling's B test

+LR	Interpretation	−LR
>10	Large	<.1
5.0-10.0	Moderate	.1-.2
2.0-5.0	Small	.2-.5
1.0-2.0	Rarely important	.5-1.0

Figure 3-27 Spurling's test.

Test and Study Quality	Description and Positive Findings	Population	Reference Standard	Sens	Spec	+LR	−LR
Spurling's A[7]	Patient is seated, the neck is sidebent toward the ipsilateral side, and 7 kg of overpressure is applied (see Fig. 3-27). Positive if symptoms are reproduced	82 consecutive patients referred to an electrophysiologic laboratory with suspected diagnosis of cervical radiculopathy or carpal tunnel syndrome	Cervical radiculopathy via needle electromyography and nerve conduction studies	.50 (.27, .73)	.86 (.77, .94)	3.5 (1.6, 7.5)	.58 (.36, .94)
Spurling's B[7]	Patient seated. Extension and sidebending/rotation to the ipsilateral side and then 7 kg of overpressure is applied (see Fig. 3-27). Positive if symptoms are reproduced			.50 (.27, .73)	.74 (.63, .85)	1.9 (1.0, 3.6)	.67 (.42, 1.1)
Spurling's test[34]	The patient's neck was extended and laterally flexed toward the involved side, and downward axial pressure was applied on the head. Positive if radicular pain or tingling in the upper limb was reproduced or aggravated	50 patients presenting to neurosurgery with neck and arm pain suggestive of radicular pain	Soft lateral cervical disc prolapse via MRI	.93 (.84, 1.0)	.95 (.86, 1.0)	18.6	.07
Spurling's test[35]	Patient sidebends and extends the neck and examiner applies compression. Positive if pain or tingling that starts in the shoulder radiates distally to the elbow	255 consecutive patients referred to a physiatrist with upper extremity nerve disorders	Cervical radiculopathy via electrodiagnostic testing	.30	.93	4.29	.75
Spurling's test[22]	Extension of the neck with rotation and sidebending to the same side. Positive if subject reported pain with procedure	75 males (22 with neck pain)	Patient reports of neck pain	.77	.92	9.63	.25

ICC or κ	Interpretation
.81-1.0	Substantial agreement
.61-.80	Moderate agreement
.41-.60	Fair agreement
.11-.40	Slight agreement
.0-.10	No agreement

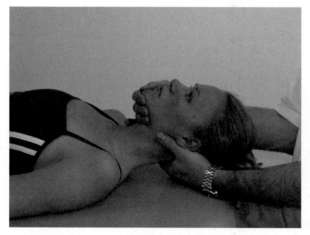

Neck distraction test

Traction test

Figure 3-28

Neck distraction and traction tests.

Test and Study	Description and Positive Findings	Population	Inter-examiner Reliability
Axial manual traction[32]	With patient supine, examiner applies axial distraction force of 10-15 kg. Positive if radicular symptoms decrease	52 patients referred for cervical myelography	κ = **.50**
Neck distraction test[7]	With patient supine, examiner grasps patient under chin and occiput while slightly flexing patient's neck while applying distraction force of 14 lb. Positive if symptoms are reduced	50 patients with suspected cervical radiculopathy or carpal tunnel syndrome	κ = **.88 (.64, 1.0)**
Traction[33]	With patient seated, examiner stands behind patient with hands underneath each maxilla and thumbs on the back of the head. Positive if symptoms are reduced during traction	100 patients with neck and/or shoulder problems with or without radiating pain	κ = **.56** without knowledge of history κ = **.41** with knowledge of history

Shoulder Abduction Test

Reliability of Shoulder Abduction Test

ICC or κ	Interpretation
.81-1.0	Substantial agreement
.61-.80	Moderate agreement
.41-.60	Fair agreement
.11-.40	Slight agreement
.0-.10	No agreement

Figure 3-29

Shoulder abduction test.

Test and Study	Description and Positive Findings	Population	Inter-examiner Reliability
Shoulder abduction test[7]	Patient is seated and asked to place the symptomatic extremity on head. Positive if symptoms are reduced	50 patients with suspected cervical radiculopathy or carpal tunnel syndrome	κ = .20 (.00, .59)
Shoulder abduction test[32]	Patient is seated and asked to raise the symptomatic extremity above the head. Positive if symptoms are reduced	52 patients referred for cervical myelography	(Right) κ = .21 (Left) κ = .40

ICC or κ	Interpretation
.81-1.0	Substantial agreement
.61-.80	Moderate agreement
.41-.60	Fair agreement
.11-.40	Slight agreement
.0-.10	No agreement

Test and Study	Description and Positive Findings	Population	Inter-examiner Reliability
Upper limb tension test A[7] ◇	With patient supine, examiner performs the following movements: 1. Scapular depression 2. Shoulder abduction 3. Forearm supination 4. Wrist and finger extension 5. Shoulder lateral rotation 6. Elbow extension 7. Contralateral/ipsilateral cervical sidebending Positive response defined by any of the following: 1. Patient symptoms reproduced 2. Side-to-side differences in elbow extension > 10° 3. Contralateral cervical sidebending increases symptoms or ipsilateral sidebending decreases symptoms	50 patients with suspected cervical radiculopathy or carpal tunnel syndrome	κ = .76 (.51, 1.0)
Upper limb tension test B[7] ◇	With patient supine and shoulder abducted 30°, examiner performs the following movements: 1. Scapular depression 2. Shoulder medial rotation 3. Full elbow extension 4. Wrist and finger flexion 5. Contralateral/ipsilateral cervical sidebending Positive response defined by any of the following: 1. Patient symptoms reproduced 2. Side-to-side differences in wrist flexion > 10° 3. Contralateral cervical sidebending increases symptoms or ipsilateral sidebending decreases symptoms		κ = .83 (.65, 1.0)
Brachial plexus test[32]	With patient supine, examiner abducts the humerus to the limit of pain-free motion, then adds lateral rotation of the arm and elbow flexion. If no limitation of motion is noted, the humerus is abducted to 90°. The appearance of symptoms is recorded	52 patients referred for cervical myelography	(Right) κ = .35 Left not calculated because prevalence of positive findings was < 10%

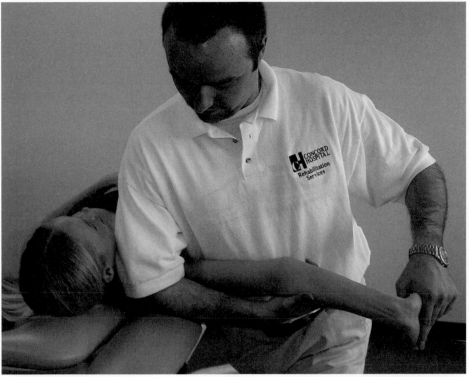

Test A

Figure 3-30
Upper limb tension tests.

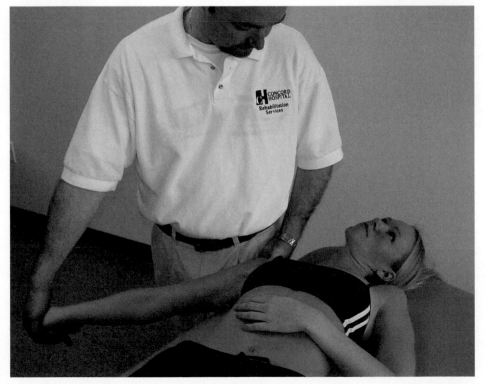

Test B

Diagnostic Utility of Neural Tension Tests for Cervical Radiculopathy

+LR	Interpretation	−LR
>10	Large	<.1
5.0-10.0	Moderate	.1-.2
2.0-5.0	Small	.2-.5
1.0-2.0	Rarely important	.5-1.0

Test and Study Quality	Description and Positive Findings	Population	Reference Standard	Sens	Spec	+LR	−LR
Upper limb tension test A[7]	With patient supine, examiner performs the following movements: 1. Scapular depression 2. Shoulder abduction 3. Forearm supination 4. Wrist and finger extension 5. Shoulder lateral rotation 6. Elbow extension 7. Contralateral and ipsilateral cervical sidebending Positive response defined by any of the following: 1. Patient symptoms reproduced 2. Side-to-side differences in elbow extension > 10° 3. Contralateral cervical sidebending increases symptoms or ipsilateral sidebending decreases symptoms	82 consecutive patients referred to an electro-physiologic laboratory with suspected diagnosis of cervical radiculopathy or carpal tunnel syndrome	Cervical radiculopathy via needle electromyography and nerve conduction studies	.97 (.90, 1.0)	.22 (.12, .33)	1.3 (1.1, 1.5)	.12 (.01, 1.9)
Upper limb tension test B[7]	With patient supine and patient's shoulder abducted 30°, examiner performs the following movements: 1. Scapular depression 2. Shoulder medial rotation 3. Full elbow extension 4. Wrist and finger flexion 5. Contralateral and ipsilateral cervical sidebending Positive response defined by any of the following: 1. Patient symptoms reproduced 2. Side-to-side differences in wrist flexion > 10° 3. Contralateral cervical sidebending increases symptoms or ipsilateral sidebending decreases symptoms			.72 (.52, .93)	.33 (.21, .45)	1.1 (.77, 1.5)	.85, (.37, 1.9)
Upper limb tension test[22]	With patient seated and arm in extension, abduction and external rotation of the glenohumeral joint, extension of the elbow, the forearm in supination, and the wrist and fingers in extension. Contralateral flexion of the neck is added. Positive if patient reported pain with procedure	75 males (22 with neck pain)	Patient reports of neck pain	.77	.94	12.83	.25

Sharp-Purser Test

Diagnostic Utility of the Sharp-Purser Test for Cervical Instability

+LR	Interpretation	−LR
>10	Large	<.1
5.0-10.0	Moderate	.1-.2
2.0-5.0	Small	.2-.5
1.0-2.0	Rarely important	.5-1.0

Figure 3-31

Sharp-purser test.

Test and Study Quality	Description and Positive Findings	Population	Reference Standard	Sens	Spec	+LR	−LR
Sharp-Purser test[36]	Patient sits with neck in a semiflexed position. Examiner places palm of one hand on patient's forehead and index finger of the other hand on the spinous process of axis. When posterior pressure is applied through the forehead, a sliding motion of the head posteriorly in relation to axis indicates a positive test for atlantoaxial instability	123 consecutive outpatients with rheumatoid arthritis	Full flexion and extension lateral radiographs. Atlantodens interval greater than 3 mm was considered abnormal	.69	.96	17.25	.32

Diagnostic Utility of Brachial Plexus Compression for Cervical Cord Compression

+LR	Interpretation	−LR
>10	Large	<.1
5.0-10.0	Moderate	.1-.2
2.0-5.0	Small	.2-.5
1.0-2.0	Rarely important	.5-1.0

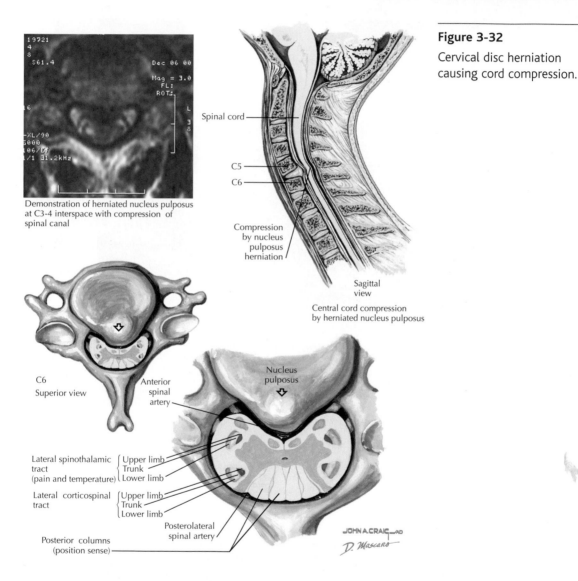

Demonstration of herniated nucleus pulposus at C3-4 interspace with compression of spinal canal

Spinal cord

C5
C6

Compression by nucleus pulposus herniation

Sagittal view

Central cord compression by herniated nucleus pulposus

C6
Superior view

Anterior spinal artery

Nucleus pulposus

Lateral spinothalamic tract (pain and temperature) — Upper limb / Trunk / Lower limb

Lateral corticospinal tract — Upper limb / Trunk / Lower limb

Posterolateral spinal artery

Posterior columns (position sense)

JOHN A.CRAIG—AD
D. Mascaro

Figure 3-32
Cervical disc herniation causing cord compression.

Test and Study Quality	Description and Positive Findings	Population	Reference Standard	Sens	Spec	+LR	−LR
Compression of brachial plexus[37] ◯	Firm compression and squeezing of the brachial plexus with the thumb. Positive only when pain radiates to the shoulder or upper extremity	65 patients who had undergone MRI of the cervical spine as a result of radiating pain	Cervical cord compression via MRI	.69	.83	4.06	.37

Combinations of Tests

Diagnostic Utility of Clusters of Tests for Cervical Radiculopathy

Wainner and colleagues[7] identified a test item cluster, or an optimal combination of clinical examination tests, to determine the likelihood of the patient presenting with cervical radiculopathy. The four predictor variables most likely to identify patients presenting with cervical radiculopathy are the upper limb tension test A, Spurling's A test, distraction test, and cervical rotation less than 60° to the ipsilateral side.

+LR	Interpretation	−LR
>10	Large	<.1
5.0–10.0	Moderate	.1–.2
2.0–5.0	Small	.2–.5
1.0–2.0	Rarely important	.5–1.0

Test and Study Quality	Description and Positive Findings	Population	Reference Standard	Sens	Spec	+LR	−LR
Upper limb tension test A + Spurling's A test + Distraction test + Cervical rotation < 60° to the ipsilateral side[7]	All 4 tests positive	82 consecutive patients referred to an electrophysiologic laboratory with suspected diagnosis of cervical radiculopathy or carpal tunnel syndrome	Cervical radiculopathy via needle electromyography and nerve conduction studies	.24 (.05, .43)	.99 (.97, 1.0)	30.3 (1.7, 38.2)	
	Any 3 tests positive			.39 (.16, .61)	.94 (.88, 1.0)	6.1 (2.0, 18.6)	
	Any 2 tests positive			.39 (.16, .61)	.56 (.43, .68)	.88 (1.5, 2.5)	Not reported

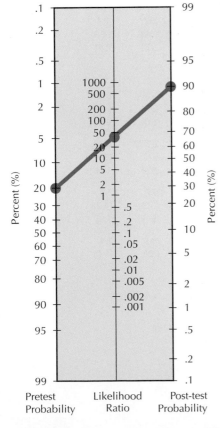

Figure 3-33

Fagan's nomogram. Considering the 20% prevalence or pretest probability of cervical radiculopathy in the study by Wainner and colleagues,[7] the nomogram demonstrates the major shifts in probability that occur when all four tests from the cluster are positive. *(Reprinted with permission from Fagan TJ. Nomogram for Bayes' theorem. N Engl J Med. 1975;293:257. Copyright 2005, Massachusetts Medical Society. All rights reserved.)*

Diagnostic Utility of Single and Combinations of Factors for Identifying Positive Short-term Clinical Outcome for Cervical Radiculopathy

We used the baseline examination and physical therapy interventions received to investigate predictors for short-term improvement in patients with cervical radiculopathy.[38] Patients were treated at the discretion of their physical therapist for a mean of 6.4 visits over an average of 28 days. In addition to identifying the single factors most strongly associated with improvement, we used logistic regression to identify the combination of factors most predictive of short-term improvement.

+LR	Interpretation	−LR
>10	Large	<.1
5.0-10.0	Moderate	.1-.2
2.0-5.0	Small	.2-.5
1.0-2.0	Rarely important	.5-1.0

Test and Study Quality	Description and Positive Findings	Population	Reference Standard	Sens	Spec	+LR	−LR
Age < 54 years[38] ◇	Self-report			.76 (.64, .89)	.52 (.38, .67)	1.5 (1.2, 2.1)	
Dominant arm is not affected[38] ◇	Self-report			.74 (.62, .86)	.52 (.38, .67)	1.5 (1.1, 2.2)	
Looking down does not worsen symptoms[38] ◇	Self-report			.68 (.55, .81)	.48 (.34, .62)	1.3 (.93, 1.8)	
>30° of cervical flexion[38] ◇	Patient sitting. Used an inclinometer after two warm-up repetitions	96 patients referred to physical therapy with cervical radiculopathy as defined by being positive on all 4 items in Wainner's diagnostic test item cluster[7](see previous)	Improvement at physical therapy discharge as defined by surpassing the minimal detectable change in all outcome measures	.56 (.42, .70)	.59 (.44, .73)	1.4 (.89, 2.1)	
Age < 54 years + Dominant arm is not affected + Looking down does not worsen symptoms + Provided with multimodal treatment including manual therapy, cervical traction, and deep neck flexor muscle strengthening for ≥ 50% of visits[38] ◇	All 4 tests positive			.18 (.07, .29)	.98 (.94, 1.0)	8.3 (1.9, 63.9)	Not reported
	Any 3 tests positive			.68 (.55, .81)	.87 (.77, .97)	5.2 (2.4, 11.3)	
	Any 2 tests positive			.94 (.87, 1.0)	.37 (.23, .51)	1.5 (1.2, 1.9)	
	Any 1 test positive			1.0 (1.0, 1.0)	.08 (.01, .2)	1.1 (1.0, 2.0)	

Interventions

Diagnostic Utility of Historical and Physical Examination Findings for Immediate Improvement with Cervical Manipulation

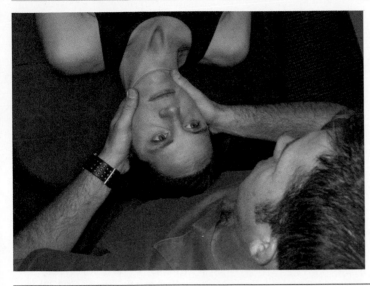

+LR	Interpretation	−LR
>10	Large	<.1
5.0-10.0	Moderate	.1-.2
2.0-5.0	Small	.2-.5
1.0-2.0	Rarely important	.5-1.0

Figure 3-34

Cervical manipulation. Delivered by Tseng and colleagues[39] at the discretion of the therapist to the most hypomobile segments. "Once a hypomobile segment was localized, the manipulator carefully flexed and sidebent the patient's neck to lock the facet joints of other spinal segments until the barrier was reached. A specific cervical manipulation with a high-velocity, low-amplitude thrust force was then exerted on the specific, manipulable lesion to gap the facet."[39]

Test and Study Quality	Description and Positive Findings	Population	Reference Standard	Sens	Spec	+LR	−LR
Initial Neck Disability Index > 11.5 + Bilateral involvement pattern + Not performing sedentary work > 5 hours/day + Feeling better while moving the neck + Without feeling worse while extending the neck + Diagnosis of spondylosis without radiculopathy[39]	5 or 6 tests positive	100 patients referred to physical therapy for neck pain	Immediate improvement after cervical manipulation as determined by any of the following: 1. ≥50% decrease in numeric pain rating 2. ≥4 (much improved) on the global rating of change scale 3. Patient satisfaction rating of "very satisfied" after manipulation.	.07 (.00, .13)	1.00 (1.00, 1.00)	Undefined	Not reported
	Any 4 tests positive			.40 (.28, .52)	.93 (.84, 1.00)	5.33 (1.72, 16.54)	
	Any 3 tests positive			.43 (.31, .56)	.78 (.65, .90)	1.93 (1.01, 3.67)	
	Any 2 tests positive			.08 (.01, .15)	.57 (.42, .73)	.20 (.08, .49)	
	Any 1 test positive			.02 (−.02, .05)	.75 (.62, .88)	.07 (.01, .50)	

Diagnostic Utility of Historical and Physical Examination Findings for Immediate Improvement with Thoracic Manipulation

+LR	Interpretation	−LR
>10	Large	<.1
5.0-10.0	Moderate	.1-.2
2.0-5.0	Small	.2-.5
1.0-2.0	Rarely important	.5-1.0

Test and Study Quality	Description and Positive Findings	Population	Reference Standard	Sens	Spec	+LR
Symptom duration < 30 days[40] ◇	Self-report	78 patients referred to physical therapy with mechanical neck pain	Improvement after several standardized thoracic manipulations and cervical ROM exercise as determined by ≥ 5 ("quite a bit better") on the global rating of change scale on the second or third visit	.36 (.22, .52)	.94 (.80, .99)	6.4 (1.60, 26.3)
No symptoms distal to the shoulder[40] ◇				.67 (.50, .80)	.53 (.36, .69)	1.4 (.94, 2.2)
FABQPA score < 12[40] ◇	Questionnaire to quantify a person's beliefs about the influence of work and activity on their neck pain			.28 (.16, .45)	.91 (.76, .98)	3.4 (1.05, 11.20)
FABQW score < 10[40] ◇				.55 (.39, .70)	.69 (.52, .83)	1.8 (1.02, 3.15)
≥3 prior episodes of neck pain[40] ◇	Self-report			.23 (.15, .35)	.83 (.54, .96)	1.9 (1.3, 2.7)
Patient reports that looking up does not aggravate symptoms[40] ◇				67 (.50, .80)	.86 (.70, .95)	4.8 (2.07, 11.03)
Exercises > 3 times/week[40] ◇				.65 (.50, .76)	.67 (.46, .83)	1.9 (1.1, 3.4)
Cervical extension ROM < 30°[40] ◇	Measured with inclinometer			.62 (.46, .76)	.75 (.57, .87)	2.5 (1.34, 4.57)
Decreased upper thoracic spine kyphosis[40] ◇	Increased convexity at T3-T5			54 (.42, .65)	.64 (.48, .78)	1.1 (.77, 1.60)
Shoulders protracted[40] ◇	Positive if acromion was noted to be anterior to the lumbar spine			.65 (.51, .77)	.76 (.52, .90)	2.7 (1.6, 3.0)

FABQPA, Fear-Avoidance Beliefs Questionnaire physical activity subscale; FABQW: Fear-Avoidance Beliefs Questionnaire work subscale. −LR not reported.

Interventions

Diagnostic Utility of a Cluster of Historical and Physical Examination Findings for Immediate Improvement with Thoracic Manipulation

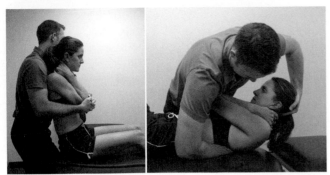

+LR	Interpretation	−LR
>10	Large	<.1
5.0-10.0	Moderate	.1-.2
2.0-5.0	Small	.2-.5
1.0-2.0	Rarely important	.5-1.0

All patients received a standardized series of 3 thrust manipulations directed at the thoracic spine. In the first technique (A), with the patient sitting, the therapist uses his or her sternum as a fulcrum on the patient's middle thoracic spine and applies a high-velocity distraction thrust in an upward direction. The second and third techniques (B) are delivered supine. The therapist uses his or her body to push down through the patient's arms to perform a high-velocity, low-amplitude thrust directed toward either T1 through T4 or T5 through T8.[40]

After the manipulations, patients were instructed in a cervical range-of-motion exercise to perform 3-4 times/day.[40]

Figure 3-35

Thoracic spine manipulation and active range of motion.

Test and Study Quality	Description and Positive Findings	Population	Reference Standard	Sens	Spec	+LR
Symptom duration < 30 days + No symptoms distal to the shoulder + FABQPA score < 12 + Patient reports that looking up does not aggravate symptoms + Cervical extension ROM < 30° + Decreased upper thoracic spine kyphosis (T3-T5)[40] ◇	All 6 tests positive	78 patients referred to physical therapy with mechanical neck pain	Improvement after several standardized thoracic manipulations and cervical ROM exercise as determined by ≥ 5 ("quite a bit better") on the global rating of change scale on the second or third visit	.05 (.00, .17)	1.0 (.97, 1.00)	Undefined
	At least 5 tests positive			.12 (.04, .25)	1.0 (.94, 1.00)	Undefined
	At least 4 tests positive			.33 (.26, .35)	.97 (.89, 1.00)	12 (2.28, 70.8)
	At least 3 tests positive			.76 (.67, .82)	.86 (.75, .93)	5.49 (2.72, 12.0)
	At least 2 tests positive			.93 (.84, .97)	.56 (.46, .61)	2.09 (1.54, 2.49)
	At least 1 test positive			1.00 (.95, 1.00)	.17 (.11, .24)	1.2 (1.06, 1.2)

FABQPA, Fear-Avoidance Beliefs Questionnaire physical activity subscale; FABQW, Fear-Avoidance Beliefs Questionnaire work subscale. −LR not reported.

Diagnostic Utility of Historical and Physical Examination Findings for Improvement with 3 Weeks of Mechanical Cervical Traction

+LR	Interpretation	−LR
>10	Large	<.1
5.0-10.0	Moderate	.1-.2
2.0-5.0	Small	.2-.5
1.0-2.0	Rarely important	.5-1.0

Test and Study Quality	Description and Positive Findings	Population	Reference Standard	Sens	Spec	+LR	−LR
Neck distraction test[41] ◇	Patient lies supine and the neck is comfortably positioned. Examiner securely grasps the patient's head under the occiput and chin and gradually applies an axial traction force up to approximately 30 lb. Positive response defined by reduction of symptoms			.83 (.66, .93)	.50 (.35, .65)	1.67 (1.18, 2.45)	.33 (.14, .73)
Shoulder abduction test[41] ◇	While sitting, the patient is instructed to place the hand of the affected extremity on the head in order to support the extremity in the scapular plane. Positive response defined by alleviation of symptoms	68 patients referred to physical therapy with neck pain with or without upper extremity symptoms	Improvement after 6 treatments over 3 weeks of mechanical cervical traction and postural/deep neck flexor strengthening exercise as determined by ≥ +7 ("A very great deal better") on the global rating of change scale	.33 (.19, .51)	.87 (.73, .94)	2.53 (1.01, 6.50)	.77 (.55, 1.00)
Positive ULTT A[41] ◇	With patient supine, examiner performs the following movements: 1. Scapular depression 2. Shoulder abduction 3. Forearm supination 4. Wrist and finger extension 5. Shoulder lateral rotation 6. Elbow extension 7. Contralateral and ipsilateral cervical sidebending Positive response defined by reproduction of symptoms			.80 (.63, .90)	.37 (.23, .53)	1.27 (.93, 1.75)	.54 (.23, 1.18)

ULTT, upper limb tension test.

Interventions

Diagnostic Utility of Historical and Physical Examination Findings for Improvement with 3 Weeks of Mechanical Cervical Traction

+LR	Interpretation	−LR
>10	Large	<.1
5.0-10.0	Moderate	.1-.2
2.0-5.0	Small	.2-.5
1.0-2.0	Rarely important	.5-1.0

Test and Study Quality	Description and Positive Findings	Population	Reference Standard	Sens	Spec	+LR	−LR
Pain with manual muscle testing[41] ◇	No details given	68 patients referred to physical therapy with neck pain with or without upper extremity symptoms	Improvement after 6 treatments over 3 weeks of mechanical cervical traction and postural/deep neck flexor strengthening exercise as determined by ≥ +7 ("A very great deal better") on the global rating of change scale	.63 (.46, .78)	.71 (.55, .83)	2.19 (1.27, 3.92)	.52 (.30, .82)
Body mass index ≥ 28.4[41] ◇				.67 (.49, .81)	.68 (.53, .81)	2.11 (1.26, 3.66)	.49 (.27, .81)
Frequency of past episodes[41] ◇				.70 (.48, .85)	.67 (.47, .82)	2.10 (1.15, 4.08)	.45 (.21, .87)
Symptoms distal to the shoulder[41] ◇				.67 (.49, .81)	.58 (.42, .72)	1.58 (1.01, 2.53)	.58 (.32, .99)
Headaches[41] ◇				.43 (.27, .61)	.55 (.40, .70)	.97 (.56, 1.65)	1.02 (.65, 1.57)
Diminished strength[41] ◇				.43 (.27, .61)	.76 (.61, .87)	1.83 (.92, 3.69)	.74 (.50, 1.04)
Peripheralization with PA C4-C7[41] ◇				.37 (.22, .54)	.82 (.67, .91)	1.99 (.90, 4.47)	.78 (.54, 1.04)
Ipsilateral rotation < 60°[41] ◇				.43 (.27, .61)	.66 (.50, .79)	1.27 (.69, 2.31)	.86 (.57, 1.26)
Patient-reported neck stiffness[41] ◇				.43 (.27, .61)	.34 (.21, .50)	.66 (.40, 1.02)	1.65 (.97, 2.88)
Flexion AROM < 55°[41] ◇				.60 (.42, .75)	.55 (.40, .70)	1.34 (.84, 2.14)	.72 (.42, 1.19)
Age ≥ 55[41] ◇				.47 (.30, .64)	.89 (.76, .96)	4.43 (1.74, 11.89)	.60 (.40, .81)
Ipsilateral sidebending < 40°[41] ◇				.73 (.56, .86)	.45 (.30-.60)	1.33 (.92, 1.93)	.60 (.29, 1.14)

PA, central posteroanterior motion testing; AROM, active range of motion.

Interventions

Diagnostic Utility of a Cluster of Historical and Physical Examination Findings for Improvement with 3 Weeks of Mechanical Cervical Traction

+LR	Interpretation	−LR
>10	Large	<.1
5.0-10.0	Moderate	.1-.2
2.0-5.0	Small	.2-.5
1.0-2.0	Rarely important	.5-1.0

Test and Study Quality	Description and Positive Findings	Population	Reference Standard	Sens	Spec	+LR	−LR
Age ≥ 55 + Positive shoulder abduction test + Positive ULTT A + Symptom peripheralization with PA at lower cervical (C4-7) spine + Positive neck distraction test[41] ◇	At least 4 tests positive	68 patients referred to physical therapy with neck pain with or without upper extremity symptoms	Improvement after 6 treatments over 3 weeks of mechanical cervical traction and postural/deep neck flexor strengthening exercise as determined by ≥ +7 ("A very great deal better") on the global rating of change scale	.30 (.17, .48)	1.0 (.91, 1.0)	23.1 (2.50, 227.9)	.71 (.53, .85)
	At least 3 tests positive			.63 (.46, .78)	.87 (.73, .94)	4.81 (2.17, 11.4)	.42 (.25, .65)
	At least 2 tests positive			.30 (.17, .48)	.97 (.87, 1.00)	1.44 (1.05, 2.03)	.40 (.16, .90)
	At least 1 test positive			.07 (.02, .21)	.97 (.87, 1.00)	1.15 (.97, 1.4)	.21 (.03, 1.23)

ULTT, upper limb tension test.

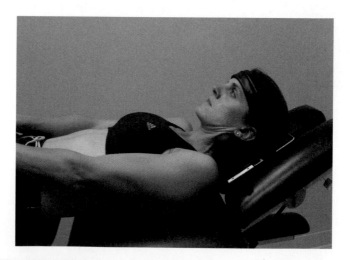

Figure 3-36

Cervical traction. The cervical traction in this study[41] was performed with patient supine and legs supported on a stool. The neck was flexed to 24 degrees for patients with full cervical range of motion, and to 15° otherwise. The traction force was set at 10 to 12 pounds initially and adjusted upward during the first treatment session to optimally relieve symptoms. Each traction session lasted approximately 15 minutes and alternated between 60 seconds of pull and 20 seconds of release at 50% force.

Outcome Measure	Scoring and Interpretation	Test-Retest Reliability	MCID
Neck Disability Index (NDI)	Users are asked to rate the difficulty of performing 10 functional tasks on a scale of 0 to 5 with different descriptors for each task. A total score out of 100 is calculated by summing each score and doubling the total. The answers provide a score between 0 and 100, with higher scores representing more disability	ICC = .50[42]	19[42]
Fear-Avoidance Beliefs Questionnaire (FABQ)	Users are asked to rate their level of agreement with statements concerning beliefs about the relationship between physical activity, work, and their back pain ("Neck" can be substituted for "back"). Level of agreement is answered on a Likert-type scale ranging from 0 (completely disagree) to 7 (completely agree). The FABQ is composed of two parts: a seven-item work subscale (FABQW), and a four-item physical activity subscale (FABQPA). Each scale is scored separately, with higher scores representing higher fear-avoidance	FABQW: ICC = .82 FABQPA: ICC = .66[43]	Not Available
Numeric Pain Rating Scale (NPRS)	Users rate their level of pain on an 11-point scale ranging from 0 to 10, with high scores representing more pain. Often asked as "current pain" and "least," "worst," and "average pain" in the past 24 hours	ICC = .76[42]	1.3[42]

MCID, minimum clinically important difference.

Quality Assessment of Diagnostic Studies Using QUADAS

	Jull 1988	Uitvlugt 1988	Viikari-Juntura 1989[44]	Uchihara 1994	Sandmark 1995	Lauder 2000	Hoffman 2000	Stiell 2001	Tong 2002	Wainner 2003
1. Was the spectrum of patients representative of the patients who will receive the test in practice?	Y	Y	N	U	N	Y	Y	Y	Y	Y
2. Were selection criteria clearly described?	Y	N	N	N	Y	Y	Y	Y	Y	Y
3. Is the reference standard likely to correctly classify the target condition?	Y	Y	U	Y	N	Y	Y	Y	Y	Y
4. Is the time period between reference standard and index test short enough to be reasonably sure that the target condition did not change between the two tests?	N	U	Y	U	U	Y	Y	U	U	U
5. Did the whole sample or a random selection of the sample, receive verification using a reference standard of diagnosis?	Y	Y	U	Y	Y	Y	Y	Y	U	Y
6. Did patients receive the same reference standard regardless of the index test result?	Y	Y	U	Y	Y	Y	Y	N	Y	Y
7. Was the reference standard independent of the index test (i.e., the index test did not form part of the reference standard)?	Y	Y	N	Y	Y	Y	Y	Y	Y	Y
8. Was the execution of the index test described in sufficient detail to permit replication of the test?	Y	Y	Y	Y	Y	Y	Y	Y	Y	Y
9. Was the execution of the reference standard described in sufficient detail to permit its replication?	Y	Y	N	Y	Y	Y	Y	Y	Y	Y
10. Were the index test results interpreted without knowledge of the results of the reference test?	Y	U	N	Y	Y	Y	Y	Y	Y	Y
11. Were the reference standard results interpreted without knowledge of the results of the index test?	U	U	N	Y	Y	U	Y	Y	U	Y
12. Were the same clinical data available when test results were interpreted as would be available when the test is used in practice?	U	Y	Y	Y	N	Y	Y	Y	Y	Y
13. Were uninterpretable/ intermediate test results reported?	Y	Y	U	Y	Y	U	Y	Y	U	U
14. Were withdrawals from the study explained?	Y	Y	U	Y	Y	U	Y	Y	U	Y
Quality summary rating:	◇	○	■	◇	○	◇	◇	◇	○	◇

Y = yes, N = no, U = unclear. ◇ Good quality (Y - N = 10 to 14)   ○ Fair quality (Y - N = 5 to 9)   ■ Poor quality (Y - N ≤ 4)

Quality Assessment of Diagnostic Studies Using QUADAS

	Bandiera 2003	Stiell 2003	Dickinson 2004	Humphreys 2004	Shah 2004	Tseng 2006	Duane 2007	Cleland 2007	King 2007	Raney 2009
1. Was the spectrum of patients representative of the patients who will receive the test in practice?	Y	Y	Y	N	Y	Y	Y	Y	Y	Y
2. Were selection criteria clearly described?	Y	Y	Y	Y	Y	Y	U	Y	Y	Y
3. Is the reference standard likely to correctly classify the target condition?	Y	Y	Y	N	Y	U	Y	Y	Y	Y
4. Is the time period between reference standard and index test short enough to be reasonably sure that the target condition did not change between the two tests?	U	U	U	U	U	Y	U	Y	U	Y
5. Did the whole sample or a random selection of the sample, receive verification using a reference standard of diagnosis?	Y	Y	Y	Y	Y	Y	Y	Y	N	Y
6. Did patients receive the same reference standard regardless of the index test result?	N	N	N	Y	Y	Y	Y	Y	Y	Y
7. Was the reference standard independent of the index test (i.e., the index test did not form part of the reference standard)?	Y	Y	Y	Y	Y	Y	Y	Y	Y	Y
8. Was the execution of the index test described in sufficient detail to permit replication of the test?	U	Y	Y	Y	Y	U	N	Y	Y	Y
9. Was the execution of the reference standard described in sufficient detail to permit its replication?	Y	Y	Y	Y	Y	Y	U	Y	Y	Y
10. Were the index test results interpreted without knowledge of the results of the reference test?	U	Y	Y	Y	U	Y	U	Y	Y	Y
11. Were the reference standard results interpreted without knowledge of the results of the index test?	U	Y	Y	Y	Y	Y	U	Y	U	Y
12. Were the same clinical data available when test results were interpreted as would be available when the test is used in practice?	Y	Y	Y	N	Y	Y	U	Y	Y	Y
13. Were uninterpretable/intermediate test results reported?	Y	Y	Y	Y	Y	Y	Y	Y	Y	U
14. Were withdrawals from the study explained?	Y	Y	Y	Y	Y	Y	Y	Y	Y	U
Quality summary rating:	◯	◇	◇	◯	◇	◇	◯	◇	◇	◇

1. Bogduk N. Neck pain. *Aust Fam Physician.* 1984;13:26-30.

2. Lord SM, Barnsley L, Wallis BJ, Bogduk N. Chronic cervical zygapophysial joint pain after whiplash. A placebo-controlled prevalence study. *Spine.* 1996;21:1737-44; discussion 1744-1745.

3. Dwyer A, Aprill C, Bogduk N. Cervical zygapophyseal joint pain patterns. I: A study in normal volunteers. *Spine.* 1990;15:453-457.

4. Fukui S, Ohseto K, Shiotani M, et al. Referred pain distribution of the cervical zygapophyseal joints and cervical dorsal rami. *Pain.* 1996;68:79-83.

5. Cooper G, Bailey B, Bogduk N. Cervical zygapophysial joint pain maps. *Pain Med.* 2007;8:344-353.

6. Cleland JA, Childs JD, Fritz JM, Whitman JM. Interrater reliability of the history and physical examination in patients with mechanical neck pain. *Arch Phys Med Rehabil.* 2006;87:1388-1395.

7. Wainner RS, Fritz JM, Irrgang JJ, et al. Reliability and diagnostic accuracy of the clinical examination and patient self-report measures for cervical radiculopathy. *Spine.* 2003;28:52-62.

8. Lauder TD, Dillingham TR, Andary M, et al. Predicting electrodiagnostic outcome in patients with upper limb symptoms: are the history and physical examination helpful? *Arch Phys Med Rehabil.* 2000;81:436-441.

9. Stiell IG, Wells GA, Vandemheen KL, et al. The Canadian C-spine rule for radiography in alert and stable trauma patients. *JAMA.* 2001;286:1841-1848.

10. Stiell IG, Clement CM, McKnight RD, et al. The Canadian C-spine rule versus the NEXUS low-risk criteria in patients with trauma. *N Engl J Med.* 2003;349:2510-2518.

11. Hoffman JR, Mower WR, Wolfson AB, et al. Validity of a set of clinical criteria to rule out injury to the cervical spine in patients with blunt trauma. National Emergency X-Radiography Utilization Study Group. *N Engl J Med.* 2000;343:94-99.

12. Dickinson G, Stiell IG, Schull M, et al. Retrospective application of the NEXUS low-risk criteria for cervical spine radiography in Canadian emergency departments. *Ann Emerg Med.* 2004;43:507-514.

13. Bandiera G, Stiell IG, Wells GA, et al. The Canadian C-spine rule performs better than unstructured physician judgment. *Ann Emerg Med.* 2003;42:395-402.

14. Duane TM, Dechert T, Wolfe LG, et al. Clinical examination and its reliability in identifying cervical spine fractures. *J Trauma.* 2007;62:1405-1410.

15. Piva SR, Erhard RE, Childs JD, Browder DA. Intertester reliability of passive intervertebral and active movements of the cervical spine. *Man Ther.* 2006;11:321-330.

16. Hoving JL, Pool JJ, van Mameren H, et al. Reproducibility of cervical range of motion in patients with neck pain. *BMC Musculoskelet Disord.* 2005;6:59.

17. Olson SL, O'Connor DP, Birmingham G, et al. Tender point sensitivity, range of motion, and perceived disability in subjects with neck pain. *J Orthop Sports Phys Ther.* 2000;30:13-20.

18. Hole DE, Cook JM, Bolton JE. Reliability and concurrent validity of two instruments for measuring cervical range of motion: effects of age and gender. *Man Ther.* 1995;1:36-42.

19. Youdas JW, Carey JR, Garrett TR. Reliability of measurements of cervical spine range of motion—comparison of three methods. *Phys Ther.* 1991;71:98-104; discussion 105-6.

20. Pool JJ, Hoving JL, de Vet HC, et al. The interexaminer reproducibility of physical examination of the cervical spine. *J Manipulative Physiol Ther.* 2004;27:84-90.

21. Van Suijlekom HA, De Vet HC, Van Den Berg SG, Weber WE. Interobserver reliability in physical examination of the cervical spine in patients with headache. *Headache.* 2000;40:581-586.

22. Sandmark H, Nisell R. Validity of five common manual neck pain provoking tests. *Scand J Rehabil Med.* 1995;27:131-136.

23. Edmondston SJ, Wallumrod ME, Macleid F, et al. Reliability of isometric muscle endurance tests in subjects with postural neck pain. *J Manipulative Physiol Ther.* 2008;31:348-354.

24. Olson LE, Millar AL, Dunker J, et al. Reliability of a clinical test for deep cervical flexor endurance. *J Manipulative Physiol Ther.* 2006;29:134-138.

25. Harris KD, Heer DM, Roy TC, et al. Reliability of a measurement of neck flexor muscle endurance. *Phys Ther.* 2005;85:1349-1355.

26. Chiu TT, Law EY, Chiu TH. Performance of the craniocervical flexion test in subjects with and without chronic neck pain. *J Orthop Sports Phys Ther.* 2005;35:567-571.

27. Kumbhare DA, Balsor B, Parkinson WL, et al. Measurement of cervical flexor endurance following whiplash. *Disabil Rehabil.* 2005;27:801-807.

28. Smedmark V, Wallin M, Arvidsson I. Inter-examiner reliability in assessing passive intervertebral motion of the cervical spine. *Man Ther.* 2000;5:97-101.

29. Humphreys BK, Delahaye M, Peterson CK. An investigation into the validity of cervical spine motion palpation using subjects with congenital block vertebrae as a 'gold standard'. *BMC Musculoskelet Disord.* 2004;5:19.

30. King W, Lau P, Lees R, Bogduk N. The validity of manual examination in assessing patients with neck pain. *Spine J.* 2007;7:22-26.

31. Jull G, Bogduk N, Marsland A. The accuracy of manual diagnosis for cervical zygapophysial joint pain syndromes. *Med J Aust.* 1988;148:233-236.

32. Viikari-Juntura E. Interexaminer reliability of observations in physical examinations of the neck. *Phys Ther*. 1987;67:1526-1532.

33. Bertilson BC, Grunnesjo M, Strender LE. Reliability of clinical tests in the assessment of patients with neck/shoulder problems—impact of history. *Spine*. 2003;28:2222-2231.

34. Shah KC, Rajshekhar V. Reliability of diagnosis of soft cervical disc prolapse using Spurling's test. *Br J Neurosurg*. 2004;18:480-483.

35. Tong HC, Haig AJ, Yamakawa K. The Spurling test and cervical radiculopathy. *Spine*. 2002;27:156-159.

36. Uitvlugt G, Indenbaum S. Clinical assessment of atlantoaxial instability using the Sharp-Purser test. *Arthritis Rheum*. 1988;31:918-922.

37. Uchihara T, Furukawa T, Tsukagoshi H. Compression of brachial plexus as a diagnostic test of cervical cord lesion. *Spine*. 1994;19:2170-2173.

38. Cleland JA, Fritz JM, Whitman JM, Heath R. Predictors of short-term outcome in people with a clinical diagnosis of cervical radiculopathy. *Phys Ther*. 2007;87:1619-1632.

39. Tseng YL, Wang WT, Chen WY, et al. Predictors for the immediate responders to cervical manipulation in patients with neck pain. *Man Ther*. 2006;11:306-315.

40. Cleland JA, Childs JD, Fritz JM, et al. Development of a clinical prediction rule for guiding treatment of a subgroup of patients with neck pain: use of thoracic spine manipulation, exercise, and patient education. *Phys Ther*. 2007;87:9-23.

41. Raney NH, Petersen EJ, Smith TA, et al. Development of a clinical prediction rule to identify patients with neck pain likely to benefit from cervical traction and exercise. *Eur Spine J*. 2009

42. Cleland JA, Childs JD, Whitman JM. Psychometric properties of the Neck Disability Index and Numeric Pain Rating Scale in patients with mechanical neck pain. *Arch Phys Med Rehabil*. 2008;89:69-74.

43. Grotle M, Brox JI, Vollestad NK. Reliability, validity and responsiveness of the fear-avoidance beliefs questionnaire: methodological aspects of the Norwegian version. *J Rehabil Med*. 2006;38:346-353.

44. Viikari-Juntura E, Porras M, Laasonen EM. Validity of clinical tests in the diagnosis of root compression in cervical disc disease. *Spine*. 1989;14:253-257.

Thoracolumbar Spine 4

CLINICAL SUMMARY AND RECOMMENDATIONS

Patient History

Complaints
- A few subjective complaints appear to be useful in identifying specific spinal pathologies. A report of "no pain when seated" is the single question with the best diagnostic utility for lumbar spinal stenosis (+likelihood ratio [LR] = 6.6). "Pain not relieved by lying down," "back pain at night," and "morning stiffness > $\frac{1}{2}$ hour" are all somewhat helpful in identifying ankylosing spondylitis (+LRs = 1.51 to 1.57). Subjective complaints of weakness, numbness, tingling, and/or burning do not appear to be especially helpful, at least in identifying lumbar radiculopathy.

Physical Examination

Neurological Screening
- Traditional neurological screening (sensation, reflex, and manual muscle testing) is reasonably useful in identifying lumbar radiculopathy. When tested in isolation, weakness with manual muscle testing, and even more so, reduced reflexes, are suggestive of lumbar radiculopathy, especially at the L3/4 spinal levels. Sensation testing (vibration and pin prick) alone does not seem to be especially useful. However, when changes in reflexes, muscular strength, and sensation are found in conjunction with a positive straight-leg raise, lumbar radiculopathy is highly likely (+LR = 6.0).

- In addition, decreased sensation (vibration and pin prick), muscle weakness, and reflex changes are each modestly helpful in identifying lumbar spinal stenosis (+LR = 2.1 to 2.8).

Range of Motion, Strength, and Manual Assessment
- Measuring both thoracolumbar range of motion (ROM) and trunk strength have consistently been shown to be very reliable, but are of unknown diagnostic utility.

- The results of studies assessing the reliability of passive intervertebral motion (PIVM) are highly variable but generally report poor reliability when assessing for limited or excessive movement and moderate reliability when assessing for pain.

- Diagnostic studies assessing PIVM suggest that abnormal segmental motion is moderately useful both in identifying radiographic hypomobility/hypermobility and for predicting the responses to certain conservative treatments. However, restricted PIVM may have little or no association with low back pain.

Special Tests
- The centralization phenomenon (movement of symptoms from distal/lateral regions to more central regions) has been shown to be both highly reliable and decidedly useful in identifying painful lumbar discs (+LR = 6.9).

- The straight-leg raise (SLR), the crossed straight-leg raise, and the slump test have all been shown to be moderately useful in identifying disc pathologies including bulges, herniations, and extrusions.

- An abundance of tests purport the ability to identify lumbar segmental instability. Reliability of these tests is highly variable, and their diagnostic utility is unknown, presumably due to a lack of an established reference standard.

- Both the Romberg test and a two-stage treadmill test have been found to be moderately useful in identifying lumbar spinal stenosis.

Interventions
- Patients with low back pain of duration less than 16 days and no symptoms distal to the knees, and/or meet at least 4 out of 5 of the Flynn and colleagues'[1] criteria, should be treated with a lumbosacral manipulation.

- Patients with low back pain that meet at least three out of five of the Hicks'[2] criteria, should be treated with lumbar stabilization exercises.

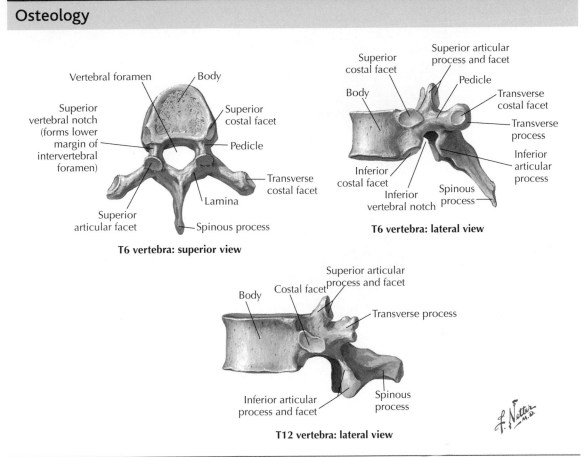

T6 vertebra: superior view

T6 vertebra: lateral view

T12 vertebra: lateral view

Figure 4-1

Thoracic vertebrae.

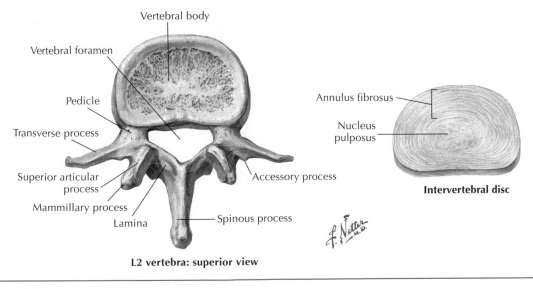

L2 vertebra: superior view

Intervertebral disc

Figure 4-2

Lumbar vertebrae.

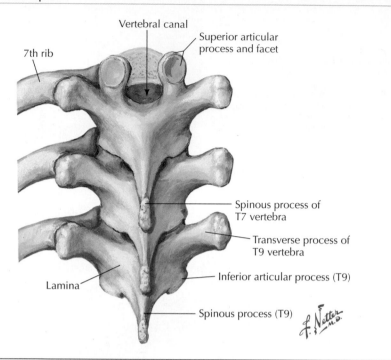

Figure 4-3

T7, T8, and T9 vertebrae, posterior view.

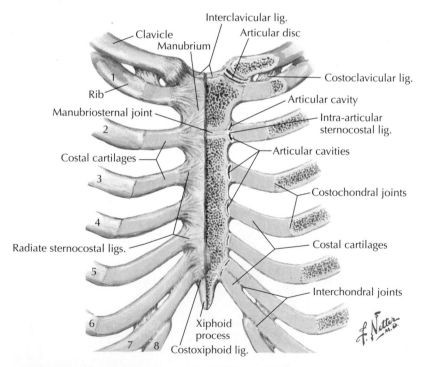

Figure 4-4

Sternocostal articulations, anterior view.

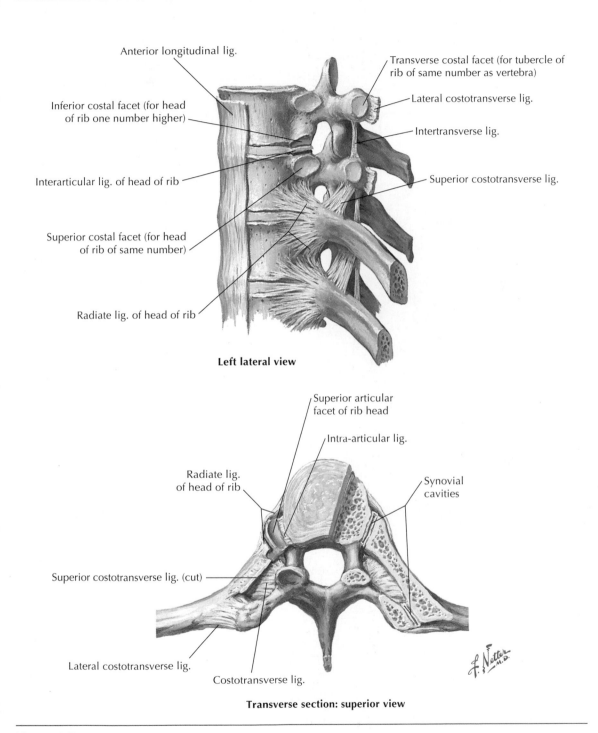

Left lateral view

Anterior longitudinal lig.

Inferior costal facet (for head of rib one number higher)

Interarticular lig. of head of rib

Superior costal facet (for head of rib of same number)

Radiate lig. of head of rib

Transverse costal facet (for tubercle of rib of same number as vertebra)

Lateral costotransverse lig.

Intertransverse lig.

Superior costotransverse lig.

Superior articular facet of rib head

Intra-articular lig.

Radiate lig. of head of rib

Synovial cavities

Superior costotransverse lig. (cut)

Lateral costotransverse lig.

Costotransverse lig.

Transverse section: superior view

Figure 4-5

Costovertebral joints.

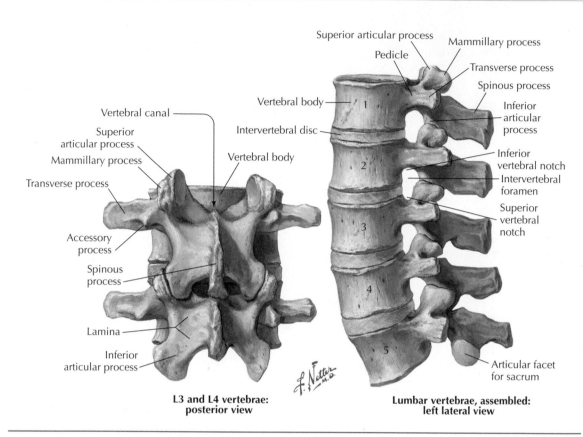

Superior articular process
Mammillary process
Pedicle
Transverse process
Spinous process
Vertebral body — 1
Inferior articular process
Vertebral canal
Intervertebral disc
Superior articular process
Mammillary process
Vertebral body
Transverse process
2
Inferior vertebral notch
Intervertebral foramen
Accessory process
Superior vertebral notch
3
Spinous process
4
Lamina
Inferior articular process
5
Articular facet for sacrum

L3 and L4 vertebrae: posterior view

Lumbar vertebrae, assembled: left lateral view

Figure 4-6

Lumbar spine.

Thoracolumbar Joints	Type and Classification	Closed Packed Position	Capsular Pattern
Zygapophyseal joints	Synovial: plane	Extension	Lumbar: significant limitation of side-bending bilaterally and limitations of flexion and extension
			Thoracic: limitation of extension, side-bending, and rotation, less limitation of flexion
Intervertebral joints	Amphiarthrodial	Not applicable	Not applicable

Thoracic Spine	Type and Classification	Closed Packed Position	Capsular Pattern
Costotransverse	Synovial	Not reported	Not reported
Costoverterbal	Synovial	Not reported	Not reported
Costochondral	Synchondroses	Not reported	Not reported
Interchondral	Synovial	Not reported	Not reported
Sternocostal			
1st joint	Amphiarthrodial	Not applicable	Not applicable
2nd-7th joint	Synovial	Not reported	Not reported

Ligaments

Costovertebral Ligaments

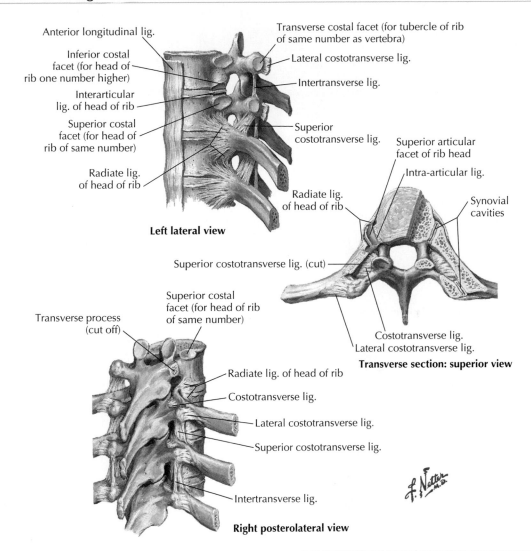

Anterior longitudinal lig.

Inferior costal facet (for head of rib one number higher)

Interarticular lig. of head of rib

Superior costal facet (for head of rib of same number)

Radiate lig. of head of rib

Left lateral view

Transverse costal facet (for tubercle of rib of same number as vertebra)

Lateral costotransverse lig.

Intertransverse lig.

Superior costotransverse lig.

Radiate lig. of head of rib

Superior articular facet of rib head

Intra-articular lig.

Synovial cavities

Superior costotransverse lig. (cut)

Costotransverse lig.
Lateral costotransverse lig.

Transverse section: superior view

Transverse process (cut off)

Superior costal facet (for head of rib of same number)

Radiate lig. of head of rib

Costotransverse lig.

Lateral costotransverse lig.

Superior costotransverse lig.

Intertransverse lig.

Right posterolateral view

Figure 4-7

Costovertebral ligaments.

Ligaments	Attachments	Function
Radiate sternocostal	Costal cartilage to the anterior and posterior aspect of the sternum	Reinforces joint capsule
Interchondral ligaments	Connect adjacent borders of articulations between 6th and 7th, 7th and 8th, and 8th and 9th costal cartilages	Reinforces joint capsule
Radiate of head of rib	Lateral vertebral body to head of rib	Prevents separation of rib head from vertebra
Costotransverse	Posterior aspect of rib to anterior aspect of transverse process of vertebra	Prevents separation of rib from transverse process
Intra-articular	Crest of the rib head to intervertebral disc	Divides joint into two cavities

Ligaments

Thoracolumbar Ligaments

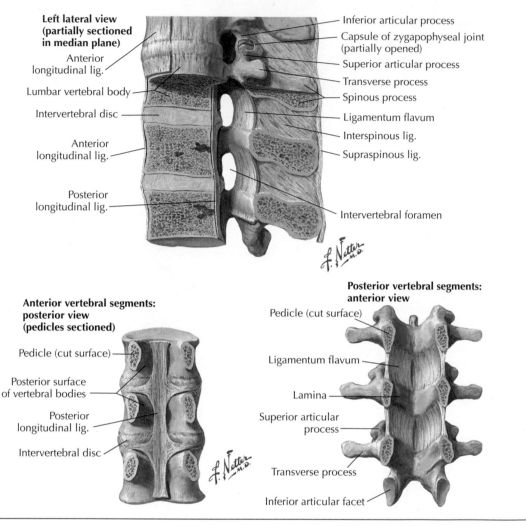

Left lateral view (partially sectioned in median plane)

- Anterior longitudinal lig.
- Lumbar vertebral body
- Intervertebral disc
- Anterior longitudinal lig.
- Posterior longitudinal lig.

- Inferior articular process
- Capsule of zygapophyseal joint (partially opened)
- Superior articular process
- Transverse process
- Spinous process
- Ligamentum flavum
- Interspinous lig.
- Supraspinous lig.
- Intervertebral foramen

Anterior vertebral segments: posterior view (pedicles sectioned)

- Pedicle (cut surface)
- Posterior surface of vertebral bodies
- Posterior longitudinal lig.
- Intervertebral disc

Posterior vertebral segments: anterior view

- Pedicle (cut surface)
- Ligamentum flavum
- Lamina
- Superior articular process
- Transverse process
- Inferior articular facet

Figure 4-8

Thoracolumbar ligaments.

Ligaments	Attachments	Function
Anterior longitudinal	Extends from anterior sacrum to anterior tubercle of C1. Connects anterolateral vertebral bodies and discs	Maintains stability and prevents excessive extension of spinal column
Posterior longitudinal	Extends from the sacrum to C2. Runs within the vertebral canal attaching the posterior vertebral bodies	Prevents excessive flexion of spinal column and posterior disc protrusion
Ligamenta flava	Binds the lamina above each vertebra to the lamina below	Prevents separation of the vertebral laminae
Supraspinous	Connect spinous processes C7-S1	Limits separation of spinous processes
Interspinous	Connect spinous processes C1-S1	Limits separation of spinous processes
Intertransverse	Connect adjacent transverse processes of vertebrae	Limits separation of transverse processes
Iliolumbar	Transverse processes of L5 to posterior aspect of iliac crest	Stabilizes L5 and prevents anterior shear

Muscles

Thoracolumbar Muscles: Superficial Layers

Muscles	Proximal Attachment	Distal Attachment	Nerve and Segmental Level	Action
Latissimus dorsi	Spinous processes T6-T12, thoracolumbar fascia, iliac crest, inferior four ribs	Intertubercular groove of humerus	Thoracodorsal nerve (C6, C7, C8)	Humerus extension, adduction and internal rotation
Trapezius				
Middle	Superior nuchal line, occipital protuberance, nuchal ligament, spinous processes T1-T12	Lateral clavicle, acromion, and spine of scapula	Accessory nerve (CN XI)	Retracts scapula
Lower				Depresses scapula
Rhomboids				
Major	Spinous processes T2-T5	Inferior medial border of scapula	Dorsal scapular nerve (C4, C5)	Retracts scapula, inferiorly rotates glenoid fossa, stabilizes scapula to thoracic wall
Minor	Spinous processes C7-T1 and nuchal ligament	Superior medial border of scapula		
Serratus posterior superior	Spinous processes C7-T3, ligamentum nuchae	Superior surface of ribs 2-4	Intercostal nerves 2-5	Elevates ribs
Serratus posterior inferior	Spinous processes T11-L2	Inferior surface of ribs 8-12	Ventral rami of thoracic spinal nerves 9-12	Depresses ribs

CN, cranial nerve.

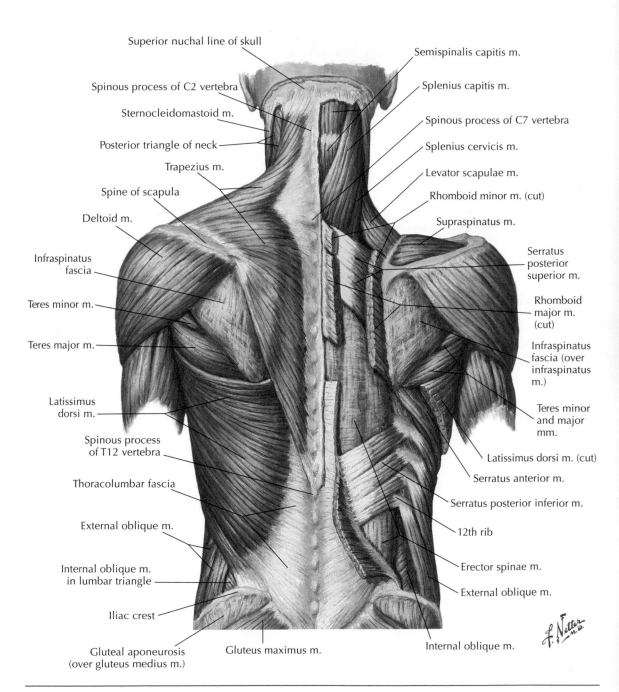

Figure 4-9

Muscles of back, superficial layers.

Thoracolumbar Muscles: Intermediate Layer

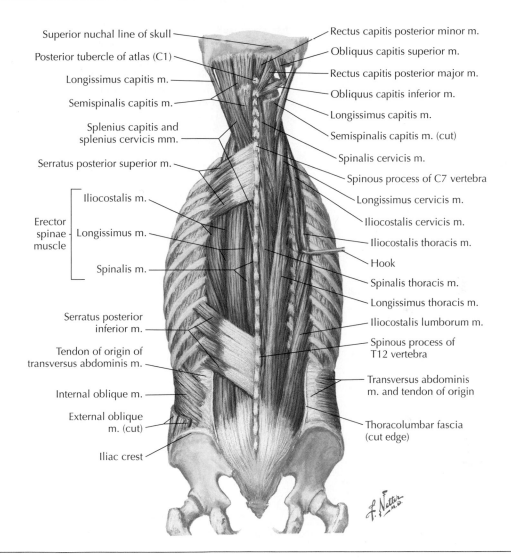

Figure 4-10

Muscles of the back, intermediate layer.

Muscles	Proximal Attachment	Distal Attachment	Nerve and Segmental Level	Action
Iliocostalis thoracis	Iliac crest, posterior sacrum, spinous processes of sacrum and inferior lumbar vertebrae, supraspinous ligament	Cervical transverse processes and superior angles of lower ribs	Dorsal rami of spinal nerves	Bilaterally: extend spinal column Unilaterally: side-bend spinal column
Iliocostalis lumborum		Inferior surface of ribs 4-12		
Longissimus thoracis		Thoracic transverse processes and superior surface of ribs		
Longissimus lumborum		Transverse process of lumbar vertebrae		
Spinalis thoracis		Upper thoracic spinous processes		

Muscles

Thoracolumbar Muscles: Deep Layer

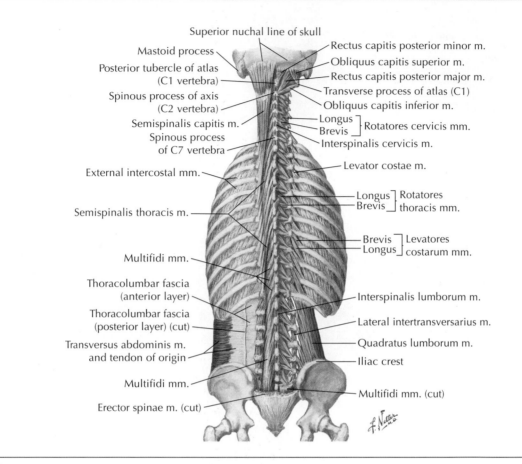

Figure 4-11

Muscles of the back, deep layer.

Muscles	Proximal Attachment	Distal Attachment	Nerve and Segmental Level	Action
Rotatores	Transverse processes of vertebrae	Spinous process of vertebra 1-2 segments above origin	Dorsal rami of spinal nerves	Vertebral stabilization, assists with rotation and extension
Interspinalis	Superior aspect of cervical and lumbar spinous processes	Inferior aspect of spinous process superior to vertebrae of origin	Dorsal rami of spinal nerves	Extension and rotation of vertebral column
Intertransversarius	Cervical and lumbar transverse processes	Transverse process of adjacent vertebrae	Dorsal and ventral rami of spinal nerves	Bilaterally stabilizes vertebral column. Ipsilaterally side-bends vertebral column
Multifidi	Sacrum, ilium, transverse processes T1-T3, articular processes C4-C7	Spinous process of vertebra 2-4 segments above origin	Dorsal rami of spinal nerves	Stabilizes vertebrae

Muscles

Anterior Abdominal Wall

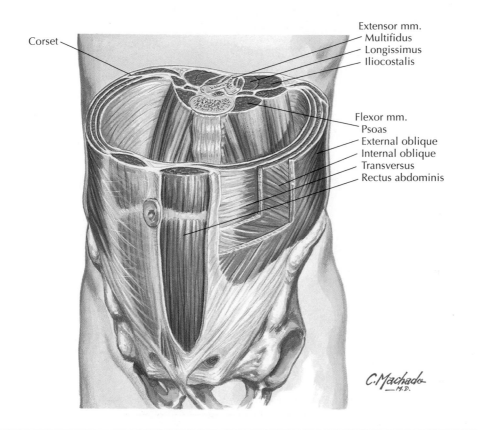

Corset

Extensor mm.
Multifidus
Longissimus
Iliocostalis

Flexor mm.
Psoas
External oblique
Internal oblique
Transversus
Rectus abdominis

C. Machado
—M.D.

Figure 4-12

Dynamic "corset" concept of lumbar stability.

Muscles	Proximal Attachment	Distal Attachment	Nerve and Segmental Level	Action
Rectus abdominis	Pubic symphysis and pubic crest	Costal cartilage 5-7 and xiphoid process	Ventral rami T6-T12	Flexes trunk
Internal oblique	Thoracolumbar fascia, anterior iliac crest, and lateral inguinal ligament	Inferior border of ribs 10-12, linea alba, and pectin pubis	Ventral rami T6-L1	Flexes and rotates trunk
External oblique	External aspect of ribs 5-12	Anterior iliac crest, linea alba, and pubic tubercle	Ventral rami T6-T12 and subcostal nerve	Flexes and rotates trunk
Transversus abdominis	Internal aspect of costal cartilage 7-12, thoracolumbar fascia, iliac crest, and lateral inguinal ligament	Linea alba, pectin pubis, and pubic crest	Ventral rami T6-L1	Supports abdominal viscera and increases intraabdominal pressure

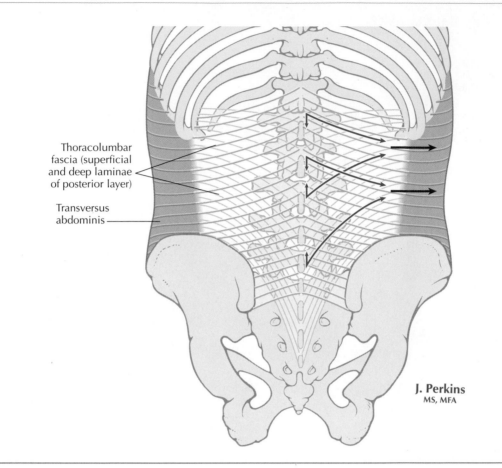

Thoracolumbar fascia (superficial and deep laminae of posterior layer)

Transversus abdominis

J. Perkins
MS, MFA

Figure 4-13

Transverse abdominis. The transverse abdominis exerts a force through the thoracolumbar fascia creating a stabilizing force through the lumbar spine.[8]

The thoracolumbar fascia is a dense layer of connective tissue running from the thoracic region to the sacrum.[3] It is comprised of three separate and distinct layers: anterior, middle, and posterior. The middle and posterior layers blend together to form a dense fascia referred to as the *lateral raphe*.[4] The posterior layer consists of two distinctly separate laminae. The superficial lamina fibers are angled downward and the deep lamina fibers are angled upward. Bergmark[5] has reported that the thoracolumbar fascia serves three purposes: (1) to transfer forces from muscles to the spine, (2) to transfer forces between spinal segments, and (3) to transfer forces from the thoracolumbar spine to the retinaculum of the erector spinae. The transverse abdominis attaches to the middle layer of the thoracolumbar fascia and exerts a force through the lateral raphe resulting in a cephalad tension through the deep layer and a caudal tension through the superficial layer of the posterior lamina.[3,4,6] The result is a stabilizing force exerted through the lumbar spine, which has been reported to provide stability and assist with controlling intersegmental motion of the lumbar spine.[7-9]

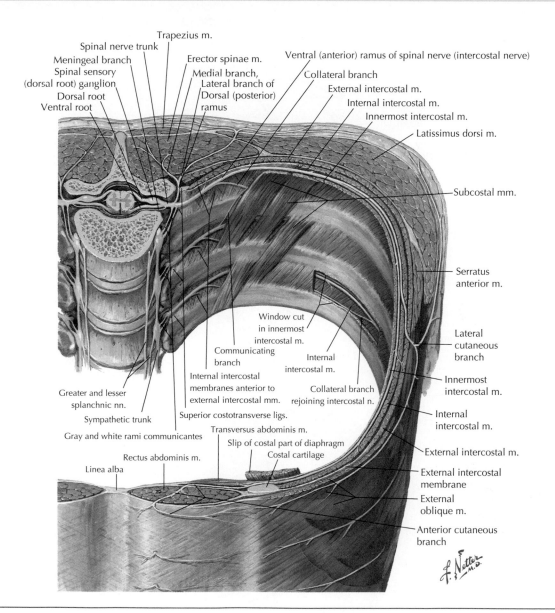

Figure 4-14

Nerves of the thoracic spine.

Nerve	Segmental Level	Sensory	Motor
Ventral Rami			
Intercostals	T1-T11	Anterior and lateral aspect of the thorax and abdomen	Intercostals, serratus posterior, levator costarum, transversus thoracis
Subcostals	T12		Part of external oblique
Dorsal rami	T1-T12	Posterior thorax and back	Splenius, iliocostalis, longissimus, spinalis, interspinales, intertransversarii, multifidi, semispinalis, rotatores

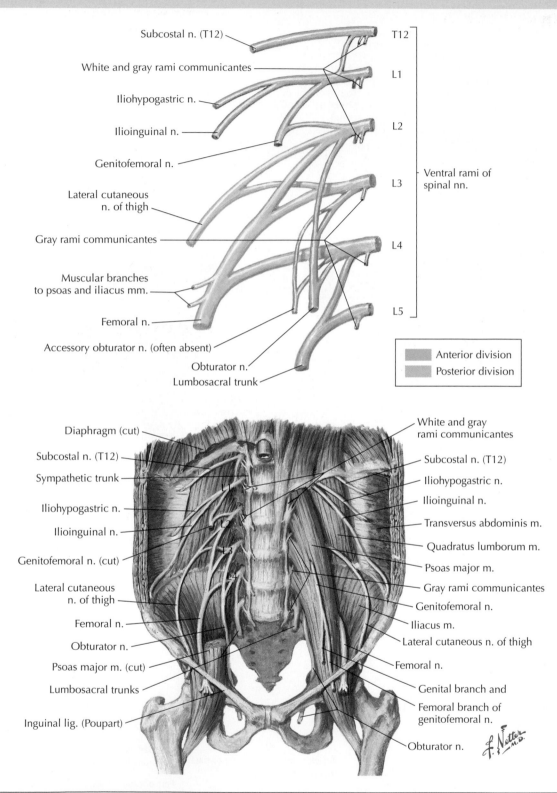

Figure 4-15

Nerves of the lumbar spine.

Nerves

Nerve	Segmental Level	Sensory	Motor
Subcostal nerve	T12	Lateral hip	External oblique
Iliohypogastric nerve	T12, L1	Posterolateral gluteal region	Internal oblique, transverse abdominis
Ilioinguinal	L1	Superior medial thigh	Internal oblique, transverse abdominis
Genitofemoral	L1, L2	Superior anterior thigh	No motor
Lateral cutaneous	L2, L3	Lateral thigh	No motor
Branch to iliacus		No sensory	Iliacus
Femoral nerve	L2, L3, L4	Thigh via cutaneus nerves	Iliacus, sartorius, quadriceps femoris, articularis genu, pectineus
Obturator nerve	L2, L3, L4	Medial thigh	Adductor longus, adductor brevis, adductor magnus (adductor part), gracilis, obturator externus
Sciatic	L4, L5, S1, S2, S3	Hip joint	Knee flexors and all muscles of the lower leg and foot

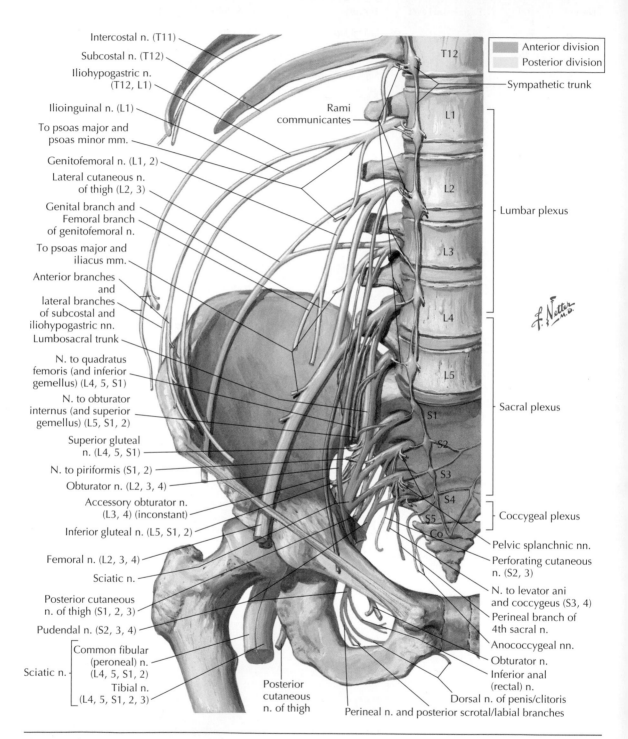

Intercostal n. (T11)
Subcostal n. (T12)
Iliohypogastric n. (T12, L1)
Ilioinguinal n. (L1)
To psoas major and psoas minor mm.
Genitofemoral n. (L1, 2)
Lateral cutaneous n. of thigh (L2, 3)
Genital branch and Femoral branch of genitofemoral n.
To psoas major and iliacus mm.
Anterior branches and lateral branches of subcostal and iliohypogastric nn.
Lumbosacral trunk
N. to quadratus femoris (and inferior gemellus) (L4, 5, S1)
N. to obturator internus (and superior gemellus) (L5, S1, 2)
Superior gluteal n. (L4, 5, S1)
N. to piriformis (S1, 2)
Obturator n. (L2, 3, 4)
Accessory obturator n. (L3, 4) (inconstant)
Inferior gluteal n. (L5, S1, 2)
Femoral n. (L2, 3, 4)
Sciatic n.
Posterior cutaneous n. of thigh (S1, 2, 3)
Pudendal n. (S2, 3, 4)

Sciatic n. — Common fibular (peroneal) n. (L4, 5, S1, 2)
Tibial n. (L4, 5, S1, 2, 3)

Posterior cutaneous n. of thigh

Rami communicantes

Anterior division
Posterior division

T12
Sympathetic trunk
L1
L2
L3
L4
L5
S1
S2
S3
S4
S5
Co

Lumbar plexus
Sacral plexus
Coccygeal plexus

Pelvic splanchnic nn.
Perforating cutaneous n. (S2, 3)
N. to levator ani and coccygeus (S3, 4)
Perineal branch of 4th sacral n.
Anococcygeal nn.
Obturator n.
Inferior anal (rectal) n.
Dorsal n. of penis/clitoris
Perineal n. and posterior scrotal/labial branches

Figure 4-16

Nerves of the lumbar spine.

PATIENT HISTORY

Initial Hypotheses Based on Patient History

History	Initial Hypothesis
Reports of restricted motion of the lumbar spine associated with low back or buttock pain exacerbated by a pattern of movement that indicates possible opening or closing joint restriction (i.e., decreased extension, right sidebending, and right rotation)	Zygapophyseal joint pain syndromes[10-12]
Reports of centralization or peripheralization of symptoms during repetitive movements or prolonged periods in certain positions	Possible discogenic pain[13]
Reports of lower extremity pain/paresthesias, which is greater than the low back pain. May report experiencing episodes of lower extremity weakness	Possible sciatica or lumbar radiculopathy[14]
Pain in the lower extremities that is exacerbated by extension and quickly relieved by flexion of the spine	Possible spinal stenosis[15]
Patient reports of recurrent locking, catching, or giving way of the low back during active motion	Possible lumbar instability[16,17]
Reports of low back pain that is exacerbated by stretch of either ligament or muscles. Might also report pain with contraction of muscular tissues	Muscle/ligamentous sprain/strain

Lumbar Zygapophyseal Joint Referral Patterns

Area of Pain Referral	Percentage of Patients Presenting with Pain (n= 176 patients with low back pain)
Left groin	15%
Right groin	3%
Left buttock	42%
Right buttock	15%
Left thigh	38%
Right thigh	38%
Left calf	27%
Right calf	15%
Left foot	31%
Right foot	8%

Prevalence of pain referral patterns in patients with zygapophyseal joint pain syndromes as confirmed by diagnostic blocks.[12] In a subsequent study,[18] it was determined that in a cohort of 63 patients with chronic low back pain, the prevalence of zygapophyseal joint pain was 40%.

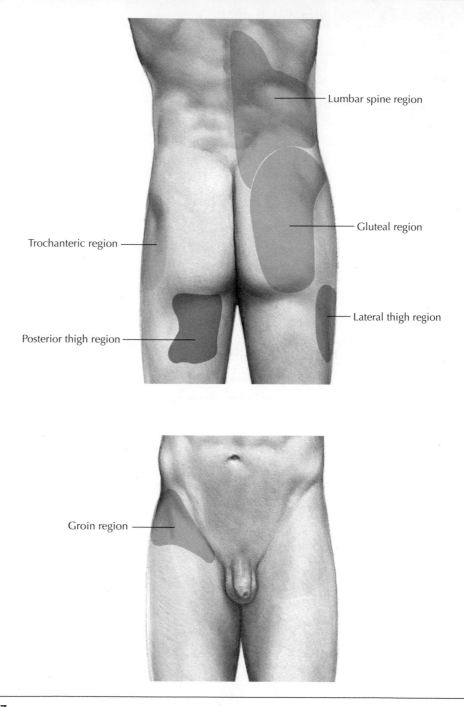

Lumbar spine region

Gluteal region

Trochanteric region

Lateral thigh region

Posterior thigh region

Groin region

Figure 4-17

Lumbar zygapophyseal joint pain referral patterns. Zygapophyseal pain patterns of the lumbar spine as described by Fukui and colleagues.[90] Lumbar zygapophyseal joints L1/2, L2/3, and L4/5 always referred pain to the lumbar spine region. Primary referral to the gluteal region was from L5/S1 (68% of the time). Levels L2/3, L3/4, L4/5, and L5/S1 occasionally referred pain to the trochanteric region (10% to 16% of the time). Primary referral to lateral thigh, posterior thigh, and groin regions were most often from L3/4, L4/5, and L5/S1 (5% to 30% of the time).

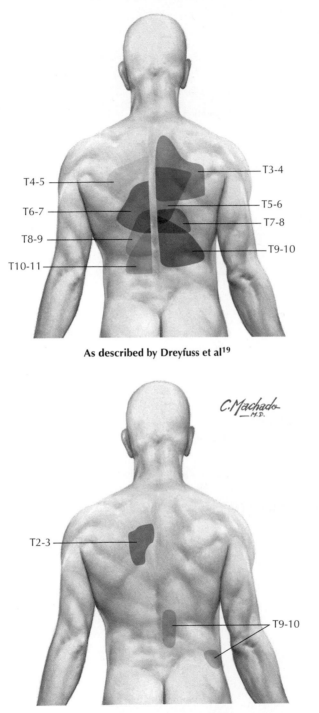

As described by Dreyfuss et al[19]

As described by Fukui et al[90]

Figure 4-18
Zygapophyseal pain patterns of the thoracic spine.

Reliability of the Historical Examination

ICC or κ	Interpretation
.81-1.0	Substantial agreement
.61-.80	Moderate agreement
.41-.60	Fair agreement
.11-.40	Slight agreement
.0-.10	No agreement

Historical Question and Study		Population	Reliability
Patient report of[21]:	Foot pain	2 separate groups of patients with low back pain ($n_1 = 50$, $n_2 = 33$).	Inter-examiner κ = .12 - .73
	Leg pain		Inter-examiner κ = .53 - .96
	Thigh pain		Inter-examiner κ = .39 - .78
	Buttock pain		Inter-examiner κ = .33 - .44
	Back pain		Inter-examiner κ = −.19 - .16
Increased pain with[22]:	Sitting	53 subjects with a primary complaint of low back pain	Test-retest κ = .46
	Standing		Test-retest κ = .70
	Walking		Test-retest κ = .67
Increased pain with[23]:	Sitting	A random selection of 91 patients with low back pain	Inter-examiner κ = .49
	Standing		Inter-examiner κ = 1.0
	Walking		Inter-examiner κ = .56
	Lying down		Inter-examiner κ = .41
Pain with sitting[24]		95 patients with low back pain	Inter-examiner κ = .99 - 1.0
Pain with bending[24]			Inter-examiner κ = .98 - .99
Pain with bending[22]		53 subjects with a primary complaint of low back pain	Test-retest κ = .65
Pain with bending[21]		2 separate groups of patients with low back pain ($n_1 = 50$, $n_2 = 33$).	Inter-examiner κ = .51 - .56
Increased pain with coughing/sneezing[23]		A random selection of 91 patients with low back pain	Inter-examiner κ = .64
Increased pain with coughing[22]		53 subjects with a primary complaint of low back pain	Test-retest κ = .75
Pain with pushing/lifting/carrying[22]			Test-retest κ = .77 - .89

Diagnostic Utility of the Patient History for Identifying Lumbar Spinal Stenosis

+LR	Interpretation	−LR
>10	Large	<.1
5.0-10.0	Moderate	.1-.2
2.0-5.0	Small	.2-.5
1.0-2.0	Rarely important	.5-1.0

Historical Question	Patient Population	Reference Standard	Sens	Spec	+ LR	− LR
Age > 65[25]	93 patients with low back pain ≥ 40 years old	Lumbar spinal stenosis per attending physician's impression; 88% also supported by computed tomography (CT) or magnetic resonance imaging (MRI)	.77 (.64, .90)	.69 (.53, .85)	2.5	.33
Pain below knees?[25]			.56 (.41, .71)	.63 (.46, .80)	1.5	.70
Pain below buttocks?[25]			.88 (.78, .98)	.34 (.18, .50)	1.3	.35
No pain when seated?[25]			.46 (.30, .62)	.93 (.84, 1.0)	6.6	.58
Severe lower extremity pain?[25]			.65 (.51, .79)	.67 (.51, .83)	2.0	.52
Symptoms improved while seated?[25]			.52 (.37, .67)	.83 (.70, .96)	3.1	.58
Worse when walking?[25]			.71 (.57, .85)	.30 (.14, .46)	1.0	.97
Numbness[25]			.63 (.49, .74)	.59 (.42, .76)	1.5	.63
Poor balance[25]			.70 (.56, .84)	.53 (.36, .70)	1.5	.57
Do you get pain in your legs with walking that is relieved by sitting?[15]	45 patients with low back and leg pain and self-reported limitations in walking tolerance	Lumbar spinal stenosis per MRI or CT imaging	.81 (.66, .96)	.16 (.00, .32)	.82 (.63, 1.1)	1.27
Are you able to walk better when holding onto a shopping cart?[15]			.63 (.42, .85)	.67 (.40, .93)	1.9 (.8, 4.5)	.55
Sitting reported as best posture with regard to symptoms[15]			.89 (.76, 1.0)	.39 (.16, .61)	1.5 (.9, 2.4)	.28
Walk/stand reported as worst posture with regard to symptoms[15]			.89 (.76, 1.0)	.33 (.12, .55)	1.3 (.8, 2.2)	.33

Diagnostic Utility of the Patient History for Identifying Lumbar Radiculopathy

+LR	Interpretation	−LR
>10	Large	<.1
5.0-10.0	Moderate	.1-.2
2.0-5.0	Small	.2-.5
1.0-2.0	Rarely important	.5-1.0

Patient Reports of	Patient Population	Reference Standard	Sens	Spec	+LR	−LR
Weakness[26]	170 patients with low back and leg symptoms	Lumbosacral radiculopathy per electrodiagnostics	.70	.41	1.19	.73
Numbness[26]			.68	.34	1.03	.94
Tingling[26]			.67	.31	.97	1.06
Burning[26]			.40	.60	1.0	1.0

Diagnostic Utility of the Patient History for Identifying Ankylosing Spondylitis

Clinical Symptom	Patient Population	Reference Standard	Sens	Spec	+LR	−LR
Pain not relieved by lying down[27]	449 randomly selected patients with low back pain	The New York criteria and radiographic confirmation of ankylosing spondylitis.	.80	.49	1.57	.41
Back pain at night[33]			.71	.53	1.51	.55
Morning stiffness > $1/2$ hour[27]			.64	.59	1.56	.68
Pain or stiffness relieved by exercise[27]			.74	.43	1.30	.60
Age of onset 40 years or less[27]			1.0	.07	1.07	.00

In early stages (sacroiliitis only), back contour may appear normal but flexion may be limited

In more advanced sacroiliac plus lower spine involvement, back is straightened with "ironed-out" appearance

Bilateral sacroiliitis is early radiographic sign. Thinning of cartilage and bone condensation on both sides of sacroiliac joints

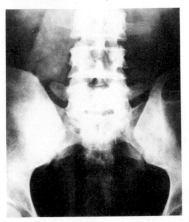

Anterior longitudinal lig.

Radiate lig. of head of rib

Costotransverse ligs.

Rib

Ossification of radiate and costotransverse ligaments limits chest expansion

Characteristic posture in late stage of disease. Measurement at nipple line demonstrates diminished chest expansion

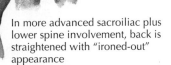

Ossification of annulus fibrosus of intervertebral discs, apophyseal joints, and anterior longitudinal and interspinal ligaments

Figure 4-19

Ankylosing spondylitis.

Diagnostic Utility of the Sensation, Manual Muscle Testing, and Reflexes for Lumbosacral Radiculopathy

+LR	Interpretation	−LR
>10	Large	<.1
5.0-10.0	Moderate	.1-.2
2.0-5.0	Small	.2-.5
1.0-2.0	Rarely important	.5-1.0

Test and Study Quality		Description and Positive Findings	Population	Reference Standard	Sens	Spec	+LR	−LR
Sensation (vibration and pin prick)[26]		Considered abnormal when either vibration or pin prick was reduced on the side of lesion			.50	.62	1.32	.81
Weakness[26]	Gastroc-soleus	Weakness was defined as any grade less than 5/5	170 patients with low back and lower extremity symptoms	Electrodiagnostic testing. Radiculopathy defined as the presence of positive sharp waves, fibrillation potentials, complex repetitive discharges, high-amplitude, long-duration motor unit potentials, reduced recruitment, or increased polyphasic motor unit potentials (>30%) in two or more muscles innervated by the same nerve root level but different peripheral nerves	S1 = .47	S1 = .76	1.96	.70
	Extensor hallucis longus				L5 = .61	L5 = .55	1.36	.71
	Hip flexors				L3-4 = .7	L3-4 = .84	4.38	.36
	Quadriceps				L3-4 = .40	L3-4 = .89	3.64	.67
Reflexes[26]	Achilles	Considered abnormal when the reflex on the side of the lesion was reduced compared with the opposite side			S1 = .47	S1 = .9	4.70	.59
	Patellar				L3-4 = .50	L3-4 = .93	7.14	.54
Reflexes + Weakness + Sensory[26]		All 3 abnormal			.12	.97	4.00	.91
Reflexes + Weakness + Sensory + Straight-leg raise[26]		All 4 abnormal			.06	.99	6.00	.95
		Any of 4 abnormal			.87	.35	1.34	.37

Diagnostic Utility of the Sensation, Manual Muscle Testing, and Reflexes for Lumbar Spinal Stenosis

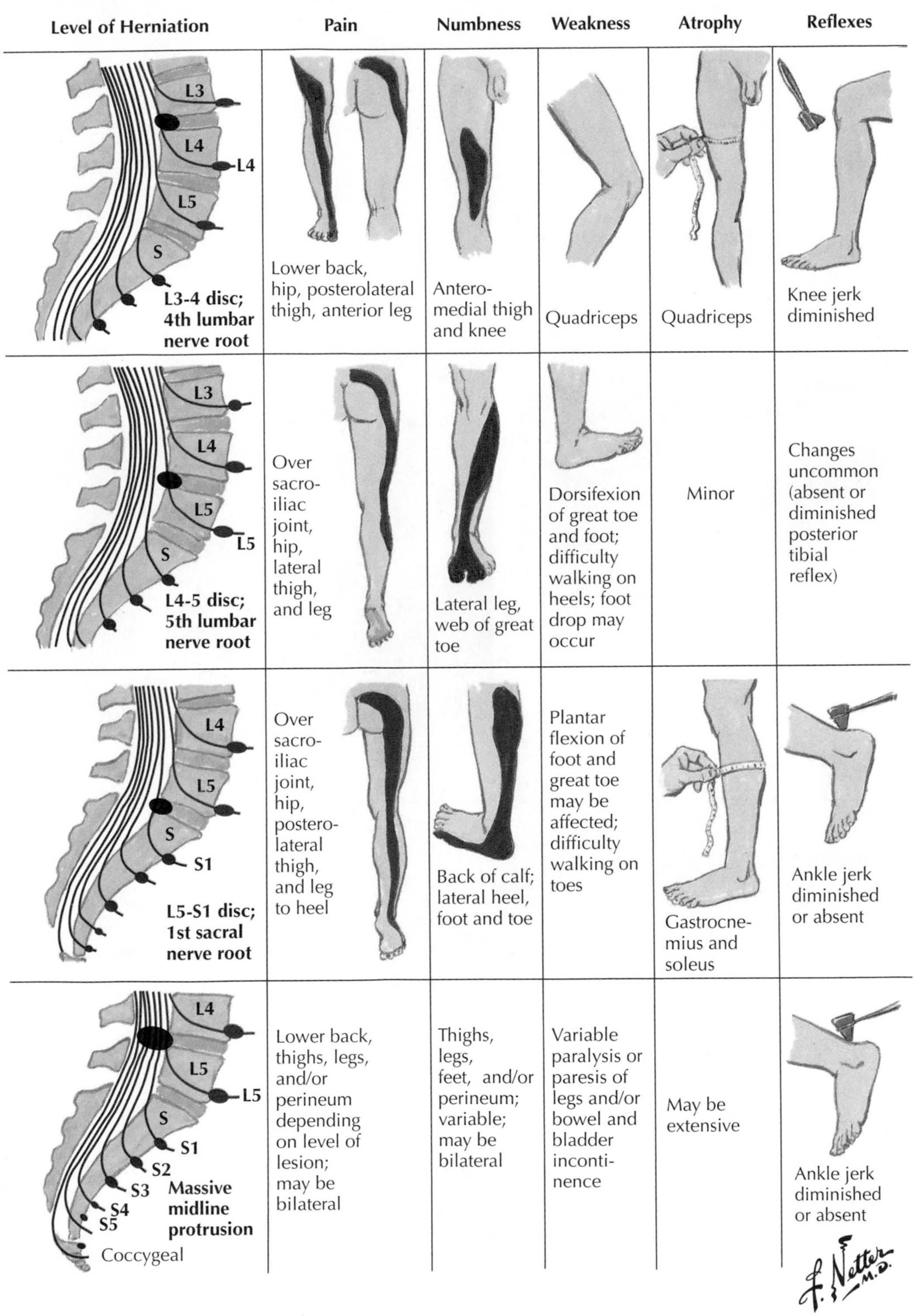

Level of Herniation	Pain	Numbness	Weakness	Atrophy	Reflexes
L3-4 disc; 4th lumbar nerve root	Lower back, hip, posterolateral thigh, anterior leg	Antero-medial thigh and knee	Quadriceps	Quadriceps	Knee jerk diminished
L4-5 disc; 5th lumbar nerve root	Over sacro-iliac joint, hip, lateral thigh, and leg	Lateral leg, web of great toe	Dorsifexion of great toe and foot; difficulty walking on heels; foot drop may occur	Minor	Changes uncommon (absent or diminished posterior tibial reflex)
L5-S1 disc; 1st sacral nerve root	Over sacro-iliac joint, hip, postero-lateral thigh, and leg to heel	Back of calf; lateral heel, foot and toe	Plantar flexion of foot and great toe may be affected; difficulty walking on toes	Gastrocne-mius and soleus	Ankle jerk diminished or absent
Massive midline protrusion	Lower back, thighs, legs, and/or perineum depending on level of lesion; may be bilateral	Thighs, legs, feet, and/or perineum; variable; may be bilateral	Variable paralysis or paresis of legs and/or bowel and bladder inconti-nence	May be extensive	Ankle jerk diminished or absent

Figure 4-20

Clinical features of herniated lumbar nucleus pulposus.

+LR	Interpretation	−LR
>10	Large	<.1
5.0-10.0	Moderate	.1-.2
2.0-5.0	Small	.2-.5
1.0-2.0	Rarely important	.5-1.0

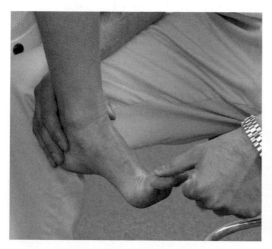

Strength testing of extensor
hallucis longus muscle

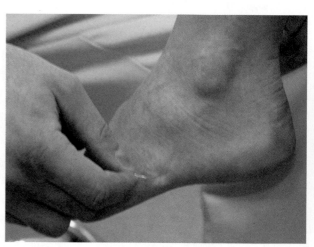

Pin prick test

Figure 4-21

Lumbar spinal stenosis testing.

Test and Study Quality	Description and Positive Findings	Population	Reference Standard	Sens	Spec	+LR	−LR
Vibration deficit[25] ◇	Assessed at the first metatarsal head with a 128-Hz tuning fork. Considered abnormal if patient did not perceive any vibration	93 patients with back pain with or without radiation to the lower extremities	Diagnosis of spinal stenosis by retrospective chart review and confirmed by MRI or CT	.53 (.38, .68)	.81 (.67, .95)	2.8	.58
Pin prick deficit[25] ◇	Sensation tested at the dorsomedial foot, dorsolateral foot, medial and lateral calf. Graded as "decreased" or "normal"			.47 (.32, .62)	.81 (.67, .95)	2.5	.65
Weakness[25] ◇	Strength of knee flexors, knee extensors, and hallucis longus were tested. Graded from 0 (no movement) to 5 (normal)			.47 (.32, .62)	.78 (.64, .92)	2.1	.68
Absent Achilles reflex[25] ◇	Reflex testing of the Achilles tendon. Graded from 0 (no response) to 4 (clonus)			.46 (.31, .61)	.78 (.64, .92)	2.1	.69

Range of Motion

Reliability of Range of Motion Measurements

ICC or κ	Interpretation
.81-1.0	Substantial agreement
.61-.80	Moderate agreement
.41-.60	Fair agreement
.11-.40	Slight agreement
.0-.10	No agreement

Measurement and Study	Instrumentation	Population	Reliability	
			Intra-examiner*	Inter-examiner
Forward bending[28]	Measured distance from fingertips to floor	30 patients with back pain and 20 asymptomatic subjects (only asymptomatic subjects were used for intra-examiner comparisons)	Intraclass correlation coefficient (ICC) = .95 (.89, .99)	ICC = .99 (.98, .10)
Lateral bending[28]	Measured distance that fingertip slid down lateral thigh		ICC (right) = .99 (.95, 1.0) ICC (left) = .94 (.82, .98)	ICC (right) = .93 (.89, .96) ICC (left) = .95 (.91, .97)
Trunk rotation[28]	Patients sit with horizontal bar on sternum. Plumb weight hung down to floor and angle was measured with a protractor		ICC (right) = .92 (.76, .97) ICC (left) = .96 (.87, .99)	ICC (right) = .82 (.70, .89) ICC (left) = .85 (.75, .91)
Modified Schober[28]	Distance between lumbosacral junction, 5 cm below, and 10 cm above, were measured in erect standing and while maximally bending forward		ICC = .87 (.68, .96)	ICC = .79 (.67, .88)
Flexion Extension Left rotation Right rotation Left sidebending Right sidebending[29]	Back range of motion instrument	47 asymptomatic students	ICC = .91 ICC = .63 ICC = .56 ICC = .57 ICC = .92 ICC = .89	ICC = .77 ICC = .35 ICC = .37 ICC = .35 ICC = .81 ICC = .89
Active rotation in standing[30]	Patients stood with a horizontal bar resting on their shoulders. A plumb weight hung from the end of the bar to the floor	24 asymptomatic golfers	ICC (right) = .86 (.70, .94) ICC (left) = .80 (.58, .92)	ICC (right) = .74 (.49, .88) ICC (left) = .78 (.56, .90)
Lumbar flexion[31]	Single inclinometer	49 patients with low back pain referred for flexion-extension radiographs	Inter-examiner ICC = .60 (.33, .79)	
Lumbar extension[31]			Inter-examiner ICC = .61 (.37, .78)	
Lumbar flexion[32]		123 patients with low back pain < 90 days	Inter-examiner ICC = .74 (.60, .84)	
Lumbar extension[32]			Inter-examiner ICC = .61 (.42, .75)	

*In the case of multiple examiners, intra-examiner estimates are presented for the first examiner only.

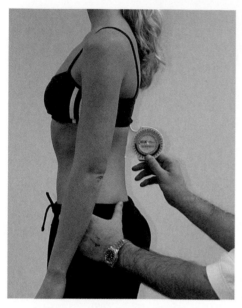

Inclinometer placement at the spinous
process of the 12th thoracic vertebra

Figure 4-22

Range of motion measurement.

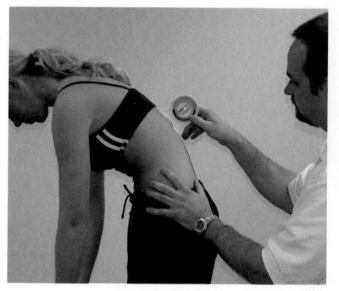

Measurement of thoracolumbar flexion

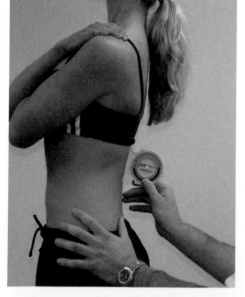

Measurement of thoracolumbar extension

Range of Motion

Reliability of Pain Provocation during Range of Motion

ICC or κ	Interpretation
.81-1.0	Substantial agreement
.61-.80	Moderate agreement
.41-.60	Fair agreement
.11-.40	Slight agreement
.0-.10	No agreement

Flexion-sidebending-rotation   Extension-sidebending-rotation

Figure 4-23

Pain provocation during active movements.

Test and Study	Description and Positive Findings	Population	Reliability
Sidebending[33]	Patient stands with arms at sides. Patient slides hand down the outside of the thigh		κ = .60 (.40, .79)
Rotation[33]	Patient stands with arms at sided. Patient rotates the trunk		κ = .17 (−.08, .42)
Sidebend-rotation[33]	Patient stands with arms at sides. Patient moves the pelvis to one side, creating a side-bend rotation to the opposite side	35 patients with low back pain	κ = .29 (.06, .51)
Flexion-sidebend-rotation[33]	Patient stands and the therapist guides the patient into lumbar flexion, then sidebending, then rotation		κ = .39 (.18, .61)
Extension-sidebend-rotation[33]	Patient stands and the therapist guides the patient into lumbar extension, then sidebending, then rotation		κ = .29 (.06, .52)
Thoracic rotation, right[34]	Patients places hands on the opposite shoulders and rotates the trunk as far as possible in each direction. Examiner then determines the effect of each movement on the patient's symptoms as "no effect," "increase symptoms," or "decreases symptoms"	22 patients with mechanical neck pain	κ = −.03 (−.11, .04)
Thoracic rotation, left[34]			κ = 0.7 (.4, 1.0)

ICC or κ	Interpretation
.81-1.0	Substantial agreement
.61-.80	Moderate agreement
.41-.60	Fair agreement
.11-.40	Slight agreement
.0-.10	No agreement

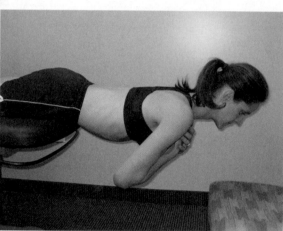

Figure 4-24

Modified Biering-Sorensen.

Measurement and Study	Description and Positive Findings	Population	Reliability
Abdominal endurance[28]	From supine hook-lying, patient curls up to touch finger tips to superior patellae and holds position for as long as possible. Time in seconds was measured with a stopwatch	30 patients with back pain and 20 asymptomatic subjects (only asymptomatic subjects used for intra-examiner comparisons)	Intra-examiner ICC = **.90** **(.75, .97)** Inter-examiner ICC = **.92** **(.87, .96)**
Modified Biering-Sorensen[28]	Patient starts prone with pelvis and legs supported on couch and trunk hanging off the edge supported by a chair. The patient then extends the trunk and holds a neutral position for as long as possible. Time in seconds was measured with a stopwatch		Intra-examiner ICC = **.92** **(.75, .97)** Inter-examiner ICC = **.91** **(.85, .95)**

Postural Assessment

Reliability of Postural Assessment

ICC or κ	Interpretation
.81-1.0	Substantial agreement
.61-.80	Moderate agreement
.41-.60	Fair agreement
.11-.40	Slight agreement
.0-.10	No agreement

Test and Study	Description and Positive Findings	Population	Inter-examiner Reliability
Forward head[34]	"Yes" if the patient's external auditory meatus was anteriorly deviated (anterior to the lumbar spine)		κ = −.10 (−.20,-.00)
Excessive shoulder protraction[34]	"Yes" if the patient's acromions were anteriorly deviated (anterior to the lumbar spine)		κ = .83 (.51, 1.0)
C7-T2 excessive kyphosis[34]	Recorded as "normal" (no deviation), "excessive kyphosis," or "diminished kyphosis." *Excessive kyphosis* was defined as an increase in the convexity, and *diminished kyphosis* was defined as a flattening of the convexity of the thoracic spine (at each segmental group)	22 patients with mechanical neck pain	κ = .79 (.51, 1.0)
T3-5 excessive kyphosis[34]			κ = .69 (.30, 1.0)
T3-5 decreased kyphosis[34]			κ = .58 (.22, .95)
T6-10 excessive kyphosis[34]			κ = .90 (.74, 1.0)
T6-10 decreased kyphosis[34]			κ = .90 (.73, 1.0)
Kyphosis[35]	With patient standing, examiner inspects posture from the side. Graded as "present" or "absent"		κ = .21
Scoliosis[35]	With patient standing, examiner runs finger along spinous processes. Patient bends over and examiner assesses height of paraspinal musculature. Graded as "present" or "absent"	111 adults age ≥ 60 with chronic low back pain and 20 asymptomatic patients	κ = .33
Functional leg length discrepancy[35]	Compare bilateral iliac crest height with patient standing. Graded as "symmetrical" or "asymmetrical"		κ = .00

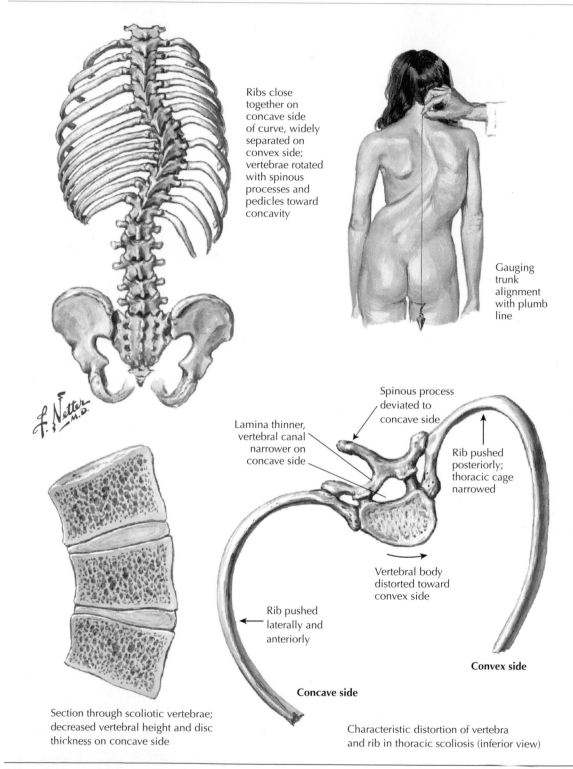

Ribs close together on concave side of curve, widely separated on convex side; vertebrae rotated with spinous processes and pedicles toward concavity

Gauging trunk alignment with plumb line

Spinous process deviated to concave side

Lamina thinner, vertebral canal narrower on concave side

Rib pushed posteriorly; thoracic cage narrowed

Vertebral body distorted toward convex side

Rib pushed laterally and anteriorly

Convex side

Concave side

Section through scoliotic vertebrae; decreased vertebral height and disc thickness on concave side

Characteristic distortion of vertebra and rib in thoracic scoliosis (inferior view)

Figure 4-25

Pathologic anatomy of scoliosis.

Passive Intervertevbral Motion

Reliability of Assessing Limited or Excessive Passive Intervertebral Motion

ICC or κ	Interpretation
.81-1.0	Substantial agreement
.61-.80	Moderate agreement
.41-.60	Fair agreement
.11-.40	Slight agreement
.0-.10	No agreement

Test and Study	Description and Positive Findings	Population	Reliability
Upper lumbar segmental mobility[36]	With patient prone, examiner applies a posteroanterior force to the spinous process and lumbar facets of each lumbar vertebra. Mobility of each segment is judged as "normal" or "restricted"	39 patients with low back pain	(Spinous) Inter-examiner κ = .02 (−.27, .32) (Left facet) Inter-examiner κ = .17 (−.14, .48) (Right facet) Inter-examiner κ = −.01 (−.33, .30)
Lower lumbar segmental mobility[36]			(Spinous) Inter-examiner κ = −.05 (−.36, .27) (Left facet) Inter-examiner κ = −.17 (−.41, .06) (Right facet) Inter-examiner κ = −.12 (−.41, .18)
Identifying the least mobile segment[37]	With patient prone, examiner applies a posteroanterior force to the spinous process of each lumbar vertebra	29 patients with central low back pain	Inter-examiner κ = .71 (.48, .94)
Identifying the most mobile segment[37]			Inter-examiner κ = .29 (−.13, .71)
Posterior to anterior (PA) stiffness[38]	Each level of the lumbar spine was evaluated for segmental dysfunction. With patient prone, examiner assessed PA stiffness and multifidus hypertonicity. With patient side lying, side flexion and ventral flexion were assessed by moving the patient's legs. After performing all four examination procedures, examiners identified the level of maximal dysfunction	60 patients with low back pain	Intra-examiner κ = .54 Intra-examiner (±1 level) κ = .64 Inter-examiner κ = .23 Inter-examiner (±1 level) κ = .52
Segmental side flexion[38]			Intra-examiner κ = .57 Intra-examiner (±1 level) κ = .69 Inter-examiner κ = .22 Inter-examiner (±1 level) κ = .45
Segmental ventral flexion[38]			Intra-examiner κ = .31 Intra-examiner (±1 level) κ = .45 Inter-examiner κ = .22 Inter-examiner (±1 level) κ = .44
Multifidus hypertonicity[38]			Intra-examiner κ = .51 Intra-examiner (±1 level) κ = .60 Inter-examiner κ = .12 Inter-examiner (±1 level) κ = .57
Maximal level of segmental dysfunction[38]			Intra-examiner κ = .60 Intra-examiner (±1 level) κ = .70 Inter-examiner κ = .21 Inter-examiner (±1 level) κ = .57
Segmental mobility[39]	With patient side-lying, examiner palpates adjacent spinous processes while moving the patient's legs to produce passive flexion and extension of the lumbar spine. Segmental mobility was graded on a 5-point scale	20 patients with low back pain	Inter-examiner κ ranged from −.25 to .53 depending on examiners and vertebral level

Reliability of Assessing Limited or Excessive Passive Intervertebral Motion

ICC or κ	Interpretation
.81-1.0	Substantial agreement
.61-.80	Moderate agreement
.41-.60	Fair agreement
.11-.40	Slight agreement
.0-.10	No agreement

Test and Study	Description and Positive Findings	Population	Reliability
Determination of segmental fixations[40]	Passive motion palpation is performed and the segment is considered fixated if a hard end-feel is noted during the assessment	60 asymptomatic volunteers	Intra-examiner κ ranged from **−.09 to .39** Inter-examiner κ ranged from **−.06 to .17**
Passive motion palpation[41]		21 symptomatic and 25 asymptomatic subjects	Inter-examiner κ = ranged from **−.03 to .23** with a mean of .07
Segmental mobility testing[42]	With patient side-lying with hips and knees flexed, examiner assesses mobility while passively moving the patient. Examiner determines whether mobility of the segment is "decreased," "normal," or "increased"	71 patients with low back pain	Inter-examiner κ = **.54**
Hypermobility at any level[31]	With patient prone, examiner applies a posteroanterior force to the spinous process of each lumbar vertebra. Mobility of each segment is judged as "normal," "hypermobile," or "hypomobile"	49 patients with low back pain referred for flexion-extension radiographs	Inter-examiner κ = **.48 (.35, .61)**
Hypomobility at any level[31]			Inter-examiner κ = **.38 (.22, .54)**
Determination of posteroanterior spinal stiffness[43]	Five raters tested lumbar spinal levels for posteroanterior mobility and graded each on an 11-point scale ranging from "markedly reduced stiffness" to "markedly increased stiffness"	40 asymptomatic individuals	Inter-examiner ICC in the first study = **.55 (.32, .79)** Inter-examiner ICC in the second study = **.77 (.57, .89)**
Posteroanterior mobility testing[44]	With the patient prone, examiner evaluates posteroanterior motion mobility. Mobility is scored on a 9-point scale ranging from "severe excess motion" to "no motion," and the presence of pain is recorded	18 patients with low back pain	Inter-examiner ICC = **.25 (.00, .39)**
Segmental mobility testing[45]	With patient prone, examiner applies an anteriorly directed force over the spinous process of the segment to be tested. Examiner grades the mobility as "hypermobile," "normal," or "hypomobile"	63 patients with current low back pain	Inter-examiner κ ranged from **−.20 to .26** depending on level tested
Identification of a misaligned vertebra[41]	Static palpation is used to determine the relationship of one vertebra to the vertebra below	21 symptomatic and 25 asymptomatic subjects	Inter-examiner κ ranged from **−.04 to .03** with a mean of **.00**
Detection of a segmental lesion T11-L5/S1[46]	Two clinicians used visual postural analysis, pain descriptions, leg length discrepancy, neurological examination, motion palpation, static palpation, and any special orthopaedic tests to determine the level of segmental lesion.	19 patients with chronic mechanical low back pain	Intra-examiner κ = **−.08 to .43** Inter-examiner κ = **−.16 to .25**

Passive Intervertebral Motion

Reliability of Assessing Painful Passive Intervertebral Motion

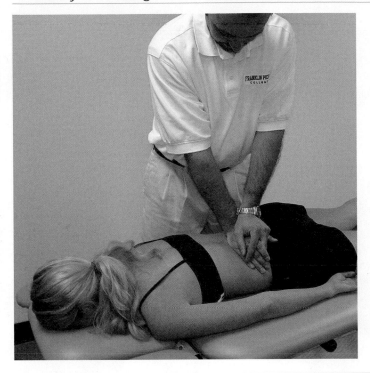

ICC or κ	Interpretation
.81-1.0	Substantial agreement
.61-.80	Moderate agreement
.41-.60	Fair agreement
.11-.40	Slight agreement
.0-.10	No agreement

Figure 4-26

Assessment of posteroanterior segmental mobility.

Test and Study	Description and Positive Findings	Population	Reliability	
			Intra-examiner	**Inter-examiner**
Spring test T10-T7[47]	With patients in the prone position the therapist applies a posteroanterior force to the spinous processes of T7-L5. The pressure of each force is held for 20 seconds. Considered positive if the force produces pain	84 subjects, of whom 53% reported experiencing low back symptoms within the last 12 months	κ = .73 (.39-1.0)	κ = .12 (−.18 -.41)
Spring test L2-T11[47]			κ = .78 (.49-1.0)	κ = .36 (.07- .66)
Spring test L5-L3[47]			κ = .56 (.18-.94)	κ = .41 (.12- .70)
Pain with upper lumbar mobility testing[36]	With patient prone, examiner applies a posteroanterior force to the spinous processes and lumbar facets of each lumbar vertebra. Response at each segment is judged as "painful" or "not painful"	39 patients with low back pain		(Spinous) Inter-examiner κ = .21 (−.10, .53) (Left facet) Inter-examiner κ = .46 (.17, .75) (Right facet) Inter-examiner κ = .38 (.06, .69)
Pain with lower lumbar mobility testing[36]				(Spinous) Inter-examiner κ = .57 (.32, .83) (Left facet) Inter-examiner κ = .73 (.51, .95) (Right facet) Inter-examiner κ = .52 (.25, .79)
Pain provocation[45]	With patient prone, examiner applies an anteriorly directed force over the spinous processes of the segment to be tested. Considered positive if pain is reproduced	63 patients with current low back pain		Inter-examiner κ ranged from **.25 to .55** depending on the segmental level tested
Pain during mobility testing[31]		49 patients with low back pain referred for flexion-extension radiographs		Inter-examiner κ = **.57 (.43, .71)**

Reliability of Assessing Limited and Painful Passive Intervertebral Motion

Motion palpation, seated

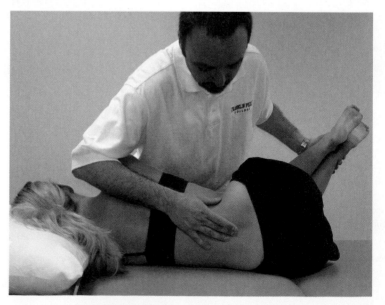

Motion palpation of sidebending, right

Figure 4-27

Segmental mobility examination.

Passive Intervertebral Motion

Diagnostic Utility of Assessing Limited and Painful Passive Intervertebral Motion

+LR	Interpretation	−LR
>10	Large	<.1
5.0-10.0	Moderate	.1-.2
2.0-5.0	Small	.2-.5
1.0-2.0	Rarely important	.5-1.0

Test and Study Quality	Description and Positive Findings	Population	Reference Standard	Sens	Spec	+LR	−LR
Active range of motion (AROM)[48] ◇	Quantity of forward bending AROM. Rated as "hypomobile," "normal," or "hypermobile"	9 patients with low back pain	Flexion and extension lateral radiographs. Segments were considered hypomobile if motion was more than 2 standard deviations from the mean of a normal population	.75 (36, 94)	.60 (27, 86)	1.88 (.57, 6.8)	.42 (.07, 1.90)
Abnormality of segmental motion (AbnROM) [48] ◇	Examiner judged presence of abnormal segmental motion during AROM. Rated as "hypomobile," "normal," or "hypermobile"			.43 (19, 71)	.88 (70, 96)	3.60 (.84, 15.38)	.65 (.28, 1.06)
Passive accessory intervertebral motion (PAIVM)[48] ◇	Examiner applies central posteroanterior pressure. Passive accessory intervertebral motion was rated as "hypomobile," "normal," or "hypermobile"			.75 (36, 94)	.35 (20, 55)	1.16 (.44, 3.03)	.71 (.12, 2.75)
Passive physiological intervertebral motion (PPIVM) [48] ◇	With patient side-lying, examiner palpates amount of PPIVM during forward bending. Rated as "hypomobile," "normal," or "hypermobile"			.42 (19, 71)	.89 (71, 96)	3.86 (.89, 16.31)	.64 (.28, 1.04)
Motion palpation[49] ○	Palpation of a motion segment during either passive or active motion. Examiners evaluated for limited motion (i.e., "fixation"). Patient's pain reaction was noted after motion palpation of each segment	184 twins	Self-reported low back pain	.42	.57	.98	1.02
Pain reaction[49] ○				.54	.77	2.35	.60

Passive Intervertebral Motion

Association of Limited Passive Intervertebral Motion with Low Back Pain

As a part of a larger epidemiological study, Leboeuf-Yde and associates[49] evaluated 184 twins as to the prevalence of restricted intervertebral motion and its relation to low back pain. As can be seen in the figure, motion restrictions were no more prevalent in people with current or recent back pain than in those who had never experienced back pain.

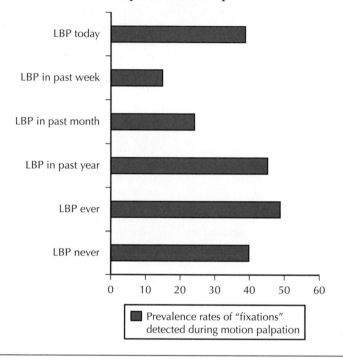

Figure 4-28

Prevalence rates of "fixations" detected during motion palpation. *(From Leboeuf-Yde C, van Dijk J, Franz C, et al. Motion palpation findings and self-reported low back pain in a population-based study sample.* J Manipulative Physiol Ther. *2002;25:80-87.)*

Passive Intervertebral Motion

Diagnostic Utility of Assessing Excessive Passive Intervertebral Motion

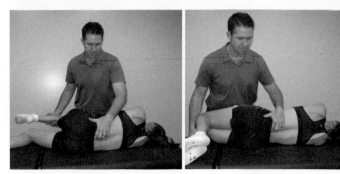

Lumbar flexion

Lumbar extension

+LR	Interpretation	−LR
>10	Large	<.1
5.0-10.0	Moderate	.1-.2
2.0-5.0	Small	.2-.5
1.0-2.0	Rarely important	.5-1.0

Figure 4-29

Assessing lumbar passive physiological intervertebral motion (PPIVM).

Test and Study Quality	Description and Positive Findings	Population	Reference Standard	Sens	Spec	+LR	−LR
Passive accessory intervertebral motion (PAIVM) [50]	Examiner applies central posteroanterior pressure. PAIVM was rated as "hypomobile," "normal," or "hypermobile"			**Rotational Lumbar Segmental Instability**			
				.33 (.12, .65)	.88 (.83, .92)	2.74 (1.01, 7.42)	.76 (.48, 1.21)
				Translational Lumbar Segmental Instability			
Flexion passive physiological intervertebral motion (PPIVM) [50]	With patient side-lying, examiner palpates amount of PPIVM during forward bending. Rated as "hypomobile," "normal," or "hypermobile"			.29 (.14, .50)	.89 (.83, .93)	2.52 (1.15, 5.53)	.81 (.61, 1.06)
			Flexion and extension lateral radiographs. Segments were considered hypermobile if motion was more than 2 standard deviations from the mean of a normal population	**Rotational Lumbar Segmental Instability**			
		Patients with a new episode of recurrent or chronic low back pain		.05 (.01, .36)	.99 (.96, 1.00)	.12 (.21, 80.3)	.96 (.83, 1.11)
				Translational Lumbar Segmental Instability			
				.05 (.01, .22)	.995 (.97, 1.00)	8.73 (.57, 134.7)	.96 (.88, 1.05)
Extension PPIVM [50]	With patient side-lying, examiner palpates amount of PPIVM during backward bending. Rated as "hypomobile," "normal," or "hypermobile"			**Rotational Lumbar Segmental Instability**			
				.22 (.06, .55)	.97 (.94, .99)	8.40 (1.88, 37.55)	.80 (.56, 1.13)
				Translational Lumbar Segmental Instability			
				.16 (.06, .38)	.98 (.94, .99)	7.07 (1.71, 29.2)	.86 (.71, 1.05)

Palpation

ICC or κ	Interpretation
.81-1.0	Substantial agreement
.61-.80	Moderate agreement
.41-.60	Fair agreement
.11-.40	Slight agreement
.0-.10	No agreement

Reliability of Identifying Segmental Levels

Procedure Performed	Description of Procedure	Patient Population	Inter-examiner Reliability
Detection of segmental levels in the lumbar spine[51]	With patient prone, examiner identifies nominated levels of the lumbar spine. Examiner marks the specific level with a pen containing ink that can only be seen under ultraviolet light	20 patients with low back pain	κ = .69
Examiner judgment of marked segmental level[44]	With the patient prone, one spinous process is arbitrarily marked on each patient. Examiners identify the level of the marked segment	18 patients with low back pain	ICC = .69 (.53, .82)

Reliability of Identifying Tenderness to Palpation

Procedure Performed	Description of Procedure	Patient Population	Inter-examiner Reliability
Lumbar paravertebral myofascial pain[35]	Reports of pain with deep thumb pressure (4 kg)		κ = .34
Piriformis myofascial pain[35]			κ = .66
Tensor fascia lata myofascial pain[35]			κ = .75
Fibromyalgia tender points[35]	Reports of pain with enough pressure to blanch thumbnail at: 1. Occiput at suboccipital muscle insertions 2. Low cervical at the anterior aspects of the intertransverse spaces at C5-C7 3. Trapezius, midpoint of upper border 4. Supraspinatus at origin 5. 2nd rib at the 2nd costochondral junction 6. 2 cm distal to the epicondyle 7. Medial fat pad of the knee 8. Greater trochanter 9. Gluteal at upper outer quadrant of buttocks	111 adults age ≥ 60 with chronic low back pain and 20 asymptomatic subjects	κ = .87
Osseous pain of each joint T11/L1 - L5/S1[41]	With the subject prone, examiner applies pressure over the bony structures of each joint	21 symptomatic and 25 asymptomatic subjects	Mean κ for all levels = .48
Intersegmental tenderness[42]	With patient prone, examiner palpates the area between the spinous processes. Increased tenderness is considered positive	71 patients with low back pain	κ = .55

Centralization Phenomena

Reliability of Identifying the Centralization Phenomena

ICC or κ	Interpretation
.81-1.0	Substantial agreement
.61-.80	Moderate agreement
.41-.60	Fair agreement
.11-.40	Slight agreement
.0-.10	No agreement

Test and Study	Description and Positive Findings	Population	Inter-examiner Reliability
Centralization and directional preference[52]	Two examiners with greater than 5 years of training in the McKenzie method evaluated all patients and determined whether centralization occurred during repeated movements. If centralization occurred the clinician recorded the directional preference	39 patients with low back pain	κ if centralization occurred = **.70** κ related to centralization and directional preference = **.90**
Judgments of centralization[53]	Therapists (without formal training in McKenzie methods) and students viewed videotapes of patients undergoing a thorough examination by one therapist. All therapists and students watching the videos were asked to make an assessment regarding the change in symptoms based on movement status	12 patients receiving physical therapy for low back pain	Between physical therapists κ = **.82 (.81, .84)** Between physical therapy students κ = **.76 (.76, .77)**
Status change with flexion in sitting[32]	10 different examiners assessed symptom change (centralization, peripheralization, or no change) with single or repeated movements	123 patients with low back pain < 90 days	κ = **.55 (.28, .81)**
Status change with repeated flexion in sitting [32]			κ = **.46 (.23, .69)**
Status change with extension[32]			κ = **.51 (.29, .72)**
Status change with repeated extension[32]			κ = **.15 (−.06, .36)**
Status change with sustained prone extension[32]			κ = **.28 (.10, .47)**

Diagnostic Utility of the Centralization Phenomena

+LR	Interpretation	−LR
>10	Large	<.1
5.0-10.0	Moderate	.1-.2
2.0-5.0	Small	.2-.5
1.0-2.0	Rarely important	.5-1.0

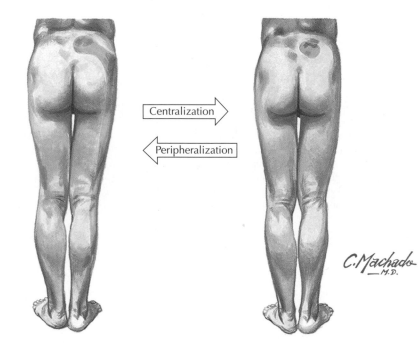

During specific movements, range of motion and movement of pain noted. Movement of pain from peripheral to central location (centralization) predicts outcome and appropriateness of therapy.

Figure 4-30

Centralization of pain.

Test and Study Quality	Description and Positive Findings	Population	Reference Standard	Sens	Spec	+LR	−LR
Centralization[54] ◇	Centralization present if pain in the furthermost region from midline was abolished or reduced with a McKenzie-styled repeated motion examination	69 patients with persistent low back pain with or without referred leg pain	At least 1 painful disc adjacent to a nonpainful disc with discography	.40 (.28, .54)	.94 (.73, .99)	6.9 (1.0, 47.3)	.63 (.49, .82)

Straight-Leg Raise Test

Reliability of the Straight-Leg Raise Test

ICC or κ	Interpretation
.81-1.0	Substantial agreement
.61-.80	Moderate agreement
.41-.60	Fair agreement
.11-.40	Slight agreement
.0-.10	No agreement

Straight-leg raise

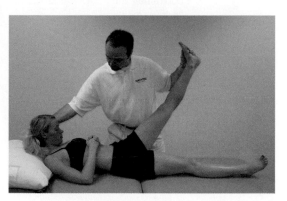

Straight-leg raise with sensitizing
maneuver of cervical flexion

Figure 4-31

Straight-leg raise.

Test and Study	Description and Positive Findings	Population	Inter-examiner Reliability
Passive straight-leg raise (SLR)[23]	With patient supine, examiner passively flexes the hip and extends the knee. Examiner measures angle of SLR and determines if symptoms occurred in a dermatomal fashion	91 patients with low back pain randomly selected	For typical dermatomal pain, κ = **.68** For any pain in the leg, κ = **.36** For SLR < 45°, κ = **.43**
Passive straight-leg raise[55]	With patient supine, examiner maintains the knee in extension while passively flexing the hip. The hip is flexed until examiner feels resistance. A range of motion measurement is recorded.	18 physiotherapy students	ICC Right = **.86**, Left = **.83**
Passive straight-leg raise[56]	Passive elevation of the leg with knee extended. Considered positive if pain in the low back or buttock is experienced	27 patients with low back pain	κ = **.32**

Diagnostic Utility of the Straight-Leg Raise for Detecting Disc Bulge or Herniation

+LR	Interpretation	−LR
>10	Large	<.1
5.0-10.0	Moderate	.1-.2
2.0-5.0	Small	.2-.5
1.0-2.0	Rarely important	.5-1.0

Deville and colleagues[68] compiled the results of 15 studies investigating the accuracy of the straight-leg raise (SLR) for detecting disc herniation. Eleven of the studies included information about both the sensitivity and specificity of the SLR and were used for statistical pooling of estimates. However, numerous variations of the SLR maneuver have been reported and no consistency was noted among the studies selected for the Deville and colleagues'[68] review. The results of each study, as well as, the pooled estimates by Deville and colleagues[68] are listed here.

SLR Study	Description and Positive Findings	Reference Standard	Sens	Spec	+LR	−LR
Albeck et al[57]	With the patient supine, the knee fully extended, and the ankle in neutral dorsiflexion, examiner then passively flexes the hip while maintaining the knee in extension. Positive test defined by reproduction of sciatic pain between 30° and 60°-75°	Herniated lumbar disc observed during surgery. Hernia was defined as extruded, protruded, and bulging disc, or sequestrated in most studies	.82 (.70, .90)	.21 (.07, .46)	1.0	.86
Charnley et al[58]			.85 (.75, .92)	.57 (.30, .81)	1.98	.26
Gurdjian et al[59]			.81 (.78, .83)	.52 (.32, .72)	1.69	.37
Hakelius et al[60]			.96 (.95, .97)	.14 (.11, .18)	1.12	.29
Hirsch et al[61]			.91 (.85, .94)	.32 (.20, .46)	1.34	2.8
Jonsson et al[62]			.87 (.81, .91)	.22 (.07, .48)	1.12	.59
Kerr et al[63]			.98 (.92, 1.00)	.44 (.28, .62)	1.75	.05
Kosteljanetz et al[64]			.89 (.75, .96)	.14 (.01, .58)	1.03	.79
Kosteljanetz et al[65]			.78 (.64, .87)	.48 (.32, .63)	1.5	.49
Knutsson et al[66]			.95 (.91, .98)	.10 (.02, .33)	1.05	.50
Spangfort et al[67]			.97 (.96, .97)	.11 (.08, .15)	1.09	.27
Pooled estimate of the above listed 11 studies as calculated by Deville et al[68]	As above	As above	.91 (.82, .94)	.26 (.16, .38)	1.23	.35
Straight-leg raise [69] ◇	With patient supine, examiner slowly lifts the symptomatic straight leg until maximal hip flexion is reached or the patient asks to stop. The angle between the leg and the table is measured. Positive if reproduction of familiar radicular pain	MRI findings of disc bulges, herniations, and/or extrusions in 75 patients with complaints of acute or recurrent low back and/or leg pain of ≤ 12 weeks' duration	.52 (.42, .58)	.89 (.79, 95)	4.73	.54

Crossed Straight-Leg Raise Test

Diagnostic Utility of the Crossed Straight-Leg Raise for Detecting Disc Bulge or Herniation

+LR	Interpretation	−LR
>10	Large	<.1
5.0-10.0	Moderate	.1-.2
2.0-5.0	Small	.2-.5
1.0-2.0	Rarely important	.5-1.0

Deville and colleagues[68] also compiled the results of eight studies investigating the accuracy of the crossed straight-leg raise (CSLR) for detecting disc herniation. Six of the studies included information about both the sensitivity and specificity of the CSLR and were used for statistical pooling of estimates. The results of each study, as well as the pooled estimates by Deville and colleagues,[68] are listed here.

CSLR Study	Description and Positive Findings	Reference Standard	Sens	Spec	+LR	−LR
Hakelius et al[60]	Performed identically to the SLR except the uninvolved lower extremity is lifted. A positive test is defined as reproducing pain in the involved lower extremity	Herniated lumbar disc observed during surgery. Hernia was defined as extruded, protruded, and bulging disc, or sequestrated in most studies	.28 (.25, .30)	.88 (.84, .90)	2.33	.82
Jonsson et al[62]			.22 (.16, .30)	.93 (.64, 1.0)	3.14	.84
Kerr et al[63]			.43 (.33, .53)	.93 (.80, .99)	6.14	.61
Kosteljanetz et al[64]			.57 (.34, .79)	1.0 (.03, 1.0)	Undefined	.43
Knutsson et al[66]			.25 (.18, .32)	.93 (.73, 1.0)	3.57	.81
Spangfort et al[67]			.23 (.21, .25)	.88 (.84, .91)	1.92	.88
Pooled estimate for the 6 studies listed above as calculated by Deville and colleagues[68]	**As above**	**As above**	.29 (.24, .34)	.88 (.86, .90)	2.42	.81

Slump Test

Reliability of the Slump Test

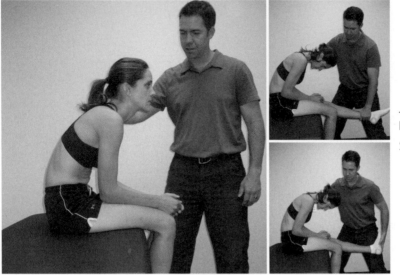

ICC or κ	Interpretation
.81-1.0	Substantial agreement
.61-.80	Moderate agreement
.41-.60	Fair agreement
.11-.40	Slight agreement
.0-.10	No agreement

Figure 4-32

Slump test.

Test and Study	Description and Positive Findings	Population	Intra-examiner Reliability
Knee extension range of motion during the slump test[70]	Subject sitting maximally slumped with 1 thigh flexed 25° to the horizontal plane. Starting with the knee at 90° and maximal ankle dorsiflexion, the knee was slowly extended to maximal discomfort and measured with an electrogoniometer	20 asymptomatic subjects	With cervical flexion: ICC = .95 With cervical extension: ICC = .95

Diagnostic Utility of the Slump Test for Detecting Disc Bulge or Herniation

+LR	Interpretation	−LR
>10	Large	<.1
5.0-10.0	Moderate	.1-.2
2.0-5.0	Small	.2-.5
1.0-2.0	Rarely important	.5-1.0

Test and Study Quality	Description and Positive Findings	Population	Reference Standard	Sens	Spec	+LR	−LR
Slump test[69] ◇	Sitting with the back straight, the patient is encouraged to slump into lumbar and thoracic flexion while looking straight ahead. Then the patient fully flexes the neck and extends 1 knee. Last, the patient dorsiflexes the ipsilateral foot. Positive if reproduction of familiar radicular pain	75 patients with complaints of acute or recurrent low back and/or leg pain of ≤ 12 weeks' duration	MRI findings of disc bulges, herniations, and/or extrusions	.84 (.74, .90)	.83 (.73, .90)	4.94	.19

Diagnostic Utility of the Slump Test for Detecting Disc Bulge/Herniation

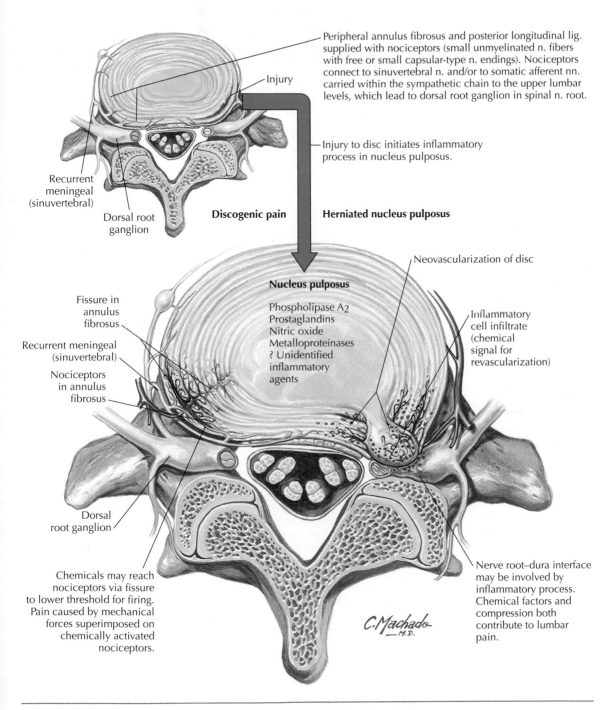

Peripheral annulus fibrosus and posterior longitudinal lig. supplied with nociceptors (small unmyelinated n. fibers with free or small capsular-type n. endings). Nociceptors connect to sinuvertebral n. and/or to somatic afferent nn. carried within the sympathetic chain to the upper lumbar levels, which lead to dorsal root ganglion in spinal n. root.

Injury

Injury to disc initiates inflammatory process in nucleus pulposus.

Recurrent meningeal (sinuvertebral)

Dorsal root ganglion

Discogenic pain

Herniated nucleus pulposus

Neovascularization of disc

Fissure in annulus fibrosus

Nucleus pulposus

Phospholipase A$_2$
Prostaglandins
Nitric oxide
Metalloproteinases
? Unidentified inflammatory agents

Inflammatory cell infiltrate (chemical signal for revascularization)

Recurrent meningeal (sinuvertebral)

Nociceptors in annulus fibrosus

Dorsal root ganglion

Chemicals may reach nociceptors via fissure to lower threshold for firing. Pain caused by mechanical forces superimposed on chemically activated nociceptors.

Nerve root–dura interface may be involved by inflammatory process. Chemical factors and compression both contribute to lumbar pain.

C.Machado
—M.D.

Figure 4-33

Role of inflammation in lumbar pain.

ICC or κ	Interpretation
.81-1.0	Substantial agreement
.61-.80	Moderate agreement
.41-.60	Fair agreement
.11-.40	Slight agreement
.0-.10	No agreement

Test and Study	Description and Positive Findings	Population	Inter-examiner Reliability
Hip extension test[71]	Prone patient extends one hip at a time. Positive if lateral shift, rotation, or hyperextension of the lumbar spine	42 patients with chronic low back pain	κ = .72 (left) κ = .76 (right)
Painful arc in flexion[45]	Patient reports symptoms at a particular point in the movement but the symptoms are not present before or after the movement		κ = .69 (.54, .84)
Painful arc on return from flexion[45]	Patient experiences symptoms when returning from the flexed position		κ = .61 (.44, .78)
Instability catch[45]	Patient experiences a sudden acclimation of deceleration of trunk movements outside the primary plane of movement	63 patients with current low back pain	κ = .25 (−.10, .60)
Gower's sign[45]	Patient pushes up from thighs with the hands when returning to upright from a flexed position		κ = .00 (−1.09, 1.09)
Reversal of lumbo-pelvic rhythm[45]	On attempting to return from the flexed position, the patient bends the knees and shifts the pelvis anteriorly		κ = .16 (−.15, .46)
Aberrant movement pattern[45]			κ = .60 (.47, .73)
Aberrant movement pattern[32]	If the patient demonstrates any of the above five possible movement patterns they are considered to be positive for an aberrant movement pattern.	123 patients with low back pain < 90 days	κ = .18 (−.07, .43)
Posterior shear test[45]	With patient standing with arms crossed over the abdomen, examiner places one hand over the patient's crossed arms while the other stabilizes the pelvis. Examiner uses the index finger to palpate the L5-S1 interspace. Examiner then applies a posterior force through the patient's crossed arms. This procedure is performed at each level. A positive test is indicated by provocation of symptoms.	63 patients with current low back pain	κ = .35 (.20, .51)
Prone instability test[45]	The patient is prone with the edge of the torso on the plinth while the legs are over the edge and feet are resting on the floor. Examiner performs a posteroanterior pressure maneuver and notes the provocation of any symptoms. The patient then lifts the feet off the floor, and examiner again performs the posteroanterior pressure maneuver. Provocation of symptoms is reported. Test is considered positive if the patient experiences symptoms while feet are on the floor, but symptoms disappear when the feet are lifted off the floor.		κ = .87 (.80, .94)
Prone instability test[32]		123 patients with low back pain < 90 days	κ = .28 (.10, .47)
Prone instability test[36]		39 patients with low back pain	κ = .46 (.15, .77)
Trendelenburg[72]	While standing, the patient flexes one hip to 30° and lifts the ipsilateral pelvis above the transiliac line. The test is positive if the patient cannot hold the position for 30 seconds or needs more than one finger for balance.	36 patients with chronic low back pain	κ = .83 (left) κ = .75 (right)
Active straight-leg raise (ASLR)[72]	The patient is supine with straight legs and feet 20 cm apart. The patient is instructed to "try to raise your legs, one after the other above the couch without bending the knee." The patient is asked to score the maneuver on a 6-point scale ranging from "not difficult at all" to "unable to do."		κ = .70 (left) κ = .71 (right)
Active straight-leg raise (ASLR)[73]		50 females with lumbo-pelvic pain	Test-retest ICC = .83

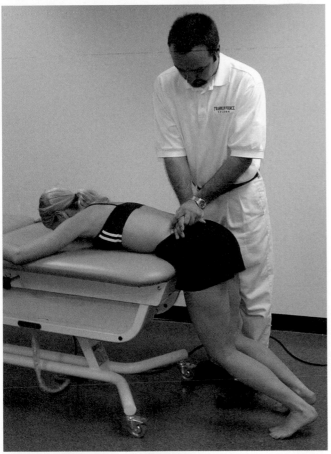

Figure 4-34
Prone instability test.

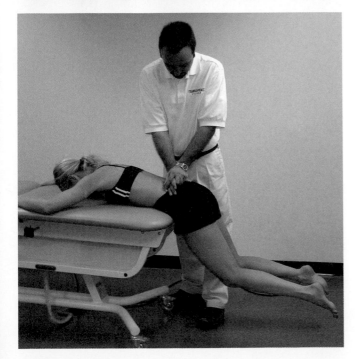

Diagnostic Utility of Tests for Lumbar Spinal Stenosis

+LR	Interpretation	−LR
>10	Large	<.1
5.0-10.0	Moderate	.1-.2
2.0-5.0	Small	.2-.5
1.0-2.0	Rarely important	.5-1.0

Test and Study Quality	Description and Positive Findings	Population	Reference Standard	Sens	Spec	+LR	−LR
Abnormal Rhomberg test[25] ◇	Patient stands with feet together and eyes closed for 10 seconds. Considered abnormal if compensatory movements were required to keep feet planted.	93 patients with back pain with or without radiation to the lower extremities	Diagnosis of spinal stenosis by retrospective chart review and confirmed by MRI or CT	.39 (.24, .54)	.91 (.81, 1.0)	4.3	.67
Thigh pain with 30 seconds of extension[25] ◇	Patient performs hip extension for 30 seconds. Positive if patient has pain in the thigh following or during extension			.51 (.36, .66)	.69 (.53, .85)	1.6	.71
Two-stage treadmill test[15] ◯	Subjects ambulate on a level and inclined (15°) treadmill for 10 minutes. The patient rests for 10 minutes while sitting upright in a chair after each treadmill test	45 subjects with low back and lower extremity pain	Diagnosis of spinal stenosis by MRI or CT scanning	Time to onset of symptoms			
				.68 (.50, .86)	.83 (.66, 1.0)	4.07 (1.40, 11.8)	.39
				Longer total walking time during the inclined test			
				.50 (.38, .63)	.92 (.78, 1.0)	6.46 (3.1, 13.5)	.54
				Prolonged recovery after level walking			
				.82 (.66 - .98)	.68 (.48, .90)	2.59 (1.3, 5.2)	.26

Degenerative Disc Disease

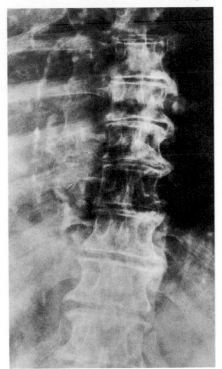

Figure 4-35

Degenerative disc disease and lumbar spinal stenosis.

Radiograph of thoracic spine shows narrowing of intervertebral spaces and spur formation.

Degeneration of lumbar intervertebral discs and hypertrophic changes at vertebral margins with spur formation. Osteophytic encroachment on intervertebral foramina compresses spinal nerves.

Lumbar Disc Herniation

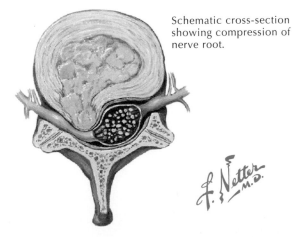

Schematic cross-section showing compression of nerve root.

+LR	Interpretation	−LR
>10	Large	<.1
5.0-10.0	Moderate	.1-.2
2.0-5.0	Small	.2-.5
1.0-2.0	Rarely important	.5-1.0

Test and Study Quality	Description and Positive Findings	Population	Reference Standard	Sens	Spec	+LR	−LR
Age < 37 years old[31]	History collected prior to physical examination			.57 (.39, .74)	.81 (.60, .92)	3.0 (1.2, 7.7)	.53 (.33, .85)
Lumbar flexion > 53°[31]	Range of motion demonstrated by single inclinometer			.68 (.49, .82)	.86 (.65, .94)	4.8 (1.6, 14.0)	.38 (.21, .66)
Total extension greater than 26°[31]	Range of motion demonstrated by single inclinometer			.50 (.33, .67)	.76 (.55, .89)	2.1 (.90, 4.9)	.66 (.42, 1.0)
Lack of hypomobility during intervertebral testing[31]	With patient prone, examiner applies a posteroanterior force to the spinous process of each lumbar vertebra. Mobility of each segment was judged as "normal," "hypermobile," or "hypomobile"	49 patients with low back pain referred for flexion-extension radiographs	Radiological findings revealed either 2 segments with rotational/translational instability or one segment with both rotational and translational instability.	.43 (.27, .61)	.95 (.77, .99)	9.0 (1.3, 63.9)	.60 (.43, .84)
Any hypermobility during intervertebral motion testing[31]				.46 (.30, .64)	.81 (.60, .92)	2.4 (.93, 6.4)	.66 (.44, .99)
Lumbar flexion greater than 53° + Lack of hypomobility during intervertebral testing[31]	Combination of both factors above			.29 (.13, .46)	.98 (.91, 1.0)	12.8 (.79, 211.6)	.72 (.55, .94)

Diagnostic Utility of Tests for Radiographic Lumbar Instability

Fritz and colleagues[74] investigated the accuracy of the clinical examination in 49 patients with radiographically determined lumbar instability. Results revealed that two predictor variables, including lack of hypomobility of the lumbar spine and lumbar flexion greater than 53°, demonstrated a +LR of 12.8 (.79, 211.6). The nomogram below represents the change in pretest probability (57% in this study) to a post-test probability of 94.3%.

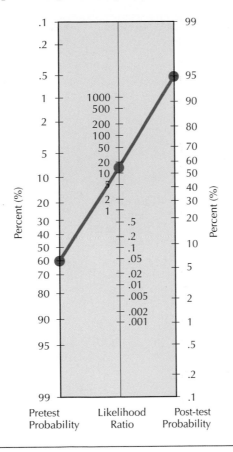

Figure 4-36

Nomogram. Nomogram representing the post-test probability of lumbar instability given the presence of hypomobility in the lumbar spine and lumbar flexion greater than 53 degrees. *(Adapted with permission from Fagan TJ. Nomogram for Baye's theorem. N Engl J Med. 1975;293-257. Copyright 2005, Massachusetts Medical Society. All rights reserved.)*

+LR	Interpretation	−LR
>10	Large	<.1
5.0-10.0	Moderate	.1-.2
2.0-5.0	Small	.2-.5
1.0-2.0	Rarely important	.5-1.0

Test and Study Quality	Description and Positive Findings	Population	Reference Standard	Sens	Spec	+LR	−LR
Measurements of chest expansion[27]	<7 cm (procedure not reported)	449 randomly selected patients with low back pain	The New York criteria and radiographic confirmation of ankylosing spondylitis	.63	.53	1.34	.70
	<2.5 cm (procedure not reported)			.91	.99	91	.09
Schober test < 4 cm[27]	With patient standing, examiner marks a point 5 cm below and 10 cm above S2. This distance is then measured in the upright position and then in full flexion. The difference between the two measurements is calculated and recorded to the closest centimeter			.30	.86	2.14	.81
Decreased lumbar lordosis[27]	Visual observation individually judged by each examiner			.36	.80	1.8	.80
Direct tenderness over sacroiliac joint[27]	Direct pressure over the joint with the patient in an upright position. Positive if patient reports pain			.27	.68	.84	1.07

Classification Methods

Reliability of Low Back Pain Classification Systems

ICC or κ	Interpretation
.81-1.0	Substantial agreement
.61-.80	Moderate agreement
.41-.60	Fair agreement
.11-.40	Slight agreement
.0-.10	No agreement

Test and Study	Description and Positive Findings	Population	Inter-examiner Reliability
McKenzie's classification for low back pain[75]	Therapists (of which only 32% had ever taken any form of McKenzie training) completed a McKenzie evaluation form and classified the patient as exhibiting a postural, dysfunction or derangement syndrome. Therapists also determined if the patient presented with a lateral shift	363 patients referred to physical therapists for the treatment of low back pain	κ for classification = **26** κ for lateral shift = **.26**
McKenzie's classification for low back pain[52]	Two examiners with greater than 5 years of training in the McKenzie method evaluated all patients. Therapists completed a McKenzie evaluation form and classified the patient as exhibiting a postural, dysfunction, or derangement syndrome. Therapists also determined if the patient presented with a lateral shift	39 patients with low back pain	κ for classification = **.70** κ for lateral shift = **.20**
McKenzie's evaluation[76]	Examination consisted of history-taking, evaluation of spinal range of motion, and specified test movements	46 consecutive patients presenting with low back pain	Classification of syndrome κ = **.70** Derangement subsyndrome κ = **.96** Presence of lateral shift κ = **.52** Deformity of sagittal plane κ = **1.0**
Movement impairment–based classification system for lumbar spine syndromes[77]	Examiners used a standardized history and physical examination to assess patients and classify them into one of five lumbar spine categories	24 patients with chronic low back pain	κ for classification = **.61**
Treatment-based classification[32]	Thirty examiners used a standardized history and physical examination to assess patients and classify them into one of three treatment-based categories	123 patients with low back pain < 90 days	κ for classification = **.61 (.56, .64)**
Treatment-based classification[74]	Examiners used a standardized history and physical examination to assess patients and classify them into one of four treatment-based categories	120 patients with low back pain	κ for classification = **.56**
Treatment-based classification[78]	Examiners used a standardized history and physical examination to assess patients and classify them into one of four treatment-based categories after a 1-day training session	45 patients with low back pain	κ for classification = **.45**

Classification Methods

Treatment-Based Classification Method[79]

Subgroup Criteria	Treatment Approach
Specific Exercise Subgroup	
Extension • Symptoms distal to the buttock • Symptoms centralize with lumbar extension • Symptoms peripheralize with lumbar flexion • Directional preference for extension	• End-range extension exercises • Mobilization to promote extension • Avoidance of flexion activities
Flexion • Older age (>50 years) • Directional preference for flexion • Imaging evidence of lumbar spine stenosis	• End-range flexion exercises • Mobilization or manipulation of the spine and/or lower extremities • Exercise to address impairments of strength or flexibility • Body weight-supported ambulation
Stabilization Subgroup	
• Age (<40 years) • Average SLR (>91°) • Aberrant movement present • Positive prone instability test	• Exercises to strengthen large spinal muscles (erector spinae, oblique abdominals) • Exercises to promote contraction of deep spinal muscles (multifidus, transversus abdominis)
Manipulation Subgroup	
• No symptoms distal to knee • Duration of symptoms < 16 days • Lumbar hypomobility • FABQW < 19 • Hip internal rotation ROM > 35°	• Manipulation techniques for the lumbopelvic region • Active lumbar range of motion exercises
Traction Subgroup	
• Symptoms extend distal to the buttock(s) • Signs of nerve root compression are present • Peripheralization occurs with extension movement or positive contralateral SLR test is present	• Prone mechanical traction • Extension specific exercise activities

Rather than attempt to classify low back pain based on pathoanatomy, the Treatment-Based Classification (TBC) system identifies subgroups of patients thought to respond to specific conservative treatment interventions. Although its initial proposal was based on experience and clinical reasoning,[80] researchers have since systematically identified many of the historical and clinical examination factors associated with each subgroup using clinical prediction rule research methodology.[1,2,81]

Interventions

Diagnostic Utility of Single Factors for Identifying Patients Likely to Benefit from Spinal Manipulation

+LR	Interpretation	−LR
>10	Large	<.1
5.0-10.0	Moderate	.1-.2
2.0-5.0	Small	.2-.5
1.0-2.0	Rarely important	.5-1.0

Test and Study Quality	Description and Criteria	Population	Reference Standard	Sens	Spec	+LR	−LR
Symptoms < 16 days[1] ◇				.56 (.39, .72)	.87 (.73, .94)	4.39 (1.83, 10.51)	
FABQ work subscale score < 19[1] ◇	Self-report			.84 (.68, .93)	.49 (.34, .64)	1.65 (1.17, 2.31)	
No symptoms distal to the knee[1] ◇		71 patients with low back pain	≥ 50% reduction in back pain related disability within 1 week as measured by the Oswestry questionnaire	.88 (.72, .95)	.36 (.23, .52)	1.36 (1.04, 1.79)	Not reported
At least one hip with > 35° internal rotation ROM[1] ◇	With patient prone, measured with standard goniometer			.50 (.34, .66)	.85 (.70, .93)	3.25 (1.44, 7.33)	
Hypomobility in the lumbar spine[1] ◇	With patient prone, examiner applies a posteroanterior force to the spinous process of each lumbar vertebra. Mobility of each segment was judged as "normal," "hypermobile," or "hypomobile"			.97 (.84, .99)	.23 (.13, .38)	1.26 (1.05, 1.51)	

Interventions

Diagnostic Utility of Combinations of Factors for Identifying Patients Likely to Benefit from Spinal Manipulation

+LR	Interpretation	−LR
>10	Large	<.1
5.0-10.0	Moderate	.1-.2
2.0-5.0	Small	.2-.5
1.0-2.0	Rarely important	.5-1.0

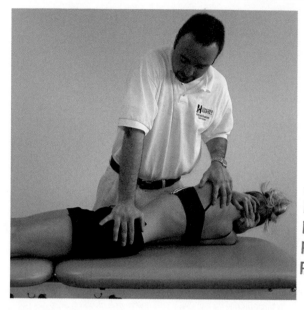

Figure 4-37

Spinal manipulation. Spinal manipulation technique used by Flynn and colleagues.[1] The patient is passively sidebent toward the side to be manipulated (away from the therapist). The therapist then rotates the patient away from the side to be manipulated (toward the therapist) and delivers a quick thrust through the anterior superior iliac spine in a posteroinferior direction.

Test and Study Quality	Description and Criteria	Population	Reference Standard	Sens	Spec	+LR	−LR
Symptoms < 16 days + No symptoms distal to the knee + Hypomobility in the lumbar spine + FABQ work subscale score < 19 + At least one hip with > 35° internal rotation ROM[1] ◇	All 5 tests positive	71 patients with low back pain	≥50% reduction in back pain related disability within 1 week as measured by the Oswestry questionnaire	.19 (.09, .35)	1.00 (.91, 1.00)	Undefined	Not reported
	≥4 tests positive			.63 (.45-.77)	.97 (.87-1.0)	24.38 (4.63-139.41)	
	≥3 tests positive			.94 (.80, .98)	.64 (.48, .77)	2.61 (1.78, 4.15)	
	≥2 tests positive			1.00 (.89, 1.0)	.15 (.07, .30)	1.18 (1.09, 1.42)	
	≥1 test positive			1.00 (.89, 1.0)	.03 (.005, .13)	1.03 (1.01, 1.15)	
Symptoms < 16 days + No symptoms distal to the knee[81] ◇	Must meet both criteria	141 patients with low back pain		.56 (.43, .67)	.92 (.84, .96)	7.2 (3.2, 16.1)	

Interventions

Diagnostic Utility of Single and Combinations of Factors for Identifying Patients Likely to Benefit from Lumbar Stabilization Exercises

+LR	Interpretation	−LR
>10	Large	<.1
5.0-10.0	Moderate	.1-.2
2.0-5.0	Small	.2-.5
1.0-2.0	Rarely important	.5-1.0

Test and Study Quality	Description and Positive Findings	Population	Reference Standard	Sens	Spec	+LR	−LR
Age < 40 years[2]	Self-report			.61 (.39, .80)	.83 (.68, .92)	3.7 (1.6, 8.3)	.47 (.26, .85)
Average straight-leg raise >91°[2]	Measured with an inclinometer			.28 (.13, .51)	.92 (.78, .97)	3.3 (.90, 12.4)	.79 (.58, 1.1)
Aberrant movement present[2]	Presence of any of the following during flexion ROM: • Instability catch • Painful arc of motion • "Thigh climbing" (Gower's sign) • Reversal of lumbopelvic rhythm	54 patients with low back pain with or without leg pain	≥50% reduction in back pain related disability after 8 weeks of lumbar stabilization exercises as measured by the Oswestry questionnaire	.78 (.55, .91)	.50 (.35, .66)	1.6 (1.0, 2.3)	.44 (.18, 1.1)
Positive prone instability test[2]	See description under Tests for Lumbar Segmental Instability			.72 (.49, .88)	.58 (.42, .73)	1.7 (1.1, 2.8)	.48 (.22, 1.1)
Combination of any 4 factors above[2]	≥3 tests positive			.56 (.34, .75)	.86 (.71, .94)	4.0 (1.6, 10.0)	.52 (.30, .88)
	≥2 tests positive			.83 (.61, .94)	.56 (.40, .71)	1.9 (1.2, 2.9)	.30 (.10, .88)
	≥1 test positive			.94 (.74, .99)	.28 (.16, .44)	1.3 (1.0, 1.6)	.20 (.03, 1.4)

Outcome Measure	Scoring and Interpretation	Test-Retest Reliability	MCID
Oswestry Disability Index (ODI)	Users are asked to rate the difficulty of performing 10 functional tasks on a scale of 0 to 5 with different descriptors for each task. A total score out of 100 is calculated by summing each score and doubling the total. The answers provide a score between 0 and 100, with higher scores representing more disability	ICC = .91[82]	11[83]
Modified Oswestry Disability Index (modified ODI)	As above, except the modified ODI replaces the sex life question with an employment/homemaking question	ICC = .90[84]	6[84]
Roland-Morris Disability Questionnaire (R-M)	Users are asked to answer 23 or 24 (depending on the version) questions about their back pain and related disability. The RMDQ is scored by adding the number of items checked by the patient, with higher numbers indicating more disability	ICC = .91[85]	5[83]
Fear-Avoidance Beliefs Questionnaire (FABQ)	Users are asked to rate their level of agreement with statements concerning beliefs about the relationship between physical activity, work, and their back pain. Level of agreement is answered on a Likert-type scale ranging from 0 (completely disagree) to 7 (completely agree). The FABQ is made of two parts: a seven-item work subscale (FABQW) and a four-item physical activity subscale (FABQPA). Each scale is scored separately, with higher scores representing greater fear-avoidance	FABQW: ICC = .82 FABQPA: ICC = .66[86]	Not Available
Numeric Pain Rating Scale (NPRS)	Users rate their level of pain on an 11-point scale ranging from 0 to 10, with high scores representing more pain. Often asked as "current pain" and "least," "worst," and "average" pain in the past 24 hours	ICC = .72[87]	2[88,89]

MCID, Minimum clinically important difference.

Quality Assessment of Diagnostic Studies Using QUADAS

	Russel 1981[91]	Blower 1984[92]	Gran 1985	Kerr 1988	Katz 1995	Phillips 1996[93]	Fritz 1997	Lauder 2000	Leboeuf-Yde 2002	Abbott 2003	Laslett 2005	Abbott 2005	Fritz 2005	Hicks 2005	Majlesi 2008
1. Was the spectrum of patients representative of the patients who will receive the test in practice?	U	Y	Y	U	Y	Y	Y	Y	N	Y	Y	Y	Y	Y	Y
2. Were selection criteria clearly described?	N	N	Y	N	Y	N	N	N	Y	Y	Y	Y	Y	Y	Y
3. Is the reference standard likely to correctly classify the target condition?	Y	Y	Y	U	N	U	Y	Y	U	U	Y	Y	Y	Y	Y
4. Is the time period between reference standard and index test short enough to be reasonably sure that the target condition did not change between the two tests?	U	U	U	U	U	N	U	U	Y	U	Y	U	Y	N	U
5. Did the whole sample or a random selection of the sample, receive verification using a reference standard of diagnosis?	Y	U	Y	N	Y	Y	Y	Y	Y	Y	Y	Y	Y	Y	Y
6. Did patients receive the same reference standard regardless of the index test result?	U	U	Y	N	Y	Y	Y	Y	Y	Y	Y	Y	Y	Y	Y
7. Was the reference standard independent of the index test (i.e., the index test did not form part of the reference standard)?	Y	Y	Y	Y	Y	Y	Y	Y	Y	Y	Y	Y	Y	Y	Y
8. Was the execution of the index test described in sufficient detail to permit replication of the test?	Y	N	Y	N	Y	U	U	Y	N	Y	Y	Y	Y	Y	U
9. Was the execution of the reference standard described in sufficient detail to permit its replication?	N	U	Y	N	Y	N	U	Y	Y	Y	Y	Y	Y	Y	U
10. Were the index test results interpreted without knowledge of the results of the reference test?	U	N	Y	U	Y	N	U	Y	U	Y	Y	Y	Y	Y	Y
11. Were the reference standard results interpreted without knowledge of the results of the index test?	U	U	Y	U	Y	Y	Y	U	U	Y	Y	Y	Y	Y	Y

Quality Assessment of Diagnostic Studies Using QUADAS

	Russel 1981[91]	Blower 1984[92]	Gran 1985	Kerr 1988	Katz 1995	Phillips 1996[93]	Fritz 1997	Lauder 2000	Leboeuf-Yde 2002	Abbott 2003	Laslett 2005	Abbott 2005	Fritz 2005	Hicks 2005	Majlesi 2008
12. Were the same clinical data available when test results were interpreted as would be available when the test is used in practice?	U	Y	Y	U	Y	U	U	Y	U	Y	Y	Y	Y	Y	Y
13. Were uninterpretable/ intermediate test results reported?	N	U	Y	U	Y	Y	Y	Y	Y	Y	Y	Y	Y	Y	U
14. Were withdrawals from the study explained?	U	Y	Y	Y	Y	Y	Y	Y	Y	Y	Y	Y	Y	Y	Y
Quality summary rating:	■	■	◇	■	◇	■	○	◇	○	◇	◇	◇	◇	◇	◇

Y = yes, N = no, U = unclear. ◇ Good quality (Y - N = 10 to 14)   ○ Fair quality (Y - N = 5 to 9)   ■ Poor quality (Y - N ≤ 4)

REFERENCES

1. Flynn T, Fritz J, Whitman J, et al. A clinical prediction rule for classifying patients with low back pain who demonstrate short-term improvement with spinal manipulation. *Spine.* 2002;27:2835-2843.

2. Hicks GE, Fritz JM, Delitto A, McGill SM. Preliminary development of a clinical prediction rule for determining which patients with low back pain will respond to a stabilization exercise program. *Arch Phys Med Rehabil.* 2005;86:1753-1762.

3. Vleeming A, Pool-Goudzwaard AL, Stoeckart R, et al. The posterior layer of the thoracolumbar fascia. Its function in load transfer from spine to legs. *Spine.* 1995;20:753-758.

4. Bogduk N. The applied anatomy of the lumbar fascia. *Spine.* 1984;9:164-170.

5. Bergmark A. Stability of the lumbar spine. A study in mechanical engineering. *Acta Orthop Scand Suppl.* 1989;230:1-54.

6. Bogduk N. *Clinical Anatomy of the Lumbar Spine and Sacrum.* London: Churchill Livingstone; 1997.

7. Evans C, Oldreive W. A study to investigate whether golfers with a history of low back pain show a reduced endurance of transversus abdominis. *J Manual Manipulative Ther.* 2000;8:162-174.

8. Kay AG. An extensive literature review of the lumbar multifidus: biomechanics. *J Manual Manipulative Therapy.* 2001;9:17-39.

9. Norris CM. Spinal stabilisation; 1. Active lumbar stabilisation—concepts. *Physiotherapy.* 1995;81:61-78.

10. Bogduk N. Neck pain. *Aust Fam Physician.* 1984;13:26-30.

11. Schwarzer AC, Aprill CN, Derby R, et al. The relative contributions of the disc and zygapophyseal joint in chronic low back pain. *Spine.* 1994;19:801-806.

12. Schwarzer AC, Aprill CN, Derby R, et al. Clinical features of patients with pain stemming from the lumbar zygapophysial joints. Is the lumbar facet syndrome a clinical entity? *Spine.* 1994;19:1132-1137.

13. McKenzie RA. Mechanical diagnosis and therapy for disorders of the low back. In: Twomay LT, Taylor JR, eds. 3rd ed. *Physical Therapy of the Low Back (5).* Philadelphia: Churchill Livingstone; 2000.141-165.

14. Morris EW, Di Paola M, Vallance R, Waddell G. Diagnosis and decision making in lumbar disc prolapse and nerve entrapment. *Spine.* 1986;11:436-439.

15. Fritz JM, Erhard RE, Delitto A, et al. Preliminary results of the use of a two-stage treadmill test as a clinical diagnostic tool in the differential diagnosis of lumbar spinal stenosis. *J Spinal Disord.* 1997;10:410-416.

16. Fritz JM, Erhard RE, Hagen BF. Segmental instability of the lumbar spine. *Phys Ther.* 1998;78:889-896.

17. O'Sullivan PB. Lumbar segmental 'instability': clinical presentation and specific stabilizing exercise management. *Man Ther.* 2000;5:2-12.

18. Schwarzer AC, Wang SC, Bogduk N, et al. Prevalence and clinical features of lumbar zygapophysial joint pain: a study in an Australian population with chronic low back pain. *Ann Rheum Dis.* 1995;54:100-106.

19. Dreyfuss P, Tibiletti C, Dreyer SJ. Thoracic zygapophyseal joint pain patterns. A study in normal volunteers. *Spine.* 1994;19:807-811.

20. Fukui S, Ohseto K, Shiotani M. Patterns of pain induced by distending the thoracic zygapophyseal joints. *Reg Anesth.* 1997;22:332-336.

21. McCombe PF, Fairbank JC, Cockersole BC, Pynsent PB. 1989 Volvo Award in clinical sciences. Reproducibility of physical signs in low-back pain. *Spine.* 1989;14:908-918.

22. Roach KE, Brown MD, Dunigan KM, et al. Test-retest reliability of patient reports of low back pain. *J Orthop Sports Phys Ther.* 1997;26:253-259.

23. Vroomen PC, de Krom MC, Knottnerus JA. Consistency of history taking and physical examination in patients with suspected lumbar nerve root involvement. *Spine.* 2000;25:91-97.

24. Van Dillen LR, Sahrmann SA, Norton BJ, et al. Reliability of physical examination items used for classification of patients with low back pain. *Phys Ther.* 1998;78:979-988.

25. Katz JN, Dalgas M, Stucki G, et al. Degenerative lumbar spinal stenosis. Diagnostic value of the history and physical examination. *Arthritis Rheum.* 1995;38:1236-1241.

26. Lauder TD, Dillingham TR, Andary M, et al. Effect of history and exam in predicting electrodiagnostic outcome among patients with suspected lumbosacral radiculopathy. *Am J Phys Med Rehabil.* 2000;79:60-68; quiz 75-76.

27. Gran JT. An epidemiological survey of the signs and symptoms of ankylosing spondylitis. *Clin Rheumatol.* 1985;4:161-169.

28. Lindell O, Eriksson L, Strender LE. The reliability of a 10-test package for patients with prolonged back and neck pain: could an examiner without formal medical education be used without loss of quality? A methodological study. *BMC Musculoskelet Disord.* 2007;8:31.

29. Breum J, Wiberg J, Bolton JE. Reliability and concurrent validity of the BROM II for measuring lumbar mobility. *J Manipulative Physiol Ther.* 1995;18:497-502.

30. Evans K, Refshauge KM, Adams R. Measurement of active rotation in standing: reliability of a simple test protocol. *Percept Mot Skills.* 2006;103:619-628.

31. Fritz JM, Piva SR, Childs JD. Accuracy of the clinical examination to predict radiographic instability of the lumbar spine. *Eur Spine J.* 2005;14:743-750.

32. Fritz JM, Brennan GP, Clifford SN, et al. An examination of the reliability of a classification algorithm for

subgrouping patients with low back pain. *Spine*. 2006;31:77-82.

33. Haswell K, Williams M, Hing W. Interexaminer reliability of symptom-provoking active sidebend, rotation and combined movement assessments of patients with low back pain. *J Manual Manipulative Ther*. 2004;12:11-20.

34. Cleland JA, Childs JD, Fritz JM, Whitman JM. Interrater reliability of the history and physical examination in patients with mechanical neck pain. *Arch Phys Med Rehabil*. 2006;87:1388-1395.

35. Weiner DK, Sakamoto S, Perera S, Breuer P. Chronic low back pain in older adults: prevalence, reliability, and validity of physical examination findings. *J Am Geriatr Soc*. 2006;54:11-20.

36. Schneider M, Erhard R, Brach J, et al. Spinal palpation for lumbar segmental mobility and pain provocation: an interexaminer reliability study. *J Manipulative Physiol Ther*. 2008;31:465-473.

37. Landel R, Kulig K, Fredericson M, et al. Intertester reliability and validity of motion assessments during lumbar spine accessory motion testing. *Phys Ther*. 2008;88:43-49.

38. Qvistgaard E, Rasmussen J, Laetgaard J, et al. Intraobserver and inter-observer agreement of the manual examination of the lumbar spine in chronic low-back pain. *Eur Spine J*. 2007;16:277-282.

39. Johansson F. Interexaminer reliability of lumbar segmental mobility tests. *Man Ther*. 2006;11:331-336.

40. Mootz RD, Keating JCJ, Kontz HP, et al. Intra- and interobserver reliability of passive motion palpation of the lumbar spine. *J Manipulative Physiol Ther*. 1989;12:440-445.

41. Keating JCJ, Bergmann TF, Jacobs GE, et al. Interexaminer reliability of eight evaluative dimensions of lumbar segmental abnormality. *J Manipulative Physiol Ther*. 1990;13:463-470.

42. Strender LE, Sjoblom A, Sundell K, et al. Interexaminer reliability in physical examination of patients with low back pain. *Spine*. 1997;22:814-820.

43. Maher CG, Latimer J, Adams R. An investigation of the reliability and validity of posteroanterior spinal stiffness judgments made using a reference-based protocol. *Phys Ther*. 1998;78:829-837.

44. Binkley J, Stratford PW, Gill C. Interrater reliability of lumbar accessory motion mobility testing. *Phys Ther*. 1995;75:786-795.

45. Hicks GE, Fritz JM, Delitto A, Mishock J. The reliability of clinical examination measures used for patients with suspected lumbar segmental instability. *Arch Phys Med Rehabil*. 2003;84:1858-1864.

46. French SD, Green S, Forbes A. Reliability of chiropractic methods commonly used to detect manipulable lesions in patients with chronic low-back pain. *J Manipulative Physiol Ther*. 2000;23:231-238.

47. Horneij E, Hemborg B, Johnsson B, Ekdahl C. Clinical tests on impairment level related to low back pain: a study of test reliability. *J Rehabil Med*. 2002;34:176-182.

48. Abbot J, Mercer S. Lumbar segmental hypomobility: criterion-related validity of clinical examination items (a pilot study). *N Z J Physiother*. 2003;31:3-9.

49. Leboeuf-Yde C, van Dijk J, Franz C, et al. Motion palpation findings and self-reported low back pain in a population-based study sample. *J Manipulative Physiol Ther*. 2002;25:80-87.

50. Abbott JH, McCane B, Herbison P, et al. Lumbar segmental instability: a criterion-related validity study of manual therapy assessment. *BMC Musculoskelet Disord*. 2005;6:56.

51. Downey BJ, Taylor NF, Niere KR. Manipulative physiotherapists can reliably palpate nominated lumbar spinal levels. *Man Ther*. 1999;4:151-156.

52. Kilpikoski S, Airaksinen O, Kankaanpaa M, et al. Interexaminer reliability of low back pain assessment using the McKenzie method. *Spine*. 2002;27:E207-E214.

53. Fritz JM, Delitto A, Vignovic M, Busse RG. Interrater reliability of judgments of the centralization phenomenon and status change during movement testing in patients with low back pain. *Arch Phys Med Rehabil*. 2000;81:57-61.

54. Laslett M, Oberg B, Aprill CN, McDonald B. Centralization as a predictor of provocation discography results in chronic low back pain, and the influence of disability and distress on diagnostic power. *Spine J*. 2005;5:370-380.

55. Rose MJ. The statistical analysis of the intra-observer repeatability of four clinical measurement techniques. *Physiotherapy*. 1991;77:89-91.

56. Viikari-Juntura E, Takala EP, Riihimaki H, et al. Standardized physical examination protocol for low back disorders: feasibility of use and validity of symptoms and signs. *J Clin Epidemiol*. 1998;51:245-255.

57. Albeck MJ. A critical assessment of clinical diagnosis of disc herniation in patients with monoradicular sciatica. *Acta Neurochir (Wien)*. 1996;138:40-44.

58. Charnley J. Orthopaedic signs in the diagnosis of disc protrusion. With special reference to the straight-leg-raising test. *Lancet*. 1951;1:186-192.

59. Gurdjian ES, Webster Je, Ostrowski AZ, et al. Herniated lumbar intervertebral discs—an analysis of 1176 operated cases. *J Trauma*. 1961;1:158-176.

60. Hakelius A, Hindmarsh J. The significance of neurological signs and myelographic findings in the diagnosis of lumbar root compression. *Acta Orthop Scand*. 1972;43:239-246.

61. Hirsch C, Nachemson A. The reliability of lumbar disc surgery. *Clin Orthop*. 1963;29:189-195.

62. Jonsson B, Stromqvist B. The straight leg raising test and the severity of symptoms in lumbar disc herniation. A preoperative evaluation. *Spine*. 1995;20:27-30.

63. Kerr RS, Cadoux-Hudson TA, Adams CB. The value of accurate clinical assessment in the surgical management of the lumbar disc protrusion. *J Neurol Neurosurg Psychiatry*. 1988;51:169-173.

64. Kosteljanetz M, Bang F, Schmidt-Olsen S. The clinical significance of straight-leg raising (Lasegue's sign) in

the diagnosis of prolapsed lumbar disc. Interobserver variation and correlation with surgical finding. *Spine.* 1988;13:393-395.

65. Kosteljanetz M, Espersen JO, Halaburt H, Miletic T. Predictive value of clinical and surgical findings in patients with lumbago-sciatica. A prospective study (Part I). *Acta Neurochir (Wien).* 1984;73:67-76.

66. Knutsson B. Comparative value of electromyographic, myelographic and clinical-neurological examinations in diagnosis of lumbar root compression syndrome. *Acta Orthop Scand Suppl.* 1961;49:1-135.

67. Spangfort EV. The lumbar disc herniation: a computer aided analysis of 2504 operations. *Acta Orthop Scand.* 1972;142:5-79.

68. Deville WL, van der Windt DA, Dzaferagic A, et al. The test of Lasegue: systematic review of the accuracy in diagnosing herniated discs. *Spine.* 2000;25:1140-1147.

69. Majlesi J, Togay H, Unalan H, Toprak S. The sensitivity and specificity of the slump and the straight leg raising tests in patients with lumbar disc herniation. *J Clin Rheumatol.* 2008;14:87-91.

70. Tucker N, Reid D, McNair P. Reliability and measurement error of active knee extension range of motion in a modified slump test position: a pilot study. *J Man Manip Ther.* 2007;15:E85-E91.

71. Murphy DR, Byfield D, McCarthy P, et al. Interexaminer reliability of the hip extension test for suspected impaired motor control of the lumbar spine. *J Manipulative Physiol Ther.* 2006;29:374-377.

72. Roussel NA, Nijs J, Truijen S, et al. Low back pain: clinimetric properties of the Trendelenburg test, active straight leg raise test, and breathing pattern during active straight leg raising. *J Manipulative Physiol Ther.* 2007;30:270-278.

73. Mens JM, Vleeming A, Snijders CJ, et al. Reliability and validity of the active straight leg raise test in posterior pelvic pain since pregnancy. *Spine.* 2001;26:1167-1171.

74. Fritz JM, George S. The use of a classification approach to identify subgroups of patients with acute low back pain. Interrater reliability and short-term treatment outcomes. *Spine.* 2000;25:106-114.

75. Riddle DL, Rothstein JM. Intertester reliability of McKenzie's classifications of the syndrome types present in patients with low back pain. *Spine.* 1993;18:1333-1344.

76. Razmjou H, Kramer JF, Yamada R. Intertester reliability of the McKenzie evaluation in assessing patients with mechanical low-back pain. *J Orthop Sports Phys Ther.* 2000;30:368-89.

77. Trudelle-Jackson E, Sarvaiya-Shah SA, Wang SS. Interrater reliability of a movement impairment-based classification system for lumbar spine syndromes in patients with chronic low back pain. *J Orthop Sports Phys Ther.* 2008;38:371-376.

78. Heiss DG, Fitch DS, Fritz JM, et al. The interrater reliability among physical therapists newly trained in a classification system for acute low back pain. *J Orthop Sports Phys Ther.* 2004;34:430-439.

79. Hebert J, Koppenhaver S, Fritz J, Parent E. Clinical prediction for success of interventions for managing low back pain. *Clin Sports Med.* 2008;27:463-479.

80. Delitto A, Erhard RE, Bowling RW. A treatment-based classification approach to low back syndrome: identifying and staging patients for conservative management. *Phys Ther.* 1995;75:470-489.

81. Fritz JM, Childs JD, Flynn TW. Pragmatic application of a clinical prediction rule in primary care to identify patients with low back pain with a good prognosis following a brief spinal manipulation intervention. *BMC Fam Pract.* 2005;6:29.

82. Lauridsen HH, Hartvigsen J, Manniche C, et al. Danish version of the Oswestry Disability Index for patients with low back pain. Part 1: Cross-cultural adaptation, reliability and validity in two different populations. *Eur Spine J.* 2006;15:1705-1716.

83. Lauridsen HH, Hartvigsen J, Manniche C, et al. Responsiveness and minimal clinically important difference for pain and disability instruments in low back pain patients. *BMC Musculoskelet Disord.* 2006;7:82.

84. Fritz JM, Irrgang JJ. A Comparison of a Modified Oswestry Disability Questionnaire and the Quebec Back Pain Disability Scale. *Phys Ther.* 2001;81:776-788.

85. Brouwer S, Kuijer W, Dijkstra PU, et al. Reliability and stability of the Roland Morris Disability Questionnaire: intra class correlation and limits of agreement. *Disabil Rehabil.* 2004;26:162-165.

86. Grotle M, Brox JI, Vollestad NK. Reliability, validity and responsiveness of the fear-avoidance beliefs questionnaire: methodological aspects of the Norwegian version. *J Rehabil Med.* 2006;38:346-353.

87. Li L, Liu X, Herr K. Postoperative pain intensity assessment: a comparison of four scales in Chinese adults. *Pain Med.* 2007;8:223-234.

88. Farrar JT, Berlin JA, Strom BL. Clinically important changes in acute pain outcome measures: a validation study. *J Pain Symptom Manage.* 2003;25:406-411.

89. Farrar JT, Portenoy RK, Berlin JA, et al. Defining the clinically important difference in pain outcome measures. *Pain.* 2000;88:287-294.

90. Fukui S, Ohseto K, Shiotani M, et al. Distribution of referred pain from the lumbar zygapophyseal joints and dorsal rami. *Clin J Pain.* 1997;13:303-307.

91. Russel AS, Maksymowych W, LeClercq S. Clinical examination of the sacroiliac joints: a prospective study. *Arthritis Rheum.* 1981;24:1575-1577.

92. Blower PW, Griffin AJ. Clinical sacroiliac tests in ankylosing spondylitis and other causes of low back pain—2 studies. *Ann Rheum Dis.* 1984;43:192-195.

93. Phillips DR, Twomey LT. A comparison of manual diagnosis with a diagnosis established by a uni-level lumbar spinal block procedure. *Man Ther.* 1996;1:82-87.

Sacroiliac Region

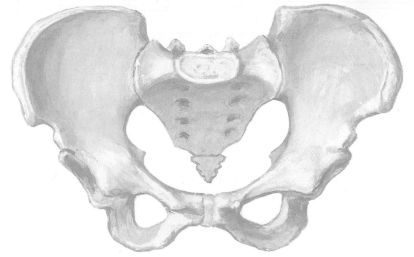

CLINICAL SUMMARY AND RECOMMENDATIONS

Patient History

Questions
- "Pain relieved by standing" is the only question studied to demonstrate some diagnostic utility (+LR of 3.5) for sacroiliac joint pain.

Pain Location
- Recent evidence suggests that patients with sacroiliac joint pain commonly experience the most intense pain around one or both sacroiliac joints with or without referral into the lateral thigh.

Physical Examination

Pain Provocation Tests
- Pain provocation tests generally demonstrate fair to moderate reliability and some exhibit moderate diagnostic utility for detecting sacroiliac joint pain.

- Clusters of pain provocation tests consistently demonstrate good diagnostic utility for detecting sacroiliac joint pain. Using a cluster of four to five tests including *distraction, thigh thrust, sacral thrust,* and *compression* after a McKenzie-type repeated motion examination seems to exhibit the best diagnostic utility (+LR of 6.97) and is recommended.

Motion Assessment and Static Palpation
- Motion assessment and static palpation tests generally demonstrate very poor reliability and almost no diagnostic utility for either sacroiliac joint pain or innominate torsion and, therefore, are not recommended for use in clinical practice.

- Lumbar hypomobility is the one exception that, although exhibiting questionable reliability, demonstrates some diagnostic utility when used as part of a cluster to determine which patients will respond to spinal manipulation.

Interventions
- Patients with low back pain of duration less than 16 days and no symptoms distal to the knees, and/or meet four out of five of the Flynn and colleagues[1] criteria, should be treated with a lumbosacral manipulation.

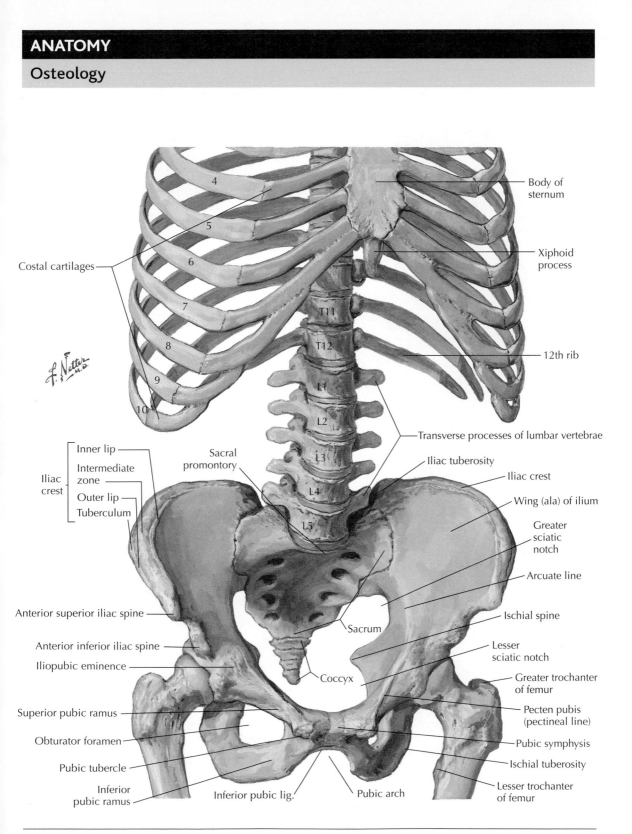

Figure 5-1 Bony framework of abdomen.

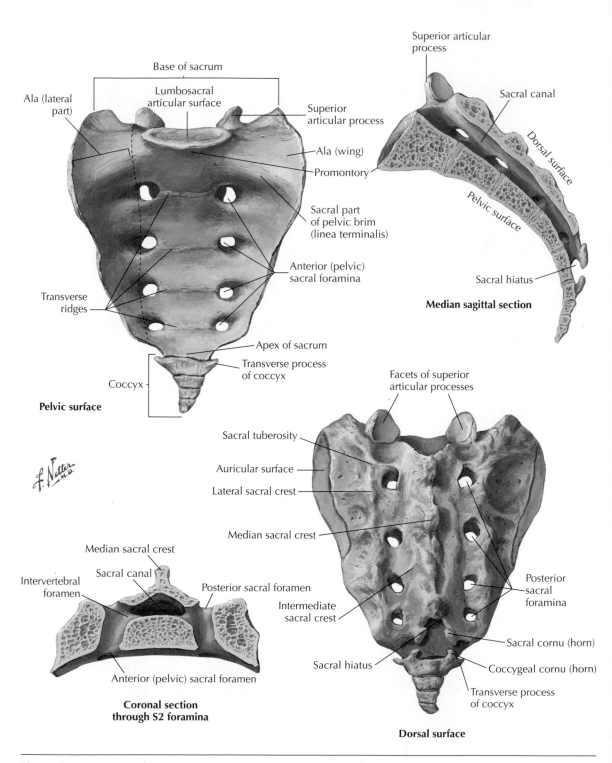

Base of sacrum

Lumbosacral articular surface

Ala (lateral part)

Superior articular process

Ala (wing)

Promontory

Sacral part of pelvic brim (linea terminalis)

Anterior (pelvic) sacral foramina

Transverse ridges

Apex of sacrum

Transverse process of coccyx

Coccyx

Pelvic surface

Superior articular process

Sacral canal

Dorsal surface

Pelvic surface

Sacral hiatus

Median sagittal section

Facets of superior articular processes

Sacral tuberosity

Auricular surface

Lateral sacral crest

Median sacral crest

Posterior sacral foramina

Intermediate sacral crest

Sacral cornu (horn)

Coccygeal cornu (horn)

Sacral hiatus

Transverse process of coccyx

Dorsal surface

Intervertebral foramen

Sacral canal

Median sacral crest

Posterior sacral foramen

Anterior (pelvic) sacral foramen

Coronal section through S2 foramina

Figure 5-2 Sacrum and coccyx.

Osteology

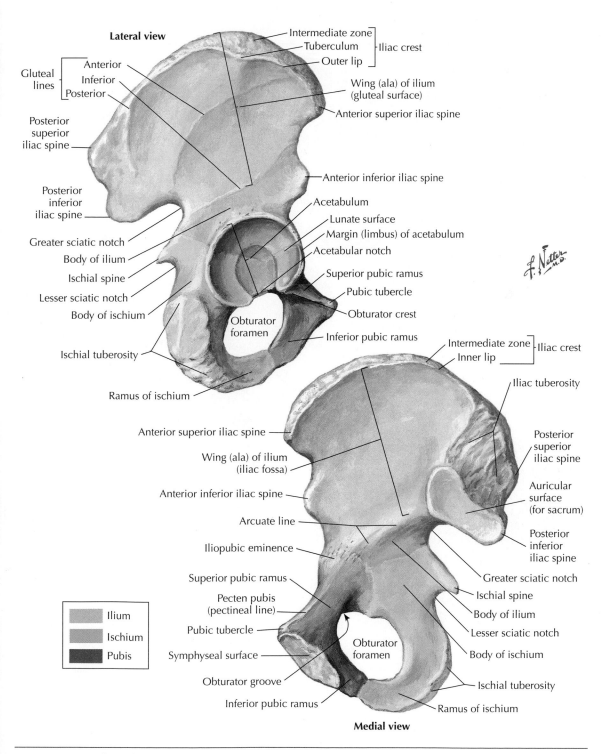

Lateral view

Gluteal lines
- Anterior
- Inferior
- Posterior

Posterior superior iliac spine

Posterior inferior iliac spine

Greater sciatic notch

Body of ilium

Ischial spine

Lesser sciatic notch

Body of ischium

Ischial tuberosity

Ramus of ischium

Intermediate zone
Tuberculum ⎫ Iliac crest
Outer lip

Wing (ala) of ilium (gluteal surface)

Anterior superior iliac spine

Anterior inferior iliac spine

Acetabulum

Lunate surface

Margin (limbus) of acetabulum

Acetabular notch

Superior pubic ramus

Pubic tubercle

Obturator crest

Obturator foramen

Inferior pubic ramus

Anterior superior iliac spine

Wing (ala) of ilium (iliac fossa)

Anterior inferior iliac spine

Arcuate line

Iliopubic eminence

Superior pubic ramus

Pecten pubis (pectineal line)

Pubic tubercle

Symphyseal surface

Obturator groove

Inferior pubic ramus

Intermediate zone ⎫ Iliac crest
Inner lip

Iliac tuberosity

Posterior superior iliac spine

Auricular surface (for sacrum)

Posterior inferior iliac spine

Greater sciatic notch

Ischial spine

Body of ilium

Lesser sciatic notch

Body of ischium

Ischial tuberosity

Ramus of ischium

Obturator foramen

Medial view

Ilium

Ischium

Pubis

Figure 5-3 Hip (coxal) bone.

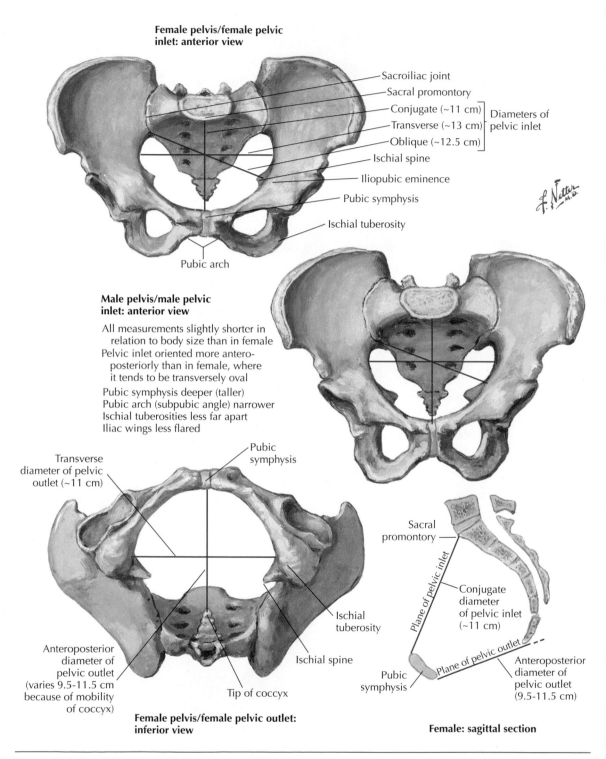

Female pelvis/female pelvic inlet: anterior view

Sacroiliac joint
Sacral promontory
Conjugate (~11 cm)
Transverse (~13 cm) — Diameters of pelvic inlet
Oblique (~12.5 cm)
Ischial spine
Iliopubic eminence
Pubic symphysis
Ischial tuberosity
Pubic arch

Male pelvis/male pelvic inlet: anterior view

All measurements slightly shorter in relation to body size than in female
Pelvic inlet oriented more antero-posteriorly than in female, where it tends to be transversely oval
Pubic symphysis deeper (taller)
Pubic arch (subpubic angle) narrower
Ischial tuberosities less far apart
Iliac wings less flared

Transverse diameter of pelvic outlet (~11 cm)
Pubic symphysis
Ischial tuberosity
Ischial spine
Anteroposterior diameter of pelvic outlet (varies 9.5-11.5 cm because of mobility of coccyx)
Tip of coccyx

Female pelvis/female pelvic outlet: inferior view

Sacral promontory
Plane of pelvic inlet
Conjugate diameter of pelvic inlet (~11 cm)
Plane of pelvic outlet
Anteroposterior diameter of pelvic outlet (9.5-11.5 cm)
Pubic symphysis

Female: sagittal section

Figure 5-4 Sex differences of pelvis.

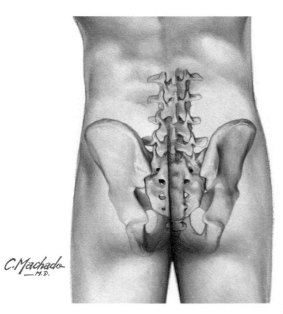

Figure 5-5 Sacroiliac joint.

Sacroiliac Region	Type and Classification	Closed Packed Position	Capsular Pattern
Sacroiliac joint	Plane synovial	Has not been described	Considered a capsular pattern if pain is provoked when joints are stressed
Lumbosacral			
Apophyseal joints	Plane synovial	Extension	Equal limitations of sidebending, flexion, and extension
Intervertebral joint	Amphiarthrodial	Not applicable	Not applicable

Ligaments

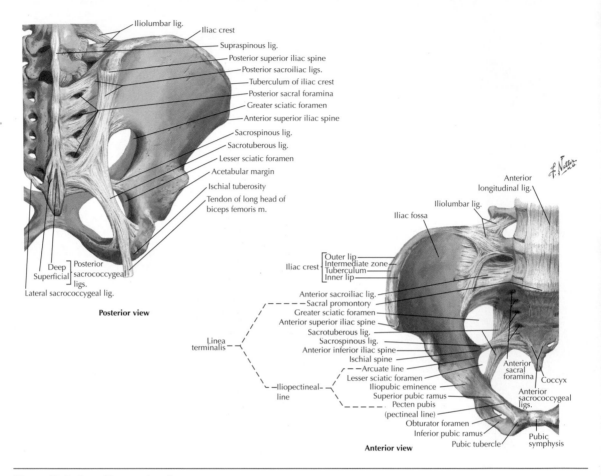

Figure 5-6 Sacroiliac region ligaments.

Sacroiliac Region Ligaments	Attachment	Function
Posterior sacroiliac	Iliac crest to tubercles of S1–S4	Limits movement of sacrum on iliac bones
Anterior sacroiliac	Anterosuperior aspect of sacrum to anterior ala of ilium	Limits movement of sacrum on iliac bones
Sacrospinous	Inferior lateral border of sacrum to ischial spine	Limits gliding and rotary movement of sacrum on iliac bones
Sacrotuberous	Middle lateral border of sacrum to ischial tuberosity	Limits gliding and rotary movement of sacrum on iliac bones
Posterior sacrococcygeal	Posterior aspect of inferior sacrum to posterior aspect of coccyx	Reinforces sacrococcygeal joint
Anterior sacrococcygeal	Anterior aspect of inferior sacrum to anterior aspect of coccyx	Reinforces sacrococcygeal joint
Lateral sacrococcygeal	Lateral aspect of inferior sacrum to lateral aspect of coccyx	Reinforces sacrococcygeal joint
Anterior longitudinal	Extends from anterior sacrum to anterior tubercle of C1. Connects anterolateral vertebral bodies and discs	Maintains stability of vertebral body joints and prevents hyperextension of vertebral column

Muscles

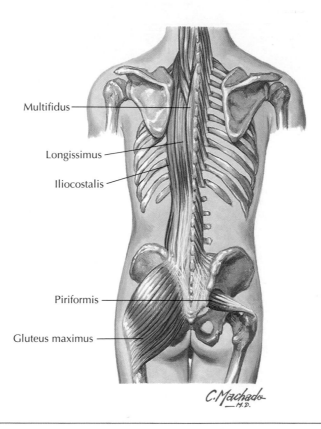

Figure 5-7 Sacroiliac region muscles. Posterior view of spine and associated musculature.

Sacroiliac Region Muscles	Proximal Attachment	Distal Attachment	Nerve and Segmental Level	Action
Gluteus maximus	Posterior border of ilium, dorsal aspect of sacrum and coccyx, and sacrotuberous ligament	Iliotibial tract of fascia lata and gluteal tuberosity of femur	Inferior gluteal nerve (L5, S1, S1)	Extension, external rotation and some abduction of the hip joint
Piriformis	Anterior aspect of sacrum and sacrotuberous ligament	Superior greater trochanter of femur	Ventral rami S1, S2	External rotation of extended hip, abduction of flexed hip
Multifidi	Sacrum, ilium, transverse processes T1-T3, articular processes C4-C7	Spinous processes of vertebrae two to four segments above origin	Dorsal rami of spinal nerves	Stabilizes vertebrae
Longissimus	Iliac crest, posterior sacrum, spinous processes of sacrum and inferior lumbar vertebrae, supraspinous ligament	Transverse processes of lumbar vertebrae	Dorsal rami of spinal nerves	Bilaterally extends vertebral column. Unilaterally sidebends spinal column
Iliocostalis		Inferior surface of ribs 4-12		

Nerves

Nerve	Segmental Level	Sensory	Motor
Superior gluteal	L4, L5, S1	No sensory	Tensor fascia latae, gluteus medius, gluteus minimus
Inferior gluteal	L5, S1, S2	No sensory	Gluteus maximus
Nerve to piriformis	S1, S2	No sensory	Piriformis
Sciatic	L4, L5, S1, S2, S3	Hip joint	Knee flexors and all muscles of leg and foot
Nerve to quadratus femoris	L5, S1, S2	No sensory	Quadratus femoris, inferior gemellus
Nerve to obturator internus	L5, S1, S2	No sensory	Obturator internus, superior gemellus
Posterior cutaneous	S2, S3	Posterior thigh	No motor
Perforating cutaneous	S2, S3	Inferior gluteal region	No motor
Pudendal	S2, S3, S4	Genitals	Perineal muscles, external urethral sphincter, external anal sphincter
Nerve to levator ani	S3, S4	No sensory	Levator ani
Perineal branch	S1, S2, S3	Genitals	No motor
Anococcygeal	S4, S5, C0	Skin in the coccygeal region	No motor
Coccygeal	S3, S4	No sensory	Coccygeus
Pelvic splanchnic	S2, S3, S4	No sensory	Pelvic viscera

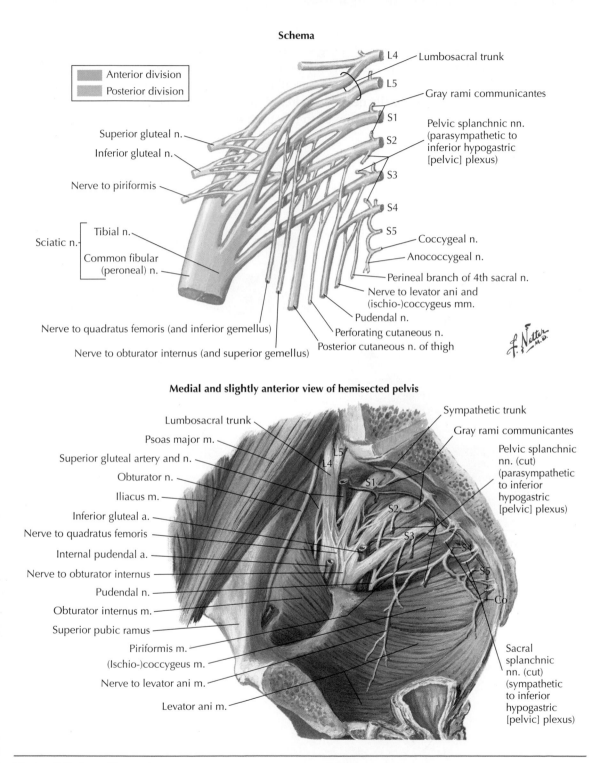

Schema

Anterior division

Posterior division

L4 — Lumbosacral trunk

L5

Gray rami communicantes

S1

S2

Pelvic splanchnic nn.
(parasympathetic to
inferior hypogastric
[pelvic] plexus)

Superior gluteal n.

Inferior gluteal n.

S3

Nerve to piriformis

S4

S5

Coccygeal n.

Sciatic n.

Tibial n.

Anococcygeal n.

Common fibular
(peroneal) n.

Perineal branch of 4th sacral n.

Nerve to levator ani and
(ischio-)coccygeus mm.

Pudendal n.

Nerve to quadratus femoris (and inferior gemellus)

Perforating cutaneous n.

Posterior cutaneous n. of thigh

Nerve to obturator internus (and superior gemellus)

Medial and slightly anterior view of hemisected pelvis

Sympathetic trunk

Lumbosacral trunk

Gray rami communicantes

Psoas major m.

Pelvic splanchnic
nn. (cut)
(parasympathetic
to inferior
hypogastric
[pelvic] plexus)

Superior gluteal artery and n.

Obturator n.

Iliacus m.

Inferior gluteal a.

Nerve to quadratus femoris

Internal pudendal a.

Nerve to obturator internus

Pudendal n.

Obturator internus m.

Superior pubic ramus

Piriformis m.

(Ischio-)coccygeus m.

Nerve to levator ani m.

Levator ani m.

Sacral
splanchnic
nn. (cut)
(sympathetic
to inferior
hypogastric
[pelvic] plexus)

Figure 5-8 Sacroiliac region nerves.

Sacroiliac Pain and Sacroiliac Dysfunction

There has been considerable controversy surrounding the contribution of the sacroiliac joint in low back pain syndromes. Recent research suggests that the sacroiliac joint can be a contributor to low back pain and disability and can certainly be a primary source of pain.[2-7] The concept of "sacroiliac joint dysfunction" is distinct from "sacroiliac joint pain" and is hypothetical at best.[3] Sacroiliac joint dysfunction is usually defined as altered joint mobility and/or malalignment,[8-10] neither of which have been consistently linked to low back or sacroiliac joint pain.

Figure 5-9 Common cause of sacroiliac injury. Falling and landing on the buttock.

Pain Location and Aggravating Factors

Dreyfuss and colleagues[2] performed a prospective study to determine the diagnostic utility of both the history and physical examination in determining pain of sacroiliac origin. The diagnostic properties for the aggravating and easing factors and patient-reported location of pain are below.

+LR	Interpretation	−LR
>10	Large	<.1
5.0-10.0	Moderate	.1-.2
2.0-5.0	Small	.2-.5
1.0-2.0	Rarely important	.5-1.0

Question and Study Quality	Population	Reference Standard	Sens	Spec	+LR	−LR
Pain relieved by standing?[2]	85 consecutive patients with low back pain referred for sacroiliac joint blocks	90% pain relief with injection of local anesthetics into sacroiliac joint	.07	.98	3.5	.95
Pain relieved by walking?[2]			.13	.77	.57	1.13
Pain relieved by sitting?[2]			.07	.8	.35	1.16
Pain relieved by lying down?[2]			.53	.49	1.04	.96
Coughing/sneezing aggravates symptoms?[2]			.45	.47	.85	1.17
Bowel movements aggravate symptoms?[2]			.38	.63	1.03	.98
Wearing heels/boots aggravates symptoms?[2]			.26	.56	.59	1.32
Job activities aggravate symptoms?[2]			.20	.74	.77	1.08

Patient Report of Pain Location and Study Quality	Population	Reference Standard	Sens	Spec	+LR	−LR
Sacroilliac joint pain[2]	85 consecutive patients with low back pain referred for sacroiliac joint blocks	90% pain relief with injection of local anesthetics into sacroiliac joint	.82*	.12*	.93	1.5
Groin pain[2]			.26*	.63*	.70	1.17
Buttock pain[2]			.78*	.18*	.95	1.22
Points to of posterior-superior iliac spine (PSIS) as main area of pain?[2]			.71*	.47*	1.34	.62

*Mean of chiropractor and physician sensitivity and specificity scores.

Figure 5-10 Jung and associates[11] determined the most common pain distribution patterns in patients with sacroiliac joint pain. They then prospectively tested the ability of the pain distribution patterns to diagnose the response to sacroiliac joint radiofrequency neurotomies in 160 patients with presumed sacroiliac joint pain. The pain distribution patterns with the best diagnostic utility are depicted in Figure 5-10.

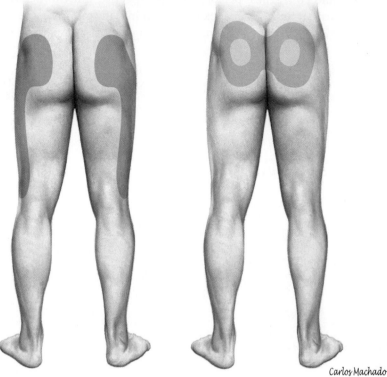

Carlos Machado

Figure 5-11 In a similar study, van der Wurff and colleagues[12] compared compiled pain distribution maps from patients that responded to double-block sacroiliac joint injections to those that didn't respond. They found no difference in the location of pain distribution, but found differences in the pain intensity locations. Patients with sacroiliac joint pain reported the highest intensity pain overlying the sacroiliac joint as depicted in Figure 5-11.

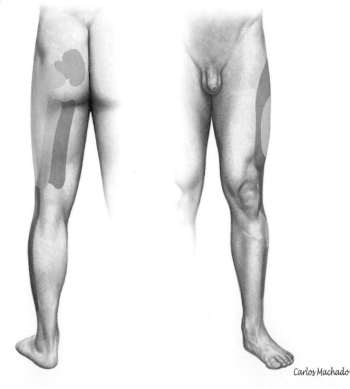

Carlos Machado

Palpation

Pain Provocation and Patient Identification of Location of Pain

+LR	Interpretation	−LR
>10	Large	<.1
5.0-10.0	Moderate	.1-.2
2.0-5.0	Small	.2-.5
1.0-2.0	Rarely important	.5-1.0

Measurement (and Study Quality)	Population	Reference Standard	Sens	Spec	+LR	−LR
Sacral sulcus tenderness only[2] ◯	85 consecutive patients with low back pain referred for sacroiliac joint blocks	90% pain relief with injection of local anesthetics into sacroiliac joint	.89*	.14	1.03*	.79*
Sacral sulcus tenderness + the patient points to the PSIS as the main site of pain[2] ◯			.63*	.50*	1.26*	.74*
Sacral sulcus tenderness + groin pain[2] ◯			.25*	.68*	.78*	1.10*
Patient points to PSIS as main site of pain + complains of groin pain[2] ◯			.16	.85	1.07	.99
Sacral sulcus tenderness + patient identifies PSIS as main site of pain + groin pain[2] ◯			.13	.86	.93	1.01

*Mean of chiropractor and physician sensitivity and specificity scores

Assessment of Symmetry of Bony Landmarks

ICC or κ	Interpretation
.81-1.0	Substantial agreement
.61-.80	Moderate agreement
.41-.60	Fair agreement
.11-.40	Slight agreement
.0-.10	No agreement

Landmark	Description and Positive Findings	Population	Reliability
Sitting PSIS[13]	With patient sitting, examiner palpates right and left PSIS. Positive if one PSIS is higher than the other	62 women recruited from obstetrics; 42 pregnant with pelvic girdle pain, and 20 who were not pregnant and were asymptomatic	Inter-examiner κ = **.26**
Sitting PSIS[9]		65 patients with low back pain	Inter-examiner κ = **.37**
Sitting PSIS[1]		71 patients with low back pain	Inter-examiner κ = **.23**
Standing PSIS[1]	Same as above with patient standing		Inter-examiner κ = **.13**
Iliac crest symmetry[1]	With patient standing, examiner palpates right and left iliac crest. Positive if one crest is higher than the other		Inter-examiner κ = **.23**
Prone PSIS[14]	With patient prone and examiner's fingers or thumbs on landmark and dominant eye over the patient's mid-sagittal plane, examiner determines if the landmarks are: • Right higher than left • Left higher than right • Equal right to left	10 asymptomatic female volunteers	Intra-examiner κ = **.33** Inter-examiner κ = **.04**
Sacral inferior lateral angle[14]			Intra-examiner κ = **.69** Inter-examiner κ = **.08**
Sacral sulcus[14]	As above, determining if the landmarks are: • Right deeper than left • Left deeper than right • Equal right to left		Intra-examiner κ = **.24** Inter-examiner κ = **.07**
Sacral sulcus[15]		25 patients with low back or sacroiliac pain	Inter-examiner κ = **.11** **(−.14, .36)**
Sacral inferior lateral angle[15]	As above, determining if the landmarks are: • Right more posterior than left • Left more posterior than right • Equal right to left		Inter-examiner κ = **.11** **(−.12, .34)**
L5 transverse process[15]			Inter-examiner κ = **.17** **(−.03, .37)**
Medial malleoli[15]	As above, determining if the landmarks are: • Right more superior than left • Left more superior than right • Equal right to left		Inter-examiner κ = **.28** **(−.01, .57)**
Medial malleoli[16]		24 patients with low back pain	Inter-examiner κ = **.21**
Anterior-superior iliac spine (ASIS)[16]	With patient supine, evaluator palpates inferior slope ASIS. Recorded as above		Inter-examiner κ = **.15**
Sacral base[16]	With patient sitting, evaluator palpates the sacral base with the patient's trunk flexed and extended. Recorded as symmetrical, left-base anterior or posterior, or right-base anterior or posterior		Inter-examiner κ = [Trunk flexion] **.37** [Trunk extension] **.05**

Potter and Rothstein[17] also studied static palpation, but were excluded because they only reported percent agreement.

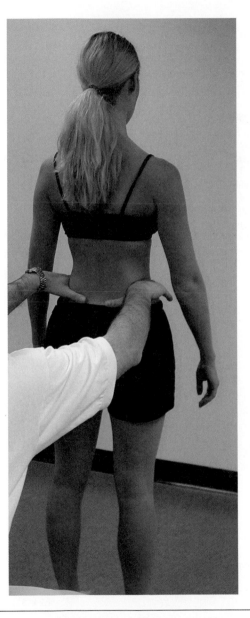

Figure 5-12 Assessment of iliac crest symmetry in standing.

Patrick Test (FABER Test)

ICC or κ	Interpretation
.81-1.0	Substantial agreement
.61-.80	Moderate agreement
.41-.60	Fair agreement
.11-.40	Slight agreement
.0-.10	No agreement

See Figure 5-13, page 221

Test and Study	Description and Positive Findings	Population	Reliability
Patrick test[18]	With patient supine, examiner brings ipsilateral knee into flexion with lateral malleolus placed over the contralateral knee, fixates the contralateral ASIS, and applies a light pressure over the ipsilateral knee. Positive if familiar pain is increased or reproduced	15 patients with ankylosing spondylitis, 30 women with postpartum pelvic pain, and 16 asymptomatic subjects	Inter-examiner κ = [Right] .60 (.39, .81) [Left] .48 (.27, .69)
Patrick test[19]		25 patients with asymmetrical low back pain	Intra-examiner* κ = [Right] .41 (.07, .78) [Left] .40 (.03, .78) Inter-examiner κ = [Right] .44 (.06, .83) [Left] .49 (.09, .89)
Patrick test[20]		40 patients with chronic low back pain	Inter-examiner κ = [Right] .60 (.35, .85) [Left] .43 (.15, .71)
Patrick test[1]		71 patients with low back pain	Inter-examiner κ = .60
Patrick test[21]		59 patients with low back pain	Inter-examiner κ = .61 (.31, −.91)
Patrick test[2]		See diagnostic table	Inter-examiner κ = .62

*Intra-examiner reliability reported for examiner #1 only.

+LR	Interpretation	−LR
>10	Large	<.1
5.0-10.0	Moderate	.1-.2
2.0-5.0	Small	.2-.5
1.0-2.0	Rarely important	.5-1.0

Test and Study Quality	Description and Positive Findings	Population	Reference Standard	Sens	Spec	+LR	−LR
Patrick test[20] ◇	With patient supine, examiner brings ipsilateral knee into flexion with lateral malleolus placed over the contralateral knee, fixates the contralateral ASIS, applying a light pressure over the ipsilateral knee. Positive if familiar pain is increased or reproduced	40 patients with chronic low back pain	Sacroiliitis apparent on magnetic resonance imaging (MRI)	**Right side**			
				.66 (.30, .90)	.51 (.33, .69)	1.37 (.76, 2.48)	.64 (.24, 1.72)
				Left side			
				.54 (.24, .81)	.62 (.42, .78)	1.43 (.70, 2.93)	.73 (.36, 1.45)
Patrick test[2] ◯		85 consecutive patients with low back pain referred for sacroiliac joint blocks	90% pain relief with injection of local anesthetics into sacroiliac joint	.68*	.29*	.96*	1.1*

*Mean of chiropractor and physician sensitivity and specificity scores.
Broadhurst and Bond[22] also investigated this test, but the study was excluded because results for all participants were positive on the test (making sensitivity = 1, and specificity = 0).

Pain Provocation

Thigh Thrust (or Posterior Shear Test or Posterior Pelvic Provocation Test)

See Figure 5-14, page 221

ICC or κ	Interpretation
.81-1.0	Substantial agreement
.61-.80	Moderate agreement
.41-.60	Fair agreement
.11-.40	Slight agreement
.0-.10	No agreement

Test and Study	Description and Positive Findings	Population	Reliability
Thigh thrust[20]	Patient supine with hip flexed to 90°. The examiner applies posteriorly directed force through the femur. Positive if familiar pain is increased or reproduced	See diagnostic table	Inter-examiner κ = [Right] **.46** (.15, .76)
Thigh thrust[18]		15 patients with ankylosing spondylitis, 30 women with postpartum pelvic pain, and 16 asymptomatic subjects	Inter-examiner κ = [Right] **.76** (.48, .86) [Left] **.74** (.57, .91)
Thigh thrust[19]	Patient supine with hip flexed to 90° and slightly adducted. One of the examiner's hands cups the sacrum and the other applies posteriorly directed force through the femur. Positive test is the production or increase of familiar symptoms	25 patients with asymmetrical low back pain	Intra-examiner* κ = [Right] **.44** (.06, .83) [Left] **.40** (.00, .82) Inter-examiner κ = [Right] **.60** (.24, .96) [Left] **.40** (.00, .82)
Thigh thrust[1]		71 patients with low back pain	Inter-examiner κ = **.70**
Thigh thrust[23]		51 patients with low back pain	Inter-examiner κ = **.88**
Thigh thrust[21]		59 patients with low back pain	Inter-examiner κ = **.67** (.46, .88)
Thigh thrust[2]		See diagnostic table	Inter-examiner κ = **.64**

*Intra-examiner reliability reported for examiner #1 only.

+LR	Interpretation	−LR
>10	Large	<.1
5.0-10.0	Moderate	.1-.2
2.0-5.0	Small	.2-.5
1.0-2.0	Rarely important	.5-1.0

Test and Study Quality	Description and Positive Findings	Population	Reference Standard	Sens	Spec	+LR	−LR
Thigh thrust[20] ◇	With patient supine with hip flexed to 90°, examiner applies posteriorly directed force through the femur. Positive if familiar pain is increased or reproduced	40 patients with chronic low back pain	Sacroiliitis apparent on MRI	**Right side**			
				.55 (.22, .84)	.70 (.51, .85)	1.91 (.85, 4.27)	.62 (.29, 1.33)
				Left side			
				.45 (.18, .75)	.86 (.67, .95)	3.29 (1.07, 10.06)	.63 (.36, 1.09)
Thigh thrust[4] ◇	With patient supine with hip flexed to 90° and slightly adducted, one of the examiner's hands cups the sacrum and the other applies posteriorly directed force through the femur. Positive if familiar symptoms are produced or increased	48 patients with chronic lumbopelvic pain referred for sacroiliac joint injection	80% pain relief with injection of local anesthetics into sacroiliac joint	.88 (.64, .97)	.69 (NR, .82)	2.8 (1.66, 4.98)	.18 (.05, 1.09)
Thigh thrust[2] ○		85 consecutive patients with low back pain referred for sacroiliac joint blocks	90% pain relief with injection of local anesthetics into sacroiliac joint	.39*	.50*	.78*	1.22*

*Mean of chiropractor and physician sensitivity and specificity scores.
Broadhurst and Bond[22] also investigated this test, but the study was excluded because results for all participants were positive on the test (making sensitivity = 1, and specificity = 0).

See Figure 5-15, page 221

ICC or κ	Interpretation
.81-1.0	Substantial agreement
.61-.80	Moderate agreement
.41-.60	Fair agreement
.11-.40	Slight agreement
.0-.10	No agreement

Test and Study	Description and Positive Findings	Population	Reliability
Compression test[18]	With patient side-lying, affected side up, with hips flexed approximately 45° and knees flexed approximately 90°, examiner applies a force vertically downward on the anterior-superior iliac crest. Positive test is the production or increase of familiar symptoms	15 patients with ankylosing spondylitis, 30 women with postpartum pelvic pain, and 16 asymptomatic subjects	Inter-examiner κ = [Right] .48 (.18, .78) [Left] .67 (.43, .91)
Compression test[20]		40 patients with chronic low back pain	Inter-examiner κ = [Right] .48 (.14, .81) [Left] .44 (.08, .79)
Compression test[23]		51 patients with low back pain	Inter-examiner κ = .73
Compression test[21]		59 patients with low back pain	Inter-examiner κ = .57 (.21, .93)
Compression test[1]		71 patients with low back pain	Inter-examiner κ = .26

+LR	Interpretation	−LR
>10	Large	<.1
5.0-10.0	Moderate	.1-.2
2.0-5.0	Small	.2-.5
1.0-2.0	Rarely important	.5-1.0

Test and Study Quality	Description and Positive Findings	Population	Reference Standard	Sens	Spec	+LR	−LR
Compression test[20] ◇	With patient side-lying, affected side up, with hips flexed approximately 45° and knees flexed approximately 90°, examiner applies a force vertically downward on the anterior-superior iliac crest. Positive test is the production or increase of familiar symptoms	40 patients with chronic low back pain	Sacroiliitis apparent on MRI	**Right side**			
				.22 (.03, .59)	.83 (.65, .93)	1.37 (.31, 5.94)	.92 (.64, 1.33)
				Left side			
				.27 (.07, .60)	.93 (.75, .98)	3.95 (.76, 20.57)	.78 (.54, 1.12)
Compression test[4] ◇		48 patients with chronic lumbopelvic pain referred for sacroiliac joint injection	80% pain relief with injection of local anesthetics into sacroiliac joint	.69 (.44, .86)	.69 (.51, NR)	2.20 (1.18, 4.09)	.46 (.20, .87)

Russel and associates[24] and Blower and Griffin[25] also investigated this test, but were excluded due to poor study quality.

Pain Provocation

Sacral Thrust Test

See Figure 5-16, page 222

ICC or κ	Interpretation
.81-1.0	Substantial agreement
.61-.80	Moderate agreement
.41-.60	Fair agreement
.11-.40	Slight agreement
.0-.10	No agreement

Test and Study	Description and Positive Findings	Population	Reliability
Sacral thrust test[20]		40 patients with chronic low back pain	Inter-examiner κ = [Right] .87 (.70, 1.0) [Left] .69 (.40, .97)
Sacral thrust test[6]	With patient prone, examiner applies a force vertically downward to the center of the sacrum. Positive test is the production or increase of familiar symptoms	71 patients with low back pain	Inter-examiner κ = .41
Sacral thrust test[23]		51 patients with low back pain	Inter-examiner κ = .56
Sacral thrust test[2]		85 patients with low back pain referred for sacroiliac joint blocks	Inter-examiner κ = .30

+LR	Interpretation	−LR
>10	Large	<.1
5.0-10.0	Moderate	.1-.2
2.0-5.0	Small	.2-.5
1.0-2.0	Rarely important	.5-1.0

Test and Study Quality	Description and Positive Findings	Population	Reference Standard	Sens	Spec	+LR	−LR
Sacral thrust test[20] ◇	With patient prone, examiner applies a force vertically downward to the center of the sacrum. Positive test is the production or increase of familiar symptoms	40 patients with chronic low back pain	Sacroiliitis apparent on MRI	Right side			
				.33 (.09, .69)	.74 (.55, .87)	1.29 (.42, 3.88)	.89 (.55, 1.45)
				Left side			
				.45 (.18, .75)	.89 (.71, .97)	4.39 (1.25, 15.36)	.60 (.35, 1.05)
Sacral thrust test[4] ◇		48 patients with chronic lumbopelvic pain referred for sacroiliac joint injection	80% pain relief with injection of local anesthetics into sacroiliac joint	.63 (.39, .82)	.75 (.58, .87)	2.5 (1.23, 5.09)	.5 (.24, .87)
Sacral thrust test[2] ◯		85 consecutive patients with low back pain referred for sacroiliac joint blocks	90% pain relief with injection of local anesthetics into sacroiliac joint	.52*	.38*	.84*	1.26*

*Mean of chiropractor and physician sensitivity and specificity scores.

Pain Provocation

Gaenslen Test

See Figure 5-17, page 222

ICC or κ	Interpretation
.81-1.0	Substantial agreement
.61-.80	Moderate agreement
.41-.60	Fair agreement
.11-.40	Slight agreement
.0-.10	No agreement

Test and Study	Description and Positive Findings	Population	Reliability
Gaenslen test[20]	With patient supine near the edge of the table and one leg hanging over the edge of the table and the other flexed toward the patient's chest, examiner applies firm pressure to both the hanging leg and the leg flexed toward the chest. Positive test is the production or increase of familiar symptoms	40 patients with chronic low back pain	Inter-examiner κ = [Right] .37 (.05, .68) [Left] .28 (0.0, .60)
Gaenslen test[1]		71 patients referred to physical therapy with a diagnosis related to the lumbosacral spine	Inter-examiner κ = .54
Gaenslen test[23]		51 patients with low back pain with or without radiation into the lower limb	Inter-examiner κ = .76
Gaenslen test[21]		59 patients with low back pain	Inter-examiner κ = .60 (.33, .88)

+LR	Interpretation	−LR
>10	Large	<.1
5.0-10.0	Moderate	.1-.2
2.0-5.0	Small	.2-.5
1.0-2.0	Rarely important	.5-1.0

Test and Study Quality	Description and Positive Findings	Population	Reference Standard	Sens	Spec	+LR	−LR
Gaenslen test[20] ◇	With patient supine near the edge of the table and one leg hanging over the edge of the table and the other flexed toward the patient's chest, examiner applies firm pressure to both the hanging leg and the leg flexed toward the chest. Positive test is the production or increase of familiar symptoms	40 patients with chronic low back pain	Sacroiliitis apparent on MRI	Right side			
				.44 (.15, .77)	.80 (.61, .91)	2.29 (.82, 6.39)	.68 (.37, 1.25)
				Left side			
				.36 (.12, .68)	.75 (.56, .88)	1.5 (.54, 4.15)	.83 (.52, 1.33)
Gaenslen test[4] ◇		48 patients with chronic lumbopelvic pain referred for sacroiliac joint injection	80% pain relief with injection of local anesthetics into sacroiliac joint	Right side			
				.53 (.30, .75)	.71 (.53, .84)	1.84 (.87, 3.74)	.66 (.34, 1.09)
				Left side			
				.50 (.27, .73)	.77 (.60, .89)	2.21 (.95, 5.0)	.65 (.34, 1.03)
Gaenslen test[2] ○		85 consecutive patients with low back pain referred for sacroiliac joint blocks	90% pain relief with injection of local anesthetics into sacroiliac joint	.68*	.29*	.96*	1.1*

*Mean of chiropractor and physician sensitivity and specificity scores.

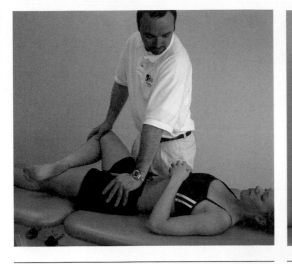

Figure 5-13 Patrick test.

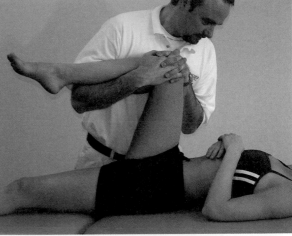

Figure 5-14 Thigh thrust.

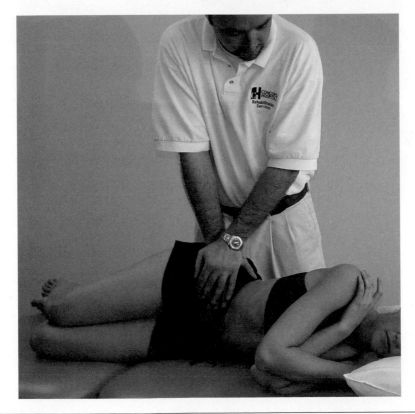

Figure 5-15 Compression test.

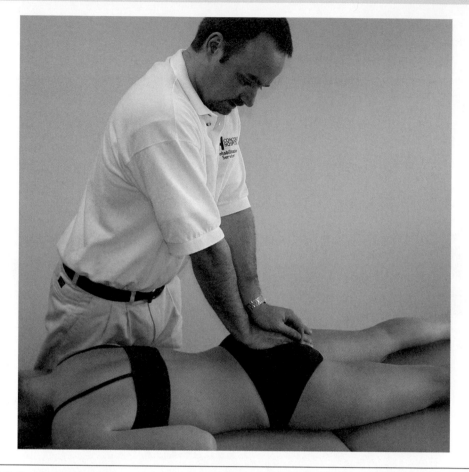

Figure 5-16 Sacral thrust test.

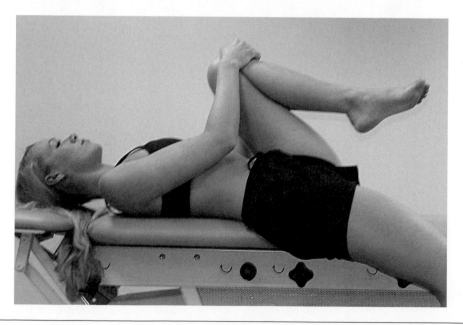

Figure 5-17 Gaenslen test.

Pain Provocation

Distraction Test

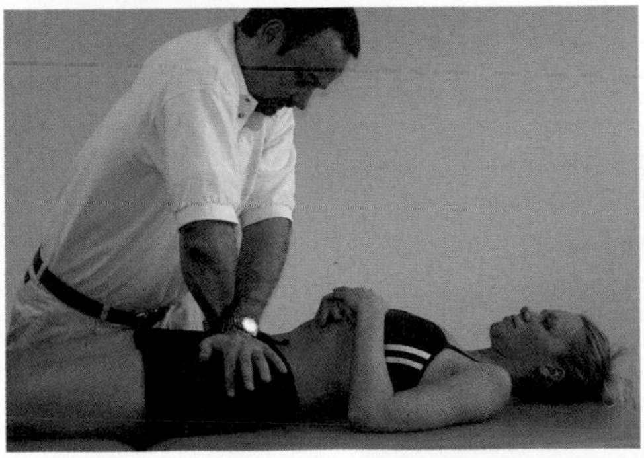

Figure 5-18 Distraction test.

Test and Study	Description and Positive Findings	Population	Reliability
Distraction test[20]	With patient supine, examiner applies cross-arm pressure to both anterior superior iliac spines. Positive test is the production or increase of familiar symptoms	40 patients with chronic low back pain	Inter-examiner κ = **.50**
Distraction test[23]		51 patients with low back pain, with or without radiation into the lower limb	Inter-examiner κ = **.69**
Distraction test[21]	With patient supine, examiner applies a posteriorly directed force to both anterior superior iliac spines. Positive test is the production or increase of familiar symptoms	59 patients with low back pain	Inter-examiner κ = **.45 (.10, .78)**
Distraction test[1]		71 patients referred to physical therapy with a diagnosis related to the lumbosacral spine	Inter-examiner κ = **.26**

Test and Study Quality	Description and Positive Findings	Population	Reference Standard	Sens	Spec	+LR	−LR
Distraction test[20] ◇	With patient supine, examiner applies cross-arm pressure to both anterior superior iliac spines. Positive test is the production or increase of familiar symptoms	40 patients with chronic low back pain	Sacroiliitis apparent on MRI	.23 (.06, .54)	.81 (.61, .92)	1.24 (.35, 4.4)	.94 (.68, 1.29)
Distraction test[4] ◇	With patient supine, examiner applies a posteriorly directed force to both anterior superior iliac spines. Positive test is the production or increase of familiar symptoms	48 patients with chronic lumbopelvic pain referred for sacroiliac joint injection	80% pain relief with injection of local anesthetics into sacroiliac joint	.60 (.36, .80)	.81 (.65, .91)	3.20 (1.42, 7.31)	.49 (.24, .83)

ICC or κ	Interpretation
.81–1.0	Substantial agreement
.61–.80	Moderate agreement
.41–.60	Fair agreement
.11–.40	Slight agreement
.0–.10	No agreement

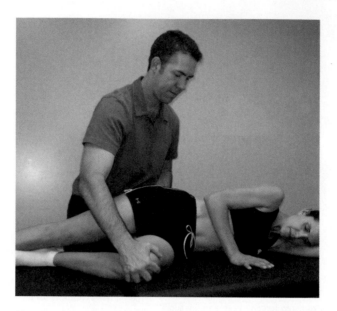

Figure 5-19 Mennell's test.

Test and Study	Description and Positive Findings	Population	Reliability
Mennell's test[20]	With patient side-lying, affected side down, with affected side hip and knee flexed toward the abdomen, examiner puts one hand over the ipsilateral buttock and iliac crest and the other hand grasps the semiflexed ipsilateral knee and lightly forces the leg into extension. Positive test is the production or increase of familiar symptoms	40 patients with chronic low back pain	Inter-examiner κ = [Right] **.54 (.26, .82)** [Left] **.50 (.20, .80)**

+LR	Interpretation	−LR
>10	Large	<.1
5.0–10.0	Moderate	.1–.2
2.0–5.0	Small	.2–.5
1.0–2.0	Rarely important	.5–1.0

Test and Study Quality	Description and Positive Findings	Population	Reference Standard	Sens	Spec	+LR	−LR
Mennell's test[20] ◇	As above	40 patients with chronic low back pain	Sacroiliitis apparent on MRI	Right side			
				.66 (.30, .90)	.80 (.61, .91)	3.44 (1.49, 8.09)	.41 (.16, 1.05)
				Left side			
				.45 (.18, 75)	.86 (.67, .95)	3.29 (1.07, 10.06)	.63 (.36, 1.09)

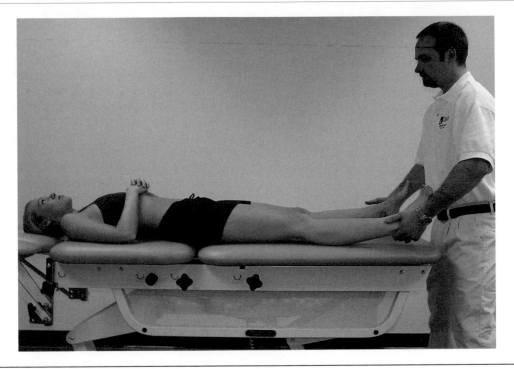

Figure 5-20 Resisted abduction of the hip.

ICC or κ	Interpretation
.81-1.0	Substantial agreement
.61-.80	Moderate agreement
.41-.60	Fair agreement
.11-.40	Slight agreement
.0-.10	No agreement

Test and Study	Description and Positive Findings	Population	Reliability
Resisted abduction test[19]	With patient supine with legs extended and abducted 30°, examiner holds the ankle and pushes medially while the patient pushes laterally. Positive test is the production or increase of familiar symptoms	25 patients with asymmetrical low back pain	Intra-examiner* κ = [Right] .48 (.07, .88) [Left] .50 (.06, .95) Inter-examiner κ = [Right] .78 (.49, 1.07) [Left] .50 (−.02, 1.03)
Resisted abduction test[1]		71 patients with low back pain	Inter-examiner κ = .41
Internal rotation of the hip[18]	With patient prone, examiner maximally internally rotates one or both femurs. Positive test is the production or increase of familiar symptoms	15 patients with ankylosing spondylitis, 30 women with postpartum pelvic pain, and 16 asymptomatic subjects	Inter-examiner κ = [Right] .78 (.60, .94) [Left] .88 (.75, 1.01) [Bilateral] .56 (.33, .79)
Drop-test[18]	With patient standing on one foot, patient lifts the heel from the floor and drops down on the heel again. Positive test is the production or increase of familiar symptoms		Inter-examiner κ = [Right] .84 (.61, 1.06) [Left] .47 (.11, .83)

*Intra-examiner reliability reported for examiner #1 only.
Broadhurst and Bond[22] investigated the diagnostic properties of the resisted abduction test, but the study was excluded because all participants were positive on the test (making sensitivity = 1, and specificity = 0).

Gillet Test (Stork Test)

ICC or κ	Interpretation
.81-1.0	Substantial agreement
.61-.80	Moderate agreement
.41-.60	Fair agreement
.11-.40	Slight agreement
.0-.10	No agreement

Test and Study	Description and Positive Findings	Population	Reliability
Gillet test[26]	With patient standing, examiner palpates the following landmarks: • L5 spinous process and PSIS • S1 tubercle and PSIS • S3 tubercle and PSIS • Sacral apex and posteromedial margin of the ischium Patient is instructed to raise the ipsilateral leg of the side of palpation. Positive if the lateral landmark fails to move posteroinferiorly with respect to medial landmark	54 asymptomatic college students	Intra-examiner mean value for all tests κ = **.31** Inter-examiner mean value for all tests κ = **.02**
Gillet test[27]	As above except using the following landmarks: • L5 spinous process and PSIS • S1 spinous process and PSIS • S3 spinous process and PSIS • Sacral hiatus and caudolateral just below the ischial spine	38 male students; 9 during the first testing procedure and 12 during the second had low back pain	Intra-examiner[*] κ = **.08 (.01, .14)** Inter-examiner κ = **−.05 (−.06, −.12)**
Gillet test[19]	With patient standing, examiner palpates the PSIS and asks patient to flex the hip and knee on the side being tested. Positive if the PSIS fails to move posteroinferiorly	25 patients with asymmetrical low back pain	Intra-examiner[*] κ = [Right] **.42 (−.01, .87)** [Left] **.49 (.09, .89)** Inter-examiner κ = [Right] **.41 (.03, .87)** [Left] **.34 (−.06, .70)**
Gillet test[28]	With patient standing, examiner palpates the S2 spinous process with one thumb and the PSIS with the other and asks patient to flex the hip and knee on the side being tested. Rated intrapelvic motion as "cephalad," "neutral," or "caudad"	33 volunteers; 15 had pelvic-girdle pain	Inter-examiner κ = [Right] **.59** [Left] **.59**
Gillet test[16]	With patient standing, examiner palpates the S2 spinous process with one thumb and the PSIS with the other and asks patient to flex the hip and knee on the side being tested. Positive if the PSIS fails to move posteroinferiorly with respect to S2	24 patients with low back pain	Inter-examiner κ = **.27**
Gillet test[2]		See diagnostic table	Inter-examiner κ = **.22**
Gillet test[6]		71 patients with low back pain	Inter-examiner κ = **.59**

*Intra-examiner reliability reported for examiner #1 only.
Potter and Rothstein[17] and Herzog and colleagues[29] also studied this test, but were excluded because they only reported percent agreement.

Gillet Test (Stork Test) (Continued)

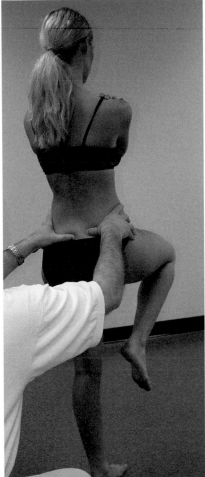

Figure 5-21 Gillet test.

+LR	Interpretation	−LR
>10	Large	<.1
5.0-10.0	Moderate	.1-.2
2.0-5.0	Small	.2-.5
1.0-2.0	Rarely important	.5-1.0

Test and Study Quality	Description and Positive Findings	Population	Reference Standard	Sens	Spec	+LR	−LR
Gillet test[2] ○	With patient standing with feet spread 12 inches apart, examiner palpates the S2 spinous process with one thumb and the posterior superior iliac spine with the other. The patient then flexes the hip and knee on the side being tested. The test is considered positive if the PSIS fails to move in a posteroinferior direction relative to S2	85 consecutive patients with low back pain referred for sacroiliac joint blocks	90% pain relief with injection of local anesthetics into sacroiliac joint	.47*	.64*	1.31*	.83*
Gillet test[30] ○		274 patients being treated for low back pain or another condition not related to the low back	Innominate torsion calculated by measured differences in pelvic landmarks	.08	.93	1.14	.99

*Mean of chiropractor and physician sensitivity and specificity scores.

Motion Assessment

Spring Test (Joint Play Assessment)

ICC or κ	Interpretation
.81-1.0	Substantial agreement
.61-.80	Moderate agreement
.41-.60	Fair agreement
.11-.40	Slight agreement
.0-.10	No agreement

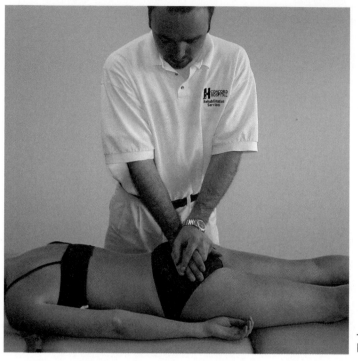

Figure 5-22 Spring test.

Test and Study	Description and Positive Findings	Population	Reliability
Spring test[18]	With patient prone, examiner uses one hand to lift the ilium while using the other hand to stabilize the sacrum and palpate the movement between the sacrum and ilium with the index finger	15 patients with ankylosing spondylitis, 30 women with postpartum pelvic pain, and 16 asymptomatic subjects	Inter-examiner κ = −.06

+LR	Interpretation	−LR
>10	Large	<.1
5.0-10.0	Moderate	.1-.2
2.0-5.0	Small	.2-.5
1.0-2.0	Rarely important	.5-1.0

Test and Study Quality	Description and Positive Findings	Population	Reference Standard	Sens	Spec	+LR	−LR
Spring test[2] ◯	Therapist's hands are placed over the superior sacrum and a posteroanterior thrust is applied while the therapist monitors the spring at the end range of motion. The asymptomatic side is compared with the symptomatic	85 consecutive patients with low back pain referred for sacroiliac joint blocks	90% pain relief with injection of local anesthetics into sacroiliac joint	.66*	.42*	1.14*	.81*

*Mean of chiropractor and physician sensitivity and specificity scores.

Motion Assessment

Long-Sit Test (Supine to Sit Test)

ICC or κ	Interpretation
.81-1.0	Substantial agreement
.61-.80	Moderate agreement
.41-.60	Fair agreement
.11-.40	Slight agreement
.0-.10	No agreement

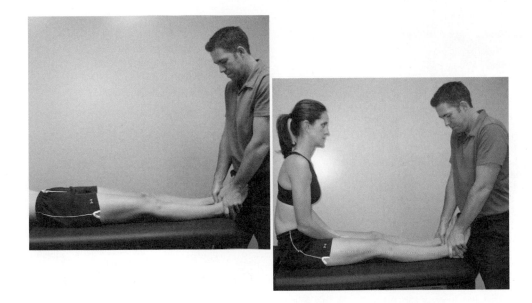

Figure 5-23 Long-sit test.

Test and Study	Description and Positive Findings	Population	Reliability
Long-sit test[1]	With patient supine, lengths of medial malleoli are compared. Patient is asked to long-sit and lengths of medial malleoli are again compared. Positive if one leg appears shorter in supine and then lengthens when the patient comes into long-sitting position	71 patients with low back pain	Inter-examiner κ = .21
Long-sit test[9]		65 patients with low back pain	Inter-examiner κ = .19

+LR	Interpretation	−LR
>10	Large	<.1
5.0-10.0	Moderate	.1-.2
2.0-5.0	Small	.2-.5
1.0-2.0	Rarely important	.5-1.0

Test and Study Quality	Description and Positive Findings	Population	Reference Standard	Sens	Spec	+LR	−LR
Long-sit test[30] ○	With patient supine, lengths of medial malleoli are compared. Patient is asked to long-sit and lengths of medial malleoli are again compared. Positive if one leg appears shorter in supine and then lengthens when the patient comes into long-sitting position	274 patients being treated for low back pain or another condition not related to the low back	Innominate torsion calculated by measured differences in pelvic landmarks	.44	.64	1.22	.88

Motion Assessment

Standing Flexion Test

ICC or κ	Interpretation
.81-1.0	Substantial agreement
.61-.80	Moderate agreement
.41-.60	Fair agreement
.11-.40	Slight agreement
.0-.10	No agreement

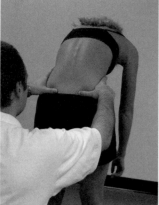

Figure 5-24 Standing flexion test.

Test and Study	Description and Positive Findings	Population	Reliability
Standing flexion test[19]		25 patients with asymmetrical low back pain	Intra-examiner* κ = [Right] **.68 (.35, 1.01)** [Left] **.61 (.27, .96)** Inter-examiner κ = [Right] **.51 (.08, .95)** [Left] **.55 (.20, .90)**
Standing flexion test[16]	With patient standing, examiner palpates inferior slope of PSIS. Patient is asked to forward bend completely. Positive for sacroiliac hypomobility if one PSIS moves more cranially than the contralateral side	24 patients with low back pain	Inter-examiner κ = **.06**
Standing flexion test[9]		65 patients currently receiving treatment for low back pain	Inter-examiner κ = **.32**
Standing flexion test[31]		14 asymptomatic graduate students	Inter-examiner κ = **.52**
Standing flexion test[10,32]		480 male construction workers; 50 had low back pain the day of the examination; 236 reported experiencing low back pain within the past 12 months	Inter-examiner κ values ranged from **.31-.67**
Standing flexion test[1]		71 patients with low back pain	Inter-examiner κ = **.08**

*Intra-examiner reliability reported for examiner #1 only.
Potter and Rothstein[17] also studied this test, but were excluded because they only reported percent agreement.

+LR	Interpretation	−LR
>10	Large	<.1
5.0-10.0	Moderate	.1-.2
2.0-5.0	Small	.2-.5
1.0-2.0	Rarely important	.5-1.0

Test and Study Quality	Description and Positive Findings	Population	Reference Standard	Sens	Spec	+LR	−LR
Standing flexion test[30] ○	with patient standing, examiner palpates inferior slope of PSIS. Patient is asked to forward bend completely. Positive for sacroiliac hypomobility if one PSIS moves more cranially than the contralateral side	274 patients being treated for low back pain or another condition not related to the low back	Innominate torsion calculated by measured differences in pelvic landmarks	.17	.79	.81	1.05

Motion Assessment

Sitting Flexion Test

ICC or κ	Interpretation
.81-1.0	Substantial agreement
.61-.80	Moderate agreement
.41-.60	Fair agreement
.11-.40	Slight agreement
.0-.10	No agreement

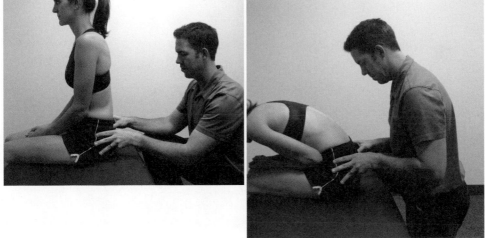

Figure 5-25 Sitting flexion test.

Test and Study	Description and Positive Findings	Population	Reliability
Sitting flexion test[19]	With patient sitting, examiner palpates inferior slope of PSIS. Patient is asked to forward bend completely. Positive for sacroiliac hypomobility if one PSIS moves more cranially than the contralateral side	25 patients with asymmetrical low back pain	Intra-examiner* κ = [Right] **.73 (.45, 1.01)** [Left] **.65 (.34, .96)** Inter-examiner κ = [Right] **.75 (.42, 1.08)** [Left] **.64 (.32, .96)**
Sitting flexion test[1]		71 patients with low back pain	Inter-examiner κ = **.21**
Sitting flexion test[16]		24 patients with low back pain	Inter-examiner κ = **.06**

*Intra-examiner reliability reported for examiner #1 only.

+LR	Interpretation	−LR
>10	Large	<.1
5.0-10.0	Moderate	.1-.2
2.0-5.0	Small	.2-.5
1.0-2.0	Rarely important	.5-1.0

Test and Study Quality	Description and Positive Findings	Population	Reference Standard	Sens	Spec	+LR	−LR
Sitting flexion test[30] ○	With patient seated, examiner palpates inferior aspect of each PSIS. Positive for sacroiliac joint dysfunction if inequality of PSIS is found	274 patients being treated for low back pain or another condition not related to the low back	Innominate torsion calculated by measured differences in pelvic landmarks	.09	.93	1.29	.98

ICC or κ	Interpretation
.81-1.0	Substantial agreement
.61-.80	Moderate agreement
.41-.60	Fair agreement
.11-.40	Slight agreement
.0-.10	No agreement

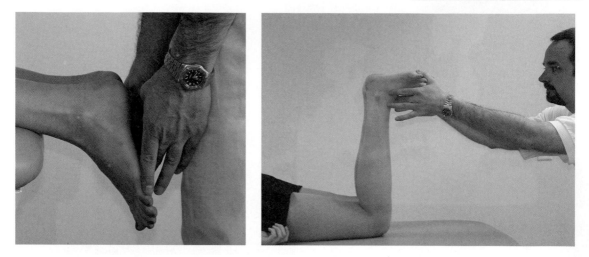

Figure 5-26 Prone knee bend test.

Test and Study	Description and Positive Findings	Population	Reliability
Prone knee bend[19]	With patient prone, examiner, looking at heels, assesses leg lengths. Knees are passively flexed to 90° and leg lengths are again assessed. Considered positive if a change in leg lengths occurs between positions	25 patients with asymmetrical low back pain	Intra-examiner* κ = [Right] **.41** (.07, .78) [Left] **.27** (−.22, .78) Inter-examiner κ = [Right] **.58** (.25, .91) [Left] **.33** (−.18, .85)
Prone knee bend[1]		71 patients with low back pain	Inter-examiner κ = **.21**
Prone knee bend[9]		65 patients with low back pain	Inter-examiner κ = **.26**

*Intra-examiner reliability reported for examiner #1 only.
Potter and Rothstein[17] also studied this test, but were excluded because they only reported percent agreement.

Other Motion Assessment Tests

Test and Study	Description and Positive Findings	Population	Reliability
Click-clack test[13]	With patient sitting and examiner's thumbs on caudal PSIS, the patient rocks pelvis forward and backward. Test is positive if one PSIS moves slower from cranial to caudal than the other	62 women recruited from obstetrics: 42 pregnant with pelvic girdle pain and 20 who were not pregnant and were asymptomatic	Inter-examiner κ = **.03**
Heel-bank test[13]	With patient sitting and examiner's thumbs on caudal PSIS, the patient raises one leg at a time and places the heel on the bench without using hands. Considered positive if the test required any effort		Inter-examiner κ = [Right] **.32** [Left] **.16**
Abduction test[13]	With patient side-lying with hips flexed 70° and knees flexed 90°, the patient is asked to lift the top leg about 20 cm. Considered positive if the test required any effort		Inter-examiner κ = [Right] **.61** [Left] **.41**

Combinations of Tests

Test and Study Quality	Description and Positive Findings	Population	Reference Standard	Sens	Spec	+LR	−LR
Mennell's test + Gaenslen's test + Thigh thrust[20] ◇	Procedures all previously described in this chapter. At least 2 of 3 tests need to be positive to indicate sacroiliitis	40 patients with chronic low back pain	**Right side**				
			Sacroiliitis apparent on MRI	.55 (.22, .84)	.83 (.65, .93)	3.44 (1.27, 9.29)	.52 (.25, 1.11)
			Left side				
				.45 (.18, .75)	.86 (.67, .95)	3.29 (1.07, 10.0)	.63 (.36, 1.09)
Distraction + Thigh thrust + Gaenslen's test + Patrick sign + Compression[33] ◇	Procedures all previously described in this chapter. At least 3 of 5 tests need to be positive to indicate sacroiliac joint pain	60 patients with chronic low back pain referred to pain clinic	50% pain relief with injection of local anesthetics into sacroiliac joint	.85 (.72, .99)	.79 (.65, .93)	4.02 (2.04, 7.89)	.19 (.07, .47)
Distraction + Thigh thrust + Sacral thrust + Compression[4] ◇	Procedures all previously described in this chapter. At least 2 of 4 tests need to be positive to indicate sacroiliac joint pain	48 patients with chronic lumbopelvic pain referred for sacroiliac joint injection	80% pain relief with injection of local anesthetics into sacroiliac joint	.88 (.64, .97)	.78 (.61, .89)	4.0 (2.13, 8.08)	.16 (.04, .47)
Distraction + Thigh thrust + Gaenslen's test + Sacral thrust + Compression[5] ◇	Procedures all previously described in this chapter. At least 3 of 5 tests need to be positive to indicate sacroiliac joint pain	48 patients with chronic lumbopelvic pain referred for diagnostic spinal injection	80% pain relief with injection of local anesthetics into sacroiliac joint	.91 (.62, −.98)	.78 (.61, .89)	4.16 (2.16, 8.39)	.12 (.02, .49)

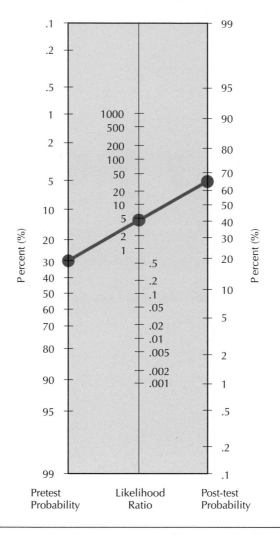

Figure 5-27 Nomogram representing the changes from pretest to post-test probability using the cluster of tests for detecting sacroiliac dysfunction. Considering a 33% pretest probability and a +LR of 4.16, the post-test probability that the patient presents with sacroiliac dysfunction is 67%. (*Adapted with permission from Fagan TJ. Nomogram for Bayes' theorem.* N Engl J Med. 1975;293-257. *Massachusetts Medical Society, 2005.*)

Combinations of Tests

Following the McKenzie Evaluation to Rule out Discogenic Pain

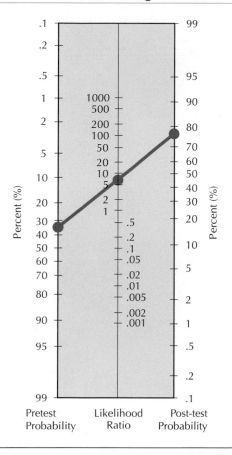

Figure 5-28 Nomogram representing the changes from pretest to post-test probability using the above cluster of tests for detecting sacroiliac pain following the exclusion of patients determined to have pain of discogenic origin as determined by a McKenzie assessment. Considering a 33% pretest probability and a +LR of 6.97, the post-test probability that the patient presents with sacroiliac pain is 77%. *(Adapted with permission from Fagan TJ. Nomogram for Bayes' theorem.* N Engl J Med. 1975;293-257. Massachusetts Medical Society, 2005.)

Laslett and associates[5] assessed the diagnostic utility of the McKenzie method of mechanical assessment combined with the following sacroiliac tests: *distraction, thigh thrust, Gaenslen, sacral thrust,* and *compression.* The McKenzie assessment consisted of flexion in standing, extension in standing, right and left side gliding, flexion in lying, and extension in lying. The movements were repeated in sets of 10, and centralization and peripheralization were recorded. If it was determined that repeated movements resulted in centralization, the patient was considered to have pain of discogenic origin. Following the use of the McKenzie method to rule out individuals presenting with discogenic pain, in terms of diagnostic utility, the cluster of these tests exhibited a sensitivity of .91 (95% CI .62, .98), specificity .87 (95% CI .68, .96), +LR of 6.97 (95% CI 2.16, 8.39), −LR .11 (95% CI .02, .44).

Identifying Patients Likely to Benefit from Spinal Manipulation

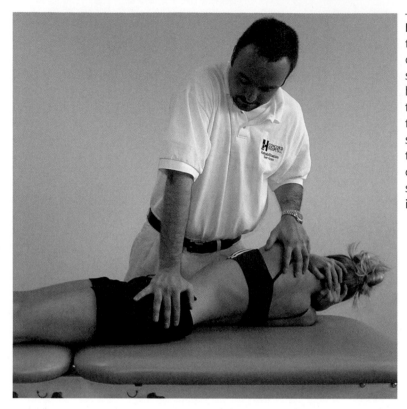

Figure 5-29 Spinal manipulation technique used by Flynn and colleagues. The patient is passively sidebent toward the side to be manipulated (away from the therapist). The therapist then rotates the patient away from the side to be manipulated (toward the therapist) and delivers a quick thrust through the anterior superior iliac spine in a postero-inferior direction.

Flynn and colleagues[1] investigated the effects of spinal manipulation technique in a heterogeneous population of patients with low back pain. They identified a number of variables that were associated with a successful outcome following the manipulation. A logistics regression equation was used to identify a cluster of signs and symptoms leading to a clinical prediction rule that could significantly enhance the likelihood of identifying patients who will achieve a successful outcome with spinal manipulation. Five variables formed the clinical prediction rule (below).

Childs and colleagues[34] tested the validity of the clinical prediction rule when applied in a separate patient population and by a variety of clinicians with varying levels of clinical experience and practicing in different settings. Consecutive patients with low back pain were randomized to receive either spinal manipulation or a lumbar stabilization program. The results of the study demonstrated that patients who satisfied the clinical prediction rule and received spinal manipulation had significantly better outcomes than patients who did not meet the clinical prediction rule but still received spinal manipulation and the group who met the clinical prediction rule but received lumbar stabilization exercises.

To make use of the clinical prediction rule more practical in a primary care environment, Fritz and colleagues[35] tested an abbreviated version consisting of only the acuity and symptom location factors. Ninety-two percent of patients with low back pain that met both criteria had successful outcomes. The results of the Childs and colleagues[34] and Fritz and associates[35] studies support the findings of Flynn and colleagues[1] and significantly increase clinician confidence in using the clinical prediction rule in decision-making regarding individual patients with low back pain.

Interventions

Test and Study Quality	Description and Criteria	Population	Reference Standard	Sens	Spec	+LR
Symptoms < 16 days + No symptoms distal to the knee + Hypomobility in the lumbar spine + FABQ work subscale score < 19 + At least 1 hip with > 35° internal rotation ROM[1] ◇	At least 4 of 5 tests needed to be positive	71 patients with low back pain	≥ 50% reduction in back pain related disability within 1 week as measured by the Oswestry questionnaire	.63 (.45-.77)	.97 (.87-1.0)	24.38 (4.63-139.41)
Symptoms < 16 days + No symptoms distal to the knee[35] ◇	Must meet both criteria	141 patients with low back pain		.56 (.43, .67)	.92 (.84, .96)	7.2 (3.2, 16.1)

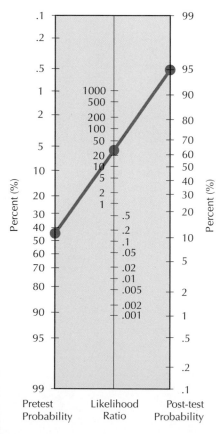

Pretest Probability — Likelihood Ratio — Post-test Probability

Figure 5-30 Nomogram representing the changes from pretest to post-test likelihood that a patient with low back pain, who satisfies four of five criteria for the rule, will have a successful outcome following spinal manipulation. The pretest likelihood that any patient with low back pain would respond favorably to sacroiliac manipulation was determined to be 45%. However, if the patient presents with four of the five predictor variables identified by Flynn and colleagues[1] (+LR 24), then the post-test probability that the patient will respond positively to spinal manipulation increases dramatically to 95%. *(Adapted with permission from Fagan TJ. Nomogram for Bayes' theorem. N Engl J Med. 1975;293-257. Massachusetts Medical Society, 2005.)*

Outcome Measure	Scoring and Interpretation	Test-Retest Reliability	MCID
Oswestry Disability Index (ODI)	Users are asked to rate the difficulty of performing 10 functional tasks on a scale of 0 to 5 with different descriptors for each task. A total score out of 100 is calculated by summing each score and doubling the total. The answers provide a score between 0 and 100, with higher scores representing more disability	ICC = .91[36]	11[37]
Modified Oswestry Disability Index (modified ODI)	As above except replaces the sex life question with an employment/homemaking question	ICC = .90[38]	6[38]
Roland-Morris Disability Questionnaire (R-M)	Users are asked to answer 23 or 24 (depending on the version) questions about their back pain and related disability. The RMDQ is scored by adding up the number of items checked by the patient, with higher numbers indicating more disability	ICC = .91[39]	5[37]
Fear-Avoidance Beliefs Questionnaire (FABQ)	Users are asked to rate their level of agreement with statements concerning beliefs about the relationship between physical activity, work, and their back pain. Level of agreement is answered on a Likert-type scale ranging from 0 (completely disagree) to 7 (completely agree). The FABQ is made of 2 parts: a 7-item work subscale (FABQW), and a 4-item physical activity subscale (FABQPA). Each scale is scored separately, with higher scores representing higher fear-avoidance	FABQW: ICC = .82 FABQPA: ICC = .66[40]	Not Available
Numeric Pain Rating Scale (NPRS)	Users rate their level of pain on an 11-point scale ranging from 0 to 10, with high scores representing more pain. Often asked as current pain and least, worst, and average pain in the past 24 hours	ICCs = .72[41]	2[42,43]

MCID, Minimum clinically important difference.

Quality Assessment of Diagnostic Studies for the Sacroiliac Region Using QUADAS

	Russel 1981	Blower 1984	Dreyfuss 1996	Broadhurst 1998	Levangie 1999	Laslett 2003	Laslett 2005	van der Wurff 2006	Jung 2007	Ozgocmen 2008	Flynn 2002	Fritz 2005
1. Was the spectrum of patients representative of the patients who will receive the test in practice?	U	Y	Y	Y	Y	Y	Y	Y	N	Y	Y	Y
2. Were selection criteria clearly described?	N	N	N	Y	Y	Y	Y	Y	Y	Y	Y	Y
3. Is the reference standard likely to correctly classify the target condition?	Y	Y	Y	Y	Y	Y	Y	Y	U	Y	Y	Y
4. Is the time period between reference standard and index test short enough to be reasonably sure that the target condition did not change between the two tests?	U	U	U	Y	U	Y	Y	Y	U	Y	Y	Y
5. Did the whole sample or a random selection of the sample, receive verification using a reference standard of diagnosis?	Y	U	Y	Y	Y	Y	Y	Y	Y	Y	Y	Y
6. Did patients receive the same reference standard regardless of the index test result?	U	U	Y	N	Y	Y	Y	Y	Y	Y	Y	Y
7. Was the reference standard independent of the index test (i.e., the index test did not form part of the reference standard)?	Y	Y	Y	Y	Y	Y	Y	Y	Y	Y	Y	Y
8. Was the execution of the index test described in sufficient detail to permit replication of the test?	Y	N	Y	Y	Y	Y	Y	Y	N	Y	Y	Y
9. Was the execution of the reference standard described in sufficient detail to permit its replication?	N	U	Y	Y	Y	Y	Y	Y	Y	Y	Y	Y
10. Were the index test results interpreted without knowledge of the results of the reference test?	U	N	Y	Y	N	Y	Y	Y	U	Y	Y	Y
11. Were the reference standard results interpreted without knowledge of the results fo the index test?	U	U	U	N	Y	Y	Y	Y	U	U	Y	U
12. Were the same clinical data available when test results were interpreted as would be available when the test is used in practice?	U	Y	U	N	N	Y	Y	N	U	N	Y	Y
13. Were uninterpretable/intermediate test results reported?	N	U	Y	Y	Y	Y	Y	Y	N	Y	Y	Y
14. Were withdrawals from the study explained?	U	Y	Y	Y	Y	Y	Y	Y	Y	Y	Y	U
Quality summary rating:	▪	▪	◯	◯	◯	◇	◇	◇	▪	◇	◇	◇

Y = yes, N = no, U = unclear.   ◇ Good quality (Y - N = 10 to 14).   ◯ Fair quality (Y - N = 5 to 9).   ▪ Poor quality (Y - N ≤ 4).

1. Flynn T, Fritz J, Whitman J, et al. A clinical prediction rule for classifying patients with low back pain who demonstrate short-term improvement with spinal manipulation. *Spine.* 2002;27:2835-2843.

2. Dreyfuss P, Michaelsen M, Pauza K, et al. The value of medical history and physical examination in diagnosing sacroiliac joint pain. *Spine.* 1996;21:2594-2602.

3. Laslett M. Pain provocation tests for diagnosis of sacroiliac joint pain. *Aust J Physiother.* 2006;52:229.

4. Laslett M, Aprill CN, McDonald B, Young SB. Diagnosis of sacroiliac joint pain: validity of individual provocation tests and composites of tests. *Man Ther.* 2005;10:207-218.

5. Laslett M, Young SB, Aprill CN, McDonald B. Diagnosing painful sacroiliac joints: a validity study of a McKenzie evaluation and sacroiliac provocation tests. *Aust J Physiother.* 2003;49:89-97.

6. Maigne JY, Aivaliklis A, Pfefer F. Results of sacroiliac joint double block and value of sacroiliac pain provocation tests in 54 patients with low back pain. *Spine.* 1996;21:1889-1892.

7. Schwarzer AC, Aprill CN, Bogduk N. The sacroiliac joint in chronic low back pain. *Spine.* 1995;20:31-37.

8. Cibulka MT, Delitto A, Koldehoff RM. Changes in innominate tilt after manipulation of the sacroiliac joint in patients with low back pain. An experimental study. *Phys Ther.* 1988;68:1359-1363.

9. Riddle DL, Freburger JK. Evaluation of the presence of sacroiliac joint region dysfunction using a combination of tests: a multicenter intertester reliability study. *Phys Ther.* 2002;82:772-781.

10. Toussaint R, Gawlik CS, Rehder U, Ruther W. Sacroiliac dysfunction in construction workers. *J Manipulative Physiol Ther.* 1999;22:134-138.

11. Jung JH, Kim HI, Shin DA, et al. Usefulness of pain distribution pattern assessment in decision-making for the patients with lumbar zygapophyseal and sacroiliac joint arthropathy. *J Korean Med Sci.* 2007;22:1048-1054.

12. van der Wurff P, Buijs EJ, Groen GJ. Intensity mapping of pain referral areas in sacroiliac joint pain patients. *J Manipulative Physiol Ther.* 2006;29:190-195.

13. van Kessel-Cobelens AM, Verhagen AP, Mens JM, et al. Pregnancy-related pelvic girdle pain: intertester reliability of 3 tests to determine asymmetric mobility of the sacroiliac joints. *J Manipulative Physiol Ther.* 2008;31:130-136.

14. O'Haire C, Gibbons P. Inter-examiner and intra-examiner agreement for assessing sacroiliac anatomical landmarks using palpation and observation: pilot study. *Man Ther.* 2000;5:13-20.

15. Holmgren U, Waling K. Inter-examiner reliability of four static palpation tests used for assessing pelvic dysfunction. *Man Ther.* 2008;13:50-56.

16. Tong HC, Heyman OG, Lado DA, Isser MM. Interexaminer reliability of three methods of combining test results to determine side of sacral restriction, sacral base position, and innominate bone position. *J Am Osteopath Assoc.* 2006;106:464-468.

17. Potter NA, Rothstein JM. Intertester reliability for selected clinical tests of the sacroiliac joint. *Phys Ther.* 1985;65:1671-1675.

18. Robinson HS, Brox JI, Robinson R, et al. The reliability of selected motion- and pain provocation tests for the sacroiliac joint. *Man Ther.* 2007;12:72-79.

19. Arab AM, Abdollahi I, Joghataei MT, et al. Inter- and intra-examiner reliability of single and composites of selected motion palpation and pain provocation tests for sacroiliac joint. *Man Ther.* 2009;14:213-221.

20. Ozgocmen S, Bozgeyik Z, Kalcik M, Yildirim A. The value of sacroiliac pain provocation tests in early active sacroiliitis. *Clin Rheumatol.* 2008;10:1275-1282.

21. Kokmeyer DJ, van der Wurff P, Aufdemkampe G, Fickenscher TC. The reliability of multitest regimens with sacroiliac pain provocation tests. *J Manipulative Physiol Ther.* 2002;25:42-48.

22. Broadhurst NA, Bond MJ. Pain provocation tests for the assessment of sacroiliac joint dysfunction. *J Spinal Disord.* 1998;11:341-345.

23. Laslett M, Williams M. The reliability of selected pain provocation tests for sacroiliac joint pathology. *Spine.* 1994;19:1243-1249.

24. Russel AS, Maksymowych W, LeClercq S. Clinical examination of the sacroiliac joints: a prospective study. *Arthritis Rheum.* 1981;24:1575-1577.

25. Blower PW, Griffin AJ. Clinical sacroiliac tests in ankylosing spondylitis and other causes of low back pain—2 studies. *Ann Rheum Dis.* 1984;43:192-195.

26. Carmichael JP. Inter- and intra-examiner reliability of palpation for sacroiliac joint dysfunction. *J Manipulative Physiol Ther.* 1987;10:164-171.

27. Meijne W, van Neerbos K, Aufdemkampe G, van der Wurff P. Intraexaminer and interexaminer reliability of the Gillet test. *J Manipulative Physiol Ther.* 1999;22:4-9.

28. Hungerford BA, Gilleard W, Moran M, Emmerson C. Evaluation of the ability of physical therapists to palpate intrapelvic motion with the Stork test on the support side. *Phys Ther.* 2007;87:879-887.

29. Herzog W, Read LJ, Conway PJ, et al. Reliability of motion palpation procedures to detect sacroiliac joint fixations. *J Manipulative Physiol Ther.* 1989;12:86-92.

30. Levangie PK. Four clinical tests of sacroiliac joint dysfunction: the association of test results with innominate torsion among patients with and without low back pain. *Phys Ther.* 1999;79:1043-1057.

31. Vincent-Smith B, Gibbons P. Inter-examiner and intra-examiner reliability of the standing flexion test. *Man Ther.* 1999;4:87-93.

32. Toussaint R, Gawlik CS, Rehder U, Ruther W. Sacroiliac joint diagnostics in the Hamburg Construction

Workers Study. *J Manipulative Physiol Ther*. 1999; 22:139-143.

33. van der Wurff P, Buijs EJ, Groen GJ. A multitest regimen of pain provocation tests as an aid to reduce unnecessary minimally invasive sacroiliac joint procedures. *Arch Phys Med Rehabil*. 2006;87:10-14.

34. Childs JD, Fritz JM, Flynn TW, et al. A clinical prediction rule to identify patients with low back pain most likely to benefit from spinal manipulation: a validation study. *Ann Intern Med*. 2004;141:920-928.

35. Fritz JM, Childs JD, Flynn TW. Pragmatic application of a clinical prediction rule in primary care to identify patients with low back pain with a good prognosis following a brief spinal manipulation intervention. *BMC Fam Pract*. 2005;6:29.

36. Lauridsen HH, Hartvigsen J, Manniche C, et al. Danish version of the Oswestry Disability Index for patients with low back pain. Part 1: Cross-cultural adaptation, reliability and validity in two different populations. *Eur Spine J*. 2006;15:1705-1716.

37. Lauridsen HH, Hartvigsen J, Manniche C, et al. Responsiveness and minimal clinically important difference for pain and disability instruments in low back pain patients. *BMC Musculoskelet Disord*. 2006;7:82.

38. Fritz JM, Irrgang JJ. A Comparison of a Modified Oswestry Disability Questionnaire and the Quebec Back Pain Disability Scale. *Phys Ther*. 2001;81:776-788.

39. Brouwer S, Kuijer W, Dijkstra PU, et al. Reliability and stability of the Roland Morris Disability Questionnaire: intra class correlation and limits of agreement. *Disabil Rehabil*. 2004;26:162-165.

40. Grotle M, Brox JI, Vollestad NK. Reliability, validity and responsiveness of the fear-avoidance beliefs questionnaire: methodological aspects of the Norwegian version. *J Rehabil Med*. 2006;38:346-353.

41. Li L, Liu X, Herr K. Postoperative pain intensity assessment: a comparison of four scales in Chinese adults. *Pain Med*. 2007;8:223-234.

42. Farrar JT, Berlin JA, Strom BL. Clinically important changes in acute pain outcome measures: a validation study. *J Pain Symptom Manage*. 2003;25:406-411.

43. Farrar JT, Portenoy RK, Berlin JA, et al. Defining the clinically important difference in pain outcome measures. *Pain*. 2000;88:287-294.

Hip and Pelvis

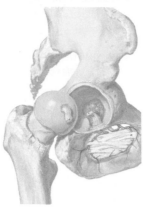

CLINICAL SUMMARY AND RECOMMENDATIONS

Patient History

Complaints
- Several complaints appear to be useful in identifying specific hip pathologies. A subjective complaint of "clicking in the hip" is strongly associated with acetabular labral tears.

- Reports of "constant low back/buttock pain" and "ipsilateral groin pain" are moderately helpful in diagnosing osteoarthritis (OA) of the hip.

Physical Examination

Range of Motion
- Measuring hip range of motion (ROM) has consistently been shown to be highly reliable and when limited in three planes can be fairly useful in identifying hip OA (+LR = 4.5 to 4.7).

- Assessing pain during ROM can be helpful in identifying both OA and lateral tendon pathology. Lateral hip pain during passive abduction is strongly suggestive of lateral tendon pathology (+LR = 8.3), whereas groin pain during active hip abduction or adduction is moderately suggestive of OA (+LR = 5.7).

- Limited hip abduction in infants can also be very helpful in identifying hip dysplasia or instability.

Strength Assessment
- Assessment of hip muscle strength has been shown to be fairly reliable, but appears to be less helpful in identifying lateral tendon pathologies than reports of pain during resisted tests, especially of the gluteus minimus and medius (+LR = 3.27).

- Similarly, a report of posterior pain with a squat is also fairly useful in identifying hip OA (+LR = 6.1).

- Although less reliable than strength tests, the Trendelenburg test is also moderately useful in identifying both lateral tendon pathologies and gluteus medius tears (+LR = 3.2 to 3.6).

Special Tests
- Generally special tests of the hip have not been demonstrated to be especially helpful in identifying specific hip pathologies. Not the Patrick's test (FABER), the flexion-internal rotation-adduction (FADIR) test, or the scour test appear to have much diagnostic utility.

- One exception is the patellar-pubic-percussion test, which is very good at detecting and ruling out hip fractures (+LR = 6.7 to 21.6, −LR = .07 to .14).

Combinations of Findings
- Patients with at least four of five signs and symptoms (*squatting aggravates symptoms, lateral pain with active hip flexion, scour test with adduction causes lateral hip or groin pain, pain with active hip extension, and passive internal rotation ≤ 25°*) are highly likely to have hip OA.

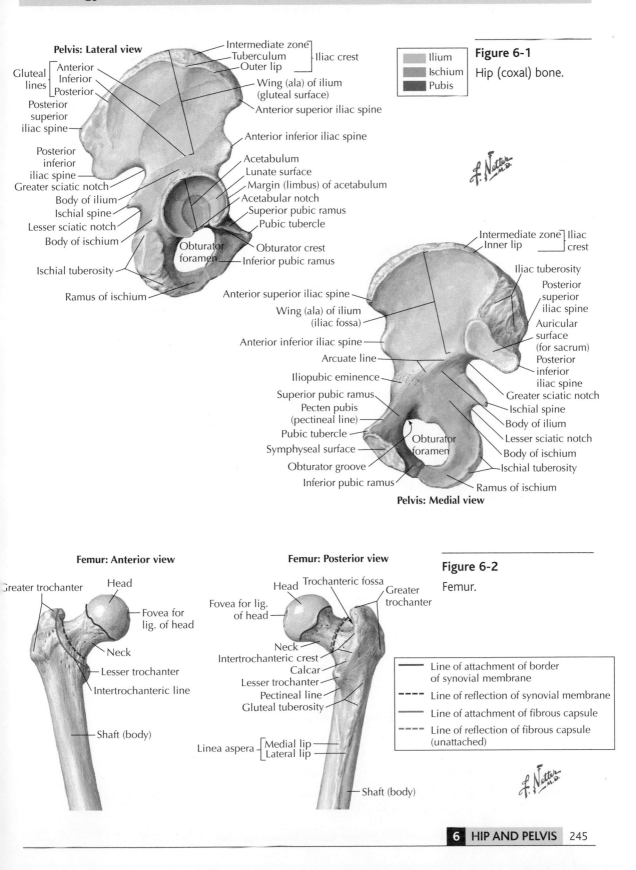

Pelvis: Lateral view

Gluteal lines
- Anterior
- Inferior
- Posterior

Intermediate zone
Tuberculum
Outer lip
} Iliac crest

Posterior superior iliac spine

Wing (ala) of ilium (gluteal surface)

Anterior superior iliac spine

Anterior inferior iliac spine

Posterior inferior iliac spine

Acetabulum
Lunate surface
Margin (limbus) of acetabulum
Acetabular notch
Superior pubic ramus
Pubic tubercle

Greater sciatic notch
Body of ilium
Ischial spine
Lesser sciatic notch
Body of ischium

Obturator foramen

Obturator crest
Inferior pubic ramus

Ischial tuberosity

Ramus of ischium

Ilium
Ischium
Pubis

Figure 6-1

Hip (coxal) bone.

Intermediate zone
Inner lip
} Iliac crest

Iliac tuberosity

Posterior superior iliac spine

Auricular surface (for sacrum)

Posterior inferior iliac spine

Greater sciatic notch
Ischial spine
Body of ilium
Lesser sciatic notch
Body of ischium
Ischial tuberosity
Ramus of ischium

Anterior superior iliac spine

Wing (ala) of ilium (iliac fossa)

Anterior inferior iliac spine
Arcuate line
Iliopubic eminence
Superior pubic ramus
Pecten pubis (pectineal line)
Pubic tubercle
Symphyseal surface
Obturator groove
Inferior pubic ramus

Obturator foramen

Pelvis: Medial view

Femur: Anterior view

Greater trochanter
Head
Fovea for lig. of head
Neck
Lesser trochanter
Intertrochanteric line
Shaft (body)

Femur: Posterior view

Head
Trochanteric fossa
Greater trochanter
Fovea for lig. of head
Neck
Intertrochanteric crest
Calcar
Lesser trochanter
Pectineal line
Gluteal tuberosity

Linea aspera
- Medial lip
- Lateral lip

Shaft (body)

Figure 6-2

Femur.

⎯⎯⎯	Line of attachment of border of synovial membrane
- - - -	Line of reflection of synovial membrane
——	Line of attachment of fibrous capsule
- - - -	Line of reflection of fibrous capsule (unattached)

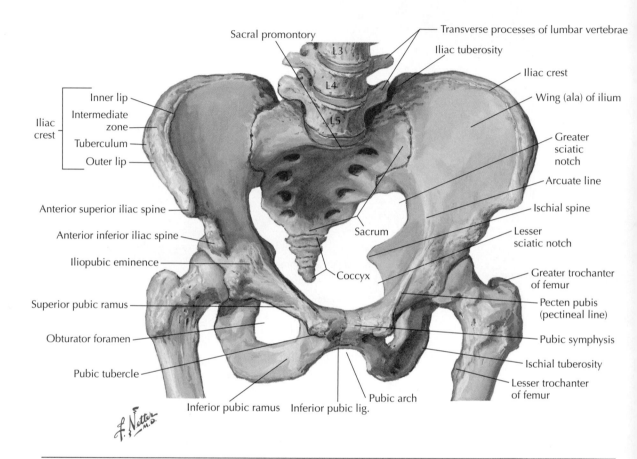

Figure 6-3

Hip and pelvis joints.

Joint	Type and Classification	Closed Packed Position	Capsular Pattern
Femoroacetabular	Synovial: Spheroidal	Full extension, some internal rotation, and abduction	Internal rotation and abduction > flexion and extension
Pubic symphysis	Amphiarthrodial	Not applicable	Not applicable
Sacroiliac	Synovial: Plane	Not documented	Not documented

Ligaments

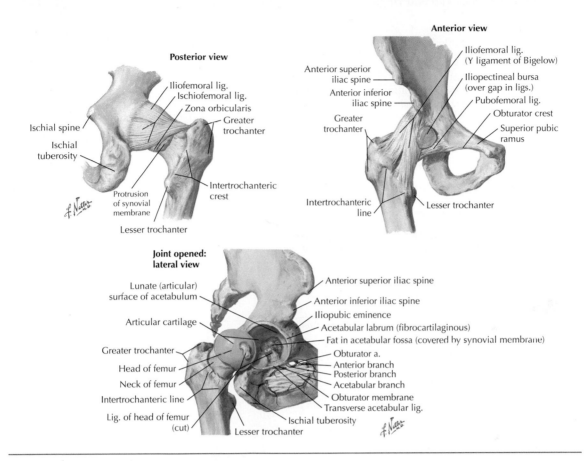

Posterior view

- Iliofemoral lig.
- Ischiofemoral lig.
- Zona orbicularis
- Greater trochanter
- Ischial spine
- Ischial tuberosity
- Protrusion of synovial membrane
- Intertrochanteric crest
- Lesser trochanter

Anterior view

- Anterior superior iliac spine
- Anterior inferior iliac spine
- Greater trochanter
- Iliofemoral lig. (Y ligament of Bigelow)
- Iliopectineal bursa (over gap in ligs.)
- Pubofemoral lig.
- Obturator crest
- Superior pubic ramus
- Intertrochanteric line
- Lesser trochanter

Joint opened: lateral view

- Lunate (articular) surface of acetabulum
- Articular cartilage
- Greater trochanter
- Head of femur
- Neck of femur
- Intertrochanteric line
- Lig. of head of femur (cut)
- Lesser trochanter
- Anterior superior iliac spine
- Anterior inferior iliac spine
- Iliopubic eminence
- Acetabular labrum (fibrocartilaginous)
- Fat in acetabular fossa (covered by synovial membrane)
- Obturator a.
- Anterior branch
- Posterior branch
- Acetabular branch
- Obturator membrane
- Transverse acetabular lig.
- Ischial tuberosity

Figure 6-4
Ligaments of the hip and pelvis.

Hip Ligaments	Attachments	Function
Iliofemoral	Anterior inferior iliac spine to intertrochanteric line of femur	Limits hip extension
Ischiofemoral	Posterior inferior acetabulum to apex of greater tubercle	Limits internal rotation, external rotation, and extension
Pubofemoral	Obturator crest of pubic bone to blend with capsule of hip and iliofemoral ligament	Limits hip hyperabduction
Ligament of head of femur	Margin of acetabular notch and transverse acetabular ligament to head of femur	Carries blood supply to head of femur
Pubic Symphysis Ligaments	**Attachments**	**Function**
Superior pubic ligament	Connects superior aspect of right and left pubic crests	Reinforces superior aspect of joint
Inferior pubic ligament	Connects inferior aspect of right and left pubic crests	Reinforces inferior aspect of joint
Posterior pubic ligament	Connects posterior aspect of right and left pubic crests	Reinforces inferior aspect of joint

Muscles

Posterior Muscles of Hip and Thigh

Muscle	Proximal Attachment	Distal Attachment	Nerve and Segmental Level	Action
Gluteus maximus	Posterior border of ilium, dorsal aspect of sacrum and coccyx, and sacrotuberous ligament	Iliotibial tract of fascia lata and gluteal tuberosity of femur	Inferior gluteal nerve (L5, S1, S2)	Extension, external rotation, and some abduction of the hip joint
Gluteus medius	External superior border of ilium and gluteal aponeurosis	Lateral aspect of greater trochanter of femur	Superior gluteal nerve (L5, S1)	Hip abduction and internal rotation; maintains level pelvis in single limb stance
Gluteus minimus	External surface of ilium and margin of greater sciatic notch	Anterior aspect of greater trochanter of femur		
Piriformis	Anterior aspect of sacrum and sacrotuberous ligament	Superior greater trochanter of femur	Ventral rami S1, S2	External rotation of extended hip, abduction of flexed hip, steady femoral head in acetabulum
Superior gemellus	Ischial spine	Trochanteric fossa of femur	Nerve to obturator internus (L5, S1)	
Inferior gemellus	Ischial tuberosity		Nerve to quadratus femoris (L5, S1)	
Obturator internus	Internal surface of obturator membrane, border of obturator foramen		Nerve to obturator internus (L5, S1)	
Quadratus femoris	Lateral border of ischial tuberosity	Quadrate tubercle of femur	Nerve to quadratus femoris (L5, S1)	Lateral rotation of hip; steadies femoral head in acetabulum
Hamstrings				
Semitendinosus	Ischial tuberosity	Superomedial aspect of tibia	Tibial division of sciatic nerve (L5, S1, S2)	Hip extension, knee flexion, medial rotation of knee in knee flexion
Semimembranosus		Posterior aspect of medial condyle of tibia		
Biceps femoris	Long head: ischial tuberosity Short head: linea aspera and lateral supracondylar line of femur	Lateral aspect of head of fibula, lateral condyle of tibia	Long head: tibial division of sciatic nerve (L5, S1, S2) Short head: common fibular division of sciatic nerve (L5, S1, S2)	Knee flexion, hip extension, and knee external rotation when knee is flexed

Posterior Muscles of Hip and Thigh

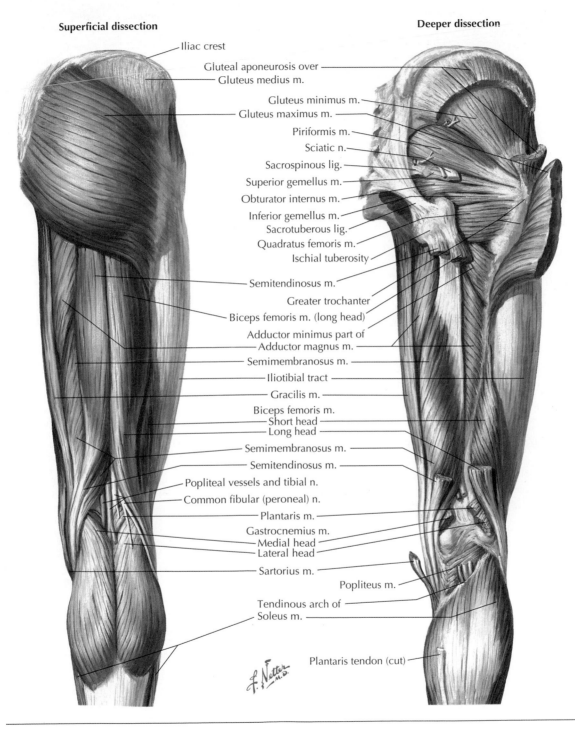

Superficial dissection

Deeper dissection

Iliac crest

Gluteal aponeurosis over
Gluteus medius m.

Gluteus minimus m.

Gluteus maximus m.

Piriformis m.

Sciatic n.

Sacrospinous lig.

Superior gemellus m.

Obturator internus m.

Inferior gemellus m.

Sacrotuberous lig.

Quadratus femoris m.

Ischial tuberosity

Semitendinosus m.

Greater trochanter

Biceps femoris m. (long head)

Adductor minimus part of
Adductor magnus m.

Semimembranosus m.

Iliotibial tract

Gracilis m.

Biceps femoris m.
Short head
Long head

Semimembranosus m.

Semitendinosus m.

Popliteal vessels and tibial n.

Common fibular (peroneal) n.

Plantaris m.

Gastrocnemius m.
Medial head
Lateral head

Sartorius m.

Popliteus m.

Tendinous arch of
Soleus m.

Plantaris tendon (cut)

Figure 6-5

Muscles of hip and thigh: posterior views.

Muscles

Anterior Muscles of Hip and Thigh

Muscle	Proximal Attachment	Distal Attachment	Nerve and Segmental Level	Action
Psoas				
Major	Lumbar transverse processes	Lesser trochanter of femur	L1-4	Flexes the hip, assists with external rotation and abduction
Minor	Lateral bodies of T12-L1	Iliopectineal eminence, and arcuate line of ileum	L1-2	Flexion of pelvis on lumbar spine
Iliacus	Superior iliac fossa, iliac crest and ala of sacrum	Lateral tendon of psoas major and distal to lesser trochanter	Femoral nerve (L1-4)	Flexes the hip, assists with external rotation and abduction
Adductors				
Longus	Inferior to pubic crest	Middle third of linea aspera of femur	Obturator nerve (L2, L3, L4)	Hip adduction
Brevis	Inferior ramus of pubis	Pectineal line and proximal linea aspera of femur	Obturator nerve (L2, L3, L4)	Hip adduction and assists with hip extension
Magnus	Adductor part: inferior pubic ramus, ramus of ischium Hamstring part: ischial tuberosity	Adductor part: gluteal tuberosity, linea aspera, medial supracondylar line Hamstring part: adductor tubercle of femur	Adductor part: obturator nerve (L2, L3, L4) Hamstring part: tibial part of sciatic nerve (L4)	Hip adduction Adductor part: hip flexion Hamstring part: hip extension
Gracilis	Inferior ramus of pubis	Superomedial aspect of tibia	Obturator nerve (L2, L3)	Hip adduction and flexion; assists with hip internal rotation
Pectineus	Superior ramus of pubis	Pectineal line of femur	Femoral nerve and obturator nerve (L2, L3, L4)	Hip adduction and flexion; assists with hip internal rotation
Tensor fasciae latae	Anterior superior iliac spine and anterior aspect of iliac crest	Iliotibial tract that attaches to lateral condyle of tibia	Superior gluteal nerve (L4, L5)	Hip abduction, internal rotation and flexion; aids in maintaining knee extension
Rectus femoris	Anterior inferior iliac spine	Base of patella and through patellar ligament to tibial tuberosity	Femoral nerve (L2, L3, L4)	Hip flexion and knee extension
Sartorius	Anterior superior iliac spine and notch just inferior	Superomedial aspect of tibia	Femoral nerve (L2, L3)	Flexes, abducts, and externally rotates hip, flexes knee
Obturator externus	Margin of obturator foramen and obturator membrane	Trochanteric fossa of femur	Obturator nerve (L3, L4)	Hip external rotation, steadies head of femur in acetabulum

Muscles (continued)

Anterior Muscles of Hip and Thigh

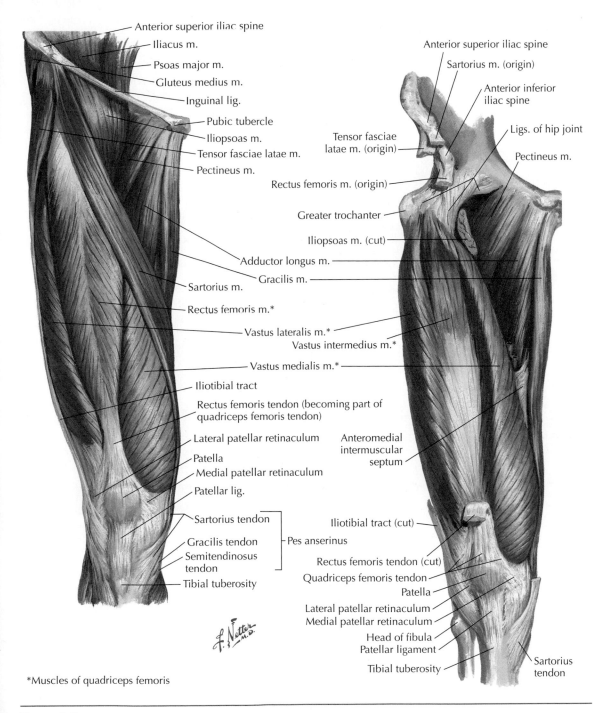

Anterior superior iliac spine

Iliacus m.

Psoas major m.

Gluteus medius m.

Inguinal lig.

Pubic tubercle

Iliopsoas m.

Tensor fasciae latae m.

Pectineus m.

Adductor longus m.

Gracilis m.

Sartorius m.

Rectus femoris m.*

Vastus lateralis m.*

Vastus intermedius m.*

Vastus medialis m.*

Iliotibial tract

Rectus femoris tendon (becoming part of quadriceps femoris tendon)

Lateral patellar retinaculum

Patella

Medial patellar retinaculum

Patellar lig.

Sartorius tendon

Gracilis tendon

Semitendinosus tendon
— Pes anserinus

Tibial tuberosity

Anterior superior iliac spine

Sartorius m. (origin)

Anterior inferior iliac spine

Ligs. of hip joint

Tensor fasciae latae m. (origin)

Pectineus m.

Rectus femoris m. (origin)

Greater trochanter

Iliopsoas m. (cut)

Anteromedial intermuscular septum

Iliotibial tract (cut)

Rectus femoris tendon (cut)

Quadriceps femoris tendon

Patella

Lateral patellar retinaculum

Medial patellar retinaculum

Head of fibula

Patellar ligament

Tibial tuberosity

Sartorius tendon

*Muscles of quadriceps femoris

Figure 6-6
Muscles of thigh: anterior view.

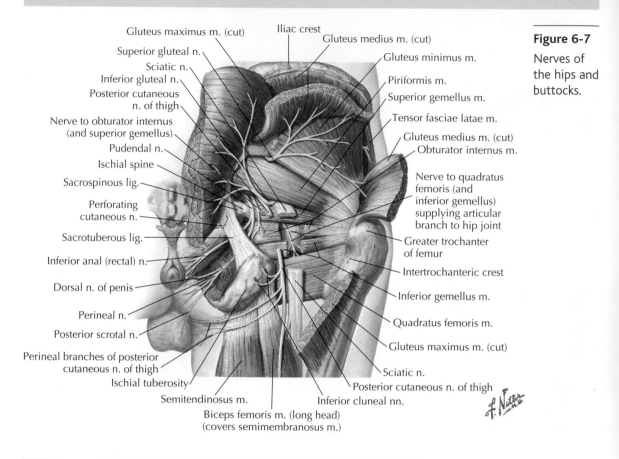

Figure 6-7

Nerves of the hips and buttocks.

Nerve	Segmental Level	Sensory	Motor
Obturator	L2, L3, L4	Medial thigh	Adductor longus, adductor brevis, adductor magnus (adductor part), gracilis, obturator externus
Saphenous	Femoral nerve	Medial leg and foot	No motor
Femoral	L2, L3, L4	Thigh via cutaneous nerves	Iliacus, sartorius, quadriceps femoris, articularis genu, pectineus
Lateral cutaneous of thigh	L2, L3	Lateral thigh	No motor
Posterior cutaneous of thigh	S2, S3	Posterior thigh	No motor
Inferior cluneal	Dorsal rami L1, L2, L3	Buttock region	No motor
Sciatic	L4, L5, S1, S2, S3	Hip joint	Knee flexors and all muscles of lower leg and foot
Superior gluteal	L4, L5, S1	No sensory	Tensor fascia latae, gluteus medius, gluteus minimus
Inferior gluteal	L5, S1, S2	No sensory	Gluteus maximus
Nerve to quadratus femoris	L5, S1, S2	No sensory	Quadratus femoris, inferior gemellus
Pudendal	S2, S3, S4	Genitals	Perineal muscles, external urethral sphincter, external anal sphincter

Deep dissection

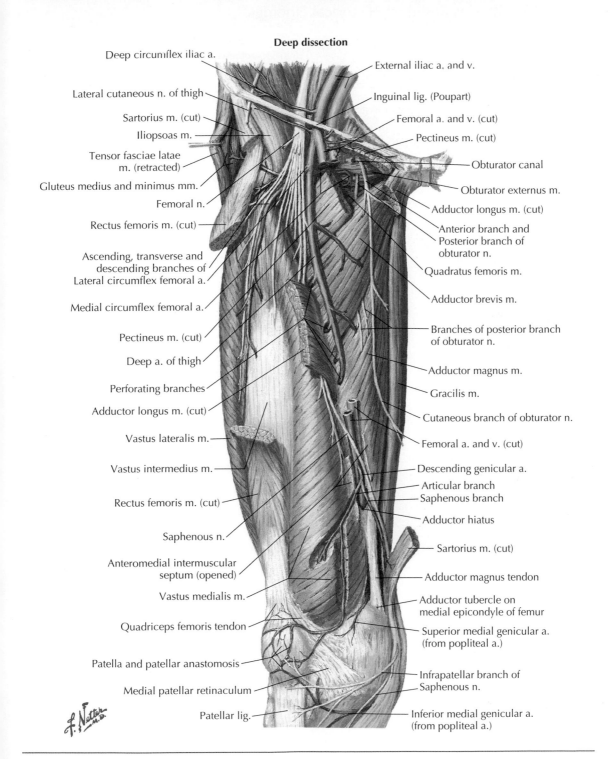

Deep circumflex iliac a.

Lateral cutaneous n. of thigh

Sartorius m. (cut)

Iliopsoas m.

Tensor fasciae latae m. (retracted)

Gluteus medius and minimus mm.

Femoral n.

Rectus femoris m. (cut)

Ascending, transverse and descending branches of Lateral circumflex femoral a.

Medial circumflex femoral a.

Pectineus m. (cut)

Deep a. of thigh

Perforating branches

Adductor longus m. (cut)

Vastus lateralis m.

Vastus intermedius m.

Rectus femoris m. (cut)

Saphenous n.

Anteromedial intermuscular septum (opened)

Vastus medialis m.

Quadriceps femoris tendon

Patella and patellar anastomosis

Medial patellar retinaculum

Patellar lig.

External iliac a. and v.

Inguinal lig. (Poupart)

Femoral a. and v. (cut)

Pectineus m. (cut)

Obturator canal

Obturator externus m.

Adductor longus m. (cut)

Anterior branch and Posterior branch of obturator n.

Quadratus femoris m.

Adductor brevis m.

Branches of posterior branch of obturator n.

Adductor magnus m.

Gracilis m.

Cutaneous branch of obturator n.

Femoral a. and v. (cut)

Descending genicular a.

Articular branch

Saphenous branch

Adductor hiatus

Sartorius m. (cut)

Adductor magnus tendon

Adductor tubercle on medial epicondyle of femur

Superior medial genicular a. (from popliteal a.)

Infrapatellar branch of Saphenous n.

Inferior medial genicular a. (from popliteal a.)

Figure 6-8

Nerves and arteries of thigh: anterior views.

Initial Hypotheses Based on Historical Findings

History	Initial Hypothesis
Reports of pain at the lateral thigh. Pain exacerbated when transferring from sitting to standing	Greater trochanteric bursitis[19] Muscle strain[2]
Age > 60. Reports of pain and stiffness in the hip with possible radiation into the groin	OA[3]
Reports of clicking or catching in the hip joint. Pain exacerbated by full flexion or extension	Labral tear[4]
Reports of a repetitive or overuse injury	Muscle sprain/strain[2]
Deep aching throb in the hip or groin. Possible history of prolonged steroid use	Avascular necrosis[4]
Sharp pain in groin. Often misdiagnosed by multiple providers	Femoroacetabular (anterior) impingement[5]
Pain in the gluteal region with occasional radiation into the posterior thigh and calf	Piriformis syndrome[6] Hamstring strain[2,4] Ischial bursitis[2]

Diagnostic Utility of the Patient History for Identifying Intra-articular Hip Pain, Osteoarthritis, and Acetabular Labral Tears

+LR	Interpretation	−LR
>10	Large	<.1
5.0-10.0	Moderate	.1-.2
2.0-5.0	Small	.2-.5
1.0-2.0	Rarely important	.5-1.0

Patient Complaint	Population	Reference Standard	Sens	Spec	+LR	−LR
Groin pain[7]	49 potential surgical patients with hip pain	Intra-articular hip pain as defined by > 50% relief with intra-articular anesthetic-steroid injection	.59 (.41, .75)	.14 (.05, .33)	.67 (.48, .98)	3.0 (.95, 9.4)
Catching[7]			.63 (.44, .78)	.54 (.35, .73)	1.39 (.81, 2.4)	.68 (.36, 1.3)
Pinching pain when sitting[7]			.48 (.31, .66)	.54 (.35, .73)	1.1 (.58, 1.9)	.95 (.56, 1.6)
No lateral thigh pain[7]			.78 (.59, .89)	.36 (.2, .57)	1.2 (.84, 1.8)	.61 (.25, 1.5)
Constant low back/ buttock pain[8]	78 patients with unilateral pain in the buttock, groin, or anterior thigh	Hip OA on radiographs using the Kellgren and Lawrence grading scale	.52 (.30, .74)	.92 (.80, .97)	6.4 (2.4, 17.4)	.52 (.33, .81)
Ipsilateral groin pain[8]			.29 (.12, .52)	.92 (.80, .97)	3.6 (1.2, 11.0)	.78 (.59, 1.00)
Squatting aggravates symptoms[8]			.76 (.52, .91)	.57 (.42, .70)	1.8 (1.2, 2.6)	.42 (.19, .93)
Patient complains of clicking in the hip[9]	18 patients with hip pain	Acetabular labral tear as determined by magnetic resonance arthrography	1.0 (.48, 1.0)	.85 (.55, .98)	6.7	.00

Reliability of Range of Motion Measurements

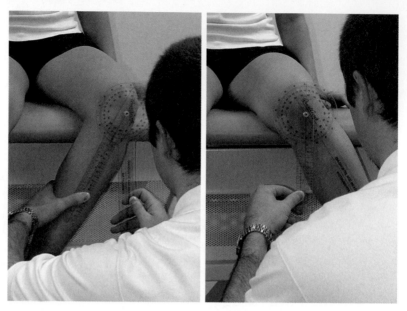

External rotation   Internal rotation

Figure 6-9

Measurement of passive range of motion.

ICC or κ	Interpretation
.81-1.0	Substantial agreement
.61-.80	Moderate agreement
.41-.60	Fair agreement
.11-.40	Slight agreement
.0-.10	No agreement

Measurements	Instrumentation	Population	Inter-examiner Reliability
External rotation (sitting) Internal rotation (sitting) External rotation (supine) Internal rotation (supine) Flexion Abduction Adduction Extension[10]	Goniometer	6 patients with hip OA	Pre/post standardization: ICC = .55/.80 ICC = .95/.94 ICC = .87/.80 ICC = .87/.94 ICC = .91/.91 ICC = .91/.88 ICC = .72/.56 ICC = **NA/.66**
Internal rotation External rotation Flexion Abduction Extension (knee flexed) Extension (knee unconstrained)[11]	Goniometer (except rotation with inclinometer)	22 patients with hip OA	ICC = .93 (.83, .97) ICC = .96 (.91, .99) ICC = .97 (.93, .99) ICC = .94 (.86, .98) ICC = .86 (.67, .94) ICC = .89 (.72, .95)

ICC, Intraclass correlation coefficient.

Range of Motion (continued)

Reliability of Range of Motion Measurements

ICC or κ	Interpretation
.81-1.0	Substantial agreement
.61-.80	Moderate agreement
.41-.60	Fair agreement
.11-.40	Slight agreement
.0-.10	No agreement

Measurements	Instrumentation	Population	Intra-examiner Reliability
Flexion Abduction Adduction External rotation Internal rotation Extension[8]	Inclinometer	78 patients with unilateral pain in the buttock, groin, or anterior thigh	ICC = .85 (.64 to .93) ICC = .85 (.68 to .93) ICC = .54 (−.19 to .81) ICC = .77 (.53 to .89) ICC = .88 (.74 to .94) ICC = .68 (.32 to .85)
Passive hip flexion[12]	Gravity inclinometer	22 patients with knee OA and 17 asymptomatic subjects	ICC = .94 (.89-.97)
Flexion Extension Abduction Adduction External Rotation Internal rotation Total hip motion[13]	Goniometer	25 subjects with radiologically verified OA of the hip	ICC = .82 ICC = .94 ICC = .86 ICC = .50 ICC = .90 ICC = .90 ICC = .85
Flexion Internal rotation External rotation Abduction Extension Adduction[14]	Goniometer	168 patients, 50 with no hip OA, 77 with unilateral hip OA, 40 with bilateral hip OA based on radiological reports	ICC = .92 ICC = .90 ICC = .58 ICC = .78 ICC = .56 ICC = .62
Hip flexion, right Hip flexion, left[15]	Goniometer	106 patients with OA of the hip or knee confirmed by a rheumatologist or orthopaedic surgeon	ICC = .82 (.26, .95) ICC = .83 (.33, .96)

Reliability of Determining Capsular and Noncapsular End-Feels

ICC or κ	Interpretation
.81-1.0	Substantial agreement
.61-.80	Moderate agreement
.41-.60	Fair agreement
.11-.40	Slight agreement
.0-.10	No agreement

Measurements	Description and Positive Finding	Population	Intra-examiner Reliability
Flexion[8]	Maximal passive ROM (PROM) was assessed. End-feels were dichotomized into "capsular" (early capsular, spasm, bone-to-bone) and "noncapsular" (soft tissue approximation, springy block, and empty) as defined by Cyriax	78 patients with unilateral pain in the buttock, groin, or anterior thigh	κ = .21 (−.22, .64)
Internal rotation[8]			κ = .51 (.19, .83)
Scour test[8]			κ = .52 (.08, .96)
FABER test[8]			κ = .47 (.12, .81)
Hip flexion test[8]			κ = .52 (.09, .96)

Diagnostic Utility of Cyriax's Capsular Pattern for Detecting Osteoarthritis

A few studies[14,16] have investigated the diagnostic utility of Cyriax's capsular pattern (greater limitation of flexion and internal rotation than of abduction, little if any limitation of adduction and external rotation) in detecting the presence of OA of the hip. Bijl and associates[16] demonstrated that hip joints with OA had significantly lower ROM values in all planes when compared with hip joints without OA. However, the magnitude of the range limitations did not follow Cyriax's capsular pattern. Similarly, Klässbo and colleagues[14] did not detect a correlation between hip OA and Cyriax's capsular pattern. In fact, they identified 138 patterns of PROM restrictions depending on the established norms used (either the mean for symptom-free hips or Kaltenborn's published norms).

Characteristic habitus and gait

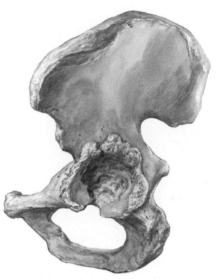

Advanced degenerative changes in acetabulum

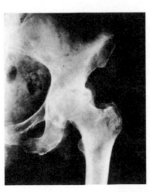

Radiograph of hip shows typical degeneration of cartilage and secondary bone changes with spurs at margins of acetabulum

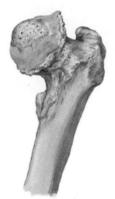

Erosion of cartilage and deformity of femoral head

Figure 6-10

Hip joint involvement in ostearthritis.

Range of Motion

Diagnostic Utility of Pain and Limited Range of Motion

+LR	Interpretation	−LR
>10	Large	<.1
5.0–10.0	Moderate	.1–.2
2.0–5.0	Small	.2–.5
1.0–2.0	Rarely important	.5–1.0

Test and Study Quality		Population	Reference Standard	Sens	Spec	+LR	−LR
Lateral pain with active hip flexion[8]		78 patients with unilateral pain in the buttock, groin, or anterior thigh	Hip OA on radiographs using the Kellgren and Lawrence grading scale	.43 (.23, .66)	.88 (.75, .95)	3.6 (1.5, 8.7)	.65 (.44, .94)
Passive internal rotation ≤ 25°[8]				.76 (.52, .91)	.61 (.46, .74)	1.9 (1.3, 3.0)	.39 (.18, .86)
Pain with active hip extension[8]				.52 (.30, .74)	.80 (.66, .90)	2.7 (1.3, 5.3)	.59 (.37, .94)
Groin pain with active abduction or adduction[8]				.33 (.15, .57)	.94 (.83, .98)	5.7 (1.7, 18.6)	.71 (.52, .96)
Decreased passive hip internal rotation ROM[17]		40 patients with unilateral lateral hip pain	Lateral hip tendon pathology via MRI	.43 (.19, .70)	.86 (.42, .99)	3.00 (.44, 20.31)	.67 (.40, 1.10)
Pain with active hip internal rotation[17]				.31 (.10, .61)	.86 (.42, .99)	2.15 (.29, 15.75)	.81 (.54, 1.22)
Pain with passive hip abduction[17]				.59 (.33, .82)	.93 (.49, 1.00)	8.31 (.56, 123.88)	.44 (.24, .81)
Pain with passive hip internal rotation[17]				.53 (.27, .78)	.86 (.42, .99)	3.73 (.57, 24.35)	.54 (.30, .98)
Number of planes with restricted movement[18]	0	195 patients presenting with first time episodes of hip pain	Radiographic evidence of mild-to-moderate OA	1.0	.00	1.0	NA
	1			.86	.54	1.87	.26
	2			.57	.77	2.48	.56
	3			.33	.93	4.71	.72
Number of planes with restricted movement[18]	0		Radiographic evidence of severe OA	1.0	.00	1.0	NA
	1			1.0	.42	1.72	NA
	2			.81	.69	2.61	.28
	3			.54	.88	4.5	.52
Pain with hip PROM[19]		21 women diagnosed with pelvic girdle pain (PGP)	PGP as defined by: • Current or recent pregnancy • Daily pain • Points to the pelvic girdle joints as the painful area • Pain during one or more of the 6 selected clinical tests (active straight leg raise [ASLR], Gaenslen, sacroiliac compression, sacroiliac distraction, thigh thrust)	.55	1.0	Undefined	.45

Diagnostic Utility of Pain and Limited Range of Motion

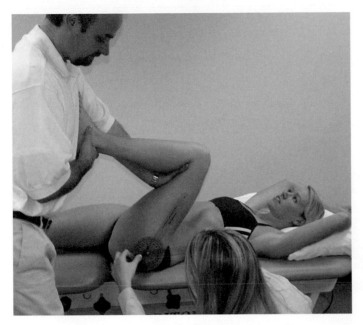

Hip flexion

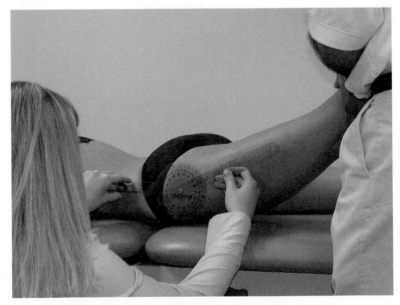

Hip extension

Figure 6-11

Passive range of motion measurement.

Diagnostic Utility of Limited Range of Motion for Detecting Avascular Necrosis

+LR	Interpretation	−LR
>10	Large	<.1
5.0-10.0	Moderate	.1-.2
2.0-5.0	Small	.2-.5
1.0-2.0	Rarely important	.5-1.0

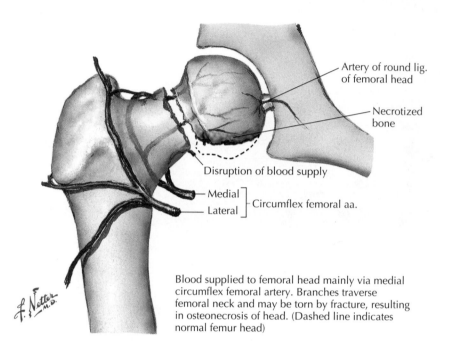

Artery of round lig. of femoral head

Necrotized bone

Disruption of blood supply

Medial
Lateral — Circumflex femoral aa.

Blood supplied to femoral head mainly via medial circumflex femoral artery. Branches traverse femoral neck and may be torn by fracture, resulting in osteonecrosis of head. (Dashed line indicates normal femur head)

Figure 6-12

Osteonecrosis.

Motion and Finding	Population	Reference Standard	Sens	Spec	+LR	−LR
PROM extension < 15°[20]			.19 (.00, .38)	.92 (.89, .95)	2.38	.88
PROM abduction < 45°[20]			.31 (.09, .54)	.85 (.82, .89)	2.07	.81
PROM internal rotation < 15°[20]	176 asymptomatic HIV-infected patients	MRI confirmation of avascular necrosis (AVN) of the hip. Ten had AVN	.50 (.26, .75)	.67 (.62, .72)	1.52	.75
PROM external rotation < 60°[20]			.38 (.14, .61)	.73 (.68, .77)	.48	.85
Pain with Internal rotation[20]			.13 (.00, .29)	.86 (.83, .89)	.93	1.01

HIV, human immunodeficiency virus; MRI: magnetic resonance imaging.

Range of Motion

Diagnostic Utility of Limited Hip Abduction for Detecting Developmental Dysplasia in Infants

+LR	Interpretation	−LR
>10	Large	<.1
5.0-10.0	Moderate	.1-.2
2.0-5.0	Small	.2-.5
1.0-2.0	Rarely important	.5-1.0

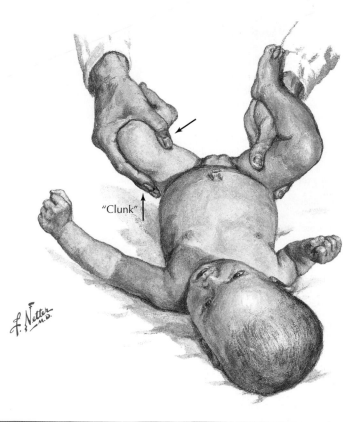

"Clunk"

Figure 6-13

Recognition of congenital dislocation of the hip.

Test		Description and Positive Findings	Population	Reference Standard	Sens	Spec	+LR	−LR
Limited hip abduction test[21] ◇	Unilateral limitation	Passive abduction of the hips performed with both hips flexed 90°. Considered positive if abduction is more than 20° greater than the contralateral side	1107 infants	Ultrasound verification of clinical instability of the hip	.70 (.60, .69)	.90 (.88, .92)	7.0	.33
	Bilateral limitation				.43 (.50, .64)	.90 (.88, .92)	4.3	.63
Limited hip abduction [22] ○		As above except considered positive if either (1) abduction < 60° or (2) asymmetry in abduction of ≥ 20°	683 infants	Hip dysplasia as detected by ultrasound	.69	.54	1.5	.57

ICC or κ	Interpretation
.81-1.0	Substantial agreement
.61-.80	Moderate agreement
.41-.60	Fair agreement
.11-.40	Slight agreement
.0-.10	No agreement

Test and Study	Description and Positive Findings	Population	Reliability Intra-examiner	Inter-examiner
Abduction strength[23]	With subject supine, patient exerts maximal isometric hip abduction force into a handheld dynamometer placed just proximal to the knee	29 football players	ICC (right/left) = .81/.84	ICC (right/left) = .73/.58
Adduction strength[23]	With subject supine, patient exerts maximal isometric hip adduction force into a sphygmomanometer placed between the knees		ICC = .81 to .94 (depending on knee angle)	ICC = .80 to .83 (depending on knee angle)
Internal rotation[23]	With subject supine and tested knee flexed to 90°, patient exerts maximal isometric rotational force into a handheld dynamometer placed just proximal to the lateral malleolus		ICC (right/left) = .67/.57	ICC (right/left) = .40/.54
External rotation[23]	As above except with the dynamometer placed just proximal to the medial malleolus		ICC (right/left) = .55/.64	ICC (right/left) = .60/.63
Abduction strength[10]	With patient supine, patient abducts bilateral hips into examiner's hands. Strength graded on scale of 0-2	6 patients with hip OA	Inter-examiner pre/post standardization: κ = .90/.86	
Adduction strength[10]	As above except patient adducts bilateral hips		Inter-examiner pre/post standardization: κ = .87/.86	
Flexion strength (sitting)[10]	With patient sitting, the patient lifts one knee against examiner's hand. Strength graded on scale of 0-2		Inter-examiner pre/post standardization: κ = .83/.95	
Flexion strength (supine)[10]	As above except supine with knees bent 90°		Inter-examiner pre/post standardization: κ = NA/.90	
Extension strength[10]	Patient prone with knee bent 90°. Lifts 1 leg against examiners hand. Strength graded on scale of 0-2		Inter-examiner pre/post standardization: κ = .85/.86	

Assessing Muscle Strength (continued)

Reliability of Detecting Pain or Weakness During Resisted Tests

ICC or κ	Interpretation
.81-1.0	Substantial agreement
.61-.80	Moderate agreement
.41-.60	Fair agreement
.11-.40	Slight agreement
.0-.10	No agreement

Test and Study	Description and Positive Findings	Population	Reliability	
			Intra-examiner	Inter-examiner
Abduction strength[23]	With subject supine, the patient exerts maximal isometric hip abduction force into a handheld dynamometer placed just proximal to the knee	29 football players	ICC (right/left) = **.81/.84**	ICC (right/left) = **.73/.58**
Adduction strength[23]	With subject supine, the patient exerts maximal isometric hip adduction force into a sphygmomanometer placed between the knees		ICC = **.81 to .94** (depending on knee angle)	ICC = **.80 to .83** (depending on knee angle)
Internal rotation[23]	With subject supine and tested knee flexed to 90°, the patient exerts maximal isometric rotational force into a handheld dynamometer placed just proximal to the lateral malleolus		ICC (right/left) = **.67/.57**	ICC (right/left) = **.40/.54**
External rotation[23]	As above except with the dynamometer placed just proximal to the medial malleolus		ICC (right/left) = **.55/.64**	ICC (right/left) = **.60/.63**
Abduction strength[10]	With patient supine, the patient abducts bilateral hips into examiner's hands. Strength graded on scale of 0-2	6 patients with hip OA	Inter-examiner pre/post standardization: κ = **.90/.86**	
Adduction strength[10]	As above except the patient adducts bilateral hips		Inter-examiner pre/post standardization: κ = **.87/.86**	
Flexion strength (sitting)[10]	With patient sitting, the patient lifts one knee against examiner's hand. Strength graded on scale of 0-2		Inter-examiner pre/post standardization: κ = **.83/.95**	
Flexion strength (supine)[10]	As above except with patient supine and knees bent 90°		Inter-examiner pre/post standardization: κ = **NA/.90**	
Extension strength[10]	With patient prone and knee bent 90°, patient lifts one leg against examiner's hand. Strength graded on scale of 0-2		Inter-examiner pre/post standardization: κ = **.85/.86**	

Assessing Muscle Strength

Diagnostic Utility of Pain or Weakness for Identifying Lateral Hip Tendon Pathology

+LR	Interpretation	−LR
>10	Large	<.1
5.0-10.0	Moderate	.1-.2
2.0-5.0	Small	.2-.5
1.0-2.0	Rarely important	.5-1.0

Test and Study Quality	Description and Positive Findings	Population	Reference Standard	Sens	Spec	+LR	−LR
Pain with resisted gluteus minimus[17] ◇	Tested isometrically as described by Kendal and colleagues. Positive if reproduction of pain	40 patients with unilateral lateral hip pain	Lateral hip tendon pathology via MRI	.47 (.22, .73)	.86 (.42, .99)	3.27 (.49, 21.70)	.62 (.37, 1.05)
Pain with resisted gluteus minimus and medius[17] ◇				.47 (.22, .73)	.86 (.42, .99)	3.27 (.49, 21.70)	.62 (.37, 1.05)
Gluteus minimus and medius weakness[17] ◇	Tested isometrically as described by Kendal and colleagues. Positive if less than 5/5			.80 (.51, .95)	.71 (.30, .95)	2.80 (.85, 9.28)	.28 (.09, .86)
Gluteus minimus weakness[17] ◇				.80 (.51, .95)	.57 (.20, .88)	1.87 (.76, 4.55)	.35 (.10, 1.19)
Pain with resisted abduction[24] ◇	With patient supine and affected hip at 45°, positive if symptoms over the greater trochanter are reproduced on resisted abduction	24 patients with lateral hip pain and tenderness over the greater trochanter	Gluteus medius tendon tear via MRI	.73	.46	1.35	.59
Pain with resisted internal rotation[24] ◇	With patient supine and affected hip at 45° and maximal external rotation, positive if symptoms over the greater trochanter are replicated on internal rotation			.55	.69	1.77	.65

Assessing Muscle Strength

Reliability of the Trendelenburg Test

ICC or κ	Interpretation
.81-1.0	Substantial agreement
.61-.80	Moderate agreement
.41-.60	Fair agreement
.11-.40	Slight agreement
.0-.10	No agreement

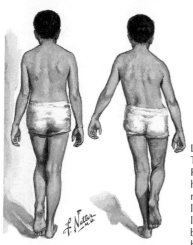

Left: patient demonstrates negative Trendelenburg test of normal right hip. Right: positive test of involved left hip. When weight is on affected side, normal hip drops, indicating weakness of left gluteus medius muscle. Trunk shifts left as patient attempts to decrease biomechanical stresses across involved hip and thereby maintain balance

Figure 6-14

Trendelenburg test.

Test and Study	Description and Positive Findings	Population	Intra-examiner Reliability
Positive Trendelenburg test[10]	Standing patient raises one foot 10 cm off the ground while examiner inspects for change in level of pelvis. Positive if pelvis drops on the un-supported side or trunk shifts to the stance side	6 patients with hip OA	κ = **.36** (pre-standardization) κ = **.06** (post-standardization)
Positive Trendelenburg test[24]	Assessed in two ways. Pelvic tilt was assessed in single leg stance on the affected leg. Pelvic movement was assessed during gait. A positive test was defined as clearly abnormal pelvic tilt during both stance and gait	24 patients with lateral hip pain and tenderness over the greater trochanter	κ = **.67 (.27, 1.08)**

Diagnostic Utility of the Trendelenburg Test for Identifying Lateral Hip Tendon Pathology

+LR	Interpretation	−LR
>10	Large	<.1
5.0-10.0	Moderate	.1-.2
2.0-5.0	Small	.2-.5
1.0-2.0	Rarely important	.5-1.0

Test and Study Quality	Description and Positive Findings	Population	Reference Standard	Sens	Spec	+LR	−LR
Positive Trendelenburg test[17] ◇	Patient lifts one foot off the ground at a time while standing. Positive if the patient is unable to elevate his/her pelvis on the nonstance side and hold the position for at least 30 sec	40 patients with unilateral lateral hip pain	Lateral hip tendon pathology via MRI	.23 (.05, .57)	.94 (.53, 1.00)	3.64 (.20, 65.86)	.82 (.59, 1.15)
Positive Trendelenburg test[24] ◇	Assessed in two ways. Pelvic tilt was assessed in single leg stance on the affected leg. Pelvic movement was assessed during gait. A positive test was defined as clearly abnormal pelvic tilt during both stance and gait	24 patients with lateral hip pain and tenderness over the greater trochanter	Gluteus medius tendon tear via MRI	.73	.77	3.17	.35

Assessing Muscle Length

Reliability of Tests for Iliotibial Band Length

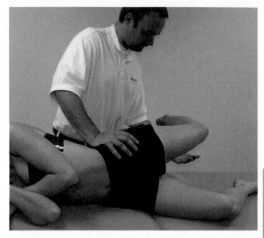

Ober test

ICC or κ	Interpretation
.81–1.0	Substantial agreement
.61–.80	Moderate agreement
.41–.60	Fair agreement
.11–.40	Slight agreement
.0–.10	No agreement

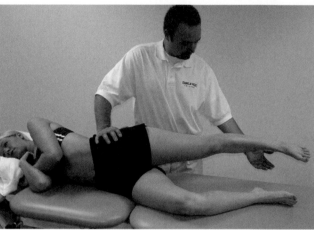

Modified Ober test

Figure 6-15

Tests for iliotibial band length.

Measurements	Test Procedure	Population	Reliability
Ober test[10]	With patient side-lying with examined leg up, examiner flexes patient's knee to 90° and abducts and extends the hip until the hip is in line with the trunk. Examiner allows gravity to adduct hip as much as possible. Positive if unable to adduct to horizontal position	6 patients with hip OA	κ = **.38** (pre-standardization) κ = **.80** (post-standardization)
Ober test[25]	As above except an inclinometer is used on the distal lateral thigh to measure hip adduction angle	30 patients with patellofemoral pain syndrome	Inter-examiner ICC = **.97** (**.93, .98**)
Ober test[26]		61 asymptomatic individuals	Intra-examiner ICC = **.90**
Modified Ober test[27]	As above but with test knee fully extended	10 patients experiencing anterior knee pain	Inter-examiner ICC = **.73** Intra-examiner ICC = **.94**
Modified Ober test[27]		61 asymptomatic individuals	Intra-examiner ICC = **.91**

Assessing Muscle Length

Reliability of the Thomas Test for Hip Flexor Contracture

ICC or κ	Interpretation
.81-1.0	Substantial agreement
.61-.80	Moderate agreement
.41-.60	Fair agreement
.11-.40	Slight agreement
.0-.10	No agreement

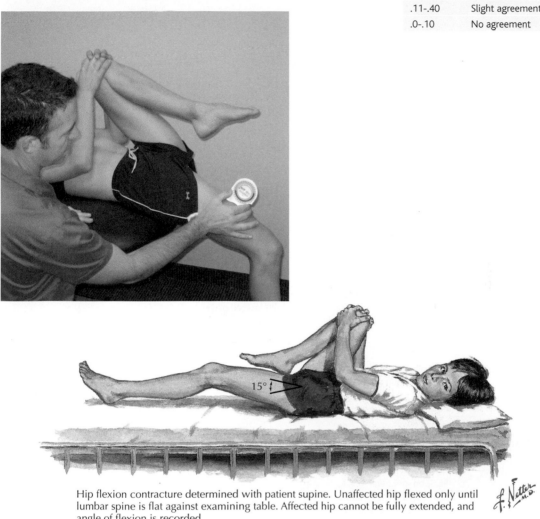

Hip flexion contracture determined with patient supine. Unaffected hip flexed only until lumbar spine is flat against examining table. Affected hip cannot be fully extended, and angle of flexion is recorded

15°

Figure 6-16

Thomas test.

Measurements	Test Procedure	Population	Reliability
Modified Thomas test[28]	With the subject sitting as close to the edge of the table as possible and holding the non-tested thigh, the patient rolls back into supine position and flexes the untested hip until the lumbar lordosis is flattened. The tested limb is allowed to hang into extension and is measured with an inclinometer or goniometer	42 asymptomatic individuals	ICC = **.92** (goniometer) ICC = **.89** (inclinometer)
Thomas test[10]	With patient supine with both hips flexed and maintaining one hip in flexion, the tested hip is extended. Positive if unable to touch posterior thigh with examination table	6 patients with hip OA	κ = **.60** (pre-standardization) κ = **.88** (post-standardization)

ICC or κ	Interpretation
.81-1.0	Substantial agreement
.61-.80	Moderate agreement
.41-.60	Fair agreement
.11-.40	Slight agreement
.0-.10	No agreement

Test and Study	Description and Positive Findings	Population	Reliability	
			Intra-examiner	Inter-examiner
Bent knee fall out (adductors)[23]	With subject supine and knees flexed to 90°, the patient lets knees fall out while keeping feet together. The distance from the fibular head to the table is measured with a tape measure		ICC (right/left) = **.90/.89**	ICC (right/left) = **.93/.91**
External rotators of the hip[23]	With subject prone and knees flexed to 90°, the patient lets feet fall outward while keeping feet together. Examiner passively flexes knee 90°. Internal rotation measurement is taken with an inclinometer	29 football players	ICC (right/left) = **.97/.96**	ICC (right/left) = **.89/.93**
Internal rotators of the hip[23]	With subject supine with nontested hip flexed and the test leg hanging over the end of the table, passive external rotation is measured with an inclinometer		ICC (right/left) = **.82/.80**	ICC (right/left) = **.64/.77**
Short hip extensors[29]	With patient supine, examiner brings hip passively into flexion while palpating posterior-superior iliac spine (PSIS) on ipsilateral side. As soon as PSIS moves posteriorly, the movement is ceased and the measurement is recorded with an inclinometer		Intra-examiner ICC = **.87**	
Short hip flexors[29]	With patient supine, lower limbs over the plinth, and both hips flexed, examiner slowly lowers the side being tested. When limb ceases to move, measurement is recorded with an inclinometer	11 asymptomatic individuals	Intra-examiner ICC = **.98**	
External rotators of the hip[29]	With patient prone, examiner passively flexes knee 90°. Examiner palpates contralateral PSIS and passively internally rotates limb. When rotation of pelvis occurs, measurement is taken with an inclinometer		Intra-examiner ICC = **.99**	
Internal rotators of the hip[29]	Same as above except examiner takes hip into external rotation		Intra-examiner ICC = **.98**	

Measurement of the length of external
rotators of the hip

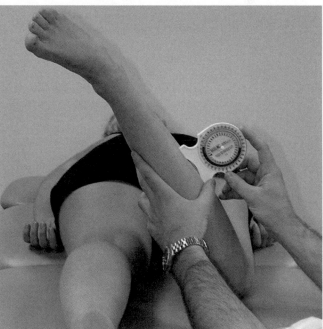

Measurement of the length of internal
rotators of the hip

Figure 6-17

Measurement of muscle length with a bubble inclinometer.

Diagnostic Utility of Pain with Functional Movements

+LR	Interpretation	−LR
>10	Large	<.1
5.0-10.0	Moderate	.1-.2
2.0-5.0	Small	.2-.5
1.0-2.0	Rarely important	.5-1.0

Test and Study Quality	Description and Positive Findings	Population	Reference Standard	Sens	Spec	+LR	−LR
Posterior pain with squat[8]◇	Patient squats as low as possible with feet 20 cm apart, trunk upright, and hands on hips	78 patients with unilateral pain in the buttock, groin, or anterior thigh	Hip OA on x-rays using the Kellgren and Lawrence grading scale	.24 (.09, .48)	.96 (.85, .99)	6.1 (1.5, 25.6)	.79 (.62, 1.00)
Step up[19]◯	No details given	21 women with pelvic girdle pain	PGP defined by: • Current or recent pregnancy • Daily pain • Points to the pelvic girdle joints as the painful area • Pain during one or more of the six selected clinical tests (ASLR, Gaenslen, sacroiliac compression, sacroiliac distraction, thigh thrust, palpation of pubic symphysis)	.29	1.0	Undefined	.71
Single leg stance[19]◯				.35	.67	1.1	.97
Lunge[19]◯				.44	.83	2.6	.68
Sit to stand[19]◯				.13	1.0	Undefined	.88
Deep squat[19]◯				.24	1.0	Undefined	.88

Palpation

Reliability of Pain with Palpation

ICC or κ	Interpretation
.81-1.0	Substantial agreement
.61-.80	Moderate agreement
.41-.60	Fair agreement
.11-.40	Slight agreement
.0-.10	No agreement

Test and Study	Description and Positive Findings	Population	Inter-examiner Reliability
Trochanteric tenderness[10]	With patient supine, firm pressure is applied to the greater trochanter. Test positive if patient's symptoms are reproduced	6 patients with hip OA	κ = **.40** (pre-standardization) κ = **.68** (post-standardization)
Trochanteric tenderness[7]		70 patients with hip pain	κ = **.66 (.48, .84)**

Diagnostic Utility of Pain with Palpation for Intra-articular Hip Pain

+LR	Interpretation	−LR
>10	Large	<.1
5.0-10.0	Moderate	.1-.2
2.0-5.0	Small	.2-.5
1.0-2.0	Rarely important	.5-1.0

Patient Complaint	Description and Positive Findings	Population	Reference Standard	Sens	Spec	+LR	−LR
Trochanteric tenderness[7] ◇	With patient supine, firm pressure is applied to the greater trochanter. Test positive if patient's symptoms are reproduced	49 potential surgical patients with hip pain	Intra-articular hip pain as defined by > 50% relief with intra-articular anesthetic-steroid injection	.57 (.39, .74)	.45 (.27, .65)	1.1 (.36, 3.6)	.93 (.49, 1.8)

Special Tests

Reliability of Patrick's (FABER) Test

ICC or κ	Interpretation
.81-1.0	Substantial agreement
.61-.80	Moderate agreement
.41-.60	Fair agreement
.11-.40	Slight agreement
.0-.10	No agreement

Test and Study	Description and Positive Findings	Population	Reliability
Patrick's test[7]	With patient supine, examiner flexes, abducts, and externally rotates the involved hip so that the lateral ankle is placed just proximal to the contralateral knee. While stabilizing the anterior superior iliac spine, the involved leg is lowered toward the table to end range. Test is positive if it reproduces the patient's symptoms	70 patients with hip pain	Intra-examiner κ = .63 (.43, .83)
Patrick's test[10]	As above except test is considered positive if the patient has inguinal pain	6 patients with hip OA	Inter-examiner κ = .78 (pre-standardization) κ = .75 (post-standardization)
Patrick's test[8]	As above except inclinometer is used 2.5 cm proximal to the patient's flexed knee	78 patients with unilateral pain in the buttock, groin, or anterior thigh	Intra-examiner ICC = .90 (.78 to .96)

Diagnostic Utility of Patrick's (FABER) Test

+LR	Interpretation	−LR
>10	Large	<.1
5.0-10.0	Moderate	.1-.2
2.0-5.0	Small	.2-.5
1.0-2.0	Rarely important	.5-1.0

Test and Study Quality	Description and Positive Findings	Population	Reference Standard	Sens	Spec	+LR	−LR
Patrick's test[7] ◇	With patient supine, examiner flexes, abducts, and externally rotates the involved hip so that the lateral ankle is placed just proximal to the contralateral knee. While stabilizing the anterior superior iliac spine, the involved leg is lowered toward the table to end range. Test is positive if it reproduces the patient's symptoms	49 potential surgical patients with hip pain	Intra-articular hip pain as defined by > 50% relief with intra-articular anesthetic-steroid injection	.60 (.41, .77)	.18 (.07, .39)	.73 (.5, 1.1)	2.2 (.8, 6.0)
Patrick's test less than 60°[8] ◇	As above, but also uses inclinometer 2.5 cm proximal to the patient's flexed knee	78 patients with unilateral pain in the buttock, groin, or anterior thigh	Hip OA on radiographs using the Kellgren and Lawrence grading scale	.57 (.34, .77)	.71 (.56, .82)	1.9 (1.1, 3.4)	.61 (.36, 1.00)

Special Tests

Reliability of Special Tests for Detecting Intra-articular Pathology

ICC or κ	Interpretation
.81-1.0	Substantial agreement
.61-.80	Moderate agreement
.41-.60	Fair agreement
.11-.40	Slight agreement
.0-.10	No agreement

Figure 6-18

Internal rotation-flexion-axial compression maneuver.

Test and Study	Description and Positive Findings	Population	Inter-examiner Reliability
Flexion-internal rotation-adduction (FADIR) impingement test[7]	With patient supine, examiner flexes, adducts, and internally rotates the involved hip to end range. Test is positive if it reproduces the patient's symptoms	70 patients with hip pain	κ = .58 (.29, .87)
Log roll[7]	With patient supine with greater trochanters in the maximally prominent position, examiner places both hands on the patient's mid thigh and passively externally rotates each hip maximally. Test is positive if greater external rotation is noted on the symptomatic side		κ = .61 (.41, .81)

Diagnostic Utility of Special Tests for Detecting Intra-articular Pathology

+LR	Interpretation	−LR
>10	Large	<.1
5.0-10.0	Moderate	.1-.2
2.0-5.0	Small	.2-.5
1.0-2.0	Rarely important	.5-1.0

Test	Description and Positive Findings	Population	Reference Standard	Sens	Spec	+LR	−LR
Scour test with adduction causes lateral hip or groin pain[8]	With patient supine, examiner passively flexes the symptomatic hip to 90° and then moves the knee toward the opposite shoulder and applies an axial load to the femur	78 patients with unilateral pain in the buttock, groin, or anterior thigh	Hip OA on radiographs using the Kellgren and Lawrence grading scale	.62 (.39, .81)	.75 (.60, .85)	2.4 (1.4, 4.3)	.51 (.29, .89)
FADIR impingement test[7]	With patient supine, examiner flexes, adducts, and internally rotates the involved hip to end range. Test is positive if it reproduces the patient's symptoms	49 potential surgical patients with hip pain	Intra-articular hip pain as defined by > 50% relief with intra-articular anesthetic-steroid injection	.78 (.59, .89)	.10 (.03, .29)	.86 (.67, 4) 1.1	.58
Internal rotation-flexion-axial compression maneuver[9]	With patient supine, examiner flexes and internally rotates the hip, then applies an axial compression force through the femur. Provocation of pain is considered positive	18 patients with hip pain	Acetabular labral tear as determined by magnetic resonance arthrography	.75 (.19, .99)	.43 (.1		

Diagnostic Utility of the Patellar-Pubic-Percussion Test for Detecting Hip Fractures

+LR	Interpretation	−LR
>10	Large	<.1
5.0-10.0	Moderate	.1-.2
2.0-5.0	Small	.2-.5
1.0-2.0	Rarely important	.5-1.0

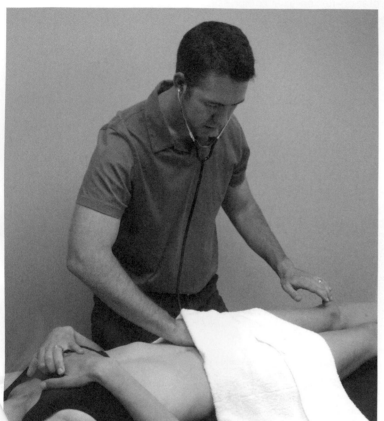

Figure 6-19

Percussion test.

and	Description and Positive Findings	Population	Reference Standard	Sens	Spec	+LR	−LR
Pa pu cuss test	With patient supine, examiner percusses (taps) one patella at a time while auscultating the pubic-pubic symphysis with a stethoscope. A positive a diminution of percussion note on ed side	290 patients with suspected radiologically occult hip fractures	Hip fracture seen on repeat radiographs, bone scintography, MRI, or computed tomography	.96 (.87, .99)	.86 (.49, .98)	6.73	.14
Patella pubic-p cussion test[31]		41 patients in the emergency department with a chief complaint of hip trauma	Hip fracture on seen on radiograph	.94	.96	21.6	.07

Intertrochanteric Fracture of Femur

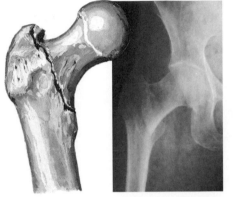

I. Nondisplaced fracture   II. Comminuted displaced fracture

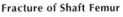

Fracture of Shaft Femur

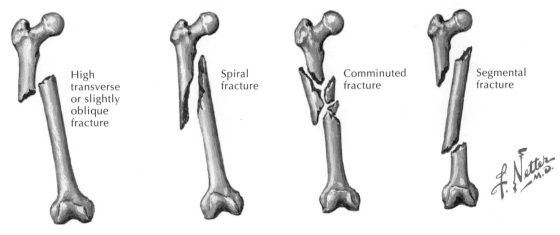

High transverse or slightly oblique fracture   Spiral fracture   Comminuted fracture   Segmental fracture

Figure 6-20

Hip fractures.

Combinations of Tests

Diagnostic Utility of Combinations of Tests for Osteoarthritis

+LR	Interpretation	−LR
>10	Large	<.1
5.0-10.0	Moderate	.1-.2
2.0-5.0	Small	.2-.5
1.0-2.0	Rarely important	.5-1.0

Test and Study Quality	Number of Variables Present	Population	Reference Standard	Sens	Spec	+LR	−LR
Squatting aggravates symptoms + Lateral pain with active hip flexion + Scour test with adduction causes lateral hip or groin pain + Pain with active hip extension + Passive internal rotation ≤ 25°8	5/5	78 patients with unilateral pain in the buttock, groin, or anterior thigh	Hip OA on radiograph using the Kellgren and Lawrence grading scale	.14 (.04, .37)	.98 (.88, 1.0)	7.3 (1.1, 49.1)	.87 (.73, 1.1)
	≥ 4/5			.48 (.26, .70)	.98 (.88, 1.0)	24.3 (4.4, 142.1)	.53 (.35, .80)
	≥ 3/5			.71 (.48, .88)	.86 (.73, .94)	5.2 (2.6, 10.9)	.33 (.17, .66)
	≥ 2/5			.81 (.57, .94)	.61 (.46, .74)	2.1 (1.4, 3.1)	.31 (.13, .78)
	≥ 1/5			.95 (.74, 1.0)	.18 (.09, .31)	1.2 (.99, 1.4)	.27 (.04, 2.0)

Outcome Measure	Scoring and Interpretation	Test-Retest Reliability	MCID
Lower Extremity Functional Scale (LEFS)	Users are asked to rate the difficulty of performing 20 functional tasks on a Likert-type scale ranging from 0 (extremely difficult or unable to perform activity) to 4 (no difficulty). A total score out of 80 is calculated by summing each score. The answers provide a score between 0 and 80, with lower scores representing more disability	ICC = .92[32]	9[33]
Western Ontario and Mc-Master Universities Osteoarthritis Index (WOMAC)	The WOMAC consists of three subscales: pain (5 items), stiffness (2 items), and physical function (17 items). Users answer the 24 condition-specific questions on a numerical rating scale ranging from 0 (no symptoms) to 10 (extreme symptoms), or alternatively on a Likert-type scale from 0 to 4. Scores from each subscale are summed with higher scores indicating more pain, stiffness, and disability	ICC = .90[32]	6.7% for improvement and 12.9% for worsening[34]
Numeric Pain Rating Scale (NPRS)	Users rate their level of pain on an 11-point scale ranging from 0 to 10, with high scores representing more pain. Often asked as "current pain" and "least," "worst," and "average pain" in the past 24 hours	ICC = .72[35]	2[36,37]

MCID, Minimum clinically important difference.

Quality Assessment of Diagnostic Studies Using QUADAS

	Altman 1991	Adams 1997	Birrell 2001	Bird 2001	Castelein 2001	Joe 2002	Jari 2002	Fishman 2002	Tiru 2002	Narvani 2003	Cook 2007	Martin 2008	Sutlive 2008	Woodley 2008
1. Was the spectrum of patients representative of the patients who will receive the test in practice?	U	U	Y	Y	Y	N	Y	U	Y	Y	Y	Y	Y	Y
2. Were selection criteria clearly described?	N	N	Y	Y	Y	N	Y	U	Y	U	Y	Y	Y	Y
3. Is the reference standard likely to correctly classify the target condition?	U	Y	Y	Y	Y	Y	Y	U	Y	Y	Y	Y	Y	Y
4. Is the time period between reference standard and index test short enough to be reasonably sure that the target condition did not change between the two tests?	U	U	Y	U	U	U	U	Y	U	N	U	U	Y	Y
5. Did the whole sample or a random selection of the sample, receive verification using a reference standard of diagnosis?	Y	Y	Y	Y	Y	Y	Y	Y	Y	Y	Y	Y	Y	Y
6. Did patients receive the same reference standard regardless of the index test result?	Y	Y	Y	Y	Y	Y	Y	Y	Y	Y	Y	Y	Y	Y
7. Was the reference standard independent of the index test (i.e., the index test did not form part of the reference standard)?	U	Y	Y	Y	Y	Y	Y	U	Y	Y	N	Y	Y	Y
8. Was the execution of the index test described in sufficient detail to permit replication of the test?	N	Y	Y	Y	N	U	Y	Y	Y	U	N	Y	Y	N
9. Was the execution of the reference standard described in sufficient detail to permit its replication?	N	U	Y	Y	Y	Y	Y	Y	U	Y	Y	Y	Y	Y
10. Were the index test results interpreted without knowledge of the results of the reference test?	U	Y	Y	Y	U	Y	U	U	U	U	U	U	Y	Y
11. Were the reference standard results interpreted without knowledge of the results of the index test?	Y	U	U	Y	U	U	U	U	U	U	U	U	Y	Y
12. Were the same clinical data available when test results were interpreted as would be available when the test is used in practice?	U	U	Y	Y	Y	Y	U	Y	U	U	U	U	Y	Y
13. Were uninterpretable/intermediate test results reported?	Y	U	U	Y	U	Y	Y	U	Y	Y	Y	Y	Y	Y
14. Were withdrawals from the study explained?	Y	U	U	Y	Y	Y	Y	U	Y	Y	Y	Y	Y	Y
Quality summary rating:	▪ Poor	○ Fair	◇ Good	◇ Good	○ Fair	○ Fair	◇ Good	○ Fair	○ Fair	○ Fair	○ Fair	◇ Good	◇ Good	◇ Good

Y = yes, N = no, U = unclear. ◇ Good quality (Y - N = 10 to 14). ○ Fair quality (Y - N = 5 to 9). ▪ Poor quality (Y - N ≤ 4).

REFERENCES

1. Hertling D, Kessler RM. *Management of Common Musculoskeletal Disorders: Physical Therapy Principles and Methods*. 3rd ed. Philadelphia: Lippincott; 1996.

2. Pecina MM, Bojanic I. *Overuse Injuries of the Musculoskeletal System*. Boca Raton: CRC Press; 1993.

3. Altman R, Alarcon G, Appelrouth D, et al. The American College of Rheumatology criteria for the classification and reporting of osteoarthritis of the hip. *Arthritis Rheum*. 1991;34:505-514.

4. Hartley A. *Practical Joint Assessment*. St Louis: Mosby; 1995.

5. Clohisy JC, Knaus ER, Hunt DM, et al. Clinical presentation of patients with symptomatic anterior hip impingement. *Clin Orthop Relat Res*. 2009;467: 638-644.

6. Fishman LM, Dombi GW, Michaelsen C, et al. Piriformis syndrome: diagnosis, treatment, and outcome—a 10-year study. *Arch Phys Med Rehabil*. 2002;83:295-301.

7. Martin RL, Irrgang JJ, Sekiya JK. The diagnostic accuracy of a clinical examination in determining intra-articular hip pain for potential hip arthroscopy candidates. *Arthroscopy*. 2008;24:1013-1018.

8. Sutlive TG, Lopez HP, Schnitker DE, et al. Development of a clinical prediction rule for diagnosing hip osteoarthritis in individuals with unilateral hip pain. *J Orthop Sports Phys Ther*. 2008;38:542-550.

9. Narvani AA, Tsiridis E, Kendall S, et al. A preliminary report on prevalence of acetabular labrum tears in sports patients with groin pain. *Knee Surg Sports Traumatol Arthrosc*. 2003;11:403-408.

10. Cibere J, Thorne A, Bellamy N, et al. Reliability of the hip examination in osteoarthritis: effect of standardization. *Arthritis Rheum*. 2008;59:373-381.

11. Pua YH, Wrigley TV, Cowan SM, Bennell KL. Intrarater test-retest reliability of hip range of motion and hip muscle strength measurements in persons with hip osteoarthritis. *Arch Phys Med Rehabil*. 2008;89: 1146-1154.

12. Cliborne AV, Wainner RS, Rhon DI, et al. Clinical hip tests and a functional squat test in patients with knee osteoarthritis: reliability, prevalence of positive test findings, and short-term response to hip mobilization. *J Orthop Sports Phys Ther*. 2004;34:676-685.

13. Holm I, Bolstad B, Lutken T, et al. Reliability of goniometric measurements and visual estimates of hip ROM in patients with osteoarthrosis. *Physiother Res Int*. 2000;5:241-248.

14. Klässbo M, Harms-Ringdahl K, Larsson G. Examination of passive ROM and capsular patterns in the hip. *Physiother Res Int*. 2003;8:1-12.

15. Lin YC, Davey RC, Cochrane T. Tests for physical function of the elderly with knee and hip osteoarthritis. *Scand J Med Sci Sports*. 2001;11:280-286.

16. Bijl D, Dekker J, van Baar ME, et al. Validity of Cyriax's concept capsular pattern for the diagnosis of osteoarthritis of hip and/or knee. *Scand J Rheumatol*. 1998;27:347-351.

17. Woodley SJ, Nicholson HD, Livingstone V, et al. Lateral hip pain: findings from magnetic resonance imaging and clinical examination. *J Orthop Sports Phys Ther*. 2008;38:313-328.

18. Birrell F, Croft P, Cooper C, et al. Predicting radiographic hip osteoarthritis from range of movement. *Rheumatology (Oxford)*. 2001;40:506-512.

19. Cook C, Massa L, Harm-Ernandes I, et al. Interrater reliability and diagnostic accuracy of pelvic girdle pain classification. *J Manipulative Physiol Ther*. 2007;30:252-258.

20. Joe G, Kovacs J, Miller K, et al. Diagnosis of avascular necrosis of the hip in asymptomatic HIV-infected patients: clinical correlation of physical examination with magnetic resonance imaging. *J Back Musculoskeletal Rehabil*. 2002;16:135-139.

21. Jari S, Paton RW, Srinivasan MS. Unilateral limitation of abduction of the hip. A valuable clinical sign for DDH? *J Bone Joint Surg Br*. 2002;84:104-107.

22. Castelein RM, Korte J. Limited hip abduction in the infant. *J Pediatr Orthop*. 2001;21:668-670.

23. Malliaras P, Hogan A, Nawrocki A, et al. Hip flexibility and strength measures: reliability and association with athletic groin pain. *Br J Sports Med*. 2009

24. Bird PA, Oakley SP, Shnier R, Kirkham BW. Prospective evaluation of magnetic resonance imaging and physical examination findings in patients with greater trochanteric pain syndrome. *Arthritis Rheum*. 2001; 44:2138-2145.

25. Piva SR, Fitzgerald K, Irrgang JJ, et al. Reliability of measures of impairments associated with patellofemoral pain syndrome. *BMC Musculoskelet Disord*. 2006; 7:33.

26. Reese NB, Bandy WD. Use of an inclinometer to measure flexibility of the iliotibial band using the Ober test and the modified Ober test: differences in magnitude and reliability of measurements. *J Orthop Sports Phys Ther*. 2003;33:326-330.

27. Melchione WE, Sullivan MS. Reliability of measurements obtained by use of an instrument designed to indirectly measure iliotibial band length. *J Orthop Sports Phys Ther*. 1993;18:511-515.

28. Clapis PA, Davis SM, Davis RO. Reliability of inclinometer and goniometric measurements of hip extension flexibility using the modified Thomas test. *Physiother Theory Pract*. 2008;24:135-141.

29. Bullock-Saxton JE, Bullock MI. Repeatability of muscle length measures around the hip. *Physiother Can*. 1994;46:105-109.

30. Tiru M, Goh SH, Low BY. Use of percussion as a screening tool in the diagnosis of occult hip fractures. *Singapore Med J.* 2002;43:467-469.
31. Adams SL, Yarnold PR. Clinical use of the patellar-pubic percussion sign in hip trauma. *Am J Emerg Med.* 1997;15:173-175.
32. Pua YH, Cowan SM, Wrigley TV, Bennell KL. The Lower Extremity Functional Scale could be an alternative to the Western Ontario and McMaster Universities Osteoarthritis Index physical function scale. *J Clin Epidemiol.* 2009
33. Binkley JM, Stratford PW, Lott SA, Riddle DL. The Lower Extremity Functional Scale (LEFS): scale development, measurement properties, and clinical application. North American Orthopaedic Rehabilitation Research Network. *Phys Ther.* 1999;79:371-383.
34. Angst F, Aeschlimann A, Stucki G. Smallest detectable and minimal clinically important differences of rehabilitation intervention with their implications for required sample sizes using WOMAC and SF-36 quality of life measurement instruments in patients with osteoarthritis of the lower extremities. *Arthritis Rheum.* 2001;45:384-391.
35. Li L, Liu X, Herr K. Postoperative pain intensity assessment: a comparison of four scales in Chinese adults. *Pain Med.* 2007;8:223-234.
36. Farrar JT, Berlin JA, Strom BL. Clinically important changes in acute pain outcome measures: a validation study. *J Pain Symptom Manage.* 2003;25:406-411.
37. Farrar JT, Portenoy RK, Berlin JA, et al. Defining the clinically important difference in pain outcome measures. *Pain.* 2000;88:287-294.

Knee 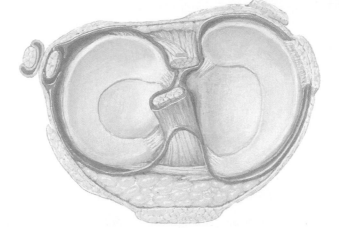 7

CLINICAL SUMMARY AND RECOMMENDATIONS

Patient History

Complaints
- Little is known about the utility of subjective complaints with knee pain. The lack of self-noticed swelling seems moderately helpful in ruling out knee joint effusion. Similarly, the absence of "weight bearing during trauma" may help rule out a meniscal tear (both $-LRs = .40$).

Physical Examination

Screening
- The Ottawa Knee Rule for Radiography is highly sensitive for knee fractures in both adults and children. When patients are younger than 55, can bear weight and flex their knee to 90°, and have no tenderness on the patella or fibular head; providers can confidently rule out a knee fracture ($-LR = .05$ to $.07$)

Range of Motion and Strength Assessment
- Measuring knee range of motion (ROM) has consistently been shown to be highly reliable but is of unknown diagnostic utility. The assessment of "end-feel" during ROM, however, is unreliable, especially between different examiners.
- Assessing strength with manual muscle testing (MMT) has been shown to accurately detect side-to-side knee extension strength deficits, at least in patients in an acute rehabilitation hospital setting.

Special Tests
- Several systematic reviews with meta-analysis have examined special tests of the knee.
- Both "joint line tenderness" and McMurray's test consistently show moderate utility in detecting and ruling out meniscal tears. More recently, the Thessaly test has been shown to be excellent at both detecting and ruling ruling our meniscal tears ($+LR = 9.0$ to 39.3, $-LR = .08$ to $.35$).
- While the anterior drawer and the pivot shift test are good at identifying anterior cruciate ligament (ACL) tears ($+LR = 2.9$ to 8.5), the Lachman test is best at ruling them out ($-LR = .10$ to $.20$).
- Varus and valgus testing, while not particularly reliable, is fairly good at ruling out medial collateral ligament (MCL) tears ($-LR = .20$ to $.30$).
- The "moving patellar apprehension test" seems to show very good diagnostic utility in both identifying and ruling out patellar instability ($+LR = 8.3$, $-LR = .00$).

Combinations of Findings
- Generally, the clinical examination and/or combinations of findings seem to be very good at identifying and ruling out various knee pathologies, including meniscal tears, ACL tears, and symptomatic plica.
- However, although the ability of several combinations of tests to identify meniscal tears have been studied, no combination seems as helpful as the Thessaly test alone.

Interventions

- In patients with patellofemoral pain syndrome, two factors (2° or more of forefoot valgus and 78° or less of great toe extension) seem to predict a favorable response to off-the-shelf foot orthoses and activity modification.
- Similarly, several factors have been identified that predict which patients with knee osteoarthritis (OA) may benefit from hip mobilizations.

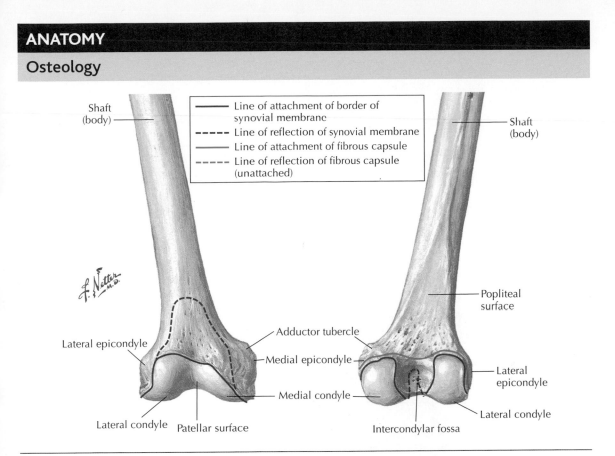

Shaft (body)

Line of attachment of border of synovial membrane
Line of reflection of synovial membrane
Line of attachment of fibrous capsule
Line of reflection of fibrous capsule (unattached)

Shaft (body)

Popliteal surface

Lateral epicondyle

Adductor tubercle

Medial epicondyle

Lateral epicondyle

Medial condyle

Lateral condyle   Patellar surface

Intercondylar fossa

Lateral condyle

Figure 7-1

Femur.

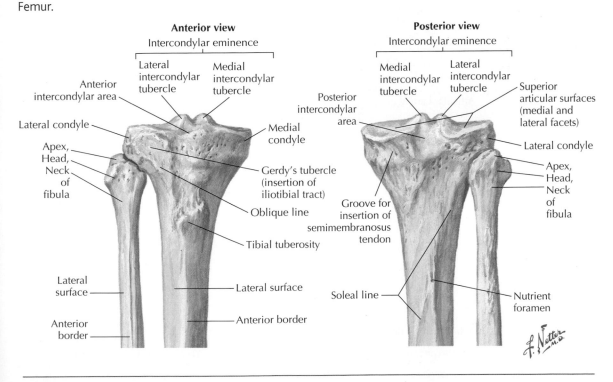

Anterior view

Intercondylar eminence

Lateral intercondylar tubercle

Medial intercondylar tubercle

Anterior intercondylar area

Lateral condyle

Medial condyle

Apex, Head, Neck of fibula

Gerdy's tubercle (insertion of iliotibial tract)

Oblique line

Tibial tuberosity

Lateral surface

Lateral surface

Anterior border

Anterior border

Posterior view

Intercondylar eminence

Medial intercondylar tubercle

Lateral intercondylar tubercle

Posterior intercondylar area

Superior articular surfaces (medial and lateral facets)

Lateral condyle

Apex, Head, Neck of fibula

Groove for insertion of semimembranosus tendon

Soleal line

Nutrient foramen

Figure 7-2

Tibia and fibula.

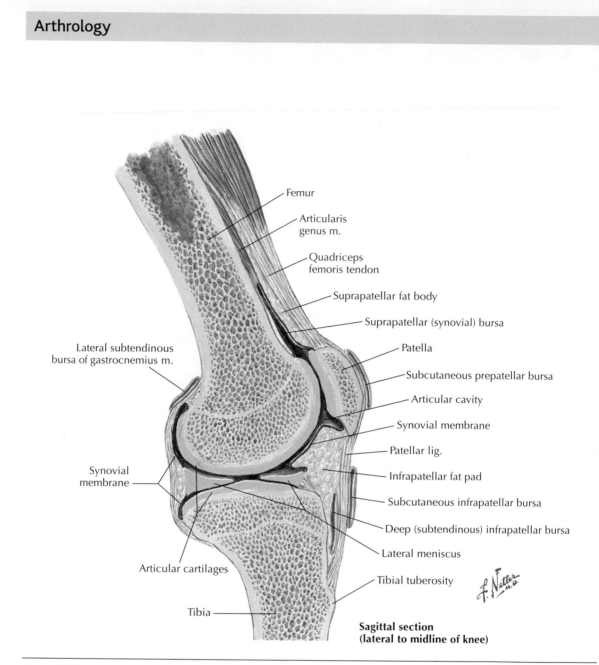

Femur

Articularis genus m.

Quadriceps femoris tendon

Suprapatellar fat body

Suprapatellar (synovial) bursa

Lateral subtendinous bursa of gastrocnemius m.

Patella

Subcutaneous prepatellar bursa

Articular cavity

Synovial membrane

Patellar lig.

Synovial membrane

Infrapatellar fat pad

Subcutaneous infrapatellar bursa

Deep (subtendinous) infrapatellar bursa

Lateral meniscus

Articular cartilages

Tibial tuberosity

Tibia

**Sagittal section
(lateral to midline of knee)**

Figure 7-3

Sagittal knee.

Joints	Type and Classification	Closed Packed Position	Capsular Pattern
Tibiofemoral	Double condyloid	Full extension	Flexion restricted greater than extension
Proximal tibiofibular	Synovial: plane	Not reported	Not reported
Patellofemoral	Synovial: plane	Full flexion	Not reported

Ligaments

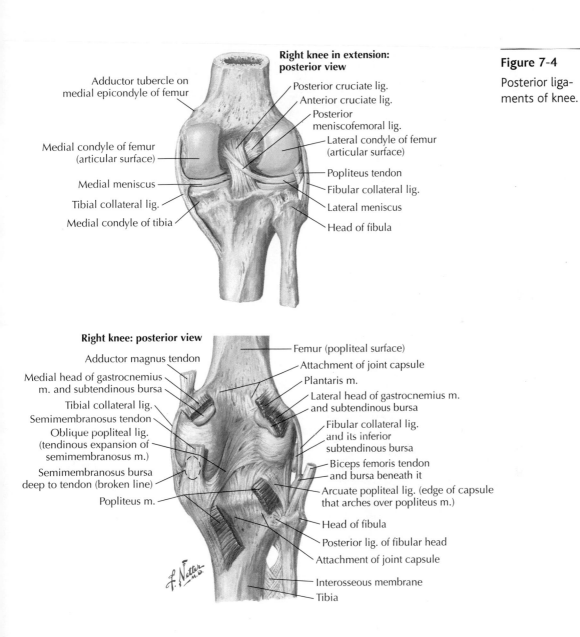

Right knee in extension: posterior view

Adductor tubercle on medial epicondyle of femur

Posterior cruciate lig.

Anterior cruciate lig.

Posterior meniscofemoral lig.

Lateral condyle of femur (articular surface)

Medial condyle of femur (articular surface)

Medial meniscus

Tibial collateral lig.

Medial condyle of tibia

Popliteus tendon

Fibular collateral lig.

Lateral meniscus

Head of fibula

Figure 7-4

Posterior ligaments of knee.

Right knee: posterior view

Adductor magnus tendon

Medial head of gastrocnemius m. and subtendinous bursa

Tibial collateral lig.

Semimembranosus tendon

Oblique popliteal lig. (tendinous expansion of semimembranosus m.)

Semimembranosus bursa deep to tendon (broken line)

Popliteus m.

Femur (popliteal surface)

Attachment of joint capsule

Plantaris m.

Lateral head of gastrocnemius m. and subtendinous bursa

Fibular collateral lig. and its inferior subtendinous bursa

Biceps femoris tendon and bursa beneath it

Arcuate popliteal lig. (edge of capsule that arches over popliteus m.)

Head of fibula

Posterior lig. of fibular head

Attachment of joint capsule

Interosseous membrane

Tibia

Ligaments	Attachments	Function
Posterior meniscofemoral	Lateral meniscus to posterior cruciate ligament (PCL) and medial femoral condyle	Reinforces posterior lateral meniscal attachment
Oblique popliteal	Posterior aspect of medial tibial condyle to posterior aspect of fibrous capsule	Strengthens posterior portion of joint capsule
Arcuate popliteal	Posterior fibular head over tendon of popliteus to posterior capsule	Strengthens posterior portion of joint capsule
Posterior ligament of fibular head	Posterior fibular head to inferior lateral tibial condyle	Reinforces posterior joint capsule

Ligaments (continued)

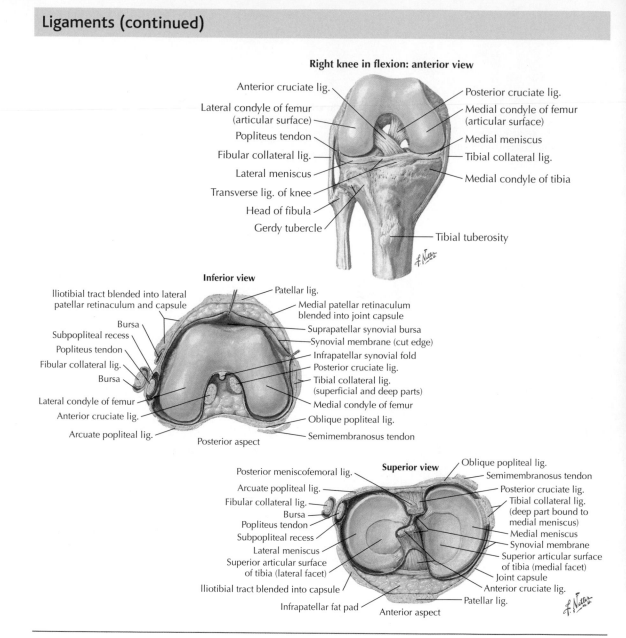

Right knee in flexion: anterior view

- Anterior cruciate lig.
- Lateral condyle of femur (articular surface)
- Popliteus tendon
- Fibular collateral lig.
- Lateral meniscus
- Transverse lig. of knee
- Head of fibula
- Gerdy tubercle
- Posterior cruciate lig.
- Medial condyle of femur (articular surface)
- Medial meniscus
- Tibial collateral lig.
- Medial condyle of tibia
- Tibial tuberosity

Inferior view

- Iliotibial tract blended into lateral patellar retinaculum and capsule
- Bursa
- Subpopliteal recess
- Popliteus tendon
- Fibular collateral lig.
- Bursa
- Lateral condyle of femur
- Anterior cruciate lig.
- Arcuate popliteal lig.
- Patellar lig.
- Medial patellar retinaculum blended into joint capsule
- Suprapatellar synovial bursa
- Synovial membrane (cut edge)
- Infrapatellar synovial fold
- Posterior cruciate lig.
- Tibial collateral lig. (superficial and deep parts)
- Medial condyle of femur
- Oblique popliteal lig.
- Semimembranosus tendon
- Posterior aspect

Superior view

- Posterior meniscofemoral lig.
- Arcuate popliteal lig.
- Fibular collateral lig.
- Bursa
- Popliteus tendon
- Subpopliteal recess
- Lateral meniscus
- Superior articular surface of tibia (lateral facet)
- Iliotibial tract blended into capsule
- Infrapatellar fat pad
- Oblique popliteal lig.
- Semimembranosus tendon
- Posterior cruciate lig.
- Tibial collateral lig. (deep part bound to medial meniscus)
- Medial meniscus
- Synovial membrane
- Superior articular surface of tibia (medial facet)
- Joint capsule
- Anterior cruciate lig.
- Patellar lig.
- Anterior aspect

Figure 7-5

Inferior and anterior ligaments of knee.

Ligaments	Attachments	Function
Anterior cruciate	Anterior intracondylar aspect of tibial plateau to posteromedial side of lateral femoral condyle	Prevents posterior translation of femur on tibia and anterior translation of tibia on femur
Posterior cruciate	Posterior intracondylar aspect of tibial plateau to anterolateral side of medial femoral condyle	Prevents anterior translation of femur on tibia and posterior translation of tibia on femur
Fibular collateral	Lateral epicondyle of femur to lateral aspect of fibular head	Protects joint from varus stress
Tibial collateral	Femoral medial epicondyle to medial condyle of tibia	Protects the joint from valgus stress
Transverse ligament of knee	Anterior edges of menisci	Allows menisci to move together during knee movement

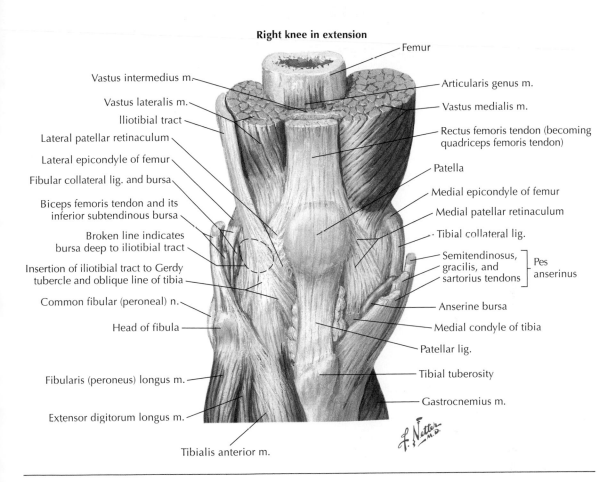

Right knee in extension

Femur

Vastus intermedius m.

Vastus lateralis m.

Iliotibial tract

Lateral patellar retinaculum

Lateral epicondyle of femur

Fibular collateral lig. and bursa

Biceps femoris tendon and its inferior subtendinous bursa

Broken line indicates bursa deep to iliotibial tract

Insertion of iliotibial tract to Gerdy tubercle and oblique line of tibia

Common fibular (peroneal) n.

Head of fibula

Fibularis (peroneus) longus m.

Extensor digitorum longus m.

Tibialis anterior m.

Articularis genus m.

Vastus medialis m.

Rectus femoris tendon (becoming quadriceps femoris tendon)

Patella

Medial epicondyle of femur

Medial patellar retinaculum

Tibial collateral lig.

Semitendinosus, gracilis, and sartorius tendons } Pes anserinus

Anserine bursa

Medial condyle of tibia

Patellar lig.

Tibial tuberosity

Gastrocnemius m.

Figure 7-6

Anterior muscles of knee.

Muscles	Proximal Attachments	Distal Attachments	Nerve and Segmental Level	Action
Quadriceps				
Rectus femoris	Anterior inferior iliac spine and ileum just superior to acetabulum	Base of patella and by patellar ligament to tibial tuberosity	Femoral nerve (L2, L3, L4)	Extends knee; rectus femoris also flexes hip and stabilizes head of femur in acetabulum
Vastus lateralis	Greater trochanter and linea aspera of femur			
Vastus medialis	Intertrochanteric line and linea aspera			
Vastus intermedius	Anterolateral aspect of shaft of femur			
Articularis genu	Anteroinferior aspect of femur	Synovial membrane of knee joint	Femoral nerve (L3, L4)	Pulls synovial membrane superiorly during knee extension to prevent pinching of membrane

Muscles (continued)

Muscles	Proximal Attachments	Distal Attachments	Nerve and Segmental Level	Action
Hamstrings				
Semimembranosus	Ischial tuberosity	Medial aspect of superior tibia	Tibial branch of sciatic nerve (L4, L5, S1, S2)	Flexes and medially rotates knee, extends and medially rotates hip
Semitendinosus	Ischial tuberosity	Posterior aspect of medial condyle of tibia		
Biceps femoris				
Short head	Lateral linea aspera and proximal two thirds of supracondylar line of femur	Lateral head of fibula and lateral tibial condyle	Fibular branch of sciatic nerve (L5, S1, S2)	Flexes and laterally rotates knee
Long head	Ischial tuberosity		Tibial branch of sciatic nerve (L5, S1-3)	Flexes and laterally rotates knee, extends and laterally rotates hip
Gracilis	Body and inferior ramus of pubis	Medial aspect of superior tibia	Obturator nerve (L2, L3)	Adducts hip, flexes and medially rotates knee
Sartorius	Anterior superior iliac spine and anterior iliac crest	Superomedial aspect of tibia	Femoral nerve (L2, L3)	Flexes, abducts, and externally rotates hip, flexes knee
Gastrocnemius				
Lateral head	Lateral femoral condyle	Posterior calcaneus	Tibial nerve (S1, S2)	Plantarflexes ankle and flexes knee
Medial head	Superior aspect of medial femoral condyle			
Popliteus	Lateral femoral condyle and lateral meniscus	Superior to soleal line on posterior tibia	Tibial nerve (L4, L5, S1)	Weak knee flexion and unlocking of knee joint
Plantaris	Lateral supracondylar line of femur and oblique popliteal ligament	Posterior calcaneus	Tibial nerve (S1, S2)	Weak assist in knee flexion and ankle plantarflexion

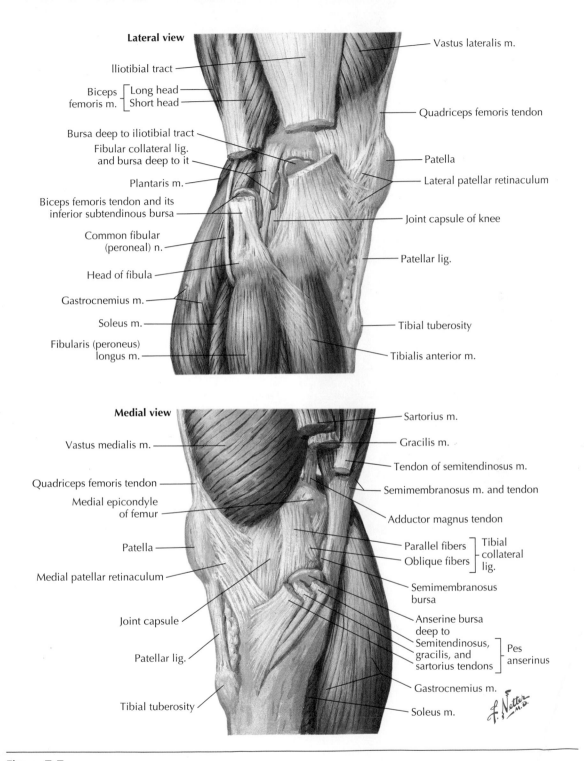

Lateral view

- Vastus lateralis m.
- Iliotibial tract
- Biceps femoris m. {Long head / Short head}
- Quadriceps femoris tendon
- Bursa deep to iliotibial tract
- Fibular collateral lig. and bursa deep to it
- Patella
- Lateral patellar retinaculum
- Plantaris m.
- Biceps femoris tendon and its inferior subtendinous bursa
- Joint capsule of knee
- Common fibular (peroneal) n.
- Patellar lig.
- Head of fibula
- Gastrocnemius m.
- Soleus m.
- Tibial tuberosity
- Fibularis (peroneus) longus m.
- Tibialis anterior m.

Medial view

- Sartorius m.
- Vastus medialis m.
- Gracilis m.
- Tendon of semitendinosus m.
- Semimembranosus m. and tendon
- Quadriceps femoris tendon
- Medial epicondyle of femur
- Adductor magnus tendon
- Patella
- Parallel fibers / Oblique fibers } Tibial collateral lig.
- Medial patellar retinaculum
- Semimembranosus bursa
- Joint capsule
- Anserine bursa deep to Semitendinosus, gracilis, and sartorius tendons } Pes anserinus
- Patellar lig.
- Gastrocnemius m.
- Tibial tuberosity
- Soleus m.

Figure 7-7

Lateral and medial muscles of knee.

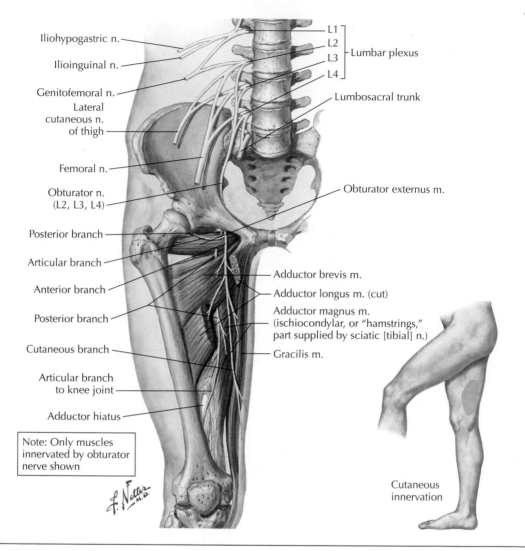

Figure 7-8

Obturator nerve.

Nerves	Segmental Level	Sensory	Motor
Femoral	L2, L3, L4	Thigh via cutaneous nerves	Iliacus, sartorius, quadriceps femoris, articularis genu, pectineus
Obturator	L2, L3, L4	Medial thigh	Adductor longus, adductor brevis, adductor magnus (adductor part), gracilis, obturator externus
Saphenous	L2, L3, L4	Medial leg and foot	No motor
Tibial nerve	L4, L5, S1, S2, S3	Posterior heel and plantar surface of foot	Semitendinosus, semimembranosus, biceps femoris, adductor magnus, gastrocnemius, soleus, plantaris, flexor hallucis longus, flexor digitorum longus, tibialis posterior
Common fibular nerve	L4, L5, S1, S2	Lateral posterior leg	Biceps femoris

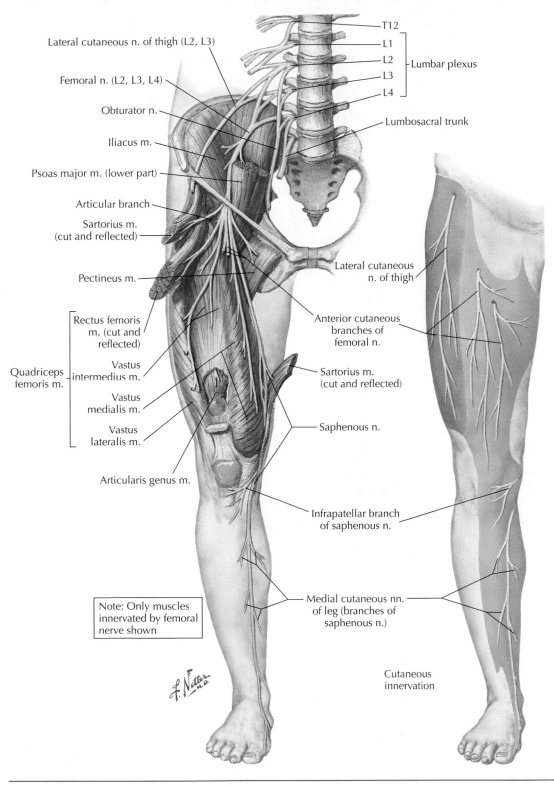

Figure 7-9

Femoral nerve and lateral femoral cutaneous nerves.

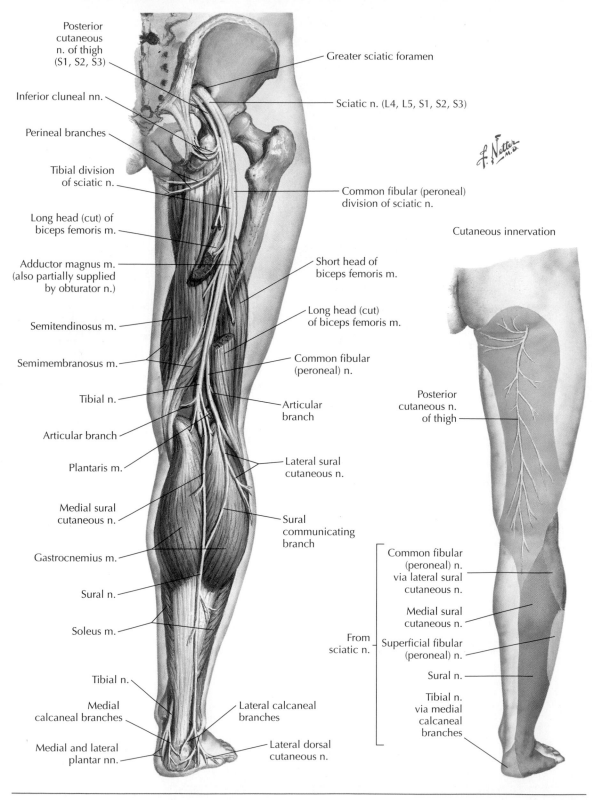

Posterior cutaneous n. of thigh (S1, S2, S3)

Inferior cluneal nn.

Perineal branches

Tibial division of sciatic n.

Long head (cut) of biceps femoris m.

Adductor magnus m. (also partially supplied by obturator n.)

Semitendinosus m.

Semimembranosus m.

Tibial n.

Articular branch

Plantaris m.

Medial sural cutaneous n.

Gastrocnemius m.

Sural n.

Soleus m.

Tibial n.

Medial calcaneal branches

Medial and lateral plantar nn.

Greater sciatic foramen

Sciatic n. (L4, L5, S1, S2, S3)

Common fibular (peroneal) division of sciatic n.

Short head of biceps femoris m.

Long head (cut) of biceps femoris m.

Common fibular (peroneal) n.

Articular branch

Lateral sural cutaneous n.

Sural communicating branch

Lateral calcaneal branches

Lateral dorsal cutaneous n.

Cutaneous innervation

Posterior cutaneous n. of thigh

From sciatic n.

Common fibular (peroneal) n. via lateral sural cutaneous n.

Medial sural cutaneous n.

Superficial fibular (peroneal) n.

Sural n.

Tibial n. via medial calcaneal branches

Figure 7-10

Sciatic nerve and posterior femoral cutaneous nerve.

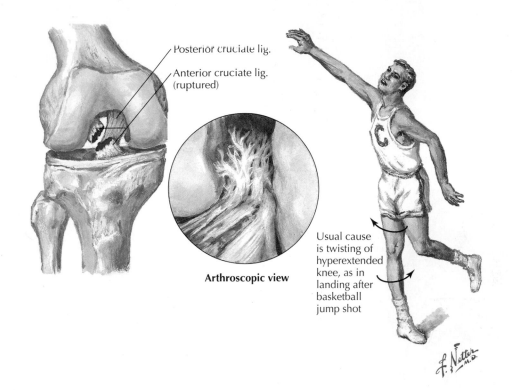

Arthroscopic view

Posterior cruciate lig.

Anterior cruciate lig. (ruptured)

Usual cause is twisting of hyperextended knee, as in landing after basketball jump shot

Figure 7-11

Anterior cruciate ligament ruptures.

Patient Reports	Initial Hypothesis
Patient reports a traumatic onset of knee pain that occurred during jumping, twisting, or changing directions with foot planted	Possible ligamentous injury (anterior cruciate)[1,2] Possible patella subluxation[2] Possible quadriceps rupture Possible meniscal tear
Patient reports traumatic injury that resulted in a posteriorly directed force to tibia with knee flexed	Possible PCL injury (posterior cruciate)[3]
Patient reports traumatic injury that resulted in a varus or valgus force exerted on knee	Possible collateral ligament injury (LCL or MCL)[3]
Patient reports anterior knee pain with jumping and full knee flexion	Possible patellar tendonitis[2,4] Possible patellofemoral pain syndrome[5,6]
Patient reports swelling in knee with occasional locking and clicking	Possible meniscal tear[7] Possible loose body within knee joint
Patient reports pain with prolonged knee flexion, during squats, and while going up and down stairs	Possible patellofemoral pain syndrome[5,6]
Patient reports pain and stiffness in morning that diminishes after a few hours	Possible OA[8,9]

Reliability of Assessing Subjective Questions in Patients with Osteoarthritis of Knee

Progressive stages in joint pathology

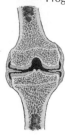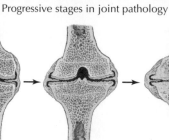

ICC or κ	Interpretation
.81-1.0	Substantial agreement
.61-.80	Moderate agreement
.41-.60	Fair agreement
.11-.40	Slight agreement
.0-.10	No agreement

Early degenerative changes with surface fraying of articular cartilages

Further erosion of cartilages, pitting, and cleft formation. Hypertrophic changes of bone at joint margins

Cartilages almost completely destroyed and joint space narrowed. Subchondral bone irregular and eburnated; spur formation at margins. Fibrosis of joint capsule

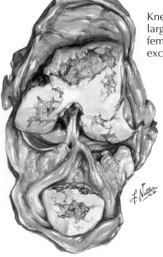

Knee joint opened anteriorly reveals large erosion of articular cartilages of femur and patella with cartilaginous excrescences at intercondylar notch

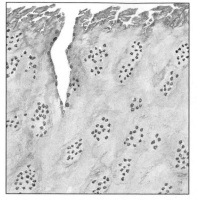

Section of articular cartilage shows fraying of surface and deep cleft. Hyaline cartilage abnormal with clumping of chondrocytes

Figure 7-12

Osteoarthritis of the knee.

History	Population	Inter-examiner Reliability
Acute injury[10]	152 patients with OA of knee	κ = .21 (.03, .39)
Swelling[10]		κ = .33 (.17, .49)
Giving way[10]		κ = .12 (−.04, .28)
Locking[10]		κ = .44 (.26, .62)
Pain, generalized[10]		κ = −.03 (.15, .21)
Pain at rest[10]		κ = .16 (.0, 32)
Pain rising from chair[10]		κ = .25 (.05, .45)
Pain climbing stairs[10]		κ = .21 (.06, .48)
Inactivity stiffness[9]	49 patients presenting to outpatient rheumatology clinics for OA of knee	κ = .90 (.74, 1.0)
Pain on using stairs[9]		κ = .86 (.70, 1.0)
Night pain[9]		κ = .81 (.66, .96)

Diagnostic Utility of the Patient History for Identifying Effusion, Meniscal Tears, and Medial Collateral Ligament Tears

+LR	Interpretation	−LR
>10	Large	<.1
5.0-10.0	Moderate	.1-.2
2.0-5.0	Small	.2-.5
1.0-2.0	Rarely important	.5-1.0

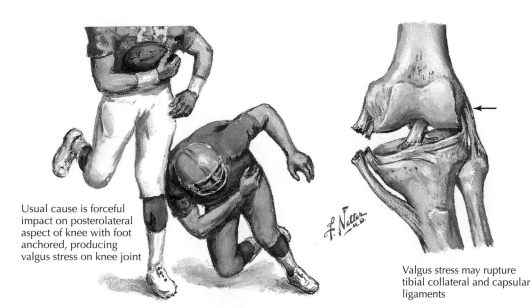

Usual cause is forceful impact on posterolateral aspect of knee with foot anchored, producing valgus stress on knee joint

Valgus stress may rupture tibial collateral and capsular ligaments

Figure 7-13

Medial collateral ligament rupture.

Patient Report and Study Quality	Population	Reference Standard	Sens	Spec	+LR	−LR
Self-noticed swelling[11] ◇		Knee joint effusion per MRI	.80 (.68, .92)	.45 (.35, .39)	1.5 (1.1, 1.9)	.40 (.20, .90)
Trauma by external force to the leg[12] ◇		MCL tear per MRI	.21 (.07, .35)	.89 (.83, .96)	2.0 (.8, 4.8)	.90 (.70, 1.1)
Rotational trauma[12] ◇	134 patients with traumatic knee complaints		.62 (.41, .83)	.63 (.51, .74)	1.7 (1.1, 2.6)	.60 (.30, 1.1)
Age > 40 years[13] ◇		Meniscal tear per MRI	.70 (.57, .83)	.64 (.54, .74)	2.0 (1.4, 2.8)	.50 (.30, .70)
Continuation of activity impossible[1] ◇			.64 (.49, .78)	.55 (.45, .66)	1.4 (1.0, 2.0)	.70 (.40, 1.0)
Weight bearing during trauma[13] ◇			.85 (.75, .96)	.35 (.24, .46)	1.3 (1.1, 1.6)	.40 (.20, .90)

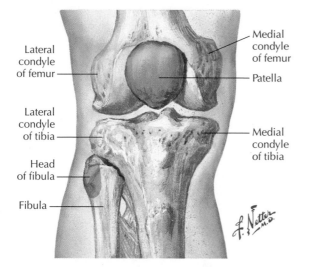

Lateral condyle of femur

Medial condyle of femur

Patella

Lateral condyle of tibia

Medial condyle of tibia

Head of fibula

Fibula

Stiell and colleagues[60,61] identified a clinical prediction rule to determine the need to order radiographs following knee trauma. If one of five variables identified were present, radiographs were required. The five variables included an age ≥55 years, isolated patellar tenderness without other bone tenderness, tenderness of the fibular head, inability to flex knee to 90°, inability to bear weight immediately after injury and in the emergency room (unable to transfer weight onto each lower extremity-regardless of limping). This rule has been validated in numerous studies in adult[14,61-63] and pediatric[64,65] populations. The inter-examiner agreement between clinicians for identification of predictor variables exhibited a kappa value of .77 with a 95% confidence interval of .65-.89.[61]

Types of distal femur fractures

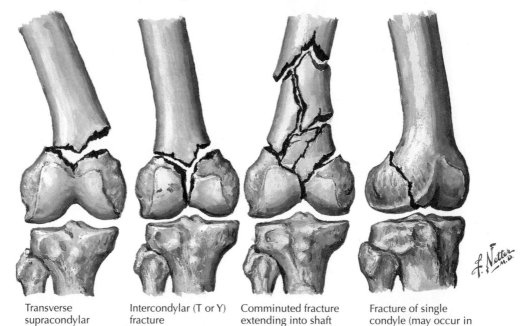

Transverse supracondylar fracture

Intercondylar (T or Y) fracture

Comminuted fracture extending into shaft

Fracture of single condyle (may occur in frontal or oblique plane)

Figure 7-14

Identifying the need to order radiographs following acute knee trauma.

Screening

Diagnostic Utility of the Ottawa Knee Rule for Radiography

+LR	Interpretation	−LR
>10	Large	<.1
5.0-10.0	Moderate	.1-.2
2.0-5.0	Small	.2-.5
1.0-2.0	Rarely important	.5-1.0

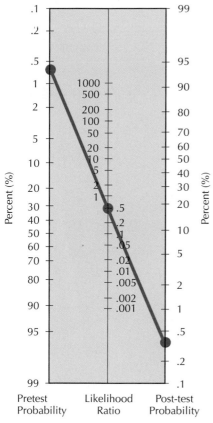

Pretest Probability   Likelihood Ratio   Post-test Probability

Figure 7-15

Nomogram. Assuming a fracture prevalence of 7% (statistically pooled from Bachmann and colleagues[14]), an adult seen in the emergency department with an acute injury whose finding was negative on the Ottawa Knee Rule would have a 0.37% (95% CI, 0.15% to 1.48%) chance of having a knee fracture. *(Adapted with permission from Fagan TJ. Nomogram for Bayes' theorem. N Engl J Med. 1975;293-257. Copyright 2005, Massachusetts Medical Society. All rights reserved.)*

Test and Study Quality	Description and Positive Findings	Population	Reference Standard	Sens	Spec	+LR	−LR
Ottawa Knee Rule for Radiography in Adults[14] **2004 Meta-analysis**	Knee x-rays ordered when patients exhibited any of the following: (1) Age ≥55 years (2) Isolated patellar tenderness without other bone tenderness (3) Tenderness of the fibular head (4) Inability to flex knee to 90° (5) Inability to bear weight immediately after injury and in the emergency department	Statistically pooled data from six high-quality studies involving 4249 adults	X-rays	.99 (.93, 1.0)	.49 (.43, .51)	1.9	.05 (.02, .23)
Ottawa Knee Rule for Radiography in Children[15] **2009 Meta-analysis**		Statistically pooled data from three high-quality studies involving 1130 children		.99 (.94, 1.0)	.46 (.43, .49)	1.9 (1.6, 2.4)	.07 (.02, .29)

Reliability of Detecting Inflammation

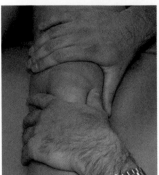

ICC or κ	Interpretation
.81-1.0	Substantial agreement
.61-.80	Moderate agreement
.41-.60	Fair agreement
.11-.40	Slight agreement
.0-.10	No agreement

Figure 7-16
Fluctuation test.

Test and Study	Description and Positive Findings	Population	Inter-examiner Reliability
Observation of swelling[16]	Not described	53 patients with knee pain	κ = −.02 to .65
Palpation for warmth[16]			κ = −.18
Palpation for swelling[16]			κ = −.11 to .11
Fluctuation test[17]	With patient supine, examiner places thumb and finger around patella while pushing any fluid from suprapatellar pouch with other hand. Positive if finger and thumb are pushed apart	152 patients with unilateral knee dysfunction	κ = .37
Patellar tap test[17]	With patient supine, examiner presses suprapatellar pouch then taps on patella. Patella remains in contact with femur if no swelling is present		κ = .21
Palpation for warmth[17]	Examiner palpates anterior aspect of knee. Results compared with uninvolved knee		κ = .66
Visual inspection for redness[17]	Examiner visually inspects involved knee for redness and compares it with uninvolved side		κ = .21

Diagnostic Utility of the Ballottement Test for Identifying Knee Joint Effusion

+LR	Interpretation	−LR
>10	Large	<.1
5.0-10.0	Moderate	.1-.2
2.0-5.0	Small	.2-.5
1.0-2.0	Rarely important	.5-1.0

Test and Study Quality	Description and Positive Findings	Population	Reference Standard	Sens	Spec	+LR	−LR
Ballottement test[11] ◇	Examiner quickly pushes the patient's patella posteriorly with 2 or 3 fingers. Positive if patella bounces off trochlea with a distinct impact	134 patients with traumatic knee complaints	Knee joint effusion per MRI	.83 (.71, .94)	.49 (.39, .59)	1.6 (1.3, 2.1)	.30 (.20, .70)
Self-noticed knee swelling + Ballottement test[11] ◇	Combination of two findings			.67 (.52, .81)	.82 (.73, .90)	3.6 (2.2, 5.9)	.40 (.30, .60)

Range of Motion

Reliability of Range of Motion Measurements

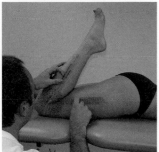

ICC or κ	Interpretation
.81-1.0	Substantial agreement
.61-.80	Moderate agreement
.41-.60	Fair agreement
.11-.40	Slight agreement
.0-.10	No agreement

Figure 7-17

Measurement of active knee flexion range of motion.

Measurements	Instrumentation	Population	Reliability				
Active flexion sitting[18]	Standard goniometer	30 patients 3 days after total knee arthroplasty	Inter-examiner ICC = **.86 (.64, .94)**				
Passive flexion sitting[18]			Inter-examiner ICC = **.88 (.69, .95)**				
Active flexion supine[18]			Inter-examiner ICC = **.89 (.78, .95)**				
Passive flexion supine[18]			Inter-examiner ICC = **.88 (.77, .94)**				
Active extension[18]			Inter-examiner ICC = **.64 (.38, .81)**				
Passive extension[18]			Inter-examiner ICC = **.62 (.28, .80)**				
Passive flexion[16]	Standard goniometer	53 patients with knee pain	Intra-examiner ICC = **.82** Inter-examiner ICC = **.68**				
Passive flexion Passive extension[19]	Standard goniometer	25 patients with knee osteoarthritis	Inter-examiner ICC = **.87 (.73, .94)** Inter-examiner ICC = **.69 (.41, .85)**				
Passive flexion and extension[20]	3 standard goniometers (metal, large plastic, and small plastic)	24 patients referred for physical therapy	Intra-examiner ICC				
					Flexion		Extension
			Metal		.97		.96
			Large		.99		.91
			Small		.99		.97
Passive flexion[21]	Standard goniometer	30 asymptomatic subjects	Inter-examiner ICC = **.99**				
Passive flexion Passive extension[22]	Standard goniometer	43 patients referred for physical therapy where examination would normally include passive ROM (PROM) measurements of knee	Intra-examiner ICC		Inter-examiner ICC		
			Flexion	.99	Flexion		.90
			Extension	.98	Extension		.86
Passive flexion Passive extension[22]	Visual estimation		Inter-examiner ICC = **.83** Inter-examiner ICC = **.82**				
Active flexion Active extension[23]	Standard goniometer	20 asymptomatic subjects	Intra-examiner ICC = **.95** Intra-examiner ICC = **.85**				
Active flexion[24]	Universal goniometer	60 healthy university students	Intra-examiner ICC = **.86-.97** Inter-examiner ICC = **.62-1.0**				
Passive flexion Passive extension[25]	Universal goniometer	79 patients with OA of knee	Intra-examiner ICC = **.95-.96** Intra-examiner ICC = **.71-.86**				
Passive flexion Passive extension[17]	Standard goniometer	152 patients with unilateral knee dysfunction	Inter-examiner ICC				
			Involved knee		Uninvolved knee		
			Flexion	.97	Flexion		.80
			Extension	.94	Extension		.72

ICC, Intraclass correlation coefficient.

Range of Motion

Reliability of Determining Capsular and Noncapsular End-Feels

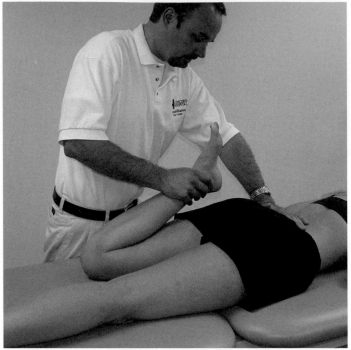

ICC or κ	Interpretation
.81-1.0	Substantial agreement
.61-.80	Moderate agreement
.41-.60	Fair agreement
.11-.40	Slight agreement
.0-.10	No agreement

Figure 7-18

Assessment of end-feel for knee flexion.

Test and Study	Description and Positive Findings	Population	Reliability
Flexion end-feel Extension end-feel[19]	End-feel is assessed at end of PROM and categorized as "normal," "empty," "stiff," or "loose"	25 patients with knee osteoarthritis	Inter-examiner ICC = **.31** **(−.53, 1.15)** Inter-examiner ICC = **.25** (−.18, .68)
Flexion end-feel Extension end-feel[25]	End-feel is assessed at end of PROM and categorized as "capsular," "tissue approximation," "springy block," "bony," "spasm," "empty"	79 patients with OA of knee	Intra-examiner κ = **.48** Intra-examiner κ = **.17**
Flexion end-feel Extension end-feel[26]	End-feel is assessed at end of PROM and graded on an 11-point scale with "capsular at end of normal range," "capsular early in range," "capsular," "tissue approximation," "springy block," "bony," "spasm," "empty"	40 patients with unilateral knee pain	Intra-examiner κ = **.76 (.55, .97)** Inter-examiner κ = **−.01 (−.36, .35)** Intra-examiner κ = **1.0 (1.0, 1.0)** Inter-examiner κ = **.43** (−.06, .92)
End-feel assessment during Lachman test[27]	Examiners asked to grade end-feel during Lachman test. End-feel graded as "hard" or "soft"	35 patients referred to physical therapy clinics for rehabilitation of knee joint	Intra-examiner κ = **.33**
End-feel of adduction stress applied to knee[28]	Examiner places knee in 0° and 30° of flexion and applies valgus force through knee. End-feel graded as "soft" or "firm"	50 patients referred to an outpatient orthopaedic clinic who would normally undergo valgus stress tests directed at knee	Inter-examiner 0° of flexion κ = **.00** 30° of flexion κ = **.33**

ICC or κ	Interpretation
.81-1.0	Substantial agreement
.61-.80	Moderate agreement
.41-.60	Fair agreement
.11-.40	Slight agreement
.0-.10	No agreement

Test and Study	Description and Positive Findings	Population	Reliability
Pain resistance sequence: Passive flexion Passive extension[25]	Pain sequence is assessed during PROM of knee. Pain is graded on a 4-point scale as "no pain," "pain occurs after resistance is felt," "pain occurs at the same time as resistance is felt," or "pain occurs before resistance is felt"	79 patients with OA of knee	Intra-examiner κ = .34 Intra-examiner κ = .36
Pain resistance sequence: Passive flexion[26]		40 patients with unilateral knee pain	Intra-examiner κ = .78 (.68, .87) Inter-examiner κ = .51
Pain resistance sequence: Passive extension[26]			Intra-examiner κ = .85 (.75, .95) Inter-examiner κ = .42
Pain resistance sequence: Passive flexion[17]	Examiner passively flexes knee. Subject is directed to report when pain is above baseline levels. Examiner reports if pain occurs before, during, or after PROM limitation has occurred	152 patients with unilateral knee dysfunction	Inter-examiner κ = .28
Assessment of pain during adduction stress applied to knee[28]	Examiner places knee in 0° and 30° of flexion and applies valgus force through knee. Pain responses recorded	50 patients referred to outpatient orthopaedic clinic who would normally undergo valgus stress tests directed at knee	Inter-examiner 0° of flexion κ = .40 30° of flexion κ = .33

bility of Strength Assessment

ICC or κ	Interpretation
.81–1.0	Substantial agreement
.61–.80	Moderate agreement
.41–.60	Fair agreement
.11–.40	Slight agreement
.0–.10	No agreement

Measurements	Instrumentation	Population	Reliability
Determination of 1 repetition maximum (1RM) knee extension[29]	With patient sitting in leg extension machine, subject performs slow knee extension from 100° to 0°. Amount of weight is systematically increased until subject can no longer complete lift. 1RM defined as the heaviest resistance that could be lifted once	27 asymptomatic adults	Inter-day (same examiner) ICC = .90 Inter-examiner ICC = .96
Isometric extensor strength[16]	Against inflated sphygmomanometer cuff	53 patients with knee pain	Intra-examiner ICC = .85 Inter-examiner ICC = .83
Isometric flexor strength[16]			Intra-examiner ICC = .89 Inter-examiner ICC = .70

Diagnostic Utility of Manual Muscle Testing for Detecting Strength Deficits

+LR	Interpretation	−LR
>10	Large	<.1
5.0–10.0	Moderate	.1–.2
2.0–5.0	Small	.2–.5
1.0–2.0	Rarely important	.5–1.0

Test and Study Quality	Description and Positive Findings	Population	Reference Standard	Sens	Spec	+LR	−LR
MMT of knee extension strength[30] ◇	Patient extends knee as forcefully as possible into examiner's hand. Strength graded on a scale of 0 to 5	107 patients from an acute rehabilitation hospital	Side-to-side difference with a handheld dynamometer of: 15% 20% 25% 30%	.63 .68 .72 .72	.89 .88 .83 .77	5.7 5.7 4.2 3.1	.42 .36 .34 .36

Assessing Muscle Length

Reliability of Assessing Muscle Length

ICC or κ	Interpretation
.81–1.0	Substantial agreement
.61–.80	Moderate agreement
.41–.60	Fair agreement
.11–.40	Slight agreement
.0–.10	No agreement

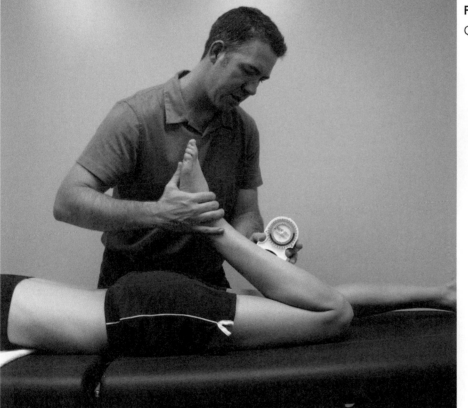

Figure 7-19
Quadriceps length.

Test and Study	Description and Positive Findings	Population	Inter-examiner Reliability
Quadriceps length[19]	Assessed with Thomas test	25 patients with knee OA	Result: κ = .18 (−.17, .53) Pain: κ = .39 (.14, .64)
Hamstring length[31]	Straight leg raise test with inclinometer		ICC = .92 (.82, .96)
ITB/TFL complex length[31]	Ober's test with inclinometer		ICC = .97 (.93, .98)
Quadriceps length[31]	Quadriceps femoris muscle angle with inclinometer	30 patients with patello-femoral pain syndrome	ICC = .91 (.80, .96)
Gastrocnemius length[31]	Dorsiflexion with knee extended and inclinometer		ICC = .92 (.83, .96)
Soleus length[31]	Dorsiflexion with knee flexed 90° and inclinometer		ICC = .86 (.71, .94)

Reliability of the Assessing Mediolateral Patellar Tilt

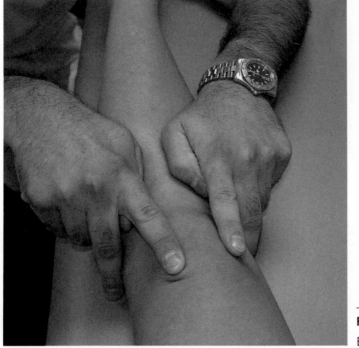

ICC or κ	Interpretation
.81–1.0	Substantial agreement
.61–.80	Moderate agreement
.41–.60	Fair agreement
.11–.40	Slight agreement
.0–.10	No agreement

Figure 7-20

Examination of mediolateral patellar tilt.

Test and Measure	Procedure	Determination of Positive Finding	Population	Reliability
Mediolateral tilt[32]	Examiner estimates patellar alignment while palpating medial and lateral aspects of patella	Patellar orientation graded using an ordinal scale extending from −2 to +2 with −2 representing a lateral tilt, 0 no appreciable tilt, and +2 a medial tilt	27 asymptomatic subjects	Intra-examiner κ = .57 Inter-examiner κ = .18
Mediolateral tilt[33]	Examiner palpates medial and lateral borders of patella with thumb and index finger	If digit palpating the medial border is higher than lateral border, then patella is considered laterally tilted. If digit palpating the lateral border is higher than patella, then patella is medially tilted	66 patients referred for physical therapy who would normally undergo an evaluation of patellofemoral alignment	Inter-examiner κ = .21
Mediolateral tilt[34]	Examiner attempts to palpate posterior surface of medial and lateral patellar borders	Scored 0, 1 or 2. 0 if examiner palpates posterior border on both medial and lateral sides. 1 if >50% of lateral border can be palpated but posterior surface cannot. 2 if <50% of lateral border can be palpated	56 subjects, 25 of whom had symptomatic knees	Intra-examiner κ = .28–.33 Inter-examiner κ = .19
Patellar tilt test[34]	Examiner lifts lateral edge of patella from lateral femoral epicondyle	Graded as having positive, neutral, or negative angle with respect to horizontal plane	99 knees, of which 26 were symptomatic	Intra-examiner κ = .44–.50 Inter-examiner κ = .20–.35

Assessing Bony Alignment

Reliability of the Assessing Patellar Orientation

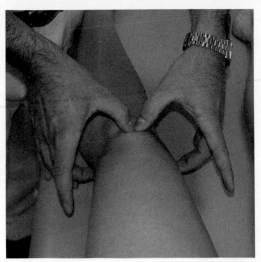

ICC or κ	Interpretation
.81-1.0	Substantial agreement
.61-.80	Moderate agreement
.41-.60	Fair agreement
.11-.40	Slight agreement
.0-.10	No agreement

Figure 7-21

Examination of mediolateral patellar orientation.

Test and Measure	Procedure	Determination of Positive Finding	Population	Reliability
Mediolateral position[32]	Examiner visually estimates patellar alignment while palpating sides of lateral epicondyles with index fingers and patella midline with thumbs	Patellar orientation graded using an ordinal scale extending from −2 to +2, with −2 representing a lateral displacement and +2 a medial displacement	27 asymptomatic subjects	Intra-examiner κ = .40 Inter-examiner κ = .03
Mediolateral orientation[35]	With patient's knee supported in 20° of flexion, examiner identifies medial and lateral epicondyle of femur and midline of patella. Examiner then marks medial and lateral epicondyle and patella midline with tape	Distances between patella midline and medial and lateral condyles are measured	20 healthy physiotherapy students	Inter-examiner Medial distance: ICC = .91 Lateral distance: ICC = .94
Mediolateral displacement[33]	Examiner palpates medial and lateral epicondyles with index fingers while simultaneously palpating midline of patella with thumbs	Distance between index fingers and thumbs should be same. When distance between index finger palpating lateral epicondyle is less, patella is laterally displaced. When distance between index finger palpating medial epicondyle is less, patella is medially displaced	66 patients referred for physical therapy who would normally undergo evaluation of patellofemoral alignment	Inter-examiner κ = .10
Mediolateral glide[34]	Examiner uses a tape measure to record distance from medial and lateral femoral condyles to mid patella	Scored 0 or 1. 0 if the distance from medial epicondyle to mid patella equals distance from lateral epicondyle to mid patella. 1 if the distance from medial epicondyle to mid patella is 0.5 cm greater than from lateral condyle to mid patella	56 subjects, 25 of whom had symptomatic knees	Intra-examiner κ = .11-.35 Inter-examiner κ = .02

Reliability of Assessing Superoinferior Patellar Tilt

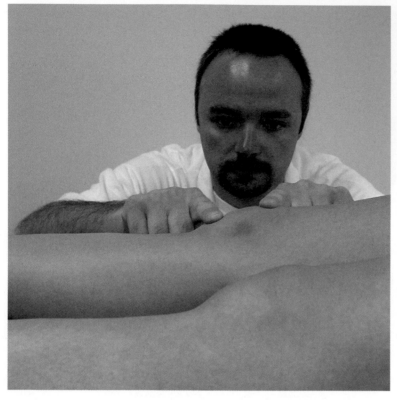

ICC or κ	Interpretation
.81-1.0	Substantial agreement
.61-.80	Moderate agreement
.41-.60	Fair agreement
.11-.40	Slight agreement
.0-.10	No agreement

Figure 7-22

Examination of anteroposterior patellar tilt.

Test and Measure	Procedure	Determination of Positive Finding	Population	Reliability
Superoinferior tilt[32]	Examiner visually estimates patellar alignment while palpating superior and inferior patellar poles	Patellar orientation graded using an ordinal scale extending from −2 to +2, with −2 representing inferior patellar pole below superior pole and +2 representing inferior patellar pole above superior pole	27 asymptomatic subjects	Intra-examiner κ = **.50** Inter-examiner κ = **.30**
Anterior tilt[33]	Examiner palpates inferior patellar pole	If examiner easily palpates inferior pole, no anterior tilt exists. If downward pressure on superior pole is required to palpate inferior pole, it is considered to have an anterior tilt	66 patients referred for physical therapy who would normally undergo evaluation of patellofemoral alignment	Inter-examiner κ = **.24**
Anteroposterior tilt component[34]	Examiner palpates inferior and superior patellar poles	Scored 0, 1, or 2. 0 if inferior patellar pole is as easily palpable as superior pole. 1 if inferior patellar pole is not as easily palpable as superior pole. 2 if inferior pole is not clearly palpable compared with superior pole	56 subjects, 25 of whom had symptomatic knees	Intra-examiner κ = **.03-.23** Inter-examiner κ = **.04**

Assessing Bony Alignment

Reliability of Assessing Patellar Rotation

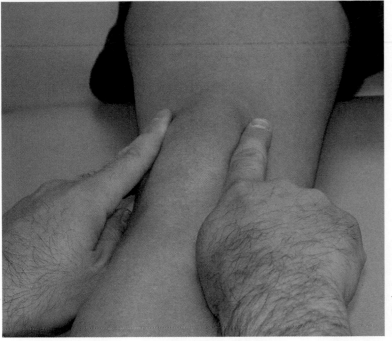

ICC or κ	Interpretation
.81-1.0	Substantial agreement
.61-.80	Moderate agreement
.41-.60	Fair agreement
.11-.40	Slight agreement
.0-.10	No agreement

Figure 7-23

Examination of patellar rotation.

Test and Measure	Procedure	Determination of Positive Finding	Population	Reliability
Rotation[32]	Examiner positions index fingers along longitudinal axes of patella and estimates acute angle formed	Graded using ordinal scale extending from −2 to +2. −2 represents longitudinal axis of patella being more lateral than axis of femur. +2 represents patella being more medial than axis of femur	27 asymptomatic subjects	Intra-examiner κ = .41 Inter-examiner κ = −.03
Patellar rotation[33]	Examiner determines relationship between longitudinal axis of patella and femur	Longitudinal axis of patella should be in line with ASIS. If distal end of patella is medial, it is considered to be medially rotated. If distal end is lateral, it is considered to be laterally rotated	66 patients referred for physical therapy who would normally undergo evaluation of patellofemoral alignment	Inter-examiner κ = .36
Patellar rotation component[34]		Scored as −1, 0, or +1. 0 when patellar long axis is parallel to long axis of femur. 1 when inferior patellar pole is lateral to axis of femur and classified as a lateral patellar rotation. −1 when inferior pole is medial to axis of femur and classified as medial patellar rotation	56 subjects, 25 of whom had symptomatic knees	Intra-examiner κ = −.06-.00 Inter-examiner κ = −.03

Reliability of Assessing Quadriceps Angle Measurements

ICC or κ	Interpretation
.81-1.0	Substantial agreement
.61-.80	Moderate agreement
.41-.60	Fair agreement
.11-.40	Slight agreement
.0-.10	No agreement

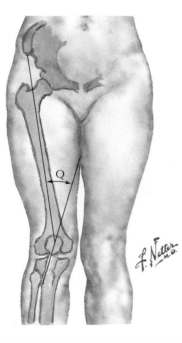

Q-angle formed by intersection of lines from anterior superioriliac spine and from tibial tuberosity through midpoint of patella. Large Q-angle predisposes to patellar subluxation

Figure 7-24

Quadriceps angle.

Test and Measure	Procedure	Population	Reliability ICC		
Q-angle[31]	Proximal arm of goniometer is aligned with ASIS, distal arm is aligned with tibial tubercle, and fulcrum is positioned over patellar midpoint	30 patients with patello-femoral pain syndrome	Inter-examiner ICC = **.70 (.46, .85)**		
Q-angle[32]		27 asymptomatic subjects	Intra-examiner ICC = **.63** Inter-examiner ICC = **.23**		
Q-angle[36]	As above. Measure with knee fully extended and in 20° of flexion	50 asymptomatic knees	Inter-examiner at full extension		
			Right ICC = **.14-.21**	Left ICC = **.08-.11**	
			Inter-examiner at 20° of knee flexion		
			Right ICC = **.04-.08**	Left ICC = **.13-.16**	

Assessing Bony Alignment

Reliability of the Assessing the Angle between the Longitudinal Axis of the Patella and the Patellar Tendon Measurements (A Angle)

ICC or κ	Interpretation
.81-1.0	Substantial agreement
.61-.80	Moderate agreement
.41-.60	Fair agreement
.11-.40	Slight agreement
.0-.10	No agreement

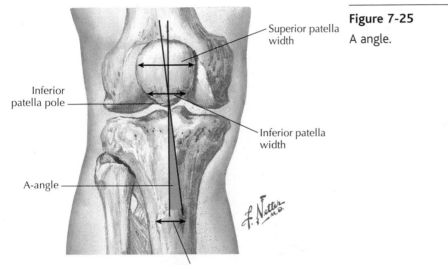

Superior patella width

Inferior patella pole

Inferior patella width

A-angle

Tibial tuberosity width

Figure 7-25

A angle.

Test and Measure	Procedure	Population	Reliability
A angle[32]	Proximal and distal goniometer arms are aligned with middle of superior patellar pole and tibial tubercle. Fulcrum is positioned over midpoint of inferior patellar pole. Angle recorded in degrees	27 asymptomatic subjects	Intra-examiner ICC = .61 Inter-examiner ICC = .49
A angle[37]	Superior patellar pole, superior patellar width, inferior patellar width, inferior patellar pole and tibial tuberosity are identified. A angle is then measured with a goniometer. Angle recorded in degrees	36 asymptomatic subjects	Intra-examiner ICC = .20-.32 Inter-examiner ICC = −.01

Reliability of the Lateral Pull Test to Assess Patellar Alignment

Test and Study	Description and Positive Findings	Population	Reliability
Lateral pull test[38]	With patient supine and knee extended, examiner asks patient to perform isometric quadriceps contraction. Examiner observes patellar tracking during contraction. Positive if patella tracks more laterally than superiorly. Negative if superior displacement is equal to lateral displacement	99 knees, 26 of which were symptomatic	Intra-examiner κ = .39-.47 Inter-examiner κ = .31

Palpation

Reliability of Pain during Palpation

ICC or κ	Interpretation
.81-1.0	Substantial agreement
.61-.80	Moderate agreement
.41-.60	Fair agreement
.11-.40	Slight agreement
.0-.10	No agreement

Palpation of lateral joint line

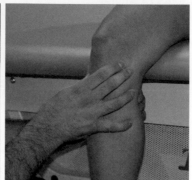

Palpation of medial joint line

Figure 7-26

Palpation of joint lines.

Physical Finding	Population	Reliability	
Palpation for tenderness[16]	53 patients with knee pain	Inter-examiner κ = **.10-.30**	
Posterior joint line tenderness[39]	71 patients with knee pain	Inter-examiner κ = **.48**	
Tenderness at medial joint line[10]	152 patients with OA of knee	Inter-examiner κ = **.21 (.01, .41)**	
Tenderness at lateral joint line[10]		Inter-examiner κ = **.25 (.07, .43)**	
Patellofemoral tenderness[9]	49 patients presenting to outpatient rheumatology clinics for OA of knee	Intra-examiner κ = **.61 (.43, .78)**	Inter-examiner κ = **.27 (.05, .48)**
Medial tibiofemoral tenderness[9]		Intra-examiner κ = **.60 (.47, .72)**	Inter-examiner κ = **.35 (.24, .45)**
Lateral tibiofemoral tenderness[9]		Intra-examiner κ = **.60 (.44, .74)**	Inter-examiner κ = **.29 (.14, .44)**
Periarticular tenderness[9]		Intra-examiner κ = **.58 (.45, .73)**	Inter-examiner κ = **.22 (.09, .36)**

Diagnostic Utility of Joint Line Tenderness

+LR	Interpretation	−LR
>10	Large	<.1
5.0-10.0	Moderate	.1-.2
2.0-5.0	Small	.2-.5
1.0-2.0	Rarely important	.5-1.0

Test and Study Quality	Description and Positive Findings	Population	Reference Standard	Sens	Spec	+LR	−LR
Joint line tenderness[40] **2008 Meta-analysis**	Depended on study, but generally: Examiner palpates joint line with patient's knee in 90° flexion. Positive if test reproduces pain	Pooled, quality adjusted estimates from eight studies*	Meniscal tears via arthroscopy or arthrotomy	.76 (.73, .80)	.77 (.64, .87)	3.3	.31
Joint line tenderness[41] **2007 Meta-analysis**		Pooled, estimates from 14 studies*	Meniscal tears via arthroscopy, arthrotomy, or MRI	.63 (.61, .66)	.77 (.76, .79)	2.7	.48

*Some of the included studies would not have met our QUADAS quality criterion for inclusion.

Special Tests

Reliability of the Lachman Test

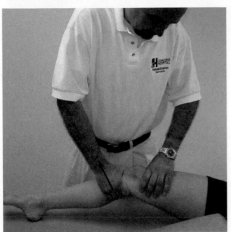

ICC or κ	Interpretation
.81-1.0	Substantial agreement
.61-.80	Moderate agreement
.41-.60	Fair agreement
.11-.40	Slight agreement
.0-.10	No agreement

Figure 7-27

Lachman test.

Test and Measure	Procedure	Determination of Positive Finding	Population	Reliability
Lachman test[27]	Examiners perform Lachman test as they would in practice	Results are graded as "positive" or "negative." Examiners also grade amount of anterior tibial translation as 0, 1+, 2+, or 3+. 0 represents no difference in tibial translation between unaffected and affected knees	35 patients referred to physical therapy clinics for rehabilitation of knee joint	For positive or negative findings Intra-examiner κ = .51 Inter-examiner κ = .19 For grading of tibial translation Intra-examiner κ = .44 -.60 Inter-examiner κ = .02 -.61
Lachman test[10]	Not specified	Not specified	152 patients with OA of knee	Inter-examiner κ = −.08 (−.12, .04)

Diagnostic Utility of the Lachman Test in Identifying Anterior Cruciate Ligament Tears

+LR	Interpretation	−LR
>10	Large	<.1
5.0-10.0	Moderate	.1-.2
2.0-5.0	Small	.2-.5
1.0-2.0	Rarely important	.5-1.0

Test and Study Quality	Description and Positive Findings	Population	Reference Standard	Sens	Spec	+LR	−LR
Lachman test (without anesthesia)[42] **2006 Meta-analysis**	Depended on study, but generally: With patient supine and knee joint flexed between 10° and 20°, examiner stabilizes femur with one hand. With other hand, examiner translates tibia anteriorly. Positive if lack of end point for tibial translation or subluxation is positive	Pooled estimates from 2276 patients from 21 studies*	ACL tears via arthroscopy, arthrotomy, or MRI	.85 (.83, .87)	.94 (.92, .95)	1.2 (4.6, 22.7)	.2 (.1, .3)
Lachman test (with anesthesia)[42] **2006 Meta-analysis**		Pooled estimates from 1174 patients from 15 studies*		.97 (.96, .98)	.93 (.89, .96)	12.9 (1.5, 108.5)	.1 (.0, .3)

*Some of the included studies would not have met our QUADAS quality criterion for inclusion.

Special Tests

Reliability of the Anterior Drawer Test

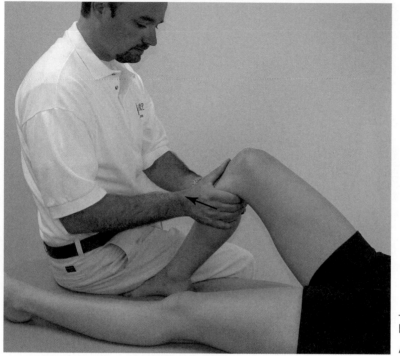

ICC or κ	Interpretation
.81-1.0	Substantial agreement
.61-.80	Moderate agreement
.41-.60	Fair agreement
.11-.40	Slight agreement
.0-.10	No agreement

Figure 7-28
Anterior drawer test.

Test and Study	Description and Positive Finding	Population	Inter-examiner Reliability
Anterior drawer test[16]	Not specified	53 patients with knee pain	κ = **.34**

Diagnostic Utility of the Anterior Drawer Test in Identifying Anterior Cruciate Ligament Tears

+LR	Interpretation	−LR
>10	Large	<.1
5.0-10.0	Moderate	.1-.2
2.0-5.0	Small	.2-.5
1.0-2.0	Rarely important	.5-1.0

Test and Study Quality	Description and Positive Findings	Population	Reference Standard	Sens	Spec	+LR	−LR
Anterior drawer test (without anesthesia)[42] **2006 Meta-analysis**	Depended on study, but generally: With patient's knee flexed between 60° and 90° with foot on examination table, examiner draws tibia anteriorly. Positive if there is anterior subluxation of > 5 mm	Pooled estimates from 1809 patients from 20 studies*	ACL tears via arthroscopy, arthrotomy, or MRI	.55 (.52, .58)	.92 (.90, .94)	7.3 (3.5, 15.2)	.5 (.4, .6)
Anterior drawer test (with anesthesia)[42] **2006 Meta-analysis**		Pooled estimates from 1306 patients from 15 studies*		.77 (.82, .91)	.87 (.82, .91)	5.9 (.9, 38.2)	.4 (.2, .8)

*Some of the included studies would not have met our QUADAS quality criterion for inclusion.

Special Tests

Diagnostic Utility of the Pivot Shift Test in Identifying Anterior Cruciate Ligament Tears

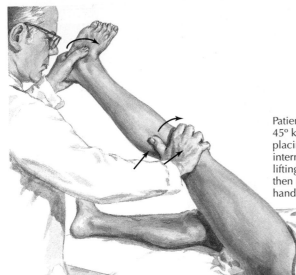

+LR	Interpretation	−LR
>10	Large	<.1
5.0-10.0	Moderate	.1-.2
2.0-5.0	Small	.2-.5
1.0-2.0	Rarely important	.5-1.0

Patient supine and relaxed. Examiner lifts heel of foot to flex hip 45° keeping knee fully extended; grasps knee with other hand, placing thumb beneath head of fibula. Examiner applies strong internal rotation to tibia and fibula at both knee and ankle while lifting proximal fibula. Knee permitted to flex about 20°; examiner then pushes medially with proximal hand and pulls with distal hand to produce a valgus force at knee

— Degrees of sprain —

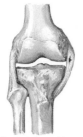 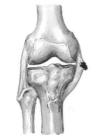 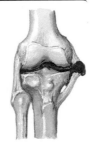

Grade I. Stretching of ligament with minimal disruption of fibers

Grade II. Tearing of up to 50% of ligament fibers; small hematoma. Hemarthrosis may be present

Grade III. Complete tear of ligament and separation of ends, hematoma, and hemarthrosis

Figure 7-29

Pivot shift test.

Test and Study Quality	Description and Positive Findings	Population	Reference Standard	Sens	Spec	+LR	−LR
Pivot shift test (without anesthesia)[42] **2006 Meta-analysis**	Depended on study, but generally: Patient's knee is placed in 10°- 20° of flexion, and tibia is rotated internally while examiner applies valgus force. Positive if lateral tibial plateau sub-luxes anteriorly	Pooled estimates from 1431 pa-tients from 15 studies*	ACL tears via arthroscopy, arthrotomy, or MRI	.24 (.21, .27)	.98 (.96, .99)	8.5 (4.7, 15.5)	.9 (.8, 1.0)
Pivot shift test (with anesthesia)[42] **2006 Meta-analysis**		Pooled estimates from 1077 pa-tients from 13 studies*		.74 (.71, .77)	.99 (.96, 1.0)	2.9 (2.8, 156.2)	.3 (.1, .7)

*Some of the included studies would not have met our QUADAS quality criterion for inclusion.

ICC or κ	Interpretation
.81-1.0	Substantial agreement
.61-.80	Moderate agreement
.41-.60	Fair agreement
.11-.40	Slight agreement
.0-.10	No agreement

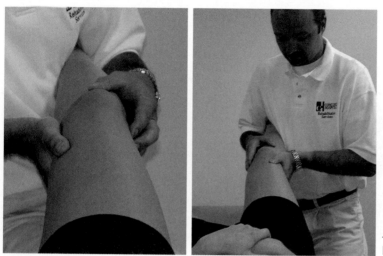

Varus stress test   Valgus stress test

Figure 7-30

Valgus and varus stress tests.

Test and Study	Description and Positive Finding	Population	Inter-examiner Reliability
Varus test[16]		53 patients with knee pain	(Laxity) κ = .24 (Pain) κ = .18
Valgus test[16]	Not specified		(Laxity) κ = .48 (Pain) κ = .37
Varus test[10]		152 patients with OA of knee	κ = 0 (−.18, .18)
Valgus test[10]			κ = .05 (−.13, 2.3)

Diagnostic Utility of Valgus Stress for Identifying Medial Collateral Ligament Tears

+LR	Interpretation	−LR
>10	Large	<.1
5.0-10.0	Moderate	.1-.2
2.0-5.0	Small	.2-.5
1.0-2.0	Rarely important	.5-1.0

Test and Study Quality	Description and Positive Findings	Population	Reference Standard	Sens	Spec	+LR	−LR
Pain with valgus stress at 30° [12] ◇	Not specifically described	134 patients with traumatic knee complaint	MCL tears per MRI	.78 (.64, .92)	.67 (.57, .76)	2.3 (1.7, .3.3)	.30 (.20, .60)
Laxity with valgus stress at 30° [12] ◇				.91 (.81, 1.0)	.49 (.39, .59)	1.8 (1.4, 2.2)	.20 (.10, .60)

Special Tests

Reliability of McMurray's Test

ICC or κ	Interpretation
.81-1.0	Substantial agreement
.61-.80	Moderate agreement
.41-.60	Fair agreement
.11-.40	Slight agreement
.0-.10	No agreement

Test and Study	Description and Positive Finding	Population	Reliability
McMurray's test[10]	Knee is passively flexed, externally rotated, and axially loaded while brought into extension. Test is repeated in IR. Positive if a palpable or audible click or pain occurs during rotation	152 patients with OA of knee	Inter-examiner κ = .16 (−.01, .33)

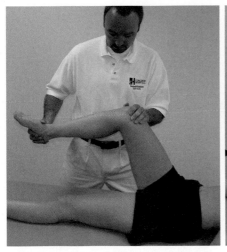

With internal rotation of tibia

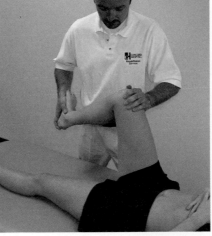

With external rotation of tibia

Figure 7-31
McMurray's test.

Diagnostic Utility of the McMurray's Test

+LR	Interpretation	−LR
>10	Large	<.1
5.0-10.0	Moderate	.1-.2
2.0-5.0	Small	.2-.5
1.0-2.0	Rarely important	.5-1.0

Test and Study Quality	Description and Positive Findings	Population	Reference Standard	Sens	Spec	+LR	−LR
McMurray's test[40] **2008 Meta-analysis**	Depended on study, but generally same as above	Pooled, quality adjusted estimates from 8 studies*	Arthroscopy or arthrotomy	.55 (.50, .60)	.77 (.62, .87)	2.4	.58
McMurray's test[41] **2007 Meta-analysis**		Pooled, estimates from 14 studies*	Arthroscopy, arthrotomy, or MRI	.71 (.67, .73)	.71 (.69, .73)	2.5	.41

*Some of the included studies would not have met our QUADAS quality criterion for inclusion.

Diagnostic Utility of Apley's Test

+LR	Interpretation	−LR
>10	Large	<.1
5.0-10.0	Moderate	.1-.2
2.0-5.0	Small	.2-.5
1.0-2.0	Rarely important	.5-1.0

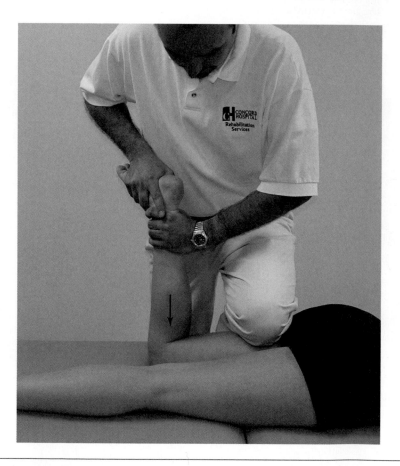

Figure 7-32 Apley's grinding test.

Test and Study Quality	Description and Positive Findings	Population	Reference Standard	Sens	Spec	+LR	−LR
Apley's test[40] 2008 Meta-analysis	Depended on study, but generally patient is prone with knee flexed to 90°. Examiner places downward pressure on foot, compressing knee, while internally and externally rotating tibia	Pooled, quality-adjusted estimates from three studies*	Arthroscopy or arthrotomy	.22 (.17, .28)	.88 (.72, .96)	1.8	.89
Apley's test[41] 2007 Meta-analysis		Pooled, estimates from seven studies*	Arthroscopy, arthrotomy, or MRI	.61 (.56, .66)	.70 (.68, .72)	2.0	.56

*Some of the included studies would not have met our QUADAS quality criterion for inclusion.

Special Tests

Diagnostic Utility of Other Tests for Identifying Meniscal Tears

+LR	Interpretation	−LR
>10	Large	<.1
5.0-10.0	Moderate	.1-.2
2.0-5.0	Small	.2-.5
1.0-2.0	Rarely important	.5-1.0

Figure 7-33 Ege's test.

Test and Study Quality	Description and Positive Findings	Population	Reference Standard	Sens	Spec	+LR	−LR
Pain with passive knee flexion[13] ◇	Not described	134 patients with traumatic knee complaint	Meniscal tear per MRI	.77 (.64, .89)	.41 (.31, .52)	1.3 (1.0, 1.7)	.60 (.30, 1.0)
Ege's test[43] ◯	Patient stands with feet 30 to 40 cm apart. To detect medial meniscal tears, the patient performs a full squat with legs maximally externally rotated. To detect	150 consecutive patients with knee symptoms related to intra-articular knee pathology	Knee arthroscopy	Medial			
				.67	.81	3.5	.41
				Lateral			
				.64	.90	6.4	.40

Special Tests

Diagnostic Utility of the Thessaly Test for Identifying Meniscal Tears

Figure 7-34 Thessaly test.

Test and Study Quality	Description and Positive Findings	Population	Reference Standard	Sens	Spec	+LR	−LR
Thessaly test[44] ◇	Patients stand on the symptomatic leg while holding the examiner's hands. They then rotate the body and leg internally and externally with the knee bent 5° and then 20°. Positive when the patient feels pain and/or a click in the joint line	213 knee injury patients and 197 asymptomatic volunteers	Meniscal tear per MRI	With knee at 5° of flexion			
				.66 MMT .81 LMT	.96 MMT .91 LMT	16.5 MMT 9.0 LMT	.35 MMT .21 LMT
				With knee at 20° of flexion			
				.89 MMT .92 LMT	.97 MMT .96 LMT	29.7 MMT 23.0 LMT	.11 MMT .08 LMT
Thessaly test[45] ○	As above, except only at 20° knee flexion	116 consecutive patients who had knee arthroscopy for suspected meniscal pathology	Meniscal tear via arthroscopy	.90	.98	39.3	.09

LMT, lateral meniscal tear; MMT, medial meniscal tear.

Special Tests

Diagnostic Utility of Moving Patellar Apprehension Test for Identifying Patellar Instability

+LR	Interpretation	−LR
>10	Large	<.1
5.0-10.0	Moderate	.1-.2
2.0-5.0	Small	.2-.5
1.0-2.0	Rarely important	.5-1.0

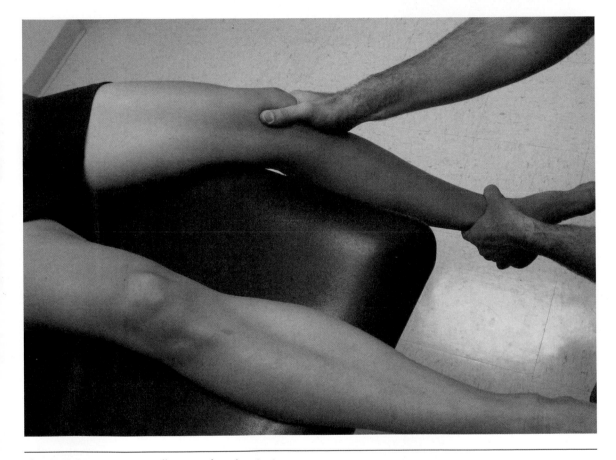

Figure 7-35 Moving patellar apprehension test.

Test and Study Quality	Description and Positive Findings	Population	Reference Standard	Sens	Spec	+LR	−LR
Moving patellar apprehension test[46]	With patient supine with ankle off examination table and knee fully extended, examiner then flexes the knee to 90° and back to extension while holding the patella in lateral translation. The procedure is then repeated with medial translation. Positive if patient exhibits apprehension and/or quadriceps contraction during lateral glide and no apprehension during medial glide	51 patients who had knee surgery and in which patellar instability was suspected	Ability to dislocate the patella when examined under anesthesia	1.0	.88	8.3	.00

Combinations of Tests

Diagnostic Utility of Combinations of Tests for Diagnosing Meniscal Tears

+LR	Interpretation	−LR
>10	Large	<.1
5.0-10.0	Moderate	.1-.2
2.0-5.0	Small	.2-.5
1.0-2.0	Rarely important	.5-1.0

Test and Study Quality	Description and Positive Findings	Population	Reference Standard	Sens	Spec	+LR	−LR
Both pain and laxity with valgus stress at 30° + Trauma by external force to the leg or rotational trauma[12]	Self-reported trauma and physical examination of valgus stress	134 patients with traumatic knee complaint	MRI	.56 (.33, .79)	.91 (.85, .98)	6.4 (2.7, 15.2)	.50 (.30, .80)
Age > 40 years + Continuation of activity impossible + Weight-bearing during trauma + Pain with passive knee flexion[13]	All four factors positive	134 patients with traumatic knee complaint	MRI	.15 (.05, .25)	.97 (.94, 1.0)	5.8 (1.3, 26.8)	.90 (.80, 1.0)
Tenderness to palpation of joint line + Bohler test + Steinmann test + Apley's grinding test + Payr test + McMurray's test[7]	If two tests are positive, then patient is considered to have meniscal lesion	36 patients scheduled to undergo arthroscopic surgery	Arthroscopic visualization	.97	.87	7.5	.03

Diagnostic Utility of Combinations of Tests for Diagnosing Meniscal Tears

+LR	Interpretation	−LR
>10	Large	<.1
5.0-10.0	Moderate	.1-.2
2.0-5.0	Small	.2-.5
1.0-2.0	Rarely important	.5-1.0

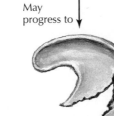

Longitudinal (vertical) tear
May progress to ↓

Radial tear
May progress to ↓

Horizontal tear (probe in cleft)
May progress to ↓

Bucket handle tear

Parrot beak tear

Flap tear

Figure 7-36 Types of meniscal tears.

Test and Study Quality	Description and Positive Findings	Population	Reference Standard	Sens	Spec	+LR	−LR
Combined historical and physical examination[47] ◇	Physical examination includes assessment of joint effusion, joint line tenderness, McMurray's test, hyperflexion test, and squat test. Exact procedures of each test not defined	100 consecutive patients who underwent arthroscopic surgery of knee	Arthroscopic visualization	.86	.83	5.06	.17
Patient history + Joint line tenderness + McMurray's test + Steinmann + Modified Apley's test[48] ○	Conclusion of examiner	50 patients with clinical diagnosis of meniscal tears and/or ACL rupture	Knee arthroscopy	Medial			
				.87	.68	2.7	.19
				Lateral			
				.75	.95	15.0	.26

Diagnostic Utility of Combinations of Tests for Diagnosing Other Knee Pathology

+LR	Interpretation	−LR
>10	Large	<.1
5.0-10.0	Moderate	.1-.2
2.0-5.0	Small	.2-.5
1.0-2.0	Rarely important	.5-1.0

Test and Study Quality	Description and Positive Findings	Population	Reference Standard	Sens	Spec	+LR	−LR
Clinical examination[49] ◯	Retrospective review of clinical examination and clinical diagnosis	698 patients who had undergone knee arthroscopy	Medial meniscal tear via arthroscopy	.92	.79	4.4	.10
			OA via arthroscopy	.75	.97	25.0	.26
			ACL tear via arthroscopy	.86	.98	43.0	.14
			Lateral meniscal tear via arthroscopy	.54	.96	13.5	.48
			Loose body via arthroscopy	.94	.98	47.0	.06
			Tight lateral retinaculum via arthroscopy	1.0	1.0	UD	.00
			Synovitis via arthroscopy	.57	1.0	UD	.43
			Lateral meniscal cyst via arthroscopy	1.0	.99	100.0	.00
Patient History + Anterior drawer + Lachman test + Pivot shift test[48] ◯	Conclusion of examiner	50 patients with clinical diagnosis of meniscal tears and/or ACL rupture	ACL rupture via arthroscopy	1.0	1.0	UD	.00
History of anteromedial knee pain + Pain primarily over the medial femoral condyle + Visible or palpable plica + Exclusion of other causes of anteromedial knee pain[50] ◯	Meet all four criteria	48 patients with anteromedial knee pain that was clinically suspected of being caused by pathological medial plicae	Pathological medial plica via arthroscopy	1.0 (.92, 1.0)	.00	1.0	UD

UD, Undefined.

Interventions

Diagnostic Utility of History and Physical Examination Findings for Predicting Favorable Response to Foot Orthoses and Activity Modification

+LR	Interpretation	−LR
>10	Large	<.1
5.0-10.0	Moderate	.1-.2
2.0-5.0	Small	.2-.5
1.0-2.0	Rarely important	.5-1.0

Sutlive and colleagues[51] have developed a clinical prediction rule that identifies individuals with patellofemoral pain who are likely to improve with an off-the-shelf foot orthosis and modified activity. The study identified a number of predictor variables.

Test and Study Quality	Population	Reference Standard	Sens	Spec	+LR	−LR
2° or more of fore-foot valgus[51]			.13 (.04, .24)	.97 (.90, 1.0)	4.0 (.7, 21.9)	.90
78° or less of great toe extension[51]			.13 (.04, .24)	.97 (.90, 1.0)	4.0 (.7, 21.9)	.90
3 mm or less of na-vicular drop[51]			.47 (.32, .61)	.80 (.67, .93)	2.4 (1.3, 4.3)	.66
5° or less valgus and any varus of relaxed calcaneal stance[51]	50 patients with patello-femoral pain syndrome	≥50% decreased pain after 3 weeks of wearing off-the-shelf foot orthoses and activ-ity modification	.36 (.17, .55)	.81 (.71, .92)	1.9 (1.0, 3.6)	.79
Tight hamstring muscles as measured by 90/90 straight-leg raise test[51]			.68 (.55, .80)	.56 (.37, .75)	1.5 (1.0, 2.3)	.57
Reports of difficulty walking[51]			.71 (.55, .86)	.48 (.33, .62)	1.4 (1.0, 1.8)	.60

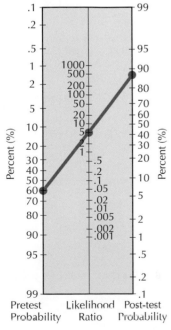

Pretest Probability — Likelihood Ratio — Post-test Probability

Figure 7-37

Nomogram. Considering a pretest probability of success of 60% (as deter-mined in the Sutlive et al[51] study), 2° or more of forefoot valgus or 78° or less of great toe extension results in a post-test probability of 85%. This means that if a patient presented with one of the two aforementioned vari-ables, the likelihood of achieving a successful outcome with off-the-shelf orthotics and activity modification would be 86%. *(Adapted with permission from Fagan TJ. Nomogram for Bayes' theorem. N Engl J Med. 1975;293-257. Copyright 2005, Massachusetts Medical Society. All rights reserved.)*

Interventions

Diagnostic Utility of History and Physical Examination Findings for Predicting Favorable Short-term Response to Hip Mobilizations

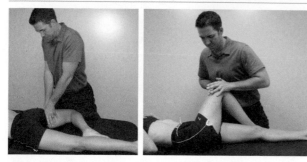

+LR	Interpretation	−LR
>10	Large	<.1
5.0-10.0	Moderate	.1-.2
2.0-5.0	Small	.2-.5
1.0-2.0	Rarely important	.5-1.0

Figure 7-38

Hip mobilization technique used in the management of patients with knee osteoarthritis. Patients were treated with one session of four different hip mobilizations including (1) posteroanterior glide with flexion, abduction, and lateral rotation (depicted left), (2) caudal glide, (3) anteroposterior glide (depicted right), and (4) posteroanterior glide.

Test and Study Quality	Population	Reference Standard	Sens	Spec	+LR	−LR
Ipsilateral anterior thigh pain[19] ◇			.27 (.13, .4)	.95 (.85, 1.05)	5.1 (.71, 36.7)	.77 (.62, .96)
Intermittent hip or groin pain[19] ◇			.15 (.05, .26)	.98 (.91, 1.04)	6.2 (.4, 104.7)	.87 (.75, 1.00)
Strengthening exercises aggravate knee pain[19] ◇			.20 (.04, .37)	.96 (.85, 1.07)	4.9 (.3, 83.7)	.83 (.65, 1.06)
Location of hip or groin pain bilaterally[19] ◇			.18 (.06, .29)	.98 (.91, 1.04)	7.1 (.4, 119.0)	.84 (.72, .99)
Side-to-side difference in hip internal rotation ROM[19] ◇		≥ 30% decreased pain or Global Rating of Change rated as "moderately better" 2 days after hip mobilizations	.98 (.93, 1.02)	.11 (−.03, .24)	1.1 (.9, 1.3)	.23 (.02, 2.40)
Empty end-feel on ipsilateral hip flexion ROM[19] ◇	60 patients with knee OA		.13 (.03, .23)	.98 (.91, 1.04)	5.2 (.3, 9.2)	.89 (.78, 1.02)
Pain with ipsilateral hip distraction[19] ◇			.13 (.03, .23)	.98 (.91, 1.04)	5.2 (.3, 9.2)	.89 (.78, 1.02)
Pain at knee on ipsilateral hip extension ROM[19] ◇			.11 (.01, .20)	.98 (.91, 1.04)	4.3 (.2, 75.8)	.92 (.81, 1.04)
Ipsilateral knee flexion PROM <122°[19] ◇			.32 (.17, .46)	.95 (.85, 1.05)	6.0 (.9, 42.8)	.72 (.57, .91)
Ipsilateral hip internal rotation PROM <17°[19] ◇			.32 (.17, .45)	.95 (.85, 1.05)	6.0 (.9, 42.8)	.72 (.57, .91)
Pain or paresthesia in ipsilateral hip or groin[19] ◇			.20 (.08, .32)	.98 (.91, 1.04)	8.1 (.5, 133.4)	.82 (.69, .97)

OUTCOME MEASURES

Outcome Measure	Scoring and Interpretation	Test-Retest Reliability	MCID
Lower Extremity Functional Scale (LEFS)	Users rate the difficulty of performing 20 functional tasks on a Likert-type scale ranging from 0 (extremely difficult or unable to perform activity) to 4 (no difficulty). A total score out of 80 is calculated by summing each score. The answers provide a score between 0 and 80, with lower scores representing more disability	ICC = .92[52]	9[53]
Western Ontario and McMaster Universities Osteoarthritis Index (WOMAC)	The WOMAC consists of three subscales: pain (5 items), stiffness (2 items), and physical function (17 items). Users answer the 24 condition-specific questions on a numerical rating scale ranging from 0 (no symptoms) to 10 (extreme symptoms), or alternatively on a Likert-type scale from 0 to 4. Scores from each subscale are summed with higher scores indicating more pain, stiffness, and disability	ICC = .90[52]	**6.7%** for improvement **12.9%** for worsening[54]
Knee Outcome Survey (KOS) Activity of Daily Living Scale (ADLS)	The KOS ADLS consists of one section on symptoms and one section on functional disability. Users rate the eight symptom items on a Likert-type scale from 5 (never have) to 0 (prevent me from all daily activity) and the eight functional items from 5 (not difficult at all) to 0 (unable to do). Scores are summed and divided by 80 to get a percentage. Higher scores represent fewer symptoms and higher function	ICC = .93[55]	**7.1%**[56]
Numeric Pain Rating Scale (NPRS)	Users rate their level of pain on an 11-point scale ranging from 0 to 10, with high scores representing more pain. Often asked as "current pain" and "least," "worst," and "average" pain in the past 24 hours	ICC = .72[57]	**2**[58,59]

MCID, Minimum clinically important difference.

Quality Assessment of Diagnostic Studies Using QUADAS

	Braunstein 1982[66]	Katz 1986[67]	Bonamo 1988	Lee 1988[68]	Fowler 1989	Cooperman 1990	Boeree 1991[69]	Evans 1993[70]	Rubinstein 1994[71]	Shelbourne 1995[72]	Stiell 1995	Stiell 1997	Muellner 1997	Khine 2001	Emparanza 2001	Ketelslegers 2002
1. Was the spectrum of patients representative of the patients who will receive the test in practice?	N	U	U	N	Y	Y	Y	N	Y	Y	Y	Y	Y	Y	Y	Y
2. Were selection criteria clearly described?	N	N	N	N	N	Y	N	N	N	N	Y	Y	Y	Y	Y	Y
3. Is the reference standard likely to correctly classify the target condition?	Y	Y	Y	Y	Y	Y	Y	Y	Y	Y	Y	Y	Y	Y	Y	Y
4. Is the time period between reference standard and index test short enough to be reasonably sure that the target condition did not change between the two tests?	U	U	U	Y	Y	U	U	U	U	U	Y	Y	U	Y	U	Y
5. Did the whole sample or a random selection of the sample, receive verification using a reference standard of diagnosis?	Y	Y	Y	Y	Y	N	Y	N	N	Y	N	Y	Y	Y	Y	Y
6. Did patients receive the same reference standard regardless of the index test result?	Y	U	U	Y	Y	N	U	Y	N	Y	N	N	Y	Y	Y	N
7. Was the reference standard independent of the index test (i.e., the index test did not form part of the reference standard)?	Y	Y	Y	Y	Y	Y	Y	Y	Y	Y	Y	Y	Y	Y	Y	Y
8. Was the execution of the index test described in sufficient detail to permit replication of the test?	Y	Y	U	Y	Y	Y	N	N	Y	Y	Y	Y	Y	Y	Y	Y
9. Was the execution of the reference standard described in sufficient detail to permit its replication?	N	Y	Y	Y	U	N	Y	Y	N	Y	Y	Y	Y	Y	Y	Y
10. Were the index test results interpreted without knowledge of the results of the reference test?	U	U	U	Y	Y	U	U	U	Y	Y	Y	Y	Y	Y	Y	Y
11. Were the reference standard results interpreted without knowledge of the results of the index test?	U	U	U	U	U	U	U	U	U	U	Y	N	Y	Y	Y	U

Quality Assessment of Diagnostic Studies Using QUADAS

	Braunstein 1982[66]	Katz 1986[67]	Bonamo 1988	Lee 1988[68]	Fowler 1989	Cooperman 1990	Boeree 1991[69]	Evans 1993[70]	Rubinstein 1994[71]	Shelbourne 1995[72]	Stiell 1995	Stiell 1997	Muellner 1997	Khine 2001	Emparanza 2001	Ketelslegers 2002
12. Were the same clinical data available when test results were interpreted as would be available when the test is used in practice?	U	U	Y	U	U	U	U	U	N	U	Y	U	U	Y	Y	U
13. Were uninterpretable/intermediate test results reported?	Y	U	Y	Y	Y	U	U	Y	Y	Y	Y	U	Y	Y	Y	Y
14. Were withdrawals from the study explained?	U	Y	Y	U	Y	Y	Y	Y	Y	Y	Y	U	Y	Y	Y	Y
Quality summary rating:	■	◯	◯	◯	◯	■	■	■	■	◯	◇	◯	◇	◇	◇	◇

Y = yes, N = no, U = unclear. ◇ Good quality (Y - N = 10 to 14). ◯ Fair quality (Y - N = 5 to 9). ■ Poor quality (Y - N ≤ 4).

Quality Assessment of Diagnostic Studies Using QUADAS

	Bulloch 2003	Eren 2003[73]	Sutlive 2004	Akseki 2004	Kocabey 2004	Bohannon 2005	Karachalios 2005	Haim 2006[74]	Shetty 2007	Currier 2007	Doberstein 2008[75]	Wagemakers 2008	Kastelein 2008	Kastelein 2009	Ahmad 2009	Nickinson 2009	Harrison 2009
1. Was the spectrum of patients representative of the patients who will receive the test in practice?	Y	Y	Y	U	U	Y	Y	U	Y	Y	N	Y	Y	Y	Y	Y	U
2. Were selection criteria clearly described?	Y	Y	Y	N	N	Y	Y	Y	U	Y	N	Y	Y	Y	U	N	N
3. Is the reference standard likely to correctly classify the target condition?	Y	Y	Y	Y	Y	Y	U	N	Y	Y	Y	U	Y	Y	Y	Y	Y
4. Is the time period between reference standard and index test short enough to be reasonably sure that the target condition did not change between the two tests?	Y	U	Y	U	U	U	U	U	U	Y	U	Y	Y	Y	U	U	U
5. Did the whole sample or a random selection of the sample, receive verification using a reference standard of diagnosis?	Y	Y	Y	Y	Y	Y	Y	U	Y	Y	Y	Y	Y	Y	Y	Y	Y
6. Did patients receive the same reference standard regardless of the index test result?	N	Y	Y	Y	Y	Y	Y	Y	Y	Y	Y	Y	Y	Y	U	Y	Y
7. Was the reference standard independent of the index test (i.e., the index test did not form part of the reference standard)?	Y	Y	Y	Y	Y	Y	Y	Y	Y	Y	Y	Y	Y	Y	Y	Y	Y
8. Was the execution of the index test described in sufficient detail to permit replication of the test?	Y	Y	Y	Y	U	Y	Y	Y	N	Y	Y	Y	Y	Y	Y	N	Y
9. Was the execution of the reference standard described in sufficient detail to permit its replication?	Y	U	Y	U	U	Y	Y	U	Y	Y	N	Y	Y	Y	N	N	U
10. Were the index test results interpreted without knowledge of the results of the reference test?	Y	Y	Y	Y	Y	U	Y	N	U	Y	U	Y	Y	Y	U	Y	Y

(Continued)

Quality Assessment of Diagnostic Studies Using QUADAS

	Bulloch 2003	Eren 2003[73]	Sutlive 2004	Akseki 2004	Kocabey 2004	Bohannon 2005	Karachalios 2005	Haim 2006[74]	Shetty 2007	Currier 2007	Doberstein 2008[75]	Wagemakers 2008	Kastelein 2008	Kastelein 2009	Ahmad 2009	Nickinson 2009	Harrison 2009
11. Were the reference standard results interpreted without knowledge of the results of the index test?	Y	U	Y	U	U	U	Y	N	U	Y	U	Y	Y	Y	U	U	U
12. Were the same clinical data available when test results were interpreted as would be available when the test is used in practice?	Y	Y	Y	Y	Y	U	Y	Y	Y	Y	U	Y	Y	Y	Y	Y	U
13. Were uninterpretable/intermediate test results reported?	Y	Y	Y	U	Y	Y	Y	Y	Y	Y	Y	Y	Y	Y	Y	U	U
14. Were withdrawals from the study explained?	Y	Y	Y	U	U	Y	Y	Y	Y	Y	Y	Y	Y	Y	Y	Y	U
Quality summary rating:	◆	◆	◆	○	○	◆	◆	■	○	◆	■	◆	◆	◆	○	○	○

Y = yes, N = no, U = unclear. ◆ Good quality (Y − N = 10 to 14). ○ Fair quality (Y − N = 5 to 9). ■ Poor quality (Y − N ≤ 4).

1. Greenfield B, Tovin BJ. Knee. *Current Concepts in Orthopedic Physical Therapy (11.2.11)*. La Crosse: Orthopaedic Section, American Physical Therapy Association; 2001.

2. Hartley A. *Practical Joint Assessment*. St Louis: Mosby; 1995.

3. DeHaven KE. Diagnosis of acute knee injuries with hemarthrosis. *Am J Sports Med*. 1980;8:9-14.

4. Cook JL, Khan KM, Kiss ZS, et al. Reproducibility and clinical utility of tendon palpation to detect patellar tendinopathy in young basketball players. Victorian Institute of Sport tendon study group. *Br J Sports Med*. 2001;35:65-69.

5. Cleland JA, McRae M. Patellofemoral pain syndrome: a critical analysis of current concepts. *Phys Ther Rev*. 2002;7:153-161.

6. Grelsamer RP, McConnell J. *The Patella: A Team Approach*. Gaithersburg: Aspen Publishers; 1998.

7. Muellner T, Weinstabl R, Schabus R, et al. The diagnosis of meniscal tears in athletes. A comparison of clinical and magnetic resonance imaging investigations. *Am J Sports Med*. 1997;25:7-12.

8. Cibere J, Bellamy N, Thorne A, et al. Reliability of the knee examination in osteoarthritis: effect of standardization. *Arthritis Rheum*. 2004;50:458-468.

9. Jones A, Hopkinson N, Pattrick M, et al. Evaluation of a method for clinically assessing osteoarthritis of the knee. *Ann Rheum Dis*. 1992;51:243-245.

10. Dervin GF, Stiell IG, Wells GA, et al. Physicians' accuracy and interrator reliability for the diagnosis of unstable meniscal tears in patients having osteoarthritis of the knee. *Can J Surg*. 2001;44:267-274.

11. Kastelein M, Luijsterburg PA, Wagemakers HP, et al. Diagnostic value of history taking and physical examination to assess effusion of the knee in traumatic knee patients in general practice. *Arch Phys Med Rehabil*. 2009;90:82-86.

12. Kastelein M, Wagemakers HP, Luijsterburg PA, et al. Assessing medial collateral ligament knee lesions in general practice. *Am J Med*. 2008;121:982-988.e2.

13. Wagemakers HP, Heintjes EM, Boks SS, et al. Diagnostic value of history-taking and physical examination for assessing meniscal tears of the knee in general practice. *Clin J Sport Med*. 2008;18:24-30.

14. Bachmann LM, Haberzeth S, Steurer J, ter Riet G. The accuracy of the Ottawa Knee Rule to rule out knee fractures: a systematic review. *Ann Intern Med*. 2004;140:121-124.

15. Vijayasankar D, Boyle AA, Atkinson P. Can the Ottawa Knee Rule be applied to children? A systematic review and meta-analysis of observational studies. *Emerg Med J*. 2009;26:250-253.

16. Wood L, Peat G, Wilkie R, et al. A study of the noninstrumented physical examination of the knee found high observer variability. *J Clin Epidemiol*. 2006;59:512-520.

17. Fritz JM, Delitto A, Erhard RE, Roman M. An examination of the selective tissue tension scheme, with evidence for the concept of a capsular pattern of the knee. *Phys Ther*. 1998;78:1046-1056; discussion 1057-1061.

18. Lenssen AF, van Dam EM, Crijns YH, et al. Reproducibility of goniometric measurement of the knee in the in-hospital phase following total knee arthroplasty. *BMC Musculoskelet Disord*. 2007;8:83.

19. Currier LL, Froehlich PJ, Carow SD, et al. Development of a clinical prediction rule to identify patients with knee pain and clinical evidence of knee osteoarthritis who demonstrate a favorable short-term response to hip mobilization. *Phys Ther*. 2007;87: 1106-1119.

20. Rothstein JM, Miller PJ, Roettger RF. Goniometric reliability in a clinical setting. Elbow and knee measurements. *Phys Ther*. 1983;63:1611-1615.

21. Gogia PP, Braatz JH, Rose SJ, Norton BJ. Reliability and validity of goniometric measurements at the knee. *Phys Ther*. 1987;67:192-195.

22. Watkins MA, Riddle DL, Lamb RL, Personius WJ. Reliability of goniometric measurements and visual estimates of knee range of motion obtained in a clinical setting. *Phys Ther*. 1991;71:90-97.

23. Clapper MP, Wolf SL. Comparison of the reliability of the Orthoranger and the standard goniometer for assessing active lower extremity range of motion. *Phys Ther*. 1988;68:214-218.

24. Brosseau L, Tousignant M, Budd J, et al. Intratester and intertester reliability and criterion validity of the parallelogram and universal goniometers for active knee flexion in healthy subjects. *Physiother Res Int*. 1997;2:150-166.

25. Hayes KW, Petersen C, Falconer J. An examination of Cyriax's passive motion tests with patients having osteoarthritis of the knee. *Phys Ther*. 1994;74:697-709.

26. Hayes KW, Petersen CM. Reliability of assessing end-feel and pain and resistance sequence in subjects with painful shoulders and knees. *J Orthop Sports Phys Ther*. 2001;31:432-445.

27. Cooperman JM, Riddle DL, Rothstein JM. Reliability and validity of judgments of the integrity of the anterior cruciate ligament of the knee using the Lachman's test. *Phys Ther*. 1990;70:225-233.

28. McClure PW, Rothstein JM, Riddle DL. Intertester reliability of clinical judgments of medial knee ligament integrity. *Phys Ther*. 1989;69:268-275.

29. Tagesson SK, Kvist J. Intra- and interrater reliability of the establishment of one repetition maximum on squat and seated knee extension. *J Strength Cond Res*. 2007;21:801-807.

30. Bohannon RW. Manual muscle testing: does it meet the standards of an adequate screening test? *Clin Rehabil*. 2005;19:662-667.

31. Piva SR, Fitzgerald K, Irrgang JJ, et al. Reliability of measures of impairments associated with patellofemoral pain syndrome. *BMC Musculoskelet Disord.* 2006;7:33.

32. Tomsich DA, Nitz AJ, Threlkeld AJ, Shapiro R. Patellofemoral alignment: reliability. *J Orthop Sports Phys Ther.* 1996;23:200-208.

33. Fitzgerald GK, McClure PW. Reliability of measurements obtained with four tests for patellofemoral alignment. *Phys Ther.* 1995;75:84-92.

34. Watson CJ, Propps M, Galt W, et al. Reliability of McConnell's classification of patellar orientation in symptomatic and asymptomatic subjects. *J Orthop Sports Phys Ther.* 1999;29:378-393.

35. Herrington LC. The inter-tester reliability of a clinical measurement used to determine the medial-lateral orientation of the patella. *Man Ther.* 2002;7:163-167.

36. Greene CC, Edwards TB, Wade MR, Carson EW. Reliability of the quadriceps angle measurement. *Am J Knee Surg.* 2001;14:97-103.

37. Ehrat M, Edwards J, Hastings D, Worrell T. Reliability of assessing patellar alignment: the A angle. *J Orthop Sports Phys Ther.* 1994;19:22-27.

38. Watson CJ, Leddy HM, Dynjan TD, Parham JL. Reliability of the lateral pull test and tilt test to assess patellar alignment in subjects with symptomatic knees: student raters. *J Orthop Sports Phys Ther.* 2001;31:368-374.

39. Wadey VM, Mohtadi NG, Bray RC, Frank CB. Positive predictive value of maximal posterior joint-line tenderness in diagnosing meniscal pathology: a pilot study. *Can J Surg.* 2007;50:96-100.

40. Meserve BB, Cleland JA, Boucher TR. A meta-analysis examining clinical test utilities for assessing meniscal injury. *Clin Rehabil.* 2008;22:143-161.

41. Hegedus EJ, Cook C, Hasselblad V, et al. Physical examination tests for assessing a torn meniscus in the knee: a systematic review with meta-analysis. *J Orthop Sports Phys Ther.* 2007;37:541-550.

42. Benjaminse A, Gokeler A, van der Schans CP. Clinical diagnosis of an anterior cruciate ligament rupture: a meta-analysis. *J Orthop Sports Phys Ther.* 2006;36:267-288.

43. Akseki D, Ozcan O, Boya H, Pinar H. A new weight-bearing meniscal test and a comparison with McMurray's test and joint line tenderness. *Arthroscopy.* 2004;20:951-958.

44. Karachalios T, Hantes M, Zibis AH, et al. Diagnostic accuracy of a new clinical test (the Thessaly test) for early detection of meniscal tears. *J Bone Joint Surg Am.* 2005;87:955-962.

45. Harrison BK, Abell BE, Gibson TW. The Thessaly test for detection of meniscal tears: validation of a new physical examination technique for primary care medicine. *Clin J Sport Med.* 2009;19:9-12.

46. Ahmad CS, McCarthy M, Gomez JA,, et al. The moving patellar apprehension test for lateral patellar instability. *Am J Sports Med.* 2009;37:791-796.

47. Bonamo JJ, Shulman G. Double contrast arthrography of the knee. A comparison to clinical diagnosis and arthroscopic findings. *Orthopedics.* 1988;11:1041-1046.

48. Kocabey Y, Tetik O, Isbell WM, et al. The value of clinical examination versus magnetic resonance imaging in the diagnosis of meniscal tears and anterior cruciate ligament rupture. *Arthroscopy.* 2004;20:696-700.

49. Nickinson R, Darrah C, Donell S. Accuracy of clinical diagnosis in patients undergoing knee arthroscopy. *Int Orthop.* 2009.

50. Shetty VD, Vowler SL, Krishnamurthy S, Halliday AE. Clinical diagnosis of medial plica syndrome of the knee: a prospective study. *J Knee Surg.* 2007;20:277-280.

51. Sutlive TG, Mitchell SD, Maxfield SN, et al. Identification of individuals with patellofemoral pain whose symptoms improved after a combined program of foot orthosis use and modified activity: a preliminary investigation. *Phys Ther.* 2004;84:49-61.

52. Pua YH, Cowan SM, Wrigley TV, Bennell KL. The Lower Extremity Functional Scale could be an alternative to the Western Ontario and McMaster Universities Osteoarthritis Index physical function scale. *J Clin Epidemiol.* 2009.

53. Binkley JM, Stratford PW, Lott SA, Riddle DL. The Lower Extremity Functional Scale (LEFS): scale development, measurement properties, and clinical application. North American Orthopaedic Rehabilitation Research Network. *Phys Ther.* 1999;79:371-383.

54. Angst F, Aeschlimann A, Stucki G. Smallest detectable and minimal clinically important differences of rehabilitation intervention with their implications for required sample sizes using WOMAC and SF-36 quality of life measurement instruments in patients with osteoarthritis of the lower extremities. *Arthritis Rheum.* 2001;45:384-391.

55. Marx RG, Jones EC, Allen AA, et al. Reliability, validity, and responsiveness of four knee outcome scales for athletic patients. *J Bone Joint Surg Am.* 2001;83-A:1459-1469.

56. Piva SR, Gil AB, Moore CG, Fitzgerald GK. Responsiveness of the activities of daily living scale of the knee outcome survey and numeric pain rating scale in patients with patellofemoral pain. *J Rehabil Med.* 2009;41:129-135.

57. Li L, Liu X, Herr K. Postoperative pain intensity assessment: a comparison of four scales in Chinese adults. *Pain Med.* 2007;8:223-234.

58. Farrar JT, Berlin JA, Strom BL. Clinically important changes in acute pain outcome measures: a validation study. *J Pain Symptom Manage.* 2003;25:406-411.

59. Farrar JT, Portenoy RK, Berlin JA, et al. Defining the clinically important difference in pain outcome measures. *Pain.* 2000;88:287-294.

60. Stiell IG, Greenberg GH, Wells GA, et al. Derivation of a decision rule for the use of radiography in acute knee injuries. *Ann Emerg Med.* 1995;26:405-413.

61. Stiell IG, Wells GA, Hoag RH, et al. Implementation of the Ottawa Knee Rule for the use of radiography in acute knee injuries. *JAMA*. 1997;278:2075-2079.

62. Emparanza JI, Aginaga JR. Validation of the Ottawa Knee Rules. *Ann Emerg Med*. 2001;38:364-368.

63. Ketelslegers E, Collard X, Vande Berg B, et al. Validation of the Ottawa Knee Rules in an emergency teaching centre. *Eur Radiol*. 2002;12:1218-1220.

64. Bulloch B, Neto G, Plint A, et al. Validation of the Ottawa Knee Rule in children: a multicenter study. *Ann Emerg Med*. 2003;42:48-55.

65. Khine H, Dorfman DH, Avner JR. Applicability of Ottawa Knee Rule for knee injury in children. *Pediatr Emerg Care*. 2001;17:401-404.

66. Braunstein EM. Anterior cruciate ligament injuries: a comparison of arthrographic and physical diagnosis. *AJR Am J Roentgenol*. 1982;138:423-425.

67. Katz JW, Fingeroth RJ. The diagnostic accuracy of ruptures of the anterior cruciate ligament comparing the Lachman test, the anterior drawer sign, and the pivot shift test in acute and chronic knee injuries. *Am J Sports Med*. 1986;14:88-91.

68. Lee JK, Yao L, Phelps CT, et al. Anterior cruciate ligament tears: MR imaging compared with arthroscopy and clinical tests. *Radiology*. 1988;166:861-864.

69. Boeree NR, Ackroyd CE. Assessment of the menisci and cruciate ligaments: an audit of clinical practice. *Injury*. 1991;22:291-294.

70. Evans PJ, Bell GD, Frank C. Prospective evaluation of the McMurray test. *Am J Sports Med*. 1993;21:604-608.

71. Rubinstein RAJ, Shelbourne KD, McCarroll JR, et al. The accuracy of the clinical examination in the setting of posterior cruciate ligament injuries. *Am J Sports Med*. 1994;22:550-557.

72. Shelbourne KD, Martini DJ, McCarroll JR, VanMeter CD. Correlation of joint line tenderness and meniscal lesions in patients with acute anterior cruciate ligament tears. *Am J Sports Med*. 1995;23:166-169.

73. Eren OT. The accuracy of joint line tenderness by physical examination in the diagnosis of meniscal tears. *Arthroscopy*. 2003;19:850-854.

74. Haim A, Yaniv M, Dekel S, Amir H. Patellofemoral pain syndrome: validity of clinical and radiological features. *Clin Orthop Relat Res*. 2006;451:223-228.

75. Doberstein ST, Romeyn RL, Reineke DM. The diagnostic value of the Clarke sign in assessing chondromalacia patella. *J Athl Train*. 2008;43:190-196.

Foot and Ankle

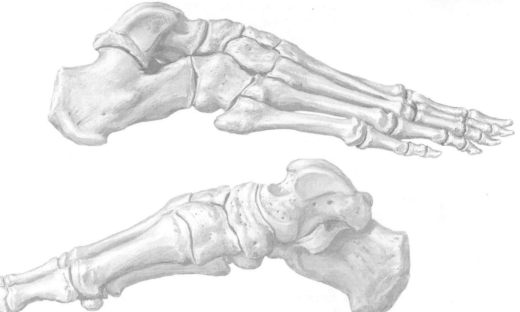

CLINICAL SUMMARY AND RECOMMENDATIONS

Patient History

Complaints
- No studies of acceptable quality have assessed either the reliability or diagnostic utility of items from the subjective history in patients with foot and ankle problems.

Physical Examination

Screening
- The Ottawa Ankle Rule for Radiography is highly sensitive for ankle and midfoot fractures in both adults and children. When patients can bear weight and have no tenderness on the malleoli, navicular, or base of the fifth metatarsal, providers can confidently rule out foot and ankle fractures ($-LR = .10$). The addition of a tuning fork may increase the specificity of the rules, especially when placed on the distal fibula.

Range of Motion and Strength Assessment
- Measuring ankle range of motion (ROM) has consistently been shown to be highly reliable when measured by the same person, but much less reliable when measured by different people.

- Calf strength can be reliably assessed using repeated calf raises. The paper grip test is a simple yet accurate method to measure toe plantarflexion strength.

Other Assessment
- Assessments of static foot alignment, sensation, swelling, proprioception, and dynamic performance have all been shown to be adequately reliable, but are of unknown diagnostic utility. Dynamic assessments of hindfoot motion during gait are likely too unreliable to be clinically useful.

Special Tests
- The "impingement sign" seems to show very good diagnostic utility in both identifying and ruling out anterolateral ankle impingement ($+LR = 7.9$, $-LR = .06$).

- The windlass test appears highly reliable, but is of unknown diagnostic utility in identifying plantar fasciitis.

- Overall there is a considerable lack of information available on diagnostic tests for the foot and ankle.

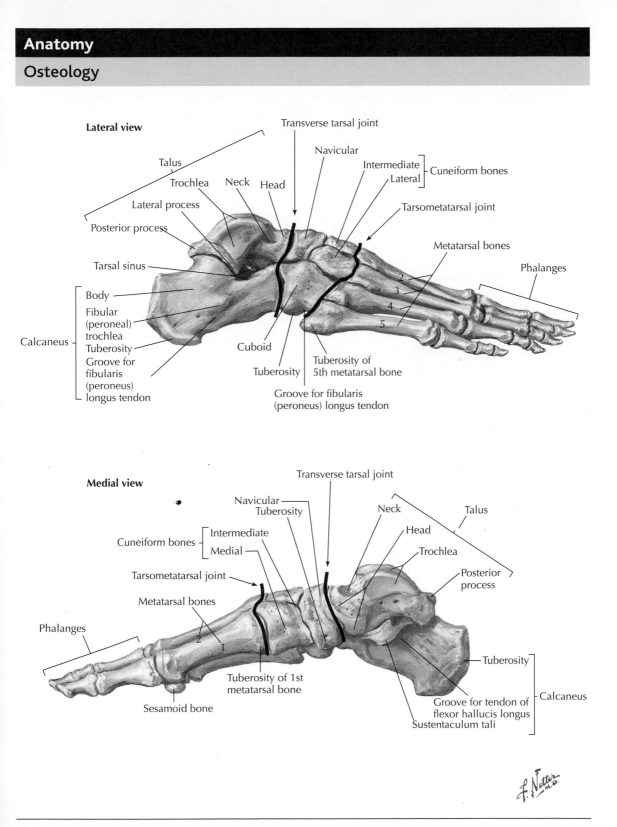

Lateral view

Transverse tarsal joint

Talus

Navicular

Trochlea Neck Head

Intermediate ⎤
Lateral ⎦ Cuneiform bones

Lateral process

Posterior process

Tarsometatarsal joint

Tarsal sinus

Metatarsal bones

Phalanges

Body

2

3

4

5

Fibular (peroneal) trochlea

Tuberosity

Groove for fibularis (peroneus) longus tendon

Calcaneus

Cuboid

Tuberosity

Tuberosity of 5th metatarsal bone

Groove for fibularis (peroneus) longus tendon

Medial view

Transverse tarsal joint

Navicular

Tuberosity

Neck

Talus

Cuneiform bones ⎡ Intermediate
⎣ Medial

Head

Trochlea

Posterior process

Tarsometatarsal joint

Metatarsal bones

2

1

Phalanges

Tuberosity of 1st metatarsal bone

Tuberosity

Calcaneus

Sesamoid bone

Groove for tendon of flexor hallucis longus
Sustentaculum tali

Figure 8-1

Bones of the foot.

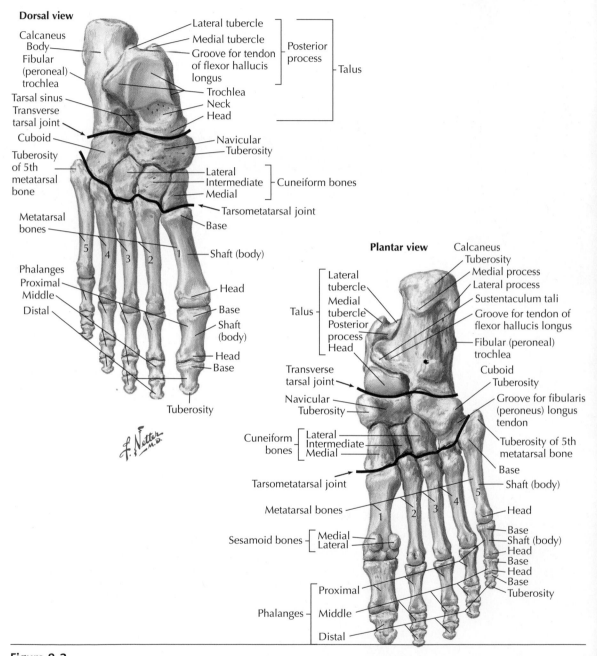

Figure 8-2

Bones of the foot.

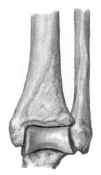

Subtalar (hinge joint)

Metatarsophalangeal (condyloid) joint

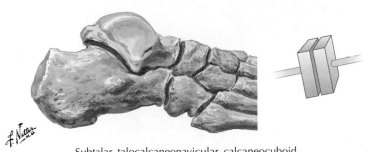

Subtalar, talocalcaneonavicular, calcaneocuboid,
transverse tarsal, and tarsometatarsal (plane) joints

Figure 8-3

Talocrural (hinge) joint.

Joint	Type and Classification	Closed Packed Position	Capsular Pattern
Talocrural	Synovial: hinge	Dorsiflexion	Plantarflexion slightly more limited than dorsiflexion
Distal tibiofibular	Syndesmosis	Not available	Not available
Subtalar	Synovial: plane	Supination	Inversion greatly restricted; eversion not restricted
Talocalcaneonavicular	Synovial: plane	Supination	Supination more limited than pronation
Calcaneocuboid	Synovial: plane	Supination	
Transverse tarsal	Synovial: plane	Supination	
Tarsometatarsal	Synovial: plane	Supination	Not available
Metatarsophalangeal (MTP)	Synovial: condyloid	Extension	Great toe: extension more limited than flexion MTP joints 2-5: variable
Interphalangeal (IP)	Synovial: hinge	Extension	Extension more limited than flexion

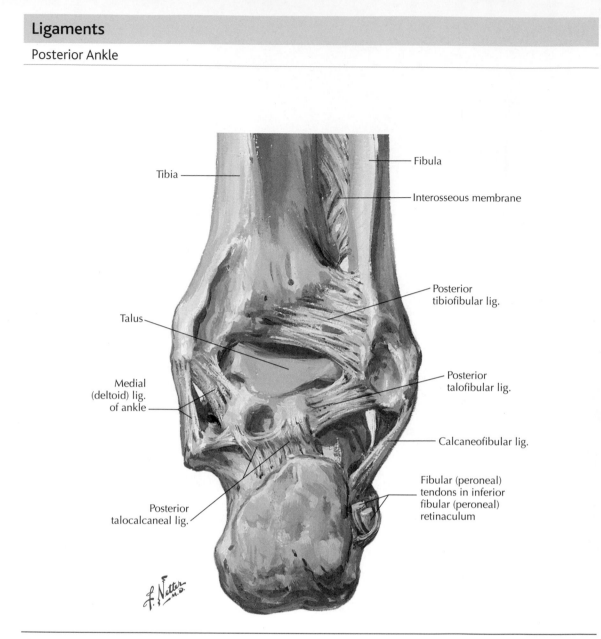

Tibia

Fibula

Interosseous membrane

Posterior tibiofibular lig.

Talus

Posterior talofibular lig.

Medial (deltoid) lig. of ankle

Calcaneofibular lig.

Fibular (peroneal) tendons in inferior fibular (peroneal) retinaculum

Posterior talocalcaneal lig.

Figure 8-4

Calcaneus: posterior view with ligaments.

Ligaments	Attachments	Function
Posterior talocalcaneal	Superior body of calcaneus to posterior process of talus	Limits posterior separation of talus from calcaneus
Posterior tibiofibular	Distal posterior tibia to distal posterior fibula	Maintains distal tibiofibular joint
Posterior talofibular	Posterior talus to posterior lateral malleolus	Limits separation of fibula from talus
Interosseous membrane	Continuous connection between tibia and fibula	Reinforces approximation between tibia and fibula

Ligaments

Lateral Ankle

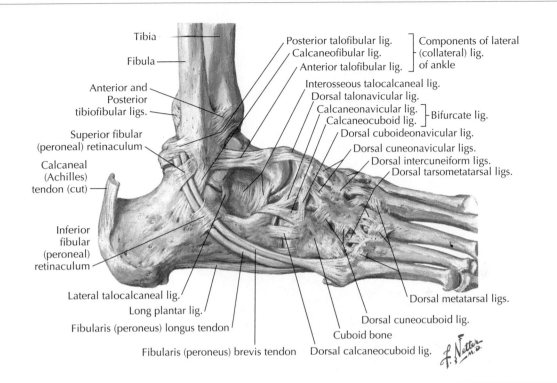

Figure 8-5

Ligaments of ankle: lateral view of right foot.

Ligaments	Attachments	Function
Anterior tibiofibular	Anterior aspect of lateral malleolus to inferior border of medial tibia	Reinforces anterior tibiofibular joint
Lateral Collateral		
Posterior talofibular	Lateral malleolus to lateral talus	Limits ankle inversion
Calcaneofibular	Lateral malleolus to lateral calcaneus	
Anterior talofibular	Lateral malleolus to talus	
Interosseous talocalcaneal	Inferior aspect of talus to superior aspect of calcaneus	Limits separation of talus from calcaneus
Dorsal talonavicular	Dorsal aspect of talus to dorsal aspect of navicular	Limits separation of navicular from talus
Bifurcate		
Calcaneonavicular	Distal calcaneus to proximal navicular	Limits separation of navicular and cuboid from calcaneus
Calcaneocuboid	Distal calcaneus to proximal cuboid	
Dorsal cubonavicular	Lateral aspect of cuboid to dorsal aspect of navicular	Limits separation of navicular from cuboid
Dorsal cuneonavicular	Navicular to three cuneiforms	Limits separation of cuneiforms from navicular
Dorsal intercuneiform	Joining of three cuneiforms	Limits separation of cuneiforms
Dorsal tarsometatarsal	Dorsal tarsal bones to corresponding metatarsal bones	Reinforces tarsometatarsal joints

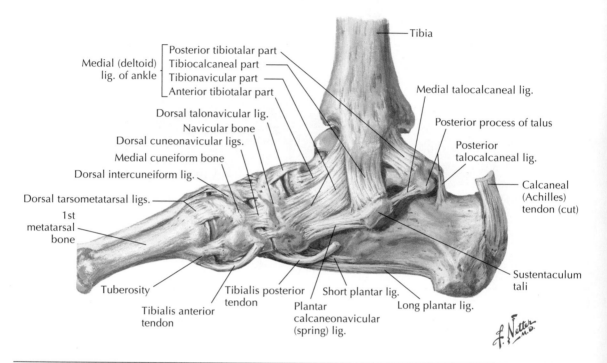

Figure 8-6

Ligaments of ankle: medial view of right foot.

Ligaments	Attachments	Function
Medial (Deltoid)		
Posterior tibiotalar	Medial malleolus to medial talus	Limits ankle eversion
Tibiocalcaneal	Anterior distal medial malleolus to sustentaculum tali	
Tibionavicular	Medial malleolus to proximal aspect of navicular	
Anterior tibiotalar	Medial malleolus to talus	
Medial talocalcaneal	Sustentaculum tali to talus	Limits posterior separation of talus on calcaneus
Plantar calcaneonavicular (spring)	Sustentaculum tali to posteroinferior navicular	Maintains longitudinal arch of foot

Ligaments

Plantar Foot

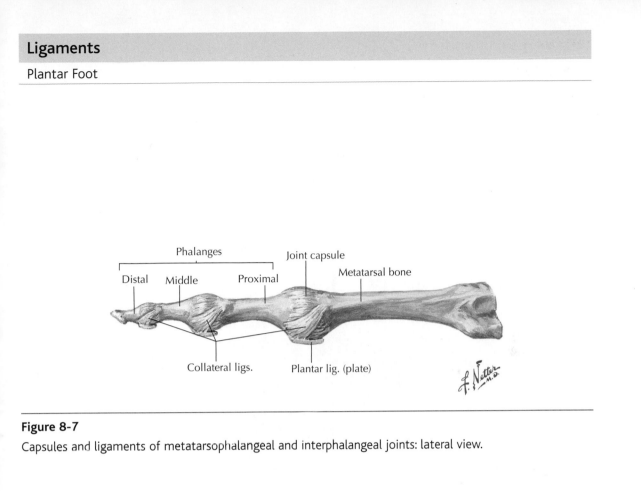

Figure 8-7

Capsules and ligaments of metatarsophalangeal and interphalangeal joints: lateral view.

Ligaments	Attachments	Function
Long plantar	Plantar of calcaneus to cuboid	Maintains arches of foot
Plantar calcaneocuboid (short plantar)	Anteroinferior aspect of calcaneus to inferior aspect of cuboid	Maintains arches of foot
Plantar calcaneonavicular (spring)	Sustentaculum tali to posteroinferior aspect of talus.	Maintains longitudinal arch of foot
Plantar cubonavicular	Inferior navicular to inferomedial cuboid	Limits separation of cuboid from navicular and supports arch
Plantar tarsometatarsal	Connects metatarsals 1-5 to corresponding tarsal on plantar aspect	Limits separation of metatarsals from corresponding tarsal bones
Collateral	Distal aspect of proximal phalanx to proximal aspect of distal phalanx	Reinforces capsule of IP joints
Plantar plate	Thickening of plantar aspect of joint capsule	Reinforces plantar aspect of IP joint
Deep transverse metatarsal	MTP joints on plantar aspect	Limits separation of MTP joints

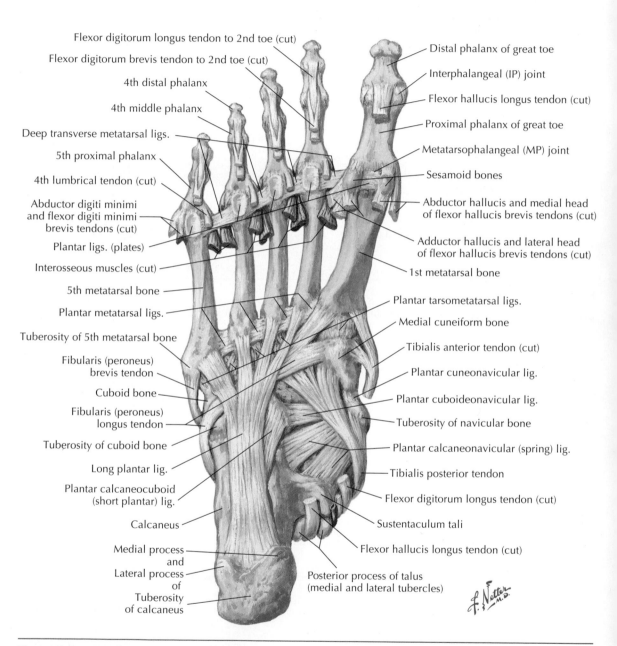

Flexor digitorum longus tendon to 2nd toe (cut)

Flexor digitorum brevis tendon to 2nd toe (cut)

4th distal phalanx

4th middle phalanx

Deep transverse metatarsal ligs.

5th proximal phalanx

4th lumbrical tendon (cut)

Abductor digiti minimi and flexor digiti minimi brevis tendons (cut)

Plantar ligs. (plates)

Interosseous muscles (cut)

5th metatarsal bone

Plantar metatarsal ligs.

Tuberosity of 5th metatarsal bone

Fibularis (peroneus) brevis tendon

Cuboid bone

Fibularis (peroneus) longus tendon

Tuberosity of cuboid bone

Long plantar lig.

Plantar calcaneocuboid (short plantar) lig.

Calcaneus

Medial process and Lateral process of Tuberosity of calcaneus

Distal phalanx of great toe

Interphalangeal (IP) joint

Flexor hallucis longus tendon (cut)

Proximal phalanx of great toe

Metatarsophalangeal (MP) joint

Sesamoid bones

Abductor hallucis and medial head of flexor hallucis brevis tendons (cut)

Adductor hallucis and lateral head of flexor hallucis brevis tendons (cut)

1st metatarsal bone

Plantar tarsometatarsal ligs.

Medial cuneiform bone

Tibialis anterior tendon (cut)

Plantar cuneonavicular lig.

Plantar cuboideonavicular lig.

Tuberosity of navicular bone

Plantar calcaneonavicular (spring) lig.

Tibialis posterior tendon

Flexor digitorum longus tendon (cut)

Sustentaculum tali

Flexor hallucis longus tendon (cut)

Posterior process of talus (medial and lateral tubercles)

Figure 8-8

Ligaments and tendons of foot: plantar view.

Muscles

Lateral Muscles of Leg

Muscles	Proximal Attachments	Distal Attachments	Nerve and Segmental Level	Action
Gastrocnemius	Lateral head: lateral femoral condyle Medial head: popliteal surface of femur	Posterior aspect of calcaneus	Tibial nerve (S1, S2)	Plantarflexes ankle and flexes knee
Soleus	Posterior aspect of head of fibula, fibular soleal line and medial aspect of tibia	Posterior aspect of calcaneus	Tibial nerve (S1, S2)	Plantarflexes ankle
Fibularis longus	Superolateral surface of fibula	Base of 1st metatarsal and medial cuneiform	Superficial fibular nerve (L5, S1, S2)	Everts foot and assists in plantarflexion
Fibularis brevis	Distal aspect of fibula	Tuberosity of base of 5th metatarsal	Superficial fibular nerve (L5, S1, S2)	Everts foot and assists in plantarflexion
Fibularis tertius	Anteroinferior aspect of fibula and interosseus membrane	Base of 5th metatarsal	Deep fibular nerve (L5, S1)	Dorsiflexes ankle and everts foot
Extensor digitorum longus	Lateral condyle of tibia, medial surface of fibula	Middle and distal phalanges of digits 2-5	Deep fibular nerve (L5, S1)	Extends digits 2-5 and assists with ankle dorsiflexion
Extensor hallucis longus	Anterior fibula and interosseus membrane	Dorsal base of distal phalanx of great toe	Deep fibular nerve (L5, S1)	Extends great toe and assists with ankle dorsiflexion
Extensor digitorum brevis	Superolateral aspect of calcaneus, extensor retinaculum	Dorsal base of middle phalanx of digits 2-5	Deep fibular nerve (L5, S1)	Extends digits 2-4 at MTP joints
Tibialis anterior	Lateral condyle and anterior surface of tibia	Inferomedial aspect of medial cuneiform and base of 1st metatarsal	Deep fibular nerve (L4, L5)	Ankle dorsiflexion and foot inversion

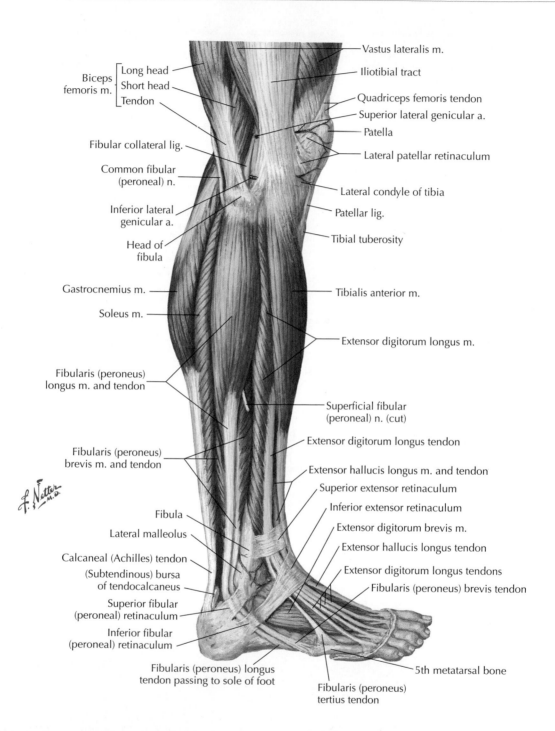

Figure 8-9

Muscles of foot and ankle: lateral view.

Muscles

Posterior Muscles of Leg

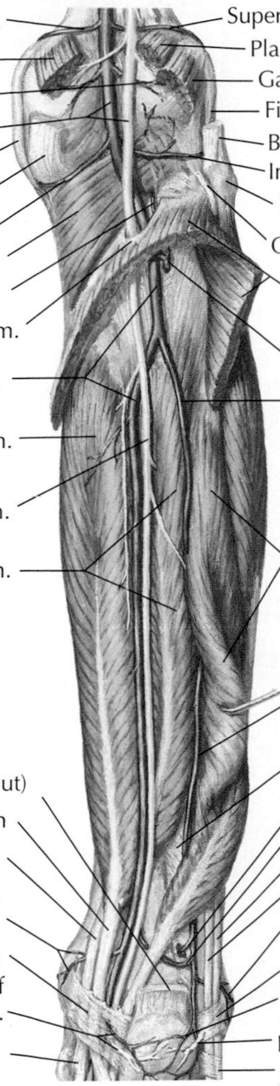

Superior medial genicular a.
Gastrocnemius m. (medial head) (cut)
Sural (muscular) branches
Popliteal a. and tibial n.
Tibial collateral lig.
Semimembranosus tendon (cut)
Inferior medial genicular a.
Popliteus m.
Posterior tibial recurrent a.
Tendinous arch of soleus m.
Posterior tibial a.
Flexor digitorum longus m.
Tibial n.
Tibialis posterior m.

Superior lateral genicular a.
Plantaris m. (cut)
Gastrocnemius m. (lateral head) (cut)
Fibular collateral lig.
Biceps femoris tendon (cut)
Inferior lateral genicular a.
Head of fibula
Common fibular (peroneal) n.
Soleus m. (cut and reflected)
Anterior tibial a.
Fibular (peroneal) a.
Flexor hallucis longus m. (retracted)
Fibular (peroneal) a.
Interosseous membrane

Calcaneal (Achilles) tendon (cut)
Flexor digitorum longus tendon
Tibialis posterior tendon
Medial malleolus and posterior medial malleolar branch of posterior tibial a.
Flexor retinaculum
Medial calcaneal branches of posterior tibial a. and tibial n.
Tibialis posterior tendon

Perforating branch — of fibular
Communicating branch — (peroneal) a.
Fibularis (peroneus) longus tendon
Fibularis (peroneus) brevis tendon
Lateral malleolus and posterior lateral malleolar branch of fibular (peroneal) a.
Superior fibular (peroneal) retinaculum
Lateral calcaneal branch of fibular (peroneal) a.
Lateral calcaneal branch of sural n.
Inferior fibular (peroneal) retinaculum

Figure 8-10

Muscles of leg: posterior view.

Muscles	Proximal Attachments	Distal Attachments	Nerve and Segmental Level	Action
Tibialis posterior	Interosseus membrane, posteroinferior aspect of tibia and posterior fibula	Navicular tuberosity, cuneiform, cuboid and bases of metatarsals 2-4	Tibial nerve (L4, L5)	Plantarflexes ankle and inverts foot
Flexor hallucis longus	Posteroinferior fibula and interosseus membrane	Base of distal phalanx of great toe	Tibial nerve (S2, S3)	Flexes great toe and assists with ankle plantarflexion
Flexor digitorum longus	Posteroinferior tibia	Bases of distal phalanges 2-5	Tibial nerve (S2, S3)	Flexes lateral four digits, plantarflexes ankle, supports longitudinal arch of foot

Superficial fibular (peroneal) n. (cut)
Fibularis (peroneus) longus tendon
Fibularis (peroneus) brevis m. and tendon
Extensor digitorum longus m. and tendon
Fibula
Perforating branch of fibular (peroneal) a.
Anterior lateral malleolar a.
Lateral malleolus
Lateral branch of deep peroneal n. (to mm. of dorsum of foot) and lateral tarsal a.
Fibularis (peroneus) longus tendon (cut)
Extensor digitorum brevis and extensor hallucis brevis mm. (cut)
Fibularis (peroneus) brevis tendon (cut)
Fibularis (peroneus) tertius tendon (cut)
Abductor digiti minimi m.
Dorsal metatarsal aa.
Metatarsal bones
Dorsal interosseous mm.
Lateral dorsal cutaneous n. (continuation of sural n.) (cut)
Anterior perforating branches from plantar metatarsal aa.
Dorsal digital aa.
Dorsal branches of proper plantar digital aa. and nn.

Soleus m.
Tibialis anterior m. and tendon
Tibia
Anterior tibial a. and deep fibular (peroneal) n.
Extensor hallucis longus m. and tendon
Anterior medial malleolar a.
Medial malleolus
Dorsalis pedis a.
Medial branch of deep fibular (peroneal) n.
Medial tarsal aa.
Tuberosity of navicular bone
Arcuate a.
Posterior perforating branches from deep plantar arch
Deep plantar a. to deep plantar arch
Abductor hallucis m.
Extensor hallucis longus tendon
Extensor hallucis brevis tendon (cut)
Extensor digitorum brevis tendons (cut)
Extensor digitorum longus tendons (cut)
Extensor expansions
Dorsal digital branches of deep fibular (peroneal) n.
Dorsal digital branches of superficial fibular (peroneal) n.

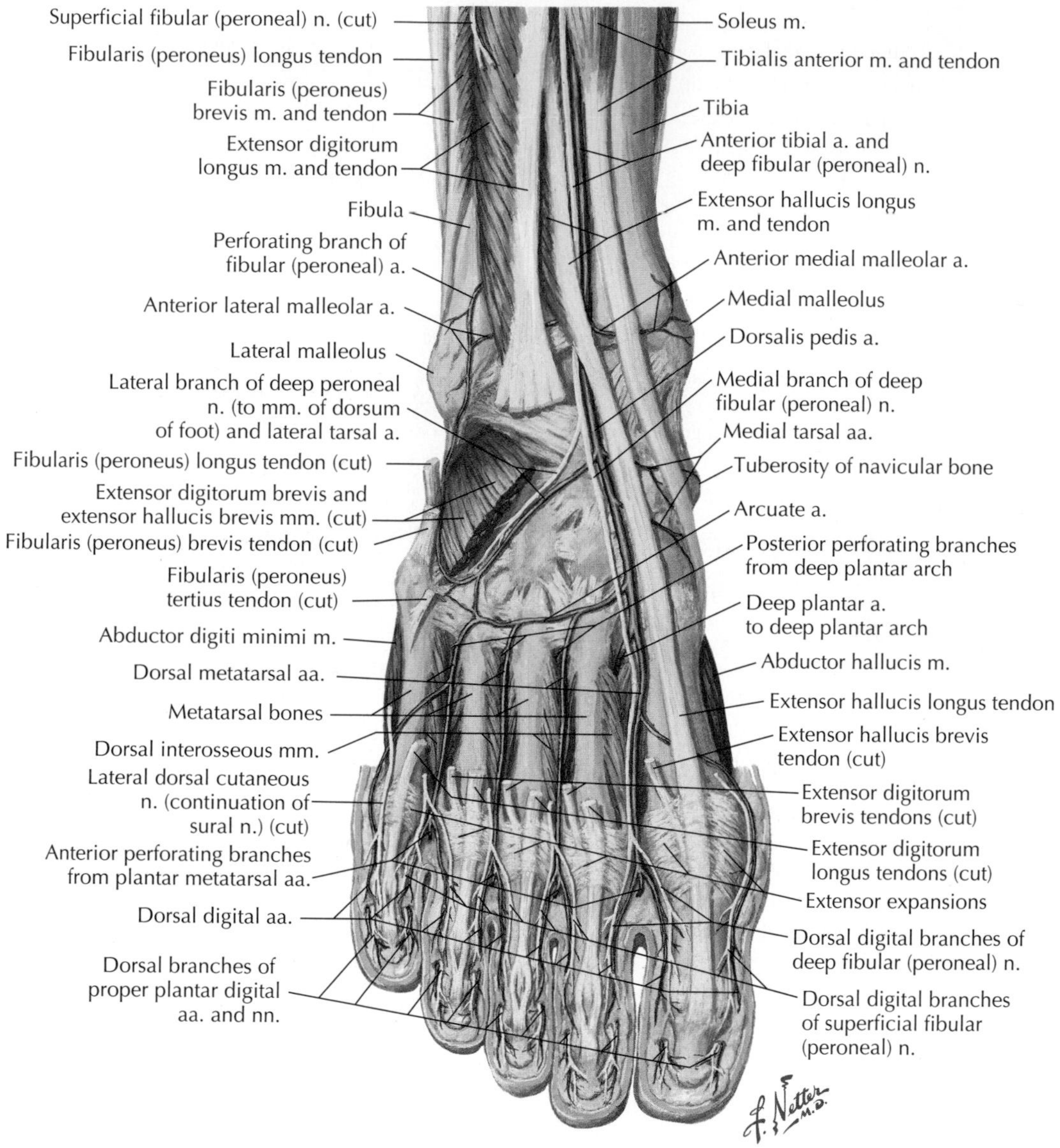

Figure 8-11

Muscles, arteries, and nerves of front of ankle and dorsum of foot: deeper dissection.

Muscles	Proximal Attachments	Distal Attachments	Nerve and Segmental Level	Action
Extensor digitorum brevis	Superolateral aspect of calcaneus and extensor retinaculum	Dorsal base of middle phalanx of digits 2-5	Deep fibular nerve (L5, S1)	Extends digits 2-4 at MTP joints
Extensor hallucis brevis	Superolateral aspect of calcaneus and extensor retinaculum	Dorsal base of proximal phalanx of great toe	Deep fibular nerve (L5, S1)	Extends great toe at MTP joints
Dorsal interossei	Sides of metatarsals 1-5	1st: medial aspect of proximal phalanx of 2nd digit 2nd-4th: lateral aspect of digits 2-4	Lateral plantar nerve (S2, S3)	Abducts digits 2-4 and flexes MTP joints

Muscles

First Layer: Sole of Foot

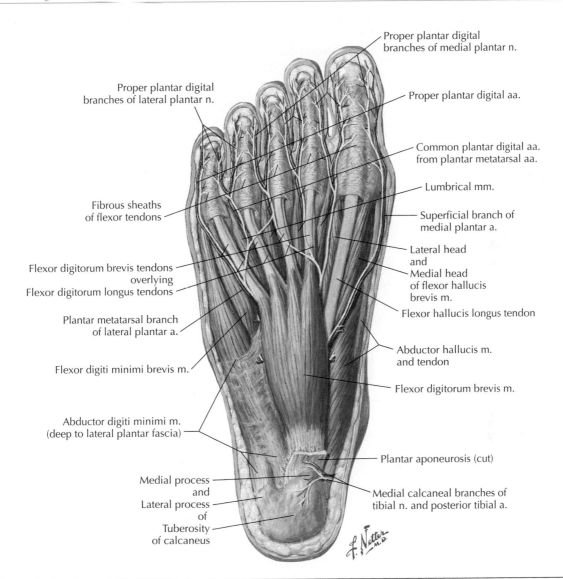

Figure 8-12

Muscles of sole of foot: first layer.

Muscles	Proximal Attachments	Distal Attachments	Nerve and Segmental Level	Action
Abductor hallucis longus	Medial calcaneal tuberosity, flexor retinaculum, and plantar aponeurosis	Base of proximal phalanx of 1st digit	Medial plantar nerve (S2, S3)	Abducts and flexes great toe
Flexor digitorum brevis	Medial calcaneal tuberosity and plantar aponeurosis	Sides of middle phalanges of digits 2-5	Medial plantar nerve (S2, S3)	Flexes digits 2-5
Abductor digiti minimi	Medial and lateral calcaneal tuberosities	Lateral aspect of base of proximal phalanx of 5th metatarsal	Lateral plantar nerve (S2, S3)	Abducts and flexes 5th digit

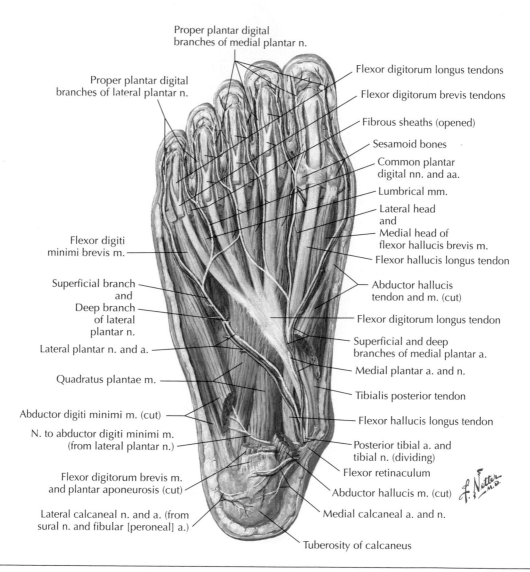

Proper plantar digital branches of medial plantar n.

Proper plantar digital branches of lateral plantar n.

Flexor digitorum longus tendons

Flexor digitorum brevis tendons

Fibrous sheaths (opened)

Sesamoid bones

Common plantar digital nn. and aa.

Lumbrical mm.

Lateral head and

Medial head of flexor hallucis brevis m.

Flexor hallucis longus tendon

Flexor digiti minimi brevis m.

Abductor hallucis tendon and m. (cut)

Superficial branch and Deep branch of lateral plantar n.

Flexor digitorum longus tendon

Superficial and deep branches of medial plantar a.

Lateral plantar n. and a.

Medial plantar a. and n.

Quadratus plantae m.

Tibialis posterior tendon

Abductor digiti minimi m. (cut)

Flexor hallucis longus tendon

N. to abductor digiti minimi m. (from lateral plantar n.)

Posterior tibial a. and tibial n. (dividing)

Flexor retinaculum

Flexor digitorum brevis m. and plantar aponeurosis (cut)

Abductor hallucis m. (cut)

Lateral calcaneal n. and a. (from sural n. and fibular [peroneal] a.)

Medial calcaneal a. and n.

Tuberosity of calcaneus

Figure 8-13

Muscles of sole of foot: second layer.

Muscles	Proximal Attachments	Distal Attachments	Nerve and Segmental Level	Action
Lumbricals	Tendons of flexor digitorum longus	Medial aspect of expansion over lateral four digits	Lateral three: lateral plantar nerve (S2, S3) Medial one: medial plantar nerve (S2, S3)	Flexes proximal phalanges and extends middle and distal phalanges of digits 2-5
Quadratus plantae	Medial and plantar aspect of calcaneus	Posterolateral aspect of tendon of flexor digitorum longus	Lateral plantar nerve (S2, S3)	Assists in flexing digits 2-5

Third Layer: Sole of Foot

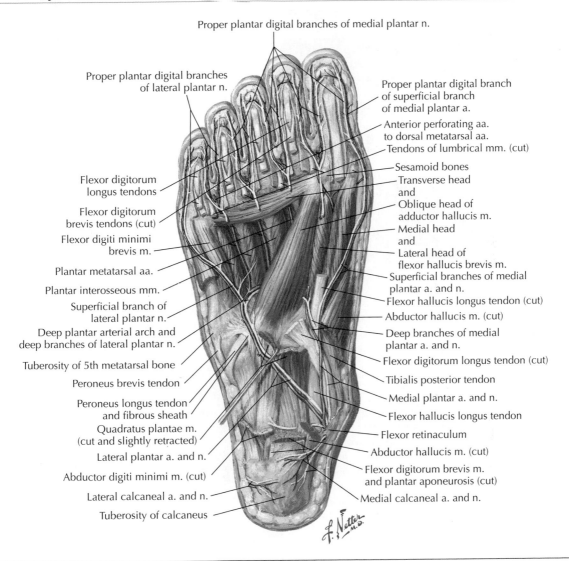

Proper plantar digital branches of medial plantar n.

Proper plantar digital branches of lateral plantar n.

Proper plantar digital branch of superficial branch of medial plantar a.

Anterior perforating aa. to dorsal metatarsal aa.

Tendons of lumbrical mm. (cut)

Flexor digitorum longus tendons

Sesamoid bones

Transverse head and

Flexor digitorum brevis tendons (cut)

Oblique head of adductor hallucis m.

Flexor digiti minimi brevis m.

Medial head and

Lateral head of flexor hallucis brevis m.

Plantar metatarsal aa.

Plantar interosseous mm.

Superficial branches of medial plantar a. and n.

Flexor hallucis longus tendon (cut)

Superficial branch of lateral plantar n.

Abductor hallucis m. (cut)

Deep plantar arterial arch and deep branches of lateral plantar n.

Deep branches of medial plantar a. and n.

Flexor digitorum longus tendon (cut)

Tuberosity of 5th metatarsal bone

Tibialis posterior tendon

Peroneus brevis tendon

Medial plantar a. and n.

Peroneus longus tendon and fibrous sheath

Flexor hallucis longus tendon

Quadratus plantae m. (cut and slightly retracted)

Flexor retinaculum

Lateral plantar a. and n.

Abductor hallucis m. (cut)

Abductor digiti minimi m. (cut)

Flexor digitorum brevis m. and plantar aponeurosis (cut)

Lateral calcaneal a. and n.

Medial calcaneal a. and n.

Tuberosity of calcaneus

Figure 8-14

Muscles of sole of foot: third layer.

Muscles	Proximal Attachments	Distal Attachments	Nerve and Segmental Level	Action
Flexor digiti minimi brevis	Base of 5th metatarsal	Base of proximal phalanx of 5th metatarsal	Superficial branch of lateral plantar nerve	Flexes proximal phalanx of fifth digit
Adductor Hallucis				
Transverse head	Plantar ligaments of MTP joints	Lateral base of proximal phalanx of great toe	Deep branch of lateral plantar nerve (S2, S3)	Adducts great toe
Oblique head	Bases of metatarsals 2-4			
Flexor hallucis brevis	Plantar cuboid and lateral cuneiforms	Sides of proximal phalanx of great toe	Medial plantar nerve (S2, S3)	Flexes proximal phalanx of great toe

Muscles

Deep Interosseous Muscles: Sole of Foot

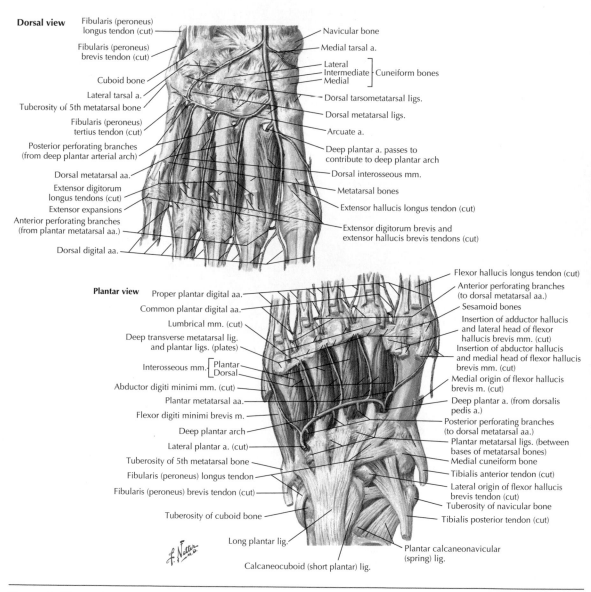

Dorsal view
- Fibularis (peroneus) longus tendon (cut)
- Fibularis (peroneus) brevis tendon (cut)
- Cuboid bone
- Lateral tarsal a.
- Tuberosity of 5th metatarsal bone
- Fibularis (peroneus) tertius tendon (cut)
- Posterior perforating branches (from deep plantar arterial arch)
- Dorsal metatarsal aa.
- Extensor digitorum longus tendons (cut)
- Extensor expansions
- Anterior perforating branches (from plantar metatarsal aa.)
- Dorsal digital aa.

- Navicular bone
- Medial tarsal a.
- Lateral / Intermediate / Medial — Cuneiform bones
- Dorsal tarsometatarsal ligs.
- Dorsal metatarsal ligs.
- Arcuate a.
- Deep plantar a. passes to contribute to deep plantar arch
- Dorsal interosseous mm.
- Metatarsal bones
- Extensor hallucis longus tendon (cut)
- Extensor digitorum brevis and extensor hallucis brevis tendons (cut)

Plantar view
- Proper plantar digital aa.
- Common plantar digital aa.
- Lumbrical mm. (cut)
- Deep transverse metatarsal lig. and plantar ligs. (plates)
- Interosseous mm. [Plantar / Dorsal]
- Abductor digiti minimi mm. (cut)
- Plantar metatarsal aa.
- Flexor digiti minimi brevis m.
- Deep plantar arch
- Lateral plantar a. (cut)
- Tuberosity of 5th metatarsal bone
- Fibularis (peroneus) longus tendon
- Fibularis (peroneus) brevis tendon (cut)
- Tuberosity of cuboid bone
- Long plantar lig.
- Calcaneocuboid (short plantar) lig.

- Flexor hallucis longus tendon (cut)
- Anterior perforating branches (to dorsal metatarsal aa.)
- Sesamoid bones
- Insertion of adductor hallucis and lateral head of flexor hallucis brevis mm. (cut)
- Insertion of abductor hallucis and medial head of flexor hallucis brevis mm. (cut)
- Medial origin of flexor hallucis brevis m. (cut)
- Deep plantar a. (from dorsalis pedis a.)
- Posterior perforating branches (to dorsal metatarsal aa.)
- Plantar metatarsal ligs. (between bases of metatarsal bones)
- Medial cuneiform bone
- Tibialis anterior tendon (cut)
- Lateral origin of flexor hallucis brevis tendon (cut)
- Tuberosity of navicular bone
- Tibialis posterior tendon (cut)
- Plantar calcaneonavicular (spring) lig.

Figure 8-15

Interosseous muscles and plantar arterial arch.

Muscles	Proximal Attachments	Distal Attachments	Nerve and Segmental Level	Action
Plantar interosseous	Bases of metatarsals 3-5	Medial bases of proximal phalanges 3-5	Lateral plantar nerve (S2, S3)	Adducts digits 2-4 and flexes MTP joints
Dorsal interosseous	Sides of metatarsals 1-5	1st: medial aspect of proximal phalanx of 2nd digit 2nd-4th: Lateral aspect of digits 2-4	Lateral plantar nerve (S2, S3)	Abducts digits 2-4 and flexes MTP joints

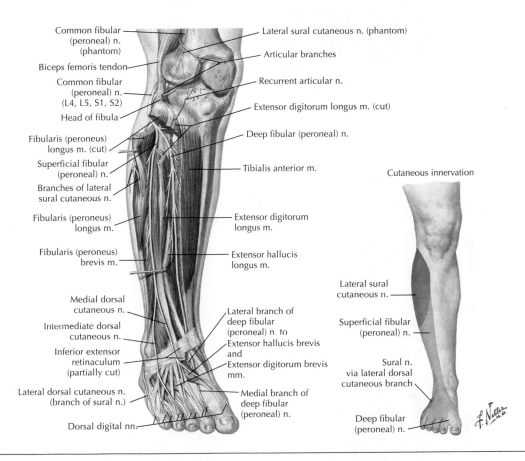

Figure 8-16

Tibial and fibular nerves: posterior view.

Nerves	Segmental Levels	Sensory	Motor
Sural	S1, S2	Posterior and lateral leg and lateral foot	No motor
Tibial	L4, L5, S1, S2, S3	Posterior heel and plantar surface of foot	Semitendinosus, semimembranosus, biceps femoris, adductor magnus, gastrocnemius, soleus, plantaris, flexor hallucis longus, flexor digitorum longus, tibialis posterior
Medial plantar	S2, S3	Medial 3 1/2 digits	Flexor hallucis brevis, abductor hallucis, flexor digitorum brevis, lumbricales
Lateral plantar	S2, S3	Lateral 1 1/2 digits	Adductor hallucis, abductor digiti minimi, quadratus plantae, lumbricales, flexor digiti minimi brevis, interossei
Saphenous	L2, L3, L4	Medial leg and foot	No motor
Deep fibular	L4, L5, S1	1st interdigital cleft	Tibialis anterior, extensor digitorum longus, extensor hallucis longus, fibularis tertius, extensor digitorum brevis, extensor hallucis brevis
Superficial fibular	L5, S1, S2	Distal anterior leg and dorsum of foot	Fibularis longus, fibularis brevis

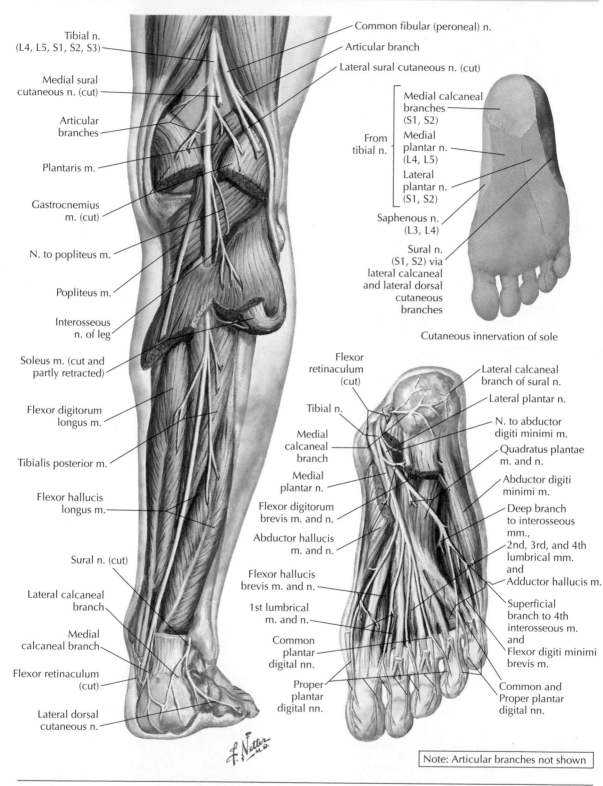

Figure 8-17

Tibial and fibular nerves: anterior view.

Initial Hypotheses Based on Historical Findings

Patient Reports	Initial Hypothesis
Patient reports a traumatic incident resulting in either forced inversion or eversion	Possible ankle sprain[1,2] Possible fracture Possible peroneal nerve involvement (if mechanism of injury is inversion)[3-5]
Patient reports trauma to ankle that included tibial rotation on a planted foot	Possible syndesmotic sprain[1]
Patient notes tenderness of anterior shin and may exhibit excessive pronation. Symptoms may be exacerbated by repetitive weight-bearing activities	Possible medial tibial stress syndrome[6]
Patient reports traumatic event resulting in inability to plantarflex ankle	Possible Achilles tendon rupture
Patient reports pain with stretch of calf muscles and during gait (toe push off)	Possible Achilles tendonitis[7] Possible Sever's disease[1]
Patient reports pain at heel with first few steps out of bed after prolonged periods of walking	Possible plantar fasciitis
Patient reports pain or paresthesias in plantar surface of foot	Possible tarsal tunnel syndrome[1] Possible sciatica Possible lumbar radiculopathy
Patient reports pain on plantar surface of foot between 3rd and 4th metatarsals. Might also state that pain is worse when walking with shoes compared with barefoot	Possible Morton's neuroma[7] Possible metatarsalgia

Evaluation Following Acute Ankle Trauma

ICC or κ	Interpretation
.81-1.0	Substantial agreement
.61-.80	Moderate agreement
.41-.60	Fair agreement
.11-.40	Slight agreement
.0-.10	No agreement

Test	Test Procedure and Determination of Positive Finding	Population	Inter-examiner Reliability
Ability to bear weight[8]			κ = .83
Bone tenderness at base of 5th metatarsal[8]			κ = .78
Bone tenderness at posterior edge of lateral malleolus[8]			κ = .75
Bone tenderness at tip of medial malleolus[8]			κ = .66
Bone tenderness at proximal fibula[8]	Tenderness calculated as tender or not. Swelling and ROM limitations dichotomized as "none-minimal" or "moderate-marked"	100 patients having sustained acute ankle trauma	κ = −.01
Combinations of bone tenderness[8]			κ = .76
Soft tissue tenderness[8]			κ = .41
Degree of swelling in area of anterior talofibular ligament[8]			κ = .18
Ecchymosis[8]			κ = .39
ROM restrictions present[8]			κ = .33
Palpation test[9]	Examiner palpates over anterior talofibular ligament. Positive if pain is reproduced		κ = .36
ER test[9]	With patient sitting over edge of plinth, passive ER stress is applied to foot and ankle. Positive if pain is reproduced over syndesmotic ligaments		κ = .75
Squeeze test[9]	With patient sitting over edge of plinth, examiner manually compresses fibula and tibia over calf midpoint. Positive if pain is reproduced over syndesmotic ligaments	53 patients presenting for treatment of ankle injury	κ = .50
Dorsiflexion-compression test[9]	With patient standing, patient actively dorsiflexes ankle while weight-bearing. Examiner applies manual compression around malleoli with patient's foot in dorsiflexed position. Positive if significant increase in ankle dorsiflexion or reduction in pain with compression		κ = .36

Evaluation Following Acute Ankle Trauma

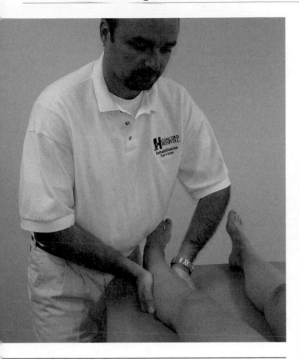

Figure 8-18
Squeeze test.

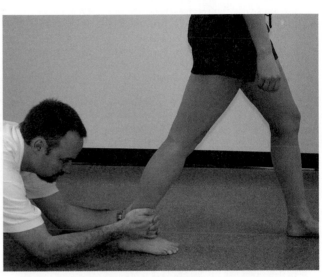

Figure 8-19
Dorsiflexion-compression test.

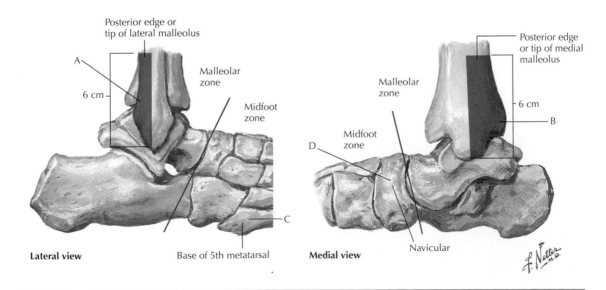

Posterior edge or tip of lateral malleolus

A

6 cm

Malleolar zone

Midfoot zone

C

Lateral view

Base of 5th metatarsal

Malleolar zone

Midfoot zone

D

Posterior edge or tip of medial malleolus

6 cm

B

Navicular

Medial view

Figure 8-20
Ottawa ankle rules.

+LR	Interpretation	−LR
>10	Large	<.1
5.0-10.0	Moderate	.1-.2
2.0-5.0	Small	.2-.5
1.0-2.0	Rarely important	.5-1.0

Test and Study Quality	Description and Positive Findings	Population	Reference Standard	Sens	Spec	+LR	−LR
Ottawa Ankle Rule for Radiography[10] **2003 Meta-analysis**	Ankle x-ray series ordered when patients have bone tenderness at A or B or C or D (see Fig. 8-20) or if the patient could not bear weight immediately after the injury or during the examination (four steps regardless of limping)	Statistically pooled data from 27 high-quality studies involving 15,581 adults and children		.98 (.97, .99)	.20	1.23	.10 (.06, .16)
Bernese ankle rules[11] ◇	Ankle x-ray series ordered when patients had pain with any of the following: (1) Indirect fibular stress applied by compressing the tibia and fibula proximal to the malleoli (2) Direct medial malleolar stress with examiner's thumb (3) Compression stress of the mid and hindfoot applied simultaneously	354 patients reporting to the emergency department after a low-energy, supination-type ankle or foot injury	Ankle or midfoot fracture on radiograph	1.0	.91	11.11	.00
Adding tuning fork to Ottawa Ankle Rule for Radiography[12] ◯	Base of a vibrating tuning fork placed on tip of lateral malleolus. Positive if patient reports discomfort or pain	49 patients reporting to emergency department after inversion ankle injury		1.0	.61	2.59	.00
	As above, but placed on distal fibular shaft.			1.0	.95	22.00	.00

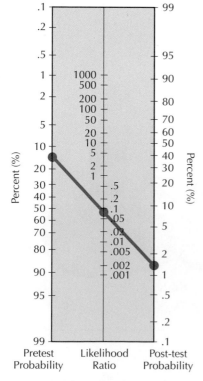

Pretest Probability — Likelihood Ratio — Post-test Probability

Figure 8-21

Nomogram. Assuming a fracture prevalence of 15% (statistically pooled from Bachmann et al[10]), an adult seen in the emergency department with an acute injury whose findings were negative on the Ottawa Ankle Rule would have a 1.4% (95% CI, 0.15% to 1.48%) chance of having an ankle and/or midfoot fracture. *(Adapted with permission from Fagan TJ. Nomogram for Bayes' theorem. N Engl J Med. 1975;293-257. Copyright 2005, Massachusetts Medical Society. All rights reserved.)*

Range of Motion

Reliability of Range of Motion Measurements

ICC or κ	Interpretation
.81-1.0	Substantial agreement
.61-.80	Moderate agreement
.41-.60	Fair agreement
.11-.40	Slight agreement
.0-.10	No agreement

Measurements	Instrumentation	Population	Reliability	
			Intra-examiner	Inter-examiner
AROM (sitting) Subtalar joint inversion Subtalar joint eversion[13]	Plastic goniometer	31 asymptomatic subjects	ICC = **.91-.96** ICC = **.82-.93**	ICC = **.73 (.61, .82)** ICC = **.62 (.49, .74)**
AROM (prone) Subtalar joint inversion Subtalar joint eversion[13]	Plastic goniometer	31 asymptomatic subjects	ICC = **.94 (.91, .96)** ICC = **.83-.94**	ICC = **.54 (.33, .70)** ICC = **.41 (.25, .56)**
AROM Ankle dorsiflexion Ankle plantar flexion[14]	Plastic goniometer	38 patients with orthopaedic disorders of ankle or knee	ICC = **.89** ICC = **.91**	ICC = **.28** ICC = **.25**
PROM Subtalar joint neutral Subtalar joint inversion Subtalar joint eversion Plantarflexion Dorsiflexion[15]	Plastic goniometer	43 patients with orthopaedic or neurologic disorders wherein measurements of foot and ankle would be appropriate in a clinical setting	ICC = **.77** ICC = **.62** ICC = **.59** ICC = **.86** ICC = **.90**	ICC = **.25** ICC = **.15** ICC = **.12** ICC = **.72** ICC = **.50**
PROM Pronation Supination Ankle dorsiflexion First ray plantarflexion First ray dorsiflexion[16]	Inclinometer	30 healthy subjects	ICC = **.89-.97** ICC = **.90-.95** ICC = **.86-.97** ICC = **.72-.97** ICC = **.90-.98**	ICC = **.46-.49** ICC = **.28-.40** ICC = **.26-.31** ICC = **.21-.91** ICC = **.14-.16**
First ray mobility[17]	Manual assessment. Graded as "hypomobile," "normal," or "hypermobile"	30 asymptomatic subjects	Not tested	κ = **.08-.20**
Dorsiflexion in a calf stretch position[18]	Digital inclinometer used to take measurements between the tibia and vertical when subject is standing in a calf stretch position with knee extended	30 healthy subjects	ICC = **.77-.91**	ICC = **.92-.95**
Dorsiflexion in a modified lunge test[19]	Inclinometer used to take measurements calculated during lunge between angle formed by fibular head and lateral malleolus	31 subjects 76 to 87 years of age recruited from general population	ICC = **.87 (.74, .94)**	**Not tested**
Open kinetic chain: Resting subtalar joint Subtalar joint neutral[20]	Inclinometer	30 asymptomatic subjects	ICC = **.85** ICC = **.85**	ICC = **.68** ICC = **.79**
Passive dorsiflexion[21]	Standard goniometer	63 healthy Navy Reserve officers	ICC = **.74**	ICC = **.65**

AROM, Active range of motion; ICC, intraclass correlation coefficient; PROM, passive range of motion.

Range of Motion

Reliability of Range of Motion Measurements

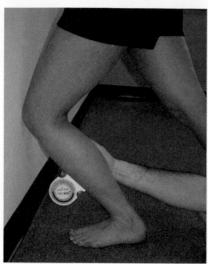

Weight-bearing lunge measurement
of ankle dorsiflexion

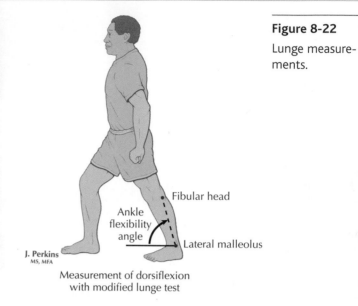

Figure 8-22
Lunge measure-
ments.

Fibular head

Ankle
flexibility
angle

Lateral malleolus

J. Perkins
MS, MFA

Measurement of dorsiflexion
with modified lunge test

Reliability of Range of Motion Measurement of Calcaneal Position

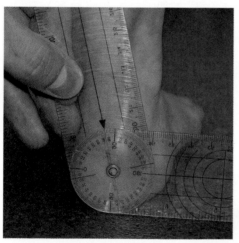

ICC or κ	Interpretation
.81-1.0	Substantial agreement
.61-.80	Moderate agreement
.41-.60	Fair agreement
.11-.40	Slight agreement
.0-.10	No agreement

Figure 8-23
Measurement of relaxed calcaneal stance.

Measurements	Instrumentation	Population	Reliability	
			Intra-examiner	Inter-examiner
Relaxed calcaneal stance position[22]	Standard goniometer	212 healthy subjects: 88 adults, 124 children	ICC = .61-.90	**Not tested**
Relaxed calcaneal stance Neutral calcaneal stance[16]	Gravity goniometer	30 healthy subjects	ICC = .95-.97 ICC = .87-.93	ICC = .61-.62 ICC = .21-.31
Rearfoot angle[21]	Standard goniometer	63 healthy Navy Reserve officers	ICC = .88	ICC = .86

Assessing Strength

Reliability of Strength Assessment

ICC or κ	Interpretation
.81-1.0	Substantial agreement
.61-.80	Moderate agreement
.41-.60	Fair agreement
.11-.40	Slight agreement
.0-.10	No agreement

Test and Measure	Test Procedure	Population	Inter-examiner Reliability
Ankle plantarflexion strength and endurance[23]	Children asked to perform as many single-leg heel-rises as possible at a rate of 1 every 2 seconds while examiner counts the repetitions	95 7- to 9-year-old children	ICC = .99

Diagnostic Utility of the Paper Grip Test for Detecting Toe Plantarflexion Strength Deficits

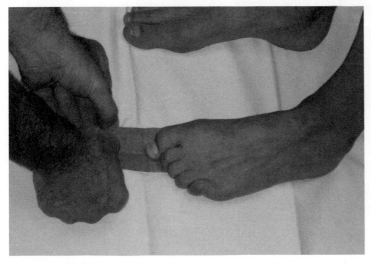

+LR	Interpretation	−LR
>10	Large	<.1
5.0-10.0	Moderate	.1-.2
2.0-5.0	Small	.2-.5
1.0-2.0	Rarely important	.5-1.0

Figure 8-24

Paper grip test.

Test and Study Quality	Description and Positive Findings	Population	Reference Standard	Sens	Spec	+LR	−LR
Paper grip test[24] ◇	With patient sitting with hips, knees, and ankles at 90° and toes on a piece of cardboard, examiner stabilizes the feet while attempting to slide cardboard away from the toes. Positive if participant cannot maintain cardboard under toes	80 asymptomatic adults	Toe plantarflexion strength as measured by a force plate system	.80	.79	3.8	.25

Measurement of Navicular Height

ICC or κ	Interpretation
.81-1.0	Substantial agreement
.61-.80	Moderate agreement
.41-.60	Fair agreement
.11-.40	Slight agreement
.0-.10	No agreement

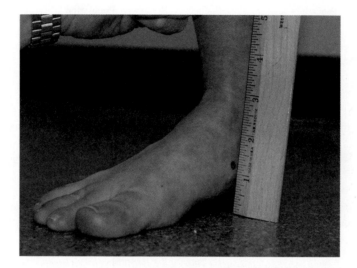

Figure 8-25

Measurement of navicular height.

Test and Measure	Test Procedure	Population	Reliability	
			Intra-examiner	Inter-examiner
Navicular height[19]	Navicular tuberosity is marked while patient is in weight-bearing position. Distance from ground to navicular tuberosity is measured	31 subjects 76 to 87 years of age recruited from general population	ICC = .64 (.38, .81)	Not tested
Navicular drop test[25]	Navicular tuberosity is marked. Difference between distance from navicular tuberosity with foot resting on ground with weight bearing mostly on contralateral lower extremity while examiner maintains subtalar joint neutral and during relaxed bilateral stance with full weight bearing is recorded	30 patients with patellofemoral pain syndrome	Not tested	ICC = .93 (.84, .97)
Navicular height technique[20]		30 asymptomatic subjects	ICC = .83	ICC = .73
Navicular drop test[26]		20 symptomatic subjects	ICC = .33-.62	ICC = .31-.40
Navicular height[27]	Height of navicular tuberosity is calculated with digital calipers	100 consecutive patients presenting to an orthopaedic foot and ankle clinic	ICC = .90	ICC = .74

Assessing Bony Alignment

Assessment of Medial Arch Height

ICC or κ	Interpretation
.81-1.0	Substantial agreement
.61-.80	Moderate agreement
.41-.60	Fair agreement
.11-.40	Slight agreement
.0-.10	No agreement

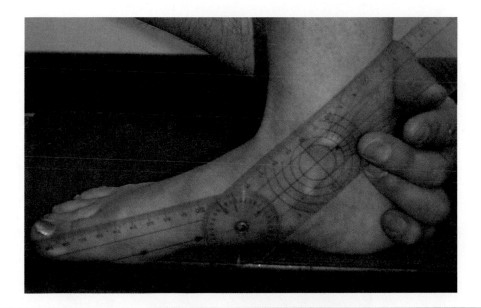

Figure 8-26

Measurement of arch angle.

Test and Measure	Test Procedure	Population	Reliability	
			Intra-examiner	Inter-examiner
Arch angle[21]	Patient in weight-bearing position. Examiner measures angle formed by line connecting medial malleolus and navicular tuberosity and angle from tuberosity to medial aspect of 1st metatarsal head with standard goniometer	63 healthy Navy Reserve officers	ICC = .90	ICC = .81
Arch height test[27]	Highest point of soft tissue margin along medial longitudinal arch recorded with a digital caliper	100 consecutive patients presenting to an orthopaedic foot and ankle clinic	ICC = .91	ICC = .76

ICC or κ	Interpretation
.81-1.0	Substantial agreement
.61-.80	Moderate agreement
.41-.60	Fair agreement
.11-.40	Slight agreement
.0-.10	No agreement

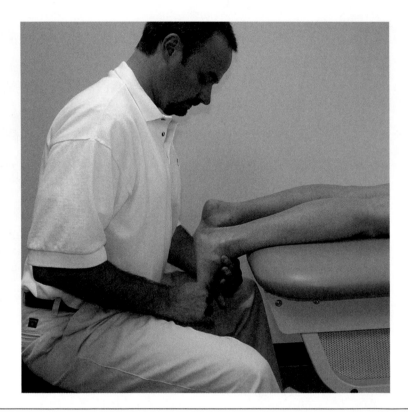

Figure 8-27

Determination of forefoot varus/valgus.

Test and Measure	Test Procedure	Population	Reliability	
			Intra-examiner	Inter-examiner
Forefoot varus[1]	With patient prone with foot over edge of table, examiner palpates medial and lateral talar head then grasps 4th and 5th metatarsals, taking up slack in midtarsal joints. Subtalar neutral is position in which medial and lateral talar head is palpated equally[28]	30 healthy subjects	ICC = .95-.99	ICC = .61

Assessing Balance and Dynamic Performance

Reliability of Assessing Balance and Proprioception

ICC or κ	Interpretation
.81-1.0	Substantial agreement
.61-.80	Moderate agreement
.41-.60	Fair agreement
.11-.40	Slight agreement
.0-.10	No agreement

Test	Procedure	Population	Reliability
Single leg balance test[29]	Participants stand on one foot, without shoes on, on a Polyform mat with eyes closed and the contralateral leg bent for 1 minute. Examiner counts number of errors (surface contract with contralateral foot or movement of the test foot)	24 male recreational athletes with functional ankle instability	Test-retest ICC = **.94**
Single leg balance test[30]	Participants stand on one foot, without shoes on, with the contralateral leg bent and not touching the tested limb. Test is positive when patient cannot remain balanced or reports a sense of imbalance	240 healthy athletes	Inter-examiner κ = **.90**
Threshold for perception of passive movement[31]	Examiner collects measurements with potentiometer	24 healthy adult subjects	Test-retest ICC = **.95**
Active-to-active reproduction of joint position[31]			Test-retest ICC = **.83**
Reproduction of movement velocity[31]			Test-retest ICC = **.79**
Reproduction of torque[31]			Test-retest ICC = (Dorsiflexion) **.86** (Plantarflexion) **.72**

ICC or κ	Interpretation
.81-1.0	Substantial agreement
.61-.80	Moderate agreement
.41-.60	Fair agreement
.11-.40	Slight agreement
.0-.10	No agreement

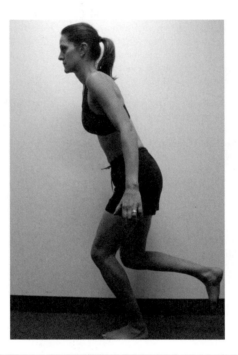

Figure 8-28

Single leg hop test.

Test and Measure	Test Procedure	Population	Reliability
Single leg hopping course[29]	Course consists of 8 squares, some of which are inclined, declined, or have a lateral inclination. Patients jump on each square on one leg as quickly as possible. Performance indicated in number of seconds taken to perform task		Test-retest ICC = **.97**
Single leg hop for distance[29]	Patients asked to hop once or three times as far as possible on one leg. Performance indicated by distance covered	24 male recreational athletes with functional ankle instability	Test-retest ICC = **.97**
Triple hop for distance[29]			Test-retest ICC = **.98**
6-meter hop for time[29]	Patients hop in a straight line or crosswise over a line, for 6 meters on one leg as quickly as possible. Performance indicated in number of seconds taken to perform task		Test-retest ICC = **.95**
Cross 6-meter hop for time[29]			Test-retest ICC = **.94**

Assessing Foot Motion during Gait

Reliability of Assessing Hindfoot Motion during Gait

ICC or κ	Interpretation
.81-1.0	Substantial agreement
.61-.80	Moderate agreement
.41-.60	Fair agreement
.11-.40	Slight agreement
.0-.10	No agreement

Test and Measure	Test Procedure	Population	Inter-examiner Reliability	
			5-Point Scale	2-Point Scale
Duration of hindfoot motion[32]	Each aspect of dynamic hindfoot motion is graded on a 2- or 5-point scale while observing participant walking barefoot on a treadmill. *5 point scale:* (1) Less than normal (2) Normal (3) Mildly abnormal (4) Moderately abnormal (5) Severely abnormal *2 point scale:* (1) Normal or less than normal (2) Greater than normal	24 healthy participants	κ = −.03-.01	κ = .14-.24
Velocity of hindfoot motion[32]			κ = −.04-.01	κ = .02-.20
Timing of hindfoot motion[32]			κ = .15-.20	κ = .19-.20
Maximum degree of hindfoot motion[32]			κ = .13-.18	κ = .27-.48
Range of hindfoot motion[32]			κ = .06-.19	κ = .15-.28

Accuracy of the Functional Hallux Limitus Test to Predict Abnormal Excessive Midtarsal Function During Gait

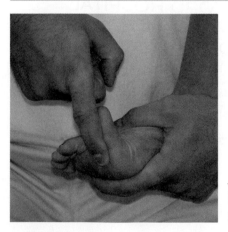

+LR	Interpretation	−LR
>10	Large	<.1
5.0-10.0	Moderate	.1-.2
2.0-5.0	Small	.2-.5
1.0-2.0	Rarely important	.5-1.0

Figure 8-29

Functional hallux: limitus test.

Test and Study Quality	Description and Positive Findings	Population	Reference Standard	Sens	Spec	+LR	−LR
Functional hallux limitus test[33] ◯	With the patient in a non–weight-bearing position, the examiner used one hand to maintaining the subtalar joint in a neutral position while maintaining the first ray in dorsiflexion. The other hand was used to dorsiflex the proximal phalanx of the hallux. The test was considered positive if examiner noted immediate plantarflexion of the first metatarsal upon dorsiflexion of the proximal phalanx	46 asymptomatic students (86 feet) with no significant orthopaedic or structural deformities of the foot	Abnormal midtarsal motion by observing if the navicular moved in a plantar direction or adducted when the heel began to lift off the ground	.72	.66	2.1	.42

ICC or κ	Interpretation
.81–1.0	Substantial agreement
.61–.80	Moderate agreement
.41–.60	Fair agreement
.11–.40	Slight agreement
.0–.10	No agreement

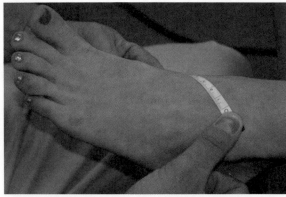

Start of figure-of-eight measurement

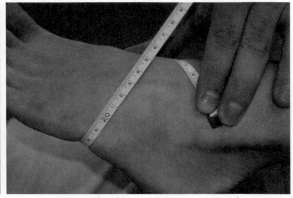

Figure-of-eight measurement continued

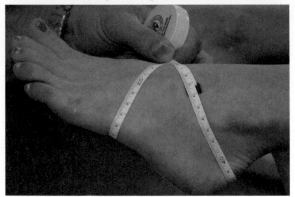

Completed figure-of-eight measurement

Figure 8-30

Figure-of-eight measurement.

Test	Procedure	Population	Reliability	
			Intra-examiner	**Inter-examiner**
Figure-of-eight method[34]	In open kinetic chain, examiner places tape measure midway between tibialis anterior tendon and lateral malleolus. Tape is then drawn medial and placed just distal to navicular tuberosity. Tape is then pulled across arch and just proximal to base of 5th metatarsal. Tape is then pulled across anterior tibialis tendon and around ankle joint just distal to medial malleolus. Tape is finally pulled across Achilles tendon and placed just distal to lateral malleolus and across start of tape	30 postoperative patients with ankle edema	ICC = .99-1.0	ICC = .99-1.0
Figure-of-eight method[35]		50 healthy subjects	ICC = .99	ICC = .99
Figure-of-eight method[36]		29 individuals with ankle swelling	ICC = .98	ICC = .98
Water volumetrics[36]	Water displacement is measured with patient's foot in a volumeter with toe tips touching front wall		ICC = .99	ICC = .99

Reliability of Assessing Protective Sensation

ICC or κ	Interpretation
.81-1.0	Substantial agreement
.61-.80	Moderate agreement
.41-.60	Fair agreement
.11-.40	Slight agreement
.0-.10	No agreement

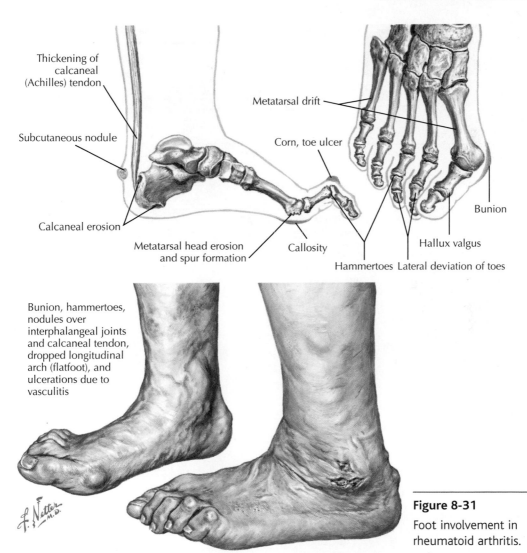

Thickening of calcaneal (Achilles) tendon

Subcutaneous nodule

Calcaneal erosion

Metatarsal head erosion and spur formation

Metatarsal drift

Corn, toe ulcer

Callosity

Hammertoes   Lateral deviation of toes

Hallux valgus

Bunion

Bunion, hammertoes, nodules over interphalangeal joints and calcaneal tendon, dropped longitudinal arch (flatfoot), and ulcerations due to vasculitis

Figure 8-31

Foot involvement in rheumatoid arthritis.

Test	Procedure	Population	Test-Retest Reliability
Sensation testing[37]	3 and 10 g Semmes Weinstein monofilaments are used to assess protective sensation. Monofilaments are applied perpendicular to the skin for approximately 1.5 seconds on six sites (plantar hallux and 1st through 5th MTP joints). With eyes closed, participants respond if they perceive pressure	51 patients with rheumatoid arthritis and 20 control subjects	(3 g) κ = **.73 (.64, .83)** (10 g) κ = **.75 (.65, .85)**

+LR	Interpretation	−LR
>10	Large	<.1
5.0-10.0	Moderate	.1-.2
2.0-5.0	Small	.2-.5
1.0-2.0	Rarely important	.5-1.0

Plantarflexion

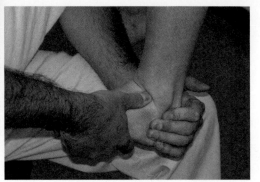

Dorsiflexion

Figure 8-32

Impingement sign.

Test	Test Procedure	Determination of Positive Finding	Population	Reference Standard	Sens	Spec	+LR	−LR
Impingement sign[38]	With patient seated, examiner grasps calcaneus with one hand and uses other hand to grasp forefoot, bringing it into plantarflexion. Examiner uses thumb to place pressure over anterolateral ankle. Foot is then brought from plantarflexion to dorsiflexion while thumb pressure is maintained	Positive if pain provoked with pressure from examiner's thumb is greater in dorsiflexion than plantarflexion	73 patients with ankle pain	Arthroscopic visualization	.95	.88	7.91	.06
History and clinical examination[39]	Examiner records aggravating factors and reports loss of motion. Examination includes observation of swelling, passive forced ankle dorsiflexion and eversion, active ROM, and double and single leg squats	Positive if five or more findings are positive: • Anterolateral ankle joint tenderness • Anterolateral ankle joint swelling • Pain with forced dorsiflexion and eversion • Pain with single leg squat • Pain with activities • Ankle instability	22 patients undergoing arthroscopic surgery for complaints of chronic ankle pain	Arthroscopic visualization	.94	.75	3.76	.08

Reliability of the Windlass Test

+LR	Interpretation	−LR
>10	Large	<.1
5.0-10.0	Moderate	.1-.2
2.0-5.0	Small	.2-.5
1.0-2.0	Rarely important	.5-1.0

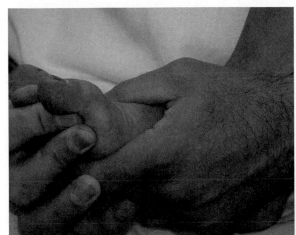

Non–weight bearing

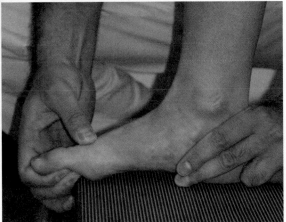

Weight bearing

Figure 8-33

Windlass test.

Test	Procedure	Population	Reliability	
			Intra-examiner	**Inter-examiner**
Windlass test[40]	Two methods of performing the windlass test: • With patient's knee flexed to 90° while in a non–weight-bearing position, examiner stabilizes the ankle and extends the MTP joint while allowing the IP joint to flex, thus preventing motion limitations due to a shortened hallucis longus muscle • With patient standing on a step stool with toes over the stool's edge, the patient's MTP joint is extended while allowing the IP joint to flex	22 patients with plantar fasciitis, 23 patients with other types of foot pain, and 30 control subjects	ICC = .99	ICC = .96

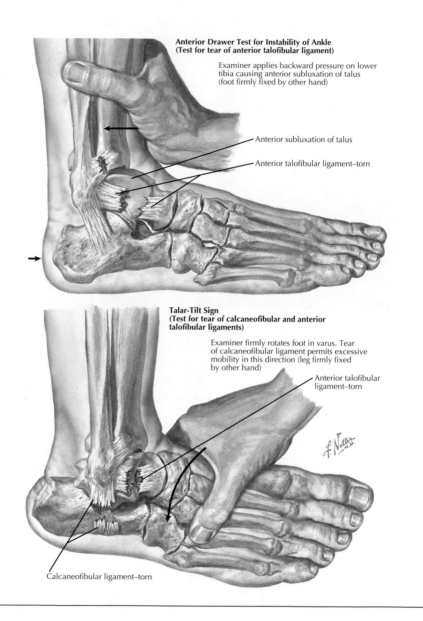

Anterior Drawer Test for Instability of Ankle
(Test for tear of anterior talofibular ligament)

Examiner applies backward pressure on lower tibia causing anterior subluxation of talus (foot firmly fixed by other hand)

Anterior subluxation of talus

Anterior talofibular ligament–torn

Talar-Tilt Sign
(Test for tear of calcaneofibular and anterior talofibular ligaments)

Examiner firmly rotates foot in varus. Tear of calcaneofibular ligament permits excessive mobility in this direction (leg firmly fixed by other hand)

Anterior talofibular ligament–torn

Calcaneofibular ligament–torn

Figure 8-34
Anterior drawer sign of ankle for test of talofibular ligaments.

No quality studies were identified that investigated the reliability or the diagnostic utility of either the talar tilt or the anterior drawer test. Their use, however, is so common in clinical practice that they are included here for completeness.

OUTCOME MEASURES

Outcome Measure		Scoring and Interpretation	Test-Retest Reliability	MCID
Lower Extremity Functional Scale (LEFS)		Users are asked to rate the difficulty of performing 20 functional tasks on a Likert-type scale ranging from 0 (extremely difficult or unable to perform activity) to 4 (no difficulty). A total score out of 80 is calculated by summing each score. The answers provide a score between 0 and 80, with lower scores representing more disability	ICC = .92[41]	9[42]
Foot Function Index (FFI)		A self-administered questionnaire consisting of 23 items divided into pain, disability, and activity restriction subscales. A score between 0 and 100 is derived by dividing the visual analog scale into 10 segments. Higher scores indicate more impairment	ICC = .85[43]	Unknown
American Orthopaedic Foot and Ankle Society (AOFAS) scales	Ankle-hindfoot	Each scale is clinician-administered and includes subjective and objective criteria including range of motion, gait abnormalities, stability, alignment, and callous assessment. The answers provide a score between 0 and 100, with lower scores representing more disability	Unknown	9[44]
	Midfoot		Unknown	12[44]
	Hallux		ICC = .95[43]	25[44]
	MTP-IP joints		ICC = .80[43]	11[44]
Numeric Pain Rating Scale (NPRS)		Users rate their level of pain on an 11-point scale ranging from 0 to 10, with high scores representing more pain. Often asked as "current pain" and "least," "worst," and "average" pain in the past 24 hours	ICC = .72[45]	2[46,47]

MCID, Minimum clinically important difference.

Quality Assessment of Diagnostic Studies Using QUADAS

	van Dijk 1996	Liu 1997	Payne 2002	De Garceau 2003	Molloy 2003	Egol 2004	Eggli 2005	Metz 2006	Dissmann 2006	Wilson 2006
1. Was the spectrum of patients representative of the patients who will receive the test in practice?	Y	Y	N	U	Y	Y	Y	Y	Y	Y
2. Were selection criteria clearly described?	Y	N	Y	N	N	Y	Y	Y	Y	U
3. Is the reference standard likely to correctly classify the target condition?	U	Y	U	U	Y	U	Y	Y	Y	U
4. Is the time period between reference standard and index test short enough to be reasonably sure that the target condition did not change between the two tests?	Y	U	U	U	U	U	Y	Y	U	U
5. Did the whole sample or a random selection of the sample, receive verification using a reference standard of diagnosis?	N	Y	Y	Y	Y	Y	Y	Y	Y	Y
6. Did patients receive the same reference standard regardless of the index test result?	N	Y	Y	U	Y	Y	Y	Y	Y	Y
7. Was the reference standard independent of the index test (i.e., the index test did not form part of the reference standard)?	N	Y	Y	U	Y	N	Y	Y	Y	U
8. Was the execution of the index test described in sufficient detail to permit replication of the test?	Y	Y	Y	Y	Y	N	U	Y	Y	Y
9. Was the execution of the reference standard described in sufficient detail to permit its replication?	U	Y	N	N	Y	Y	Y	Y	U	N
10. Were the index test results interpreted without knowledge of the results of the reference test?	U	Y	Y	U	Y	U	Y	U	U	U
11. Were the reference standard results interpreted without knowledge of the results of the index test?	U	U	U	U	U	U	U	U	U	U
12. Were the same clinical data available when test results were interpreted as would be available when the test is used in practice?	U	Y	U	U	U	Y	U	U	U	Y
13. Were uninterpretable/intermediate test results reported?	U	U	U	U	U	U	U	U	U	U
14. Were withdrawals from the study explained?	U	U	Y	U	U	U	Y	Y	U	U
Quality summary rating:	■	○	○	■	○	■	◆	◆	○	■

Y = yes, N = no, U = unclear.   ◆ Good quality (Y - N = 10 to 14).   ○ Fair quality (Y - N = 5 to 9).   ■ Poor quality (Y - N ≤ 4).

REFERENCES

1. Appling SA. *Foot and Ankle. Current Concepts of Orthopaedic Physical Therapy.* La Crosse: Orthopaedic Section, American Physical Therapy Association; 2001.

2. Hartley A. *Practical Joint Assessment.* St.. Louis: Mosby; 1995.

3. Hunt GC. Injuries of peripheral nerves of the leg, foot and ankle: an often unrecognized consequence of ankle sprains. *Foot.* 2003;13:14-18.

4. Hunt GC. Ankle sprain in a 14-year-old-girl. In: Jones MA, Rivett DA, eds. *Clinical Reasoning for Manual Therapists (8).* Edinburgh: Butterworth Heinemann; 2004.123-134.

5. Hunt GC, Sneed T, Hamann H, et al. Biomechanical and histological considerations for development of plantar fasciitis and evaluation of arch taping as a treatment option to control associated plantar heel pain: a single-subject design. *Foot.* 2004.

6. Bennett JE, Reinking MF, Pluemer B, et al. Factors contributing to the development of medial tibial stress syndrome in high school runners. *J Orthop Sports Phys Ther.* 2001;31:504-510.

7. Wooden MJ. Foot overuse syndromes of the foot and ankle. In: Wadsworth C, Kestel L, eds. *Orthopaedic Physical Therapy Home Study Course.* La Crosse: Orthopaedic Section, American Physical Therapy Association; 1995.

8. Stiell IG, McKnight RD, Greenberg GH, et al. Interobserver agreement in the examination of acute ankle injury patients. *Am J Emerg Med.* 1992;10:14-17.

9. Alonso A, Khoury L, Adams R. Clinical tests for ankle syndesmosis injury: reliability and prediction of return to function. *J Orthop Sports Phys Ther.* 1998;27:276-284.

10. Bachmann LM, Kolb E, Koller MT, et al. Accuracy of Ottawa ankle rules to exclude fractures of the ankle and mid-foot: systematic review. *BMJ.* 2003;326:417.

11. Eggli S, Sclabas GM, Eggli S, et al. The Bernese ankle rules: a fast, reliable test after low-energy, supination-type malleolar and midfoot trauma. *J Trauma.* 2005;59: 1268-1271.

12. Dissmann PD, Han KH. The tuning fork test—a useful tool for improving specificity in "Ottawa positive" patients after ankle inversion injury. *Emerg Med J.* 2006;23:788-790.

13. Menadue C, Raymond J, Kilbreath SL, et al. Reliability of two goniometric methods of measuring active inversion and eversion range of motion at the ankle. *BMC Musculoskelet Disord.* 2006;7:60.

14. Youdas JW, Bogard CL, Suman VJ. Reliability of goniometric measurements and visual estimates of ankle joint active range of motion obtained in a clinical setting. *Arch Phys Med Rehabil.* 1993;74:1113-1118.

15. Elveru RA, Rothstein JM, Lamb RL. Goniometric reliability in a clinical setting. Subtalar and ankle joint measurements. *Phys Ther.* 1988;68:672-677.

16. Van Gheluwe B, Kirby KA, Roosen P, Phillips RD. Reliability and accuracy of biomechanical measurements of the lower extremities. *J Am Podiatr Med Assoc.* 2002;92:317-326.

17. Cornwall MW, Fishco WD, McPoil TG, et al. Reliability and validity of clinically assessing first-ray mobility of the foot. *J Am Podiatr Med Assoc.* 2004;94:470-476.

18. Munteanu SE, Strawhorn AB, Landorf KB, et al. A weightbearing technique for the measurement of ankle joint dorsiflexion with the knee extended is reliable. *J Sci Med Sport.* 2009;12:54-59.

19. Menz HB, Tiedemann A, Kwan MM, et al. Reliability of clinical tests of foot and ankle characteristics in older people. *J Am Podiatr Med Assoc.* 2003;93:380-387.

20. Sell KE, Verity TM, Worrell TW, et al. Two measurement techniques for assessing subtalar joint position: a reliability study. *J Orthop Sports Phys Ther.* 1994;19: 162-167.

21. Jonson SR, Gross MT. Intraexaminer reliability, interexaminer reliability, and mean values for nine lower extremity skeletal measures in healthy naval midshipmen. *J Orthop Sports Phys Ther.* 1997;25:253-263.

22. Sobel E, Levitz SJ, Caselli MA, et al. Reevaluation of the relaxed calcaneal stance position. Reliability and normal values in children and adults. *J Am Podiatr Med Assoc.* 1999;89:258-264.

23. Maurer C, Finley A, Martel J, et al. Ankle plantarflexor strength and endurance in 7-9 year old children as measured by the standing single leg heel-rise test. *Phys Occupat Ther Pediatr.* 2007;27:37-54.

24. Menz HB, Zammit GV, Munteanu SE, Scott G. Plantarflexion strength of the toes: age and gender differences and evaluation of a clinical screening test. *Foot Ankle Int.* 2006;27:1103-1108.

25. Piva SR, Fitzgerald K, Irrgang JJ, et al. Reliability of measures of impairments associated with patellofemoral pain syndrome. *BMC Musculoskelet Disord.* 2006;7:33.

26. Vinicombe A, Raspovic A, Menz HB. Reliability of navicular displacement measurement as a clinical indicator of foot posture. *J Am Podiatr Med Assoc.* 2001;91:262-268.

27. Saltzman CL, Nawoczenski DA, Talbot KD. Measurement of the medial longitudinal arch. *Arch Phys Med Rehabil.* 1995;76:45-49.

28. Root ML, Orien WP, Weed JH. *Biomechanical Examination of the Foot.* Los Angeles: Clinical Biomechanics Corp; 1971.

29. Sekir U, Yildiz Y, Hazneci B, et al. Reliability of a functional test battery evaluating functionality, proprioception, and strength in recreational athletes with functional ankle instability. *Eur J Phys Rehabil Med.* 2008;44:407-415.

30. Trojian TH, McKeag DB. Single leg balance test to identify risk of ankle sprains. *Br J Sports Med.* 2006;40:610-613.

31. Deshpande N, Connelly DM, Culham EG, Costigan PA. Reliability and validity of ankle proprioceptive measures. *Arch Phys Med Rehabil.* 2003;84:883-889.

32. Keenan AM, Bach TM. Clinicians' assessment of the hindfoot: a study of reliability. *Foot Ankle Int.* 2006;27:451-460.

33. Payne C, Chuter V, Miller K. Sensitivity and specificity of the functional hallux limitus test to predict foot function. *J Am Podiatr Med Assoc.* 2002;92:269-271.

34. Rohner-Spengler M, Mannion AF, Babst R. Reliability and minimal detectable change for the figure-of-eight-20 method of measurement of ankle edema. *J Orthop Sports Phys Ther.* 2007;37:199-205.

35. Tatro-Adams D, McGann SF, Carbone W. Reliability of the figure-of-eight method of ankle measurement. *J Orthop Sports Phys Ther.* 1995;22:161-163.

36. Petersen EJ, Irish SM, Lyons CL, et al. Reliability of water volumetry and the figure of eight method on subjects with ankle joint swelling. *J Orthop Sports Phys Ther.* 1999;29:609-615.

37. Wilson O, Kirwan JR. Measuring sensation in the feet of patients with rheumatoid arthritis. *Musculoskeletal Care.* 2006;4:12-23.

38. Molloy S, Solan MC, Bendall SP. Synovial impingement in the ankle. A new physical sign. *J Bone Joint Surg Br.* 2003;85:330-333.

39. Liu SH, Nuccion SL, Finerman G. Diagnosis of anterolateral ankle impingement. Comparison between magnetic resonance imaging and clinical examination. *Am J Sports Med.* 1997;25:389-393.

40. De Garceau D, Dean D, Requejo SM, Thordarson DB. The association between diagnosis of plantar fasciitis and windlass test results. *Foot Ankle Int.* 2003;24:251-255.

41. Pua YH, Cowan SM, Wrigley TV, Bennell KL. The lower extremity functional scale could be an alternative to the Western Ontario and McMaster Universities Osteoarthritis Index physical function scale. *J Clin Epidemiol.* 2009

42. Binkley JM, Stratford PW, Lott SA, Riddle DL. The Lower Extremity Functional Scale (LEFS): scale development, measurement properties, and clinical application. North American Orthopaedic Rehabilitation Research Network. *Phys Ther.* 1999;79:371-383.

43. Baumhauer JF, Nawoczenski DA, DiGiovanni BF, Wilding GE. Reliability and validity of the American Orthopaedic Foot and Ankle Society Clinical Rating Scale: a pilot study for the hallux and lesser toes. *Foot Ankle Int.* 2006;27:1014-1019.

44. Dawson J, Doll H, Coffey J, Jenkinson C. Responsiveness and minimally important change for the Manchester-Oxford foot questionnaire (MOXFQ) compared with AOFAS and SF-36 assessments following surgery for hallux valgus. *Osteoarthritis Cartilage.* 2007;15:918-931.

45. Li L, Liu X, Herr K. Postoperative pain intensity assessment: a comparison of four scales in Chinese adults. *Pain Med.* 2007;8:223-234.

46. Farrar JT, Berlin JA, Strom BL. Clinically important changes in acute pain outcome measures: a validation study. *J Pain Symptom Manage.* 2003;25:406-411.

47. Farrar JT, Portenoy RK, Berlin JA, et al. Defining the clinically important difference in pain outcome measures. *Pain.* 2000;88:287-294.

Shoulder 9

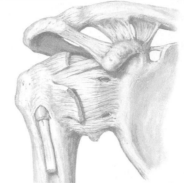

CLINICAL SUMMARY AND RECOMMENDATIONS

Patient History

Complaints
- Little is known about the utility of subjective complaints with shoulder pain. While a report of trauma does not seem clinically useful, a history of popping, clicking, or catching may be minimally helpful in diagnosing a labral tear (+LRs = 2.0).

Physical Examination

Range of Motion, Strength, and Muscle Length Assessment
- Measuring shoulder range of motion (ROM) has consistently been shown to be highly reliable but is of unknown diagnostic utility. Visual assessments and functional tests of ROM are more variable and may be adequately reliable in some instances.

- Assessing strength with manual muscle testing (MMT) appears to be reliable. Weak abduction and/or external rotation may be fairly useful in identifying subacromial impingement and/or full thickness rotator cuff tears. Weak internal rotation appears very helpful in identifying subscapularis tears (+LR = 7.5 to 20.0).

- Assessments of shoulder muscle tightness are moderately reliable. However, the single study[1] done to test associated diagnostic utility found tight pectoralis minor muscles in all 90 participants regardless of whether they had shoulder problems or not (100% sensitivity, 0% specificity).

Special Tests
- The apprehension test appears to be the most useful test in identifying shoulder instability, especially when defining a positive test by an "apprehensive response" (+LR = 7.1 to 20.2, −LR = .00 to .29) as opposed to "pain" (+LR = 1.1 to 3.1, −LR = .69 to .90). To a lesser extent, it may also be helpful in diagnosing labral tears.

- Results of studies examining the diagnostic utility of tests to identify labral tears are highly variable. Even though most single tests do not appear very useful, one study found both the Kim test and the Jerk test to be very good at identifying labral tears (+LRs of 13.3 and 36.5, respectively). The same author also found the biceps load test I and II to be very effective at identifying superior labrum anterior posterior (SLAP) lesions (+LR = 30 for both).

- A 2008 meta-analysis found both the Hawkins-Kennedy and Neer test to be minimally helpful for both ruling in and ruling out subacromial impingement. The presence of a "painful arc" during elevation may additionally be helpful in identifying the condition (+LR = .39, −LR = .32).

- In addition to rotator cuff muscle weakness (above), the external and internal rotation lag signs appear to be very helpful at identifying infraspinatus and subscapularis tears respectively. Several other tests (bear-hug, belly-press, Napoleon) appear to be also very useful in diagnosing subscapularis tears.

- Whereas several signs and symptoms are helpful in identifying brachial plexus nerve root avulsions, the shoulder protraction test appears to be the most useful (+LR = 4.8, −LR = .05).

Combinations of Findings
- Even though combinations of tests are generally better than single tests, combinations of tests are only moderately helpful in identifying labral tears. The most efficient pair seems to be the anterior apprehension and Jobe relocation tests (+LR = 5.4).

- Another study[2] reported even better diagnostic utility when specific combinations of three tests were used. By selecting two highly sensitive tests (compression rotation, anterior apprehension, and O'Brien tests) and one highly specific tests (Yergason, biceps load II, and Speed's tests), users can be fairly confident in both ruling out and ruling in SLAP lesions.

Osteology

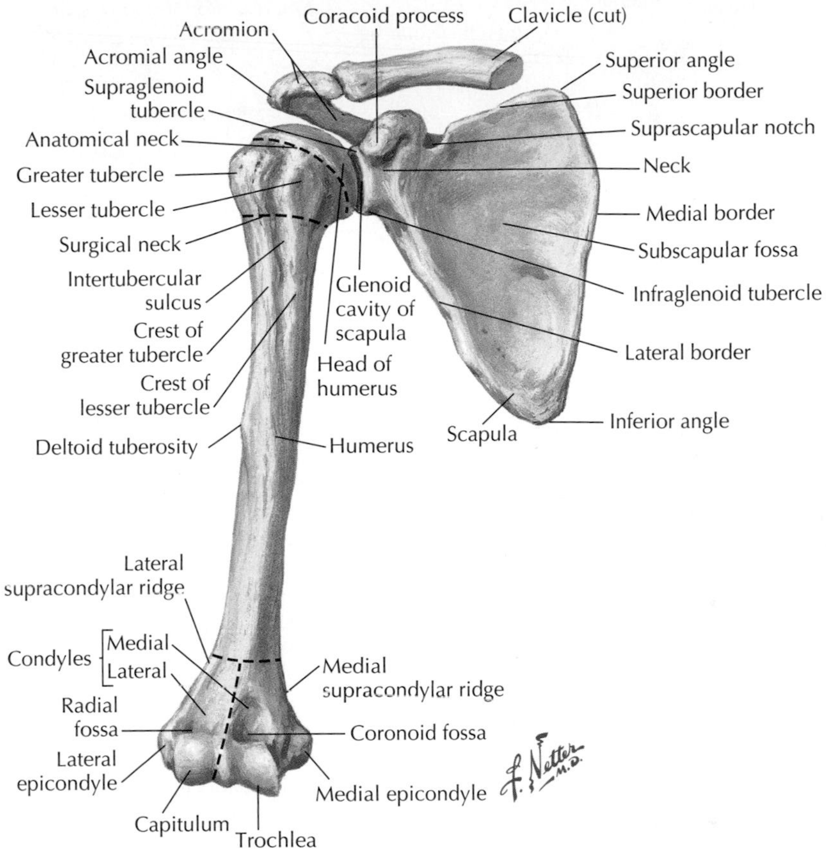

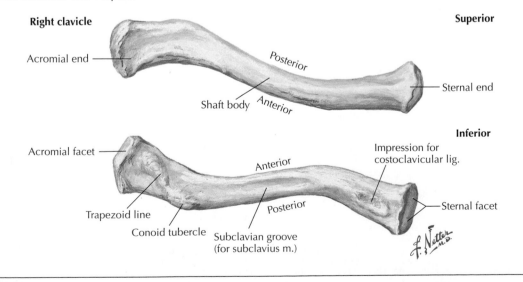

Figure 9-1
Anterior humerus and scapula.

Figure 9-2
Superior and inferior surface of clavicle.

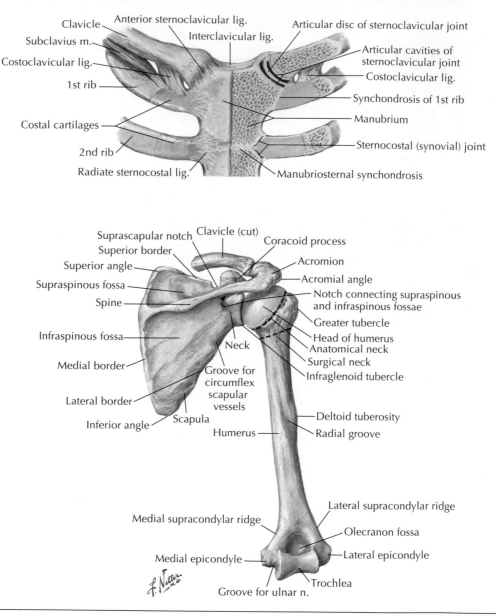

Figure 9-3

Sternoclavicular joint.

Joint	Type and Classification	Closed Packed Position	Capsular Pattern
Glenohumeral	Spheroidal	Full abduction and external rotation	ER limited more than abduction, limited more than internal rotation and flexion
Sternoclavicular	Saddle	Arm abducted to 90°	Not reported
Acromioclavicular	Plane synovial	Arm abducted to 90°	
Scapulothoracic	Not a true articulation	Not available	Not available

Scapulohumeral Rhythm

Scapulohumeral rhythm consists of integrated movements of the glenohumeral, scapulothoracic, acromioclavicular (AC), and sternoclavicular joints, and occurs in sequential fashion to allow full functional motion of the shoulder complex. Scapulohumeral rhythm serves three functional purposes: It allows for greater overall shoulder ROM, it maintains optimal contact between the humeral head and glenoid fossa, and it assists with maintaining an optimal length-tension relationship of the glenohumeral muscles.[3] To complete 180° of abduction, the overall ratio of glenohumeral to scapulothoracic, AC, and sternoclavicular motion is 2:1.

Inman and colleagues[4] were the first to explain scapulohumeral rhythm and described it as two phases that the shoulder complex completes to move through full abduction. The first phase (0°-90°) entails the scapula setting against the thorax to provide initial stability as the humerus abducts to 30°.[3,4] From 30° to 90° of abduction, the glenohumeral joint contributes another 30° of ROM while the scapula upwardly rotates 30°. The upward rotation results from clavicular elevation through the sternoclavicular and AC joints. The second phase (90°-180°) entails 60° of glenohumeral abduction and 30° of scapula upward rotation. The scapula rotation is associated with 5° of elevation at the sternoclavicular joint and 25° of rotation at the AC joint.[4,5]

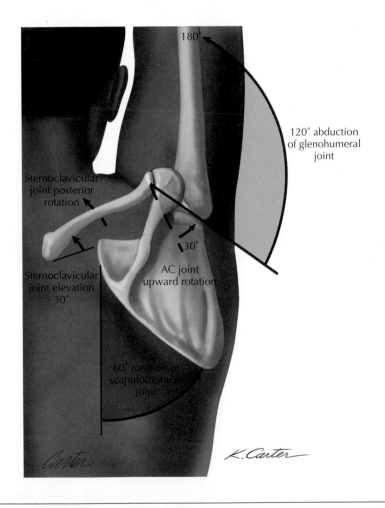

Figure 9-4
Scapulohumeral rhythm.

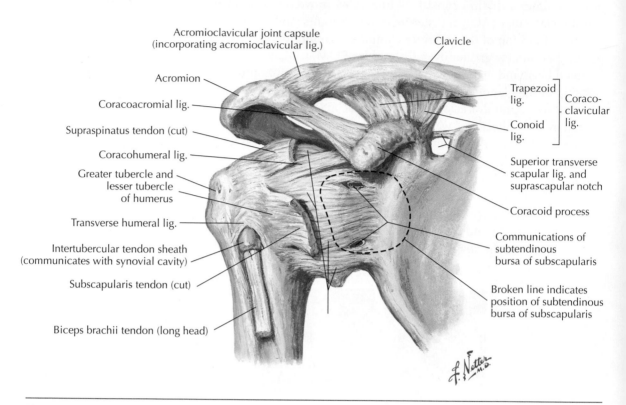

Figure 9-5

Shoulder ligaments: anterior view.

Ligaments	Attachments	Function
Glenohumeral	Glenoid labrum to neck of humerus	Reinforces anterior glenohumeral joint capsule
Coracohumeral	Coracoid process to greater tubercle of humerus	Strengthens superior glenohumeral joint capsule
Coracoclavicular		
Trapezoid	Superior aspect of coracoid process to inferior aspect of clavicle	Anchors clavicle to coracoid process
Conoid	Coracoid process to conoid tubercle on inferior clavicle	
Acromioclavicular	Acromion to clavicle	Strengthens AC joint superiorly
Coracoacromial	Coracoid process to acromion	Prevents superior displacement of humeral head
Sternoclavicular	Clavicular notch of manubrium to medial base of clavicle anteriorly and posteriorly	Reinforces sternoclavicular joint anteriorly and posteriorly
Interclavicular	Medial end of one clavicle to medial end of other clavicle	Strengthens superior sternoclavicular joint capsule
Costoclavicular	Superior aspect of costal cartilage of first rib to inferior border of medial clavicle	Anchors medial end of clavicle to first rib

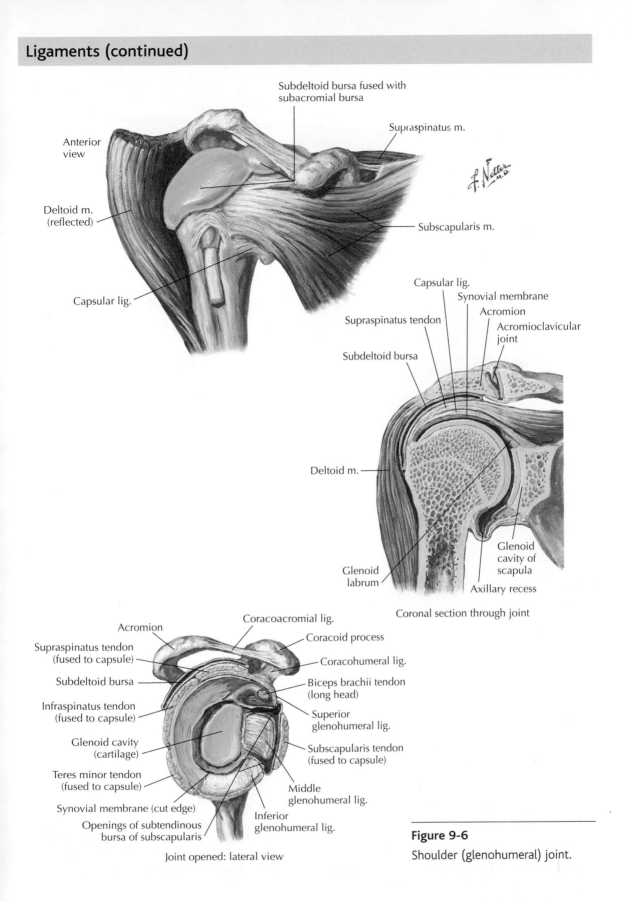

Subdeltoid bursa fused with subacromial bursa

Supraspinatus m.

Anterior view

Deltoid m. (reflected)

Capsular lig.

Subscapularis m.

Capsular lig.

Synovial membrane

Acromion

Acromioclavicular joint

Supraspinatus tendon

Subdeltoid bursa

Deltoid m.

Glenoid labrum

Glenoid cavity of scapula

Axillary recess

Coronal section through joint

Acromion

Coracoacromial lig.

Coracoid process

Supraspinatus tendon (fused to capsule)

Coracohumeral lig.

Subdeltoid bursa

Biceps brachii tendon (long head)

Infraspinatus tendon (fused to capsule)

Superior glenohumeral lig.

Glenoid cavity (cartilage)

Subscapularis tendon (fused to capsule)

Teres minor tendon (fused to capsule)

Middle glenohumeral lig.

Synovial membrane (cut edge)

Inferior glenohumeral lig.

Openings of subtendinous bursa of subscapularis

Joint opened: lateral view

Figure 9-6

Shoulder (glenohumeral) joint.

Muscles

Posterior Muscles of Shoulder

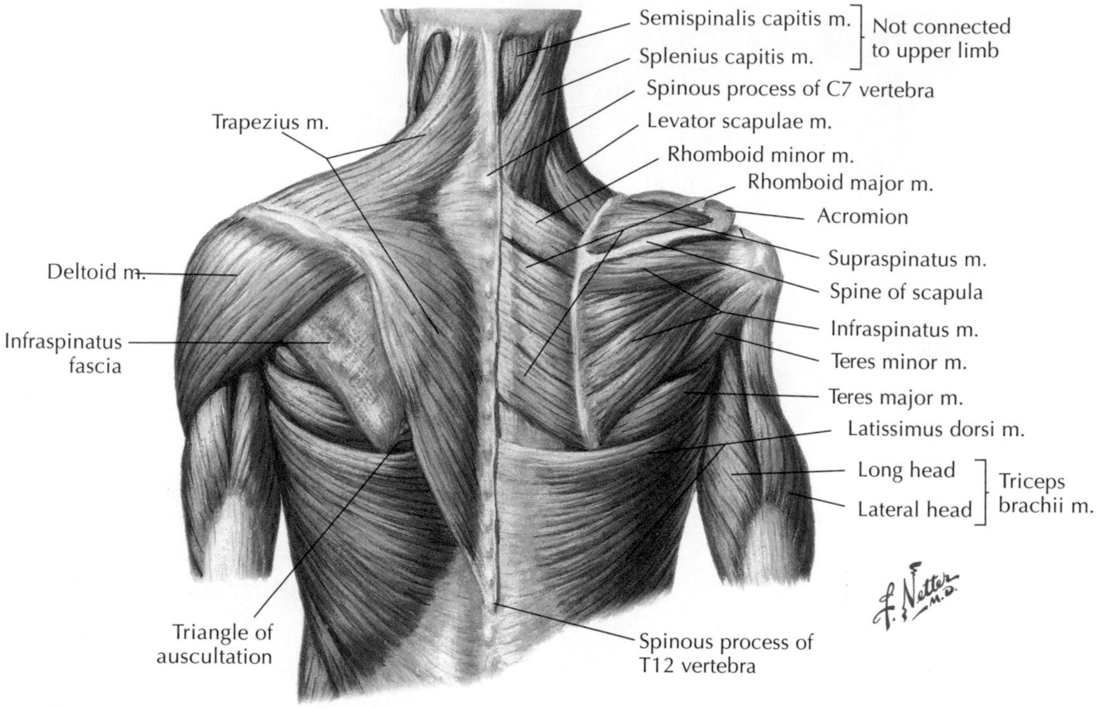

Figure 9-7

Muscles of the shoulder: posterior view.

Muscles	Origin	Insertion	Nerve and Segmental Level	Action
Upper trapezius	Occipital protuberance, nuchal line, ligamentum nuchae	Lateral clavicle and acromion	Cranial nerve XI and C2-C4	Rotates glenoid fossa upwardly, elevates scapular
Middle trapezius	Spinous process of T1-T5	Acromion and spine of scapula	Cranial nerve XI and C2-4	Retracts scapular
Lower trapezius	Spinous process of T6-T12	Apex of spine of scapula	Cranial nerve XI and C2-C4	Upward rotation of glenoid fossa, scapular depression
Levator scapulae	Transverse processes of C1-C4	Superior medial scapula	Dorsal scapular (C3-C5)	Elevates and adducts scapula
Rhomboids	Ligamentum nuchae and spinous processes C7-T5	Medial scapular border	Dorsal scapular (C4-C5)	Retracts scapula
Latissimus dorsi	Inferior thoracic vertebrae, thoracolumbar fascia, iliac crest, and inferior ribs 3-4	Intertubercular groove of humerus	Thoracodorsal (C6-C8)	Internally rotates, adducts, and extends humerus
Serratus anterior	Ribs 1-8	Anterior medial scapula	Long thoracic (C5-C8)	Protracts and upwardly rotates scapula

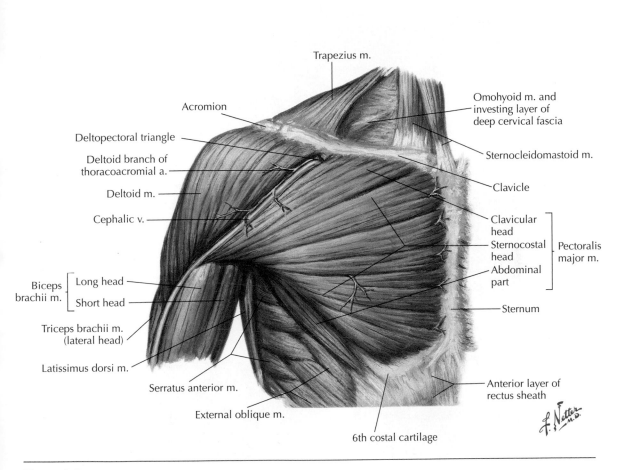

Figure 9-8

Muscles of the shoulder: anterior view.

Muscles	Origin	Insertion	Nerve and Segmental Level	Action
Deltoid	Clavicle, acromion, spine of scapular	Deltoid tuberosity of humerus	Axillary (C5-C6)	Abducts arm
Pectoralis major				
Clavicular head	Anterior medial clavicle	Intertubercular groove of humerus	Lateral and medial pectoral nerves (C5, C6, C7, C8, T1)	Adducts and internally rotates humerus
Sternocostal head	Lateral border of sternum, superior six costal cartilages and fascia of external oblique muscle			
Pectoralis minor	Just lateral to costal cartilage of ribs 3 to 5	Coracoid process	Medial pectoral nerve (C8, T1)	Stabilizes scapula

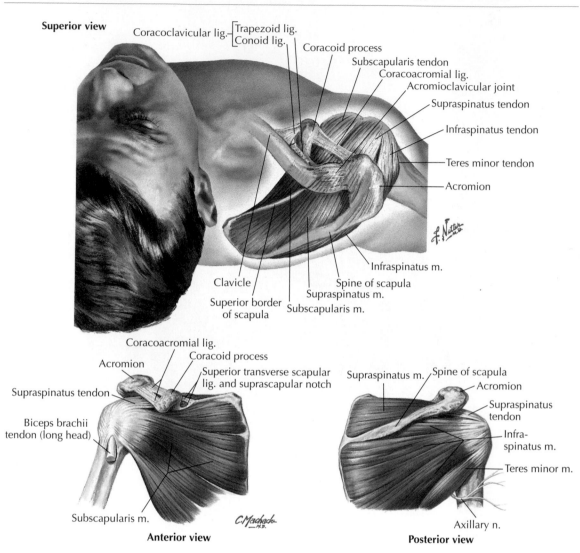

Superior view

Coracoclavicular lig.—[Trapezoid lig. / Conoid lig.]
Coracoid process
Subscapularis tendon
Coracoacromial lig.
Acromioclavicular joint
Supraspinatus tendon
Infraspinatus tendon
Teres minor tendon
Acromion
Infraspinatus m.
Spine of scapula
Supraspinatus m.
Subscapularis m.
Superior border of scapula
Clavicle

Coracoacromial lig.
Coracoid process
Acromion
Superior transverse scapular lig. and suprascapular notch
Supraspinatus tendon
Biceps brachii tendon (long head)
Subscapularis m.

Anterior view

Supraspinatus m. Spine of scapula
Acromion
Supraspinatus tendon
Infra-spinatus m.
Teres minor m.
Axillary n.

Posterior view

Figure 9-9

Muscles of the shoulder: rotator cuff.

Muscles	Origin	Insertion	Nerve and Segmental Level	Action
Supraspinatus	Supraspinous fossa of scapula	Greater tubercle of humerus	Suprascapular (C4-C6)	Assists deltoid in abduction of humerus
Infraspinatus	Infraspinatus fossa of scapula	Greater tubercle of humerus	Suprascapular (C5-C6)	Externally rotates humerus
Teres minor	Lateral border of scapula	Greater tubercle of humerus	Axillary (C5-C6)	Externally rotates humerus
Subscapularis	Subscapular fossa of scapula	Lesser tubercle of humerus	Upper and lower subscapular (C5-C6)	Internally rotates humerus
Teres major	Inferior angle of scapula	Intertubercular groove of humerus	Lower subscapular (C5-C6)	Internally rotates and adducts humerus

Nerves

Nerves	Segmental Levels	Sensory	Motor
Radial	C5, C6, C7, C8, T1	Posterior aspect of forearm	Triceps brachii, anconeus, brachioradialis, extensor muscles of forearm
Ulnar	C7, C8, T1	Medial hand including medial half of 4th digit	Flexor carpi ulnaris, medial half of flexor digitorum profundus, and most small muscles in hand
Musculocutaneous	C5, C6, C7	Becomes lateral antebrachial cutaneous nerve	Coracobrachialis, biceps brachii, brachialis
Axillary	C5, C6	Lateral shoulder	Teres minor, deltoid
Suprascapular	C4, C5, C6	No sensory	Supraspinatus, infraspinatus
Dorsal scapular	Ventral rami C4, C5	No sensory	Rhomboids, levator scapulae
Lateral pectoral	C5, C6, C7	No sensory	Pectoralis major pectoralis minor
Medial pectoral	C8, T1	No sensory	Pectoralis minor
Long thoracic	Ventral rami C5, C6, C7	No sensory	Serratus anterior
Upper subscapular	C5, C6	No sensory	Subscapularis
Lower subscapular	C5, C6	No sensory	Teres major, subscapularis
Medial cutaneous of arm	C8, T1	Medial arm	No motor

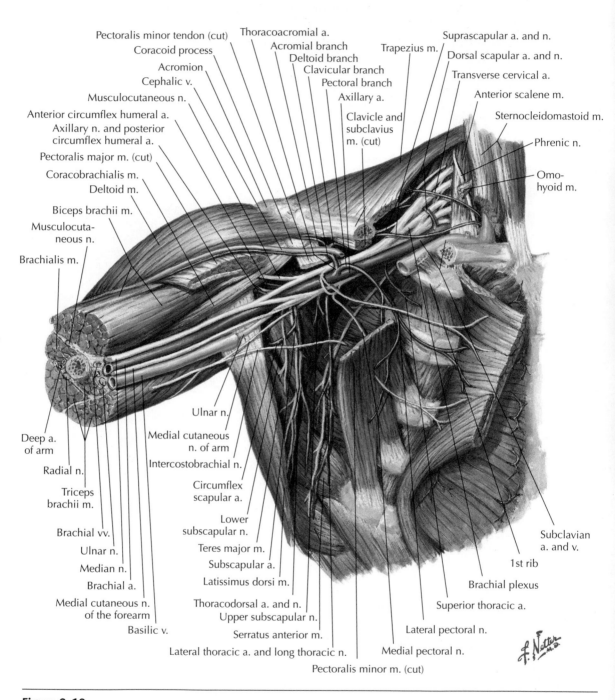

Figure 9-10

Anterior axilla.

Initial Hypotheses Based on Historical Findings

History	Initial Hypothesis
Patient reports lateral/anterior shoulder pain with overhead activities or exhibits a painful arc	Possible subacromial impingement[6,7] Possible tendinitis[8] Possible bursitis[8]
Patient reports of instability, apprehension, and pain with activities, most often when shoulder is abducted and externally rotated	Shoulder instability[6] Possible labral tear if clicking is present[9,10]
Decreased ROM and pain with resistance	Possible rotator cuff or long head of the biceps tendinitis[11]
Patient reports of pain and weakness with muscle loading, night pain. Age > 60	Possible rotator cuff tear[11]
Patient reports poorly located shoulder pain with occasional radiation into elbow. Pain is usually aggravated by movement and relieved by rest. Age > 45. Females more often affected than males	Possible adhesive capsulitis[12]
Patient reports fall on shoulder followed by pain over AC joint	Possible AC sprain[6]
Patient reports upper extremity heaviness or numbness with prolonged postures and when laying on involved side	Possible thoracic outlet syndrome[13,14] Possible cervical radiculopathy[15]

Diagnostic Utility of the Patient History for Identifying Labrum and Rotator Cuff Tears

+LR	Interpretation	−LR
>10	Large	<.1
5.0-10.0	Moderate	.1-.2
2.0-5.0	Small	.2-.5
1.0-2.0	Rarely important	.5-1.0

Patient Report and Study Quality	Population	Reference Standard	Sens	Spec	+LR	−LR
History of trauma[16]	55 patients with shoulder pain scheduled for arthroscopy	Glenoid labral tear observed during arthroscopy	.50 (.35, .65)	.36 (.08, .65)	.79 (.46, 1.34)	1.38 (.6, 3.17)
History of pop, click, or catch[16]			.55 (.4, .69)	.73 (.46, .99)	2.0 (.73, 5.45)	.63 (.38, 1.02)
History of trauma[11]	448 patients with shoulder pain scheduled for arthroscopy	Rotator cuff tear observed during arthroscopy	.36	.73	1.33	.88
Reports of night pain[11]			.88	.20	1.10	.60

Reliability of Range of Motion Measurements

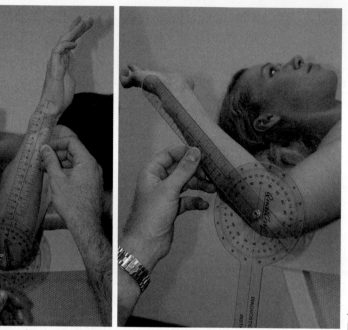

Measurment of internal rotation in 90° of abduction

Measurment of external rotation in 90° of abduction

ICC or κ	Interpretation
.81-1.0	Substantial agreement
.61-.80	Moderate agreement
.41-.60	Fair agreement
.11-.40	Slight agreement
.0-.10	No agreement

Figure 9-11

Range of motion measurements.

Test Procedure	Instrumentation	Population	Reliability
Passive flexion[17]	Universal goniometer	100 patients referred for physical therapy for shoulder impairments	Intra-examiner: ICC = **.98** Inter-examiner: ICC = **.89**
Passive extension[17]			Intra-examiner: ICC = **.94** Inter-examiner: ICC = **.27**
Passive abduction[17]			Intra-examiner: ICC = **.98** Inter-examiner: ICC = **.87**
Active elevation[18]	Visual estimation of ROM	201 patients with shoulder pain	Affected side: ICC = **.88 (.84, .91)*** Unaffected side: ICC = **.76 (.67, .82)***
Passive elevation[18]			Affected side: ICC = **.87 (.83, .90)*** Unaffected side: ICC = **.73 (.66, .79)***
Passive external rotation[18]			Affected side: ICC = **.73 (.22, .88)*** Unaffected side: ICC = **.34 (.00, .65)***
Passive horizontal adduction[18]			Affected side: ICC = **.36 (.22, .48)*** Unaffected side: ICC = **.18 (.04, .32)***

*Inter-examiner only.
ICC, Intraclass correlation coefficient;

Range of Motion

Reliability of Functional Range of Motion Tests

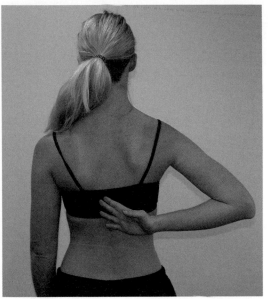

ICC or κ	Interpretation
.81–1.0	Substantial agreement
.61–.80	Moderate agreement
.41–.60	Fair agreement
.11–.40	Slight agreement
.0–.10	No agreement

Figure 9-12

Hand behind back (functional internal rotation of shoulder test).

Test and Measure	Test Procedure	Population	Inter-examiner Reliability
Hand to neck[19]	Visual estimation of ROM graded on a scale of 0 to 3 or 4	46 patients with shoulder pain	Intra-examiner: ICC = .80 (.63, .93) Inter-examiner: ICC = .90 (.69, .96)
Hand to scapula[19]			Intra-examiner: ICC = .90 (.72, .92) Inter-examiner: ICC = .90 (.69, .94)
Hand to opposite scapula[19]			Intra-examiner: ICC = .86 (.65, .90) Inter-examiner: ICC = .83 (.75, .96)
Active abduction[20]	ROM assessed visually to nearest 5°. Pain assessed as "no pain," "little pain," "much pain," and "excruciating pain"	91 patients with shoulder pain	ROM: ICC = .96 Pain: κ = .65
Passive abduction[20]			ROM: ICC = .96 Pain: κ = .69
Painful arc with active abduction[20]			Presence of: κ = .46 Starting ROM: ICC = .72 Ending ROM: ICC = .57
Painful arc with passive abduction[20]			Presence of: κ = .52 Starting ROM: ICC = .54 Ending ROM: ICC = .72
Passive external rotation[20]			ROM: ICC = .70 Pain: κ = .50
Hand behind back[20]	As above except ROM graded on a scale of 0 to 7		ROM: κ = .73 Pain: κ = .35
Hand in neck[20]			ROM: κ = .52 Pain: κ = .52
Springing test 1st rib[20]	Examiner exerts force with the 2nd metacarpophalangeal joint on the 1st rib of the patient, assessing ROM (normal or restricted), pain (present or absent), and joint stiffness (present or absent)		ROM: κ = .26 Stiffness: κ = .09 Pain: κ = .66

Assessing Strength and Proprioception

ICC or κ	Interpretation
.81-1.0	Substantial agreement
.61-.80	Moderate agreement
.41-.60	Fair agreement
.11-.40	Slight agreement
.0-.10	No agreement

Reliability of Assessing Strength

Test and Measure	Test Procedure	Population	Test-Retest Reliability	
			Within-Day	Between-Days
Serratus anterior strength[21]	With subject supine with arm at 90° of shoulder flexion and 105° of shoulder horizontal adduction, subject presses toward ceiling while holding weighted apparatus	30 asymptomatic students	Inter-examiner ICC = .90-.93	ICC = .83-.89
Serratus anterior endurance[21]	As above, with patient holding weight equal to 15% of body weight		Inter-examiner ICC = .71-.76	ICC = .44-.62
Lower trapezius[22]	With patient prone and using a handheld dynamometer on the spine of the scapula, resistance is applied to scapular adduction and depression		ICC = .93 (.89, .96)	ICC = .89 (.68, .95)
Serratus anterior[22]	With patient supine with shoulder and elbow at 90° and using handheld dynamometer on the elbow, resistance is applied to scapular protraction	40 patients with shoulder pain	ICC = .93 (.88, .96)	ICC = .94 (.88, .97)
Middle trapezius[22]	With patient prone and using a handheld dynamometer on the spine of the scapula, resistance is applied to scapular retraction		ICC = .94 (.90, .97)	ICC = .94 (.82, .97)
Upper trapezius[22]	With patient sitting and using a handheld dynamometer on the superior scapula, resistance is applied to scapular elevation		ICC = .95 (.92, .97)	ICC = .96 (.91, .98)

Reliability of Assessing Proprioception

Test and Measure	Test Procedure	Population	Test-Retest Reliability
Joint position sense[23]	With patient standing, examiner measures full external rotation (ER) and internal rotation (IR) of shoulder with inclinometer. Target angles are determined as 90% of IR and 90% of ER. With patient blindfolded, examiner guides patient's arm into target angle position and holds it for 3 sec. The patient's arm is returned to neutral. The patient is instructed to return the arm to target angle. Examiner takes measurement with inclinometer	31 asymptomatic subjects	IR ICC = .98 ER ICC = .98

Muscle Length

Reliability of Determining Length of Pectoralis Minor

ICC or κ	Interpretation
.81-1.0	Substantial agreement
.61-.80	Moderate agreement
.41-.60	Fair agreement
.11-.40	Slight agreement
.0-.10	No agreement

Test and Measure		Test Procedure	Population	Test-Retest Reliability
Posterior shoulder tightness[24]	Side-lying horizontal adduction	The humerus is passively taken into horizontal adduction. The limit of posterior shoulder flexibility is considered the onset of scapula movement or humerus rotation out of neutral. An assistant using a carpenter's square measures the distance from the top of the plinth to the medial epicondyle	37 patients with shoulder impingement syndrome and 22 control subjects (measurements taken 8 to 12 weeks apart)	Patients: ICC = **.40 (.09, .64)** Controls: ICC = **.63 (.29, .83)**
	Supine horizontal adduction	Degree of rotation is recorded at the palpable onset of scapular motion away from the plinth		Patients: ICC = **.79 (.63, .89)** Controls: ICC = **.74 (.47, .88)**
	Supine internal rotation	With an assistant preventing scapular movement, degrees of rotation are recorded at the end of passive motion		Patients: ICC = **.67 (.45, .82)** Controls: ICC = **.79 (.55, .91)**
Pectoralis minor length[1]		With the participant supine with hands resting on the abdomen, examiner measures the linear distance from the treatment table to the posterior aspect of the acromion using a plastic right angle	45 patients with shoulder pain and 45 asymptomatic persons	Single measure: ICC = **.90-.93** Mean of 3 measures: ICC = **.92-.97**

Diagnostic Utility of Tight Pectoralis Minor in Identifying Shoulder Pain

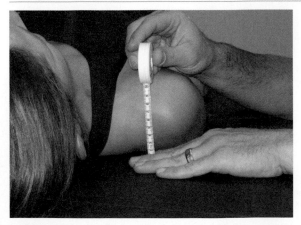

+LR	Interpretation	−LR
>10	Large	<.1
5.0-10.0	Moderate	.1-.2
2.0-5.0	Small	.2-.5
1.0-2.0	Rarely important	.5-1.0

Figure 9-13

Measuring pectoralis minor muscle strength.

Test and Study Quality	Description and Positive Findings	Population	Reference Standard	Sens	Spec	+LR	−LR
Tight pectoralis minor[1] ○	As above with a positive test being a measurement < 2.6 cm (1 inch).	45 patients with shoulder pain and 45 asymptomatic persons	Self-report of shoulder pain and/or restriction of shoulder movement	1.0*	0.0*	1.0	Undefined

*These results are due to the fact that at all 90 symptomatic and asymptomatic participants were classified as "tight" using this definition.

Palpation

Reliability of Palpating the Subacromial Space

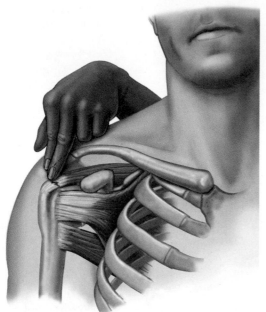

ICC or κ	Interpretation
.81-1.0	Substantial agreement
.61-.80	Moderate agreement
.41-.60	Fair agreement
.11-.40	Slight agreement
.0-.10	No agreement

Figure 9-14

Palpation of subacromial space.

Test and Measure	Test Procedure	Population	Reliability
Palpation of subacromial space[25]	Examiner palpates subacromial space and estimates distance as $^1/_4$, $^1/_2$, $^3/_4$, or whole finger's breadth	36 patients with shoulder subluxation	Intra-examiner ICC = .90-.94 Inter-examiner ICC = .77-.89

Diagnostic Utility of Palpation in Identifying Labral Tears

+LR	Interpretation	−LR
>10	Large	<.1
5.0-10.0	Moderate	.1-.2
2.0-5.0	Small	.2-.5
1.0-2.0	Rarely important	.5-1.0

Test and Study Quality	Description and Positive Findings	Population	Reference Standard	Sens	Spec	+LR	−LR
Bicipital groove tenderness[2] ◇	Examiner gently presses the biceps groove with shoulder adducted 10°. Positive if pain	68 patients with type II SLAP lesions and 78 age-matched controls who underwent shoulder arthroscopy	Type II SLAP lesion visualized during arthroscopy	.27	.66	.80	1.11
Biceps palpation[26] ◇	Point tenderness of the biceps tendon in the biceps groove 3-6 cm below anterior acromion	847 patients who underwent diagnostic arthroscopy of the shoulder	Partial biceps tendon tear visualized during arthroscopy	.53	.54	1.2	.87
Bicipital groove tenderness[27] ◯	Not reported	62 shoulders scheduled to undergo arthroscopy	SLAP lesion visualized during arthroscopy	.44	.40	.73	1.40
Bicipital groove tenderness [28] ◯	Not described	54 throwing athletes with shoulder pain		.25	.80	1.3	.94

Assessing Alignment

Reliability of Assessing Scapular Asymmetry during Static and Dynamic Activity

ICC or κ	Interpretation
.81–1.0	Substantial agreement
.61–.80	Moderate agreement
.41–.60	Fair agreement
.11–.40	Slight agreement
.0–.10	No agreement

Test and Measure		Test Procedure	Population	Reliability Intra-examiner	Inter-examiner
Lateral scapular slide test[29]	Position 1	With patient standing, examiner records measurement between inferior angle of scapula and spinous process of thoracic vertebra at same horizontal level in three positions. *Position 1:* with glenohumeral joint in neutral *Position 2:* 45° of shoulder abduction and IR *Position 3:* with upper extremity in 90° of abduction and full IR. A difference between sides >1 cm is considered scapular asymmetry	29 patients with shoulder pain	Not reported	ICC = .82 (left) ICC = .96 (right)
	Position 2			Not reported	ICC = .85 (left) ICC = .95 (right)
	Position 3			Not reported	ICC = .70 (left) ICC = .85 (right)
Lateral scapular slide test[30]	Position 1		46 subjects with shoulder dysfunction and 26 subjects without shoulder dysfunction	With dysfunction ICC = .52 (.10, .74) Without dysfunction ICC = .75 (.56, .85)	With dysfunction ICC = .79 (.46, .91) Without dysfunction ICC = .67 (.25, .85)
	Position 2			With dysfunction ICC = .66 (.36, .82) Without dysfunction ICC = .58 (.60, .86)	With dysfunction ICC = .45 (−.38, .78) Without dysfunction ICC = .43 (−.29, .75)
	Position 3			With dysfunction ICC = .62 (.27, .79) Without dysfunction ICC = .80 (.65, .88)	With dysfunction ICC = .57 (−.23, .85) Without dysfunction ICC = .74 (.41, .88)
Position of posterior acromion[29]		Measured from the posterior border of the acromion and the table surface with the patient supine	29 patients with shoulder pain	Not reported	ICC = .88–.94
Position of medial scapular border[29]		Measured from the medial scapular border to T4 spinous process		Not reported	ICC = .50–.80
Movement evaluation during abduction[31]		Examiner classifies scapular movement during shoulder abduction into categories 1-4. *Category 1* = inferior angle tilts dorsally compared with contralateral side *Category 2* = medial border tilts dorsally compared with contralateral side *Category 3* = shoulder shrug initiates movement *Category 4* = scapulae move symmetrically	20 subjects with shoulder injuries and 6 asymptomatic subjects	κ = .42	Not reported

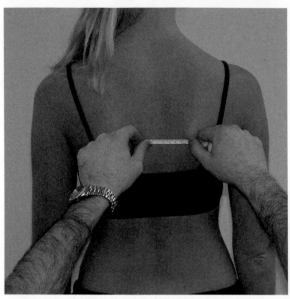

Lateral slide test position 1

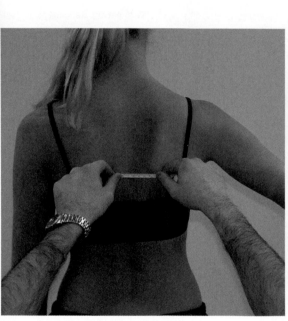

Lateral slide test position 2

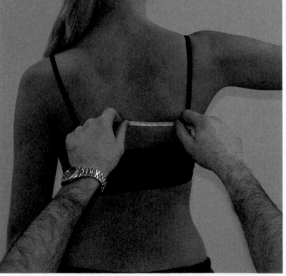

Lateral slide test position 3

Figure 9-15

Detecting scapular asymmetry.

Classifying Shoulder Disorders

Reliability of Classifying Shoulder Disorders

ICC or κ	Interpretation
.81-1.0	Substantial agreement
.61-.80	Moderate agreement
.41-.60	Fair agreement
.11-.40	Slight agreement
.0-.10	No agreement

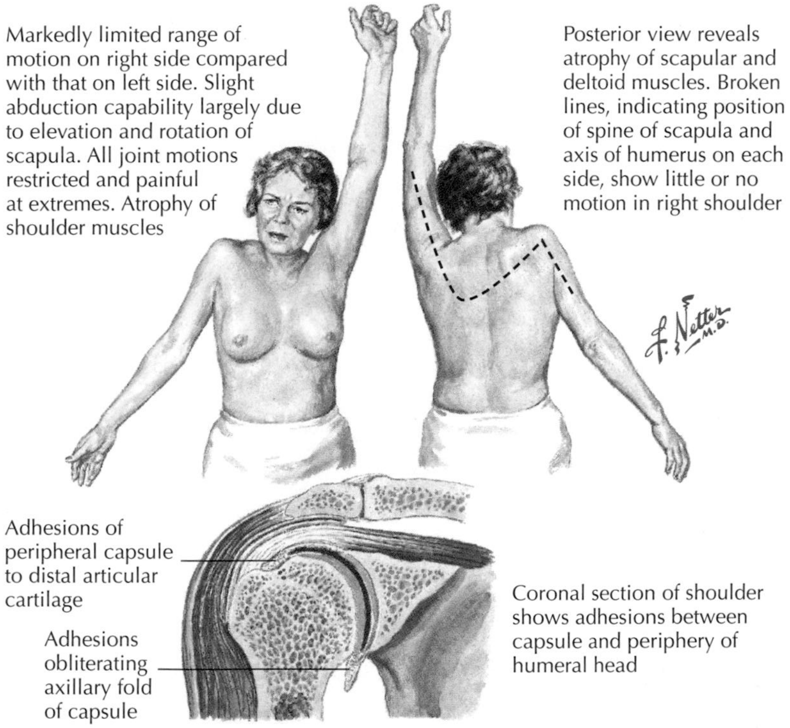

Markedly limited range of motion on right side compared with that on left side. Slight abduction capability largely due to elevation and rotation of scapula. All joint motions restricted and painful at extremes. Atrophy of shoulder muscles
Posterior view reveals atrophy of scapular and deltoid muscles. Broken lines, indicating position of spine of scapula and axis of humerus on each side, show little or no motion in right shoulder
F. Netter M.D.
Adhesions of peripheral capsule to distal articular cartilage
Adhesions obliterating axillary fold of capsule
Coronal section of shoulder shows adhesions between capsule and periphery of humeral head

Figure 9-16
Adhesive capsulitis of the shoulder.

Classification	Description of Procedure	Population	Inter-examiner Reliability
Bursitis[32]	Examiners use patient history combined with "selective tissue tension" examination during active movements, passive movements, and isometric strength assessments	56 painful shoulders	κ = **.35-.58**
Capsulitis[32]			κ = **.63-.82**
Rotator cuff lesion[32]			κ = **.71-.79**
Other diagnosis[32]			κ = **.69-.78**
Capsular syndrome[33]	Examiner obtains patient history. Physical examination consists of active, passive, and resistive movements. Determination of ROM, presence of painful arc or capsular pattern, and degree of muscle weakness are identified	201 patients with shoulder pain	κ = **.63 (.50, .76)**
Acute bursitis[33]			κ = **.50 (−.10, 1.0)**
AC syndrome[33]			κ = **.24 (−.06, .53)**
Subacromial syndrome[33]			κ = **.56 (.45, .68)**
Rest group (does not fit any category above)[33]			κ = **.39 (.24, .54)**
Mixed group (patient presents with two or more above classifications)[33]			κ = **.14 (−.03, .30)**

ICC or κ	Interpretation
.81-1.0	Substantial agreement
.61-.80	Moderate agreement
.41-.60	Fair agreement
.11-.40	Slight agreement
.0-.10	No agreement

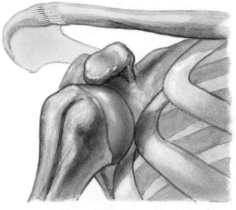

Subcoracoid dislocation (most common)

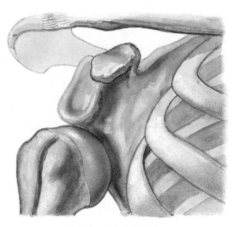

Subglenoid dislocation

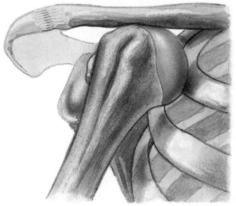

Subclavicular dislocation (uncommon).
Very rarely, humeral head penetrates
between ribs, producing intrathoracic
dislocation

Figure 9-17

Shoulder instability.

Test and Measure	Test Procedure	Population	Reliability	
Sulcus sign[34]	With patient supine, examiner applies inferior distraction to shoulder. Amount of laxity is graded on a 0-3+ scale. 0 represents no laxity. 3+ represents maximum laxity	43 healthy college athletes	Inter-examiner κ = **.03-.06**	Intra-examiner κ = **.01-.20**

Special Tests—Instability

Diagnostic Utility of the Apprehension Test in Identifying Shoulder Instability

+LR	Interpretation	−LR
>10	Large	<.1
5.0-10.0	Moderate	.1-.2
2.0-5.0	Small	.2-.5
1.0-2.0	Rarely important	.5-1.0

Figure 9-18

Apprehension test.

Test and Study Quality	Description and Positive Findings	Population	Reference Standard	Sens	Spec	+LR	−LR
Bony apprehension test[35] ◇	With patient standing, examiner places the arm in a position of ≤ 45° of abduction and ≤ 45° of external rotation. Positive if patient appears apprehensive	29 patients with symptoms of instability undergoing shoulder surgery	Arthroscopic evidence of significant bony lesion causing instability of the shoulder	1.0	.86	7.1	.00
Anterior apprehension test[2] ◇	With patient supine, examiner passively abducts and externally rotates humerus. Positive if complaints of pain or instability	68 patients with type II SLAP lesions and 78 age-matched controls who underwent shoulder arthroscopy	Type II SLAP lesion visualized during arthroscopy	.62	.42	1.1	.90
Anterior apprehension test[27] ◯	As above. Positive if pain is produced with ER	62 shoulders scheduled to undergo arthroscopy	Labral tear via arthroscopic visualization	.40	.87	3.08	.69
Apprehension test (pain)[36] ◯	With patient standing, examiner places both arms in 90° of abduction and 90° of ER. Positive if patient appears apprehensive and/or reports pain	363 patients undergoing shoulder surgery	Either radiographic documentation of an anterior shoulder dislocation after trauma or demonstration of a Hill-Sachs lesion, a Bankart lesion, or a humeral avulsion of the glenohumeral ligament at the time of arthroscopy	.50	.56	1.1	.90
Apprehension test (apprehension)[36] ◯				.72	.96	20.2	.29
Anterior apprehension test[27] ◯	With patient supine, examiner passively abducts and externally rotates humerus. Positive if pain is produced with ER	62 shoulders scheduled to undergo arthroscopy	Labral tear via arthroscopic visualization	.40	.87	3.1	.69

Diagnostic Utility of the Apprehension and Relocation Tests in Identifying Shoulder Instability

+LR	Interpretation	−LR
>10	Large	<.1
5.0-10.0	Moderate	.1-.2
2.0-5.0	Small	.2-.5
1.0-2.0	Rarely important	.5-1.0

Figure 9-19

Relocation test.

Test and Study Quality	Description and Positive Findings	Population	Reference Standard	Sens	Spec	+LR	−LR
Relocation test[2]		68 patients with type II SLAP lesions and 78 age-matched controls who underwent shoulder arthroscopy	Type II SLAP lesion visualized during arthroscopy	.44	.54	1.0	1.04
Relocation test (pain)[36]	With patient supine with glenohumeral joint at edge of table, examiner places arm in 90° of abduction, full external rotation, and 90° of elbow flexion. Examiner then applies a posterior force on head of humerus. Positive if patient's pain or apprehension diminishes with applied force	363 patients undergoing shoulder surgery	Either radiographic documentation of an anterior shoulder dislocation after trauma or demonstration of a Hill-Sachs lesion, a Bankart lesion, or a humeral avulsion of the glenohumeral ligament at the time of arthroscopy	.30	.90	3.0	.77
Relocation test (apprehension)[36]				.81	.92	10.4	.20
Jobe relocation test (pain)[27]		62 shoulders scheduled to undergo arthroscopy	Arthroscopic visualization	.44	.87	3.38	.64
Relocation test (pain)[37]				.30	.58	.71	1.21
Relocation test (apprehension)[37]	Relocation test performed as above. Following relocation test, examiner applies anteriorly directed force to proximal humerus	100 patients undergoing shoulder surgery	Surgical observation	.57	1.0	Undefined	.43
Anterior relocation test (pain)[37]				.54	.44	.96	1.05
Anterior relocation test (apprehension)[37]				.68	1.0	Undefined	.32

Diagnostic Utility of the Anterior Drawer Test in Identifying Shoulder Instability

+LR	Interpretation	−LR
>10	Large	<.1
5.0-10.0	Moderate	.1-.2
2.0-5.0	Small	.2-.5
1.0-2.0	Rarely important	.5-1.0

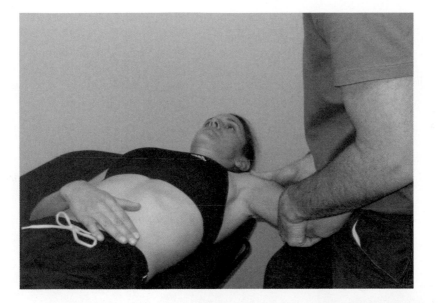

Figure 9-20

Anterior drawer test.

Test and Study Quality	Description and Positive Findings	Population	Reference Standard	Sens	Spec	+LR	−LR
Anterior drawer test (pain)[36] ◯	With patient supine with glenohumeral joint at edge of table, examiner places arm in 60°-80° of abduction and neutral rotation, and then translates the humeral head anteriorly. Positive if patient reports pain or reproduction of instability symptoms	363 patients scheduled to undergo shoulder surgery	Either radiographic documentation of an anterior shoulder dislocation after trauma or demonstration of a Hill-Sachs lesion, a Bankart lesion, or a humeral avulsion of the glenohumeral ligament at the time of arthroscopy	.28	.71	1.0	1.01
Anterior drawer test (instability symptoms)[36] ◯				.53	.85	3.6	.56

ICC or κ	Interpretation
.81–1.0	Substantial agreement
.61–.80	Moderate agreement
.41–.60	Fair agreement
.11–.40	Slight agreement
.0–.10	No agreement

Figure 9-21

Crank test.

Test	Description	Population	Inter-examiner Reliability
Crank test[16]	See page 403	55 patients with shoulder pain scheduled for arthroscopic surgery	κ = .20 (−.05, .46)

Diagnostic Utility of the Crank Test in Identifying Labral Tears

+LR	Interpretation	−LR
>10	Large	<.1
5.0–10.0	Moderate	.1–.2
2.0–5.0	Small	.2–.5
1.0–2.0	Rarely important	.5–1.0

Test and Study Quality	Description and Positive Findings	Population	Reference Standard	Sens	Spec	+LR	−LR
Crank test[26] ◆	Not described	847 patients who underwent diagnostic arthroscopy of the shoulder	Partial biceps tendon tear visualized during arthroscopy	.34	.77	1.5	.86
Crank test[16] ◆	Patient is supine while examiner elevates humerus 160° in scapular plane. Axial load is applied to humerus while shoulder is internally and externally rotated. Positive if pain is elicited	55 patients with shoulder pain scheduled for arthroscopic surgery		.61 (.47, .76)	.55 (.25, .84)	1.35 (.68, 2.69)	.71 (.37, 1.36)
Crank test[38] ◆		132 patients scheduled to undergo shoulder arthroscopy		.13	.83	.8	1.05
Crank test[39] ◆		40 athletes with shoulder pain		.35	.70	1.2	.93
Crank test[28]	Not described	54 throwing athletes with should pain		.58	.72	2.1	.58
Crank test[40] ○	Patient is supine while examiner elevates humerus 160° in scapular plane. Axial load is applied to humerus while shoulder is internally and externally rotated. Positive if pain is elicited	65 patients with symptoms of shoulder pain	Glenoid labral tear observed during arthroscopy	.46	.56	1.1	.96
Crank test[10] ○		62 patients scheduled to undergo arthroscopic shoulder surgery		.91	.93	13.0	.10
Crank test[27] ○	Patient is supine. Examiner fully abducts humerus and internally and externally rotates arm while applying axial force through glenohumeral joint. Positive if pain or clicking is elicited	62 shoulders undergoing arthroscopy		.40	.73	1.5	.82

+LR	Interpretation	−LR
>10	Large	<.1
5.0-10.0	Moderate	.1-.2
2.0-5.0	Small	.2-.5
1.0-2.0	Rarely important	.5-1.0

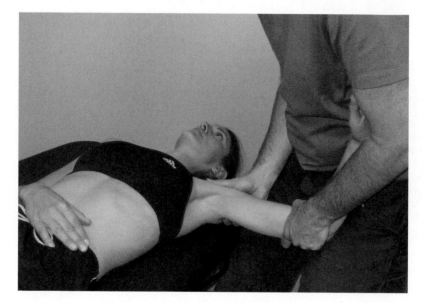

Figure 9-22

Compression rotation test.

Test and Study Quality	Description and Positive Findings	Population	Reference Standard	Sens	Spec	+LR	−LR
Compression rotation test[2] ◇	With patient supine with arm abducted to 90° and elbow flexed to 90°, examiner applies axial force to humerus. Humerus is circumducted and rotated. Positive if pain or clicking is elicited	68 patients with type II SLAP lesions and 78 age-matched controls who underwent shoulder arthroscopy	Type II SLAP lesion visualized during arthroscopy	.61	.54	1.3	.72
Compression rotation test[41] ◇		426 patients who had undergone shoulder arthroscopy	Labral tear visualized during arthroscopy	.24	.76	1.0	1.0
Compression rotation test[28] ○	Not described	54 throwing athletes with shoulder pain		.25	1.0	Undefined	.75

Diagnostic Utility of Speed's Test in Identifying Superior Labrum Anterior Posterior Lesions

+LR	Interpretation	−LR
>10	Large	<.1
5.0 10.0	Moderate	.1-.2
2.0-5.0	Small	.2-.5
1.0-2.0	Rarely important	.5-1.0

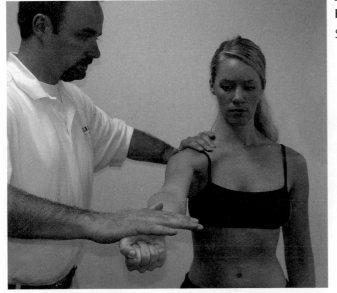

Figure 9-23
Speed's test.

Test and Study Quality	Description and Positive Findings	Population	Reference Standard	Sens	Spec	+LR	−LR
Speed's test[42] **2008 Meta-analysis**		Pooled estimates from 4 high-quality studies		.32 (.24, .42)	.61 (.54, .68)	.8	1.11
Speed's test[43] ◇	Patient elevates humerus to 90° with elbow flexion and forearm supination. Patient holds this position while examiner applies resistance against elevation. Positive if pain is elicited in the bicipital groove area	133 patients who underwent diagnostic arthroscopy of the shoulder	SLAP lesion visualized during arthroscopy	.60	.38	1.0	1.05
Speed's test[2] ◇		68 patients with type II SLAP lesions and 78 age-matched controls who underwent shoulder arthroscopy		.32	.66	.9	1.03
Speed's test[26] ◇		847 patients who underwent diagnostic arthroscopy of the shoulder	Partial biceps tendon tear visualized during arthroscopy	.50	.67	1.5	.75

Only studies published after the meta-analysis were included.

Reliability of the Active Compression/O'Brien Test

ICC or κ	Interpretation
.81-1.0	Substantial agreement
.61-.80	Moderate agreement
.41-.60	Fair agreement
.11-.40	Slight agreement
.0-.10	No agreement

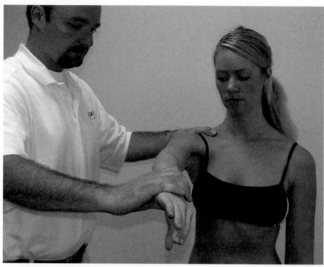

Active compression test with internal rotation

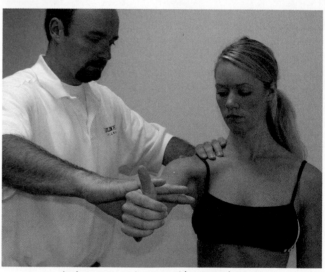

Active compression test with external rotation

Figure 9-24

Active compression test.

Test	Description	Population	Inter-examiner Reliability
Active compression test[16]	See page 407	55 patients with shoulder pain scheduled for arthroscopic surgery	κ = .24 (−.02, .50)

Diagnostic Utility of the Active Compression/O'Brien Test

+LR	Interpretation	−LR
>10	Large	<.1
5.0–10.0	Moderate	.1–.2
2.0–5.0	Small	.2–.5
1.0–2.0	Rarely important	.5–1.0

Test and Study Quality	Description and Positive Findings	Population	Reference Standard	Sens	Spec	+LR	−LR
Active compression test[16] ◆		55 patients with shoulder pain scheduled for arthroscopic surgery	Glenoid labral tear observed during arthroscopy	.55 (.4, .69)	.18 (−.05, .41)	.67 (.45, .98)	2.5 (.68, 9.13)
O'Brien test[43] ◆	Patient stands and flexes arm to 90° with elbow in full extension. Patient then adducts arm 10° internally and rotates humerus. Examiner applies downward force to arm as patient resists. Patient then fully supinates arm and repeats procedure. Positive if pain is elicited with first maneuver and reduced with second maneuver	133 patients who underwent diagnostic arthroscopy of the shoulder	SLAP lesion visualized during arthroscopy	.94	.28	1.3	.21
O'Brien test[2] ◆		68 patients with SLAP lesions and 78 age-matched controls		.63	.53	1.3	.70
Active compression test[38] ◆		132 patients scheduled to undergo shoulder arthroscopy		.63	.50	1.3	.74
Active compression test[39] ◆		40 athletes with shoulder pain		.78	.11	.1	2.00
Active compression test[41] ◆		426 patients who had undergone shoulder arthroscopy		.47	.55	1.0	.96
Active compression test (palm down)[26] ◆	As above except positive if pain is elicited in tested position	847 patients who underwent diagnostic arthroscopy of the shoulder		.68	.46	1.3	.70
Active compression test (palm up)[26] ◆				.40	.57	.9	1.1
O'Brien test[40] ○	As above except patient is seated	65 patients with symptoms of shoulder pain	Partial biceps tendon tear visualized during arthroscopy	.54	.31	.78	1.48
O'Brien test[27] ○		62 shoulders undergoing arthroscopy		.63	.73	2.3	.51
O'Brien test[28] ○	Not described	54 throwing athletes with shoulder pain		.54	.60	1.4	.77

Diagnostic Utility of the Yergason Test in Identifying Labral Tears

+LR	Interpretation	−LR
>10	Large	<.1
5.0-10.0	Moderate	.1-.2
2.0-5.0	Small	.2-.5
1.0-2.0	Rarely important	.5-1.0

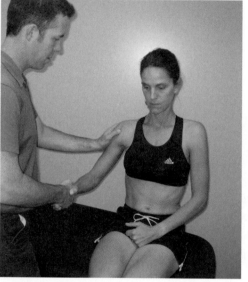

Figure 9-25

Yergason test.

Test and Study Quality	Description and Positive Findings	Population	Reference Standard	Sens	Spec	+LR	−LR
Yergason test[2] ◇		68 patients with type II SLAP lesions and 78 age-matched controls who underwent shoulder arthroscopy		.12	.87	.9	1.01
Yergason test[38] ◇	With patient standing with elbow at 90°, patient supinates forearm against examiner's resistance. During procedure, examiner palpates long head of biceps tendon. Positive if pain at biceps tendon	132 patients scheduled to undergo shoulder arthroscopy	SLAP lesion visualized during arthroscopy	.13	.94	2.2	.93
Yergason test[27] ○		62 shoulders scheduled to undergo arthroscopy		.09	.93	1.29	.98
Yergason test[28] ○		54 throwing athletes with shoulder pain		.13	1.0	Undefined	.87
Yergason test[44] ○		152 subjects with shoulder pain scheduled to undergo surgery	Biceps tendon and/or labral tear visualized during arthroscopy	.43	.79	2.05	.72

Special Tests—Labral Tears

Reliability of the Anterior Slide Test/Kibler Test

ICC or κ	Interpretation
.81-1.0	Substantial agreement
.61-.80	Moderate agreement
.41-.60	Fair agreement
.11-.40	Slight agreement
.0-.10	No agreement

Test	Description	Population	Inter-examiner Reliability
Anterior slide test[16]	See below	55 patients with shoulder pain scheduled for arthroscopic surgery	κ = .21 (−.05, .46)

Diagnostic Utility of the Anterior Slide Test/Kibler Test in Identifying Labral Tears

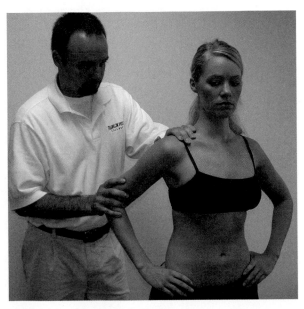

+LR	Interpretation	−LR
>10	Large	<.1
5.0-10.0	Moderate	.1-.2
2.0-5.0	Small	.2-.5
1.0-2.0	Rarely important	.5-1.0

Figure 9-26

Anterior slide test/Kibler test.

Test and Study Quality	Description and Positive Findings	Population	Reference Standard	Sens	Spec	+LR	−LR
Anterior slide test[16] ◇		55 patients with shoulder pain scheduled for arthroscopic surgery	Glenoid labral tear observed during arthroscopy	.43 (.29, .58)	.82 (.59, 1.05)	2.38 (.65, 8.7)	.69 (.48, 1.01)
Anterior slide test (Kibler test)[2] ◇	With patient standing or sitting with hands on hips, thumbs facing posteriorly, examiner stabilizes scapula with one hand and, with other hand on elbow, applies anteriorly and superiorly directed force through humerus. Patient pushes back against force. Positive if pain or click is elicited in anterior shoulder	68 patients with type II SLAP lesions and 78 age-matched controls who underwent shoulder arthroscopy	Type II SLAP lesion visualized during arthroscopy	.21	.70	.7	1.13
Anterior slide test (Kibler test)[26] ◇		847 patients who underwent diagnostic arthroscopy of the shoulder	Partial biceps tendon tear visualized during arthroscopy	.23	.84	1.4	.92
Anterior slide test[41] ◇		426 patients who had undergone shoulder arthroscopy	SLAP lesion visualized during arthroscopy	.08	.84	.56	1.1

ICC or κ	Interpretation
.81-1.0	Substantial agreement
.61-.80	Moderate agreement
.41-.60	Fair agreement
.11-.40	Slight agreement
.0-.10	No agreement

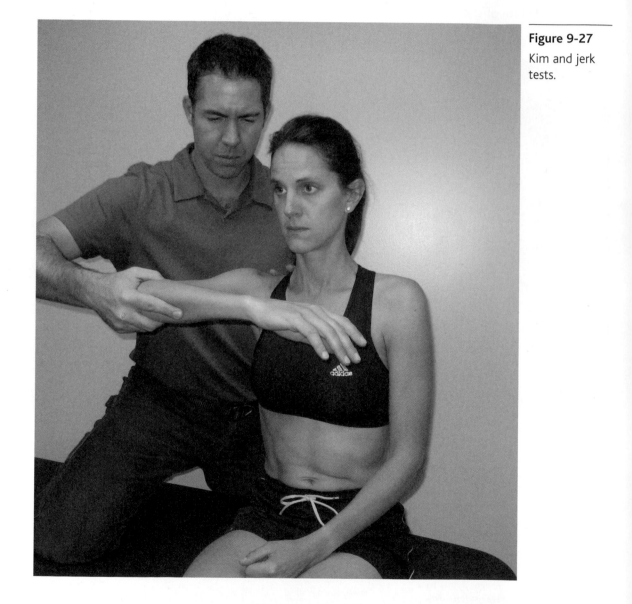

Figure 9-27
Kim and jerk tests.

Test	Description	Population	Reliability
Passive compression test[45]	See page 411	61 patients undergoing arthroscopy for shoulder pain	Inter-examiner κ = **.77**
Kim test[46]	See page 411	172 painful shoulders	Inter-examiner κ = **.91**

Diagnostic Utility of Various Tests in Identifying Labral Tears

+LR	Interpretation	−LR
>10	Large	<.1
5.0-10.0	Moderate	.1-.2
2.0-5.0	Small	.2-.5
1.0-2.0	Rarely important	.5-1.0

Test and Study Quality	Description and Positive Findings	Population	Reference Standard	Sens	Spec	+LR	−LR
Passive compression test[45] ◇	With patient side lying with affected side up, examiner places one hand over the AC joint to stabilize the shoulder and the other hand on the elbow. Examiner then externally rotates the shoulder in 30° abduction and gives axial compression while extending the arm. Positive if pain	61 patients undergoing arthroscopy for shoulder pain	SLAP lesion visualized during arthroscopy	.82	.86	5.90	.21
Kim test[46] ◇	With patient sitting with arm abducted 90°, examiner holds the elbow and lateral aspect of the proximal arm and applies a strong axial loading force. Examiner then elevates the arm to 135° and adds a posterior/inferior force. Positive if sudden onset of posterior shoulder pain	172 painful shoulders	Labral tear visualized during arthroscopy	.80	.94	13.3	.21
Jerk test[46] ◇	With patient sitting, examiner holds scapula with one hand and internally rotates and abducts the patient's arm to 90° with the other. Examiner then horizontally adducts the arm while applying an axial loading force. Sharp pain indicates a positive test			.73	.98	36.5	.28
Supine flexion resistance test[43] ◇	With patient supine with arm resting in full flexion and palm up, examiner grasps patient's arm just distal to the elbow and asks the patient to lift the arm as if throwing. Positive if pain is felt deep inside the shoulder joint	133 patients who underwent diagnostic arthroscopy of the shoulder	SLAP lesion visualized during arthroscopy	.80	.69	2.6	.29
Resisted supination external rotation test[39] ◇	With patient supine with arm abducted 90° and elbow flexed 70°, examiner supports the arm by the elbow. Examiner resists supination and gently maximally externally rotates the shoulder. Positive if shoulder pain, clicking, or catching is elicited	40 athletes with shoulder pain		.83	.82	4.6	.21

(Continued)

Diagnostic Utility of Various Tests in Identifying Labral Tears

+LR	Interpretation	−LR
>10	Large	<.1
5.0-10.0	Moderate	.1-.2
2.0-5.0	Small	.2-.5
1.0-2.0	Rarely important	.5-1.0

Test and Study Quality	Description and Positive Findings	Population	Reference Standard	Sens	Spec	+LR	−LR
Whipple test[2] ◇	The arm is flexed 90° and adducted until the hand is opposite the other shoulder. The patient resists while examiner pushes downward on the arm. Positive if pain	68 patients with type II SLAP lesions and 78 age-matched controls who underwent shoulder arthroscopy	Type II SLAP lesion visualized during arthroscopy	.65	.42	1.1	.83
Biceps load test II[2] ◇	With patient supine, examiner grasps wrist and elbow. Arm is elevated 120° and fully externally rotated with elbow held in 90° of flexion and forearm supinated. Examiner then resists elbow flexion by patient. Positive if resisted elbow flexion causes pain	68 patients with type II SLAP lesions and 78 age-matched controls who underwent shoulder arthroscopy		.30	.78	1.4	.90
Biceps load test II[47] ◯		127 patients experiencing shoulder pain scheduled to undergo arthroscopy		.90	.97	30	.10
Posterior jerk test[28] ◯	Not described	54 throwing athletes with shoulder pain		.25	.80	1.3	.72
Biceps load test[48] ◯	With patient supine, examiner grasps wrist and elbow. Arm is abducted to 90° with elbow flexed to 90° and forearm supinated. Examiner externally rotates arm until patient becomes apprehensive at which time ER is stopped. Patient flexes elbow against examiner's resistance. Positive if patient's apprehension remains or pain is produced	75 patients with unilateral recurrent anterior shoulder dislocations		.90	.97	30	.10

Special Tests—Subacromial Impingement

Reliability of Hawkins-Kennedy Test

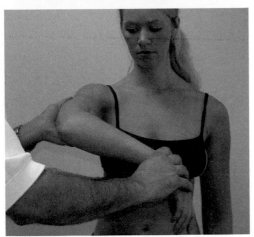

ICC or κ	Interpretation
.81-1.0	Substantial agreement
.61-.80	Moderate agreement
.41-.60	Fair agreement
.11-.40	Slight agreement
.0-.10	No agreement

Figure 9-28

Hawkins-Kennedy test.

Test	Description	Population	Reliability
Hawkins-Kennedy test[49]	See below	33 patients with shoulder pain	Test-retest κ = **1.0** Inter-examiner κ = **.91**

Diagnostic Utility of Hawkins-Kennedy Test in Identifying Subacromial Impingement

+LR	Interpretation	−LR
>10	Large	<.1
5.0-10.0	Moderate	.1-.2
2.0-5.0	Small	.2-.5
1.0-2.0	Rarely important	.5-1.0

Test and Study Quality	Description and Positive Findings	Population	Reference Standard	Sens	Spec	+LR	−LR
Hawkins-Kennedy test[4] **2008 Meta-analysis** ◯		Pooled estimates from 4 high-quality studies	Impingement syndrome diagnosed from sub-acromial injection or surgery	.79 (.75, .82)	.59 (.53, .64)	1.9	.36
Hawkins-Kennedy test[50] ◇	Patient is standing. The affected arm is forward-flexed 90° and then forcibly medially rotated. Positive if the patient complains of pain.	30 patients with new onset shoulder pain	Magnetic resonance imaging (MRI) con-firmed subacromial impingement	.74	.40	1.2 (.7, 2.3)	.65
			MRI confirmed subacro-mial bursitis	.80	.43	1.4 (.8, 2.4)	.47
Hawkins-Kennedy test[26] ◇		847 patients who underwent diag-nostic arthroscopy of the shoulder	Partial biceps tendon tear visualized during arthroscopy	.55	.38	.9	1.18

Only studies published after the meta-analysis were included.

Special Tests—Subacromial Impingement

Reliability of the Neer Test

ICC or κ	Interpretation
.81-1.0	Substantial agreement
.61-.80	Moderate agreement
.41-.60	Fair agreement
.11-.40	Slight agreement
.0-.10	No agreement

Test	Description	Population	Reliability
Neer test[49]	See below	33 patients with shoulder pain	Test-retest κ = **1.0** Inter-examiner κ = **1.0**

Diagnostic Utility of the Neer Test in Identifying Subacromial Impingement

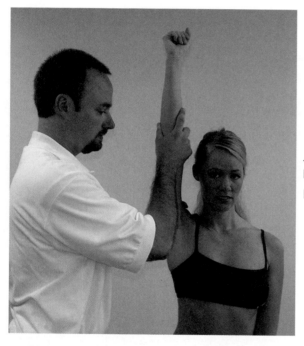

Figure 9-29

Neer test.

+LR	Interpretation	−LR
>10	Large	<.1
5.0-10.0	Moderate	.1-.2
2.0-5.0	Small	.2-.5
1.0-2.0	Rarely important	.5-1.0

Test and Study Quality	Description and Positive Findings	Population	Reference Standard	Sens	Spec	+LR	−LR
Neer test[42] **2008 Meta-analysis**		Pooled estimates from 4 high-quality studies	Impingement syndrome diagnosed from subacromial injection or surgery	.79 (.75, .82)	.53 (.48, .58)	1.7	.40
Neer test[50] ◇	Examiner forces patient's internally rotated arm into maximal elevation. Positive if pain is produced	30 patients with new-onset shoulder pain	MRI confirmed subacromial impingement	.68	.30	1.0 (.6, 1.6)	1.07
			MRI confirmed subacromial bursitis	.80	.43	1.4 (.8, 2.4)	.47
Neer test[26] ◇		847 patients who underwent diagnostic arthroscopy of the shoulder	Partial biceps tendon tear visualized during arthroscopy	.64	.41	1.1	.88

Only studies published after the meta-analysis were included.

Special Tests—Subacromial Impingement

Diagnostic Utility of Various Tests in Identifying Subacromial Impingement

+LR	Interpretation	−LR
>10	Large	<.1
5.0-10.0	Moderate	.1-.2
2.0-5.0	Small	.2-.5
1.0-2.0	Rarely important	.5-1.0

Test and Study Quality	Description and Positive Findings	Population	Reference Standard	Sens	Spec	+LR	−LR
Painful arc sign[51] ◆	Patient actively elevates arm in scapular plane to full elevation. Positive if patient experiences pain between 60° and 120°	552 patients with shoulder pain	Arthroscopic visualization • All impingement • Bursitis • Partial thickness RCT • Full thickness RCT	.74 .71 .67 .76	.81 .47 .47 .72	3.9 1.3 1.3 2.7	.32 .62 .70 .33
Cross-body adduction test[51] ◆	Arm at 90° of flexion. Examiner then adducts arm across the patient's body. Positive if shoulder pain is produced	552 patients with shoulder pain	Arthroscopic visualization • All impingement • Bursitis • Partial thickness RCT • Full thickness RCT	.23 .25 .17 .23	.82 .80 .79 .81	1.3 1.3 .8 1.2	.94 .94 1.05 .95
Lift-off test (Gerber's test)[50] ◆	Patient attempts to lift the affected arm off the back. Positive if unable to lift off back	30 patients with new-onset shoulder pain	MRI confirmed subacromial impingement	.68	.50	1.4 (.7, 2.7)	.64
			MRI confirmed subacromial bursitis	.93	.71	3.3 (1.4, 7.6)	.10
Lift-off test (Gerber's test)[26] ◆		847 patients who underwent diagnostic arthroscopy of the shoulder	Partial biceps tendon tear visualized during arthroscopy	.28	.89	2.5	.81
Yocum test[50] ◆	With patient seated or standing, patient places hand of involved shoulder on contralateral shoulder and raises elbow. Positive if pain is elicited	30 patients with new-onset shoulder pain	MRI confirmed subacromial impingement	.79	.40	1.3 (.8, 2.3)	.53
			MRI confirmed subacromial bursitis	.80	.36	1.2 (.08, 2.0)	.56
Horizontal adduction test[52] ○	Examiner forces patient's arm into horizontal adduction while elbow is flexed. Positive if pain is elicited	125 painful shoulders	Subacromial impingement via subacromial injection	.82	.28	1.14	.64
The painful arc test[52] ○	Patient is instructed to perform straight plane abduction throughout full ROM. Positive if pain occurs between 60° and 100° of abduction			.33	.81	1.74	.83

(Continued)

Diagnostic Utility of Various Tests in Identifying Subacromial Impingement

Test and Study Quality	Description and Positive Findings	Population	Reference Standard	Sens	Spec	+LR	−LR
Drop arm test[52] ○	Patient is instructed to abduct shoulder to 90° and then lower it slowly to neutral position. Positive if patient is unable to do this because of pain	125 painful shoulders	Subacromial impingement via subacromial injection	.08	.97	2.67	.95

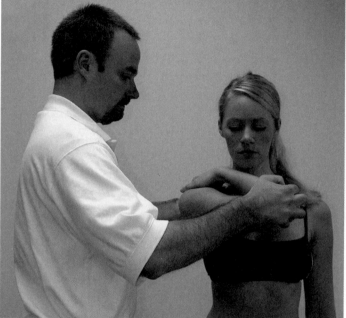

Figure 9-30

Horizontal adduction test.

Figure 9-31

Yocum test.

Diagnostic Utility of Internal Rotation Resistance Strength Test in Differentiating Subacromial Impingement versus Intra-articular Pathology

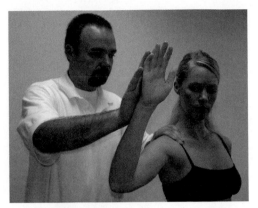

Resistance against external rotation

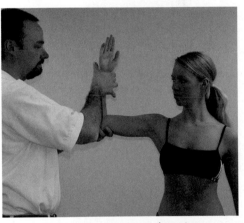

Resistance against internal rotation

Figure 9-32

Internal rotation resistance strength test.

Zaslav[53] investigated the internal rotation resistance strength (IRRS) test's ability to delineate intra-articular pathology from impingement syndrome in a group of 115 patients who underwent arthroscopic shoulder surgery. The IRRS test is performed with the patient standing. The examiner positions the patient's arm in 90° abduction and 80° ER. The examiner applies resistance against ER and then IR in the same position. The test is considered positive for intra-articular pathology if the patient exhibits greater weakness in IR when compared with ER. If the patient demonstrated greater weakness with ER, they were considered positive for impingement syndrome. The IRRS test demonstrated a sensitivity of .88, a specificity of .96, a positive LR of 22.0, and a negative LR of .13.

Special Tests—Rotator Cuff Tears

Reliability of Special Tests for Identifying Supraspinatus and/or Infraspinatus Tears

ICC or κ	Interpretation
.81–1.0	Substantial agreement
.61–.80	Moderate agreement
.41–.60	Fair agreement
.11–.40	Slight agreement
.0–.10	No agreement

Test	Description	Population	Reliability
Supraspinatus muscle test (empty can)[49]	Shoulder and elbow at 90° with arm internally rotated. Examiner then resists internal rotation force. Positive if patient gives way	33 patients with shoulder pain	Test-retest κ = **1.0** Inter-examiner κ = **.94**
Patte maneuver[49]			Test-retest κ = **1.0** Inter-examiner κ = **1.0**

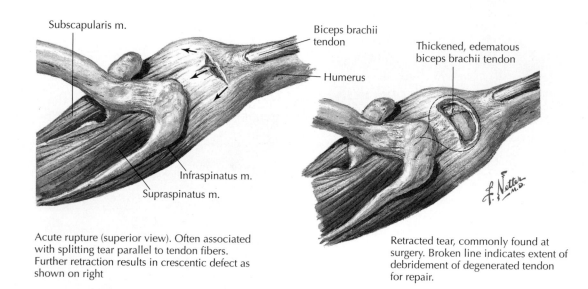

Acute rupture (superior view). Often associated with splitting tear parallel to tendon fibers. Further retraction results in crescentic defect as shown on right

Retracted tear, commonly found at surgery. Broken line indicates extent of debridement of degenerated tendon for repair.

Figure 9-33

Superior rotator cuff tear.

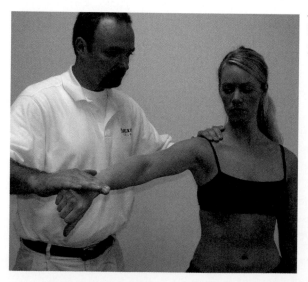

Figure 9-34

Supraspinatus muscle test (empty can).

Diagnostic Utility of Special Tests for Identifying Supraspinatus and/or Infraspinatus Tears

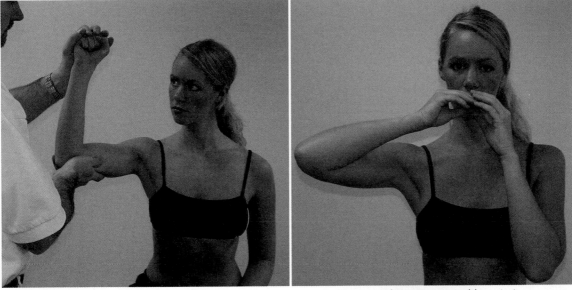

Patients with a positive Hornblower's sign
often have difficulty raising their hand to
their mouth without abducting the shoulder

Figure 9-35

Hornblower's sign.

+LR	Interpretation	−LR
>10	Large	<.1
5.0-10.0	Moderate	.1-.2
2.0-5.0	Small	.2-.5
1.0-2.0	Rarely important	.5-1.0

Test and Study Quality	Description and Positive Findings	Population	Reference Standard	Sens	Spec	+LR	−LR
Weakness with elevation (empty can)[11] ◇	With patient standing with arms elevated to shoulder level in scapular plane, thumbs pointing down, examiner applies downward force and patient resists. Positive if weakness is present	448 patients undergoing arthrography	Arthrographic confirmation of complete or partial rotator cuff tear	.64	.65	1.83	.55
Weakness with elevation (empty can)[50] ◇		30 patients with new onset shoulder pain	MRI confirmed • Subacromial impingement • Subacromial bursitis	.74 .73	.30 .29	1.1 1.0	.87 .93

(Continued)

Test and Study Quality	Description and Positive Findings	Population	Reference Standard	Sens	Spec	+LR	−LR
Supraspinatus muscle test[50] ◆	Examiner resists abduction of the arm at 90° with patient's arm neutral or internally rotated. Positive if patient gives way	30 patients with new onset shoulder pain	MRI confirmed • Subacromial impingement • Subacromial bursitis	.58 .73	.20 .43	.7 1.3	2.10 .63
Supraspinatus muscle test[51] ◆		552 patients with shoulder pain	Arthroscopic visualization • All impingement • Bursitis • Partial thickness RCT • Full thickness RCT	.44 .25 .32 .53	.90 .67 .68 .82	4.4 .80 1.0 2.9	.62 1.12 1.00 .57
Drop-arm test[51] ◆	Patient elevates fully and then slowly lowers arm. Positive if the arm suddenly drops or patient has severe pain	552 patients with shoulder pain	Arthroscopic visualization • All impingement • Bursitis • Partial thickness RCT • Full thickness RCT	.27 .14 .14 .35	.88 .77 .78 .88	2.3 .60 .60 2.9	.83 1.12 1.10 .74
Infraspinatus muscle test (Patte test)[50] ◆	Elbow at 90° with arm neutrally rotated and adducted to the trunk. Examiner then resists internal rotation force. Positive if patient gives way	30 patients with new-onset shoulder pain	MRI confirmed • Subacromial impingement • Subacromial bursitis	.58 .73	.60 .71	1.5 2.5	.70 .38
Infraspinatus muscle test[51] ◆		552 patients with shoulder pain	Arthroscopic visualization • All impingement • Bursitis • Partial thickness RCT • Full-thickness RCT	.42 .25 .19 .51	.90 .69 .69 .84	4.2 .80 .60 3.2	.64 1.09 1.17 .58
External rotation lag sign[54] ◆	With patient sitting, examiner holds the arm in 20° shoulder elevation (in the scapular plane), 5° from full external rotation, and 90° elbow extension. Patient maintains the position when examiner releases arm. Positive if unable to hold position	37 patients with shoulder pain	Supraspinatus or infraspinatus tear via ultrasound	.46	.94	7.2 (1.7, 31.0)	.60 (.40, .90)
Drop sign[54] ◆	With patient sitting, examiner holds the arm in 90° abduction and full external rotation. Patient is asked to maintain the position when examiner releases arm. Positive if unable to hold position			.73	.77	3.2 (1.5, 6.7)	.30 (.20, .80)

(Continued)

+LR	Interpretation	−LR
>10	Large	<.1
5.0-10.0	Moderate	.1-.2
2.0-5.0	Small	.2-.5
1.0-2.0	Rarely important	.5-1.0

Test and Study Quality	Description and Positive Findings	Population	Reference Standard	Sens	Spec	+LR	−LR
Passive elevation less than 170°[11] ◇	With patient supine, examiner maximally elevates shoulder	448 patients undergoing arthrography	Arthrographic confirmation of complete or partial rotator cuff tear	.30	.78	1.36	.90
Passive ER less than 70°[11] ◇	With patient supine with arm at side, examiner externally rotates arm			.19	.84	1.19	.96
Arc of pain sign[11] ◇	With patient standing, examiner passively abducts arm to 170°. Patient then slowly lowers arm to side. Positive if patient reports pain at 120° to 70° of abduction			.98	.10	1.09	.20
Atrophy of the supraspinatus muscle[11] ◇	Examiner determines atrophy through visual inspection			.56	.73	2.07	.60
Atrophy of the infraspinatus muscle[11] ◇				.56	.73	2.07	.60
Hornblower's signs (teres minor)[55] ○	With patient seated, examiner places patient's arm in 90° of scaption and patient externally rotates against resistance. Positive if patient is unable to externally rotate shoulder	54 patients who underwent shoulder surgery to repair rotator cuff	Stage of fatty degeneration of infraspinatus as determined by CT scan	1.0	.93	14.29	.00
Dropping sign (infraspinatus)[55] ○	With patient seated, examiner places patient's shoulder in 0° of abduction and 45° of ER with elbow flexed to 90°. Patient holds position when examiner releases forearm. Positive if patient is unable to hold position and arm returns to 0° of ER			1.0	1.0	Undefined	.00

(Continued)

Diagnostic Utility of Special Tests for Identifying Supraspinatus and/or Infraspinatus Tears

Test and Study Quality		Description and Positive Findings	Population	Reference Standard	Sens	Spec	+LR	−LR
Supra-spinatus test[56] ⚪	Tendinitis or partial thickness tear*	With patient standing and shoulders abducted to 90° in scapular plane and IR of humerus, examiner applies isometric resistance. Strength of involved side is compared with uninvolved side. Positive if weakness or pain	50 patients with shoulder pain scheduled to undergo surgery	Supraspinatus tear via arthroscopic visualization	.62 (.49, .75)	.54 (.40, .68)	1.35	.70
	Full thickness tear†				.41 (.27, .55)	.70 (.57, .83)	1.37	.84
	Large or massive full thickness tear†				.88 (.79, .97)	.70 (.58, .82)	2.93	.17
ER lag sign[57] ⚪		With patient seated, examiner passively flexes elbow to 90° and elevates shoulder to 20° in scapular plane. Examiner then places shoulder in near maximal rotation (5° from full). Patient maintains position of ER when examiner releases arm. Positive if patient is unable to maintain ER	74 patients scheduled to undergo arthroscopic shoulder surgery	Supraspinatus or infraspinatus tear via arthroscopic visualization	.70	1.0	Undefined	.30

*Tendinitis defined as inflammation or fraying of supraspinatus tendon. Partial thickness defined as partial tear of supraspinatus tendon.
†Full thickness tear categorized as small, moderate, large, or massive. Small indicates tear < 1 cm, moderate indicates tear 1 to 3 cm that includes infraspinatus, large indicates tear 3 to 5 cm that includes infraspinatus and teres minor, and massive indicates a tear > 5 cm that includes infraspinatus, teres minor, and subscapularis.

Diagnostic Utility of Special Tests for Identifying Subscapularis Tears

+LR	Interpretation	−LR
>10	Large	<.1
5.0-10.0	Moderate	.1-.2
2.0-5.0	Small	.2-.5
1.0-2.0	Rarely important	.5-1.0

Test and Study Quality	Description and Positive Findings	Population	Reference Standard	Sens	Spec	+LR	−LR
Internal rotation lag sign[54] ◆	With patient sitting, examiner holds hand behind the lumbar region into full IR. Patient maintains the position when examiner releases arm. Positive if unable to hold position	37 patients with shoulder pain	Subscapularis tear via ultrasound	1.0	.84	6.2 (1.9, 12.0)	.00 (.00, 2.50)
Bear-hug test[58] ○	Patient places palm of involved side on opposite shoulder and fingers extended. Examiner then attempts to pull the hand off the shoulder into ER while the patient resists. Positive if unable to maintain hand on shoulder or weakness > 20° compared to the other side	68 shoulders scheduled to undergo arthroscopic shoulder surgery	Subscapularis tear via arthroscopic visualization	.60	.92	7.5	.43
Belly-press test[58] ○	With elbow at 90° and hand on belly, patient forcefully presses into a tensiometer on the belly. Positive if weak compared to other side or if patient uses elbow or shoulder extension to push			.40	.98	20.0	.61
Lift-off test[58] ○	Patients places the hand of the affected arm on the back (at the position of the mid-lumbar spine) and then attempts to internally rotate the arm to lift the hand posteriorly off of the back. Positive if unable to lift the arm off the back or if patient performs the lifting maneuver by extending the elbow or the shoulder			.18	1.0	Undefined	.82
Napoleon test[58] ○	Same as the belly-press test except without a tensiometer. Positive if patient uses wrist flexion > 30° to press into belly			.25	.98	12.5	.77

Diagnostic Utility of Special Tests for Identifying Subscapularis Tears

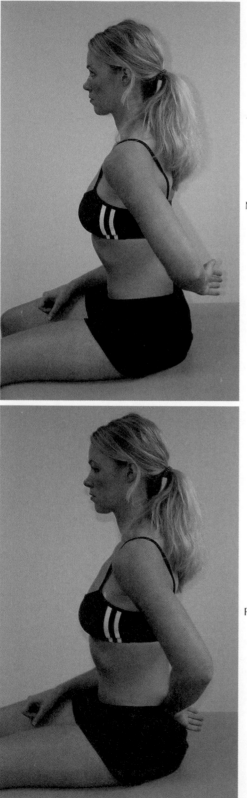

Figure 9-36

Lift-off test.

Negative test

Positive test

Special Tests—Brachial Plexus Palsy

Diagnostic Utility of Special Tests for Identifying Nerve Root Avulsion in People with Brachial Plexus Palsy

+LR	Interpretation	−LR
>10	Large	<.1
5.0-10.0	Moderate	.1-.2
2.0-5.0	Small	.2-.5
1.0-2.0	Rarely important	.5-1.0

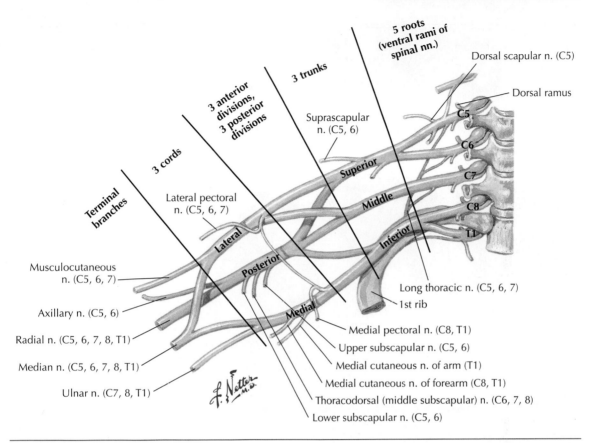

Figure 9-37

Brachial plexus: schema.

Test and Study Quality	Description and Positive Findings	Population	Reference Standard	Sens	Spec	+LR	−LR
Tinel sign C-5[59] ⃝	Gentle percussion on the supraclavicular region. Positive if painful paresthesias radiating into forearm			.85	.67	2.6	.22
Tinel sign C-6[59] ⃝	As above except painful paresthesias radiating into hand			.50	.81	2.6	.62
Shoulder protraction test[59] ⃝	From supine position, patients protract their shoulder while being resisted by the examiner's hand placed on their anterior shoulder. Positive if weaker than opposite side	32 patients with complete brachial plexus palsy	CT myelography agreement with surgical findings	.96	.80	4.8	.05
Hand pain[59] ⃝	Positive if reported as severe burning or crushing sensation			.86	.75	3.4	.19

Diagnostic Utility of Special Tests for Identifying Acromioclavicular Lesions

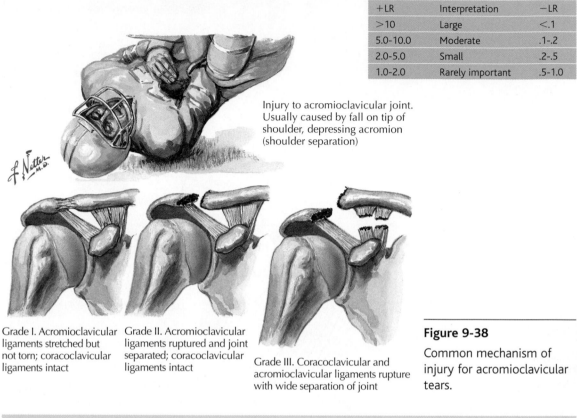

+LR	Interpretation	−LR
>10	Large	<.1
5.0-10.0	Moderate	.1-.2
2.0-5.0	Small	.2-.5
1.0-2.0	Rarely important	.5-1.0

Injury to acromioclavicular joint. Usually caused by fall on tip of shoulder, depressing acromion (shoulder separation)

Grade I. Acromioclavicular ligaments stretched but not torn; coracoclavicular ligaments intact

Grade II. Acromioclavicular ligaments ruptured and joint separated; coracoclavicular ligaments intact

Grade III. Coracoclavicular and acromioclavicular ligaments rupture with wide separation of joint

Figure 9-38

Common mechanism of injury for acromioclavicular tears.

Test and Study Quality	Description and Positive Findings	Population	Reference Standard	Sens	Spec	+LR	−LR
O'Brien sign[60] ◇	Patient is standing. Examiner asks patient to flex arm to 90° with elbow in full extension. Patient then adducts arm 10° and internally rotates humerus. Examiner applies downward force to arm as patient resists. Patient fully supinates arm and repeats procedure. Positive if pain localized to AC joint	1013 patients with pain between mid clavicle and deltoid	AC joint infiltration test: patients were injected with lidocaine in AC joint. Those who experienced at least a 50% reduction in symptoms within 10 minutes were considered to have AC pathology	.16	.90	1.6	.93
Paxinos sign[60] ◇	Patient sits with arm by side. With one hand, examiner places thumb over posterolateral aspect of acromion and index finger superior to midportion of clavicle. Examiner then applies compressive force. Positive if pain is reported in area of AC joint			.79	.50	1.58	.42
Palpation of the AC joint[60] ◇	Not reported			.96	.10	1.07	.40

Combination of Tests

Diagnostic Utility of Combinations of Tests for Identifying Glenoid Labral Tears

+LR	Interpretation	−LR
>10	Large	<.1
5.0-10.0	Moderate	.1-.2
2.0-5.0	Small	.2-.5
1.0-2.0	Rarely important	.5-1.0

Test and Study Quality	Patient Population	Reference Standard	Sens	Spec	+LR	−LR
Pop + crank[16] ◆	55 patients with shoulder pain scheduled for arthroscopic surgery	Glenoid labral tear observed during arthroscopy	.27 (.14, .4)	.91 (.74, 1.08)	3.0 (.44, 20.67)	.8 (.62, 1.04)
Pop + anterior slide[16] ◆			.16 (.05, .27)	1.0 (1.0, 1.0)	Undefined	.84 (.74, .96)
Active compression + Anterior slide[16] ◆			.25 (.12, .38)	.91 (.74, 1.08)	2.75 (.4, 19.09)	.83 (.64, 1.06)
Anterior slide + Crank[16] ◆			.34 (.2, .48)	.91 (.74, 1.08)	3.75 (.55, 25.41)	.73 (.55, .96)
Crank test + Apprehension test + Relocation test + Load and shift test + Inferior sulcus sign[10] ◯	54 patients with shoulder pain	Arthroscopic visualization	.90	.85	6.0	.12
Jobe relocation + O'Brien[27] ◯	62 shoulders scheduled to undergo arthroscopy	As above	.41	.91	4.56	.65
Jobe relocation + Anterior apprehension[27] ◯			.38	.93	5.43	.67
O'Brien + Anterior apprehension[27] ◯			.38	.82	2.11	.76
Jobe + O'Brien + Apprehension[27] ◯			.34	.91	3.78	.73

See test descriptions under single tests.

Combination of Tests

Diagnostic Utility of Combinations of Tests for Identifying SLAP Lesions

Oh and colleagues[2] studied the ability of combinations of two and three special tests to identify type II SLAP lesions. While no combinations of two tests substantially increased the overall diagnostic utility, several combinations of three tests did. When two tests were chosen from the group with relatively high sensitivities, and one from the group with relatively high specificities, the sensitivities of the three "or" combinations were approximately 75%, and the specificities of the three "and" combinations were approximately 90%.

High Sensitivity (choose 2)	High Specificity (choose 1)
Compression rotation	Yergason
+	+
Anterior apprehension	Biceps load test II
+	+
O'Brien	Speed

Diagnostic Utility of Combinations of Tests for Identifying Subacromial Impingement

+LR	Interpretation	−LR
>10	Large	<.1
5.0-10.0	Moderate	.1-.2
2.0-5.0	Small	.2-.5
1.0-2.0	Rarely important	.5-1.0

Test and Study Quality	Test Combination	Population	Reference Standard	Sens	Spec	+LR	−LR
Hawkins-Kennedy impingement test + Painful arc sign + Infraspinatus muscle test[51] ◆	All 3 tests positive	552 patients with shoulder pain	Arthroscopic visualization • Any impingement • Full thickness RCT	.26 .33	.98 .98	10.6 15.9	.75 .69
	2/3 tests positive		Arthroscopic visualization • Any impingement • Full thickness RCT	.26 .35	.98 .90	10.6 3.6	.75 .72
Neer test + Hawkins test + Horizontal adduction test + Painful arc test + Drop arm test + Yergason test + Speed's test[52] ○	All 7 positive	125 painful shoulders	Impingement via subacromial injection test	.04	.97	1.33	.99
	At least 6 positive			.30	.89	2.73	.79
	At least 5 positive			.38	.86	2.71	.72
	At least 4 positive			.70	.67	2.12	.45
	At least 3 positive			.84	.44	1.95	.28

See test descriptions under single tests.

OUTCOME MEASURES

Outcome Measure	Scoring and Interpretation	Test-Retest Reliability	MCID
Upper Extremity Functional Index	Users are asked to rate the difficulty of performing 20 functional tasks on a Likert-type scale ranging from 0 (extremely difficult or unable to perform activity) to 4 (no difficulty). A total score out of 80 is calculated by summing each score. The answers provide a score between 0 and 80, with lower scores representing more disability	ICC = .95[61]	Unknown (MDC = 9.1)[61]
Disabilities of the Arm, Shoulder, and Hand (DASH)	Users are asked to rate the difficulty of performing 30 functional tasks on a Likert-type scale. Twenty-one items relate to physical function, 5 items relate to pain symptoms, and 4 items related to emotional and social functioning. A total score out of 100 is calculated with higher scores representing more disability	ICC = .90[62]	10.2[62]
Shortened Disabilities of the Arm, Shoulder, and Hand Questionnaire (QuickDASH)	Users are asked to rate an 11-item questionnaire that addresses symptoms and physical function. A total score out of 100 is calculated with higher scores representing more disability	ICC = .90[63]	8.0[63]
Shoulder Pain and Disability Index (SPADI)	Users are asked to rate their shoulder pain and disability on 13 items, each on a visual analog scale from 0 (no pain/difficulty) to 100 (worst pain imaginable/ so difficult requires help). Eight items relate to physical function and 5 items relate to pain symptoms. A total score out of 100 is calculated with higher scores representing more disability	ICC = .89[62]	13.1[62]
American Shoulder and Elbow Surgeons (ASES) score	Users are asked to rate their shoulder pain on a 1-item and visual analog scale and functional ability on 10 items on a Likert-type scale ranging from 0 to 4. Pain and function are equally weighted to create a total score out of 100. Lower scores represent more pain and disability	ICC = .91[62]	6.4[62]
Numeric Pain Rating Scale (NPRS)	Users rate their level of pain on an 11-point scale ranging from 0 to 10, with high scores representing more pain. Often asked as "current pain" and "least," "worst," and "average" pain in the past 24 hours	ICC = .72[64]	2[65,66]

ICC, Intraclass correlation coefficient; MDC, minimal detectable change; MCID, minimum clinically important difference.

Quality Assessment of Diagnostic Studies Using QUADAS

	Lyons 1992[67]	Speer 1994	Kibler 1995[68]	Leroux 1995[69]	Hertel 1996	Liu 1996	Gross 1997[70]	O'Brien 1998[71]	Walch 1998	Itoi 1999[72]	Kim 1999	Mimori 1999[73]	Calis 2000	Litaker 2000	Kim 2001
1. Was the spectrum of patients representative of the patients who will receive the test in practice?	U	U	U	Y	U	Y	U	U	U	U	U	U	Y	Y	U
2. Were selection criteria clearly described?	N	N	N	N	N	N	N	N	Y	N	N	N	Y	Y	U
3. Is the reference standard likely to correctly classify the target condition?	Y	Y	Y	Y	U	Y	Y	U	U	U	Y	Y	Y	Y	Y
4. Is the time period between reference standard and index test short enough to be reasonably sure that the target condition did not change between the two tests?	U	Y	U	U	U	U	U	U	U	U	U	U	U	U	U
5. Did the whole sample or a random selection of the sample, receive verification using a reference standard of diagnosis?	Y	Y	N	Y	U	Y	U	Y	Y	Y	Y	Y	Y	Y	Y
6. Did patients receive the same reference standard regardless of the index test result?	Y	Y	N	Y	U	Y	U	N	Y	Y	Y	N	U	Y	Y
7. Was the reference standard independent of the index test (i.e., the index test did not form part of the reference standard)?	Y	Y	Y	Y	U	Y	Y	U	Y	Y	Y	Y	Y	Y	Y
8. Was the execution of the index test described in sufficient detail to permit replication of the test?	N	Y	Y	Y	Y	Y	Y	Y	Y	N	Y	Y	Y	Y	Y
9. Was the execution of the reference standard described in sufficient detail to permit its replication?	N	U	N	N	N	N	U	N	U	U	N	Y	Y	U	N
10. Were the index test results interpreted without knowledge of the results of the reference test?	U	U	U	Y	U	U	U	Y	U	U	Y	U	U	Y	Y
11. Were the reference standard results interpreted without knowledge of the results of the index test?	U	U	U	U	U	U	U	U	U	U	Y	U	U	U	Y

(Continued)

Quality Assessment of Diagnostic Studies Using QUADAS

	Lyons 1992[67]	Speer 1994	Kibler 1995[68]	Leroux 1995[69]	Hertel 1996	Liu 1996	Gross 1997[70]	O'Brien 1998[71]	Walch 1998	Itoi 1999[72]	Kim 1999	Mimori 1999[73]	Calis 2000	Litaker 2000	Kim 2001
12. Were the same clinical data available when test results were interpreted as would be available when the test is used in practice?	U	U	U	U	U	Y	U	U	U	U	U	U	U	Y	N
13. Were uninterpretable/ intermediate test results reported?	U	U	U	Y	U	U	U	U	U	U	U	U	U	Y	U
14. Were withdrawals from the study explained?	U	U	U	Y	U	U	U	U	U	U	U	U	U	Y	U
Quality summary rating:	◼	◯	◼	◯	◼	◯	◼	◼	◯	◼	◯	◼	◯	◆	◯

Y = yes, N = no, U = unclear. ◆ Good quality (Y - N = 10 to 14). ◯ Fair quality (Y - N = 5 to 9). ◼ Poor quality (Y - N ≤ 4).

Quality Assessment of Diagnostic Studies Using QUADAS

	Murrell 2001[74]	Wolf 2001[75]	Zaslav 2001	McFarland 2002	Stetson 2002	Guanche 2003	Chronopoulos 2004	Holtby 2004[44]	Holtby 2004[56]	Lo 2004	Walton 2004	Kim 2005	Park 2005	Myers 2005	Nakagawa 2005
1. Was the spectrum of patients representative of the patients who will receive the test in practice?	U	U	U	U	U	U	U	Y	Y	Y	Y	Y	Y	Y	Y
2. Were selection criteria clearly described?	N	N	N	U	N	U	N	Y	Y	Y	Y	Y	Y	U	Y
3. Is the reference standard likely to correctly classify the target condition?	Y	U	Y	Y	Y	Y	Y	Y	Y	U	Y	Y	Y	Y	Y
4. Is the time period between reference standard and index test short enough to be reasonably sure that the target condition did not change between the two tests?	U	U	U	Y	U	Y	U	U	U	U	U	U	Y	U	U
5. Did the whole sample or a random selection of the sample, receive verification using a reference standard of diagnosis?	Y	Y	Y	Y	Y	Y	Y	U	Y	U	Y	Y	Y	Y	Y
6. Did patients receive the same reference standard regardless of the index test result?	U	U	Y	Y	Y	Y	U	U	Y	N	Y	Y	Y	Y	Y
7. Was the reference standard independent of the index test (i.e., the index test did not form part of the reference standard)?	Y	U	Y	Y	Y	Y	U	U	Y	U	Y	Y	Y	Y	Y
8. Was the execution of the index test described in sufficient detail to permit replication of the test?	N	Y	Y	Y	Y	N	Y	N	N	Y	Y	Y	Y	Y	N
9. Was the execution of the reference standard described in sufficient detail to permit its replication?	N	N	Y	Y	Y	Y	N	Y	Y	N	Y	Y	Y	Y	N
10. Were the index test results interpreted without knowledge of the results of the reference test?	U	Y	Y	Y	Y	U	U	Y	Y	Y	Y	Y	Y	Y	Y
11. Were the reference standard results interpreted without knowledge of the results of the index test?	U	U	U	U	U	U	U	U	Y	U	Y	Y	U	Y	Y

(Continued)

Quality Assessment of Diagnostic Studies Using QUADAS

	Murrell 2001[74]	Wolf 2001[75]	Zaslav 2001	McFarland 2002	Stetson 2002	Guanche 2003	Chronopoulos 2004	Holtby 2004[44]	Holtby 2004[56]	Lo 2004	Walton 2004	Kim 2005	Park 2005	Myers 2005	Nakagawa 2005
12. Were the same clinical data available when test results were interpreted as would be available when the test is used in practice?	U	U	Y	Y	Y	Y	U	Y	U	U	Y	U	Y	Y	U
13. Were uninterpretable/ intermediate test results reported?	U	U	U	U	U	U	U	U	U	U	U	U	Y	U	U
14. Were withdrawals from the study explained?	U	U	U	Y	U	Y	U	U	U	U	Y	U	Y	Y	U
Quality summary rating:	■	■	○	◆	○	○	■	○	○	■	◆	◆	◆	◆	○

Y = yes, N = no, U = unclear. ◆ Good quality (Y - N = 10 to 14). ○ Fair quality (Y - N = 5 to 9). ■ Poor quality (Y - N ≤ 4).

	Barth 2006	Bertelli 2006	Parentis 2006	Farber 2006	Gill 2007	Kim 2007	Lewis 2007	Miller 2008	Bushnell 2008	Oh 2008	Silva 2008	Ebinger 2008	Walsworth 2008	Kibler 2009[76]	Levy 2009[77]
1. Was the spectrum of patients representative of the patients who will receive the test in practice?	Y	U	Y	Y	U	Y	Y	Y	Y	Y	Y	Y	Y	U	U
2. Were selection criteria clearly described?	U	U	Y	N	Y	Y	Y	Y	Y	Y	Y	U	U	U	U
3. Is the reference standard likely to correctly classify the target condition?	Y	Y	Y	Y	Y	Y	N	Y	Y	Y	U	Y	Y	Y	Y
4. Is the time period between reference standard and index test short enough to be reasonably sure that the target condition did not change between the two tests?	U	U	U	U	U	U	Y	Y	U	Y	Y	Y	U	U	U
5. Did the whole sample or a random selection of the sample, receive verification using a reference standard of diagnosis?	Y	Y	Y	Y	Y	Y	Y	Y	Y	Y	Y	Y	Y	N	Y
6. Did patients receive the same reference standard regardless of the index test result?	Y	Y	Y	Y	Y	Y	Y	Y	Y	Y	Y	Y	Y	N	Y
7. Was the reference standard independent of the index test (i.e., the index test did not form part of the reference standard)?	Y	Y	Y	Y	Y	Y	Y	Y	Y	Y	Y	Y	Y	Y	Y
8. Was the execution of the index test described in sufficient detail to permit replication of the test?	Y	Y	Y	Y	Y	Y	Y	Y	Y	Y	Y	Y	Y	Y	U
9. Was the execution of the reference standard described in sufficient detail to permit its replication?	Y	Y	U	Y	Y	Y	U	Y	Y	Y	Y	Y	Y	Y	U
10. Were the index test results interpreted without knowledge of the results of the reference test?	Y	Y	Y	Y	Y	Y	U	Y	Y	Y	Y	Y	Y	Y	Y
11. Were the reference standard results interpreted without knowledge of the results of the index test?	U	U	U	U	U	U	U	Y	U	U	Y	Y	U	Y	U

(Continued)

Quality Assessment of Diagnostic Studies Using QUADAS

	Barth 2006	Bertelli 2006	Parentis 2006	Farber 2006	Gill 2007	Kim 2007	Lewis 2007	Miller 2008	Bushnell 2008	Oh 2008	Silva 2008	Ebinger 2008	Walsworth 2008	Kibler 2009[76]	Levy 2009[77]
12. Were the same clinical data available when test results were interpreted as would be available when the test is used in practice?	U	U	Y	Y	Y	N	U	Y	Y	Y	Y	Y	Y	Y	N
13. Were uninterpretable/ intermediate test results reported?	U	U	Y	U	Y	Y	U	U	U	U	U	U	Y	U	U
14. Were withdrawals from the study explained?	U	U	U	U	Y	Y	Y	Y	U	Y	Y	Y	Y	U	U
Quality summary rating:	◯	◯	◇	◯	◇	◇	◯	◇	◇	◇	◇	◇	◇	■	■

Y = yes, N = no, U = unclear. ◇ Good quality (Y - N = 10 to 14). ◯ Fair quality (Y - N = 5 to 9). ■ Poor quality (Y - N ≤ 4).

REFERENCES

1. Lewis JS, Valentine RE. The pectoralis minor length test: a study of the intra-rater reliability and diagnostic accuracy in subjects with and without shoulder symptoms. *BMC Musculoskelet Disord*. 2007;8:64.

2. Oh JH, Kim JY, Kim WS, et al. The evaluation of various physical examinations for the diagnosis of type II superior labrum anterior and posterior lesion. *Am J Sports Med*. 2008;36:353-359.

3. Norkin CC, Levangie PK. The shoulder complex. In: *Joint Structure and Function: A Comprehensive Analysis*. 2nd ed. Philadelphia: FA Davis; 1992.240-261.

4. Inman VT, Saunders SJB, Abbott LC. Observations on the function of the shoulder joint. 1944. *Clin Orthop*. 1996;330:3-12.

5. Neumann DA. Shoulder complex. In: *Kinesiology of Musculoskeletal System: Foundations for Physical Rehabilitation*. St. Louis: Mosby; 2002.189-248.

6. Brody LT. Shoulder. *Current Concepts of Orthopaedic Physical Therapy (11.2.6)*. La Crosse, WI: Orthopaedic Section, American Physical Therapy Association; 2001.

7. Michener LA, Walsworth MK, Burnet EN. Effectiveness of rehabilitation for patients with subacromial impingement syndrome: a systematic review. *J Hand Ther*. 2004;17:152-164.

8. Hartley A. *Practical Joint Assessment*. St Louis: Mosby; 1995.

9. Berg EE, Ciullo JV. A clinical test for superior glenoid labral or "SLAP" lesions. *Clin J Sport Med*. 1998;8:121-123.

10. Liu SH, Henry MH, Nuccion SL. A prospective evaluation of a new physical examination in predicting glenoid labral tears. *Am J Sports Med*. 1996;24:721-725.

11. Litaker D, Pioro M, El Bilbeisi H, et al. Returning to the bedside: using the history and physical examination to identify rotator cuff tears. *J Am Geriatr Soc*. 2000;48:1633-1637.

12. Cleland J, Durall CJ. Physical therapy for adhesive capsulitis. *Physiotherapy*. 2002;88:450-457.

13. Rayan GM, Jensen C. Thoracic outlet syndrome: provocative examination maneuvers in a typical population. *J Shoulder Elbow Surg*. 1995;4:113-117.

14. Winsor T, Brow R. Costoclavicular syndrome: its diagnosis and treatment. *JAMA*. 2004;196:109-111.

15. Wainner RS, Gill H. Diagnosis and nonoperative management of cervical radiculopathy. *J Orthop Sports Phys Ther*. 2000;30:728-744.

16. Walsworth MK, Doukas WC, Murphy KP, et al. Reliability and diagnostic accuracy of history and physical examination for diagnosing glenoid labral tears. *Am J Sports Med*. 2008;36:162-168.

17. Riddle DL, Rothstein JM, Lamb RL. Goniometric reliability in a clinical setting. Shoulder measurements. *Phys Ther*. 1987;67:668-673.

18. Terwee CB, de Winter AF, Scholten RJ, et al. Interobsever reproducibility of the visual estimation of range of motion of the shoulder. *Arch Phys Med Rehabil*. 2005;86:1356-1361.

19. Yang JL, Lin JJ. Reliability of function-related tests in patients with shoulder pathologies. *J Orthop Sports Phys Ther*. 2006;36:572-576.

20. Nomden JG, Slagers AJ, Bergman GJ, et al. Interobserver reliability of physical examination of shoulder girdle. *Man Ther*. 2009;14:152-159.

21. Wang SS, Normile SO, Lawshe BT. Reliability and smallest detectable change determination for serratus anterior muscle strength and endurance tests. *Physiother Theory Pract*. 2006;22:33-42.

22. Michener LA, Boardman ND, Pidcoe PE, Frith AM. Scapular muscle tests in subjects with shoulder pain and functional loss: reliability and construct validity. *Phys Ther*. 2005;85:1128-1138.

23. Dover G, Powers ME. Reliability of joint position sense and force-reproduction measures during internal and external rotation of the shoulder. *J Athl Train*. 2003;38:304-310.

24. Borstad JD, Mathiowetz KM, Minday LE, et al. Clinical measurement of posterior shoulder flexibility. *Man Ther*. 2007;12:386-389.

25. Boyd EA, Torrance GM. Clinical measures of shoulder subluxation: their reliability. *Can J Public Health*. 1992;83(Suppl 2):S24-S28.

26. Gill HS, El Rassi G, Bahk MS, et al. Physical examination for partial tears of the biceps tendon. *Am J Sports Med*. 2007;35:1334-1340.

27. Guanche CA, Jones DC. Clinical testing for tears of the glenoid labrum. *Arthroscopy*. 2003;19:517-523.

28. Nakagawa S, Yoneda M, Hayashida K, et al. Forced shoulder abduction and elbow flexion test: a new simple clinical test to detect superior labral injury in the throwing shoulder. *Arthroscopy*. 2005;21:1290-1295A.

29. Nijs J, Roussel N, Vermeulen K, et al. Scapular positioning in patients with shoulder pain: a study examining the reliability and clinical importance of 3 clinical tests. *Arch Phys Med Rehabil*. 2005;86:1349-1355.

30. Odom CJ, Taylor AB, Hurd CE, et al. Measurement of scapular asymmetry and assessment of shoulder dysfunction using the Lateral Scapular Slide Test: a reliability and validity study. *Phys Ther*. 2001;81:799-809.

31. Kibler WB, Uhl TL, Maddux JW, et al. Qualitative clinical evaluation of scapular dysfunction: A reliability study. *J Shoulder Elbow Surg*. 2002;11:550-556.

32. Hanchard NC, Howe TE, Gilbert MM. Diagnosis of shoulder pain by history and selective tissue tension: agreement between assessors. *J Orthop Sports Phys Ther*. 2005;35:147-153.

33. de Winter AF, Jans MP, Scholten RJ, et al. Diagnostic classification of shoulder disorders: interobserver agreement and determinants of disagreement. *Ann Rheum Dis*. 1999;58:272-277.

34. Levy AS, Lintner S, Kenter K, et al. Intra- and interobserver reproducibility of the shoulder laxity examination. *Am J Sports Med.* 1999;27:460-463.

35. Bushnell BD, Creighton RA, Herring MM. The bony apprehension test for instability of the shoulder: a prospective pilot analysis. *Arthroscopy.* 2008;24:974-982.

36. Farber AJ, Castillo R, Clough M, et al. Clinical assessment of three common tests for traumatic anterior shoulder instability. *J Bone Joint Surg Am.* 2006;88:1467-1474.

37. Speer KP, Hannafin JA, Altchek DW, Warren RF. An evaluation of the shoulder relocation test. *Am J Sports Med.* 1994;22:177-183.

38. Parentis MA, Glousman RE, Mohr KS, et al. An evaluation of the provocative tests for superior labral anterior posterior lesions. *Am J Sports Med.* 2006;34:265-268.

39. Myers TH, Zemanovic JR, Andrews JR. The resisted supination external rotation test: a new test for the diagnosis of superior labral anterior posterior lesions. *Am J Sports Med.* 2005;33:1315-1320.

40. Stetson WB, Templin K. The crank test, the O'Brien test, and routine magnetic resonance imaging scans in the diagnosis of labral tears. *Am J Sports Med.* 2002;30:806-809.

41. McFarland EG, Kim TK, Savino RM. Clinical assessment of three common tests for superior labral anterior-posterior lesions. *Am J Sports Med.* 2002;30:810-815.

42. Hegedus EJ, Goode A, Campbell S, et al. Physical examination tests of the shoulder: a systematic review with meta-analysis of individual tests. *Br J Sports Med.* 2008;42:80-92; discussion 92.

43. Ebinger N, Magosch P, Lichtenberg S, Habermeyer P. A new SLAP test: the supine flexion resistance test. *Arthroscopy.* 2008;24:500-505.

44. Holtby R, Razmjou H. Accuracy of the Speed's and Yergason's tests in detecting biceps pathology and SLAP lesions: comparison with arthroscopic findings. *Arthroscopy.* 2004;20:231-236.

45. Kim YS, Kim JM, Ha KY, et al. The passive compression test: a new clinical test for superior labral tears of the shoulder. *Am J Sports Med.* 2007;35:1489-1494.

46. Kim SH, Park JS, Jeong WK, et al. The Kim test: a novel test for posteroinferior labral lesion of the shoulder—a comparison to the jerk test. *Am J Sports Med.* 2005;33:1188-1192.

47. Kim SH, Ha KI, Ahn JH, et al. Biceps load test II: a clinical test for SLAP lesions of the shoulder. *Arthroscopy.* 2001;17:160-164.

48. Kim SH, Ha KI, Han KY. Biceps load test: a clinical test for superior labrum anterior and posterior lesions in shoulders with recurrent anterior dislocations. *Am J Sports Med.* 1999;27:300-303.

49. Johansson K, Ivarson S. Intra- and interexaminer reliability of four manual shoulder maneuvers used to identify subacromial pain. *Man Ther.* 2009;14:231-239.

50. Silva L, Andreu JL, Munoz P et al. Accuracy of physical examination in subacromial impingement syndrome. *Rheumatology (Oxford).* 2008;47:679-683.

51. Park HB, Yokota A, Gill HS, et al. Diagnostic accuracy of clinical tests for the different degrees of subacromial impingement syndrome. *J Bone Joint Surg Am.* 2005;87:1446-1455.

52. Calis M, Akgun K, Birtane M, et al. Diagnostic values of clinical diagnostic tests in subacromial impingement syndrome. *Ann Rheum Dis.* 2000;59:44-47.

53. Zaslav KR. Internal rotation resistance strength test: a new diagnostic test to differentiate intra-articular pathology fropm outlet (Neer) impingement syndrome in the shoulder. *J Shoulder Elbow Surg.* 2001;10:23-27.

54. Miller CA, Forrester GA, Lewis JS. The validity of the lag signs in diagnosing full-thickness tears of the rotator cuff: a preliminary investigation. *Arch Phys Med Rehabil.* 2008;89:1162-1168.

55. Walch G, Boulahia A, Calderone S, et al. The "dropping" and "hornblower's" signs in evaluation of rotator-cuff tears. *J Bone Joint Surg Br.* 1998;80:624-628.

56. Holtby R, Razmjou H. Validity of the supraspinatus test as a single clinical test in diagnosing patients with rotator cuff pathology. *J Orthop Sports Phys Ther.* 2004;34:194-200.

57. Hertel R, Ballmer FT, Lombert SM, Gerber C. Lag signs in the diagnosis of rotator cuff rupture. *J Shoulder Elbow Surg.* 1996;5:307-313.

58. Barth JR, Burkhart SS, De Beer JF. The bear-hug test: a new and sensitive test for diagnosing a subscapularis tear. *Arthroscopy.* 2006;22:1076-1084.

59. Bertelli JA, Ghizoni MF. Use of clinical signs and computed tomography myelography findings in detecting and excluding nerve root avulsion in complete brachial plexus palsy. *J Neurosurg.* 2006;105:835-842.

60. Walton J, Mahajan S, Paxinos A, et al. Diagnostic values of tests for acromioclavicular joint pain. *J Bone Joint Surg Am.* 2004;86-A:807-812.

61. Stratford PW, Binkley JM, Stratford DM. Development and initial validation of the upper extremity functional index. *Physiotherapy Canada.* 2001;53:259-263.

62. Roy JS, MacDermid JC, Woodhouse LJ. Measuring shoulder function: a systematic review of four questionnaires. *Arthritis Rheum.* 2009;61:623-632.

63. Mintken PE, Glynn P, Cleland JA. Psychometric properties of the shortened disabilities of the Arm, Shoulder, and Hand Questionnaire (QuickDASH) and Numeric Pain Rating Scale in patients with shoulder pain. *J Shoulder Elbow Surg.* 2009

64. Li L, Liu X, Herr K. Postoperative pain intensity assessment: a comparison of four scales in Chinese adults. *Pain Med.* 2007;8:223-234.

65. Farrar JT, Berlin JA, Strom BL. Clinically important changes in acute pain outcome measures: a validation study. *J Pain Symptom Manage.* 2003;25:406-411.

66. Farrar JT, Portenoy RK, Berlin JA, et al. Defining the clinically important difference in pain outcome measures. *Pain.* 2000;88:287-294.

67. Lyons AR, Tomlinson JE. Clinical diagnosis of tears of the rotator cuff. *J Bone Joint Surg Br*. 1992;74:414-415.

68. Kibler WB. Specificity and sensitivity of the anterior slide test in throwing athletes with superior glenoid labral tears. *Arthroscopy*. 1995;11:296-300.

69. Leroux JL, Thomas E, Bonnel F, Blotman F. Diagnostic value of clinical tests for shoulder impingement syndrome. *Rev Rhum Engl Ed*. 1995;62:423-428.

70. Gross ML, Distefano MC. Anterior release test. A new test for occult shoulder instability. *Clin Orthop Relat Res*. 1997;105-108.

71. O'Brien SJ, Pagnani MJ, Fealy S, et al. The active compression test: a new and effective test for diagnosing labral tears and acromioclavicular joint abnormality. *Am J Sports Med*. 1998;26:610-613.

72. Itoi E, Kido T, Sano A, et al. Which is more useful, the "full can test" or the "empty can test" in detecting the torn supraspinatus tendon? *Am J Sports Med*. 1999;27:65-68.

73. Mimori K, Muneta T, Nakagawa T, Shinomiya K. A new pain provocation test for superior labral tears of the shoulder. *Am J Sports Med*. 1999;27:137-142.

74. Murrell GA, Walton JR. Diagnosis of rotator cuff tears. *Lancet*. 2001;357:769-770.

75. Wolf EM, Agrawal V. Transdeltoid palpation (the rent test) in the diagnosis of rotator cuff tears. *J Shoulder Elbow Surg*. 2001;10:470-473.

76. Kibler WB, Sciascia AD, Hester P, et al. Clinical utility of traditional and new tests in the diagnosis of biceps tendon injuries and superior labrum anterior and posterior lesions in the shoulder. *Am J Sports Med*. 2009;37:1840-1847.

77. Levy O, Relwani JG, Mullett H, et al. The active elevation lag sign and the triangle sign: new clinical signs of trapezius palsy. *J Shoulder Elbow Surg*. 2009;18:573-576.

Elbow and Forearm

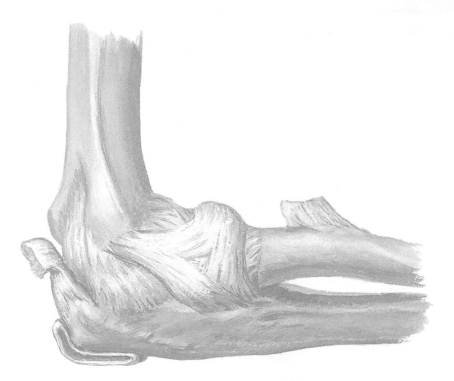

CLINICAL SUMMARY AND RECOMMENDATIONS

Patient History	
Complaints	• Little is known about the utility of subjective complaints with elbow pain.

Physical Examination	
Range of Motion	• Measuring elbow range of motion (ROM) has consistently been shown to exhibit good to high reliability for flexion, extension, supination, and pronation.
Strength Assessment	• Grip strength testing in patients with lateral epicondylalgia exhibits high inter-rater reliability.
Special Tests	• In general few studies have examined the diagnostic utility for special tests of the elbow. • The elbow extension test has been consistently been shown to be an excellent test to rule out the presence of bony or joint injury (sensitivity values between .91 and .97 and −LR values between exhibit .04 and .13). • The pressure provocation test, the flexion test, and the Tinel sign at the elbow have been found to be useful tests for identifying the presence of cubital tunnel syndrome. • The moving valgus stress test has been shown to exhibit superior diagnostic accuracy when compared with the valgus stress test for identifying a medial collateral tear. • No studies to date have examined the utility of the varus stress test for identifying the presence of a lateral collateral tear.

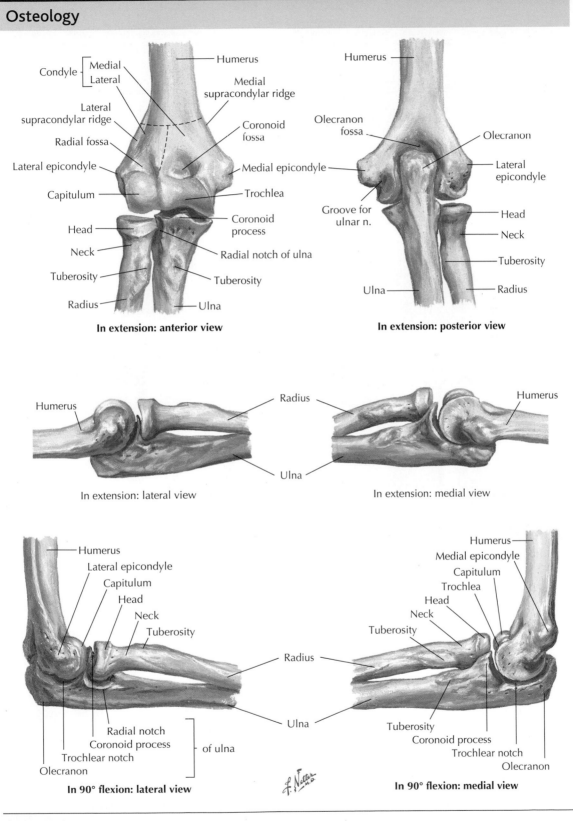

In extension: anterior view

In extension: posterior view

In extension: lateral view

In extension: medial view

In 90° flexion: lateral view

In 90° flexion: medial view

Figure 10-1

Bones of elbow.

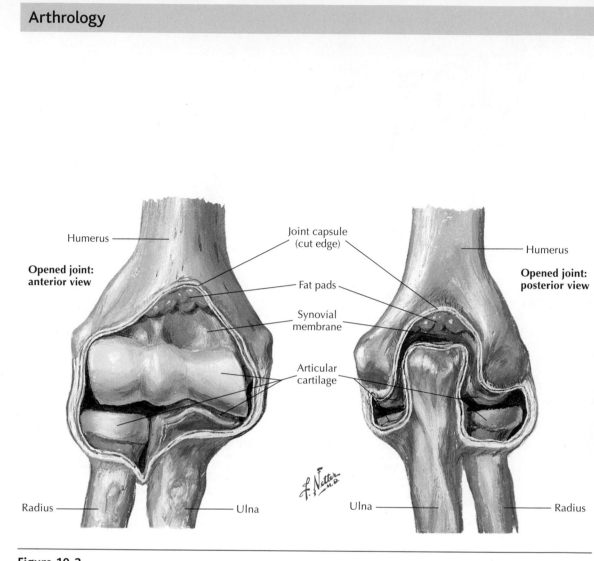

Figure 10-2
Anterior and posterior opened elbow joint.

Joint	Type and Classification	Closed Packed Position	Capsular Pattern
Humeroulnar	Synovial: hinge	Elbow extension	Flexion is limited more than extension
Humeroradial	Synovial: condyloid	0° of flexion, 5° of supination	Flexion is limited more than extension
Proximal radioulnar	Synovial: trochoid	5° of supination	Pronation = supination
Distal radioulnar	Synovial: trochoid	5° of supination	Pronation = supination

Ligaments

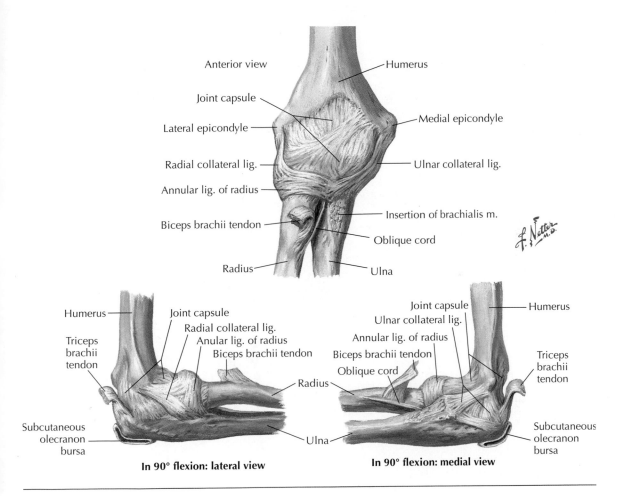

Figure 10-3

Ligaments of the elbow.

Ligaments	Attachments	Function
Radial collateral	Lateral epicondyle of humerus to annular ligament of radius	Resists varus stress
Annular ligament of radius	Coronoid process of ulna, around radial head to lateral border of radial notch of ulna	Holds head of radius in radial notch of ulna and allows forearm supination and pronation
Ulnar collateral	Medial epicondyle of humerus to coronoid process and olecranon of ulna	Resists valgus stress

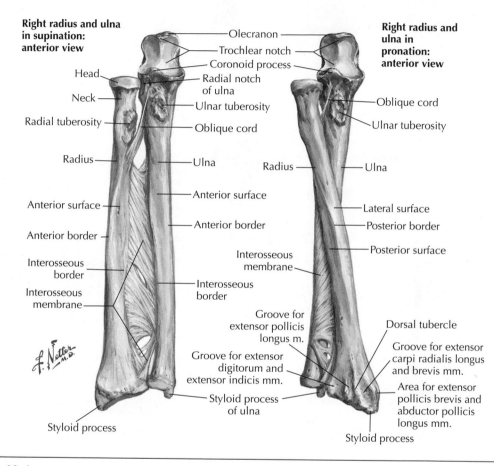

Right radius and ulna in supination: anterior view

Olecranon
Trochlear notch
Coronoid process
Radial notch of ulna
Head
Neck
Ulnar tuberosity
Radial tuberosity
Oblique cord
Radius
Ulna
Anterior surface
Anterior surface
Anterior border
Anterior border
Interosseous border
Interosseous membrane
Interosseous border
Interosseous membrane
Groove for extensor pollicis longus m.
Groove for extensor digitorum and extensor indicis mm.
Styloid process of ulna
Styloid process

Right radius and ulna in pronation: anterior view

Oblique cord
Ulnar tuberosity
Radius
Ulna
Lateral surface
Posterior border
Posterior surface
Dorsal tubercle
Groove for extensor carpi radialis longus and brevis mm.
Area for extensor pollicis brevis and abductor pollicis longus mm.
Styloid process

Figure 10-4

Ligaments of the forearm.

Ligaments	Attachments	Function
Oblique cord	Tuberosity of ulna to just distal to tuberosity of radius	Transfers forces from radius to ulna and reinforces proximity of ulna to radius
Interosseous membrane	Lateral border of ulna to medial border of radius	Transfers force from radius to ulna and reinforces proximity of ulna to radius

Muscles

Anterior and Posterior Muscles of Arm

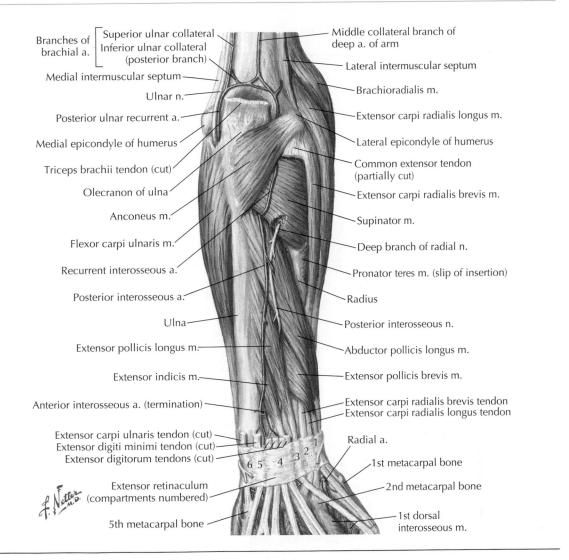

Branches of brachial a. [Superior ulnar collateral
Inferior ulnar collateral
(posterior branch)

Medial intermuscular septum

Ulnar n.

Posterior ulnar recurrent a.

Medial epicondyle of humerus

Triceps brachii tendon (cut)

Olecranon of ulna

Anconeus m.

Flexor carpi ulnaris m.

Recurrent interosseous a.

Posterior interosseous a.

Ulna

Extensor pollicis longus m.

Extensor indicis m.

Anterior interosseous a. (termination)

Extensor carpi ulnaris tendon (cut)
Extensor digiti minimi tendon (cut)
Extensor digitorum tendons (cut)

Extensor retinaculum
(compartments numbered)

5th metacarpal bone

Middle collateral branch of
deep a. of arm

Lateral intermuscular septum

Brachioradialis m.

Extensor carpi radialis longus m.

Lateral epicondyle of humerus

Common extensor tendon
(partially cut)

Extensor carpi radialis brevis m.

Supinator m.

Deep branch of radial n.

Pronator teres m. (slip of insertion)

Radius

Posterior interosseous n.

Abductor pollicis longus m.

Extensor pollicis brevis m.

Extensor carpi radialis brevis tendon
Extensor carpi radialis longus tendon

Radial a.

1st metacarpal bone

2nd metacarpal bone

1st dorsal
interosseous m.

Figure 10-5

Muscles of forearm: posterior view.

Muscle	Proximal Attachment	Distal Attachment	Nerve and Segmental Level	Action
Triceps brachii				
Long head	Infraglenoid tubercle of scapula	Olecranon process of ulna	Radial nerve (C6, C7, C8)	Extends elbow
Lateral head	Superior to radial groove of humerus			
Medial head	Inferior to radial grove of humerus			
Anconeus	Lateral epicondyle of humerus	Superoposterior aspect of ulna	Radial nerve (C7, C8, T1)	Assists in elbow extension, stabilizes elbow joint

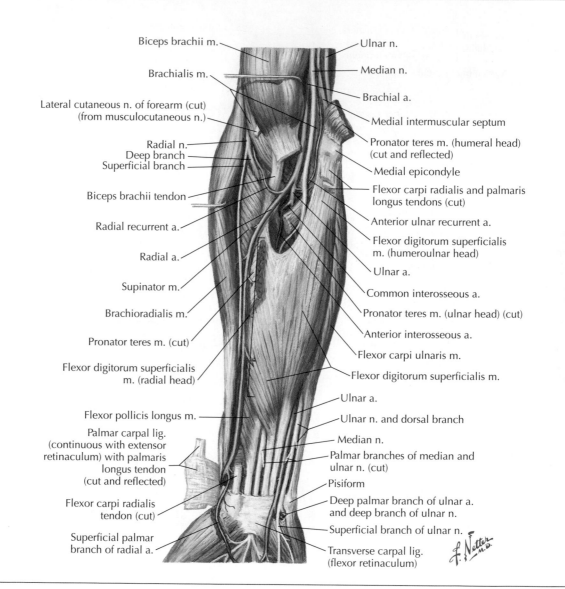

Biceps brachii m.

Brachialis m.

Lateral cutaneous n. of forearm (cut)
(from musculocutaneous n.)

Radial n.
Deep branch
Superficial branch

Biceps brachii tendon

Radial recurrent a.

Radial a.

Supinator m.

Brachioradialis m.

Pronator teres m. (cut)

Flexor digitorum superficialis
m. (radial head)

Flexor pollicis longus m.

Palmar carpal lig.
(continuous with extensor
retinaculum) with palmaris
longus tendon
(cut and reflected)

Flexor carpi radialis
tendon (cut)

Superficial palmar
branch of radial a.

Ulnar n.

Median n.

Brachial a.

Medial intermuscular septum

Pronator teres m. (humeral head)
(cut and reflected)

Medial epicondyle

Flexor carpi radialis and palmaris
longus tendons (cut)

Anterior ulnar recurrent a.

Flexor digitorum superficialis
m. (humeroulnar head)

Ulnar a.

Common interosseous a.

Pronator teres m. (ulnar head) (cut)

Anterior interosseous a.

Flexor carpi ulnaris m.

Flexor digitorum superficialis m.

Ulnar a.

Ulnar n. and dorsal branch

Median n.

Palmar branches of median and
ulnar n. (cut)

Pisiform

Deep palmar branch of ulnar a.
and deep branch of ulnar n.

Superficial branch of ulnar n.

Transverse carpal lig.
(flexor retinaculum)

Figure 10-6

Muscles of forearm: anterior view.

Muscle	Proximal Attachment	Distal Attachment	Nerve and Segmental Level	Action
Biceps brachii				
Short head	Coronoid process of scapula	Radial tuberosity and fascia of forearm	Musculocutaneus nerve (C5, C6)	Supinates forearm and flex elbow
Long head	Supraglenoid tubercle of scapula			
Brachialis	Distal aspect of humerus	Coronoid process and tuberosity of ulna	Musculocutaneus nerve (C5, C6)	Flexes elbow

Muscles

Supinators and Pronators of the Forearm

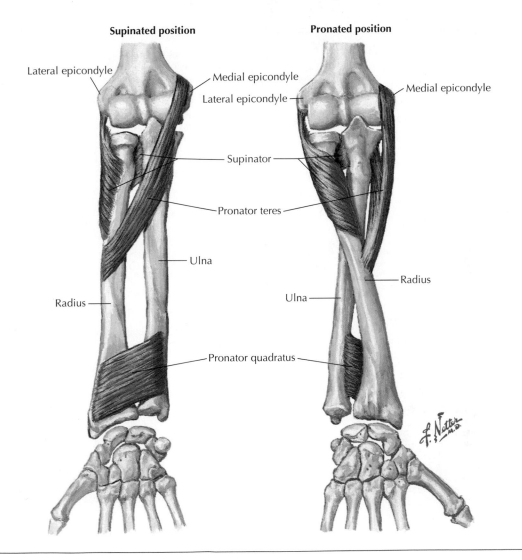

Supinated position

Pronated position

Lateral epicondyle

Medial epicondyle

Lateral epicondyle

Medial epicondyle

Supinator

Pronator teres

Ulna

Radius

Radius

Ulna

Pronator quadratus

Figure 10-7
Individual muscles of forearm: rotators of radius.

Muscle	Proximal Attachment	Distal Attachment	Nerve and Segmental Level	Action
Supinator	Lateral epicondyle of humerus, supinator fossa, and crest of ulna	Proximal aspect of radius	Deep branch of radial nerve (C5, C6)	Supinates forearm
Pronator teres	Medial epicondyle of humerus and coronoid process of ulna	Lateral aspect of radius	Median nerve (C6, C7)	Pronates forearm and flexes elbow
Pronator quadratus	Distal anterior aspect of ulna	Distal anterior aspect of radius	Anterior interosseus nerve (C8, T1)	Pronates forearm

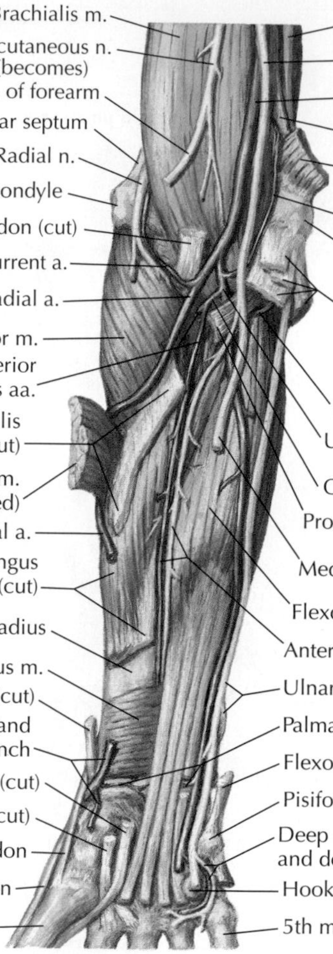

Figure 10-8

Nerves of forearm: anterior view.

Brachialis m.
Musculocutaneous n. (becomes)
Lateral cutaneous n. of forearm
Lateral intermuscular septum
Radial n.
Lateral epicondyle
Biceps brachii tendon (cut)
Radial recurrent a.
Radial a.
Supinator m.
Posterior and anterior interosseous aa.
Flexor digitorum superficialis m. (radial head) (cut)
Pronator teres m. (cut and reflected)
Radial a.
Flexor pollicis longus m. and tendon (cut)
Radius
Pronator quadratus m.
Brachioradialis tendon (cut)
Radial a. and superficial palmar branch
Flexor pollicis longus tendon (cut)
Flexor carpi radialis tendon (cut)
Abductor pollicis longus tendon
Extensor pollicis brevis tendon
1st metacarpal bone

Ulnar n.
Median n.
Brachial a.
Medial intermuscular septum
Pronator teres m. (cut and reflected)
Anterior ulnar recurrent a.
Medial epicondyle of humerus
Flexor carpi radialis, palmaris longus, flexor digitorum superficialis (humeroulnar head) and flexor carpi ulnaris mm. (cut)
Posterior ulnar recurrent a.
Ulnar a.
Common interosseous a.
Pronator teres m. (ulnar head) (cut)
Median n. (cut)
Flexor digitorum profundus m.
Anterior interosseous a. and n.
Ulnar n. and dorsal branch
Palmar carpal branches of radial and ulnar aa.
Flexor carpi ulnaris tendon (cut)
Pisiform
Deep palmar branch of ulnar a. and deep branch of ulnar n.
Hook of hamate
5th metacarpal bone

Nerves	Segmental Levels	Sensory	Motor
Musculocutaneus	C5, C6, C7	Lateral antebrachial cutaneous nerve	Coracobrachialis, biceps brachii, brachialis
Lateral cutaneous of forearm	C5, C6, C7	Lateral forearm	No motor
Median	C6, C7, C8, T1	Palmar and distal dorsal aspects of lateral 3$\frac{1}{2}$ digits and lateral palm	Flexor carpi radialis, flexor digitorum superficialis, lateral $\frac{1}{2}$ of flexor digitorum profundus, flexor pollicis longus, pronator quadratus, pronator teres, most thenar muscles, and lateral lumbricales
Anterior interosseous	C6, C7, C8, T1	No sensory	Flexor digitorum profundus, flexor pollicis longus, pronator quadratus
Ulnar	C7, C8, T1	Medial hand including medial $\frac{1}{2}$ of 4th digit	Flexor carpi ulnaris, medial $\frac{1}{2}$ of flexor digitorum profundus, and most small muscles in hand
Radial	C5, C6, C7, C8, T1	Posterior aspect of forearm	Triceps brachii, anconeus, brachioradialis, extensor muscles of forearm
Posterior interosseous	C5, C6, C7, C8, T1	None	Abductor pollicis longus, extensor pollicis brevis and longus, extensor digitorum communis, extensor indicis, extensor digiti minimi

Initial Hypotheses Based on History

History	Initial Hypothesis
Pain over lateral elbow during gripping activities	Possible lateral epicondylitis[1-4] Possible radial tunnel syndrome[5-7]
Pain over medial elbow during wrist flexion and pronation	Possible medial epicondylitis[8,9]
Reports of numbness and tingling in ulnar nerve distribution distal to elbow	Possible cubital tunnel syndrome[9,10]
Pain in anterior aspect of elbow and forearm that is exacerbated by wrist flexion combined with elbow flexion and forearm pronation	Possible pronator syndrome[11]
Reports of pain during movement with sensations of catching or instability	Possible rotatory instability[11]
Reports of posterior elbow pain during elbow hyperextension	Possible valgus extension overload syndrome[11]

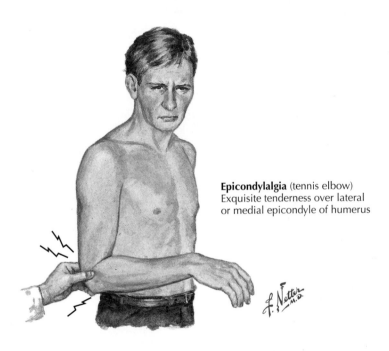

Epicondylalgia (tennis elbow)
Exquisite tenderness over lateral
or medial epicondyle of humerus

Figure 10-9

Palpation of lateral epicondyle.

Reliability of Elbow Flexion and Extension Measurements

ICC or κ	Interpretation
.81-1.0	Substantial agreement
.61-.80	Moderate agreement
.41-.60	Fair agreement
.11-.40	Slight agreement
.0-.10	No agreement

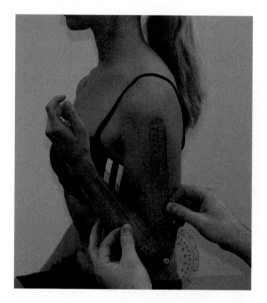

Figure 10-10

Measurement of elbow flexion.

Test and Measure	Instrumentation	Population	Reliability ICC	
			Intra-examiner	**Inter-examiner**
Active ROM (AROM) elbow flexion[12]	12-inch metal goniometer	24 patients referred to physical therapy in whom ROM measurements of elbow were appropriate	.94	.89
	10-inch plastic goniometer		.97	.96
	6-inch plastic goniometer		.96	.90
AROM elbow extension[12]	12-inch metal goniometer		.86	.96
	10-inch plastic goniometer		.96	.94
	6-inch plastic goniometer		.99	.93
AROM elbow flexion[13]	Universal standard goniometer	38 patients who had undergone a surgical procedure for injury at elbow, forearm, or wrist	.55-.98	.58-.62
AROM elbow extension[13]			.45-.98	.58-.87
AROM elbow flexion[14]	Universal plastic goniometer	30 healthy subjects	**Not reported**	.53
	Fluid-filled bubble inclinometer		**Not reported**	.92

Range of Motion

Reliability of Forearm Supination and Pronation Measurements

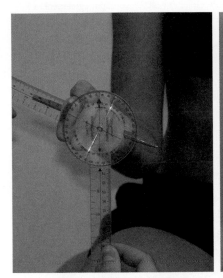

Measurement of forearm supination

Measurement of forearm pronation

Figure 10-11

Forearm supination and pronation measurements.

Test and Measure		Instrumentation	Population		Reliability ICC	
					Intra-examiner	Inter-examiner
AROM[13]	Supination	Universal standard goniometer	38 patients who had undergone a surgical procedure for elbow, forearm, or wrist injury		.96 -.99	.90-.93
	Pronation				.96-.99	.83 -.86
AROM[15]	Supination	14.5-cm plastic goniometer	40 subjects, 20 injured and 20 non-injured	injured	.98	.96
				non-injured	.96	.94
	Pronation			injured	.95-.97	.95
				non-injured	.86-.98	.92
	Supination	Plumb line goniometer: a 14.5-cm single arm plastic goniometer with a plumb line attached to the center of its 360°		injured	.98	.96
				non-injured	.94-.98	.96
	Pronation			injured	.96-.98	.92
				non-injured	.95-.97	.91
AROM Supination/pronation[16]		8-inch steel goniometer	31 asymptomatic subjects		.81-.97	Not reported
Passive ROM (PROM)[17]	Supination	Plumb line goniometer	30 hand therapy patients		.95	Not reported
	Pronation				.87	Not reported
	Supination	Standard goniometer			.95	Not reported
	Pronation				.79	Not reported

ICC, Intraclass correlation coefficient.

End-Feel Classification

Reliability of Classification on End-Feel for Elbow Flexion and Extension

ICC or κ	Interpretation
.81-1.0	Substantial agreement
.61-.80	Moderate agreement
.41-.60	Fair agreement
.11-.40	Slight agreement
.0-.10	No agreement

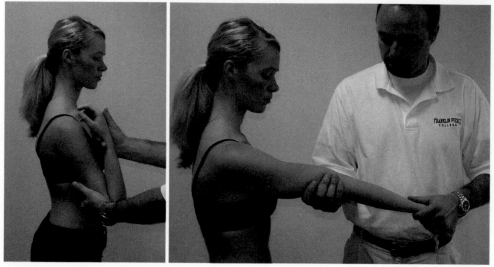

Assessment of flexion end-feel   Assessment of extension end-feel

Figure 10-12

End-feel for elbow flexion and extension assessment.

Test and Measure	Test Procedure	Population	Inter-examiner Reliability
Flexion/extension[18]	With patient standing, examiner stabilizes humerus with one hand and maintains forearm in neutral with the other hand. Examiner extends or flexes elbow and assesses end-feel. End-feel is graded as "soft tissue approximation," "muscular," "cartilage," "capsule," or "ligament"	20 asymptomatic subjects	Flexion κ = **.40** Extension κ = **.73**

Assessing Strength

Reliability of Grip Strength Testing in Patients with Lateral Epicondylalgia

Grip Strength	Test Procedure	Population	Inter-examiner Reliability
Pain-free[19]	With patient standing with elbow extended and forearm in neutral, patient squeezes dynamometer until discomfort is felt	50 patients diagnosed with lateral epicondylalgia on clinical examination	ICC = **.97**
Maximum[19]	As above except patient is instructed to squeeze dynamometer as hard as possible		ICC = **.98**

Indication of Bony or Joint Injury: Elbow Extension Test

+LR	Interpretation	−LR
>10	Large	<.1
5.0-10.0	Moderate	.1-.2
2.0-5.0	Small	.2-.5
1.0-2.0	Rarely important	.5-1.0

Test	Test Procedure	Determination of Findings	Population	Reference Standard	Sens (95% CI)	Spec (95% CI)	+LR	−LR
Elbow extension test[22] ◇	With patient seated with arms supinated, patient flexes shoulders to 90° then extends both elbows	Positive if the involved elbow has less extension than the contralateral side	2127 adults and children presenting to the emergency department	Radiographic evaluation and/or a 7-to 10-day phone call follow-up	96.8 (95.0, 98.2)	48.5 (45.6, 51.4)	1.88 (1.78, 1.99)	.06 (.04, .10)
Elbow extension test[20] ◯	Supine patient fully extends elbow	Positive if patient is unable to fully extend elbow	114 patients with acute elbow injuries	Radiographic evaluation	.97	.69	3.13	.04
Elbow extension test[21] ◯	As above except patient is standing	As above	100 patients presenting to an emergency department with elbow injury	As above	.91 (.81, 1.0)	.70 (.61, .78)	3.03	.13

+LR	Interpretation	−LR
>10	Large	<.1
5.0-10.0	Moderate	.1-.2
2.0-5.0	Small	.2-.5
1.0-2.0	Rarely important	.5-1.0

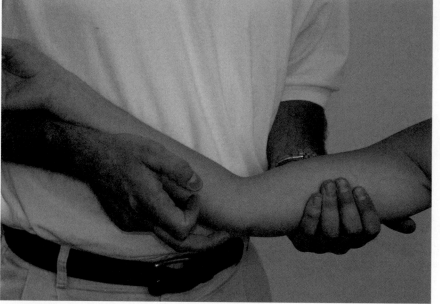

Figure 10-13
Tinel's sign.

Test and Measure	Test Procedure	Determination of Positive Findings	Population	Reference Standard	Sens	Spec	+LR	−LR
Pressure provocative test[23]	With patient's elbow in 20° of flexion and forearm supination, examiner applies pressure to ulnar nerve just proximal to cubital tunnel for 60 sec	Positive if patient reports symptoms in distribution of ulnar nerve			.89	.98	44.5	.11
Flexion test[23]	Patient's elbow is placed in maximum flexion with full supination of forearm and wrist in neutral. Position is held for 60 sec	As above	55 subjects, 32 with cubital tunnel syndrome and 33 asymptomatic subjects	Electro-diagnostically proven cubital tunnel syndrome	.75	.99	75	.25
Combined pressure and flexion provocative test[23]	Patient's arm is in maximum elbow flexion and forearm supination. Examiner applies pressure on ulnar nerve just proximal to cubital tunnel. Pressure is held for 60 sec	As above			.98	.95	19.6	.02
Tinel's sign[23]	Examiner applies 4 to 6 taps to patient's ulnar nerve just proximal to cubital tunnel	Positive if tingling sensation in distribution of ulnar nerve			.70	.98	35	.31

Special Tests

Detecting Medial Collateral Tears

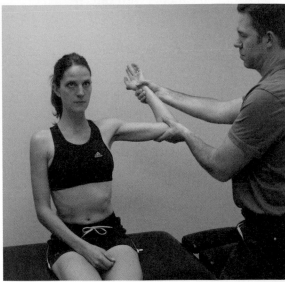

+LR	Interpretation	−LR
>10	Large	<.1
5.0-10.0	Moderate	.1-.2
2.0-5.0	Small	.2-.5
1.0-2.0	Rarely important	.5-1.0

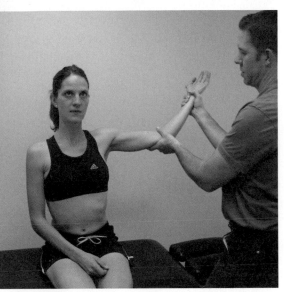

With the shoulder at 90 degrees of abduction and full external rotation, the clinician maximally flexes the patient's elbow while simultaneously applying a valgus force.

The clinician quickly extends the patient's elbow.

Figure 10-14

Moving valgus stress test.

Test and Measure	Test Procedure	Determination of Positive Findings	Patient Population	Reference Standard	Sens	Spec	+LR	−LR
Moving valgus stress test[24] ◇	Patient's shoulder is abducted to 90° with maximal external rotation. Clinician maximally flexes the elbow and applies a valgus stress. The clinician quickly extends the elbow to 30°	If patient experiences maximal medial elbow pain between 120° and 70° of elbow flexion, test is considered positive	21 patients referred with chronic medial collateral ligament injuries	Surgical visualization	1.0 (81,100)	.75 (.19, .99)	4.0 (.73, 21.8)	.04 (.00, .72)
Valgus stress test at 30°, 60°, 70°, or 90° of elbow flexion[24] ◇	Valgus stress is applied to the elbow at 30°, 60°, 70°, and 90° of elbow flexion	If the clinician identifies laxity or the patient reports pain, the test is considered positive	21 patients referred with chronic medial collateral ligament injuries	Surgical visualization	Pain .65 (.38, .86) Laxity .19 (.04, .46)	Pain .50 (.70, .93) Laxity 1.0 (.40, 1.0)	Pain 1.3 Laxity Undefined	Pain .70 Laxity .81

Diagnostic Utility of History and Physical Examination Findings for Predicting Favorable Short-Term Response to Mobilization with Movement and Exercise in Patients with Lateral Epicondylalgia

+LR	Interpretation	−LR
>10	Large	<.1
5.0-10.0	Moderate	.1-.2
2.0-5.0	Small	.2-.5
1.0-2.0	Rarely important	.5-1.0

Vicenzino and colleagues[25] have developed a preliminary clinical prediction rule to identify individuals with lateral epicondylalgia who are likely to benefit from mobilization with movement and exercise. The study identified a number of predictor variables.

Test and Study Quality	Population	Reference Standard	Sens	Spec	+LR
Age < 49 years[25]	62 patients with lateral epicondylalgia	A global perceived effect of improved, much improved, or completely recovered	.61 (.46, .74)	.77 (.46, .94)	2.6 (.96, 7.3)
Affected pain-free grip > 112 N[25]			.53 (.38, .67)	.77 (.46, .93)	2.3 (.82, 6.4)
Unaffected pain-free grip < 336 N[25]			.49 (.35, .63)	.77 (.46, .94)	2.1 (.76, 6.0)
Change in pain-free grip following the mobilization with movement > 25%[25]			.75 (.58, .87)	.5 (.78, 2.9)	1.5 (.78, 2.9)

The following three variables formed the clinical prediction rule:
1. < 49 years
2. Affected pain free grip > 112 N
3. Unaffected pain free grip < 336 N

Diagnostic accuracy for the clinical prediction rule is as follows:			
Number of variables present	Sens	Spec	+LR
3	.01 (.03, .20)	1.0 (.7, 1.0)	Undefined
2	.57 (.42, .71)	.85 (.54, .97)	3.7 (1.0, 13.6)
1	.98 (.88, .99)	.46 (.20, .74)	1.8 (1.1, 3.0)

OUTCOME MEASURES

Outcome Measure	Scoring and Interpretation	Test-Retest Reliability	MCID
Upper Extremity Functional Index	Users are asked to rate the difficulty of performing 20 functional tasks on a Likert-type scale ranging from 0 (extremely difficult or unable to perform activity) to 4 (no difficulty). A total score out of 80 is calculated by summing each score. The answers provide a score between 0 and 80, with lower scores representing more disability	ICC = .95[26]	Not reported; however, the MDC has been determined. MDC = 9.1 points[26]
Patient-Rated Tennis Elbow Evaluation	Users are asked to rate their levels of pain and function on two subscales. The pain subscale includes five questions and each is scored from 0 to 10 (0 = no pain, 10 = worst pain imaginable). The sum of the score on the five items is recorded as the pain score with a maximum of 50 with higher scores indicating greater levels of pain. The function subscale has 10 items and each is scored from 0 to 10 (0 = no difficulty, 10 = unable to do). The sum of the 10 items is divided by 2 and the patient can score a maximum of 50 on the functional scale with higher scores representing greater disability. To compute a total score (out of a 100) the sum of the pain and functional scales are computed	Pain ICC = .89-.99[27-29] Function ICC = .83-.99[27-29] Total ICC = .89-.99[27-29]	Not reported
Numeric Pain Rating Scale (NPRS)	Users rate their level of pain on an 11-point scale ranging from 0 to 10, with high scores representing more pain. Often asked as "current pain" and "least," "worst," and "average" pain in the past 24 hours	ICC = .72[30]	2[31,32]

MCID, Minimum clinically important difference; MDC, minimal detectable change.

Quality Assessment of Diagnostic Studies Using QUADAS

	Hawksworth 1991	Novak 1994	O'Driscoll 1995	Docherty 2002	Appelboam 2008
1. Was the spectrum of patients representative of the patients who will receive the test in practice?	Y	U	Y	Y	Y
2. Were selection criteria clearly described?	N	N	Y	Y	Y
3. Is the reference standard likely to correctly classify the target condition?	Y	Y	Y	Y	Y
4. Is the time period between reference standard and index test short enough to be reasonably sure that the target condition did not change between the two tests?	U	U	Y	Y	Y
5. Did the whole sample, or a random selection of the sample, receive verification using a reference standard of diagnosis?	Y	Y	Y	N	Y
6. Did patients receive the same reference standard regardless of the index test result?	U	Y	Y	N	N
7. Was the reference standard independent of the index test (i.e., the index test did not form part of the reference standard)?	Y	Y	Y	Y	Y
8. Was the execution of the index test described in sufficient detail to permit replication of the test?	Y	Y	Y	Y	Y
9. Was the execution of the reference standard described in sufficient detail to permit its replication?	N	Y	Y	N	N
10. Were the index test results interpreted without knowledge of the results of the reference test?	Y	U	U	Y	Y
11. Were the reference standard results interpreted without knowledge of the results of the index test?	Y	U	U	Y	Y
12. Were the same clinical data available when test results were interpreted as would be available when the test is used in practice?	Y	Y	Y	Y	Y
13. Were uninterpretable/ intermediate test results reported?	Y	U	Y	Y	Y
14. Were withdrawals from the study explained?	Y	U	Y	Y	Y
Quality summary rating:	◯	◯	◈	◯	◈

Y = yes, N = no, U = unclear. ◈ Good quality (Y - N = 10 to 14). ◯ Fair quality (Y - N = 5 to 9). ▨ Poor quality (Y - N ≤ 4).

REFERENCES

1. Baquie P. Tennis elbow. Principles of ongoing management. *Aust Fam Physician.* 1999;28:724-725.
2. Borkholder CD, Hill VA, Fess EE. The efficacy of splinting for lateral epicondylitis: a systematic review. *J Hand Ther.* 2004;17:181-199.
3. Vicenzino B. Lateral epicondylalgia: a musculoskeletal physiotherapy perspective. *Man Ther.* 2003;8:66-79.
4. Vicenzino B, Wright A. Lateral epicondylalgia I: epidemiology, pathophysiology, aetiology and natural history. *Phys Ther Rev.* 1996;1:23-34.
5. Pecina MM, Bojanic I. *Overuse Injuries of the Musculoskeletal System*, CRC Press. 1993.
6. Ellenbecker TS, Mattalino AJ. *The Elbow in Sport*, Human Kinetics. 1997.
7. Ekstrom R, Holden K. Examination of and intervention for a patient with chronic lateral elbow pain with signs of nerve entrapment. *Phys Ther.* 2002;82:1077-1086.
8. Pienimäki TT, Siira PT, Vanharanta H. Chronic medial and lateral epicondylitis: a comparison of pain, disability, and function. *Arch Phys Med Rehabil.* 2002;83:317-321.
9. Hertling D, Kessler RM. The elbow and forearm. In: *Management of Common Musculoskeletal Disorders: Physical Therapy Principles and Methods.* (3rd ed). Lippincott; 1990:217-242.
10. Kingery WS, Park KS, Wu PB, Date ES. Electromyographic motor Tinel's sign in ulnar mononeuropathies at the elbow. *Am J Phys Med Rehabil.* 1995;74:419-426.
11. Ryan J. Elbow. In *Current Concepts of Orthopaedic Physical Therapy*, Orthopaedic Section, American Physical Therapy Association. 2001.
12. Rothstein JM, Miller PJ, Roettger RF. Goniometric reliability in a clinical setting. Elbow and knee measurements. *Phys Ther.* 1983;63:1611-1615.
13. Armstrong AD, MacDermid JC, Chinchalkar S, et al. Reliability of range-of-motion measurement in the elbow. *J Elbow Shoulder Surg.* 1998;7:573-580.
14. Petherick M, Rheault W, Kimble S, et al. Concurrent validity and intertester reliability of universal and fluid-based goniometers for active elbow range of motion. *Phys Ther.* 1988;68:966-969.
15. Karagiannopoulos C, Sitler M, Michlovitz S. Reliability of 2 functional goniometric methods for measuring forearm pronation and supination active range of motion. *J Orthop Sports Phys Ther.* 2003;33:523-531.
16. Gajdosik RL. Comparison and reliability of three goniometric methods for measuring forearm supination and pronation. *Percept Mot Skills.* 2001;93:353-355.
17. Flowers KR, Stephens-Chisar J, LaStayo P, Galante BL. Intrarater reliability of a new method and instrumentation for measuring passive supination and pronation. *J Hand Ther.* 2001;14:30-35.
18. Patla C, Paris S. Reliability of interpretation of the Paris classification of normal end feel for elbow flexion and extension. *J Man Manipulative Ther.* 1993;1:60-66.
19. Smidt N, van der Windt DA, Assendelft WJ, et al. Interobserver reproducibility of the assessment of severity of complaints, grip strength, and pain pressure threshold in patients with lateral epicondylitis. *Arch Phys Med Rehabil.* 2002;83:1145-1150.
20. Docherty MA, Schwab RA, Ma OJ. Can elbow extension be used as a test of clinically significant injury? *South Med J.* 2002;95:539-541.
21. Hawksworth CR, Freeland P. Inability to fully extend the injured elbow: an indicator of significant injury. *Arch Emerg Med.* 1991;8:253-256.
22. Appelboam A, Reuben AD, Benger JR, et al. Elbow extension test to rule out elbow fracture: multicentre, prospective validation and observational study of diagnostic accuracy in adults and children. *Br Med J.* 2008;337:a2428.
23. Novak CB, Lee GW, Mackinnon SE, Lay L. Provocative testing for cubital tunnel syndrome. *J Hand Surg Am.* 1994;19:817-820.
24. O'Driscoll SW, Lawton RL, Smith AM. The "moving valgus stress test" for medial collateral ligament tears of the elbow. *Am J Sports Med.* 2005;33:231-239.
25. Vicenzino B, Smith D, Cleland J, Bisset L. Development of a clinical prediction rule to identify initial responders to mobilisation with movement and exercise for lateral epicondylalgia. *Man Ther.* 2009;14:550-554.
26. Stratford PW, et al. Development and initial validation of the upper extremity functional index. *Physiotherapy Canada.* 2001;259-267.
27. Leung HB, Yen CH, Tse PY. Reliability of Hong Kong Chinese version of the Patient-rated Forearm Evaluation Questionnaire for lateral epicondylitis. *Hong Kong Med J.* 2004;10:172-177.
28. Newcomer KL, Martinez-Silvestrini JA, Schaefer MP, et al. Sensitivity of the Patient-Rated Forearm Evaluation Questionnaire in lateral epicondylitis. *J Hand Ther.* 2005;18:400-406.
29. Overend TJ, Wuori-Fearn JL, Kramer JF, MacDermid JC. Reliability of a patient-rated forearm evaluation questionnaire for patients with lateral epicondylitis. *J Hand Ther.* 1999;12:31-37.
30. Li L, Liu X, Herr K. et al. Postoperative pain intensity assessment: a comparison of four scales in Chinese adults. *Pain Med.* 2007;8:223-234.
31. Farrar JT, Young JP Jr, LaMoreaux L, et al. Clinical importance of changes in chronic pain intensity measured on an 11-point numerical pain rating scale. *Pain.* 2001;94:149-158.
32. Farrar JT, Portenoy RK, Berlin JA, et al. Defining the clinically important difference in pain outcome measures. *Pain.* 2000;88:287-294.

Wrist and Hand

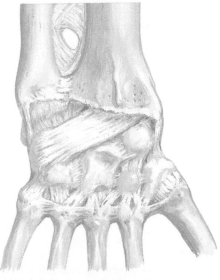

CLINICAL SUMMARY AND RECOMMENDATIONS

Patient History

Complaints
- Overall subjective complaints do not appear useful in identifying carpal tunnel syndrome. Only reports of "dropping objects" and "shaking hand improves symptoms" statistically altered the probability of diagnosis, and then only minimally (+LR = 1.7 to 1.9, −LR = .34 to .47).

Physical Examination

Screening
- Scaphoid fractures can effectively be both ruled in and ruled out by testing for *snuff box tenderness, pain with resisted supination, and pain with longitudinal compression* after an injury, suggesting possible fracture (each approximately +LR = 50, −LR = 0.0).

- The physical examination appears less effective at identifying other wrist fractures, at least in children.

Range of Motion, Strength, and Sensation Assessment
- Measuring wrist range of motion (ROM) appears to be highly reliable but is of unknown diagnostic utility. Measuring finger and thumb ROM is less reliable even when performed by the same examiner.

- Assessing strength with dynamometry has consistently been shown to be highly reliable, but again, is of unknown diagnostic utility. Manual muscle testing of the abductor pollicis brevis muscle does not appear to be very helpful in identifying carpal tunnel syndrome.

- Sensory testing of the hand is of poor to moderate reliability. Only *sensory loss at the pad of the thumb* appears helpful in identifying carpal tunnel syndrome, and then only minimally (+LR = 2.2, −LR = .49).

Special Tests
- Evidence on the diagnostic utility of Tinel's sign, Phalen's test, and carpal tunnel compression test is highly variable. The highest quality studies of each suggest that none of the three tests is particularly helpful in identifying carpal tunnel syndrome. Additionally, one study[1] found all three tests to be both more sensitive and more specific in identifying tenosynovitis than carpal tunnel syndrome.

- A new test, the ulnar fovea sign, appears to be very good at both ruling in and ruling out foveal disruption of the distal radioulnar ligaments and ulnotriquetral ligament injuries (+LR = 7.1, −LR - .06).

Combinations of Findings
- Although not yet validated, a clinical prediction rule appears to be very effective at identifying carpal tunnel syndrome. The presence of 5 variables *(a Hand Severity Scale score of > 1.9, a wrist ratio index > .67, a patient report of shaking the hand for symptom relief, diminished sensation on the thumb pad, and age older than 45)* was found to be associated with a +LR of 18.3.

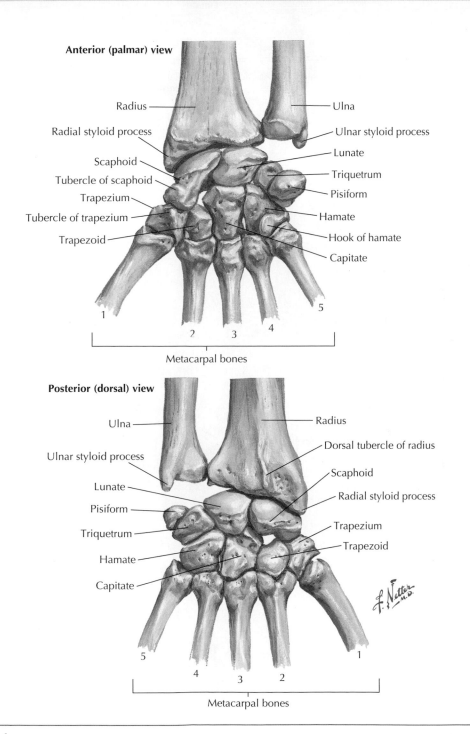

Anterior (palmar) view

- Radius
- Radial styloid process
- Scaphoid
- Tubercle of scaphoid
- Trapezium
- Tubercle of trapezium
- Trapezoid
- Ulna
- Ulnar styloid process
- Lunate
- Triquetrum
- Pisiform
- Hamate
- Hook of hamate
- Capitate

1 2 3 4 5

Metacarpal bones

Posterior (dorsal) view

- Ulna
- Ulnar styloid process
- Lunate
- Pisiform
- Triquetrum
- Hamate
- Capitate
- Radius
- Dorsal tubercle of radius
- Scaphoid
- Radial styloid process
- Trapezium
- Trapezoid

5 4 3 2 1

Metacarpal bones

Figure 11-1

Carpal bones.

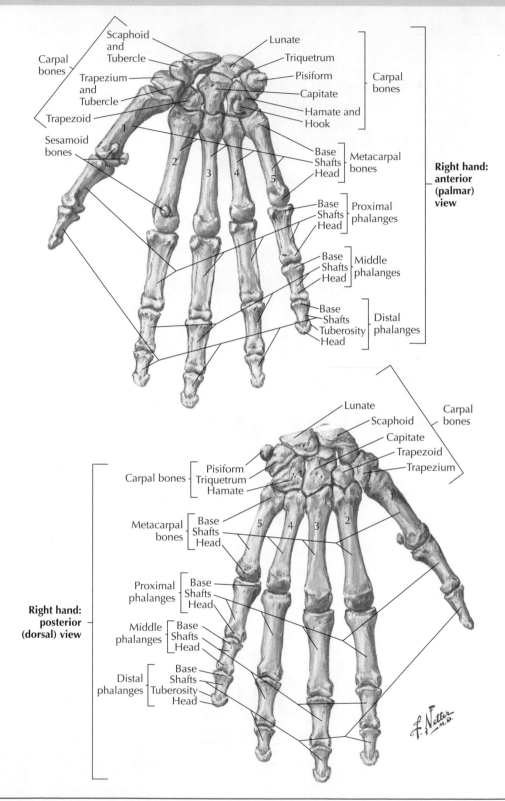

Figure 11-2

Bones of wrist and hand.

Arthrology

Coronal section: dorsal view

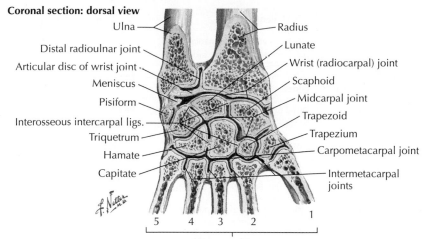

Ulna — Radius

Distal radioulnar joint — Lunate

Articular disc of wrist joint — Wrist (radiocarpal) joint

Meniscus — Scaphoid

Pisiform — Midcarpal joint

Interosseous intercarpal ligs. — Trapezoid

Triquetrum — Trapezium

Hamate — Carpometacarpal joint

Capitate — Intermetacarpal joints

5 4 3 2 1

Metacarpal bones

Sagittal sections through wrist and first finger

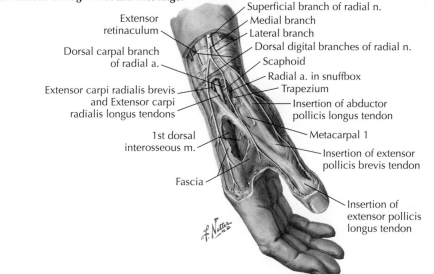

Extensor retinaculum — Superficial branch of radial n.

Medial branch

Lateral branch

Dorsal carpal branch of radial a. — Dorsal digital branches of radial n.

Scaphoid

Extensor carpi radialis brevis and Extensor carpi radialis longus tendons — Radial a. in snuffbox

Trapezium

Insertion of abductor pollicis longus tendon

1st dorsal interosseous m. — Metacarpal 1

Insertion of extensor pollicis brevis tendon

Fascia

Insertion of extensor pollicis longus tendon

Figure 11-3

Wrist joint.

Joints	Type and Classification	Closed Packed Position	Capsular Pattern
Radiocarpal	Synovial: condyloid	Full extension	Limitation equal in all directions
Intercarpal	Synovial: plane	Extension	Limitation equal in all directions
Carpometacarpal (CMC)	Synovial: plane, except for 1st CMC, which is sellar	Full opposition	Limitation equal in all directions
Metacarpophalangeal (MCP)	Synovial: condyloid	Extension except for 1st digit	Limitation equal in all directions
Interphalangeal (IP)	Synovial: hinge	Extension	Flexion greater than extension

Ligaments

Palmar Ligaments of Wrist

Ligaments	Attachments	Function
Transverse carpal	Hamate and pisiform medially, and scaphoid and trapezium laterally	Prevents bowstringing of finger flexor tendons
Palmar radiocarpal (radioscapho-lunate and radiocapitate portions)	Distal radius to both rows of carpal bones	Reinforces fibrous capsule of wrist volarly
Palmar ulnocarpal (ulnolunate and ulnotriquetral portions)	Distal ulna to both rows of carpal bones	Reinforces fibrous capsule of wrist volarly
Palmar radioulnar	Distal radius to distal ulna	Reinforces volar aspect of distal radioulnar joint
Radial collateral	Radial styloid process to scaphoid	Reinforces fibrous capsule of wrist laterally
Ulnar collateral	Ulnar styloid process to triquetrum	Reinforces fibrous capsule of wrist medially
Pisometacarpal	Pisiform to base of 5th metacarpal	Reinforces 5th carpometacarpal joint
Pisohamate	Pisiform to hook of hamate	Maintains proximity of pisiform and hamate
Capitotriquetral	Capitate to triquetrum	Maintains proximity of capitates and triquetrum
Palmar carpometacarpal	Palmar aspect of carpals to bases of metacarpals 2-5	Reinforces volar aspect of carpometacarpal joints 2-5
Palmar metacarpal	Attaches bases of metacarpals 2-+5	Maintains proximity between metacarpals

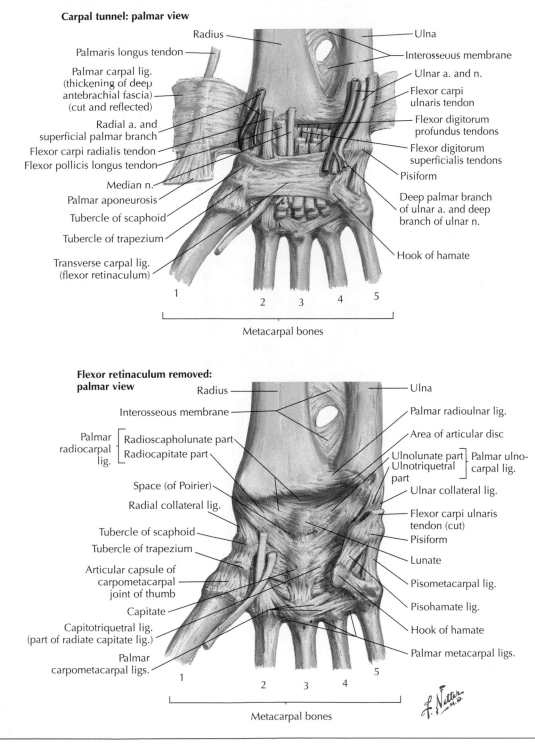

Carpal tunnel: palmar view

Radius

Palmaris longus tendon

Palmar carpal lig. (thickening of deep antebrachial fascia) (cut and reflected)

Radial a. and superficial palmar branch

Flexor carpi radialis tendon

Flexor pollicis longus tendon

Median n.

Palmar aponeurosis

Tubercle of scaphoid

Tubercle of trapezium

Transverse carpal lig. (flexor retinaculum)

Ulna

Interosseous membrane

Ulnar a. and n.

Flexor carpi ulnaris tendon

Flexor digitorum profundus tendons

Flexor digitorum superficialis tendons

Pisiform

Deep palmar branch of ulnar a. and deep branch of ulnar n.

Hook of hamate

Metacarpal bones

Flexor retinaculum removed: palmar view

Radius

Interosseous membrane

Palmar radiocarpal lig.
- Radioscapholunate part
- Radiocapitate part

Space (of Poirier)

Radial collateral lig.

Tubercle of scaphoid

Tubercle of trapezium

Articular capsule of carpometacarpal joint of thumb

Capitate

Capitotriquetral lig. (part of radiate capitate lig.)

Palmar carpometacarpal ligs.

Ulna

Palmar radioulnar lig.

Area of articular disc

Ulnolunate part
Ulnotriquetral part
— Palmar ulno-carpal lig.

Ulnar collateral lig.

Flexor carpi ulnaris tendon (cut)

Pisiform

Lunate

Pisometacarpal lig.

Pisohamate lig.

Hook of hamate

Palmar metacarpal ligs.

Metacarpal bones

Figure 11-4

Palmar ligaments of wrist.

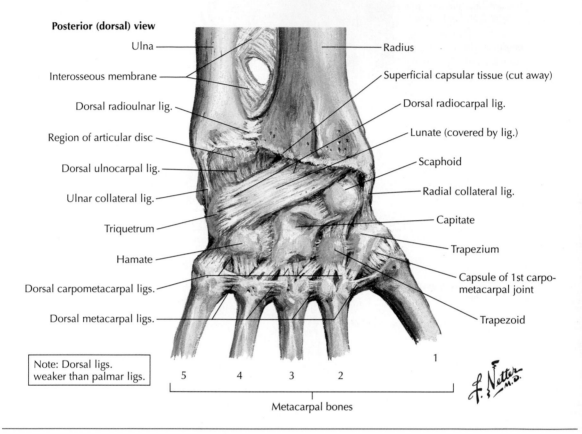

Posterior (dorsal) view

- Ulna
- Interosseous membrane
- Dorsal radioulnar lig.
- Region of articular disc
- Dorsal ulnocarpal lig.
- Ulnar collateral lig.
- Triquetrum
- Hamate
- Dorsal carpometacarpal ligs.
- Dorsal metacarpal ligs.

- Radius
- Superficial capsular tissue (cut away)
- Dorsal radiocarpal lig.
- Lunate (covered by lig.)
- Scaphoid
- Radial collateral lig.
- Capitate
- Trapezium
- Capsule of 1st carpometacarpal joint
- Trapezoid

Note: Dorsal ligs. weaker than palmar ligs.

5 4 3 2 1

Metacarpal bones

Figure 11-5

Posterior ligaments of wrist.

Ligaments	Attachments	Function
Dorsal radioulnar	Distal radius to distal ulnar	Reinforces dorsal aspect of distal radioulnar joint
Dorsal radiocarpal	Distal radius to both rows of carpal bones	Reinforces fibrous capsule of wrist dorsally
Dorsal carpometacarpal	Dorsal aspect of carpals to bases of metacarpals 2-5	Reinforces dorsal aspect of carpometacarpal joint 2-5
Dorsal metacarpal	Attaches bases of metacarpals 2-5	Maintains proximity between metacarpals

Ligaments (continued)

Metacarpophalangeal and Interphalangeal Ligaments

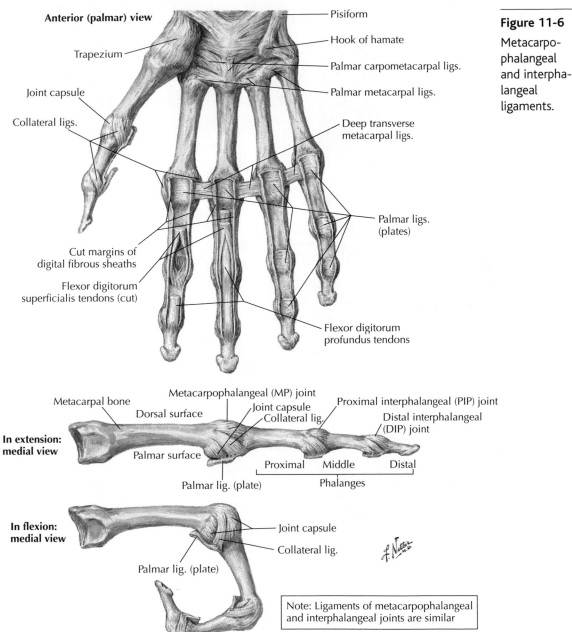

Anterior (palmar) view

Trapezium

Joint capsule

Collateral ligs.

Pisiform

Hook of hamate

Palmar carpometacarpal ligs.

Palmar metacarpal ligs.

Deep transverse metacarpal ligs.

Palmar ligs. (plates)

Cut margins of digital fibrous sheaths

Flexor digitorum superficialis tendons (cut)

Flexor digitorum profundus tendons

In extension: medial view

Metacarpal bone

Dorsal surface

Palmar surface

Palmar lig. (plate)

Metacarpophalangeal (MP) joint

Joint capsule

Collateral lig.

Proximal interphalangeal (PIP) joint

Distal interphalangeal (DIP) joint

Proximal   Middle   Distal

Phalanges

In flexion: medial view

Joint capsule

Collateral lig.

Palmar lig. (plate)

Note: Ligaments of metacarpophalangeal and interphalangeal joints are similar

Figure 11-6

Metacarpophalangeal and interphalangeal ligaments.

Ligaments	Attachments	Function
Collateral ligaments of IP joints	Sides of distal aspect of proximal phalanx to proximal aspect of distal phalanx	Reinforces medial and lateral capsules of IP joints
Deep transverse metacarpal ligaments	Connects adjacent MCP joints	Reinforces MCP joints
Palmar ligament (volar plate)	Individual plates attach to palmar aspect of MCP and IP joints	Reinforces palmar aspect of MCP and IP joints

Extensor of Wrist and Digits

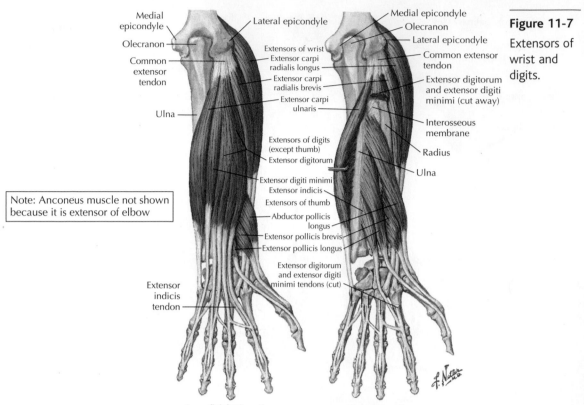

Figure 11-7
Extensors of wrist and digits.

Note: Anconeus muscle not shown because it is extensor of elbow

Superficial Dissection   Deep Dissection

Muscles	Proximal Attachments	Distal Attachments	Nerve and Segmental level	Action
Extensor carpi radialis longus	Lateral supracondylar ridge of humerus	Base of 2nd metacarpal	Radial nerve (C6, C7)	Extends and radially deviates wrist
Extensor carpi radialis brevis	Lateral epicondyle of humerus	Base of 3rd metacarpal	Deep branch of radial nerve (C7, C8)	Extends and radially deviates wrist
Extensor carpi ulnaris	Lateral epicondyle of humerus	Base of 5th metacarpal	Radial nerve (C6, C7, C8)	Extends and ulnarly deviates wrist
Extensor digitorum	Lateral epicondyle of humerus	Extensor expansions of digits 2-5	Posterior interosseous nerve (C7, C8)	Extends digits 2-5 at MCP and IP joints
Extensor digits minimi	Lateral epicondyle of humerus	Extensor expansion of 5th digit	Posterior interosseous nerve (C7, C8)	Extends 5th digit at MCP and IP joint
Extensor indicis	Posterior aspect of ulna and interosseous membrane	Extensor expansion of 2nd digit	Posterior interosseous nerve (C7, C8)	Extends 2nd digit and assists with wrist extension
Abductor pollicis longus	Posterior aspect of ulnar, radius, and interosseous membrane	Base of 1st metacarpal	Posterior interosseous nerve (C7, C8)	Abducts and extends thumb
Extensor pollicis brevis	Posterior aspect of radius and interosseous membrane	Base of proximal phalanx of thumb	Posterior interosseous nerve (C7, C8)	Extends thumb
Extensor pollicis longus	Posterior aspect of ulnar and interosseous membrane	Base of distal phalanx of thumb	Posterior interosseous nerve (C7, C8)	Extends distal phalanx of thumb at MCP and IP joints

Muscles (continued)

Flexors of Wrist and Digits

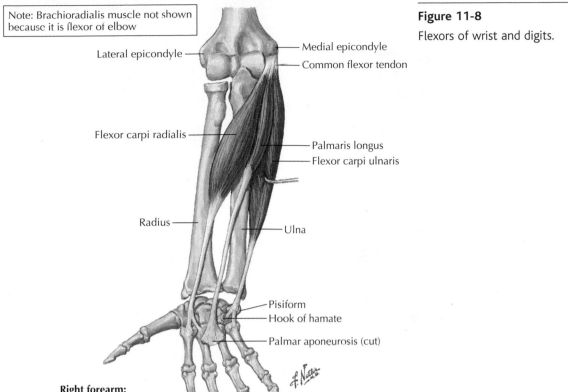

Note: Brachioradialis muscle not shown because it is flexor of elbow

Lateral epicondyle

Medial epicondyle

Common flexor tendon

Flexor carpi radialis

Palmaris longus

Flexor carpi ulnaris

Radius

Ulna

Pisiform

Hook of hamate

Palmar aponeurosis (cut)

Right forearm: anterior (palmar) view

Figure 11-8

Flexors of wrist and digits.

Muscles	Proximal Attachments	Distal Attachments	Nerve and Segmental Level	Action
Flexor carpi radialis	Medial epicondyle of humerus	Base of 2nd metacarpal bone	Median nerve (C6, C7)	Flexes and radially deviates hand
Flexor carpi ulnaris	Medial epicondyle of humerus and olecranon and posterior border of ulna	Pisiform, hook of hamate and 5th metacarpal	Ulnar nerve (C7, C8)	Flexes and ulnarly deviates hand
Palmaris longus	Medial epicondyle of humerus	Distal aspect of flexor retinaculum and palmar aponeurosis	Median nerve (C7, C8)	Flexes hand and tightens palmar aponeurosis
Flexor digitorum superficialis				
Humeroulnar head	Medial epicondyle of humerus, ulnar collateral ligament, coronoid process of ulna	Bodes of middle phalanges of digits 2-5	Median nerve (C7. C8, T1)	Flexes digits at proximal IP joints 2-5 and at MCP joints 2-5
Radial head	Superoanterior border of radius			
Flexor digitorum profundus				
Median portion	Proximal anteromedial aspect of ulnar and interosseous membrane	Bases of distal phalanges of digits 2-5	Ulnar nerve (C8, T1)	Flexes digits at distal IP joints 2-5 and assists with flexion of hand
Lateral portion			Median nerve (C8, T1)	
Flexor pollicis longus	Anterior aspect of radius and interosseous membrane	Base of distal phalanx of thumb	Anterior interosseous nerve (C8, T1)	Flexes phalanges of 1st digit

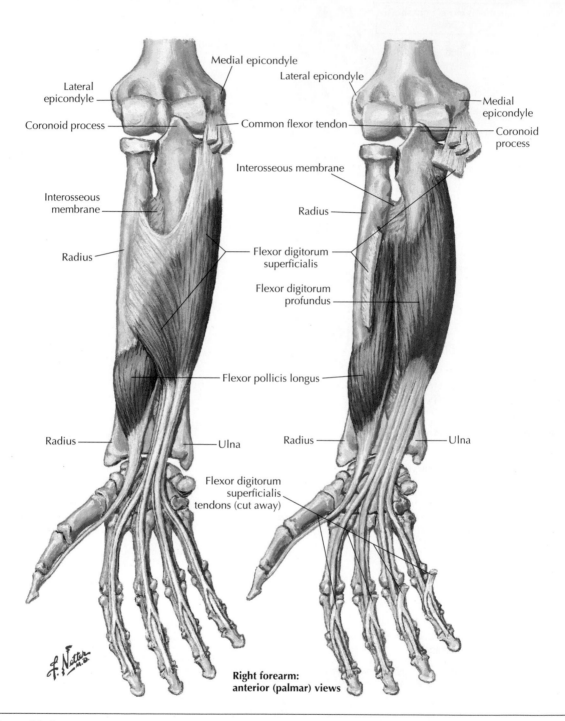

Lateral epicondyle

Medial epicondyle

Lateral epicondyle

Medial epicondyle

Coronoid process

Common flexor tendon

Coronoid process

Interosseous membrane

Interosseous membrane

Radius

Radius

Flexor digitorum superficialis

Radius

Flexor digitorum profundus

Flexor pollicis longus

Radius

Ulna

Radius

Ulna

Flexor digitorum superficialis tendons (cut away)

Right forearm: anterior (palmar) views

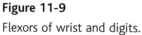

Figure 11-9

Flexors of wrist and digits.

Muscles (continued)

Intrinsic Muscles of Hand

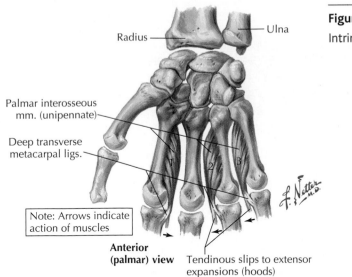

Radius — — Ulna

Palmar interosseous
mm. (unipennate)

Deep transverse
metacarpal ligs.

Note: Arrows indicate
action of muscles

**Anterior
(palmar) view**

Tendinous slips to extensor
expansions (hoods)

Figure 11-10

Intrinsic muscles of hand.

Muscles	Proximal Attachments	Distal Attachments	Nerve and Segmental Level	Action
Opponens pollicis	Flexor retinaculum, scaphoid, and trapezium	Lateral aspect of 1st metacarpal	Median nerve (C8, T1)	Opposes and medially rotates thumb
Abductor pollicis brevis		Lateral aspect of base of proximal phalanx of thumb		Abducts thumb and assists in thumb opposition
Flexor pollicis brevis				Flexes thumb
Adductor pollicis				
Oblique head	Bases of metacarpals 2 and 3 and capitates	Medial aspect of base of proximal phalanx of thumb		Adducts thumb
Transverse head	Anterior aspect of 3rd metacarpal			
Abductor digit minimi	Pisiform	Medial aspect of base of proximal phalanx of 5th digit	Deep branch of ulnar nerve (C8, T1)	Abducts 5th digit
Flexor digiti minimi	Hook of hamate and flexor retinaculum			Flexes proximal phalanx of 5th digit
Opponens digit minimi		Medial aspect of 5th metacarpal		Draws 5th digit at MCP joints, and extends IP joints
Lumbricals				
Lateral	Tendons of flexor digitorum profundus	Lateral sides of extensor expansions 2-5	Median nerve (C8, T1)	Flexes digits at MCP joints, and extends IP joints
Medial			Deep branch of ulnar nerve (C8, T1)	
Doral interosseous	Adjacent sides of two metacarpals	Bases of proximal phalanges 2-4 and extensor expansion	Deep branch of ulnar nerve (C8, T1)	Abducts digits and assists with action of lumbricals
Palmar interosseous	Palmar aspect of metacarpals 2, 4, and 5	Bases of proximal phalanges 2, 4, and 5 and extensor expansion		Adducts digits and assists with action of lumbricals

Muscles (continued)

Intrinsic Muscles of Hand

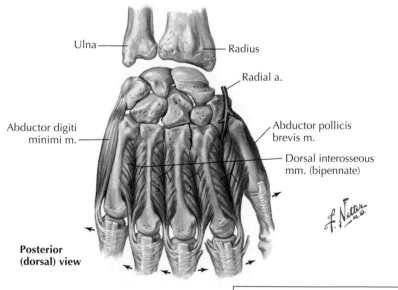

Radial a. and palmar carpal branch

Radius

Superficial palmar branch of radial a.

Transverse carpal lig.
(flexor retinaculum) (reflected)

Opponens pollicis m.

Branches of median n.
to thenar mm. and to 1st
and 2nd lumbrical mm.

Abductor pollicis
brevis m. (cut)

Flexor pollicis brevis m.

Adductor pollicis m.

1st dorsal
interosseous m.

Branches from deep branch
of ulnar n. to 3rd and 4th
lumbrical mm. and to all
interosseous mm.

Lumbrical mm. (reflected)

Pronator quadratus m.

Ulnar n.

Ulnar a. and palmar carpal branch

Flexor carpi ulnaris tendon

Palmar carpal arterial arch

Pisiform

Median n.

Abductor digiti minimi m. (cut)

Deep palmar branch of ulnar
a. and deep branch of ulnar n.

Flexor digiti minimi brevis m. (cut)

Opponens digiti minimi m.

Deep palmar (arterial) arch

Palmar metacarpal aa.

Common palmar digital aa.

Deep transverse metacarpal ligs.

Anterior (palmar) view

Ulna

Radius

Radial a.

Abductor digiti
minimi m.

Abductor pollicis
brevis m.

Dorsal interosseous
mm. (bipennate)

**Posterior
(dorsal) view**

Note: Arrows indicate action of muscles

Figure 11-11

Intrinsic muscles of hand.

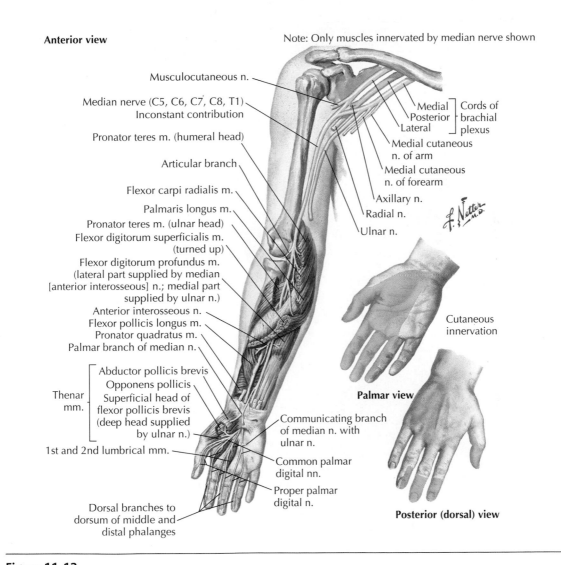

Anterior view

Note: Only muscles innervated by median nerve shown

Musculocutaneous n.

Median nerve (C5, C6, C7, C8, T1)
Inconstant contribution

Pronator teres m. (humeral head)

Articular branch

Flexor carpi radialis m.

Palmaris longus m.

Pronator teres m. (ulnar head)
Flexor digitorum superficialis m.
(turned up)

Flexor digitorum profundus m.
(lateral part supplied by median
[anterior interosseous] n.; medial part
supplied by ulnar n.)

Anterior interosseous n.
Flexor pollicis longus m.
Pronator quadratus m.
Palmar branch of median n.

Thenar mm. {
Abductor pollicis brevis
Opponens pollicis
Superficial head of
flexor pollicis brevis
(deep head supplied
by ulnar n.)

1st and 2nd lumbrical mm.

Dorsal branches to
dorsum of middle and
distal phalanges

Medial
Posterior } Cords of brachial plexus
Lateral

Medial cutaneous
n. of arm
Medial cutaneous
n. of forearm
Axillary n.
Radial n.
Ulnar n.

Cutaneous
innervation

Palmar view

Communicating branch
of median n. with
ulnar n.

Common palmar
digital nn.

Proper palmar
digital n.

Posterior (dorsal) view

Figure 11-12

Median nerve.

Nerves	Segmental Level	Sensory	Motor
Median nerve	C6, C7, C8, T1	Palmar and distal dorsal aspects of lateral 3½ digits and lateral palm	Abductor pollicis brevis, opponens pollicis, flexor pollicis brevis, lateral lumbricals

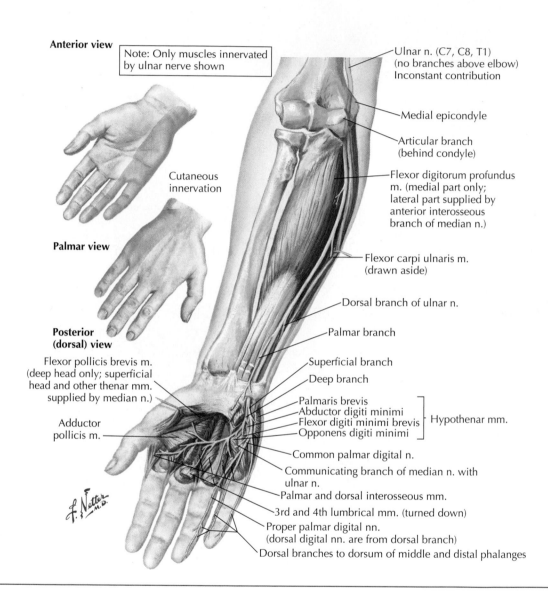

Anterior view

Note: Only muscles innervated by ulnar nerve shown

Ulnar n. (C7, C8, T1)
(no branches above elbow)
Inconstant contribution

Medial epicondyle

Articular branch
(behind condyle)

Flexor digitorum profundus
m. (medial part only;
lateral part supplied by
anterior interosseous
branch of median n.)

Cutaneous
innervation

Palmar view

Flexor carpi ulnaris m.
(drawn aside)

Dorsal branch of ulnar n.

Palmar branch

**Posterior
(dorsal) view**

Flexor pollicis brevis m.
(deep head only; superficial
head and other thenar mm.
supplied by median n.)

Adductor
pollicis m.

Superficial branch

Deep branch

Palmaris brevis
Abductor digiti minimi
Flexor digiti minimi brevis
Opponens digiti minimi

Hypothenar mm.

Common palmar digital n.

Communicating branch of median n. with
ulnar n.

Palmar and dorsal interosseous mm.

3rd and 4th lumbrical mm. (turned down)

Proper palmar digital nn.
(dorsal digital nn. are from dorsal branch)

Dorsal branches to dorsum of middle and distal phalanges

Figure 11-13

Ulnar nerve.

Nerves	Segmental Level	Sensory	Motor
Ulnar nerve	C7, C8, T1	Palmar and distal dorsal aspects of medial 1½ digits and medial palm	Interosseous, adductor pollicis, flexor pollicis brevis, medial lumbricals, abductor digiti minimi, flexor digit minimi brevis, opponens digit minimi

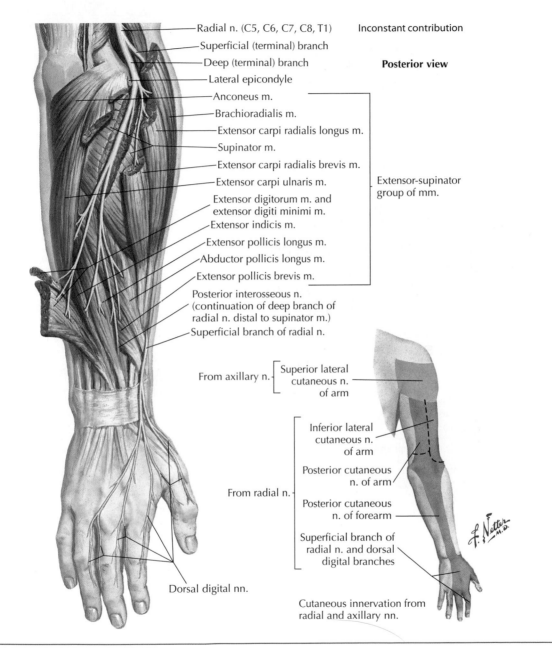

Radial n. (C5, C6, C7, C8, T1)   Inconstant contribution

Superficial (terminal) branch

Deep (terminal) branch   **Posterior view**

Lateral epicondyle

Anconeus m.

Brachioradialis m.

Extensor carpi radialis longus m.

Supinator m.

Extensor carpi radialis brevis m.

Extensor carpi ulnaris m.   Extensor-supinator
                                 group of mm.
Extensor digitorum m. and
extensor digiti minimi m.

Extensor indicis m.

Extensor pollicis longus m.

Abductor pollicis longus m.

Extensor pollicis brevis m.

Posterior interosseous n.
(continuation of deep branch of
radial n. distal to supinator m.)

Superficial branch of radial n.

From axillary n. { Superior lateral
                   cutaneous n.
                   of arm

                   Inferior lateral
                   cutaneous n.
                   of arm

                   Posterior cutaneous
                   n. of arm

From radial n. {

                   Posterior cutaneous
                   n. of forearm

                   Superficial branch of
                   radial n. and dorsal
                   digital branches

Dorsal digital nn.

Cutaneous innervation from
radial and axillary nn.

Figure 11-14
Radial nerve.

Nerves	Segmental level	Sensory	Motor
Radial nerve	C5, C6, C7, C8, T1	Dorsal aspect of lateral hand, excluding digits	No motor in hand

Initial Hypotheses Based on Patient History

History	Initial Hypothesis
Pain over radial styloid process with gripping activities	Possible de Quervain's syndrome[2]
Reports of an insidious onset of numbness and tingling in 1st three fingers; may complain of worse pain at night	Possible carpal tunnel syndrome[3-5]
Reports of paresthesias over dorsal aspect of ulnar border of hand and fingers 4-5	Possible ulnar nerve compression at canal of Guyon[6-8]
Patient reports inability to extend metacarpophalangeal of IP joints	Possible Dupuytren's contracture[8] Possible trigger finger[9]
Reports of falling on hand with wrist hyperextended; complains of pain with loading of wrist	Possible scaphoid fracture[10,11] Possible carpal instability[9]

Reliability of the Historical Examination

ICC or κ	Interpretation
.81-1.0	Substantial agreement
.61-.80	Moderate agreement
.41-.60	Fair agreement
.11-.40	Slight agreement
.0-.10	No agreement

History	Population	Inter-examiner Reliability
Most bothersome symptom pain, numbness, tingling, loss of sensation?[12]	82 patients presenting to primary care clinic, orthopaedic department, or electrophysiology laboratory with suspected cervical radiculopathy or carpal tunnel syndrome	κ = .74 (.55, .93)
Location of most bothersome symptom?[12]		κ = .82 (.68, .96)
Symptoms intermittent, variable, or constant?[12]		κ = .57 (.35, .79)
Hand swollen?[12]		κ = .85 (.68, 1.0)
Dropping objects?[12]		κ = .95 (.85, 1.0)
Entire limb goes numb?[12]		κ = .53 (.26, .81)
Nocturnal symptoms wake patient?[12]		κ = .83 (.60, 1.0)
Shaking hand improves symptoms?[12]		κ = .90 (.75, 1.0)
Symptoms exacerbated with activities that require gripping?[12]		κ = .72 (.49, .95)

Diagnostic Utility of the Patient History in Identifying Carpal Tunnel Syndrome

+LR	Interpretation	−LR
>10	Large	<.1
5.0-10.0	Moderate	.1-.2
2.0-5.0	Small	.2-.5
1.0-2.0	Rarely important	.5-1.0

History	Population	Reference Standard	Sens	Spec	+LR	−LR
Age > 45[12]	82 patients presenting to a primary care clinic, orthopaedic department, or electrophysiology laboratory with suspected cervical radiculopathy or carpal tunnel syndrome	Needle electromyography and nerve conduction studies	.64 (.47, .82)	.59 (.47, .72)	1.58 (.46, 2.4)	.60 (.35, 1.0)
Most bothersome symptom pain, numbness, tingling, loss of sensation[12]			.04 (−.04, .11)	.91 (.83, .98)	.42 (.05, 3.4)	1.1 (.94, 1.2)
Location of most bothersome symptom[12]			.35 (.16, .53)	.40 (.27, .54)	.58 (.33, 1.0)	1.6 (1.1, 2.5)
Symptoms intermittent, variable, or constant[12]			.23 (.07, .39)	.89 (.81, .97)	2.1 (.74, 5.8)	.87 (.69, 1.4)
Reports of hand becoming swollen[12]			.38 (.20, .57)	.63 (.50, .76)	1.0 (.57, 1.9)	.98 (.68, 1.4)
Dropping objects[12]			.73 (.56, .90)	.57 (.44, .71)	1.7 (1.2, 2.5)	.47 (.24, .92)
Entire limb goes numb[12]			.38 (.20, .57)	.80 (.69, .90)	1.9 (.92, 3.9)	.77 (.55, 1.1)
Nocturnal symptoms wake patient[12]			.73 (.56, .90)	.31 (.19, .44)	1.1 (.79, 1.4)	.86 (.41, 1.8)
Shaking hand improves symptoms[12]			.81 (.66, .96)	.57 (.43, .70)	1.9 (1.3, 2.7)	.34 (.15, .77)
Symptoms exacerbated with activities that require gripping[12]			.77 (.61, .93)	.37 (.24, .50)	1.2 (.91, 1.6)	.62 (.28, 1.4)
Age ≥ 40 years[13]	110 patients referred to laboratory for electrophysiologic examination	Nerve conduction tests	.80	.42	1.38	.48
Nocturnal symptoms[13]			.77	.28	1.07	.82
Bilateral symptoms[13]			.61	.58	1.45	.67

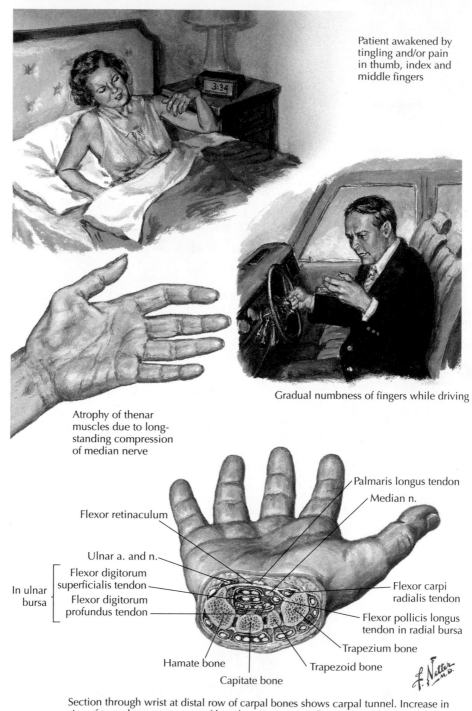

Patient awakened by tingling and/or pain in thumb, index and middle fingers

Gradual numbness of fingers while driving

Atrophy of thenar muscles due to long-standing compression of median nerve

Palmaris longus tendon

Median n.

Flexor retinaculum

Ulnar a. and n.

In ulnar bursa
- Flexor digitorum superficialis tendon
- Flexor digitorum profundus tendon

Flexor carpi radialis tendon

Flexor pollicis longus tendon in radial bursa

Trapezium bone

Hamate bone

Trapezoid bone

Capitate bone

Section through wrist at distal row of carpal bones shows carpal tunnel. Increase in size of tunnel structures caused by edema (trauma), inflammation (rheumatoid disease); ganglion, amyloid deposits, or diabetic neuropathy may compress median nerve

Figure 11-15

Carpal tunnel syndrome.

Diagnostic Utility of Tests to Identify Scaphoid Fractures

+LR	Interpretation	−LR
>10	Large	<.1
5.0–10.0	Moderate	.1–.2
2.0–5.0	Small	.2–.5
1.0–2.0	Rarely important	.5–1.0

Test and Study Quality	Description and Positive Findings	Population	Reference Standard	Sens	Spec	+LR	−LR
Snuff box tenderness[14] ◇	Examiner palpates anatomical snuff box. Positive if pain is elicited	85 patients presenting to emergency department with mechanism of injury suggesting possible scaphoid fracture	Radiographic confirmation of scaphoid fracture	1.0	.98	50.0	.00
Pain with supination against resistance[14] ◇	Examiner holds patient's hand in hand-shake position and directs patient to resist supination of forearm. Positive if pain is elicited			1.0	.98	50.0	.00
Pain with longitudinal compression of thumb[14] ◇	Examiner holds patient's thumb and applies long axis compression through metacarpal bone into scaphoid. Positive if pain is elicited			.98	.98	49.0	.02
Anatomical snuff box tenderness[15] ○	Examiner palpates anatomical snuff box. Positive if pain is elicited	221 patients with a suspected scaphoid injury		1.0	.29 (.23, .35)	1.41	.00
Scaphoid tubercle tenderness[15] ○	Examiner applies pressure to scaphoid tubercle. Positive if pain is elicited			.83 (.70, .96)	.51 (.44, .58)	1.69	.33
Scaphoid compression tenderness[15] ○	Examiner holds patient's thumb and applies long axis compression through metacarpal bone into scaphoid. Positive if pain is elicited			1.0	.80 (.74, .86)	5.0	.00

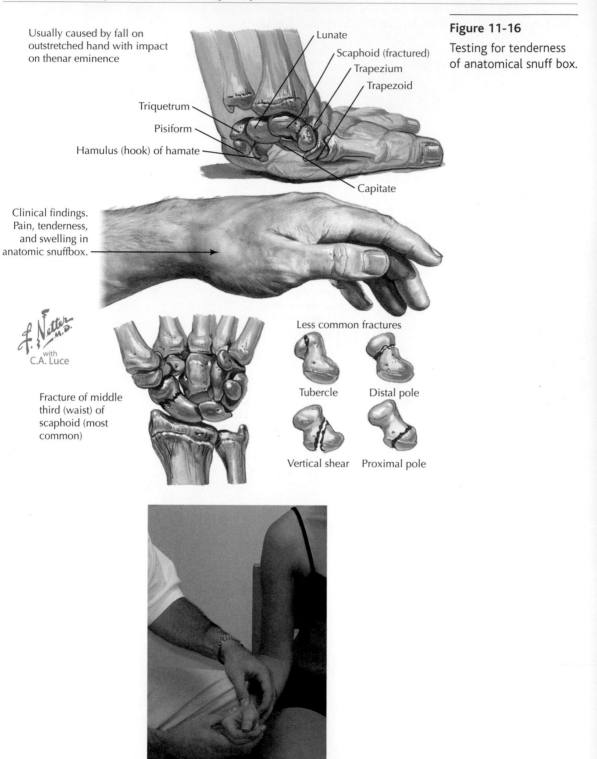

Usually caused by fall on outstretched hand with impact on thenar eminence

Lunate

Scaphoid (fractured)

Trapezium

Trapezoid

Triquetrum

Pisiform

Hamulus (hook) of hamate

Capitate

Figure 11-16

Testing for tenderness of anatomical snuff box.

Clinical findings. Pain, tenderness, and swelling in anatomic snuffbox.

F. Netter M.D.
with
C.A. Luce

Less common fractures

Fracture of middle third (waist) of scaphoid (most common)

Tubercle

Distal pole

Vertical shear

Proximal pole

Testing for tenderness of anatomical snuff box

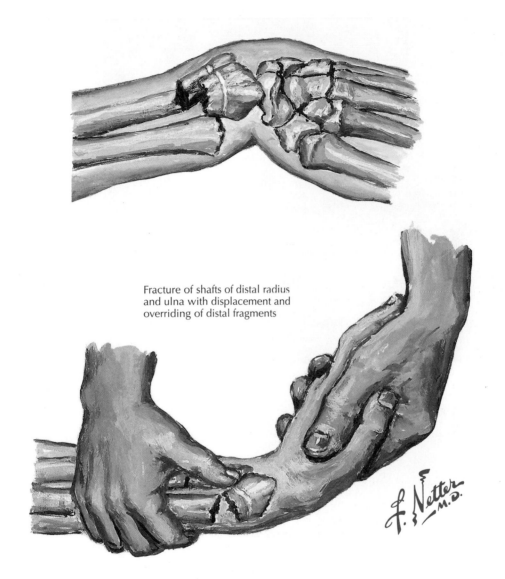

Fracture of shafts of distal radius
and ulna with displacement and
overriding of distal fragments

Figure 11-17
Fracture of forearm bones in children.

Pershad and colleagues[16] developed a clinical prediction rule to identify acute pediatric wrist injuries. Predictor variables included reduction in grip strength $\geq$ 20% compared with the opposite side and distal radius point tenderness. The rule exhibited a sensitivity of 79%, a specificity of 63%, a +LR of 2.14, and a −LR of .33.

Range of Motion

Reliability of Wrist Range of Motion Measurements

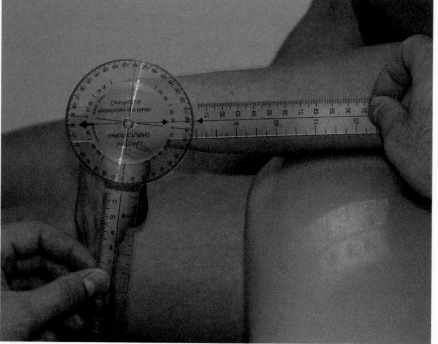

Measurement of wrist flexion

Figure 11-18

Wrist range of motion.

Test and Measure	Instrumentation	Population	Reliability			
			Intra-examiner	ICC	Inter-examiner	ICC
Active ROM (AROM)[17]	8 in plastic goniometer	48 patients in whom measurements of the wrist would normally be included in examination	Wrist flexion	.96	Wrist flexion	.90
			Wrist extension	.96	Wrist extension	.85
			Radial deviation	.90	Radial deviation	.86
			Ulnar deviation	.92	Ulnar deviation	.78
Passive ROM (PROM)[17]			Wrist flexion	.96	Wrist flexion	.86
			Wrist extension	.96	Wrist extension	.84
			Radial deviation	.91	Radial deviation	.66
			Ulnar deviation	.94	Ulnar deviation	.83
PROM[18]	Alignment of plastic 6 in goniometer	140 patients in whom passive ROM of wrist would be included in standard evaluation	Radial flexion	.86	Radial flexion	.88
			Ulnar flexion	.87	Ulnar flexion	.89
			Dorsal flexion	.92	Dorsal flexion	.93
			Radial extension	.80	Radial extension	.80
			Ulnar extension	.80	Ulnar extension	.80
			Dorsal extension	.84	Dorsal extension	.84

ICC, Intraclass correlation coefficient.

Range of Motion (continued)

Reliability of Wrist Range of Motion Measurements

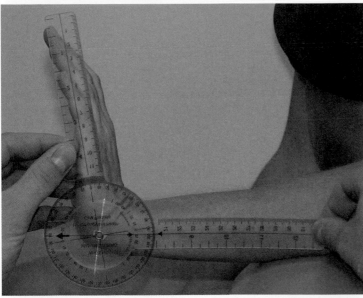

Measurement of wrist extension

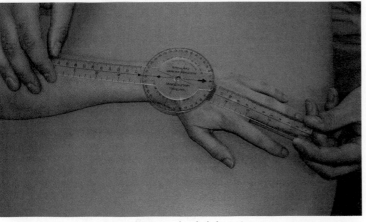

Measurement of radial deviation

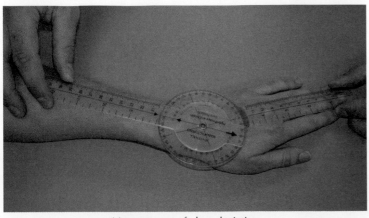

Measurement of ulnar deviation

Figure 11-19

Wrist range of motion.

ICC or κ	Interpretation
.81-1.0	Substantial agreement
.61-.80	Moderate agreement
.41-.60	Fair agreement
.11-.40	Slight agreement
.0-.10	No agreement

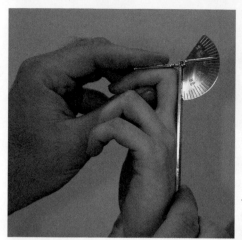

Figure 11-20

Measurement of proximal interphalangeal joint flexion.

Test and Measure	Instrumentation	Population	Test-Retest Reliability ICC			
Metacarpophalangeal joints[19]	Goniometer	20 healthy subjects 1 week apart	Flexed position = .74 Extended position = .83			
Proximal interphalangeal joints[19]			Flexed position = .80 Extended position = .80			
Distal interphalangeal joints[19]			Flexed position = .58 Extended position = .63			
Metacarpophalangeal joints[19]	Compangle		Flexed position = .76 Extended position = .83			
Proximal interphalangeal joints[19]			Flexed position = .89 Extended position = .90			
Distal interphalangeal joints[19]			Flexed position = .73 Extended position = .71			
Total AROM of IP flexion and extension[20]	Finger goniometer	30 patients with hand injuries	Intra-examiner = .97-.98 Inter-examiner = .97			
Palmar abduction[21]		25 healthy subjects	Intra-examiner		Inter-examiner	
			Active	Passive	Active	Passive
	• Goniometer		.55 (.34, .87)	.76 (.69, .94)	.31 (−.18, .77)	.37 (−.42, .79)
	• Pollexograph-thumb		.71 (.62, .93)	.82 (.78, .96)	.66 (.53, .91)	.59 (.42, .89)
	• Pollexograph-metacarpal		.82 (.78, .96)	.81 (.76, .95)	.57 (.38, .88)	.61 (.45, .89)
	• American Medical Association method		.72 (.63, .92)	.65 (.51, .90)	.24 (−.40, .73)	.52 (.28, .86)
	• American Society of Hand Therapists method		.78 (.72, .94)	.72 (.63, .93)	.55 (.34, .87)	.52 (.29, .86)
	• Intermetacarpal distance		.95 (.95, .99)	.92 (.90, .98)	.82 (.79, .96)	.79 (.78, .96)

Assessing Strength

Intra-examiner Reliability of Assessing Strength

Figure 11-21

Measurement of grip strength.

Procedure Performed	Instrumentation	Population	Test-Retest Reliability (ICCs)
Wrist extensors (mean of two efforts)[22]	Dynamometer	40 patients with suspected myopathy	Dominant side = .88 (.79, .94) Non-dominant side = .94 (.90, .97)
Wrist extensors (max of two efforts)[22]		40 patients with suspected myopathy	Dominant side = .87 (.76, .93) Non-dominant side = .94 (.88, .97)
Grip[23]		21 healthy older volunteers	Left = .95 (.89, .98) Right = .91 (.78, .96)
Grip[24]		22 asymptomatic subjects	One trial: .95 (.89, .98) Mean of three trials: .85 (.67, .94) Highest of three trials: .95 (.89, .98)
		22 patients after carpal tunnel decompression	One trial: .97, (.94, .99) Mean of three trials: .94 (.80, .98) Highest of three trials: .97 (.92, .99)
		22 patients after carpal tunnel decompression	One trial: .96 (.91, .98) Mean of three trials: .98 (.96, .99) Highest of three trials: .97 (.90, .99)
Grip[25]		104 healthy primary school children	Dominant side = .97 (.95, .98) Non-dominant side = .95 (.92, .96)
	Vigorimeter		Dominant side = .84 (.77, .89) Non-dominant side = .86 (.80, .90)

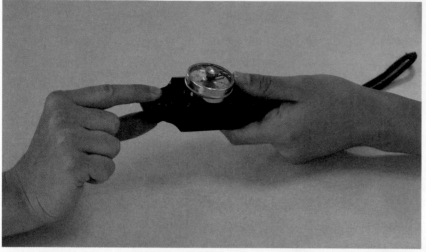

Figure 11-22
Measurement of pinch strength.

Measurement of tip pinch strength

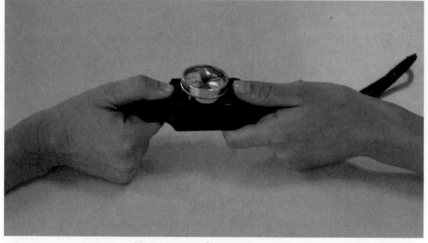

Measurement of key pinch strength

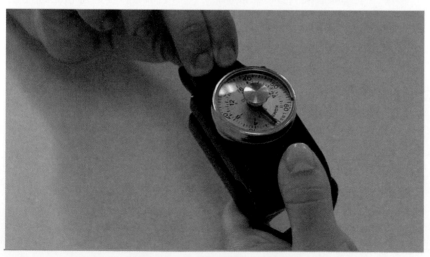

Measurement of tripod pinch strength

Assessing Strength (continued)

Inter-examiner Reliability of Assessing Strength

ICC or κ	Interpretation
.81-1.0	Substantial agreement
.61-.80	Moderate agreement
.41-.60	Fair agreement
.11-.40	Slight agreement
.0-.10	No agreement

Procedure Performed	Instrumentation	Population	Inter-Examiner Reliability (ICCs)	
Grip Palmar pinch Key pinch Tip pinch[26]	Pinch gauge	27 healthy volunteers	Right .99 .98 .99 .99	Left .99 .99 .98 .99
Grip Tip pinch Key pinch[27]	Hand and pinch grip dynamometers	33 patients with a unilateral hand injury	Injured .93-.97 .89 .94	Non-injured .92-.94 .84 .86
Grip Tip pinch Jaw pinch[20]	Grip dynamometer and pinch gauge	30 patients with hand injuries	Intra-examiner .96 .86-.94 .88-.93	Inter-examiner .95 .91 .89
Grip Tripod Key pinch[28]	Dynamometer and pinch gauge	38 patients receiving physical therapy for hand impairments	Symptomatic .93 (.86, .96) 88 (.78, .96) .94 (.88, .97)	Asymptomatic .94 (.89, .97) .87 (.74, .93) .93 (.86, .96)
Abductor pollicis strength[12]	Examiner performs manual muscle testing of abductor pollicis. Graded as "markedly reduced," "reduced," or "normal" compared with contralateral extremity	82 patients with suspected cervical radiculopathy or carpal tunnel syndrome	κ = .39 (.00, .80)	
Wrist extensors[2]	Dynamometer	30 patients presenting to a physical therapy clinic	.94	
Wrist flexion Wrist extension[29]	Dynamometer	20 healthy subjects	Wrist flexion .85 Wrist extension .91	

Diagnostic Utility of Weakness in Identifying Carpal Tunnel Syndrome

+LR	Interpretation	−LR
>10	Large	<.1
5.0-10.0	Moderate	.1-.2
2.0-5.0	Small	.2-.5
1.0-2.0	Rarely important	.5-1.0

Test and Study Quality	Description and Positive Findings	Population	Reference Standard	Sens	Spec	+LR	−LR
Strength of abductor pollicis brevis[12] ◇	Strength of abductor pollicis brevis is tested by placing thumb in a position of abduction and applying a force in direction of adduction at proximal phalanx. Positive if strength is reduced or markedly reduced compared with contralateral extremity	82 patients with suspected cervical radiculopathy or carpal tunnel syndrome	Needle electromyography and nerve conduction studies	.19 (.04, .34)	.89 (.81, .90)	1.7 (.58, 5.2)	.91 (.74, 1.1)
Abductor pollicis brevis weakness[30] ◇	Patient is instructed to touch pads of thumb and 5th digit together. Examiner applies posteriorly directed force over thumb IP joint towards palm. Positive if weakness is detected	228 hands referred for electrodiagnostic consultation with suspected carpal tunnel syndrome	Nerve conduction studies	.66	.66	1.94	.52

Assessing Wrist Anthropometry

Reliability of Measuring Wrist Anthropometry

ICC or κ	Interpretation
.81-1.0	Substantial agreement
.61-.80	Moderate agreement
.41-.60	Fair agreement
.11-.40	Slight agreement
.0-.10	No agreement

Test and Measure	Test Procedure and Determination of Positive Findings	Population	Inter-examiner Reliability
Wrist anterior-posterior width[12]	Width of wrist is measured in centimeters with pair of calipers	82 patients with suspected cervical radiculopathy or carpal tunnel syndrome	ICC = .77 (.62, .87)
Wrist medial-lateral width[12]			ICC = .86 (.75, .92)

Diagnostic Utility of Wrist Anthropometry in Identifying Carpal Tunnel Syndrome

+LR	Interpretation	−LR
>10	Large	<.1
5.0-10.0	Moderate	.1-.2
2.0-5.0	Small	.2-.5
1.0-2.0	Rarely important	.5-1.0

Test and Study Quality	Description and Positive Findings	Population	Reference Standard	Sens	Spec	+LR	−LR
Wrist-ratio index greater than .67[12] ◇	Anteroposterior width of wrist is measured and divided by medio-lateral width. Positive if ratio is greater than .67	82 patients with suspected cervical radiculopathy or carpal tunnel syndrome	Needle electromyography and nerve conduction studies	.93 (.83, 1.0)	.26 (.14, .38)	1.3 (1.0, 1.5)	.29 (.07, 1.2)
The square-shaped wrist[30] ◇	Anteroposterior and mediolateral dimensions of wrist are measured at distal flexor wrist crease using standard caliper. Positive if wrist ratio (anteroposterior dimension divided by mediolateral dimension) is ≥ .70	228 hands referred for electrodiagnostic consultation with suspected carpal tunnel syndrome	Nerve conduction studies	.69	.73	2.56	.42

Assessing Swelling

Reliability of Assessing Swelling

ICC or κ	Interpretation
.81–1.0	Substantial agreement
.61–.80	Moderate agreement
.41–.60	Fair agreement
.11–.40	Slight agreement
.0–.10	No agreement

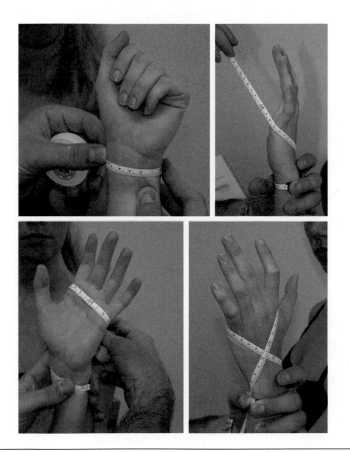

Figure 11-23

Figure-of-eight measurement.

Test and Measure	Test Procedure	Population	Reliability	
			Intra-examiner	Inter-examiner
Figure-of-eight[31]	Examiner places zero mark on distal aspect of ulnar styloid process. Tape measure is then brought across ventral surface of wrist to most distal aspect of radial styloid process. Next, tape is brought diagonally across dorsum of hand and over 5th MCP joint line, brought over ventral surface of MCP joints, and wrapped diagonally across dorsum to meet start of tape	24 individuals (33 hands) with pathologies affecting hand	ICC = .99	ICC =.99
Volumetric[31]	Hand is placed vertically in standard volumeter		ICC = .99	Not reported

Testing Sensation

Reliability of Sensory Testing

ICC or κ	Interpretation
.81-1.0	Substantial agreement
.61-.80	Moderate agreement
.41-.60	Fair agreement
.11-.40	Slight agreement
.0-.10	No agreement

Test and Measure	Test Procedure and Determination of Positive Findings	Population	Inter-examiner Reliability
Semmes-Weinstein monofilament test[28]	Sensory test is performed on pulp of thumb, index, long, and small fingertips	36 hands with carpal tunnel syndrome	κ = .22 (.26, .42)
Median sensory field deficit of thumb pad[12]	Sensation is tested with straight end of paper clip. Graded as "absent," "reduced," "normal," or "hyperesthetic"	82 patients presenting to a primary care clinic, orthopaedic department, or electrophysiology laboratory with suspected cervical radiculopathy or carpal tunnel syndrome	κ = .48 (.23, .73)
Median sensory field deficit of index finger pad[12]			κ = .50 (.25, .75)
Median sensory field deficit[12]			κ = .40 (.12, .68)

Diagnostic Utility of Diminished Sensation in Identifying Carpal Tunnel Syndrome

+LR	Interpretation	−LR
>10	Large	<.1
5.0-10.0	Moderate	.1-.2
2.0-5.0	Small	.2-.5
1.0-2.0	Rarely important	.5-1.0

Test and Study Quality	Description and Positive Findings	Population	Reference Standard	Sens	Spec	+LR	−LR
Sensory loss at pad of thumb[12] ◇	Sensation is tested with straight end of a paper clip. Positive if sensation is absent or reduced	82 patients presenting to a primary care clinic, orthopaedic department, or electrophysiology laboratory with suspected cervical radiculopathy or carpal tunnel syndrome	Needle electromyography and nerve conduction studies	.65 (.47, .84)	.70 (.47, .84)	2.2 (1.3, 3.6)	.49 (.28, .46)
Sensory loss at pad of index finger[12] ◇				.52 (.32, .72)	.67 (.32, .72)	1.6 (.92, 2.7)	.72 (.86, 1.1)
Sensory loss at pad of medial finger[12] ◇				.44 (.26, .63)	.74 (.26, .63)	1.7 (.58, .52)	.75 (.86, 1.1)
Moving two-point discrimination[13] ◯	Examiner strokes tip of index and 5th finger five times with either one or two caliber tips. Positive if patient is unable to identify number of tips performed on at least one stroke	110 patients referred to laboratory for electrophysiologic examination	Nerve conduction tests	.32	.81	1.68	.84

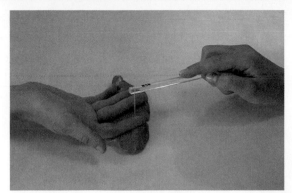

Semmes-Weinstein monofilament testing

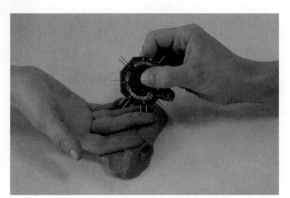

Two-point discrimination

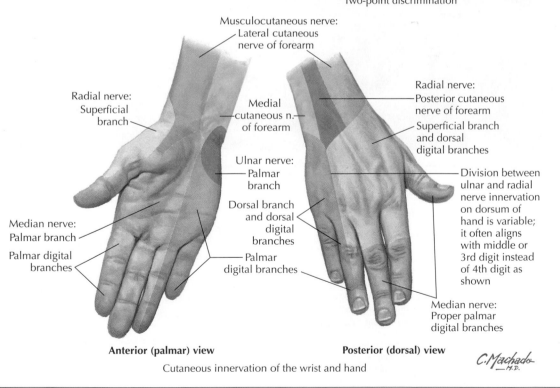

Musculocutaneous nerve:
Lateral cutaneous
nerve of forearm

Radial nerve:
Superficial
branch

Radial nerve:
Posterior cutaneous
nerve of forearm

Medial
cutaneous n.
of forearm

Superficial branch
and dorsal
digital branches

Ulnar nerve:
Palmar
branch

Division between
ulnar and radial
nerve innervation
on dorsum of
hand is variable;
it often aligns
with middle or
3rd digit instead
of 4th digit as
shown

Dorsal branch
and dorsal
digital
branches

Median nerve:
Palmar branch

Palmar digital
branches

Palmar
digital branches

Palmar
digital branches

Median nerve:
Proper palmar
digital branches

Anterior (palmar) view

Posterior (dorsal) view

C. Machado
_M.D._

Cutaneous innervation of the wrist and hand

Figure 11-24

Testing sensation.

ICC or κ	Interpretation
.81-1.0	Substantial agreement
.61-.80	Moderate agreement
.41-.60	Fair agreement
.11-.40	Slight agreement
.0-.10	No agreement

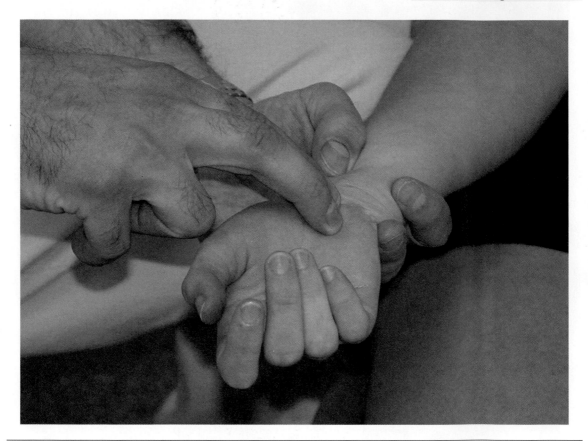

Figure 11-25

Tinel's sign.

Test and Measure	Test Procedure	Population	Inter-examiner Reliability
Tinel A[12]	With patient seated with elbow flexed 30°, forearm supinated, and wrist in neutral, examiner allows a reflex hammer to fall from a height of 6 inches along median nerve between tendons at proximal wrist crease. Positive if patient reports a nonpainful tingling sensation along course of median nerve	82 patients with suspected cervical radiculopathy or carpal tunnel syndrome	κ = .47 (.21, .72)
Tinel B[12]	As Tinel A above except examiner attempts to elicit symptoms using mild-moderate force with reflex hammer. Positive if pain is exacerbated along course of median nerve		κ = .35 (.10, .60)
Tinel's sign[28]	Examiner percusses over palm from proximal palmar crease to distal wrist crease. Positive if symptoms are elicited in distribution of median nerve	36 hands with carpal tunnel syndrome	κ = .81 (.66, .98)

Diagnostic Utility of Tinel's Sign in Identifying Carpal Tunnel Syndrome

+LR	Interpretation	−LR
>10	Large	<.1
5.0-10.0	Moderate	.1-.2
2.0-5.0	Small	.2-.5
1.0-2.0	Rarely important	.5-1.0

Test and Study Quality	Description and Positive Findings	Population	Reference Standard	Sens	Spec	+LR	−LR
Tinel's sign[32] ◇	Examiner taps median nerve at wrist with fingers. Positive if patient reports pain or paresthesias in distribution of median nerve	142 patients referred for electrodiagnostic testing	Electrodiagnostic testing	.27 (.18, .36)	.91 (.84, 1.0)	3.0	.80
Tinel's sign[30] ◇		228 hands referred for electrodiagnostic consultation with suspected carpal tunnel syndrome	Nerve conduction studies	.23	.87	1.77	.89
Tinel A[12] ◇	With patient seated with elbow flexed 30°, forearm supinated, and wrist in neutral, examiner allows reflex hammer to fall from height of 6 inches along median nerve between tendons at proximal wrist crease. Positive if patient reports nonpainful tingling sensation along course of median nerve	82 patients with suspected cervical radiculopathy or carpal tunnel syndrome	Needle electromyography and nerve conduction studies	.41 (.22, .59)	.58 (.45, .72)	.98 (.56, 1.7)	1.0 (.69, 1.5)
Tinel B[12] ◇	As Tinel A above except examiner attempts to elicit symptoms using mild-to-moderate force with reflex hammer. Positive if pain is exacerbated along course of median nerve			.48 (.29, .67)	.67 (.54, .79)	1.4 (.84, 2.5)	.78 (.52, 1.2)
Tinel's test[33] ○	Positive if percussion of the median nerve at the wrist caused tingling in the median nerve distribution	162 hands from 81 patients seeking treatment for carpal tunnel syndrome	Electrodiagnostic testing*	.90	.81	4.7	.12
Tinel's test[1] ○	Percussion of the median nerve at the wrist (no other details)	232 patients with carpal tunnel syndrome manifestations and 182 controls	Carpal tunnel syndrome via clinical examination	.30 (.24, .36)	.65 (.58, .71)	.9	1.10
			Tenosynovitis via ultrasonography	.46 (.41, .53)	.85 (.80, .89)	3.1	.64
Tinel's sign[13] ○	Examiner drops square end of reflex hammer on distal wrist crease from height of 12 cm. Positive if patient reports pain or paresthesias in at least one finger innervated by median nerve	110 patients referred to laboratory for electrophysiologic examination	Nerve conduction tests	.60	.67	1.82	.60

*Also used latent class analysis to define reference standard diagnosis of carpal tunnel syndrome, but doing so resulted in study being excluded for poor quality because the reference standard was then not independent of index tests.

ICC or κ	Interpretation
.81-1.0	Substantial agreement
.61-.80	Moderate agreement
.41-.60	Fair agreement
.11-.40	Slight agreement
.0-.10	No agreement

Phalen's test

Reverse Phalen's test

Figure 11-26

Phalen's test.

Test and Measure	Test Procedure	Population	Inter-examiner Reliability
Phalen's test[28]	Patient places dorsal aspects of hands together, maintaining maximal wrist flexion for 60 seconds. Positive if symptoms are elicited in distribution of median nerve	36 hands with carpal tunnel syndrome	κ = .88 (.77-.98)
Phalen's test[12]	With patient seated with elbow flexed 30° and forearm supinated, examiner places the wrists in maximal flexion for 60 sec. Positive if patient experiences exacerbation of symptoms in median nerve distribution	82 patients with suspected cervical radiculopathy or carpal tunnel syndrome	κ = .79 (.59. 1.0)
Wrist extension test[28]	Patient places palmar aspects of hands together maintaining maximal wrist extension for 60 sec. Positive if symptoms are elicited in distribution of median nerve	36 hands with carpal tunnel syndrome	κ = .72 (.55, .88)

Diagnostic Utility of Phalen's Test in Identifying Carpal Tunnel Syndrome

+LR	Interpretation	−LR
>10	Large	<.1
5.0-10.0	Moderate	.1-.2
2.0-5.0	Small	.2-.5
1.0-2.0	Rarely important	.5-1.0

Test and Study Quality	Description and Positive Findings	Population	Reference Standard	Sens	Spec	+LR	−LR
Phalen's test[12] ◇	With patient seated with elbow flexed 30° and forearm supinated, examiner places wrist in maximal flexion for 60 sec. Positive if patient experiences exacerbation of symptoms in median nerve distribution	82 patients with suspected cervical radiculopathy or carpal tunnel syndrome	Needle electromyography and nerve conduction studies	.77 (.61, .93)	.40 (.26, .53)	1.3 (.94, 1.7)	.58 (.27, 1.3)
Phalen's test[32] ◇		142 patients referred for electrodiagnostic testing	Electrodiagnostic testing	.34 (.24, .43)	.74 (.62, .87)	1.31	.89
Phalen's test[30] ◇	Patient maximally flexes wrist and holds position for 60 sec. Positive if symptoms are produced	228 hands referred for electrodiagnostic consultation with suspected CTS	Nerve conduction studies	.51	.76	2.13	.64
Phalen's test[33] ◯		162 hands from 81 patients seeking treatment for CTS	Electrodiagnostic testing*	.85	.79	4.0	.19
Phalen's test[1] ◯	Complete wrist flexion for 60 sec. (no other details)		Carpal tunnel syndrome via clinical examination	.47 (.41, .54)	.17 (.13, .23)	.6	3.12
		232 patients with carpal tunnel syndrome manifestations and 182 controls	Tenosynovitis via ultrasonography	.92 (.36, .49)	.87 (.82, .91)	7.1	.09
Reverse Phalen's test[1] ◯	Complete wrist extension for 60 sec (no other details)		Carpal tunnel syndrome via clinical examination	.42 (.36, .49)	.35 (.29, .42)	.6	1.66
			Tenosynovitis via ultrasonography	.75 (.69, .80)	.85 (.80, .89)	5.0	.29
Phalen's test[13] ◯	Patient flexes both wrists to 90° with dorsal aspects of hands held in opposition for 60 sec. Positive if patient reports pain or paresthesias in at least one finger innervated by median nerve	110 patients referred to laboratory for electrophysiologic examination	Nerve conduction tests	.74	.47	1.4	.55
Phalen's test[34] ◯	Patient holds forearms in pronation with elbows resting on examination table, forearms vertical, and wrists in gravity-assisted flexion. Positive if symptoms are produced	132 patients with pain of upper limb	Electrophysiologic confirmation	.79	.92	9.88	.23

*Also used latent class analysis to define reference standard diagnosis of carpal tunnel syndrome, but doing so resulted in study being excluded for poor quality because the reference standard was then not independent of index tests.

Special Tests (continued)

Reliability of Carpal Compression Test

ICC or κ	Interpretation
.81-1.0	Substantial agreement
.61-.80	Moderate agreement
.41-.60	Fair agreement
.11-.40	Slight agreement
.0-.10	No agreement

Test and Measure	Test Procedure	Population	Inter-examiner Reliability
Carpal compression test[12]	With patient seated with elbow flexed 30°, forearm supinated, and wrist in neutral., examiner places both thumbs over transverse carpal ligament and applies 6 lb of pressure for 30 sec maximum. Positive if patient experiences exacerbation of symptoms in median nerve distribution	36 hands with carpal tunnel syndrome	κ = .77 (.58, .96)

Diagnostic Utility of Carpal Compression Test in Identifying Carpal Tunnel Syndrome

Figure 11-27

Carpal compression test.

+LR	Interpretation	−LR
>10	Large	<.1
5.0-10.0	Moderate	.1-.2
2.0-5.0	Small	.2-.5
1.0-2.0	Rarely important	.5-1.0

Test and Study Quality	Description and Positive Findings	Population	Reference Standard	Sens	Spec	+LR	−LR
Carpal compression test[12] ◇	With patient seated with elbow flexed 30°, forearm supinated, and wrist in neutral, examiner places both thumbs over transverse carpal ligament and applies 6 lb of pressure for 30 sec maximum. Positive if patient experiences exacerbation of symptoms in median nerve distribution	82 patients presenting to a primary care clinic, orthopaedic department, or electrophysiology laboratory with suspected cervical radiculopathy or carpal tunnel syndrome	Needle electromyography and nerve conduction studies	.64 (.45, .83)	.30 (.17, .42)	.91 (.65, 1.3)	1.2 (.62, 2.4)
Carpal compression test[30] ◇	Examiner applies moderate pressure over median nerve just distal to distal flexor wrist crease for 5 sec. Considered positive if pain, paresthesia, or numbness is reproduced	228 hands referred for electrodiagnostic consultation with suspected carpal tunnel syndrome	Nerve conduction studies	.28	.74	1.08	.97
Carpal tunnel compression test[1] ◯	Examiner exerts even pressure on the space between the thenar and hypothenar eminence for 30 sec while arm is supinated. Patient is questioned regarding symptoms every 15 sec	232 patients with carpal tunnel syndrome manifestations and 182 controls	Carpal tunnel syndrome via clinical examination	.46 (.40, .53)	.25 (.20, .31)	.6	2.16
			Tenosynovitis via ultrasonography	.95 (.91, .97)	.97 (.94, .99)	31.7	.05
Carpal compression test[34] ◯	Examiner applies moderate pressure with thumbs over transverse carpal ligament with wrist in neutral for 30 sec. Considered positive if pain, paresthesia, or numbness is reproduced	132 patients with pain of upper limb	Electrophysiologic confirmation	.83	.92	10.38	.18

Reliability of Upper Limb Tension Tests

ICC or κ	Interpretation
.81-1.0	Substantial agreement
.61-.80	Moderate agreement
.41-.60	Fair agreement
.11-.40	Slight agreement
.0-.10	No agreement

Test and Measure	Description and Positive Findings	Population	Inter-examiner Reliability
Upper limb tension test A[12]	See below	82 patients with suspected cervical radiculopathy or carpal tunnel syndrome	κ = .76 (.51, 1.0)
Upper limb tension test B[12]			κ = .83 (.65, 1.0)

Diagnostic Utility of Upper Limb Tension Tests in Identifying Carpal Tunnel Syndrome

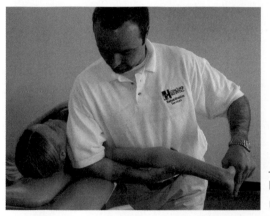

+LR	Interpretation	−LR
>10	Large	<.1
5.0-10.0	Moderate	.1-.2
2.0-5.0	Small	.2-.5
1.0-2.0	Rarely important	.5-1.0

Figure 11-28

Upper limb tension test A.

Test and Study Quality	Description and Positive Findings	Population	Reference Standard	Sens	Spec	+LR	−LR
Upper limb tension test A[12] ◇	Patient is supine. Examiner performs scapular depression, shoulder abduction, forearm supination, wrist and finger extension, shoulder lateral rotation, elbow extension, and contralateral/ipsilateral cervical sidebending. Positive if symptoms are reproduced, side-to-side difference in elbow extension greater than 10°, contralateral neck sidebending increases symptoms or ipsilateral sidebending decreases symptoms	82 patients with suspected cervical radiculopathy or carpal tunnel syndrome	Needle electromyography and nerve conduction studies	.75 (.58, .92)	.13 (.04, .22)	.86 (.67, 1.1)	1.9 (.72, 5.1)
Upper limb tension test B[12] ◇	With patient supine with shoulder abducted 30°, examiner performs scapular depression, shoulder medial rotation, full elbow extension, wrist and finger flexion, and contralateral/ipsilateral cervical sidebending. Positive if symptoms are reproduced, side-to-side difference in wrist flexion >10°, contralateral neck sidebending increases symptoms, or ipsilateral sidebending decreases symptoms			.64 (.45, .83)	.30 (.17, .42)	.91 (.65, 1.3)	1.2 (.62, 2.4)

Diagnostic Utility of Special Tests in Identifying Carpal Instability

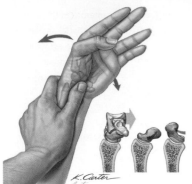

+LR	Interpretation	−LR
>10	Large	<.1
5.0-10.0	Moderate	.1-.2
2.0-5.0	Small	.2-.5
1.0-2.0	Rarely important	.5-1.0

Figure 11-29

Scaphoid shift test.

Test and Measure	Test Procedure	Determination of Positive Findings	Population	Reference Standard	Sens	Spec	+LR	−LR
Scaphoid shift test[35]	With patient's elbow stabilized on table with forearm in slight pronation, with one hand, examiner grasps radial side of patient's wrist with thumb on palmar prominence of scaphoid. With other hand, examiner grasps patient's hand at metacarpal level to stabilize wrist. Examiner maintains pressure on scaphoid tubercle and moves patient's wrist into ulnar deviation with slight extension and then radial deviation with slight flexion. Examiner releases pressure on scaphoid while wrist is in radial deviation and flexion	Positive for instability of scaphoid if scaphoid shifts, test elicits a "thunk," or patient's symptoms are reproduced when scaphoid is released			.69	.66	2.03	.47
Ballottement test[35]	Examiner stabilizes patient's lunate bone between thumb and index finger of one hand while other hand moves pisotriquetral complex in a palmar and dorsal direction	Positive for instability of luno-triquetral joint if patient's symptoms are reproduced or excessive laxity of joint is revealed	50 painful wrists undergoing arthroscopy	Arthroscopic visualization	.64	.44	1.14	.82
Ulnomeniscotriquetral dorsal glide[35]	With patient seated with elbow on table and forearm neutral, examiner places thumb over head of distal ulna. Examiner then places radial side of index PIP joint over palmar surface of patient's pisotriquetral complex. Examiner squeezes thumb and index finger together, creating a dorsal glide of pisotriquetral complex	Considered positive for ulnomeniscotriquetral complex instability if the patient's symptoms are reproduced or excessive laxity of the joint is revealed			.66	.64	1.69	.56

Reliability of Miscellaneous Special Tests

ICC or κ	Interpretation
.81-1.0	Substantial agreement
.61-.80	Moderate agreement
.41-.60	Fair agreement
.11-.40	Slight agreement
.0-.10	No agreement

Test and Measure	Test Procedure and Determination of Positive Findings	Population	Inter-examiner Reliability
Tethered median nerve test[28]	Examiner passively extends patient's index finger while patient's forearm is in supination and wrist is in full extension. Position is maintained for 15 sec. Positive if symptoms are elicited in distribution of median nerve	36 hands with carpal tunnel syndrome	κ = .49 (.26, .71)
Pinch test[28]	Patient actively pinches a piece of paper between tip of thumb, index, and long fingers using MP flexion and IP extension. Positive if symptoms are elicited in distribution of median nerve	36 hands with carpal tunnel syndrome	κ = .76 (.62, .91)

Diagnostic Utility of Miscellaneous Special Tests

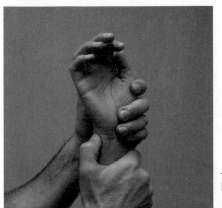

+LR	Interpretation	−LR
>10	Large	<.1
5.0-10.0	Moderate	.1-.2
2.0-5.0	Small	.2-.5
1.0-2.0	Rarely important	.5-1.0

Figure 11-30

Ulnar fovea sign.

Test and Study Quality	Description and Positive Findings	Population	Reference Standard	Sens	Spec	+LR	−LR
The flick maneuver[32] ◇	Patient demonstrates hand motions or positions patient uses when pain is most severe. Positive if patient demonstrates a flicking down of hands similar to shaking a thermometer	142 patients referred for electrodiagnostic testing	Carpal tunnel syndrome via electrodiagnostic testing	.37 (.27, .46)	.74 (.62, .87)	1.42	.85
Lumbrical provocation test[36] ◯	Patient makes a fist for 60 sec. Considered positive if the patient reports paresthesia in the distribution of the median nerve	96 consecutive patients referred for electrodiagnostic testing		.37	.71	1.28	.89
Ulnar fovea sign[37] ◯	Examiner presses thumb distally and deep into the "soft spot" between the ulnar styloid process and flexor carpi ulnaris tendon. Positive if exquisite tenderness similar to experienced wrist pain	272 consecutive patients undergoing wrist arthroscopy	Foveal disruption of the distal radioulnar ligaments and ulnotriquetral ligament injuries observed arthroscopy	.95 (.90, .98)	.87 (.79, .92)	7.1 (4.5, 11.0)	.06 (.03, .11)

Wainner and colleagues[12] developed a clinical prediction rule for detecting carpal tunnel syndrome. The result of their study demonstrated that if 5 variables (a Brigham and Women's Hospital Hand Severity Scale score of > 1.9, a wrist ratio index > .67, a patient report of shaking the hand for symptom relief, diminished sensation on the thumb pad, and age older than 45) were present, the +LR was 18.3 (95% CI 1.0, 328.3). This clinical prediction rule results in a post-test probability of 90% that the patient has carpal tunnel syndrome.

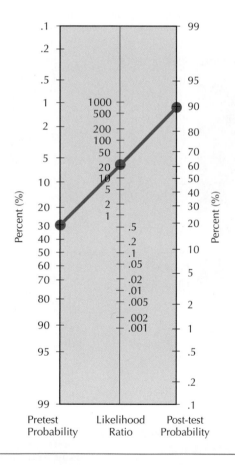

Figure 11-31

Nomogram representing the change in pretest (34% in this study) to post-test probability given the clinical prediction rule. *(Adapted with permission from Fagan TJ. Nomogram for Bayes' theorem. N Engl J Med. 1975;293:257. Copyright 2005, Massachusetts Medical Society. All rights reserved.)*

Outcome Measure	Scoring and Interpretation	Test-Retest Reliability	MCID
Upper Extremity Functional Index	Users are asked to rate the difficulty of performing 20 functional tasks on a Likert-type scale ranging from 0 (extremely difficult or unable to perform activity) to 4 (no difficulty). A total score out of 80 is calculated by summing each score. The answers provide a score between 0 and 80, with lower scores representing more disability	ICC = .95[38]	Unknown (MDC = 9.1)[38]
Disabilities of the Arm, Shoulder, and Hand (DASH)	Users are asked to rate the difficulty of performing 30 functional tasks on a Likert-type scale; 21 items relate to physical function, 5 items relate to pain symptoms, and 4 items related to emotional and social functioning. A total score out of 100 is calculated with higher scores representing more disability	ICC = .90[39]	10.2[39]
Michigan Hand Outcomes Questionnaire (MHQ)	Consists of 37 items on 6 scales: (1) overall hand function, (2) activities of daily living (ADL), (3) work performance, (4) pain, (5) aesthetics, and (6) satisfaction with hand function. Users rate each item on a 5-point Likert-type scale. Answers provide a total score between 0 and 100 with higher score indicating better hand performance	ICC = .95[40]	Pain = 23 Function = 13 ADL = 11 Work = 8[41]
Numeric Pain Rating Scale (NPRS)	Users rate their level of pain on an 11-point scale ranging from 0 to 10, with high scores representing more pain. Often asked as "current pain" and "least," "worst," and "average" pain in the past 24 hours	ICC = .72[42]	2[43,44]

MCID, Minimum clinically important difference; MDC, minimal detectable change.

APPENDIX

Quality Assessment of Diagnostic Studies Using QUADAS

	Heller 1986[45]	Gellman 1986[46]	Waeckerle 1987	Powell 1988[47]	Katz 1990	Koris 1990[48]	Durkan 1991[49]	Williams 1992[50]	LaStayo 1995	Grover 1996	Gonzalez del Pino 1997[51]	Gunnarsson 1997[52]	Kuhlman 1997	Fertl 1998
1. Was the spectrum of patients representative of the patients who will receive the test in practice?	Y	N	Y	Y	Y	N	N	N	Y	Y	N	Y	Y	N
2. Were selection criteria clearly described?	N	N	Y	N	N	N	N	U	Y	Y	N	U	Y	N
3. Is the reference standard likely to correctly classify the target condition?	Y	Y	Y	Y	Y	U	Y	U	Y	U	Y	Y	Y	Y
4. Is the time period between reference standard and index test short enough to be reasonably sure that the target condition did not change between the two tests?	U	U	Y	U	U	U	U	U	U	Y	U	U	Y	U
5. Did the whole sample or a random selection of the sample, receive verification using a reference standard of diagnosis?	Y	N	Y	U	Y	Y	Y	N	Y	Y	Y	N	Y	Y
6. Did patients receive the same reference standard regardless of the index test result?	Y	N	Y	U	Y	N	Y	N	Y	Y	U	U	Y	Y
7. Was the reference standard independent of the index test (i.e., the index test did not form part of the reference standard)?	Y	Y	Y	Y	Y	U	Y	U	Y	N	Y	U	Y	Y
8. Was the execution of the index test described in sufficient detail to permit replication of the test?	N	Y	Y	Y	Y	Y	Y	Y	Y	Y	Y	Y	Y	Y
9. Was the execution of the reference standard described in sufficient detail to permit its replication?	Y	Y	Y	N	Y	N	N	N	Y	Y	Y	Y	Y	Y
10. Were the index test results interpreted without knowledge of the results of the reference test?	U	U	Y	Y	Y	U	U	Y	U	Y	Y	Y	Y	Y
11. Were the reference standard results interpreted without knowledge of the results of the index test?	U	U	N	U	Y	U	U	Y	U	Y	U	U	U	U
12. Were the same clinical data available when test results were interpreted as would be available when the test is used in practice?	U	U	U	U	Y	U	U	U	Y	U	U	Y	U	Y
13. Were uninterpretable/ intermediate test results reported?	U	U	U	U	U	U	U	U	U	U	U	U	Y	Y
14. Were withdrawals from the study explained?	U	U	Y	U	U	U	U	U	U	U	N	N	Y	Y
Quality summary rating:	■	■	◇	■	○	■	■	■	○	○	■	■	◇	○

Y = yes, N = no, U = unclear.   ◇ Good quality (Y − N = 10 to 14).   ○ Fair quality (Y − N = 5 to 9).   ■ Poor quality (Y − N ≤ 4).

Quality Assessment of Diagnostic Studies Using QUADAS

	Tetro 1998[53]	Szabo 1999	Pershad 2000	Ahn 2001[54]	Karl 2001	Mondelli 2001[55]	Hansen 2004	Lajoie 2005	Wainner 2005	Amirfeyz 2005[56]	Tay 2007	El Miedany 2008	Cheng 2003[57]
1. Was the spectrum of patients representative of the patients who will receive the test in practice?	N	N	Y	N	Y	N	Y	Y	Y	N	Y	N	N
2. Were selection criteria clearly described?	Y	N	Y	N	Y	U	Y	U	Y	Y	U	Y	Y
3. Is the reference standard likely to correctly classify the target condition?	Y	U	Y	U	Y	Y	Y	Y	Y	Y	Y	Y	Y
4. Is the time period between reference standard and index test short enough to be reasonably sure that the target condition did not change between the two tests?	U	U	Y	U	U	U	Y	Y	Y	Y	U	U	U
5. Did the whole sample, or a random selection of the sample, receive verification using a reference standard of diagnosis?	N	N	Y	Y	Y	N	Y	Y	Y	N	Y	Y	Y
6. Did patients receive the same reference standard regardless of the index test result?	N	N	Y	U	Y	N	Y	Y	Y	N	U	Y	N
7. Was the reference standard independent of the index test (i.e., the index test did not form part of the reference standard)?	Y	U	Y	U	Y	U	Y	Y	Y	Y	Y	Y	Y
8. Was the execution of the index test described in sufficient detail to permit replication of the test?	Y	Y	Y	Y	Y	Y	Y	Y	Y	Y	Y	Y	Y
9. Was the execution of the reference standard described in sufficient detail to permit its replication?	Y	Y	Y	N	Y	N	Y	N	Y	Y	N	Y	Y
10. Were the index test results interpreted without knowledge of the results of the reference test?	U	U	Y	U	Y	U	Y	U	U	Y	Y	U	U
11. Were the reference standard results interpreted without knowledge of the results of the index test?	U	U	U	U	U	U	U	U	Y	U	U	U	U
12. Were the same clinical data available when test results were interpreted as would be available when the test is used in practice?	U	Y	Y	U	U	U	U	U	Y	U	Y	Y	U
13. Were uninterpretable/ intermediate test results reported?	U	U	Y	U	U	U	U	U	Y	U	U	U	U
14. Were withdrawals from the study explained?	U	U	Y	U	U	U	Y	U	Y	U	U	U	U
Quality summary rating:	■	■	◇	■	○	■	◇	○	◇	■	○	○	■

Y = yes, N = no, U = unclear. ◇ Good quality (Y − N = 10 to 14). ○ Fair quality (Y − N = 5 to 9). ■ Poor quality (Y − N ≤ 4).

1. El Miedany Y, Ashour S, Youssef S, et al. Clinical diagnosis of carpal tunnel syndrome: old tests-new concepts. *Joint Bone Spine.* 2008;75:451-457.

2. Bohannon RW, Andrews AW. Interrater reliability of hand-held dynamometry. *Phys Ther.* 1987;67:931-933.

3. D'Arcy CA, McGee S. The rational clinical examination. Does this patient have carpal tunnel syndrome? *JAMA.* 2000;283:3110-3117.

4. MacDermid JC, Wessel J. Clinical diagnosis of carpal tunnel syndrome: a systematic review. *J Hand Ther.* 2004;17:309-319.

5. Szabo RM, Slater RRJ, Farver TB, et al. The value of diagnostic testing in carpal tunnel syndrome. *J Hand Surg Am.* 1999;24:704-714.

6. Skirven T. Tendon and nerve injuries of the wrist and hand. *The Wrist and Hand.* La Crosse, WI: Orthopaedic Section, American Physical Therapy Association; 1995.

7. Wadsworth C. Cumulative trauma disorders of the wrist and hand. *The Wrist and Hand.* La Crosse, WI: Orthopaedic Section, American Physical Therapy Association; 1995.

8. Wadsworth C. Current concepts in orthopaedic physical therapy. *The Wrist and Hand.* La Crosse, WI: Orthopaedic Section, American Physical Therapy Association; 2001.

9. Placzek JD, Boyce DA. *Orthopaedic Physical Therapy Secrets.* Philadelphia: Hanley and Belfus; 2001.

10. Cole IC. Fractures and ligament injuries of the wrist and hand. *The Wrist and Hand.* La Crosse, WI: Orthopaedic Section, American Physical Therapy Association; 1995.

11. Hartley A. *Practical Joint Assessment.* St. Louis: Mosby; 1995.

12. Wainner RS, Fritz JM, Irrgang JJ, et al. Development of a clinical prediction rule for the diagnosis of carpal tunnel syndrome. *Arch Phys Med Rehabil.* 2005;86:609-618.

13. Katz JN, Larson MG, Sabra A et al. The carpal tunnel syndrome: diagnostic utility of the history and physical examination findings. *Ann Intern Med.* 1990;112:321-327.

14. Waeckerle JF. A prospective study identifying the sensitivity of radiographic findings and the efficacy of clinical findings in carpal navicular fractures. *Ann Emerg Med.* 1987;16:733-737.

15. Grover R. Clinical assessment of scaphoid injuries and the detection of fractures. *J Hand Surg Br.* 1996;21:341-343.

16. Pershad J, Monroe K, King W, et al. Can clinical parameters predict fractures in acute pediatric wrist injuries? *Acad Emerg Med.* 2000;7:1152-1155.

17. Horger MM. The reliability of goniometric measurements of active and passive wrist motions. *Am J Occup Ther.* 1990;44:342-348.

18. LaStayo PC, Wheeler DL. Reliability of passive wrist flexion and extension goniometric measurements: a multicenter study. *Phys Ther.* 1994;74:162-176.

19. Stam HJ, Ardon MS, den Ouden AC, et al. The compangle: a new goniometer for joint angle measurements of the hand. A technical note. *Eura Medicophys.* 2006;42:37-40.

20. Brown A, Cramer LD, Eckhaus D, et al. Validity and reliability of the dexter hand evaluation and therapy system in hand-injured patients. *J Hand Ther.* 2000;13:37-45.

21. de Kraker M, Selles RW, Schreuders TA, et al. Palmar abduction: reliability of 6 measurement methods in healthy adults. *J Hand Surg Am.* 2009;34:523-530.

22. van den Beld WA, van der Sanden GA, Sengers RC, et al. Validity and reproducibility of hand-held dynamometry in children aged 4-11 years. *J Rehabil Med.* 2006;38:57-64.

23. Bohannon RW, Schaubert KL. Test-retest reliability of grip-strength measures obtained over a 12-week interval from community-dwelling elders. *J Hand Ther.* 2005;18:426-428.

24. Coldham F, Lewis J, Lee H. The reliability of one vs. three grip trials in symptomatic and asymptomatic subjects. *J Hand Ther.* 2006;19:318-327.

25. Molenaar HM, Zuidam JM, Selles RW, et al. Age-specific reliability of two grip-strength dynamometers when used by children. *J Bone Joint Surg Am.* 2008;90:1053-1059.

26. Mathiowetz V, Weber K, Volland G, Kashman N. Reliability and validity of grip and pinch strength evaluations. *J Hand Surg Am.* 1984;9:222-226.

27. Schreuders TA, Roebroeck ME, Goumans J, et al. Measurement error in grip and pinch force measurements in patients with hand injuries. *Phys Ther.* 2003;83:806-815.

28. MacDermid JC, Kramer JF, Woodbury MG, et al. Interrater reliability of pinch and grip strength measurements in patients with cumulative trauma disorders. *J Hand Ther.* 1994;7:10-14.

29. Rheault W, Beal JL, Kubik KR, et al. Intertester reliability of the hand-held dynamometer for wrist flexion and extension. *Arch Phys Med Rehabil.* 1989;70:907-910.

30. Kuhlman KA, Hennessey WJ. Sensitivity and specificity of carpal tunnel syndrome signs. *Am J Phys Med Rehabil.* 1997;76:451-457.

31. Leard JS, Breglio L, Fraga L, et al. Reliability and concurrent validity of the figure-of-eight method of measuring hand size in patients with hand pathology. *J Orthop Sports Phys Ther.* 2004;34:335-340.

32. Hansen PA, Micklesen P, Robinson LR. Clinical utility of the flick maneuver in diagnosing carpal tunnel syndrome. *Am J Phys Med Rehabil.* 2004;83:363-367.

33. LaJoie AS, McCabe SJ, Thomas B, Edgell SE. Determining the sensitivity and specificity of common diagnostic tests for carpal tunnel syndrome using latent class analysis. *Plast Reconstr Surg.* 2005;116:502-507.

34. Fertl E, Wober C, Zeitlhofer J. The serial use of two provocative tests in the clinical diagnosis of carpal tunnel syndrome. *Acta Neurol Scand.* 1998;98:328-332.

35. LaStayo P, Howell J. Clinical provocative tests used in evaluating wrist pain: a descriptive study. *J Hand Ther.* 1995;8:10-17.

36. Karl AI, Carney ML, Kaul MP. The lumbrical provocation test in subjects with median inclusive paresthesia. *Arch Phys Med Rehabil.* 2001;82:935-937.

37. Tay SC, Tomita K, Berger RA. The "ulnar fovea sign" for defining ulnar wrist pain: an analysis of sensitivity and specificity. *J Hand Surg Am.* 2007;32:438-444.

38. Stratford PW, Binkley JM, Riddle DL. Development and initial validation of the upper extremity functional index. *Physiother Can.* 2001;53:259-263.

39. Roy JS, MacDermid JC, Woodhouse LJ. Measuring shoulder function: a systematic review of four questionnaires. *Arthritis Rheum.* 2009;61:623-632.

40. Massy-Westropp N, Krishnan J, Ahern M. Comparing the AUSCAN Osteoarthritis Hand Index, Michigan Hand Outcomes Questionnaire, and Sequential Occupational Dexterity Assessment for patients with rheumatoid arthritis. *J Rheumatol.* 2004;31:1996-2001.

41. Shauver MJ, Chung KC. The minimal clinically important difference of the Michigan hand outcomes questionnaire. *J Hand Surg Am.* 2009;34:509-514.

42. Li L, Liu X, Herr K. Postoperative pain intensity assessment: a comparison of four scales in Chinese adults. *Pain Med.* 2007;8:223-234.

43. Farrar JT, Berlin JA, Strom BL. Clinically important changes in acute pain outcome measures: A validation study. *J Pain Symptom Manage.* 2003;25:406-411.

44. Farrar JT, Portenoy RK, Berlin JA, et al. Defining the clinically important difference in pain outcome measures. *Pain.* 2000;88:287-294.

45. Heller L, Ring H, Costeff PS. Evaluation of Tinel's and Phalen's sign in diagnosis of the carpal tunnel syndrome. *Eur Neurol.* 1986;25:40-42.

46. Gellman H, Gelberman RH, Tan AM, Botte MJ. Carpal tunnel syndrome. An evaluation of the provocative diagnostic tests. *J Bone Joint Surg Am.* 1986;68:735-737.

47. Powell JM, Lloyd GJ, Rintoul RF. New clinical test for fracture of the scaphoid. *Can J Surg.* 1988;31:237-238.

48. Koris M, Gelberman RH, Duncan K, et al. Carpal tunnel syndrome. Evaluation of a quantitative provocational diagnostic test. *Clin Orthop Relat Res.* 1990;157-161.

49. Durkan JA. A new diagnostic test for carpal tunnel syndrome. *J Bone Joint Surg Am.* 1991;73:535-538.

50. Williams TM, Mackinnon SE, Novak CB, et al. Verification of the pressure provocative test in carpal tunnel syndrome. *Ann Plast Surg.* 1992;29:8-11.

51. Gonzalez del Pino J, Delgado-Martinez AD, Gonzalez Gonzalez I, Lovic A. Value of the carpal compression test in the diagnosis of carpal tunnel syndrome. *J Hand Surg Br.* 1997;22:38-41.

52. Gunnarsson LG, Amilon A, Hellstrand P, et al. The diagnosis of carpal tunnel syndrome. Sensitivity and specificity of some clinical and electrophysiological tests. *J Hand Surg Br.* 1997;22:34-37.

53. Tetro AM, Evanoff BA, Hollstien SB, Gelberman RH. A new provocative test for carpal tunnel syndrome. Assessment of wrist flexion and nerve compression. *J Bone Joint Surg Br.* 1998;80:493-498.

54. Ahn DS. Hand elevation: a new test for carpal tunnel syndrome. *Ann Plast Surg.* 2001;46:120-124.

55. Mondelli M, Passero S, Giannini F. Provocative tests in different stages of carpal tunnel syndrome. *Clin Neurol Neurosurg.* 2001;103:178-183.

56. Amirfeyz R, Gozzard C, Leslie IJ. Hand elevation test for assessment of carpal tunnel syndrome. *J Hand Surg Br.* 2005;30:361-364.

57. Cheng CJ, Mackinnon-Patterson B, Beck JL, Mackinnon SE. Scratch collapse test for evaluation of carpal and cubital tunnel syndrome. *J Hand Surg Am.* 2008;33:1518-1524.

Index

Adductor muscles, of hip and thigh, 250t, 251f
  length assessment of, 270t
Adductor pollicis muscle, 473t, 474f
  innervation of, 476f
  oblique head of, 473t
  transverse head of, 473t
Adductor tubercle, of femur, 285f
  on medial epicondyle, 253f, 287f
Adhesions
  in shoulder joint, 397f
  in temporomandibular joint arthrosis, 32f
Adhesive capsulitis, of shoulder, 389t, 397f, 397t
ADLS (Activity of Daily Living Scale), in knee outcomes, 327t
Afferent nerves, somatic, lumbar disc herniation and, 179f
Ala (wing)
  of ilium, 201f, 202f, 246f
    female vs. male, 204f
    gluteal surface of, 201f, 203f
    iliac fossa, 203f, 245f
  of sphenoid bone, greater, 19f
Alar ligament, 70f, 70t
Algometer, for TMJ pressure pain thresholds, 38t
Alignment assessment
  of bones. See Bony alignment assessment.
  dynamic. See Dynamic movements.
  static. See Static alignment.
Alveolar artery, inferior, 25f
  mylohyoid branch of, 21f
Alveolar nerve, inferior, 21f, 23f, 25f, 26f
  entering mandibular foramen, 26f
Alveolar process, of maxilla, 19f, 67f
American Orthopaedic Foot and Ankle Society (AOFAS) scale, 373t
American Shoulder and Elbow Surgeons (ASES) score, 429t
Anal (rectal) nerve, inferior, 148f, 252f
Anconeus muscle, 445f, 445t
  innervation of, 477f
Anesthetic injection, for sacroiliac pain, 211t, 213t
  double-block, referral patterns with, 212, 212f
  motion testing and, 227t, 228t, 233t
  provocative testing and, 216t, 217t, 218t, 219t, 220t, 223t
Anesthetic-steroid injection, for intra-articular hip pain, 273t, 274t, 275t

Angle between longitudinal axis of patella and patellar tendon (A angle), 311, 311f, 311t
Ankle, 335-376. See also Foot and ankle.
  anterolateral impingement in, 336
    detection of, 370, 370f, 370t
  pain in. See Foot and ankle pain.
  ROM measurements of, 359-360
  trauma to
    fractures as, 358f, 358t
    patient report of, 355t
    screening for, 356, 358
    x-rays of. See Ottawa Ankle Rule for Radiography.
Ankle flexibility angle, 360f
Ankle-hindfoot, AOFAS scale for, 373t
Ankylosing spondylitis
  of sacroiliac joint, 216t, 217t, 218t, 225t
  of thoracolumbar spine, 149, 186t
    patient history in, 154, 154t, 155f
Annular ligament of radius, 443f, 443t
Annulus fibrosus, of lumbar intervertebral disc, 133f
  fissure in, 179f
  nociceptors in, disc herniation and, 179f
  ossification of, in ankylosing spondylitis, 155f
Anococcygeal nerve, 148f, 208t, 209f
Anserine bursa, 289f, 291f
Anterior apprehension test, of shoulder, 399f, 399t
  combined with other tests, 427t, 428t
Anterior cruciate ligament (ACL), 287f, 288f, 288t
  degrees of sprain of, 315f
  ruptures of, 295f, 295t
  tears of, 284, 313t, 314t
    combination of tests for, 324t
    pivot shift test for, 315, 315f, 315t
Anterior disc displacement, in TMJ disorders
  deviation tests of, 46, 46t, 55t, 57t
  diagnostic criteria for, 31, 32f
    reliability and utility of, 33t, 40t, 45t
  patient history in, 21, 29
  range of motion and, 45, 45f, 45t
  with reduction, 33t, 54, 58t, 59t
  without reduction, 33t, 56

Anterior drawer test
  of ankle, 372, 372f
  of knee, 284, 314, 314f, 314t
  of shoulder, 401, 401f, 401t
Anterior relocation test, of shoulder, 400t
  combined with other tests, 378, 427t
Anterior slide test, for glenoid labral tears, 409, 409f, 409t
  combined with other tests, 427t
Anterior view
  of axis, 68f
  of carpal bones, 463f
  of cervical spine arthrology, 69f
  of cervical spine ligaments, 71f
  of elbow bones, in extension, 441f
  of elbow joint, opened, 442f
  of elbow ligaments, 443f
  of female pelvic inlet, 204f
  of female pelvis, 204f
  of femur, 245f
  of fibular nerves, 353f, 353t
  of forearm ligaments, in supination vs. pronation, 444f
  of forearm nerves, 448f
  of hip and pelvis ligaments, 247f
  of humerus, 379f
  of knee muscles, 289f
  of male pelvic inlet, 204f
  of male pelvis, 204f
  of metacarpophalangeal and interphalangeal ligaments, 469, 469f, 469t
  of rotator cuff muscles, 386f
  of sacroiliac region ligaments, 206f
  of scapula, 379f
  of shoulder ligaments, 382f, 383f
  of shoulder muscles, 385, 385f, 385t
  of sternocostal articulations, 134f
  of thigh nerves and arteries, 253f
  of tibia and fibula, 285f
  of tibial nerves, 353f, 353t
  of wrist and hand bones, 464f
  of wrist and hand muscles, 471f, 472f, 473f, 474f
  of wrist and hand nerves, 475f, 476f
Anterior-posterior width, of wrist, 490t
  in carpal tunnel syndrome, 490t
Anterior-superior iliac spine (ASIS)
  in hip testing, 274t
  as sacroiliac bony landmark, 214t
  in sacroiliac pain provocation, 216t, 218t, 223t
Anteroinferior view, of mouth floor muscles, 25f

Anteroposterior diameter, of pelvic outlet, 204f
Anteroposterior glide technique, for hip mobilization, 326f
Anthropometry measurements, of wrist, 490, 490t
　carpal tunnel syndrome identification with, 490, 490f, 490t
AOFAS (American Orthopaedic Foot and Ankle Society) scale, 373t
Apical ligament, 70f, 70t
Apley's grinding test, of knee, 318, 318f, 318t
　combined with other tests, 322t, 323t
Aponeuroses
　epicranial, 77f
　gluteal, 140f, 249f
　palmar, 467f, 471f
　plantar, 349f, 350f, 351f
Apophyseal joints
　cervical spine, 69t
　lumbar, ossification of, 155f
　lumbosacral, 205t
Apprehension test(s)
　moving patellar, 284, 321, 321f, 321t
　of shoulder, 378, 399, 399f
　　anterior, 399t
　　combined with other tests, 378, 427t
　　bony, 399t
　　relocation, 400t
Arc of pain sign. See Painful arc sign.
Arch angle, 363f, 363t
Arch drop, longitudinal, 369f
Arch height test, 363f
　medial, 362, 363t
Arcuate artery, 348f, 352f
　posterior perforating branches of, 348f, 352f
Arcuate line, 201f, 203f, 206f, 245f, 246f
Arm. See Forearm/arm.
Arteries. See also Named artery, e.g., Carotid artery(ies).
　of foot and ankle, 346f, 347f, 348f
　of forearm, 445f
　of hip and pelvis, 247f
　of leg, 347f
　of mandible, 21f, 22f, 23f
　of neck, 68f, 71f, 72f, 73f, 75f, 77f
　of sacroiliac region, 209f
　of shoulder, 385f, 388f
　of skull, 19f
　of sole of foot, 349f, 350f, 351f, 352f
　of thigh, 253f
　of wrist and hand, 467f, 474f

Arthralgia, in TMJ disorders, 31, 33t
Arthrography, of rotator cuff tears, 422t
Arthrology
　of cervical spine, 69
　of elbow, 442
　of foot and ankle, 339
　of hip and pelvis, 246
　of knee, 286
　of lumbar spine, 136
　of sacroiliac region, 205, 205f, 205t
　of shoulder, 380
　　integrated movements in, 381, 381f
　of temporomandibular, 20
　　jaw closed, 20, 20f
　　jaw slightly opened, 20f
　　jaw widely opened, 20f
　of thoracic spine, 134
　　1st, 136t
　　2nd-7th, 136t
　　joint classifications, 136t
　of wrist and hand, 465
Arthroscopic view, of ACL rupture, 295f
Arthroscopy
　of rotator cuff tears, 422t
　of shoulder
　　combination of tests vs., 427t, 428t
　　IRRS test following, 408, 417, 417f
　　physical examination vs., 394t, 399t, 400t, 403t, 404t, 405t, 406t, 407t, 408t, 409t, 410t, 411t-412t
　of wrist and hand, 500t, 501t
Arthrosis. See Osteoarthrosis.
Articular cartilage
　in elbow, 442f
　in hip and pelvis, 247f
　　erosion of, 259f, 296f
　in knee, 286f
　　erosion of, 296f
　in shoulder, 397f
Articular cavities
　of knee, 286f
　of sternoclavicular joint, 380f
　sternocostal, 134f
Articular discs
　of mandible, 20, 20f, 22f, 23f
　of sternoclavicular joint, 380f
　sternocostal, 134f
Articular facets
　of atlas
　　for dens, 68f
　　posterior, 69f
　of axis

Articular facets (Continued)
　anterior, for atlas, 68f
　inferior, for C3, 68f
　posterior, for atlas, 68f
　superior, for atlas, 68f
　of C4, superior, 68f
　of C7, superior, 68f
　of cervical spine, tenderness with palpation of, 105t
　for dens, 68f
　of dens, posterior, 70f
　of lumbar vertebrae, in physical examination, 167t
　of rib head, superior, 135f, 137f
　for sacrum, 136f, 202f
　of thoracic vertebrae
　　inferior, 133f, 138f
　　superior, 133f, 134f
Articular nerve, recurrent, 353f
　articular branches of, 353f
Articular pillar, of cervical vertebrae, 69f
Articular processes
　of axis, inferior, 68f
　of C4, inferior, 68f
　of C7, inferior, 68f
　of cervical vertebrae, 69f
　of lumbar vertebrae
　　inferior, 136f, 138f
　　superior, 133f, 136f, 138f
　of sacrum and coccyx, superior, 202f
　　facets of, 202f
　of T9 vertebra, inferior, 134f
　of thoracic vertebrae, inferior vs. superior, 133f, 134f, 138f
Articular surfaces
　of acetabulum, 247f
　of atlas, inferior vs. superior, for occipital condyle, 69f
　　lateral mass, 68f
　of femur, medial vs. lateral, 287f, 288f
　of sacrum and coccyx, 202f
　　lumbosacral, 202f
　　facets of, 202f
　of tibia, superior, 285f, 288f
Articular tubercles
　of mandible, 20f, 23f
　of radius, dorsal, 444f
　of temporal bone, 19f
Articularis genus muscle, 286f, 289t, 293f
Articulations. See Joints; specific articulation, e.g., Sterno-costal articulations.
ASES (American Shoulder and Elbow Surgeons) score, 429t

Elbow and forearm (Continued)
reliability of examination
end-feel classification, 452,
452f, 452t
flexion and extension measurements, 450, 450f, 450t
grip strength testing, 452, 452t
supination and pronation measurements, 451, 451f,
451t
Elbow pain
epicondylar. See Tennis elbow.
neuropathic. See Cubital tunnel
syndrome.
patient history in, 449, 449t
Electrodiagnostics
for cervical radiculopathy, 83t,
84t, 86t, 88t, 89t, 109t,
114t, 117t
for lumbar radiculopathy, 154t,
156t
for wrist and hand disorders, 478t,
479t, 489t, 490t, 492t,
495t, 497t, 498t, 501t
Elevation tests, of shoulder, 390t
for rotator cuff tears, 422t
Empty can test, for supraspinatus
tears, 418f, 418t, 422t
End-feel assessment
of elbow, 452, 452f, 452t
of hip and pelvis, capsular and
noncapsular, 258, 258f,
258t
of knee, capsular and noncapsular, 284, 302
extension vs. flexion, 302f,
302t, 326t
of temporomandibular joint, 44,
44f, 44t
of thoracolumbar spine, 166t
Endurance testing
of cervical spine flexors, 99, 99f, 99t
of serratus anterior muscle, 392t
of thoracolumbar spine, 162,
162f, 162t
Epicondylalgia. See Tennis elbow.
Epicondyles
of femur
lateral, 285f, 289f
medial, 285f, 289f, 291f
adductor tubercle on, 253f,
287f
in physical examination, 306t,
307t
of humerus, lateral vs. medial, 379f,
380f, 441f, 443f, 445f,
446f, 447f, 448f, 470f,
471f, 472f, 476f, 477f
palpation of, 449f

Epicondyles (Continued)
tenderness over. See Tennis
elbow.
Epicondylitis, of elbow, lateral vs.
medial, 449t
Epiglottis, 17f, 67f
Erector spinae muscle, 140f, 141f,
142f, 145f
Ethmoid bone, 19f
Eversion, subtalar joint, 359t
Evidence-based practice, 2
Excursions, of temporomandibular
joint, 43t, 47t, 48t
Exercise therapy
stabilizing, for low back pain. See
Stabilization exercises.
for strength. See Strengthening
exercises.
for tennis elbow, 456, 456t
Extension view
of anterior knee muscles, 289f
of posterior knee ligaments, 287f
Extension/extension tests
of cervical spine, 94f, 95t, 96t
limited passive, 100t, 103t
pain during, 97t, 98t
in slump test, 178f, 178t
of elbow, 440, 453, 453t
for carpal tunnel syndrome,
499t
end-feel classification, 452,
452f, 452t
ROM measurements, 450, 450f,
450t
of fingers, for carpal tunnel syndrome, 499t
of great toe, in predicting success
of patellofemoral pain
interventions, 325f, 325t
of hip, 256t, 257t, 261f
in flexor contracture test, 269f,
269t
length assessment with, 268t,
270t
for lumbar segmental instability, 180t
for lumbar spinal stenosis, 182t
mobilizations effect on, 326t
osteonecrosis detection with,
262t
pain during, 260t, 278t
strength assessment with, 264t,
265t
of knee
measurement of
active vs. passive, 301t
end-feel, 302t, 326t
pain during, 303t
for strength, 304t

Extension/extension tests (Continued)
in pivot shift test, 315f
in slump test, 178f, 178t
of lumbar spine, 159t
centralization phenomena and,
173t
lying, 171f, 171t
radiography with, for instability, 184t
of sacroiliac joint
lying, 235
standing, 235
of shoulder, 390t
for labral tears, 407t
of thoracolumbar spine, 159t, 160f
in low back pain classifications,
188t
pain during, 161, 161f, 161t
of wrist, 484t, 485f, 487t, 489t
for carpal tunnel syndrome,
496t, 497t, 499t, 501t
Extensor carpi radialis brevis muscle, 445f, 470f, 470t
groove on radius for, 444f
innervation of, 477f
manual testing of, for cervical radiculopathy, 88t
Extensor carpi radialis brevis tendon, 445f, 465f
Extensor carpi radialis longus muscle, 445f, 470f, 470t
groove on radius for, 444f
innervation of, 477f
manual testing of, for cervical radiculopathy, 88t
Extensor carpi radialis longus tendon, 445f, 465f
Extensor carpi ulnaris muscle, 470f,
470t
innervation of, 477f
Extensor carpi ulnaris tendon, 445f
Extensor digiti minimi muscle, 470f,
470t
innervation of, 477f
Extensor digiti minimi tendon, 445f,
470f, 470t
Extensor digitorum brevis muscle,
345t, 346f, 347f, 348t,
353f
Extensor digitorum brevis tendon,
348f, 352f
Extensor digitorum longus muscle,
289f, 345t, 346f, 348f,
353f
Extensor digitorum longus tendon,
346f, 348f, 352f
Extensor digitorum muscle, 470f, 470t
groove on radius for, 444f
innervation of, 477f

Foot rotation test, internal, for TMJ disorders
  diagnostic utility of, 53, 53f, 53t
  reliability of, 53, 53f, 53t
Foramen. *See specific anatomy, e.g.,* Intervertebral foramen.
Foramen ovale, 26f, 67f
Foramen spinosum, 26f, 67f
Force
  high-velocity thrust, in spinal manipulation, for cervical radiculopathy, 119f, 121f
  mechanical, in lumbar pain, 179f
  posteroanterior, for lumbar pain provocation, 167t
  in shoulder tests
    for instability, 400t
    for labral tears, 403t, 404t, 407t, 409t, 411t-412t
  transfer of
    in knee injuries, 297f, 297t
    by thoracolumbar fascia, 144, 144f
  in wrist and hand tests, for instability, 494t, 495t
Forearm/arm, 439-460. *See also* Elbow and forearm.
  bones of. *See* Humerus; Radius; Ulna.
  fractures of, in children, 483, 483f
  ligaments of, 443, 444f, 444t
  muscles of, 445
    anterior vs. posterior, 445, 445f
    anterior view of, 446f, 446t
    posterior view of, 445f, 445t
    supinators vs. pronators, 447, 447f, 447t
  nerves of, 387t, 388f, 448, 448f, 448t
    in hand and wrist, 493f
    in neural tension tests, 112t, 114t, 499t
  pain in, with cervical compression test, 108f, 108t
Forefoot alignment/position, 364, 364f, 364t
Forward bending, of thoracolumbar spine, 159t
Fossa. *See specific anatomy, e.g.,* Iliac fossa.
Foveal disruption, of radioulnar ligaments, 462
  testing for, 501t
Fractures
  of cervical spine
    screening for, 66, 91, 92t-93t, 305t
    types of, 90f

Fractures *(Continued)*
  of femur
    distal, 298f
    intertrochanteric, 277f
    shaft, 277f, 298f
  of foot and ankle, 336, 355t
    screening for, 336, 358f, 358t
  of forearm/arm, in children, 483, 483f
  of hip, 244
    patellar-pubic percussion test for, 276, 276f, 276t
    types of, 277f
  of knee, 284, 298-299, 299t
    distal femur and, 298f
  of wrist and hand, screening for, 462, 481-483, 481t, 482f, 483f
Frontal bone, 19f
Functional hallux limitus test, during gait, 367, 367f, 367t
Functional impairment, with TMJ disorders, 16t, 31, 31t, 60t
Functional movements. *See also* Dynamic movements.
  of sacroiliac region, 200
    assessment tests for, 226-227, 228-229, 230-231, 232
    combinations of, 233-234, 235
      dysfunction vs. pain detection with, 234-235, 234f, 235f
  of shoulder, assessment tests for, 391, 391f, 391t
Functional outcomes. *See* Outcome measures.

G

Gaenslen test
  for pelvic pain, 260t, 272t
  of sacroiliac joint, 220, 222f
    combined with other tests, 233t, 235
    diagnostic utility of, 220f, 220t
    reliability of, 220f, 220t
Gait
  characteristic, with hip osteoarthritis, 259f, 267t
  functional hallux limitus test during, 367, 367f, 367t
  hindfoot motion during, dynamic assessment of, 367, 367f, 367t
Galea aponeurotica muscle, 77f
Ganglion
  otic, 21f, 23f, 26f
  semilunar (trigeminal), 26f

Ganglion *(Continued)*
  sensory
    of lumbar spine nerves, 179f
    of thoracic spine nerves, 145f
  submandibular, 26f
Gastrocnemius muscle, 289f, 291f, 294f, 345t, 346f, 354f
  atrophy of, with herniated lumbar nucleus pulposus, 157f
  lateral head of, 249f, 286f, 287f, 290t, 347f
  length assessment of, 305t
  medial head of, 249f, 287f, 290t, 347f
  neurological examination of, 156t
  plantaris part of, 290t
  popliteus part of, 290t
  subtendinous bursa of
    lateral, 286f, 287f
    medial, 287f
Gastroc-soleus complex, neurological examination of, 156t
Gemellus muscle, inferior vs. superior, 248t, 249f, 252f
  nerves to, 148f, 208t, 209f, 252f
Genicular arteries
  articular branch of, 253f
  descending, 253f
  inferior lateral vs. superior lateral, 346f, 347f
  inferior medial vs. superior medial, 253f, 347f
Genioglossus muscle, superior mental spine for, 25f
Geniohyoid muscle, 24t, 25f, 35f, 73f, 74f
Genitofemoral nerve, 146f, 147t, 148f, 292f
  femoral branch of, 146f, 148f
  genital branch of, 148f
Gerber's test, for subacromial impingement, 415t-416t
Gerdy's tubercle, 285f, 288f
  iliotibial tract insertion to, 289f
Gillet test, 226-227, 226f, 227f, 227t
Glabella, of frontal bone, 19f
Glasgow Coma Score, with cervical spine trauma, 85t, 87t, 96t, 104t
Glenohumeral joint, 136t
  integrated movements of, 381, 381f
  in neural tension tests, 114t
  in physical examination, 395t, 400t, 401t
Glenohumeral ligaments, 382f, 382t
  avulsions of, 399t, 400t, 401t
  inferior vs. middle vs. superior, 383f

Head and neck. *See also* Neck.
bony framework of
in relation to cervical spine, 67f
in relation to TMJ, 17f
Headaches, cervical spine and, 97t,
104t
Heel-bank test, of sacroiliac joint,
232t
Herniation, of intervertebral discs.
See Disc herniation.
Hill-Sachs lesion, of shoulder, 399t,
400t, 401t
Hindfoot, in physical examination,
358t
Hindfoot motion, during gait, dynamic assessment of,
367, 367f, 367t
Hinge joints, temporomandibular,
20, 20f
Hip abduction/abduction tests, 244,
256t, 257t
length assessment with, 268t
limited, developmental dysplasia
in infants and, 244, 263,
263f, 263t
osteonecrosis detection with,
262t
pain during, 260t, 266t
resisted, for sacroiliac pain provocation, 225f, 225t
strength assessment with, 264t,
265t
Hip adduction/adduction tests, 244,
256t, 257t
for impingement. *See* Flexion–
internal rotation–
adduction (FADIR)
impingement test.
length assessment with, 268t
pain during, 260t, 278t
strength assessment with, 264t,
265t
Hip and pelvis, 243-282
arthritis of. *See* Osteoarthritis (OA).
arthrology of, 246
clinical summary and recommen-
dations, 244-280
diagnostic utility of examination
avascular necrosis detection
with limited ROM, 262,
262f, 262t
combination of tests for osteoarthritis, 278, 278f, 278t
Cyriax's capsular pattern for
detecting osteoarthritis,
258, 259f
developmental dysplasia detection in infants, 244,
263, 263f, 263t

Hip and pelvis (*Continued*)
hip fracture detection, 276,
276f, 276t, 277f
intra-articular pathology
detection, 275, 275f,
275t
lateral tendon pathology identification, 266, 266f,
266t, 267f, 267t
pain during limited ROM, 260,
260f, 260t, 261f
pain with functional movements, 272, 272f, 272t
pain with palpation, 273, 273f,
273t
patellar-pubic percussion test,
276, 276f, 276t, 277f
patient history, 255, 255f,
255t
Patrick's (FABER) test, 274,
274f, 274t
Trendelenburg test, 267, 267f,
267t
fractures of, 244, 277f
patellar-pubic percussion test
for, 276, 276f, 276t
ligaments of, 247, 247f, 247t
mobilization strategies for, for
knee osteoarthritis, 284,
326, 326f, 326t
muscles of, 248
anterior, 250, 250t, 251f
posterior, 248, 248t, 249f
nerves of, 248t, 252
and buttocks, 252, 252f, 252t
and thigh, 249f, 252t, 253f
osteology of, 245
femur, 245f
hip (coxal) bone, 245f
outcome measures of, 279, 279t
palpation of, 273
patient history and, 244, 255
initial hypotheses based on,
254, 254t
physical examination of, 244t,
256-278
quality assessment of diagnostic
studies, 280, 280t
range of motion of
passive measurements of, 256,
256f, 256t, 257t, 258t,
261f
physical examination of, 258,
260, 262-263
reliability of examination
capsular and noncapsular end-
feels, 258, 258f, 258t
intra-articular pathology detection, 275, 275f, 275t

Hip and pelvis (*Continued*)
muscle length assessment, 268-
269, 270
flexion contracture in, 269,
269f, 269t
iliotibial band length in, 268,
268f, 268t
measurements in, 270, 270f,
270t, 271f
Ober tests, 268f, 268t
pain with palpation, 273, 273f,
273t
Patrick's (FABER) test, 274,
274f, 274t
ROM measurements, 256, 256f,
256t, 257f, 257t
Thomas test, 269, 269f, 269t
Trendelenburg test, 267, 267f,
267t
in straight-leg raise test, 176t
Hip (coxal) bone, 203f
auricular surface of, for sacrum,
203f
osteology of, 245f
Hip pain. *See also* Sacroiliac pain.
combined tests for, 278t
during functional movements,
272, 272t
intra-articular
anesthetic-steroid injection for,
273t, 274t, 275t
palpation for, 273, 273t
patient report of, 244t, 254t,
255, 255t
special tests for, 274t, 275t
diagnostic utility of, 275,
275f
reliability of, 275, 275f
knee interventions and, 326t
lateral tendon pathology and,
266, 266t, 267t
physical examination for, 244,
256-278, 268t
during resistance tests, 264, 264t,
265t
History, in clinical examination. *See*
Patient history.
Hook (anatomy). *See* Hamulus
(hook).
Hook (tool), in thoracolumbar muscles, 141f
Horizontal adduction test, for subacromial impingement,
415t-416t, 416f
combined with other tests, 428t
Horizontal (cleft) tear, of meniscus,
323f
Hornblower's sign, with rotator cuff
tears, 419f, 422t

Inclinometer
in cervical spine assessment, 94f, 95t, 96t, 118t
in elbow and forearm assessment, 450t
in foot and ankle assessment, 359t
in hip and pelvis assessment, 256t, 257t, 268t, 269t, 274t
in muscle length assessment
of hip, 268t, 270t, 271f
of knee, 305f, 305t
in shoulder assessment, 392t
in thoracolumbar spine assessment, 159t, 160f, 184t, 191t
Infants, limited hip abduction in, 244
with developmental dysplasia, 263, 263f, 263t
Inferior view
of atlas, 68f
of female pelvic outlet, 204f
of mouth floor muscles, 24f
Inflammation. *See also* Swelling.
of knee, 300, 300t
lumbar pain and, 179f
Infraglenoid tubercle
of humerus, 380f
of scapula, 379f
Infrahyoid muscles, fascia of, 72f
Infrapatellar bursa
deep (subtendinous), 286f
subcutaneous, 286f
Infrapatellar fat pad, 286f, 288f
Infrapatellar synovial fold, 288f
Infraspinatus fascia, 140f, 384t
Infraspinatus muscle, 140f, 384f, 386f, 386t
tears of, 418, 418f, 418t, 419-422, 419f, 422t
Infraspinatus tendon, 383f, 386f
Infraspinatus test, for rotator cuff tears, 422t
combined with other tests, 428t
Infraspinous fossae, 380f
notch connecting, 380f
Infratemporal fossa, 67f
Inguinal ligament, 146f, 251f, 253f
Inguinal (groin) pain
in hip examination, 274t, 275t, 278t
ipsilateral, 244, 255t
knee interventions and, 326t
as lumbar zygapophyseal joint pain referral, 149t, 150f
patient report of, 254t, 255t
physical examination for, 257t
sacroiliac pain and, 211t, 213t

Injuries. *See* Trauma; *specific injury, e.g.,* Fractures.
Innominate torsion, of sacroiliac region, 200, 227t, 229t, 230t, 231t
Instability. *See* Stability/instability.
Interalveolar septa, of mandible, 18f
Interarticular ligament, of rib head, 135f, 137f
Intercarpal joint, 465t
Intercarpal ligaments, interosseous, 465f
Interchondral joints, of thoracic spine, 134f, 136t
Interchondral ligaments, 137t
Interclavicular ligament, 134f, 380f, 382t
Intercondylar area, of tibia, anterior vs. posterior, 285f
Intercondylar eminence, of tibia, 285f
Intercondylar fossa, of femur, 285f
Intercondylar (T or Y) fracture, of femur, 298f
Intercondylar notch, of femur, cartilaginous excrescences at, 285f
Intercondylar tubercle, of tibia, lateral vs. medial, 285f
Intercostal muscle, external, 142f
Intercostal nerves/membranes
1st, 79f
of thoracic spine, 145t, 148f
external, 145f
innermost, 145f
window cut in, 145f
internal, 145f
anterior to external, 145f
as ventral (anterior) ramus of spinal nerve, 145f
Intercostobrachial nerve, 388f
Intercuneiform ligaments, dorsal, 341f, 341t
Intermetacarpal joints, 465f
in palmar abduction, 486t
Intermuscular septum
of forearm, medial vs. lateral, 445f, 448f
of hip and pelvis, anteromedial, 251f, 253f
Internal rotation (IR) lag sign, in shoulder, 423t
Internal rotation resistance strength (IRRS) test, of shoulder, 408, 417, 417f
Internal rotation (IR) test, of foot, for TMJ disorders
diagnostic utility of, 53, 53f, 53t
reliability of, 53, 53f, 53t

Internal rotation–flexion–axial compression maneuver, for intra-articular hip pathology, 275t
Interosseous artery
common, 446f, 448f
posterior vs. anterior, 445f, 446f, 448f
recurrent, 445f
Interosseous border
of radius, 444f
of ulna, 444f
Interosseous ligaments, intercarpal, 465f
Interosseous membrane
of ankle joint, 340f, 340t, 347f
of forearm, 444f, 444t, 470f, 472f
1st dorsal, 445f
of knee joint, 287f
of wrist joint, 467f, 468f
1st dorsal, 465f
Interosseous nerve
of foot, 354f
of forearm
anterior, 448f, 448t, 471t, 475f
posterior, 445f, 448t, 470t, 477f
Interosseus muscles, 344f
of foot and ankle
4th, superficial branch of tibial nerve to, 354f
deep branch of tibial nerve to, 354f
dorsal, 347f, 348t, 352f, 352t
manual testing of, 87f
for cervical radiculopathy, 88t
plantar, 351f, 352f, 352t
of wrist and hand
1st dorsal, 474f
deep branch of ulnar nerve to, 474f
dorsal (bipennate), 473t, 474f
innervation of, 476f
palmar (unipennate), 473f, 473t
innervation of, 476f
Interphalangeal (IP) joints, 339t, 344f, 465t
AOFAS scale for, 373t
capsules and ligaments of, 343, 343f, 343t, 344f
distal, 469f
ligaments of, 469, 469f, 469t
nodules over, 369f
in physical examination, 371t, 501t
proximal, 500t
proximal, 469f, 500t
ROM measurements of, proximal vs. distal, 486f, 486t

Painful arc sign, in shoulder, 378, 389t, 391t, 397t, 415t-416t
combined with other tests, 428t
with rotator cuff tears, 422t
Painful arc test, for subacromial impingement, 415t-416t
combined with other tests, 428t
Palatine bone, pyramidal process of, 67f
Palmar abduction, 486t
Palmar (arterial) arch, carpal, 474f
Palmar ligaments, volar plate of, 469f, 469t
Palmar nerves
digital. See Digital nerves/branches.
median, 493f
Palmar pinch strength, 489t
Palmar view
of carpal bones, 463f
of wrist and hand bones, 464f
of wrist and hand muscles, 471f, 472f, 473f, 474f
of wrist ligaments, carpal tunnel vs. flexor retinaculum removed, 466, 466t, 467f
Palmaris brevis muscle, innervation of, 476f
Palmaris longus muscle, 448f, 471f, 471t
innervation of, 475f
Palmaris longus tendon, 446f, 467f
in carpal tunnel syndrome, 480f
Palpation
of cervical spine, pain during, 104-105, 104t, 105t
without patient history, 105, 105t
of foot and ankle, for trauma screening, 356t
of hip, 273
diagnostic utility for intra-articular pain, 273, 273f, 273t
reliability of, 273, 273f, 273t
of humerus, lateral epicondyle, 449f
of knee
for inflammation detection, 300f, 300t
lateral vs. medial joint line, 312f, 312t
pain during, 312, 312t, 322t
of sacroiliac region, 213
bony landmark symmetry assessment, 214, 214f, 214t, 215f

Palpation (Continued)
pain location identification with, 213, 213f, 213t
static, 200
of shoulder
labral tears identification with, 394, 394t
subacromial space in, 394, 394f, 394t
of temporomandibular joint, 16t, 31t, 34
conditions identified by, 37
extraoral, 34t
intraoral, 34t
lateral, 35t, 36f, 37t
muscle, 34, 35t
posterior, 35t, 36f, 37t
pressure pain thresholds, 38
regional, 35
tests, 36f
of thoracolumbar spine, 172
segmental level identification with, 172, 172f, 172t
segmental mobility identification with, 166t, 168f, 169t, 170f, 171f, 171t
tenderness identification with, 172, 172t
Paper grip test, for toe strength, 336, 361f, 361t
Paraspinal joints, tenderness with palpation of, 105t
Paraspinal muscles, tenderness with palpation of, 105t
Parasympathetic nerves, of sacroiliac region, 209f
Paresthesias. See also Radiculopathy.
in foot and ankle, 355t
in lower extremity, with lumbar pain, 149t, 154t, 157f
in upper extremity
with brachial plexus palsy, 425t
with neck pain, 66, 80t, 82t, 83f, 83t, 84t
patient report of, 66, 80t, 82t, 83f, 83t, 84t
during ROM, 97t
in wrist and hand, 495t, 498t, 501t
with brachial plexus palsy, 425t
patient report of, 478t, 479t, 480f
Parietal bone, 19f
temporal lines of, inferior vs. superior, 19f
Parotid duct, 22f, 23f
Parotid gland, 72f
Parrot beak tear, of meniscus, 323f
Passive intervertebral motion (PIVM)
of cervical spine, limited, 100, 100f, 100t

Passive intervertebral motion (PIVM) (Continued)
pain during, 101, 101t, 102f, 102t
of lumbar spine
accessory, 169t, 171t
limited vs. excessive, 165, 165t, 166t, 171, 171t
pain with, 132, 167, 167t, 169t, 170f
physiological, 169t
flexion vs. extension, 171t
radiography with, for instability, 184t
Patella, 251f, 253f, 286f, 289f, 291f, 346f
alignment of. See also Patellar tilt.
A angle in, 311, 311f, 311t
lateral pull test for, 311, 311t
Q-angle in, 310, 310f, 310t
angle between longitudinal axis of, and patellar tendon, 311, 311f, 311t
articular cartilage of, erosion of, 296f
displacement of
lateral pull test for, 311t
mediolateral, 307t
instability of, 284
bony assessment of, 306-307, 308-309, 310-311
in physical examination, 298f, 299t, 300t
subluxation of, 295t, 310f
tenderness of, in trauma screening, 298f, 299t
Patella poles, inferior vs. superior, in alignment assessment, 308t, 309t, 311f, 311t
Patellar anastomosis, 253f
Patellar apprehension test, moving, 284, 321, 321f, 321t
Patellar ligament, 251f, 253f, 286f, 288f, 289f, 291f, 346f
Patellar orientation/position
assessment of, 307, 307f, 307t
mediolateral, 307f, 307t
Patellar retinaculum
lateral, 251f, 289f, 291f, 346f
iliotibial tract blended into, 288f
tight, 324t
medial, 251f, 253f, 289f, 291f
blended into joint capsule, 288f
Patellar rotation, 309, 309f, 309t
Patellar surface, of femur, 285f

Supination measurement/tests
 of elbow, 451, 451f, 451t
  for cubital tunnel syndrome, 454f, 454t
  of forearm, for carpal tunnel syndrome, 499t
  of shoulder, for labral tears, 407t, 408t, 411t-412t
  of wrist and hand
   for carpal tunnel syndrome, 498f, 498t
   median nerve and, 501t
   for scaphoid fractures, 481t
Supinator muscle, 445f, 446f, 447, 447f, 447t, 448f
 innervation of, 477f
Supracondylar fracture, of femur, transverse, 298f
Supracondylar ridge, of humerus, medial vs. lateral, 379f, 380f, 441f
Supraglenoid tubercle, of scapula, 379f
Supraorbital notch (foramen), of frontal bone, 19f
Suprapatellar fat body, 286f
Suprapatellar synovial bursa, 286f, 288f
Suprascapular nerve, 78t, 79f, 386t, 387t, 388f
 upper vs. lower, 386t
Suprascapular notch, 379f, 380f, 382f, 386f
Suprascapular tenderness, with palpation, 104t
Supraspinatus muscle, 140f, 383f, 384f, 386f, 386t
 tears of, 418, 418f, 418t, 419-422, 419f, 422t
Supraspinatus tendon, 382f, 383f, 386f
 subtendinous bursa of, 382f
 communications of, 382f
Supraspinatus tests, of rotator cuff tears, 422t
Supraspinous fossa, 380f
 notch connecting, 380f
Supraspinous ligament, 206f
 of cervical spine, 71t
 of thoracolumbar spine, 138f, 138t
Suprasternal space, 72f
Sural cutaneous nerve
 lateral, 294f, 353f, 354f
  branches of, 348f, 353f, 354f
  phantom, 353f
  lateral calcaneal nerve from, 350f
 medial, 294f, 354f
  from sciatic nerve, 294f
  via lateral dorsal cutaneous branch, 353f

Sural nerve, 294f, 353t, 354f
 communicating branches of, 294f
 cutaneous. See Sural cutaneous nerve.
 lateral calcaneal branches of, 294f, 347f, 354f
 muscular branches of, 347f
Sustentaculum tali, 337f, 338f, 342f, 344f
Swelling
 in foot and ankle
  impingement sign with, 370t
  measurement of, 368, 368f, 368t
  in trauma screening, 356t
 in knee
  patient report of, 295t, 296t, 297t, 300t
  in trauma screening, 300, 300t
 in wrist and hand
  measurement of, 491, 491f, 491t
  patient report of, 478t, 479t
  in trauma screening, 482f
Sympathetic nerves
 of lumbar spine, 146f, 148f
 of sacroiliac region, 209f
 of thoracic spine, 145f
Symphyseal surface, of hip bone, 203f, 245f
Synchondrosis
 of 1st rib, 380f
 manubriosternal, 380f
Syndesmotic ligaments, 356t
Synovial bursa, suprapatellar, 286f, 288f
Synovial cavities
 costovertebral, 137f, 380f
 of thoracic vertebrae, 135f
Synovial fold, infrapatellar, 288f
Synovial joint, of sternum, 380f
Synovial membrane
 of acetabular fossa, 247f
 of elbow, 442f
 of femur
  line of attachment of, 245f, 285f
  line of reflection of, 245f, 285f
 of knee, 286f, 288f
 protrusion of, in hip, 247t
 of shoulder, 383f
Synovitis, of knee, 324t

T

T1 vertebra
 arthrology of, 69f, 71f
 in kyphosis, 106t, 163t
 limited and painful passive motion of, 100t, 101t
 nerves of, 78t, 79f, 445t, 447t, 471t, 473t, 476t, 477t
  brachial plexus schema, 425f

T1 vertebra *(Continued)*
 osteology of, 17f, 67f
 tenderness with palpation of, 105t
 in upper limb dermatomes, 85f, 86t
T2 vertebra
 in kyphosis, 106t, 163t
 nerves of, 79f
 tenderness with palpation of, 105t
 in zygapophyseal pain referral pattern, 151f
T3 vertebra
 in kyphosis, 106t, 163t
 tenderness with palpation of, 105t
 in zygapophyseal pain referral pattern, 151f
T4 vertebra
 in kyphosis, 106t, 163t
 in zygapophyseal pain referral pattern, 151f
T5 vertebra
 in kyphosis, 106t, 163t
 in zygapophyseal pain referral pattern, 151f
T6 vertebra
 in kyphosis, 106t, 163t
 osteology of
  lateral view of, 133f
  superior view of, 133f
 in zygapophyseal pain referral pattern, 151f
T7 vertebra
 arthrology of, 134f
 in kyphosis, 106t, 163t
 spinous processes of, 134f
 in zygapophyseal pain referral pattern, 151f
T8 vertebra
 arthrology of, 134f
 in kyphosis, 106t, 163t
 in zygapophyseal pain referral pattern, 151f
T9 vertebra
 arthrology of, 134f
 in kyphosis, 106t, 163t
 transverse process of, 134f
 in zygapophyseal pain referral pattern, 151f
T10 vertebra
 in kyphosis, 106t, 163t
 in zygapophyseal pain referral pattern, 151f
T11 vertebra
 osteology of, 201f
 in zygapophyseal pain referral pattern, 151f
T12 vertebra
 nerves of, 146f, 147t, 148f, 293f
 osteology of, 201f
  lateral view of, 133f

Temporomandibular joint (TMJ)
(Continued)
pain during regional palpation,
35, 35f, 35t
pain during resistance tests, 48,
48f, 48t
patient history, 27-28, 28f, 28t,
30
RDC/TMD diagnoses, 33f, 33t
ROM measurements, 43, 43f,
43t
Research Diagnostic Criteria for,
31-32, 33
anterior disc displacement, 32f
arthrosis, 32f
diagnoses list, 31
diagnostic utility of, 33f, 33t
examination procedures, 31t
reliability of, 33f, 33t
Temporomandibular ligament, 21,
21f
Temporomandibular pain
diagnostic criteria for, 31
during dynamic movements, 47
conditions identified by, 50-51
joint play and, 49
resistance tests, 48
myofascial, 31
diagnostic criteria for, 33t
during palpation, 34
patient report of, 28, 30, 30t
rating scales for, 28f, 28t, 60t
Tenderness. See Pain; specific anatomy, e.g., Joint line tenderness.
Tendocalcaneus, subtendinous
bursa of, 346f
Tendonitis, of shoulder, 389t, 422t
Tendons
of foot and ankle, 337f, 340f, 341f,
342f, 344f, 346f, 347f
ruptures of, 355t
in sole, 348f, 349f, 350f, 351f
of knee, 249f, 285f, 286f, 287f,
288f, 289f, 291f
of lateral hip, identifying pathology of, 266-267, 266t,
267t
of leg, 347f
of neck, 24f, 25f, 72f, 73f
of sacroiliac region, 206f
of shoulder, 382f, 383f, 388f
of temporomandibular joint, 24f,
24t, 25f, 34t
of thigh, 251f
of thoracolumbar spine, 141f, 142f
of wrist and hand, 448f, 465f,
467f, 469f, 470f, 471f,
472f, 473f, 474f, 501t

Tennis elbow
grip strength with, 452, 452t
mobilization interventions for,
456, 456t
patient history in, 449t
patient-rated evaluation of, 457t
Tenosynovitis, in wrist and hand,
462, 495t, 497t, 498t
Tension tests, neural. See Upper
limb tension tests
(ULTTs).
Tensor fasciae latae muscle, 250t,
251f, 252f, 253f
Tensor fasciae latae myofascial pain,
172t
Tensor tympani muscle, 26f
Tensor tympani nerve, 26f
Tensor veli palatini muscle, 23f,
26f
Tensor veli palatini nerve, 26f
Teres major muscle, 140f, 384f, 386t,
388f
Teres minor muscle, 140f, 384f,
386f, 386t
tears of, 422t
Teres minor tendon, 383f, 386f
Test(s)/testing. See specific test or
under specific anatomy,
disorder, or component.
Tethered median nerve test, 501t
Thenar eminence
in carpal compression test, 498t
impact of fall on, 482f
Thenar muscles, innervation of,
474f, 475f, 476f
Thessaly test, of knee, 284
for meniscal tears, 320, 320f
Thigh
ligaments of, 253f
muscles of, 248
anterior, 250, 250t, 251f
posterior, 248, 248t, 249f
nerves of, 208t, 249f
cutaneous localization of, 292f,
293f, 294f
lateral cutaneous, 146f, 147t,
148f, 252f, 252t, 253f,
292f, 293f
posterior cutaneous, 148f, 252f,
252t, 294f
perineal branches of, 294f
Thigh pain
with herniated lumbar nucleus
pulposus, 157f
in hip examination, 274t
knee interventions and, 326t
as lumbar zygapophyseal joint
pain referral, 149t, 150f
patient report of, 254t, 255t

Thigh thrust test, 200, 217, 221f
combined with other tests, 233t,
235
diagnostic utility of, 217f, 217t
for pelvic pain, 260t, 272t
reliability of, 217f, 217t
Thomas test, 305t
for hip flexor contracture, 269,
269f, 269t
modified, 269t
Thoracic artery, superior, 388f
Thoracic manipulation, for cervical
radiculopathy, 120,
120f, 120t
cluster of findings, 121, 121f, 121t
neck pain and, 66
Thoracic nerve
collateral branch of, 145f
rejoining intercostal nerve, 145f
communicating branch of, 145f
cutaneous branches of
anterior, 145f
lateral, 145f
dorsal vs. ventral root of, 145f
long, 71f, 78t, 79f, 387f, 388f
in brachial plexus schema, 425f
meningeal branch of, 145f
sensory ganglion of, 145f
subcostal branches of, 145f, 145t,
146f, 147t, 148f
Thoracic outlet syndrome, 389t
Thoracic spine
arthrology of, 134
1st, 136t
2nd-7th, 136t
joint classifications, 136t
fascia of, 140f, 141f, 144
kyphosis of, 163t
postural assessment for, 106f,
106t, 163t
ligaments of, 134f, 135f, 137
costovertebral, 137, 137f, 137t
thoracolumbar, 138, 138f, 138t
muscles of, 139
nerves of, 145. See also Thoracic
nerve.
osteology of, 133f
in relation to temporomandibular joint, 17f
pain in. See Thoracolumbar pain.
scoliosis of, 163t, 164f
Thoracic vertebrae. See also specific
vertebra, e.g., T4
vertebra.
articular facets of
inferior, 133f, 138f
superior, 133f, 134f
articular processes of, inferior vs.
superior, 133f, 134f, 138f